Pilgrims and Sultans

Pilgrims and Sultans

The Hajj under the Ottomans
1517–1683

SURAIYA FAROQHI

I.B.Tauris & Co Ltd
Publishers
London · New York

For Andreas Tietze
with respect and affection

Published in 1994 by
I.B.Tauris & Co Ltd
45 Bloomsbury Square
London WC1A 2HY
Paperback edition 1996

175 Fifth Avenue
New York
NY 10010

In the United States of America
and Canada distributed by
St Martin's Press
175 Fifth Avenue
New York
NY 10010

ISBN 1–86064–033–8

Typeset by Photoprint, Torquay, Devon
Printed and bound in Great Britain by
WBC Ltd, Bridgend, Mid Glamorgan

Contents

Preface

Every book is ultimately a collective work, and cooperation begins at an early stage, when the author begins to develop the chosen topic. Not all those who at some point suggested directions to take, and aspects to cover, will necessarily agree with the final result. Nevertheless, I am grateful to a number of people who helped along my thinking – such as it is – and suggested sources to consult. Of course, none of them can be held to the slightest degree responsible for the deficiencies of this book.

Doris Behrens-Abouseif helped with the Arabic sources, and gave generously of her time and patience. Time and again, I have profited from the rich experience and erudition of Andreas Tietze. I owe references to many Ottoman sources to Mehmet Genç; more importantly, I am grateful for his pertinent observations on the functioning of Ottoman state and society. Engin Akarlı, Halis Akder, Cornell Fleischer, Christoph Neumann and Isenbike Togan read through individual chapters and made valuable suggestions. Rifa'at Abou-El-Haj redirected my attention to the forest when the trees pressed too close; I have also profited from his ability to 'brush the fur of a text against the nap', teasing out information that the author of a given primary source may have included without being aware of the fact.

Among the people who helped me locate sources, the officials of the Başbakanlık Arşivi-Osmanlı Arşivi in Istanbul deserve special mention; they have helped in many different ways. I am especially grateful to my old teacher Mithat Sertoğlu, former director-general of the archives; he first made me feel the excitement of working with a rich and underexploited body of documentary evidence. Veli Tola and

viii *Pilgrims and Sultans*

Mesude Çorbacıoğlu were also very helpful. Hafez K. Shehab (Princeton), Tosun Arıcanlı (Harvard) and Winfried Riesterer (Munich) helped me locate important printed sources, while Andreas Tietze made it possible to procure microfilms from the Vienna National Library.

The present book is somewhat different from the German edition which preceded it. The introduction is rather more explicit. Profiting from the counsel of reviewers, I have gladly eliminated the last chapter, which took the story to the present day but was based exclusively on published material. The space thus gained allowed me to discuss financial affairs in a more detailed fashion, and to treat Meccan society as reflected in the Ottoman documents somewhat more fully. The book's new title reflects these various changes.

Christl Catanzaro and Giorgios Salakides produced the index, and I am grateful to them.

Note on Transliteration and Abbreviations

TRANSLITERATION

The present transcription is that employed by the *Encyclopedia of Islam*. Long vowels are marked by a line: ā, ī, ū. To maintain consistency, composite names such as Sa'd al-Dīn or 'Abd al-Rahīm have also been spelt according to *EI* rules, although in Turkish they are pronounced Sadettin and Abdürrahim. But otherwise the *EI* convention of treating Arabic or Persian loans in Turkish as if they were still part of their original languages has not been followed. An Ottoman would therefore be called Aḥmed or Meḥmed, while a non-Ottoman bearing this name is referred to as Aḥmad or Muḥammad. Certain doubtful cases exist, in which I have normally adopted Turkish pronunciation.

Geographical terms still in use today have been spelt according to common usage. Names no longer in use have been transcribed. Words like shaykh, Sultan or Pasha which have entered the English language have been spelt in the customary fashion.

ABBREVIATIONS

EI   *Encyclopedia of Islam*
IA   *Islam Ansiklopedisi*
IFM *Istanbul Üniversitesi Iktisat Fakültesi Mecmuası*

MD   Mühimme Defterleri (section in the Prime Minister's Archives in Istanbul)

MM   Maliyeden Müdevver (section in the Prime Minister's Archives in Istanbul)

MZ   Mühimme Zeyli (section in the Prime Minister's Archives in Istanbul)

List of Tables

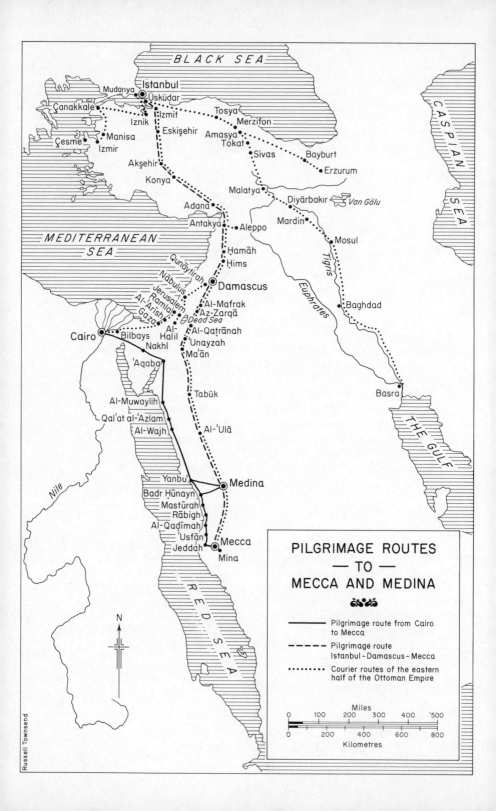

BLACK SEA

Mudanya
Istanbul
Üsküdar
Çanakkale
Iznik
Izmit
Eskişehir
Çeşme
Manisa
Izmir
Akşehir
Konya
Adana
Antakya

Tosya
Merzifon
Amasya
Tokat
Sivas
Bayburt
Erzurum

Malatya
Diyārbakır
Van Gölü
Mardin
Mosul

CASPIAN SEA

Aleppo

MEDITERRANEAN SEA

Qunāytirah
Nābulus
Jerusalem
Ramla
Al-ʿArīsh
Gaza

Ḥamāh
Ḥims

Damascus

Al-Mafrak
Az-Zarqā
Dead Sea
Al-Qaṭrānah
ʿUnayzah
Maʿān

Tigris

Euphrates

Baghdad

Cairo
Bilbays
Nakhl
Al-Halīl
ʿAqaba

Tabūk

Basra

THE GULF

Al-Muwaylih
Qalʿat al-ʿAzlam
Al-Wajh

Al-ʿUlā

Nile

Yanbu
Badr Hūnayn
Mastūrah
Rābigh
Al-Qadīmah
ʿUsfān
Jeddah

Medina

Mecca
Mina

RED SEA

N

PILGRIMAGE ROUTES
— TO —
MECCA AND MEDINA

——— Pilgrimage route from Cairo to Mecca

– – – Pilgrimage route Istanbul–Damascus–Mecca

········· Courier routes of the eastern half of the Ottoman Empire

Miles
0   100   200   300   400   500
0   200   400   600   800
Kilometres

Russell Townsend

Introduction

European and American readers who first encounter the word 'pilgrimage' will think of medieval men and women on their way to Rome, Santiago da Compostela or Jerusalem, or possibly of modern Catholics visiting Lourdes and Fatima. But for a Muslim, pilgrimage to Mecca plays a much more central role in the practice of his or her belief. Apart from a limited number of instances in which pilgrimage was prescribed for the atonement of sins by the medieval and early modern Catholic Church, Christian pilgrimages to Jerusalem are voluntary. In Islam, however, pilgrimage to Mecca is obligatory for all believers wealthy enough to afford it, even though at all times the majority of Muslims have been unable to fulfil this obligation for financial and other reasons. This practical difficulty does not however diminish the religious importance of the pilgrimage.

Moreover, the pilgrimage in Islam is fundamentally different from the experience with which Christians are familiar. The Ka'aba with its Black Stone, which the pilgrims kiss whenever they can come close enough, is by no means a relic, even though the pilgrims commemorate Abraham/Ibrāhīm, the builder of the 'Ancient House', one of the names of the Ka'aba. The latter structure possesses a religious significance unequalled even by the most venerated holy places in Christianity. When devoting himself or herself to the rites of the pilgrimage, the Muslim meditates the might and mercy of God, and also forswears the devil and all his works.

The rites of visitation are also quite different from those practised by Christian churches. The Muslim pilgrim does not necessarily enter the Ka'aba, even though this is possible at certain times of the year. The pilgrimage is valid even if the Ka'aba was beheld only from the

1

outside, while in most Christian places of pilgrimage, pious visitors are expected to enter the church or shrine. A visit to the grave of the Prophet Muḥammad in Medina is by no means an obligation, even though many pilgrims will combine a stay in the second Holy City of the Hejaz with their pilgrimage to Mecca, and some will even affirm that they had a more profound religious experience in Medina. Before the nineteenth century most pilgrims who came to Medina probably visited the graves of members of the Prophet's family and those of various venerated figures from the first centuries of Islam, and many do so even today. But quite a few religious scholars disapprove of such visits, as detracting from the veneration due to God alone. Moreover, these visits have no connection with the pilgrimage itself. There is no cult of relics connected with the Ka'aba, even though many pilgrims expect certain blessings when they drink water from the well Zamzam located inside the Meccan sanctuary. Many religious scholars even disapprove of the popular custom of carrying back a bit of Meccan earth as a pilgrimage memento.[1]

THE PILGRIMAGE AS A SOCIAL AND POLITICAL PHENOMENON

The present study has a fairly modest aim. In the first place, it is meant to deal with the pilgrimage as a political and social, rather than a religious phenomenon. These different aspects were of course closely linked in real life; to quote just one example among thousands, the pilgrimage caravans travelled at a greater or lesser speed according to the amount of time left until the prayer meeting on the plateau of 'Arafat. For if that was missed, the entire pilgrimage was invalid, and the pilgrims' effort wasted. This latter consideration is without doubt a religious phenomenon, but greater speed on the part of tardy pilgrims might lead to a severe loss of camels. This, in turn, could give rise not only to economic difficulties, when replacements had to be purchased, but also to political conflict, if the caravan commander tried to force desert dwellers to supply the caravan with riding animals. We also need to keep in mind that pilgrims of the sixteenth century did not separate the economic and social aspects of their activities from the religious side, which to them doubtlessly constituted the essential reason for undergoing the trouble and sacrifices entailed by the journey. But for today's researcher, this division into socio-economic and religious domains is a great convenience, if only because religious and legal texts concerning the pilgrimage demand different skills from the researcher trying to evaluate them than do archival materials. Given the limitations of most specialists, including the present author, the two sets of skills are rarely encountered in the same person.

Secondly, we are concerned with a fairly limited period, namely the first two centuries of Ottoman control over the Hejaz. Our study begins in 922/1517, the year in which Sultan Selīm I conquered Cairo; for the purposes of this study, this event will be taken as the end of the medieval period and the beginning of the early modern age. The first two centuries of Ottoman control merit detailed study for a variety of reasons. First of all, we have become accustomed to view this period of extraordinary political and cultural florescence almost exclusively either from the perspective of Istanbul and the central Ottoman lands, or from the 'national history' point of view. In the latter perspective, Ottoman history is regarded as important because it forms a necessary preliminary to Syrian, Hungarian or of course Turkish national history. Yet such a perspective is especially inappropriate when applied to the pilgrimage cities of Mecca and Medina, whose enduring religious significance far outweighs their role in the formation of the modern state of which they form a part. In discussing relations of the Ottoman central government with a remote province, we are thus induced to study problems which have little relation to future nation building, but touch a number of issues crucial for the functioning of the Ottoman Empire during the sixteenth and seventeenth centuries.

TRAVEL AND COMMUNICATION

When we study the pilgrimage as a phenomenon of political and social history, it forms part of the history of human communication, of the transfer of both material and immaterial resources; the relative economic strengths and weaknesses of different regions also have a major part to play in such a model. Communication took place at different levels: on the basic level, the pilgrims during their stay in the Holy Cities had a unique opportunity to affirm their faith and to communicate this experience to their fellow pilgrims. The importance of this aspect emerges most clearly from the pilgrimage account of Ibn Djubayr, an Andalusian of the late twelfth century CE.[2] Less visible in the surviving sources, but certainly not of less importance, is the communication between returning pilgrims and their neighbours who did not have a chance to visit the Holy Cities. Remote little towns of fifteenth-century Anatolia often boasted very large numbers of people who called themselves hajjis, that is, returned pilgrims. For our purposes it is quite irrelevant whether these people had really been to Mecca. If they had not, if most hajjis owed their title to the fact that it had become part of a given name, or was accorded out of general respect for age and experience, the message was even clearer: the pilgrimage constituted something uniquely blessed and desirable, which people hoped their children might accomplish even if they themselves had not had the opportunity.[3] Or if an outlying Ottoman town somewhere in the Balkans housed a modest foundation benefiting the poor of Medina, this must have brought home to the townsmen that there was in fact such a city, with men and women living in it who no doubt spent their days in pious meditation. In an otherwise highly localized society, in which most people cultivated a garden and produced for a limited market, this message must have broadened horizons considerably.

The transfer of immaterial resources should be viewed in the same context: to the inhabitants not only of Cairo, but also of fairly remote Anatolian towns, the annual return of the pilgrims was a major event, to be celebrated by a procession that at times became so exuberant that the authorities issued prohibitions.[4] It would appear that the fellow townsmen of the pilgrims thought that the latter brought something valuable into the community, something that was worth welcoming by a special feast. And that this valuable, albeit immaterial resource was brought in from a distant place again counterbalanced all those elements in the lifestyle of Ottoman towns which made for extreme localization.

FOOD, PRECIOUS METALS AND POLITICS

Other transfers concerned material resources such as food and money. If twentieth-century historians dealing with the seventeenth-century rebel Ḳatırdjıoghlu have correctly read the evidence, this local magnate was well aware of the transfer aspect of the pilgrimage.[5] He was supposedly much opposed to the outflow of gold and silver carried to the Hejaz by the hajjis, and therefore robbed their caravans with special relish. Since we do not know who attributed this bullionist motivation to Ḳatırdjıoghlu, whether it was invented by his enemies or whether he himself espoused it, this story should not be made to carry the weight of excessive interpretation. But it can still serve as a warning that popular approval for the transfer of money and grain to the Hejaz was perhaps not as unanimous as one might assume.

In spite of the possibility of occasional protests, the transfer of gold, silver and grain to the Beduins of the Syrian and Arabian deserts and to the inhabitants of the Holy Cities continued apace. In the Ottoman core lands of Anatolia and Rumelia, gold was not much used even in the larger transactions of the townsmen, and European traders, too, mainly dealt in silver. Therefore the gold was probably supplied largely by the Ottoman government, which received it in the shape of tributes, or by the Egyptian treasury and Egyptian taxpayers; for in this province, access to the gold of Africa was easier than elsewhere. As we shall see, however, these resources sometimes were insufficient, and then silver was remitted, much to the dissatisfaction of the Hejazi recipients. This preference for gold may be connected with the growing importance in the commercial exchanges of the Arabian peninsula of Indian traders, who usually demanded payment in gold.[6]

In the Middle Ages, Mecca apparently sometimes received supplies from Yemen, but by the time of the Ottoman conquest, Egypt was almost the sole source of grain consumed in the Hejaz. In the later fifteenth century, when the Egyptian economy and particularly its agriculture were in crisis, this should have made food supplies in the Hejaz precarious.[7] Yet contemporary sources apparently did not regard the matter in those terms, or else the public foundations which supplied most of the grains exported to the Hejaz were under less fiscal pressure and therefore more productive than ordinary Egyptian villages. On the other hand, it is assumed that the first century of Ottoman rule over Egypt was a time in which abandoned villages were resettled, and population increased – but this fact is not reflected in the supply situation of Mecca, either: the chronicler Ḳuṭb al-Dīn complained of the declining yields of Egyptian foundation villages. Was Ḳuṭb al-Dīn a partisan of the Mamluks or simply an elderly man who thought everything was better in his youth, or is there something wrong with the assessments of present-day historians?[8]

The overwhelming importance of Egypt in supplying the Hejaz was due to the productivity of the region, and, more importantly, to the fact that water-borne transport was available most of the way. In spite of the atrocious reputation of Red Sea ships and their owners, documented from the twelfth up to the nineteenth century, land transport of major quantities of supplies was avoided as far as possible. This is true even though a large share of the grain was donated and not sold, making minimization of costs theoretically less important than in the commercial sector.[9] Presumably Syrian grain was of limited importance, as there was no Suez Canal – even though Ottoman administrators of the sixteenth century once planned to dig one, and the seventeenth-century traveller Ewliyā Čelebi waxed enthusiastic over the possibility of such an undertaking.[10] The spurts of activity observed in the town of Suez, which possessed a well-frequented port even though its lack of water made permanent habitation difficult, are nevertheless connected with the need to transport grain by ship.

ANCIENT PROBLEMS AND NEW DEPARTURES

Many of the problems of Ottoman administrators had confronted earlier rulers as well, and continue to demand solution today. To begin with, there was the question of supplies. Pilgrims normally were responsible for their own food, mounts and other necessities. But since the pilgrims could not possibly bring all they needed from their often remote home towns, the Ottoman administration had to ensure that they could purchase grain, blankets and riding gear along the way. Water had to be supplied in wells and cisterns along the main routes; this was not only a technical but also a political problem, as the Beduins inhabiting the desert equally needed water, and could not be persuaded to share it without some compensation. Pilgrims whose resources gave out had to be accorded some emergency aid; in the Holy Cities, a degree of provision had to be made for those people who were unable to find shelter for themselves, as well as for the sick. The safety of desert routes and sea lanes could not be procured by individuals at all, even though some groups, particularly the Maghribis, made efforts in that direction.

Certain solutions to these problems had been worked out before the Ottomans arrived, and were modified according to changing circumstances. Thus, even in Mamluk times, the needs of the permanent inhabitants of the Holy Cities had been taken care of by supplying them with grain from public foundations located in Egypt. But by the early sixteenth century these no longer sufficed, and new ones were instituted by Süleymān the Lawgiver, also known as the Magnificent, and some of his successors.[11] A contemporary chronicler indicated that this was due to declining tax yields in Egypt, but it is also possible that the number of pilgrims to Mecca increased during the expansive years of the mid-sixteenth century. A quite new problem, on the other hand, was posed by the Ottoman *'ilmiye* (juridical and religious scholars), who by the sixteenth century had become strongly bureaucratized. The *ḳāḍī*s of Mecca and Medina were high-level functionaries of an imperial state whose centre was situated thousands of miles away. To a member of the religious and juridical establishment of the time, taking a position in the Hejaz might appear as an obstacle to further advancement. To ensure that officials of standing accepted these positions nonetheless, in the seventeenth century former *ḳāḍī*s of the Holy Cities were offered special inducements in the form of seniority rights, which allowed many of these high-level officials rapid promotion after their return from the Hejaz.[12] Thus Ottoman rule meant both novel departures and the continuation of policies devised centuries before, and this imbrication of old and new arrangements will be a recurrent topic of the present study.

PILGRIMS AND RULERS: THE PROBLEM OF LEGITIMACY

All pilgrims, both male and female, were responsible for their own sustenance during the pilgrimage. Therefore, wives could not demand to be taken along as a matter of course if their husbands decided to travel to the Hejaz. In the *ḳāḍī* registers of certain Ottoman towns we occasionally find wives who promised their husbands a piece of property in return for being taken along on the pilgrimage.[13] Sometimes we also encounter the complaints of women who had been abandoned en route in spite of such a payment. Even for wealthy inhabitants of Anatolian or Rumelian towns, a pilgrimage entailed grave financial sacrifices. Wealthy people tried to earn extra money by taking along trade goods, while poor pilgrims were sometimes reduced to beggary. In case of calamities such as droughts, food scarcities and Beduin attacks, many pilgrims perished of thirst, hunger and exposure.

As long as the Ummayad and Abbasid caliphs held power (661–750 and 750–1258 CE), these rulers claimed the protection of the pilgrims as both a duty and a right. This function involved the setting of rules the pilgrims were expected to follow. In extreme cases the caliph might even proclaim that no pilgrimage would take place in a given year, and absolve the faithful from their obligation for the time being. This happened in 1047 and 1048 CE, when a famine in the Hejaz made it impossible to accommodate any further influx of people. But whether such an admission of failure undermined the legitimacy of the ruling caliph remains an open question.[14]

From the sixteenth century onward, the failure of a pilgrimage caravan to reach Mecca and return home safely constituted a severe political liability to the Sultan currently occupying the Ottoman throne. The same applied to major Beduin attacks or uprisings in the Holy Cities. To put it differently, such events occasioned a crisis of legitimacy. Sultanic legitimacy was also upheld by the construction and repair of pious foundations. The mere right to put up public buildings in Mecca and Medina was considered a privilege.[15] The local rulers of Mecca (known as Sherifs due to their descent from the Prophet Muḥammad), who controlled the city's day-to-day destinies from the tenth to the twentieth century, in pre-Ottoman times demanded a fee from every aspiring donor which equalled the sum of money to be spent on the construction itself. This state of affairs indicates a degree of competition between the Sherifs and their suzerains the Sultans residing in Cairo until 1517, and in Istanbul thereafter. Many Mamluk and Ottoman Sultans were surely motivated by reasons of personal piety when they put up magnificent buildings in Mecca and Medina. But, in addition, they were also staking their claim to a preeminent political position in the Holy Cities. Construction activities therefore are treated at some length in this book, which focuses on the ways and means of legitimizing sultanic power through the pilgrimage.

Ottoman Sultans' activities and responsibilities in the Hejaz are discussed in official documents with some frequency, but practically no texts have come to my attention which link the Sultan's role in this matter to his responsibilities as caliph. While the example of certain Mamluk Sultans is sometimes cited, Ottoman documents of the sixteenth and seventeenth centuries never evoke the image of Hārūn al-Rashīd and his consort Zubayda, who built the water conduits that Ottoman Sultans spent much time and money repairing. This is all the more remarkable as the munificence of the royal couple Süleymān the Lawgiver and Khurrem Sultan (Roxolana), who instituted major foundations in Mecca and Medina, would seem to have invited such a comparison. Ottoman official discourse was oriented toward the present and recent past, rather than toward the already very remote history of early Islam.

The annual preparation of the pilgrimage and public construction in the Holy Cities were very costly; and for at least part of the year they also demanded the concerted efforts of numerous Ottoman officials. We may visualize pilgrimage affairs as a set of interlocking mechanisms, whose component parts were meant to balance one another. Thus the Sherif in Ottoman times was allowed many of the trappings of an independent ruler, but his authority was counterbalanced by the Ottoman governor of Jeddah, a highly prestigious official. The Ottoman central administration instituted a complicated set of measures, some of which (such as gifts and tax exemptions) were meant to ensure the support of Beduins residing near the pilgrimage route.[16] Free deliveries of grain secured the cooperation of the year-round inhabitants of the Holy Cities. These measures could only be effective if their application was properly supervised, and the bureaucratic positions needed for this purpose were a source of patronage and therefore a further means of mobilizing support.

When the linkages between different socio-political groups and fields of activity were so numerous, a single failure could make the whole mechanism grind to a standstill. If gifts to Beduin tribes along the desert routes were omitted or not paid in full, or if disputes within the provincial governments of Egypt or Syria prevented the mobilization of support to the caravan from among the desert tribes, the pilgrims had to prepare to protect themselves – and they did not always succeed in doing this.[17] If discontented Beduins attacked the caravans, food scarcities in Mecca and Medina might be the result, and the pilgrims also suffered; for in the case of shortages, the locals often were better placed to secure supplies. Similar problems occurred when the Beduins and their camels were decimated by droughts and epidemics. Not only were needed supplies held back in Jeddah or Yanbu', but desperate men were likely to attack caravans and thus contribute to the general insecurity. The whole set-up could only work if the Ottoman administration kept on channelling resources even from remote territories to the Hejaz and the Red Sea region.

At the same time this mechanism – an exchange of gifts and prestations linking not only Istanbul, but also settlements on the Rumelian frontier with Mecca and Medina – also served as a powerful integrating device. In pre-industrial societies it was usually difficult to set up a governing apparatus affordable by the as yet weakly developed productive forces of the society in question, and yet strong enough to hold together a large territory. Viewed from Istanbul, the state apparatus for the support of the pilgrimage had the great virtue of being flexible and multi-purpose. The Ottoman state protected the pilgrimage because this was an activity demanded by the Muslim religion, and because this protection legitimized the Sultan. At the same time, through the soldiers and foundation officials that were sent to the Hejaz to ensure the safety of pilgrims, the Ottoman state maintained a presence in some of its most remote border provinces. Often control was loose; sometimes it was almost symbolic. The Ottoman state nonetheless managed to maintain itself in the Hejaz with only one fairly brief interruption during the Wahabi wars of the early nineteenth century, and the mechanisms supporting the pilgrimage significantly contributed to this success.

A study dealing with the views and policies of the Ottoman central administration with respect to the hajj inevitably touches upon the images and representations then current in the upper reaches of Ottoman society, and from there diffused into the population at large. The Sultan, as a generous benefactor of the inhabitants of Mecca and Medina and as the organizer and protector of the pilgrimage, constituted a dominant image. This imparts a special colouring to even mundane matters such as the clogged water pipes leading from 'Arafat to Mecca, and a certain unity to the changing policies of Sultans and viziers. Large sums of money were spent upon the pilgrimage every year, and most of these expenditures yielded no economic return. This fact alone indicates that the Sultan's title 'Servant of the Holy Places' was more than a matter of rhetoric, and formed an important aspect of the Ottoman state's legitimation *vis à vis* the society it governed.

SOURCES

A discussion of these issues becomes possible because, by the middle of the sixteenth century, the Ottoman Empire possessed a developed bureaucratic structure and well-functioning state archives.[18] Everyday issues concerning food supplies, military security, public construction and many other matters were documented at length; and the Registers of Important Affairs (Mühimme Defterleri) in the Ottoman archives in Istanbul contain hundreds of sultanic commands concerned in one way or another with pilgrimage affairs. Some of these valuable sources have been used in specialized articles, often published in conference proceedings difficult to locate even for the specialist, but most of the Ottoman archival material concerning the pilgrimage has remained completely untouched so far.

From the beginning of the Registers of Important Affairs in the middle of the sixteenth century down to 1018/1609–10, more than fifty volumes were found to contain material on the hajj, on an average ten rescripts to each register. More often than might be expected, the rescripts preserved in the Mühimme Defterleri contain quantitative data, such as the sums of money spent on various repair and rebuilding projects in and around the Great Mosque of Mecca. Even more significant are the accounts of negotiations which preceded political action in the Hejaz, and which inform us of the manner in which the Ottoman administration bargained for political support in the Red Sea region.

Many pilgrimage-related activities were financed out of the resources of Egypt and Syria, and are thus documented in provincial financial accounts, of which we possess a few samples from late-sixteenth century Egypt and a larger number from seventeenth-century Syria. These documents contain information on the military expenditures connected with the caravan. Particular attention was paid to the soldiers' equipment, such as the cannons regarded as indispensable for any desert campaign. Moreover, the Ottoman administration's attempt to obtain a measure of control over the numerous endowments supporting the poor of Mecca and Medina resulted in the compilation of inventories which list all the relevant foundations existing at the end of the sixteenth century. These inventories mention the revenues each foundation was expected to send to the Hejaz, and thus allow us to assess the contribution of different regions to the hajj effort.

Among narrative accounts, our main source is the pilgrimage report of Ewliyā Čelebi.[19] Strangely enough, this text has all but escaped the attention of historians, although many other sections of his great travel narrative have been studied intensively. On the surface, Ewliyā's account is intended to help pilgrims fulfil their religious duties, and therefore occasionally mentions the prayers to recite at the various stations in a pilgrim's itinerary. Like the other sections of his narrative, however, Ewliyā's account of his pilgrimage concentrates upon a description of the larger cities and their inhabitants. Here are the experiences of a vibrant and adventurous Ottoman gentleman among Beduins, robbers and doughty pashas, and the serious purpose of the pilgrimage does not prevent him from describing humorous or satirical scenes.

A unique narrative account is that of Süheylī.[20] About his life nothing is known, except that he was a Damascene or Syrian living in the seventeenth century. He has left an account, in straightforward Ottoman, of the restoration of the Ka'aba under Sultan Murād IV, after the building had collapsed in a disastrous rainstorm in 1039/ 1630. Süheylī gives a stone-by-stone account of what happened on the site during the construction period, but also describes the manner in which the Egyptian official Ridwān Beg, who headed the project, managed to short-circuit all opposition to his way of running the affair; if Süheylī's impression is correct, the Istanbul authorities avoided all direct involvement.

Another important narrative source is the life story of Mehmed Agha, one of the two full-length biographies of Ottoman architects of the classical period.[21] This text has recently become available in English. The author is a certain Dja'fer Efendi, about whom we know almost nothing except that his father was named Shaykh Behrām and that he belonged to Mehmed Agha's clientele. In Dja'fer Efendi's account, Mehmed Agha is described in a style vaguely reminiscent of popular hagiography. For our purposes the biography is important because Mehmed Agha was responsible for major restorations in Mecca, and Dja'fer Agha presents certain clues concerning the manner in which educated Ottomans regarded projects of this kind. A poem in praise of Medina, which concludes the chapter on Mehmed Agha's activities in the Holy Cities, is also of interest in this context.

In the following chapter we will accompany some of the more famous pilgrims of the Middle Ages, particularly Ibn Djubayr, the twelfth-century Andalusian who has left a most detailed and lively description of his experiences in the Hejaz. This will give us the opportunity to discuss the major elements of the pilgrimage ritual and the localities which the pilgrims visited. This brief account of medieval pilgrimages is intended, however, as a mere backdrop for a discussion of the sixteenth and seventeenth centuries, in which pilgrims such as Ewliyā Čelebi and Meḥmed Edīb, provincial administrators such as the Egyptian Mamluk Riḍwān Beg, and rulers such as Süleymān the Lawgiver (1520–66) and Aḥmed I (1603–17) constitute the focus of our attention.[22]

1

The Pilgrimage to Mecca in Pre-Ottoman Times

With the expansion of the islamicate empire under the first four caliphs (632–61 CE) and the Ummayad dynasty (661–750 CE), an area reaching from Spain to Iran had come under Muslim sway.[1] The centre of this empire was first located in Medina, but soon moved to Damascus. The conquerors were all Muslims, and many members of the conquered people soon adopted their religion. Even though the islamization of the Iranian ruling class was not complete until the end of the eighth century, a multitude of pilgrims from a variety of linguistic and cultural backgrounds were already arriving in Mecca by the end of the seventh century CE. The area from which pilgrims travelled to Mecca expanded even further during the subsequent centuries: in the tenth century Maḥmūd of Ghazni, famed for the support which he gave to the poet Ferdosi, conquered part of northern India. The islamization of large numbers of Central Asian Turks also took place during this period. In the thirteenth century, the Mongol conquests at first resulted in a setback, as Chingiz Khan and his immediate successors did not adopt Islam, while favouring non-Muslims as a counterweight to entrenched Muslim elites. But, in the long run, the Mongols established in the Middle East did adopt Islam, while the Tatars, who dominated Russia for several centuries, also became Muslims. The islamicate world thus expanded impressively in the aftermath of the Mongol conquests. A fifteenth-century pilgrim crowd in Mecca would have included, apart from Arabs and Iranians, Turks from Anatolia and the Balkans, Tatars from what is today southern Russia, Central Asians, Indians and even the occasional African king.

13

A POET'S PILGRIMAGE HANDBOOK

For the history of the pilgrimage in the medieval period down to 1517, the accounts of travellers constitute the most important sources. These texts were written with a practical purpose in mind, namely to help a pilgrim find his way to the sanctuaries and perform the pilgrimage rites in a correct and dignified manner. Many of these accounts contain historical information, much of it referring to the major mosques. This historical and art historical detail was not considered in any way frivolous or futile. Events such as the activities of the Prophet and his companions were of major significance to the believer. Therefore the pilgrimage guides should be regarded both as pious works and as descriptions of actions and things located in time and space. Religious motivation and minute attention to mundane detail in no way excluded one another. Unfortunately, the pilgrimage accounts almost never contain information permitting us to estimate the number of people participating.

The poet Naṣīr-i Khosraw, who lived in the eleventh century CE, has left a detailed account of his pilgrimage.[2] Naṣīr-i Khosraw came from the town of Balkh in modern Afghanistan, and undertook the pilgrimage after a major religious experience, which induced him to transform his hitherto rather worldly style of life. While visiting Egypt, he was greatly impressed by the florescence this country experienced under the Fāṭimid caliphs. He converted to the Ismā'īlī version of Shi'ism which the Fāṭimids propounded, and ultimately achieved high rank in the spiritual hierarchy of this faith. Naṣīr-i Khosraw's first visit to Mecca fell in the year 1047, a time of drought and famine. Not only the Hejaz but Iraq was affected, so that outside support was not forthcoming, and no pilgrimage caravan could be sent. The Fāṭimid ruler dispatched an embassy, no more, to escort the covering for the Ka'aba, which even at this early period was sent every year from Cairo, and Naṣīr-i Khosraw formed part of this embassy. After crossing the Red Sea, the travellers visited the Prophet's mosque in Medina, then followed the pilgrimage route through the desert. They found the Holy City all but abandoned, but as the time for the hajj had just arrived, Naṣīr-i Khosraw was able to perform the rites of the pilgrimage. Yet the calamities of that year permitted no more than a short stay; the author admits to having spent but two days in Medina, and he probably remained no longer in Mecca than strictly necessary. He was able to return in later years, however, and his pilgrimage account refers to his second, more leisurely visit.

Naṣīr-i Khosraw's intention is to provide orientation to the pilgrim with no previous experience of the Holy City, and he therefore begins with an account of its geographical location. He then discusses the manner in which the city fits into the landscape. His description leads us to the walls which close off the wadis leading into Mecca and the very few trees growing within the city limits. He also evokes the hills of Ṣafā and Marwa, between which the pilgrims rush back and forth, thereby completing an essential part of the ritual – which is discussed in detail, so that the pilgrim knows where to go at different stages of his visit. Naṣīr's account also includes the hospices of Mecca and provides information about water supplies, presumably with practical purposes in mind. At the same time, he avoids any discussion of his personal religious experience.

After returning from the pilgrimage, Naṣīr-i K̲h̲osraw led an adventurous life in the service of the Fāṭimids and their particular variety of Shi'ism; in the end he was killed in the mountains of Badakhshan. But for many other scholars and literati, the pilgrimage was the beginning of a more conventional career. In Neyshapur, during the eleventh and twelfth centuries, scholars often visited Mecca before embarking on careers as teachers and judges. For these people, the pilgrimage was an occasion on which to visit centres of Islamic learning, and pursue their studies in Islamic law and the Prophet's words and deeds (*ḥadīth*). Some of them also taught for a while in the mosques and theological schools (*madrasa*) of the cities they visited, the caliphal city of Bag̲h̲dad being especially popular in this respect. Upon their return to Neyshapur, these scholars, who were usually the scions of prominent families, had gained additional prestige due to their knowledge and piety, even though the hajj was not an indispensable precondition for an official career.[3] Unfortunately, we do not possess a pilgrimage account by a Neyshapuri traveller. All our information stems from brief notices in the biographical dictionaries of the time, whose aim was not to provide a record of pilgrimage and travel, but to document the reliability of individual scholars in the transfer of religious knowledge throughout the centuries. We therefore have no way of knowing what the Neyshapuri scholars brought home as their most important experiences.

ON THE ROAD TO MECCA

Matters are somewhat different when we turn to the pilgrimage account of Abū'l-Ḥusayn Muḥammad b. D̲j̲ubayr, usually known as Ibn D̲j̲ubayr.[4] He was a courtier and secretary in the service of the governor of Granada, and famed for his literary talents. But while participating in court life he had allowed himself to be persuaded to drink wine, and afterwards he much regretted this breach of Islamic law. His patron was moved by Ibn Djubayr's scruples, and not only gave him leave to undertake the pilgrimage, but also a generous allowance for his expenses.

Ibn Djubayr's pilgrimage was quite dramatic. In 1183 he travelled to the Moroccan city of Ceuta, where he embarked on a Genoese ship which took him to Alexandria in Egypt. He probably chose a Genoese ship because, during the period of the crusades, the Italian cities dominated Mediterranean trade and their ships were thus comparatively secure from pirate attacks. This use of European ships by Muslim pilgrims from the western Mediterranean was to persist throughout the centuries. Even in the seventeenth century, Algerians, Tunisians and Tripolitanians often travelled on English or French ships as far as Alexandria, and then joined the pilgrimage caravan in Cairo.[5] When Ibn Djubayr arrived in Egypt, the country was governed by Sultan Saladin (Ṣalāḥ al-Dīn Ayyūbī), who much impressed the author by his energetic rule and generous programme of public construction. Ibn Djubayr then journeyed to the Upper Egyptian port of Aydhāb, which at that time was still a major commercial centre, though it was to lose most of its importance by the fifteenth century.[6]

Ibn Djubayr's impressions of Aydhab and its inhabitants were mostly negative. An account of the pearl fisheries located near the city he concludes with the words: 'But indeed these folk are closer to wild beasts than they are to men.'[7] His bad impressions were probably prompted by the treatment meted out to pilgrims: the ships on which the latter were made to cross the Red Sea were always perilously overloaded, so that the passengers were squeezed together like chickens in a basket. In this fashion, the owners of the boats attempted to maximize their earnings without any regard for the safety of the passengers: some even said in so many words that the owner only provided the ship, responsibility for safe arrival resting with the passengers alone. Ibn Djubayr warns all pilgrims against the use of this route and suggests a long detour as an alternative. A pilgrim coming from the western Mediterranean region is advised to travel first to Baghdad by way of Syria, and continue his journey with the Baghdad pilgrimage caravan. 'And should he find this circling road to be too long, it will be easy in comparison with what he would meet in Aydhab and places like it.'[8] Ibn Djubayr also mentions a pilgrimage route near the coast, which led from Egypt to the Sinai and from there to Medina by way of 'Aqaba, and which probably corresponded to the route followed by seventeenth-century Egyptian pilgrims. In Ibn Djubayr's time, however, this route was impassable due to a Frankish crusader castle located nearby.

Ibn Djubayr's short voyage across the Red Sea was so troublesome that his negative reactions are easy to understand. (On his return journey, he did in fact travel by way of Baghdad, although we do not know whether this decision was motivated by security considerations alone.) Shortly before landing in Jeddah, his ship was caught in a severe storm and swept off its course, so that eight days were needed to cover the short distance between Aydhab and Jeddah. Nor were the pilgrims' troubles at an end once they reached the port of Mecca, which at that time was still a modest settlement with houses built mostly of reeds. Ibn D̲jubayr complains bitterly about the inhabitants of the Hejaz, who for the most part ruthlessly exploited the pilgrims and used all manner of stratagems to deprive them of their food and money. His worst experiences were with the amir of Mecca. Sultan Saladin at this time was trying to alleviate the difficulties of the pilgrims by assigning the amir grants of money and foodstuffs. In return, the amir was to forgo the customs duties he had hitherto demanded from pilgrims. The amir however viewed the pilgrims as no more than a source of revenue which he was legitimately entitled to exploit, and when Sultan Saladin's grant was slow to arrive, the wealthy traveller from Andalusia seemed as good a substitute as any. Ibn D̲jubayr was detained, and he and his companions were made to serve as hostages to guarantee the continuing prestation of Egyptian wheat and money. This experience caused Ibn D̲jubayr to pen a few harsh comments on the Shi'i beliefs of the Hejazis, whom he regarded as heretics. He wished that their lands might be conquered by the Spanish Sunni dynasty of the Muwahhidun/Almohads, and the inhabitants themselves be punished for their numerous sins and heretical practices. Yet even when expressing his anger, Ibn D̲jubayr uses moderation. Certainly the amir of Mecca acted unjustly and, as a ruler, was much inferior to Sultan Saladin of Egypt. Even so, he remained a descendant of the Prophet Muḥammad and, as such, was respected by the pious Ibn D̲jubayr.[9]

THE RITES OF THE PILGRIMAGE

On the short trip from Jeddah to Mecca, the company of pilgrims stopped to change into pilgrims' garb (*iḥrām*). This has remained more or less unchanged since the Prophet's time, and for men consists of two seamless pieces of white cloth. One of them covers the loins, reaching down to the knee; the other is worn on the shoulder.[10] The pilgrims wear sandals that leave the instep bare, or, if unavoidable, ordinary shoes. There are no special features to the women pilgrims' garb. The English traveller Richard Burton, who saw mid-nineteenth-century women pilgrims, remarks that the face covering should not touch the face and that the women therefore wore masks made out of palm leaves; but present-day photographs show that almost all pilgrims leave their faces uncovered.[11] Many theologians believe that this uniform garb symbolizes the equality of all believers in the sight of God.

Pilgrim behaviour is governed by a set of rules which emphasize the special status of the Mecca pilgrim. According to many theologians, these rules express the pilgrims' separation from wordly concerns and their complete dedication to God. The most important rule is the prohibition against killing living beings of any kind, apart from the ritual sacrifice at the end of the pilgrimage. Hunting is accordingly forbidden, and armed men through the centuries have expressed their peaceful intentions by entering the Holy City wearing the *iḥrām*. Marital relations and even the conclusion of marriage contracts are likewise prohibited, and the same applies to disputes and discussions. No perfumes are to be used, nor are pilgrims to cut their hair or their nails. Men are required to let their beards grow. Bathing is permitted, and the pilgrims take a bath before donning the *iḥrām*. At the end of the pilgrimage, when the pilgrim, now a hajji, reenters ordinary life, he cuts his hair, beard and nails.

For the rites of pilgrimage to be valid, pilgrims have to make a declaration of intent stating whether they wish to undertake the hajj or merely the lesser pilgrimage or *'umra*. The hajj, which includes a visit to the 'Arafat as mentioned above, can only be performed once a year; most pilgrims coming to Mecca from afar have this purpose in mind. The time for the pilgrimage is the ninth day of the twelfth month of the Islamic lunar year, known as Dhū al-Ḥidjdja. The *'umra* rites are limited to the perimeter of Mecca and can be undertaken at any time of the year.

Ibn Djubayr and his companions donned the *iḥrām* at a predetermined spot between Jeddah and Mecca. Pilgrims arriving from other directions also knew exactly where they were to change into pilgrims' clothing. The seventeenth-century Ottoman traveller Ewliyā Čelebi approached Mecca from the direction of Medina and stated that the pilgrims of his time put on the *iḥrām* in a place called Bi'r 'Alī, not very far from Medina.[12] Today, pilgrims who travel to Mecca from Medina change their clothing in Dhū al-Ḥulayfa, sometimes called Ābār 'Alī, which is probably identical with Ewliyā Čelebi's Bi'r 'Alī. Pilgrims who wish to avoid the discomfort of travelling through the desert dressed only in an *iḥrām* can wear their ordinary clothes until they get to the locality known as Makām al-'Umra. They are, however, expected to compensate for this indulgence by a supplementary sacrifice. Pilgrimage guides, who showed the new arrivals the rites and sites as their successors do to the present day, came to Makām al-'Umra to meet their charges. In Ewliyā's time there was a pond at this place, which received water by means of a water wheel and was surrounded by rooms in which pilgrims could refresh themselves. This complex was still rather new, having been founded by a governor of Egypt in 1662–3, less than ten years before Ewliyā's visit. Pilgrims approaching the Holy City by sea donned the *iḥrām* in a place about the same distance away from Mecca as the locations in which this ceremony is performed today. Those who arrived from the south changed into the *iḥrām* when they first saw Mount Yalamlam, which lies about 54 kilometres to the south of Mecca.

THE KA'ABA

Ibn Djubayr has left a most vivid account of the pious emotions of the pilgrims when they entered Mecca and saw the Ka'aba for the first time.[13] It was already night, and from all sides he heard prayers and invocations of God, particularly the 'here my God, here I am' which forms part of the ritual used on this occasion. After entering the mosque, the pilgrims circumambulated the Ka'aba seven times and touched its covering at a certain place, hoping for an answer to their prayers. If in spite of the crowd it was possible to approach the Black Stone, they kissed it. 'Alī b. Abī Bakr al-Ḥarawī, a contemporary of Ibn Djubayr, has left a matter-of-fact description of the Mecca and Medina sanctuaries.[14] He includes an account of the history of the building, which was a matter of interest to Muslim scholars and on which a considerable body of evidence had therefore been collected. His 'Inventory of Pilgrimage Sites' recounts that the original Ka'aba was built by the Prophet Ibrāhīm. This building remained more or less in its original state until one of the most important tribes of Mecca, namely the Kuraysh, rebuilt it in the seventh century, at the time of the Prophet Muḥammad. The latter was himself a member of the Kuraysh. It was assumed that he had intervened in person by solving a dispute over precedence which concerned the placing of the Black Stone, one of the most important elements of the structure.

During the civil wars of the early Ummayad period the Ka'aba was burned down. Ibn Zubayr, who for a time reigned as caliph in Mecca, rebuilt and enlarged it. The structure now could be entered by two doors; but when Ibn Zubayr had been deposed by the Ummayad governor al-Ḥadjdjādj, the latter tore down what his defeated rival had constructed and rebuilt the Ka'aba according to what was known of the building which had existed in the time of the Prophet Muḥammad. This new building was smaller than its predecessor, one of the doors had been walled up, and the floor was covered with stones taken from the previous building. The new structure thus was four cubits higher than ground level. This was the building seen by Ibn Djubayr and al-Harawī. In later times, however, the Ka'aba was to undergo extensive repairs, which in one case amounted to a total reconstruction. With this aspect of the Ka'aba's history, which coincided with the reigns of the Ottoman Sultans Ahmed I and Murād IV (1603–17 and 1623–40), we will deal in Chapter 5.

When Ibn Djubayr visited the Ka'aba, the building was richly decorated with the precious gifts of various Muslim rulers.[15] The door and its posts were made of silver gilt, while the lintel was of pure gold. The interior was decorated in coloured marble, and three teak columns supported the roof. A silver band surrounded the building on the outside. The flat and slightly inclined roof, as well as the walls, were covered with fine tissues of silk and cotton cloth. In Ibn Djubayr's time, the covering of the Ka'aba was green and set off with red bands, decorated with the name of the caliph then reigning, al-Nāṣir li-Dīn Allāh (1180–1225).[16] One of the last Abbasids to play an active political role, he attempted to reorganize the *fityān*, associations of pugnacious young men recruited from among the poorer city dwellers, as a base of his own power. Al-Nāṣir's name, mentioned in highly visible form as servitor of the Holy Places (*khadīm al-haramayn*) was noted by pious visitors like Ibn Djubayr, and his symbolic presence at the Ka'aba considerably enhanced his political reputation. He did not, however, succeed in his attempt to establish himself as ruler of Mecca and Medina in a more concrete political sense.

Ibn Djubayr also visited the stone on which Ibrāhīm supposedly stood when building the Ka'aba. A small annexe had been specially built to accommodate it: Ibn Djubayr informs us that originally it had been kept in a separate wooden building, then transferred to this annexe for its better protection. The Andalusian pilgrim has also left a detailed description of the other buildings in the courtyard of the Great Mosque. Thus, even though his visit was not a part of obligatory pilgrimage ritual, he described the well Zamzam, whose water is highly esteemed and considered a cure for many diseases. After refreshing themselves at the well, Ibn Djubayr and his companions undertook the seven ritual courses between the hills of Safā and Marwa, both located within the city proper. These courses serve as a commemoration of the plight of Hādjar/Hagar, after she had been cast out of the household of Ibrāhīm along with her infant son Ismā'īl, and reduced to a desperate search for water to keep her son and herself alive. With this rite, the *'umra* or lesser pilgrimage was at an end.

As the time of the hajj was as yet several months away, the pilgrims changed into their ordinary clothes, and began their lives as temporary residents of the Holy City. The pilgrims could repeat the *'umra* whenever they felt the desire to do so; in that case, they left the city and travelled to the spot where the regular inhabitants of Mecca donned the *iḥrām*. Being a wealthy man, Ibn Djubayr could afford to make himself comfortable while waiting for the month of the pilgrimage. He participated in local festivities and apparently liked the sweetmeats on sale in Mecca, as he confesses that he spent a lot of money in the confectioners' shops. His appartment was well-appointed, and offered a spectacular view of the Great Mosque and the Ka'aba. Ibn Djubayr probably used these months to collect the information on the buildings of Mecca which served to make his account into our principal source for the medieval pilgrimage.

THE HAJJ CEREMONIES

The Islamic calendar is lunar; the dates of religious festivals are determined on the basis of statements on the part of credible witnesses, who testify that they did in fact observe the new moon. In 1184, when Ibn Djubayr was in the Hejaz, the determination was more difficult than it normally is in the latitude of Mecca. At the time the new moon should have appeared, the sky was overcast and nothing was visible. On the other hand, many pilgrims ardently wished for the ritual 'station' on 'Arafat (*wakfa*), the plateau to the east of Mecca, to take place on a Friday. For a saying attributed to the Prophet Muḥammad promises that whenever this central ritual of the pilgrimage, which takes place on the ninth day of Dhū al-Ḥidjdja, falls on a Friday, the pilgrims can expect much greater blessings than in an ordinary year. Therefore quite a few people came forward claiming to have seen the new moon, even though, physically speaking, this was an impossibility. The *ḳāḍī* of Mecca insisted on rejecting their testimonies, and was not exactly gentle with the over-zealous witnesses.[17] Apparently he commented that 'those Maghribis [several of the claimants were Maghribis] are deranged. A hair escapes from their eyelashes, they see something, and immediately they think it to be the new moon.' Ibn Djubayr approved of the *ḳāḍī*'s attitude, as he thought the pilgrimage was not amenable to what he felt to be frivolous manipulation. In his view, the pilgrims' devotion was bound to suffer if even minor details were not handled with the appropriate seriousness. In the end the *ḳāḍī* devised a compromise which satisfied both sides. He ordered the ritual station on the 'Arafat to begin on Friday afternoon and continue into Saturday.

Just before the day appointed for the *wakfa*, new groups of pilgrims entered the Holy City. Ibn Djubayr mentions the Yemenis and a

former prince of Aden recently deposed.[18] On the 7 D̲h̲ū al-Ḥidjdja a
messenger arrived from the Iraqi pilgrimage caravan which was still
on its way. Thereupon the *ḳāḍī* preached a solemn sermon in front of
the pilgrims assembled in the city, in which he explained the ritual of
the hajj. He announced that on the next day the caravan would move
to Mina, the first stop on the way to 'Arafat. On Thursday a large
crowd set out; however the pilgrims hurried more than seemed
desirable to Ibn D̲j̲ubayr, as there was a constant danger of being
attacked by Beduin marauders. As western Catholics of the fourteenth century felt few scruples when they enslaved Greek Christians,
and many Beduins, even though they had been Muslims for centuries,
did not hesitate to rob unwary pilgrims on their way to and from the
sanctuary. Travellers who attempted to resist were often killed.
Whoever claimed to rule the Hejaz, therefore, above everything else
needed to protect the pilgrims from attack. According to Ibn
D̲j̲ubayr's testimony, the ruling amir of Mecca was quite successful in
this task – which legitimized him in the eyes of the Andalusian
traveller and, no doubt, in the view of a wider public.

The pilgrims spent their first night after leaving Mecca in an
uninhabited locality called Muzdalifa where there was an abundant
supply of water. This was due to the munificence of Hārūn al-
Ras̲h̲īd's wife Zubayda, who in the ninth century had built a number
of water reservoirs in this place. The 'Arafat plateau was reached the
next day. At this locality, surmounted by the 'Mount of Mercy'
(D̲j̲abal al-Raḥmat), the pilgrims prayed in a number of mosques or at
prayer niches in the open air. Here the assembly which constitutes the
core of the pilgrimage took place. Ibn D̲j̲ubayr says very little about
this event, so that we have to supplement his story with other, much
more recent information. According to the Ottoman traveller Ewliyā
Čelebi, who participated in the 'station' at 'Arafat in 1672, the
pilgrims prayed in the Mosque of Ibrāhīm and waited on the plateau
for the *ḳāḍī* of Mecca to begin his solemn sermon.[19] In Ewliyā's time,
the pilgrims assembled according to their region of origin; the
Anatolians to the west, the Abyssinians, Yemenis, Iraqis and Hejazis
at other prearranged places. This custom was already centuries old
when Ewliyā Čelebi wrote, for Ibn D̲j̲ubayr also noted that the
Yemenis assembled by tribe, and that no tribe ever transgressed on
the territory assigned to another.[20] Both Ibn D̲j̲ubayr and Ewliyā were
full of admiration for the large number of pilgrims who had
assembled on 'Arafat. Ibn D̲j̲ubayr particularly mentions the non-
Arabs of high rank, both men and women. But unfortunately neither
of these two writers, nor any other travellers from the time before the
nineteenth century, have made an attempt to estimate the number of
participants.

To ensure the validity of the *wakfa* on 'Arafat, it was necessary to adhere to certain rules. The territory known as 'Arafat, where the pilgrims absolutely needed to sojourn, was set off from the outside world by a line of boundary stones. The time factor was also significant, as apparent from the dispute between the *kadi* of Mecca and the over-zealous Maghribis. It was essential that the pilgrims arrive at 'Arafat on time, that is while the preacher was still speaking. Ewliyā recounts how for that very reason his own caravan pressed forward in hurried marches, spending only the briefest possible time in Medina. That year, the Basra caravan was also in trouble; 1671–2 fell in a period of widespread political tension, and in such years Beduin tribes tended to be especially aggressive. The Basra pilgrimage caravan was set upon, but reinforcements sent from Mecca helped to repel the attackers. The unlucky caravan almost missed the meeting at 'Arafat. 'They [the Basra pilgrims] entered [the site of 'Arafat] at the boundary stones [marking off the site in the direction of] Iraq. They also brought along their dead to the *wakfa*. Thank God, they were able to perform their pilgrimage: If they had arrived but a short time later, it would have been invalid.'[21]

At the beginning of the meeting, many people called out 'Here my God, here I am', and Ewliyā says that this continued for an hour. According to the same source, the *kadi*'s sermon concerned the further course of the pilgrimage. The pilgrims were instructed how to behave when sacrificing and throwing stones at the rocks of Mina, which in this context symbolize the devil. When the sermon ended, the pilgrims hurriedly left the site of the meeting. As it was already turning dark, this procedure gave rise to a certain amount of confusion. At Muzdalifa the pilgrims assembled for another ritual 'station', which this time took place by night and was particularly impressive due to the many candles lit by the Khorasanis. The pilgrims collected pebbles which they would need the next day for the stoning of the devil. Most pilgrims left Muzdalifa by night so as to perform the morning prayer in Mina and subsequently throw their seven stones against a specially designated rock. After that, those who could afford it sacrificed an animal, and thereby fulfilled their religious obligations for the day.

Ibn Djubayr does not tell us how the pilgrims spent their free time in Mina.[22] Today it is customary for pilgrims to return to Mecca, which is close by, and to circle the Ka'aba seven times (*tawāf al-ifāda*) before taking off the pilgrim's garb.[23] The men shave, and everybody returns to Mina dressed in his or her best clothes. However, both Ibn Djubayr and Ewliyā Čelebi are describing pilgrimages performed in unsettled times, in which people may have put off their visit to the Ka'aba to the time of their final return to the Holy City.

In Mina a large fair was held at this time. Ewliyā Čelebi, who calls this place 'Mine pazarı' ('the market of Mina'), records that many goods were on sale here, 'from precious pearls to the coarsest of glass'. Ewliyā's story is confirmed by an anonymous source from the sixteenth century. The Bahrain pearls, which Ibn Djubayr and Ewliyā both mention, were the most remarkable speciality of this fair. In addition a good many foods and beverages were on sale. The pilgrims, who during their stay in Mina were excused from most of the restrictions which they had imposed on themselves upon approaching the Holy City, now visited with one another and made merry. On the two following days the lapidations were repeated, most pilgrims throwing forty-nine stones in all. Ibn Djubayr explains that originally the pilgrims had spent an additional day in Mina, further extending the lapidations, but in his time the ritual had been abridged because of the unsafe conditions obtaining in the area.

When the pilgrims reentered the city after an absence of several days, they performed the concluding rite of their pilgrimage, namely the final circumambulation of the Ka'aba. For this occasion, Ibn Djubayr changes his perspective, thereby contributing to the liveliness of his tale. While up to this point he has recounted mainly his own experiences, he now concentrates upon the behaviour of his fellow pilgrims. He was particularly interested in the Khorasanis, who must have seemed most exotic both to him and to his readers, in all likelihood mainly educated Andalusians and North Africans. We learn that on this occasion the covering of the Ka'aba had to be pulled up, as otherwise it would certainly have been ruined by the pilgrims who threw themselves upon the covering and clung to it. This form of devotion was foreign to Ibn Djubayr, but he describes it with equanimity and tolerance. This is particularly obvious when he discusses the women pilgrims, who threw themselves into the crowd, hoping for a chance to visit the interior of the Ka'aba, and reemerged rather the worse for wear.[24] Ibn Djubayr also comments favourably on the Khorasani preachers, who could speak most impressively both in Arabic and Persian. He also approved of the Khorasanis' custom of soliciting questions from the congregation after their sermons; many of these question-and-answer sessions developed into an outright examination of the preacher by his listeners.

IBN DJUBAYR'S IDEAS CONCERNING THE PILGRIMAGE

In the course of his narrative, Ibn Djubayr quite frequently discusses his own reactions to different aspects of the pilgrimage. We already know that he had a strong sense of reality, and did not believe that manipulation for pious ends was a good thing. As a highly educated man, Ibn Djubayr must have known very well that many religious scholars believed pilgrims derived greater blessings if they performed the *wakfa* on a Friday, yet he insists that God's mercy can be expected by any pilgrim. To put it differently, Ibn Djubayr recommends that the pilgrims use the opportunity provided by the pilgrimage to reflect upon God's mercy, and avoid being overly anxious about the details of the ritual. He thus remarks that the Beduins of the Yemen lack even an elementary knowledge of the Islamic ritual, but possess an abundance of good intentions.[25] Ibn Djubayr concludes his account of Beduin religious life, which includes an enumeration of the many mistakes these people make when saying their prayers, with a saying ascribed to the Prophet Muḥammad: 'Teach them ritual prayer, and they will teach you the prayer of the heart.'[26]

On a more personal level, Ibn Djubayr also discusses his religious experiences in the course of the pilgrimage. He praises the night when his caravan first entered Mecca, and thanks his Creator for the grace of pilgrimage, for now he feels included in the community of those who may hope for the intercession of the Prophet Ibrāhīm. The humble invocations by which pilgrims acknowledged their being in God's presence are mentioned as an awesome experience, and the nightly prayers held in the Great Mosque during the fast of Ramadān made a profound impression on Ibn Djubayr.

Concerning the Prophet's miracles, Ibn Djubayr occasionally mentions them and does not express any doubts on that score. But it is obvious from his account of the Meccan sanctuaries outside the Great Mosque, often associated with the personal and family history of the Prophet, that miracles play a very subordinate role in his style of piety. As to assorted practices pilgrims engage in for the sake of obtaining blessings (*baraka*), Ibn Djubayr is quite critical. Thus he describes pilgrims who try to pass through a narrow opening in a cave because the Prophet allegedly did the same, and remarks that they are likely to get themselves into trouble: apart from looking ridiculous, trying to wriggle out of the narrow opening is painful as well.[27]

At the core of the Meccan pilgrimage rituals there survive pre-Islamic practices which have interested both scholars of the early Islamic period and twentieth-century specialists in comparative religious studies. These rituals have been transformed by the Prophet Muḥammad and his immediate successors, however, and reinterpreted in a strictly monotheistic sense. Ibn Djubayr's account permits us to see how a pious and learned person of the twelfth century who possessed a strong critical sense, viewed the rituals of the pilgrimage. Pilgrims of his calibre took the hajj as a way toward a more profound understanding of their monotheistic religion. Ibn Djubayr stressed the importance of an interior life, and had no time for an overly ritualistic approach. Certainly the author, who was a courtier in addition to being a scholar, came from an elite milieu, and his understanding of the pilgrimage may well have been a minority phenomenon. But we are fortunate that at least one writer of the twelfth century has been so explicit about his thoughts and feelings.

THE PROPHET'S MOSQUE IN MEDINA

The Prophet Muḥammad died in Medina in 632 CE, in the year 10 according to the Muslim reckoning. He was buried in his former dwelling place, soon to be rebuilt as a mosque.[28] Later, other important personages of early Islamic history were buried there, including his first two successors Abū Bakr (reigned 632–4) and 'Umar (reigned 634–44). During the years immediately following the death of the Prophet, Medina was the capital of the Islamic empire which was then expanding rapidly. But with the reign of Mu'āwiya (661–80) the empire's political centre moved to Syria and Iraq, and Medina became a city inhabited by religious scholars, who developed and elaborated Islamic law. Throughout the history of Islam the city has held a particular attraction for pious people. Although a visit to Medina does not form part of the Islamic pilgrimage ritual, many visitors to the Hejaz use the opportunity to pray at the Prophet's grave, either when travelling to Mecca or else on the return trip.

Naṣīr-i Khosraw, when visiting the Hejaz in 1048, also paid a visit to the Prophet's mosque in Medina, and has left a brief description of the sanctuary.[29] In his time, the building consisted mainly of the following parts: a chamber with an adjacent court, an enclosed and partly roofed area in which the Prophet's grave was located, the preacher's chair and the hall named the 'Garden' (*Rawḍa*) which separates the preacher's chair from the Prophet's grave. Naṣīr-i Khosraw even mentions the net, which closed off the unroofed parts of the mosque, so birds could not get in. But we possess even older descriptions, one of the most remarkable being that of Ibn 'Abd Rabbih, written in the tenth century. Ibn 'Abd Rabbih relies almost completely on his own observations and seems to have paid but scant attention to the work of his predecessors. He came from the same region as Ibn Djubayr, namely Andalusia, and was a courtier like his successor, active in the entourage of the caliph 'Abd al-Raḥmān III; to his contemporaries he was mainly known as a poet and literary man.

Ibn 'Abd Rabbih's description is extremely careful and detailed, so that his text has often been used by modern scholars attempting to reconstruct the appearance of the Prophet's mosque in the early centuries of its existence.[30] The author gives an account of the columns carrying the roof of the gallery and of the windows, which he compares to those of the Great Mosque of Cordoba; he also cites the text of the inscription which decorated one of the mosque walls. In Ibn 'Abd Rabbih's time a mirror hung on the mosque wall, which purportedly had belonged to 'Ay<u>sh</u>a, the Prophet's favourite wife, who was very active in politics after her husband's death. The preacher's chair used by the Prophet struck the observer by its simplicity, lacking any adornment or special elegance. The platform used by the preacher had been closed off by a slab of wood, so that the seat of the Prophet was not used by the preachers of Ibn 'Abd Rabbih's time. The author did not doubt the authenticity of the chair, but with respect to the other mementoes preserved in the mosque, he merely comments 'and God knows best'.[31]

The most detailed description of the Prophet's mosque dates from the concluding years of the fifteenth century.[32] Its author is the Egyptian scholar al-Samhūdī, and it is a critical and carefully documented account. Al-Samhūdī has located a great many sources concerning the mosque and compares them so as to arrive at a realistic reconstruction. He also discusses the buildings originally located in the vicinity, which in the course of various building campaigns were included in the mosque itself. We find a moving description of the weeping and lamentations with which the pious people of Medina reacted to the decision of the caliph Walīd b. 'Abd al-Mālik (reigned 705–15) who had the modest habitations of the Prophet's wives torn down to make room for the enlarged mosque. Apparently many devout people felt that these dwellings should have been preserved to demonstrate the extreme modesty and lack of ostentation practised by the Prophet, at a time when all the treasures of this world were readily accessible to him.[33]

From al-Samhūdī's description we understand that in Ummayad times, the Great Mosque of Medina was built of hewn stone. The stones were held together by the application of plaster, and several loads of shells had been used in the decoration of the building. Only the roof was made of gilt palm wood. In the eighth century the mosque did not yet possess any minarets; the latter were added later and had to be rebuilt several times because of lightning damage. When al-Samhūdī wrote, however, little remained of the mosque of Ummayad times, as it had been struck by two devastating fires, in 1256 and 1481. After the first fire only casual repairs could be undertaken due to lack of means, for two years after this event, in 1258, the Mongols conquered Baghdad, killed the Abbasid caliph and destroyed the city. With no help forthcoming from that quarter, major repairs had to wait for the Mamluk Sultans of Egypt to stabilize their

position. Repairs were finally undertaken by Sultan Ḳā'it Bāy
(reigned 1468–96), who was also active as a builder in Mecca. In
Medina, Ḳā'it Bāy twice sponsored the rebuilding of the Prophet's
mosque, as the fire of 1481 destroyed most of what had been built a
few years previously. This Sultan had the wooden dome over the
Prophet's grave taken down and a cupola of stone erected in its place.
Little trace remains of Ḳā'it Bāy's buildings today, as a further
campaign of restoration, or indeed rebuilding, was undertaken in the
time of the Ottoman Sultan 'Abd ül-Medjīd (reigned 1839–61). The
medieval mosque therefore needs to be reconstructed from written
sources.

Ibn 'Abd Rabbih had little to say on the grave of the Prophet
proper, which in his time bore only modest decorations. This is in
accordance with the views of certain Islamic schools of law, which
recommend this simplicity even today. Ibn 'Abd Rabbih simply
discussed the prayers to be performed at the Prophet's grave, and
recommended that worshippers observe a certain decorum. Particularly, pilgrims should not cling to the grave, behaviour which in the
author's view is characteristic of the ignorant. When visiting the
Prophet's grave, the principal concern was to offer prayers to God,
even though visitors were free to invoke the intercession of the
Prophet as well.

THE HOLY CITIES IN THE LATER MIDDLE AGES

For the late Middle Ages, that is the period preceding the Ottoman
conquest of Egypt in 1517, we possess a comprehensive history of
Medina and a series of Meccan chronicles. These texts document the
tensions between the Mamluk Sultans of Egypt, who exercised
suzerainty over the Sherifs of Mecca (functioning as local rulers), and
other important princes of the Islamic world. These rivalries
sometimes had repercussions upon ceremonial life in the Holy
Cities.[34] Thus, in 1424–34, the Egyptian Sultan Barsbāy refused
the demands of Shāhrukh, son and successor of Timur Lenk, who
repeatedly requested the privilege of being permitted to donate a
covering for the Ka'aba. Meḥmed the Conqueror (reigned 1451–81)
was likewise refused when he made a similar offer. Difficulties of this
kind had a long tradition: a full century earlier, amir Čūbān (died
1327), one of the most powerful figures at the court of the Ilkhanid
Abū Sa'īd, had undertaken to construct a waterpipe to alleviate the
lack of water in Mecca, which had grown ever more serious with the
passage of time.[35] Amir Čoban donated 50,000 gold coins for this
purpose. Conditions of work on this line, which led from Ḥunayn

over 'Arafat to the Holy City, were reputed highly satisfactory, and many Beduins, including their womenfolk, accepted employment on the construction site. Work was completed within four months, but the reaction of the Egyptian Sultan to a project initiated by a rival court was decidedly negative. Luckily a skilled negotiator, who previously had been in charge of the construction site, managed to make the whole affair palatable to the Egyptian Sultan. The latter contented himself with the construction of a second pipeline next to the one built by amir Čūbān, without taking revenge for the flouting of his authority.

In addition to the rulers of Egypt and Iran, the Sultan of Yemen occasionally claimed suzerainty over Mecca.[36] Thus the Sultan al-Mudjāhid performed the pilgrimage several times and built a major complex of pious foundations in Mecca. But while sojourning in the Holy City on his second pilgrimage in 1351, he was arrested because he insisted upon his rights as an independent sovereign, *vis à vis* both the Sherifs of Mecca and the envoy of the Egyptian Sultan. The next years were filled with extraordinary adventures. Due to his arrest, al-Mudjāhid was unable to complete the requirements for his second pilgrimage. Instead he was brought to Egypt, where the ruling Sultan treated him in a manner befitting his station and soon released him. Al-Mudjāhid was already on his way back to Yemen when the Egyptian authorities changed their minds and decided to hold the Yemeni ruler captive as a possible rival. This time he was held in a castle not far from the Dead Sea, but soon released when a former fellow prisoner, who had once again achieved a powerful position in Cairo, interceded for him. While in this region, al-Mudjāhid demonstrated his piety by visiting the Muslim sanctuaries of Jerusalem and Khalīl al-Raḥmān (Hebron) and ultimately managed to return to Yemen by way of the Red Sea (1352). The chronicler who reported all these events evidently felt some sympathy for al-Mudjāhid. He reports that the offended ruler took revenge by prohibiting all trade with Mecca, which must have increased the perennial supply problems of the Holy City. Unfortunately the account does not tell us whether al-Mudjāhid really had the intention of annexing Mecca, or whether these designs had merely been imputed to him by his opponents. Be that as it may, the Sultans of Yemen certainly attempted to establish a presence in Mecca; thirty years after the adventures of al-Mudjāhid, a new conflict ensued, when a Yemeni ruler sent a covering for the Ka'aba, a gesture which the Egyptian rulers apparently regarded as their own exclusive prerogative.

During the fifteenth century, the last hundred years of Mamluk domination over Mecca, several large-scale building projects were undertaken. A fire which had broken out in a hospice near the Great Mosque had spread to the northern and western galleries of the sanctuary, and 130 columns had collapsed.[37] This part of the Meccan Great Mosque was completely rebuilt – even the foundations were dug out and reinforced. The new columns consisted of several pieces of stone held together by iron rods and crowned by marble capitals. The latter carried a wooden roof, gilt and painted in bright colours. The lack of suitable timber in the Hejaz greatly retarded the completion of the project, however, as supplies had to be imported from India or Asia Minor.

In the third quarter of the fifteenth century the Egyptian Sultan Ḳāʾit Bāy and his amirs sponsored further large construction projects, many of them quite controversial.[38] Thus Ibn al-Zamin, a close friend of the Sultan, built a hospice which created a serious obstruction on the way between Ṣafā and Marwa, which all pilgrims had to traverse many times in the course of their sojourn. A *ḳāḍī* of Mecca and other religious scholars protested in Cairo against the project, but Ibn al-Zamin had the ear of the Sultan, and the hospice was built anyway. The authorities were so worried about public disturbances, however, that construction could only go on by night.

Sultan Ḳāʾit Bāy also built a theological school and a hospice in the immediate vicinity of the Great Mosque, and several private houses and hospices were torn down for that purpose.[39] The new complex, named Ashrafiya, was built of multi-coloured marble and contained a library; due to the negligence of librarians and users, however, a few decades later the latter had lost many of its books. An Indian scholar named Ḳuṭb al-Dīn, who lived in Mecca in the sixteenth century, was in charge at that time and in his chronicle of the city of Mecca has left a graphic account of the desolate conditions he found at the beginning of his tenure of office. He also describes how he attempted to improve them, tracking down the people who had borrowed library books and in some cases securing their return. He also had many damaged volumes restored and rebound. To repair damage to the building fabric was apparently not within his power, however.[40] As we will see in the following chapters, the Ottoman Sultans of the sixteenth century were more concerned about establishing new foundations than restoring old ones. The only exceptions to this rule were the Great Mosques of Mecca and Medina.

Ḳuṭb al-Dīn has also left an account of the manner in which the Ottomans took over the Hejaz in 1517.[41] In the first stages of Ottoman rule, changes were limited in scope. At this time the Holy Cities were already totally dependent on Egyptian foodstuffs.[42] As a result, even short interruptions of the connection between the two regions, which occasionally occurred in the early sixteenth century owing to Portuguese incursions into the Red Sea, led to panics and uncontrolled price rises. Given this situation, the Sherif of Mecca sent his young son to Cairo to offer the Ottoman Sultan Selīm I (reigned 1512–20) suzerainty over the Hejaz. Selīm I accepted this proposition and, for the stretch of four centuries, Mecca and Medina became part of the Ottoman Empire. The following chapters will deal with the structures and networks which during the first two centuries of Ottoman rule ensured the survival of pilgrims and Hejazis. The interplay of long-term structures and *ad hoc* improvisation will constitute the dominant theme of our account.

2

Caravan Routes

With the Ottoman takeover of the Hejaz, the two Holy Cities came to depend on the protection of a Sultan whose capital and principal scenes of activity were much more remote, both geographically and in terms of language, than had been the case in Mamluk times. Ties between the Holy Cities on the one hand and Damascus and Cairo on the other continued to exist, but Cairo was now no more than a provincial centre. Major political decisions, such as the institution and occasionally deposition of the Sherifs of Mecca, were from now on made in Istanbul. Officials of the Sultan residing in the Ottoman capital also decided whether new buildings were to be erected in the Holy Cities, or whether the grain supply to the Hejaz should be increased by adding further Egyptian villages to the public foundations inherited from Mamluk times. However the caravan routes linking the Hejaz to Cairo and Damascus in no way lost their previous importance, for connections between the Holy Cities and Istanbul continued to pass through either one of these two provincial capitals. From Alexandria, the seaport of Cairo, a short and under normal circumstances reasonably comfortable voyage took the traveller to Rhodes, an Ottoman possession since Sultan Süleymān had conquered the island from the Knights of St John in 1522. From Damascus Istanbul was reached by way of a long but well-travelled caravan route, which passed through northern Syria and then entered Anatolia by a narrow defile between the mountains and the Mediterranean. Caravans stopped in Adana, then crossed the Taurus Mountains and the dry central Anatolian steppe before the next major staging post, Konya. Ultimately the Sea of Marmara was reached, and skirting it the caravans came to Üsküdar, which in the sixteenth

32

century was still an independent town and not merely a suburb of Istanbul. If the extant pilgrimage accounts reflect the real preferences of travellers, most pilgrims coming from Anatolia and Rumelia journeyed by way of Damascus.

The present chapter deals with the two official pigrimage caravans, which every year left Cairo and Damascus for the Hejaz. In addition, a Yemeni pilgrimage caravan must have existed, but almost no information on this matter can be found in the Ottoman records. At certain times a separate caravan from Basra on the Persian Gulf crossed the Arabian peninsula from east to west, but political conflicts between Ottomans and Safawids often closed this route. Certain pilgrims doubtless reached Mecca on their own, without the protection of an officially sponsored caravan. The Maghribis, particularly, often travelled in this fashion, and the same probably applied to many pilgrims living on the Arabian peninsula.[1] Since these unofficial caravans have left few traces in Ottoman government records, however, very little is known about them.

The two main caravans, on the other hand, are abundantly documented. We can trace the history of the Cairo and Damascus caravans back to the time of the Abbasid caliphs: Hārūn al-Rashīd (reigned 786–809), a contemporary of the Byzantine empress Irene (reigned 797–802) and Charlemagne (reigned 768–814), performed the pilgrimage nine times.[2] While most of his successors did not travel to Mecca personally, they regularly sent high-level officials to represent them at the pilgrimage. The pilgrimage caravans that we know from the Ottoman documentation of the sixteenth and seventeenth centuries, however, took shape under the Mamluk Sultans, between 1250 and 1517. Sixteenth- and seventeenth-century authors, dealing with the Ottoman Sultans in their role of protectors to the pilgrimage, have often measured Ottoman performance against the yardstick of what had been done, really or presumedly, by their Mamluk predecessors. This explains why Ottoman Sultans adhered as closely as they could to the practices connected with the names of Kā'it Bāy (reigned 1468–96) and Kānṣūh al-Ghūrī (reigned 1501–16).

THE CAIRO PILGRIMAGE CARAVAN

The Cairo caravan has frequently been described. One of the most valuable accounts was written by the Egyptian 'Abd al-Kādir al-Djazarī in the middle of the sixteenth century.[3] This writer was able to draw upon extensive personal and family experience with respect to the administration of pilgrimage caravans, as both he and his father

had worked in this line. As al-Djazarī's account has been published
and extensively studied, a summary of its main points will be sufficient for our present purpose.

Down to 1406–7, there was no fixed order in the Cairo caravan,
which resulted in a good deal of confusion when crossing narrow
defiles. An order of precedence was then instituted, which in al-
Djazarī's opinion had become unavoidable due to the large number of
pilgrims. It had the disadvantage, however, that the better-off among
them, who were able to afford faster mounts, secured places in the
front or middle of the caravan, leaving the poorer pilgrims in the
caravan's rear, the most vulnerable section. The caravan commander
was in charge of assigning the pilgrims their places; he normally
joined the caravan at 'Adjrūd, five stops away from Cairo and not far
from Suez. Apparently the officials who planned the trip back in
Cairo believed that the really difficult part of the desert journey only
began at this spot. Al-Djazarī describes the caravan as divided up into
several subsections, which he calls *kaṭārs*. Their number varied with
the size of the caravan; in a large one, there might be as many as
nine.[4]

At the very head of the caravan travelled the 'desert pilots', who
were often Beduins and thoroughly familiar with the stretch of desert
to be traversed. They were followed by water carriers and notables.
Next came the cash supplies carried by the caravan, namely donations
to the inhabitants of Mecca and Medina provided by the public
foundations instituted by different Mamluk Sultans, along with
subsidies to be paid to Beduins providing various services to the
pilgrims (see Chapters 3 and 4). The cash was guarded by soldiers,
and the caravan's artillery travelled in the immediate vicinity. A troop
of soldiers had special orders to march on that side of the caravan
which faced not the Red Sea but the mountains, which on this route
are often located close to the seashore. Since navigation on the Red
Sea with its many coral reefs was highly dangerous, an attack from
that direction was much less likely. The next section of the caravan
consisted of another treasury, which belonged to the Mamluk Sultans
and presumably was meant for the ordinary expenditures of the
caravan. Sharpshooters armed with bows and arrows as well as
torchbearers were responsible for the security of this section of the
caravan. Merchants carrying valuable goods usually travelled close to
the treasuries, while ordinary pilgrims made up the rear.

Among the numerous officials accompanying the Cairo caravan, the
commander's secretary occupied a key position.[5] He had to be
consulted whenever important decisions were taken, and he was
responsible for the payment of subsidies to the Beduins who travelled
with the caravan and thus ensured its safety. A *kāḍī* settled disputes

among the pilgrims. Al-Djazarī liked to praise past times in contrast to a present which he regarded as much less brilliant; he claimed that the office of caravan *kāḍī* had lost much of its previous lustre and now was almost always filled by Turks. Quite possibly his opinion is coloured by his own disappointment with his career. After all, he was the descendant of a family well-established both in Cairo and Medina, yet had to content himself with a fairly modest position. The caravan *kāḍī* was accompanied by a number of subordinates. Pilgrims wishing to conclude contracts or make their wills needed men of irreproachable lifestyle to act as witnesses; moreover, these men had to be found readily if ever their testimony was needed. To ensure that they were available in such cases, al-Djazarī's father had begun to assign them stipends.

In addition to his secretary the caravan commander employed a second scribe, and this office was filled by al-Djazarī's father and later by the author himself. Al-Djazarī thought that the scribes had a most important role to play, since the Mamluks – in contrast to later Ottoman practice – never allowed an amir to act as caravan commander more than once; therefore his scribes were responsible for ensuring continuity. Other officials were in charge of supervising the camels and horses as well as the official stores of food, fodder and water. The pilgrimage caravan of the late Mamluk and early Ottoman periods thus should not be envisaged as a simple crowd of pilgrims and soldiers. It appears more reasonable to regard it as a well-organized enterprise, in some ways comparable to an army on the march, with its commander as a temporary ruler holding court, and accompanied by his treasuries, scribes, subordinate officers, soldiers and Beduin auxiliaries.

THE ORGANIZATION OF THE DAMASCENE CARAVAN

For the Syrian caravan we do not possess an account even remotely comparable to the work of al-Djazarī. However, a mass of official documents have survived, including a large number of sultanic rescripts from the second half of the sixteenth century, and a significant number of account books covering the years 1600 to 1683. The Damascus caravan resembled its Cairo counterpart in possessing a well-defined structure, which did not change much in the course of the period under investigation. Presumably the Ottomans also followed Mamluk models quite closely in this case.

Syrian provincial budgets of the seventeenth century routinely contain figures concerning expenditures on behalf of the officials forming part of the caravan.[6] A number of officials travelling with the pilgrimage were assigned camels for their journeys. The numbers of mounts varied according to the rank of the official involved. We thus gain an idea of the caravan hierarchy. As an example, we may study the records of 1636–7: the commander was granted the use of eight camels, while his substitute, the *ketkhüdā* had two at his disposal.[7] It was the latter's job to distribute the pilgrims among the different subsections of the caravan; if the Damascus caravan resembled its Egyptian counterpart, this task was not always an easy one. In addition there was an amir in charge of stopping points, also assigned two camels; this official probably coordinated the movements of the different subsections of the caravan whenever the latter settled down to rest or began a new stretch of the journey. This, too, was probably a difficult job: at the end of a long day, many people – all thirsty, tired and nervous, and for the most part armed – competed for scanty water supplies, and the amir had to ensure that disputes did not degenerate into violence. The Master of the Stables (*mirākhōr*) was in charge of the horses and camels of soldiers and officials; he also helped the *ketkhüdā* of the commander to keep the caravan in order. There was also an *emīn* in charge of finances; he had a scribe at his disposal, and thereby ranked lower than his colleague in charge of supplies, who was aided by two scribes. But possibly the difference in this case was not a matter of rank, but simply reflected the fact that supplies were more cumbersome to handle than cash. The Damascus caravan also possessed a *kāḍī* and a supervisor (*nāzır*). The latter's duties remain unspecified; however, the supervisor was a high-ranking official with two camels at his disposal, and thereby comparable to the *kāḍī*. He also required the services of a scribe. There was also a supervisor in charge of 'the poor'. It was probably the supervisor's job to administer the alms to be distributed among poor pilgrims on the Sultan's behalf; but this official, along with prayer leaders and muezzins, only possessed a comparatively modest status. All these men were assigned a single camel per person. The same applied to the official who confiscated heirless estates for the Sultan's treasury, and also to musicians, messengers and other service personnel.

Seventeenth-century accounts permit us to identify yet other officials. The Damascene caravan was accompanied by several *poursuivants*, who as a group were granted five camels, an official who administered the gifts of the Sultan to the population of Mecca and Medina and a police officer (*ṣūbashı*). When the caravan was about to leave Istanbul, the official dealing with largesse to the Hejaz was received by the ruler in a private audience. But in the older account books his office does not even occur, possibly because his expenses were paid from Istanbul directly and therefore did not concern the finance department of Damascus. While most officials accompanying the caravan were chosen from among the notables of Syria, the official in charge of imperial largesse directly represented the Ottoman Sultan.

CEREMONIES ACCOMPANYING DEPARTURES AND RETURNS

In the Ottoman Empire, festivities connected with the pilgrimage served to emphasize the position of the ruler, his capacity to win victories and the continuing florescence of the dynasty in a form easily accessible to the subject population. These festivities were for the most part public, and thus comparable to the *joyeuses entrées* and other ceremonies of medieval and early Renaissance Europe.[8] From the sixteenth century onward, however, European festivities increasingly retreated into a non-public space, accessible to the ruler and his courtiers or to the patriciate of a city, while the public celebrations lost much of their previous lustre. A comparable development was less obvious in the Ottoman context, where public festivities remained important; and among the occasions celebrated on the streets of Istanbul, Damascus and particularly Cairo, the departure and return of the pilgrimage caravans constituted one of the most brilliant events.

These festivities have been recorded extensively by the Ottoman traveller Ewliyā Čelebi, who lived in Cairo for about a decade and therefore had the opportunity to observe them in minute detail. His testimony gains in significance because he was a product of the Ottoman Palace school and therefore intimately acquainted with imperial ceremonial. This latter qualification does not apply to European visitors, who have also left accounts of these festivities. Ewliyā's description, therefore, has been employed as the basis of our study.

The high point of the departure ceremony came when the caravan commander appeared on the square of Ḳara Meydān, which was normally used for military exercises and parades.[9] He was accompanied by a numerous suite of soldiers and officers, while the band played, and janissaries and other soldiers saluted their commander. The caravan commander then visited the governor of Egypt in his tent, which must have been put up in this place for the occasion. Now artillery was brought to the square, presumably the cannons which the commander was to take along with him on his desert journey. The flag of the Prophet, a major relic, was paraded about the grounds along with the palanquin symbolizing the Sultan's presence, which was to accompany the caravan to Mecca; the palanquin was carried by a camel. At the formal audience, with all the notables of Cairo present, the Pasha asked the caravan commander whether he had received the money he was going to need – subsidies for the Beduin shaykhs along the desert route and for the Sherif of Mecca, donations to people living in the Holy Cities, and ready cash for all the other needs of the caravan. The caravan commander formally acknowledged that everything had been handed over, 'down to the last grain and the last cloak', certain gifts taking the shape of clothing. The Pasha instructed a judge to record the matter in his register and then, with a ritual invocation of God, rose from his seat and walked up to the camel carrying the palanquin. After rubbing his face and hands against this symbol of the Sultan's presence, he once again invoked God and took the camel's silver chain to lead the animal around the Kara Meydān. Ewliyā states that by this gesture he proclaimed himself the Prophet's camel driver, or humble servant, and the author states that the audience was much moved when watching this gesture of humility. In the meantime, the soldiers in a loud voice invoked the intercession of the Prophet. Then the Pasha turned to the caravan commander, affirming that the Ottoman Sultan controlled Mecca and Medina, acting as servitor of the two Holy Places. He, as the Pasha, was at once the Sultan's representative and the ruler's slave. Acting in his official capacity, with the force and impressiveness required by his office, the Pasha now handed over the palanquin to the caravan commander and commended the pilgrims to the protection of God, wishing them a victorious and safe return. The Pasha then returned to his seat in the tent, and now it was the turn of the caravan commander to parade the palanquin. After that, the caravan set out on its way.

As to the ceremonies accompanying the return of the pilgrimage caravan, Ewliyā describes them so to say as a participant observer, as he presumably entered Cairo as a member of the suite of the caravan commander. After completing the pilgrimage in 1672, Ewliyā did not return to Damascus where he had spent time before, but took the opportunity of travelling to Cairo, where he seems to have resided for most of the remaining years of his life.[10] When the caravan had reached Birkat al-Ḥadjdj the last stop before Cairo, the commander stayed in this locality overnight, and gave a feast for the notables and officers of Cairo. The soldiers fired their muskets and cannons, and at the end there were fireworks which Ewliyā greatly admired. The next morning's principal event was the ceremonial entry into the city. The notables of Cairo and the palanquin preceded the commander, who stopped at the tents of various officers to salute them. At the entrance to the city, by the gate of Bāb Nāṣir, the governor's soldiers awaited the returning pilgrims. Leaving his suite behind, the Pasha galloped ahead to meet the arriving palanquin. He then dismounted, and for forty or fifty steps ran beside the camel carrying the symbol of the sultanic presence. Invoking the prayers of the Prophet, the governor kissed the palanquin's covering. The caravan commander now welcomed his illustrious visitor with military music, and dismounted to rub his face against the foot of the Pasha, who thereupon honoured the new arrival with a gown of honour lined with sable. In response, the caravan commander kissed the ground, then entered the city by the gate of Bāb Nāṣir. He spent the night as a visitor to the mosque of Djānbulāt, while the governor remained in 'Adiliya. At this time, the people of Cairo came to the mosque to pay their respects to the palanquin. At night religious scholars, pious people and derwish shaykhs assembled in the mosque and recited prayers in honour of the Prophet.

We observe certain obvious parallels between the two ceremonies; in both instances, the two principal actors were the caravan commander and the Pasha of Egypt. The initial ceremony of handing over the money to be spent on the pilgrimage had its parallel in an equally official encounter at the end, in which the caravan commander gave an account of how he had spent the money entrusted to him. These two ceremonies emphasized the delegation of power and responsibility from the Pasha to the caravan commander. But at the same time the ultimate sources of power and responsibility were made vividly apparent. When the Pasha led about the camel with the sacred palanquin, he declared that he was the Prophet's camel driver, and thereby established a close, albeit subordinate relationship to the founder of the Muslim religion. Since Ewliyā's contemporaries believed that the palanquin, a symbol of the sovereignty of Islamic rulers, was directly connected to the practice of the Prophet, the religious aura of this ceremony was reinforced.[11] According to Ewliyā, the palanquin originally had contained the most indispensable personal belongings of the Prophet, namely his gown, a toothbrush manufactured from the twig of a tree, wooden clogs and a ewer for religious ablutions (since clay apparently was not available, the latter consisted of basketware made impermeable by a coat of pitch). The Prophet's favourite spouse 'Aysha also supposedly had travelled in this palanquin. When the Pasha played the role of the Prophet's camel driver, literate contemporaries may have been reminded of another event, this time pertaining to Mamluk history. When Sultan Baybars (reigned 1260–71) wanted to perform this same gesture of humility and lead the camel around, a saint intervened and performed the office himself.[12] Given all these motifs from Islamic sacred history, the Ottoman ruler and his governor were firmly linked to the religious sphere and legitimized by this connection.

On the other hand, a major misunderstanding had to be avoided: since the Sultan was far away in Istanbul and the Pasha represented him with the appropriate pomp and circumstance, the spectator might easily assume that the governor was the successor of the Mamluk Sultans, particularly since the caravan commander continually emphasized his subordination to the Pasha. Given the long tradition of Mamluk independence, that particular misunderstanding had to be avoided at all costs. This was achieved by the Pasha's public proclamation that he derived his power from the Sultan. Not the governor of Egypt, but the Ottoman ruler was the servitor of the Holy Places. Moreover, the Pasha explicitly declared that he was the Sultan's *ḳul*, his servitor, who owed his position entirely to the ruler's pleasure and whose inheritance was to return to the latter's treasury at his death. Such was the normal status of a high-level Ottoman official.[13] Probably these very explicit declarations were meant to balance the impression generated by the ceremony, namely that the governor possessed an independent source of religious legitimation due to his role as protector of the pilgrimage.

The ceremonies at the departure and return of the caravan also emphasized the ties of the pilgrims to their respective regions of origin, from which they were absent for months or sometimes even years, and to which some of them would never return. The ceremonies accompanying the departure of the caravan diluted the traumatic moments of departure and return by dividing them up into a sequence of events. For both those who departed and those who stayed behind, the separation thus was made more bearable. The caravan was not like a ship which at a given moment has left port and sailed out onto the high seas. After leaving Damascus, the Syrian caravan spent considerable time at the stopping place of Muzayrib, where pilgrims did their shopping in preparation of the journey.[14] In the Egyptian case, part of the ceremonies of departure and arrival took place at Birkat al-Hadjdj, the first stop after Cairo. Of course, there were practical reasons for this arrangement, which was popular in other Ottoman commercial centres as well.[15] If the caravan did not travel very far on the first day, latecomers could join it at the last moment, while travellers could send for items which they had forgotten. On the other hand, during the last stages of the return journey, the pilgrims and their animals were exhausted, so that it was of vital importance that they should be met by supply caravans while still in the desert, and relatives and friends of the pilgrims often joined the merchants and officials making up these caravans. But beyond this utilitarian consideration, the 'slicing up' of departure and return also had a symbolic significance.

TRAVEL ROUTES

The travel routes between Cairo and Damascus on the one hand, and Mecca on the other, are well known from a variety of pilgrimage accounts, the handbook compiled by 'Abd al-Kādir al-Djazarī, and a few Ottoman official documents. Apart from al-Djazarī's account, all these sources pertain to the seventeenth century (compare map).[16] Particularly interesting is a document from the year 1647, which permits us to view the pilgrimage roads in connection with the major courier routes traversing the eastern half of the Ottoman Empire.[17] Anatolia was crossed by three important routes, which Ottoman sources describe as 'right', 'left' and 'centre'.

The right-hand route (the designation assumes a traveller turning his back to Istanbul) led from the capital to Aleppo and Damascus, crossing Anatolia from northwest to southeast.[18] From Damascus to Mecca, the pilgrimage route and that used by official couriers were virtually identical, as the lack of water severely limited choices. As it was, couriers would often have had trouble procuring horses even on the pilgrimage route, for some of the stopping points, such as Tabūk according to Ewliyā Čelebi, only consisted of an open space where water was to be found, and fodder was probably scarce.[19] Even in some of the desert forts along the hajj route, garrisons were unable to maintain themselves, and it is hard to imagine how the officials responsible for the couriers' mounts protected the animals from thieves. Probably special arrangements were made whenever an official messenger was sent outside the pilgrimage season. Moreover, the 1647 document does not tell us how a courier travelled between Cairo and Mecca, although such couriers needed to be sent with reasonable frequency. We do, however, possess evidence for a courier route leading from Damascus to Cairo by way of Ramla, Ghazzah and Bilbays, and also for a connection between Damascus and the pilgrimage centres of Jerusalem and Khalīl al-Raḥmān (Hebron, al-Khalil).

The courier route from Istanbul by way of Damascus to Mecca constituted one of the three major routes of the eastern Ottoman Empire.[20] In the empire as a whole, the Istanbul–Mecca route was one of seven, for in the Rumelian part of the empire three major routes also radiated from Istanbul. One of them was the successor to the Via Egnatia of Roman times, linking the Ottoman capital to the Adriatic coast. The central route led to Hungary, which at this time was still an Ottoman province, while for an observer turning his back to the capital, the right-hand route led through Moldavia and Walachia into southern Poland. Moreover, due to the recently increased importance of Izmir as a trade centre frequented by

European merchants, a new courier route to this city had been instituted not long before. Unfortunately, we have no way of knowing whether the Istanbul–Damascus–Mecca road was more or less frequented than the other courier routes. But given the numerous sultanic rescripts to recipients in the Hejaz made out by the Ottoman chancery and recorded in the Registers of Important Affairs, this route, at least in peacetime, must have been among the most frequented courier routes. Apart from correspondence with the Sherif of Mecca, the central administration needed to maintain liaison with the *emīn* of Jeddah, who directly represented the Ottoman Sultan in the region, aided by the *kādīs* of the two Holy Cities and a host of lesser functionaries. Both *kādīs*, as high Ottoman officials, maintained their own correspondence with the central administration. Since the affairs of the pilgrimage were considered so important by the Ottoman government, Mecca and Medina were supervised much more closely than would otherwise have been true of two remote towns separated from the core of the empire by vast stretches of desert.

SERVICES TO PILGRIMS AND SOLDIERS

In principle, every pilgrim was responsible for his or her own supplies. Only pilgrims who had fallen on hard times were, at least to some extent, under the care of the staff of the caravan commander. But soldiers and officials who accompanied the caravan as part of their official duties had to be supplied with food and water out of public resources. A special bureau was in charge of this business, called 'The Sultan's Larder for the Noble Pilgrimage'. The servitors of this bureau made sure that water was carried along in skins whenever there was reason to assume that there would be a shortage at the next stopping point. From the 1636–7 accounts of the Damascus caravan we learn that a hundred camels had been set aside merely for this purpose.[21] Presumably this was a year of drought, but even in normal years the Damascus caravan took along at least fifty camels to ensure an adequate water supply.

The Egyptian caravan also often had trouble securing the water it required, even though occasionally pilgrims were assisted by foreign Muslim rulers. Thus in 1543–4 an Indian prince, Maḥmūd Shāh, sent a quantity of ivory with the proviso that it be sold to finance the digging of wells for the Egyptian pilgrimage caravan. The project proved difficult to execute, however, and al-Djazarī was not greatly impressed by the success of the enterprise.[22] This author also reports that, on one of his numerous trips to Mecca, he unsuccessfully tried to persuade the caravan commander to hand over some of the water meant for soldiers and officials to the poor. But the caravan commander apparently was worried about the possibility that the soldiers might run out of water themselves. A thoroughly organized caravan with a well-oiled bureaucratic machine no doubt made life easier for ordinary pilgrims. At the same time, the privileges of high-level officials and the high operating costs of the bureaucratic apparatus often made it impossible to give poor pilgrims help when they most needed it.

Food for the return journey was sometimes deposited in desert forts protecting the caravan's stopping points. If these supplies were not in the meantime plundered by Beduins, this was a convenient arrangement. Sometimes, however, more complicated transactions were needed. Thus Ewliyā reports that, in 1672, supplies belonging to the Sultan's Larder were entrusted in Muzayrib to Beduins who undertook to transport them to al-'Ulā.[23] Other Beduins, probably the allies of those encountered in Muzayrib, then returned the supplies to the caravan in the locality previously agreed upon. We do not know whether the grain was physically transported, or whether the Beduins of al-'Ulā owned stocks from which they supplied the caravan. Given the fact that in a year of unseasonable rains Beduins would have had almost as much trouble getting the grain to al-'Ulā as the caravan itself, the second possibility seems more likely. Because the caravan represented a formidable accumulation of military and political power by desert standards, such arrangements could be made without taking too great a risk.

For charitable services to poor pilgrims, 60 camels were set aside in the Damascus caravan of the late sixteenth century.[24] Twenty of them carried foodstuffs, particularly ship's biscuits, while the remaining camels were intended to mount pilgrims in cases of emergency. Whenever the caravan stopped, a special tent was set up for the poor, who also received a warm meal out of the Sultan's bounty. A rescript from the year 1576–7 shows that this kitchen did not always function in the manner intended: sometimes the meals were cooked so late that the poor had no chance to eat before the caravan set out again.[25] At times the poor also received alms in cash, or were issued new trousers and shoes. We also hear of indigent pilgrims being buried in shrouds which had been donated by pious persons. Some of the foundations disbursing alms to poor pilgrims went back to Mamluk times. Thus in 1580–1 a charity established by the last major Mamluk Sultan Kānsūh al-Ghūrī (reigned 1501–17) was still operating. It regularly provided twelve loads of ship's biscuits to the poor.[26]

However the administration in Istanbul needed to supervise these foundations constantly to make sure that they did, in fact, serve the poor. As it was customary to allow various dignitaries (*wādjib al-re'āyet*) the use of officially financed mounts, abuse was especially easy with respect to camels. In 1579–80 the governor of Damascus was threatened by the central government that he would have to foot the bill out of his own pocket if he insisted on assigning camels to people not entitled to them.[27] These admonitions, however, were only moderately successful. An account book of the Damascus caravan from the year 1647 shows that various influential people were permitted the use of no less than 349 camels. In the seventeenth century, however, this merely meant the payment of a subsidy, as the finances of the state no longer permitted major largesse; and the dignitaries thus honoured had to foot a good part of the bill themselves. But in the sixteenth century, the cost of renting camels for a sizable number of influential people had been paid by the Ottoman treasury.

SUPPLYING CARAVANS ON THE RETURN TRIP

More effective than the provisions in favour of poor pilgrims were the auxiliary caravans which, on a commercial basis, supplied the travellers with food, fodder and mounts. When this seemed necessary, the caravan commander demanded supplies for the return journey. Thus in 1567–8 the commander reported that food and camels would urgently be required in al-'Ulā, for all supplies would be exhausted by the time the caravan reached this settlement.[28] In such cases the governors of provinces along the pilgrimage route were solicited for help. Moreover, the place where pilgrimage and supply caravans were to meet was advanced further into the desert, and the treasurer of Damascus province was given the right to contract a loan in order to supply the caravan. In particularly urgent cases, he had the right to spend extra money on the caravan without first obtaining the consent of the chief treasurer.[29]

The provincial administrators in Egypt and Syria were obviously not in a position to check the references of those people who volunteered to meet the pilgrimage caravan in al-'Ulā or Kal'at al-'Azlam. As a result, legitimate traders and camel drivers were accompanied by a number of less welcome visitors. Ewliyā Čelebi claimed that the pilgrims, exhausted after their long trek, were often unable to guard their possessions against the thieves of Cairo, who 'will steal one's eye from under the eye makeup'.[30] Apart from thieves there were also outright robbers, whom the disgusted traveller compares with the 'Black Scribe' (Kara Yazıdjı) and Djānbulādoghlu, some of the major robbers and rebels from the crisis years before and after 1600. Every now and then travellers were awakened by cries of 'Don't let him get away!' and 'Now he is gone!'[31] The streets and markets of Cairo, on the other hand, must have been unusually quiet during these last weeks of the pilgrimage season.

A PERMANENT SOURCE OF TROUBLE: THE ESTATES OF DECEASED PILGRIMS

To the average Ottoman pilgrim, protecting life and property from thieves was difficult enough. Things got worse if a companion died on the road. Great courage, skill and finesse were needed to protect the estate of the deceased from the depredations of the official in charge of securing heirless property on behalf of the Ottoman fisc, and hand it over to the legal heirs. The general rule was that heirless property accrued to the fisc. But in the context of the pilgrimage caravans this often was taken to mean that property could be confiscated if none of the heirs was present in the caravan. Heirs who had stayed at home must have complained about these abuses, for the central administtration issued not a few rescripts to bring the situation under control. Pilgrims were explicitly permitted to choose an executor who could take charge of the estate.[32] If a pilgrim died without appointing an executor, in the Egyptian caravan the fisc took over. In the Syrian caravan a more liberal rule applied, and fellow villagers or townsmen of the deceased could also take charge of the estate.[33] Only if such people could not be located either, did the deceased's property fall to the Ottoman fisc.

Yet these rulings were not always applied in practice, as the officials dealing with heirless property had paid appreciable sums for their appointments, and therefore tried to maximize profits during their limited tenure. Temptations were numerous, as many pilgrims carried sizable quantities of money or goods to defray travel expenses. Some officials made a terrible reputation for themselves: 'When a Muslim pilgrim dies, his tent companions are afraid of the fiscal official, the scribe and the *ḳāḍī*. In order to avoid harm to property and honour, they do not wash the dead person and do not wrap him/her into a shroud, nor do they pray the prayers for the dead', as prescribed by Islamic ritual.[34] Instead, the body was furtively buried in the deceased's tent. Repeated attempts to curb the misbehaviour of fiscal officials met with only modest success, and these people probably were among the most detested members of the caravan.

THE NUMBER OF PILGRIMS

Even though the Ottoman state of the sixteenth and seventeenth centuries possessed a well-organized financial bureaucracy and frequently counted its taxpayers, there was never any attempt to count the pilgrims to Mecca. So we are limited to a few more or less informed guesses. The detailed description of the Cairo pilgrimage caravan which we owe to al-Djazarī claims that, in 1279, 40,000 Egyptians and as many Syrians and Iraqis undertook the pilgrimage.[35] A Christian pilgrim from the fourteenth century, Jacobo of Verona, encountered a single hajj caravan in the desert and estimated it at 17,000 people. In an anonymous account from the year 1580, probably written by a Portuguese, we find the figure of 50,000 participants for the Egyptian caravan alone.[36]

We also possess some late medieval figures concerning the number of camels in pilgrimage caravans. These appear more reliable, as camels are easier to count than people. A major Syrian or Egyptian caravan might be made up of more than 11,000 camels, but a small Iraqi caravan consisted of no more than four to five hundred. The Italian traveller Ludovico di Varthéma, who converted to Islam and visited the Holy Cities in 1503 as a Mamluk, reports that his caravan carried 16,000 camel loads of water. Ludovico di Varthéma travelled with the Damascus pilgrims; the Cairo caravan arrived in Mecca just before he did and, according to his estimate, it consisted of 64,000 animals. The Portuguese anonymous author believes that the Cairo caravan in about 1580 was made up of at least 40,000 camels. Unfortunately, it is all but impossible to compute the number of human beings from the number of camels, for many of the wealthier pilgrims brought along several loads of supplies and trade goods.

Very few eye witnesses of the prayer meeting at 'Arafat have recorded numerical data. Ludovico di Varthéma states that, in 1503, wealthy people sacrificed a total of 30,000 sheep; however, quite a few of them offered more than one animal. Supposedly 30,000 poor people were assembled on this occasion, and they consumed the meat of the sacrificial animals. According to the anonymous Portuguese author, 200,000 people and 300,000 animals participated in a late sixteenth-century prayer meeting at 'Arafat.[37] The Spaniard 'Alī Beg, who visited Mecca in 1807, mentions 80,000 men, 2000 women and a thousand children.[38] Seven years later, John Lewis Burckhardt estimated that about 70,000 people participated in the prayer meeting at 'Arafat.[39] This total includes not only the pilgrims who had come with the Cairo and Damascus caravans, but also Africans, Indians and

Afghans who had travelled by a variety of land and sea routes. In addition, there were people from Medina present, while the Meccans themselves probably constituted the majority of all pilgrims. Obviously, these estimates are not based on counts and therefore should be treated with caution.

FINANCIAL ADMINISTRATORS IN THE PILGRIMAGE CARAVAN

In this section we will not deal with the resources, both official and private, which ultimately paid for the pilgrimage (see Chapter 4), but with the day-to-day business of the caravans' financial administrators. The activities of these modest but indispensable personages are recorded in the accounts of the Damascus caravan, particularly the so-called daybooks (*rūznāmdje*). A daybook from 1592–3 records, in the case of each expenditure, the function of the official who had ordered it.[40] Usually no cash changed hands in the office of the caravan administration itself. The head of the 'Sultan's Larder for the Noble Pilgrimage' or other officials gave the payees pieces of paper with their seals, which the latter then presented to the financial administration for payment. Some people who had delivered goods to the caravan brought along a document from the *ḳāḍī* attesting their claims. ·

In procuring supplies for the Damascus caravan, the governor of the province played a central role. At times his chief doorkeeper deputized for him, but the more important payments were made in the governor's presence. The Pasha also checked the accounts of the pilgrimage caravan if there was any suspicion of irregularities.[41] In case such a suspicion was confirmed, the official responsible was required to make good the damage; after the accounts had been settled, a note to that effect was included in the registers.

Most caravan expenses had been met before the pilgrims left Damascus; but occasionally additional purchases became necessary en route. Sometimes the caravan ran out of cash, and pilgrims and merchants were required to raise the money needed. This arrangement was familiar from merchant caravans, money being raised *ad hoc* when the caravan had to pay customs and tolls.[42] In other instances officials borrowed money from wealthy pilgrims and merchants who happened to be travelling with the pilgrimage caravan. Often these debts were only repaid after a long lapse of time, particularly when a member of the caravan administration had reason to think that his expenditures might be questioned. In 1578–9 a former official of the Damascus caravan made sure that he went on campaign when the day of reckoning approached, and 5600 gold pieces had to be returned to a creditor of the caravan.[43]

Many caravans owed considerable amounts of money. In 1656–7, debts amounted to 23,000 *esedī ghurush* (Dutch silver coins, a popular means of payment in the seventeenth-century Ottoman Empire). In this case, some of the creditors were tax collectors active in Tripoli (Syria) and Safed (Palestine).[44] Other creditors had something to do with the port town of Saydā (Sidon), but the document does not specify the nature of the relationship.[45] Since many French traders visited Saydā, it is possible that the creditors in question were long-distance merchants dealing on the one hand with the Hejaz, and on the other with their European opposite numbers. Even the head of a craft guild was listed among the creditors of the caravan administration.

There was a good deal of variation among the sums advanced by individual creditors. One of the tax collectors had lent 6066 *esedī ghurush*, and two of the presumed Saydā merchants 2000 each. But other creditors were owed only a few hundred *ghurush* each; probably, they had delivered goods for which they had not yet received payment.

CAMELS AMD CAMEL ENTREPRENEURS

Securing camels in the appropriate quantity and quality constituted one of the most difficult problems confronting the caravan administration. Soldiers and officials by themselves needed more than 600 animals. In addition, a large number of spare camels had to be taken along, as losses on the long route to Mecca were quite high. This was merely the official part of the caravan, and thousands of camels were procured privately by pilgrims and merchants.

In order to encourage Beduins to supply the caravan with camels, their elders were sometimes granted the right to exhibit the flag of the Sultan.[46] These honours occasionally turned out to be counter-productive, as they intensified rivalries between different groups, and if the latter degenerated into fights, the supply of camels was adversely affected. To be less dependent on such eventualities, the Ottoman administration purchased its own camels and sometimes even sent them to the greener pastures of Anatolia to keep them in good condition.[47] Moreover, Sultan Murād III's Grand Vizier in 1586–7 experimented with a new solution to the problem of camel supply.[48] Ibrāhīm Pasha established a pious foundation in favour of the Damascus pilgrimage caravan, and donated 600 camels to the new establishment. The animals were placed at the disposal of the caravan commander. The provincial treasury of Damascus was very much opposed to the whole project, however, claiming that the money needed for the upkeep of the animals constituted a needless long-term commitment of resources. As a result, the foundation did not continue long in operation.

This attitude of the Damascene finance administration may have had something to do with the fact that a number of established entrepreneurs in the city made a living by renting out camels. The document which recounts the sad fate of Ibrāhīm Pasha's foundation is quite explicit in this respect: camel entrepreneurs (*mukawwim*), fearing for their profits, made sure that the foundation's herd was soon dispersed. However, the *mukawwim*s probably made most of their money from pilgrims and merchants, while the service of the Sultan was not a very profitable venture. In 1578–9 pilgrims paid between 50 and 55 gold pieces to get from Damascus to Mecca, while the Ottoman administration disbursed no more than 28 gold pieces for the same service.[49] In the seventeenth century, prices remained at about the same level; ordinary animals cost the Ottoman administration 26 gold pieces each, while the more expensive camels ridden by dignitaries rated 30 gold pieces per trip.[50] Admittedly, the camel entrepreneurs may have received some money over and above the sums officially assigned to them. But private persons certainly were the more lucrative customers.

In the sixteenth century the Ottoman administration several times tried to secure the services of camel entrepreneurs without any cash disbursement at all. Instead the latter were offered military prebends (*timār, ze'āmet*) of the kind which supported Ottoman cavalry troops.[51] This novelty did not work out very well; in 1578–9 the governor and finance director of Damascus were asked to determine whether the Ottoman treasury could expect to save money by giving out such grants, or whether entrepreneurs would continue to demand cash from the Ottoman administration even after receiving *timār*s and *ze'āmet*s. Apparently the whole business was given up soon after, for in seventeenth-century accounts we find no further trace of it.

Before the Damascus hajj caravan left the fair of Muzayrib, located a few days' travel to the south of the city, camel entrepreneurs working for the state received an advance payment in cash. Further advances were often made in the course of the journey, and if the entrepreneurs were not able to obtain money from the caravan authorities, they took a leaf out of the caravan commander's book and put pressure on merchants accompanying the caravan in order to obtain a loan.[52] Accounts were settled upon return to Damascus. Other entrepreneurs managed to secure payment before even leaving for Mecca, but that in no way prevented them from demanding loans from the caravan treasury.[53] Even though this procedure was illegal, many camel entrepreneurs managed to obtain about the same amount in loans and advances as they had received as regular payments. A popular pretext was the need to purchase grain and other foodstuffs, even though assignments from the 'Sultan's Larder for the Noble Pilgrimage' had already been obtained.

Not all entrepreneurs managed to make a profit, however, as risks were considerable even in 'good' years. A camel entrepreneur returning to Damascus might discover that he owed the administration money, because the amount received as advances surpassed the total price the authorities were willing to pay.[54] Some entrepreneurs devised quite remarkable strategies when they found themselves in this plight. One man, who died deeply in debt, was found to have sold his possessions or turned them into a pious foundation; he must have hoped to avoid confiscation in that way. The case was submitted to the Council of State (*diwān-i humāyūn*), which decided that a person with debts to the Treasury had no right to constitute a pious foundation. Sale and foundation deeds were therefore declared invalid.[55] Other bankrupt entrepreneurs fled to remote provinces, such as Egypt or the Yemen.

One of the risks that camel entrepreneurs had to bear was the high mortality of their beasts, for presumably they had to provide substitutes whenever one of their customers lost his mount. At least, this was the rule in late nineteenth- and early twentieth-century Damascus, and although sixteenth-century documents say nothing explicit on this point, indirect evidence makes it seem likely that this rule existed in earlier times as well.[56] Camel entrepreneurs often complained of soldiers and officials mistreating the mounts entrusted to their care by overloading them with trade goods.[57] When the animals then collapsed, the entrepreneurs were asked to foot the bill. These complaints induced the Ottoman administration to issue a rescript setting maxima for camel loads. But rules of this kind were often broken, and the problem remained.

Certain entrepreneurs invested large sums of money in the camel business, while others were discouraged by the high risks and provided camels as a sideline only. In 1591–2 some of the larger entrepreneurs supplied 100–120 beasts.[58] We have little information about camel prices, but in 1578–9 an animal could be bought for 60–70 Ottoman gold pieces.[59] Between 1578–9 and 1591–2 the Ottoman gold coin remained stable; thus a large entrepreneur of the late sixteenth century invested between 6000 and 8500 gold pieces. But sums of this magnitude were the exception rather than the rule; in the account books we find payments to quite a few entrepreneurs who had provided no more than a few dozen animals.

INVOLUNTARY SERVICES

In some instances camel entrepreneurs did not willingly furnish their animals to Ottoman dignitaries on official business, but were forced to do so. In 1591–2 some Damascus notables managed to avoid this unwelcome responsibility by bribing the caravan commander, and that year there were not enough entrepreneurs with the requisite capital.[60] The following year a Damascene named Hekīmoghlu Aḥmed, whom rumour granted a fortune of five million *akče* (or 41,667 gold pieces according to the official exchange rate), was ordered to furnish the caravan with one hundred camels. If the rumour was correct, Hekīmoghlu was meant to invest about 15 per cent of his fortune. Whether he did so or not is impossible to determine, however, and documents from the seventeenth century make no further mention of entrepreneurs rendering forced services to the pilgrimage.

Even though this case seems to have been exceptional in the history of the Damascus caravan, it conformed to late sixteenth-century Ottoman administrative practice as documented for Anatolia and Rumelia.[61] To provide meat for the inhabitants of Istanbul, and particularly the court and janissaries, wealthy inhabitants of the Balkans were obliged to furnish a set number of sheep at officially determined prices. Some of the people involved (*djeleb*) possessed large flocks. But others drastically had to change their patterns of investment so as to comply with official demands.

If Ewliyā Čelebi's evaluation is at all realistic, some of the *djeleb* managed to make a profit out of their involuntary investment.[62] But sixteenth- and seventeenth-century archival materials show that many *djeleb* attempted to avoid service, so that new people constantly needed to be recruited; apparently, most *djeleb* worked at a loss. Even less popular was service as a butcher in Istanbul, at least during the second half of the sixteenth century, when wealthy provincials who had made themselves unpopular by usury were often drafted to perform this service. For political reasons, Istanbul meat prices during this period were set at so low a level that they did not cover costs, and many butchers sustained heavy losses or even went bankrupt. In the long run, however, the Ottoman government did not continue this policy, probably because it became more and more difficult to find people with the requisite fortunes who were not in the employ of the Sultan and thereby exempt from services of this kind. In the seventeenth century, Istanbul meat prices were allowed to find a level that permitted butchers to live off their trade. Only the forced deliveries of sheep continued.

In the case of Hekīmoghlu, there is no evidence that the camel hire to which he was entitled was fixed at a punitively low level. In fact there is no evidence at all that the Ottoman administration interfered in the formation of camel prices. However, such an interference probably did occur: between the sixteenth and eighteenth centuries, officially administered prices were very much part of Ottoman economic life.[63] Even in the nineteenth and early twentieth centuries, the governor of Damascus and the Sherif of Mecca promulgated the prices camel entrepreneurs could charge for the outgoing and return trips respectively.[64] Admittedly entrepreneurs could try to charge higher prices under a variety of pretexts. But these men did not possess a monopoly, as at least the wealthier pilgrims could and did buy their own camels. Camel suppliers could not pass on all their losses to the pilgrims, therefore, and bankruptcies were not a rare occurrence.

CONTINUITY AND LONG-TERM CHANGE

If we compare the information provided by 'Abd al-Ḳādir al-Djazarī concerning the late Mamluk and early Ottoman pilgrimage caravans with the data provided by late sixteenth- and early seventeenth-century archival material, elements of continuity strike the eye. Whatever change occurred from Mamluk to Ottoman times happened gradually, and the Ottoman administration's approach was strictly pragmatic. In the late sixteenth century, the Registers of Important Affairs every year contained rescripts concerned with concrete complaints. We learn of a caravan commander who refused to stop the caravan at prayer time, so that pilgrims neglected their daily worship for fear of being left behind.[65] Other pilgrims were given to the enjoyment of fireworks, which disturbed the pious concentration of their more restrained brethren. After their return to Damascus, Istanbul or Cairo, or even while still travelling, pilgrims probably made an official record of their complaints and deposited it with the relevant ḳāḍī or in the offices of the provincial governor. Moreover, secretaries of the caravan commander, who like al-Djazarī were concerned with the affairs of the pilgrimage on a full-time basis, probably collected, organized and passed on these complaints to Istanbul. Admittedly we have no proof that this is what occurred. But if this assumption were totally false, the authorities in Istanbul could not have been as well-informed as our records show them to have been. The experience accumulated in Istanbul constituted the base of new regulations and, in the long run, modified previous practice. But this was by no means a universal rule. As we have seen, the attempt to force rich men to furnish the caravan with camels ended in failure, and it would be a mistake to believe that every Sultan's command was automatically obeyed.

Other changes were caused more by the general political situation than by the specific needs of the caravan. In the eighteenth century, the Pasha of Damascus was normally appointed commander of the pilgrimage, while in the sixteenth and seventeenth centuries he had intervened only in urgent matters and otherwise limited himself to a supervisory role.[66] This change was due to a different distribution of power in the province. Before the fall of the Druze amir Fakhr al-Dīn Ma'ān in 1635, a number of families with power bases in rural Syria had played a significant role in provincial politics, and were integrated into the Ottoman system by receiving the honour of commanding the pilgrimage caravan. But when these families were marginalized in the later seventeenth century, a caravan commander chosen from among their midst did not benefit either the Ottoman central government or the pilgrims themselves. On the other hand, the early eighteenth century was a period of political reform, when the Ottoman administration tried to reassert control over the pilgrimage route, which had slipped away during the Habsburg–Ottoman war of 1683–99. Thus it must have seemed expedient to grant a single figure sweeping powers, and this happened to be the governor of Damascus. As a result, we should imagine the pilgrims moving through a political terrain where they had no control over the main actors, even though in day-to-day matters at least the wealthiest and best-connected among the pilgrims were not unable to influence events to their own advantage. This situation will become even clearer when we analyse the institutions concerned with the military protection of the pilgrimage caravan.

3

Caravan Security

It was one of the obligations of the Sultan as 'Servant of the Holy Places' to protect the pilgrims during their long journey through the Syrian and Arabian deserts. This was not an easy task, as the deserts were controlled by the Ottoman Sultan only to a limited extent. The Yemenis travelled through a vast region where even nominal control by the Pādi<u>sh</u>āh in Istanbul ended in the 1630s. Moreover, the pilgrims who arrived from Basra in a special caravan needed to traverse a desert over which Ottoman control was all but non-existent, even though Basra itself formed part of the Ottoman Empire. It was not possible to secure the safety of the pilgrims by stationing major bodies of troops in the area. Quite apart from the expenses involved, large garrisons would have used up much of the water urgently needed by the pilgrims and the Beduins who constituted the permanent inhabitants of the desert region.

The pilgrimage caravan was accompanied by a detachment of janissaries and, in the case of the Syrian caravan, by cavalrymen in receipt of a military tax assignment (*timār*). Only in case of disturbances in the desert or the Holy Cities was this detachment increased to a more impressive size. For the most part, the safety of the pilgrimage caravan was assured by official subsidies to the Beduins living along the hajj route (*ṣürre*). In Ottoman government circles, these payments were interpreted as a counterpart to the food and water which the Beduins delivered to the caravan. But when the payments in question were not made on time or did not satisfy the recipients in terms of quantity or quality, the Beduins felt justified in attacking the pilgrims and thus securing their subsidies *manu militari*. Therefore the *ṣürre* should be regarded not as a mere payment for services rendered, but as a means of protecting the caravan from Beduin attack.

BEDUIN SUBSIDIES

For the late sixteenth and early seventeenth centuries we possess accounts of the Syrian and Egyptian provincial finance administrations, which record official expenses related to the caravan (see Chapter 2). In the secondary literature it has become customary to call these accounts 'budgets' even though they record past expenses, and do not constitute a guide for future behaviour as is true of regular budgets.[1] Some of these provincial accounts have even been published. But they were intended to serve strictly practical purposes and in no way to stand as scientific statistics. Therefore the headings under which expenditures were recorded differ from one account to the next without formal redefinition of the relevant categories. Officials of the time knew exactly what they were documenting, but very often we do not, and therefore accounts a few years or decades apart are often difficult to compare. Minor differences between years, therefore, should not be made to carry the weight of too much interpretation. But, even so, the provincial accounts are of great significance because they allow us to establish an order of magnitude with respect to the expenses of the pilgrimage caravan's official section.

A further difficulty stems from the fact that Ottoman accounts of the sixteenth and seventeenth centuries use a variety of coins, which exchanged at different rates in different parts of the country. Only for some of the major cities do we possess lists of the relevant exchange rates, and even these lists are often incomplete.[2] Extrapolations are therefore unavoidable, which increases the possibility of mistakes. But similar problems are quite familiar to the historian of the European Middle Ages or the Early Modern period. We thus have no alternative but to use the accounts with a degree of scepticism and to assume that even dubious statistics are better than none at all.

The Egyptian budget of 1596–7 contains the names of individuals and tribal units receiving subsidies.[3] Presumably the individuals recorded did not receive grants for their own exclusive use, but also represented groups of Beduins. Sometimes the provincial accounts inform us of the stretch of road for which the recipients were responsible. In Table 1 we have attempted to separate subsidies in the narrow sense of the word from the recompense for goods and services furnished. Payments for the provision of camels have been eliminated

Table 1 *Payments to Beduins from Egyptian Provincial Budgets, to Facilitate Hajj Travel*

Year	Recipients	Payment in pāra	Payment in gold (sikke-i ḥasene)
1005–6/ 1596–7[1]	Beduins, unspecified[2]	211,451	5286
1009/ 1600	Beduins, unspecified	206,170	5154
1010–11/ 1601–2	Beduins, unspecified (only payments not in compensation for specific services)	208,455	5211
1020/ 1611–12	Beduins, unspecified	222,945	5574
1023–4/ 1614–15	as in 1020/ 1611–12	222,945	5574

1 Shaw (1968), p. 158 ff.
2 The Banū Ḥusayn, descendants of the Prophet, were for the most part townsmen and not desert dwellers. But the accounts do not always permit us to distinguish subsidies to the Banū Ḥusayn, so they have been included in the total.

whenever recognizable as such. But often a tidy separation was impossible, because the accounts contain nothing but global figures. As far as Ottoman treasury officials were concerned, the difference between payment for services rendered and subsidies was quite irrelevant. In both cases, the ultimate aim was identical, namely to provide for the safe transit of the pilgrimage caravan. In the relationship of Ottoman administrators and pilgrims on the one hand, and Beduins on the other, political and economic factors were so closely intertwined as to be inextricable. The Ottoman administration obliged the Beduins to provide goods and services, but payments were especially generous so as to cement political loyalties.

Between 1596–7 and 1614–15, 5100–5800 Ottoman gold coins were assigned every year from Egyptian provincial revenues as *şürre* payments to Beduins. Oscillations are moderate and must have had local reasons which we cannot now determine. In the Syrian case, changes from year to year are much more dramatic (see Table 2).[4] Payments to tribes whose names appear in the table, such as the 'Anaza or Waḥīdāt probably constituted only a share of total subsidy

Table 2 *Payments to Beduins from Syrian Provincial Budgets, to Facilitate Hajj Travel*

Year	Recipients	Payment in pāra	Payment in gold (sikke-i ḥasene)	Payment in esedī ghurush
1005/ 1596–7	Rashīd, Nu'aym, Salāma (Beduins)	101,280	2532	
1018/ 1609–10	Beduins, unspecified		9057	
1019/ 1610–11	Beduins, unspecified		9268	
1020/ 1611–12	Beduins, unspecified		11,678	
1085/ 1674–5	Beduins: Banū Ṣakhr,[1] 'Urbān-i-Karak, 'Anaza, Waḥīdāt, al-'Umr		4271	9076
	Payment to Salāma, for transportation		2220	4718
	Total (1674–5)		6491[2]	13,794

1 On the Banū Ṣakhr, see Hütteroth and Abdulfattah (1977), p. 169 f. Evliya Çelebi (1896–1938), vol. 9, p. 571, gives a list of Beduin groups in receipt of subsidies in the late seventeenth century. On the 'Anaza, see Rafeq (1970), *passim*.

2 This is no longer the *sikke-i ḥasene*, but a later and less valuable gold coin known as *sherīfī*. Since our data are insufficient, conversion is approximate.

payments, albeit an important one. For although the Rashīd, Nu'aym and Salāma were influential tribes frequently mentioned in the context of the pilgrimage, the provincial accounts do not mention them as *ṣürre* recipients. It is probable, however, that the increase in *ṣürre* payments by the beginning of the seventeenth century (see Table 2) is more than a mere optical illusion due to the dubious character of the older data. For during those years the Kurdish Pasha Djānbulā-doghlu 'Alī and the Druze prince Fakhr al-Dīn 'Alī II were both trying to seize power in the Syrian provinces.[5] As a result of the ensuing unrest, the Beduins living along the hajj route were able to demand higher *ṣürre* payments than was customary. The Ottoman administration having entrusted the Beduin notable Aḥmad b. Ṭurabāy with the task of breaking Fakhr al-Dīn's resistance, many tribal units were induced to abandon their normal routes of migration, and needed to be compensated by increased subsidies.[6] Nor were the 1670s a particularly calm period; but if the accounts of 1674–5 reflect reality to some extent, disturbances were less dramatic and *sürre* increases accordingly less marked than at the beginning of the century.

For 1681–3 we possess a further group of Syrian provincial accounts, which unfortunately contain only lump sums for all expenses connected with the Damascus pilgrimage caravan, so that the height of Beduin subsidies cannot be determined.[7] But in spite of all these gaps in our information we can conclude that payments from Syrian revenue sources were usually higher than those derived from Egypt.

Given the much more limited Syrian revenues, subsidies to the Beduins supplying and protecting the hajj caravan constituted a major item in the provincial 'budget'. At the beginning of the seventeenth century, the Ottoman administration paid out between 15,000 and 17,000 gold pieces to the Beduins residing in the vicinity of the caravan route; a sizable share, however, was handed over in the shape of silver coins. Thus the Beduins were able to purchase certain goods in urban markets, such as arms and textiles, and thereby were integrated into the Ottoman economic structure.

THE COMMANDER OF THE PILGRIMAGE CARAVAN

In the long run, the political situation in the desert, but also in the cultivated regions of Egypt and Syria, determined the height of *sürre* payments. In the short run, however, the amount of money to be paid over was determined in annual negotiations.[8] On the Ottoman side, the negotiators were the commanders of the Syrian and Egyptian pilgrimage caravans, supported by the central administration in Istanbul. The Beduins were represented by their tribal leaders, often allied to the Sherifs of Mecca by ties which were more or less solid according to circumstances. Since Beduin leaders did not put down their impressions in writing, documentation concerning the negotiation process is one-sided. There are not even any neutral observers, for Ottoman writers not in an official position at the time of their pilgrimage, such as Ewliyā Čelebi or 'Abd al-Raḥmān Ḥibrī, were close enough to the bureaucracy to reflect the official point of view.[9] Ewliyā and other authors have drawn heroic images of caravan commanders and military governors; but these accounts should be taken as part of the self-image of the Ottoman bureaucracy and not necessarily as a faithful depiction of reality.

Particularly the Egyptian records show us the caravan commander as responsible for the purchasing of supplies.[10] In addition he was in charge of distributing subsidies to the Beduins and commander of the detachment accompanying the caravan. He decided how long the caravan was to remain at different resting places. In case of danger he could order a detour or withdrawal to a fortified town or camp. Finally it was his responsibility to bring the Sultan's pious donations safely to Mecca and Medina. These basic responsibilities of the caravan commander had been determined in Mamluk times and did not change during the sixteenth and seventeenth centuries; this continuity becomes obvious when we study the sequence of appointment documents contained in the Mühimme Defterleri. In 1591–2, when Ahmed Beg, governor of the sub-province of Gaza, was appointed commander of the pilgrimage, the importance of continuity was specifically invoked, and a major reason for the appointment was the fact that Ahmed Beg had successfully commanded pilgrimage caravans in the past.[11] The appointment document particularly recognized his merits in procuring supplies for the caravan and having them transported to diverse stopping points. According to al-Djazarī's account of the caravan in late Mamluk times, similar administrative and political skills had been demanded of earlier caravan commanders.[12]

In the appointment document concerning the provincial governor of Gaza, only one of the customary duties of the caravan commander is not mentioned, namely the safe delivery of the Sultan's gifts to Mecca and Medina. In practical life, however, some caravan commanders considered this their principal responsibility. When Ewliyā Čelebi travelled to the Hejaz in 1671–2, the Syrian caravan was caught in a rainstorm only a few miles south of Damascus. Soon the desert was transformed into a sea of mud, in which the camels were unable to move.[13] A delegation of pilgrims visited the caravan commander, who in that particular year happened to be the governor of Damascus, to discuss what should be done next. The governor received them most ungraciously, and declared that if need be he would abandon the pilgrims to their fate in the middle of the desert. His own responsibility, he declared, was limited to the safe transport of the Sultan's gifts to Mecca and Medina, and of the state palanquin symbolizing the Sultan's presence to 'Arafat.[14] Now this was an unusual situation, as the governor had been charged with a punitive expedition against the rebellious Sherif of Mecca. In this particular year, therefore, political and military considerations must have been more important than in normal years. But this incident demonstrates that individual caravan commanders possessed, or thought they possessed, some leeway in determining the relative weight of their different responsibilities.

In the first half of the sixteenth century, when Ottoman rule over Egypt was still being established, the authorities in Istanbul were careful not to appoint a Mamluk to the office of caravan commander. This fact is worth noting, as at the time local administration remained solidly in Mamluk hands; the central government was anxious to avoid anything that might endanger the regular collection of revenues.[15] But the caravan commander was not concerned with tax collection, and it was considered necessary to establish a balance between Mamluk and non-Mamluk officials. These conditions were of special significance as the governor of the pilgrimage caravan had reasonable expectations of being appointed governor of Egypt in the future.

Beyond general considerations of this type, the factors which had a role to play in the appointment of a caravan commander are recognizable only from documentation pertaining to the second half of the sixteenth century. Candidates willing to subsidize the caravan out of their own fortunes apparently had an advantage over their competitors. Thus in 1560–1 Ḳara Shāhīn Muṣṭafā Pasha, who as a governor of Yemen had been severely criticized for his avarice, declared himself willing to conduct the caravan with an official budget of only 14 'purses' of *akče*.[16] Possibly Muṣṭafā Pasha was trying to counterbalance the impact of the complaints levied against him by a show of generosity. At the same time officials in Istanbul commented that the Pasha's family lived in Cairo and that he was willing to pay in hard cash for the privilege of being reunited with them. All these special circumstances obviously did not apply to Muṣṭafā Pasha's successor. But the responsible authorities in the capital pretended to believe that future caravan commanders would also be willing to run the caravan on a budget of 14 'purses', even though before Muṣṭafā Pasha's tenure of office, 18 'purses' had been the going rate.[17] The document we possess concerns the negotiations which preceded the appointment of Muṣṭafā Pasha's successor. The governor of Egypt pleaded that 16 'purses' constituted the minimum sum on which the caravan could be conducted. If the sum offered lay below this limit, Özdemiroghlu 'Othmān Pasha, known as a most successful military commander, would be unable to accept the appointment.[18] This argument induced the authorities in Istanbul to increase their offer to 16 'purses', but the governor was emphatically informed that a higher offer was totally out of the question. Other considerations which might determine an appointment involved relations between the two caravan commanders, at times a thorny issue. In the second half of the sixteenth century, disputes between soldiers of the Syrian and

Egyptian caravans occurred frequently, particularly when the two groups escorted the Sultan's palanquin (*maḥmal*). The subject of these disputes were mainly questions of precedence at 'Arafat, and usually occurred at the time when the prayer meeting which constitutes the high point of the pilgrimage had been completed and the pilgrims hurriedly left the site.[19] In Mamluk times, the Cairo *maḥmal* had enjoyed precedence, but toward the end of the sixteenth century the Ottoman central administration decided that the two *maḥmal*s should leave 'Arafat at the same time. This rule if anything exacerbated disputes. In 1570–1 the quarrel even degenerated into a brawl in which the Egyptian caravan commander was wounded in the head.

Given this situation, the responsible officials in Istanbul attempted to defuse matters by appointing caravan commanders who were on good terms with their opposite numbers. In 1580–1 Ķānṣūh Beg, long-time commander of the Damascene pilgrimage caravan, had nothing but praise for his colleague 'Alī Beg, former governor of Jerusalem, who had just brought the caravan safely back under very difficult conditions.[20] 'Alī Beg therefore was reappointed commander of the Cairo caravan, and only his death shortly before the pilgrims were due to leave Egypt prevented him from actually filling the office.

Occasionally the authorities in Istanbul appointed two men to command the Damascus pilgrimage in one and the same year. These appointments may reflect disputes between Syrian amirs, in which the central government preferred not to take sides. By appointing the representative first of one faction and then of the other, the central power probably intended to play off the two sides against one another and thereby retain control of the situation. In certain instances, however, such a policy severely inconvenienced the pilgrims, for they risked attack by the partisans of the man disappointed in his hopes for preferment and more than ready to prove his rival's ineffectiveness. In other instances, Istanbul might appoint two candidates when the central administration's officials did not feel well enough informed about the distribution of power in the Syrian desert to make a choice. In that case, the decision was left to the governor of Damascus, who was in a better position to judge the situation even though he generally held office for a short time only. Thus we possess a rescript from the Ottoman Sultan dated 1570–1, in which the governor of Damascus is asked to choose between the governor of Gaza, Riḍwān Beg, and his own finance director, 'Alī Beg.[21]

Somewhat more complicated was the case recorded in 1585–6. Once more a governor of Gaza had been appointed commander of the Syrian pilgrimage caravan, this office in the sixteenth century being much more important than the location of Gaza would seem to warrant.[22] Quite frequently, this particular governorship was a stepping stone to more important positions, for instance the *pashalık* of Yemen.[23] Yet when the candidate realized he was competing against Ḳānṣūh Beg, an old but very powerful man and for most of his life governor of the fortress of 'Adjlun on the edge of the Syrian desert, he withdrew his candidacy. It must be admitted that Ḳānṣūh Beg's candidacy was merely symbolic, as at the time he was in Istanbul, after having been called there to give an account of his manifold and, from the administration's point of view, problematic activities. He thus had been appointed caravan commander as a mark of the Sultan's favour after having cleared himself, and not as a practical proposition.[24] As a result the Damascus caravan was left without any commander at all, a situation which much impeded travel preparations. The rescript we possess was meant to clarify this situation; the governor of Gaza was told that the appointment of his competitor was a mere formality and that he was to make sure preparations were completed on time. In this case, the governor of Damascus was not asked for his opinion; the officials in Istanbul felt sufficiently in control to make the decision on their own.

FROM THE BIOGRAPHY OF A CARAVAN COMMANDER

In order to understand why the governor of Gaza did not believe that he stood a realistic chance of becoming caravan commander in competition against Ḳānṣūh Beg of 'Adjlun, we need to take a closer look at the latter's biography.[25] Ḳānṣūh Beg came from an old family, but although throughout his life he maintained close connections to the Beduins, his own relatives were village dwellers. In sixteenth- and seventeenth-century Syria it was common enough for influential families to maintain rural seats which under propitious circumstances might be passed on for a few generations within the same family. The fortress of 'Adjlun, which still stands today, was just such a family seat.[26] Well known in the Crusader period and destroyed during the Mongol wars, it was rebuilt and entered the hands of Ibn Sā'id's family in the later Mamluk period.

Ḳānṣūh's ancestor Ibn Sā'īd had even, at times when he was fighting it out with the Mamluk governor of Syria, used 'Adjlun's strategic location to deny passage to the pilgrimage caravans. However, the family had trouble adapting to the changed situation after the Ottoman conquest of Syria, and one of Ibn Sā'īd's sons as well as one of his grandsons were executed. In later life Ibn Sā'īd seems to have lost all his power, and the chroniclers do not even report how he met his end. The family survived this temporary fall from favour, however, and in the second half of the sixteenth century we find its members again established in and around 'Adjlun – it seems the family never lost its main seat, or at least managed to regain it in fairly short order.

We do not know for certain whether Ķānṣūh Beg was a son, grandson or other relative of Ibn Sā'īd's. In a document dating from the year 1581 he is said to be eighty years old.[27] Allowing for the fact that the Islamic year is a lunar year, Ķānṣūh would have been born about 1504–5, so that he may perfectly well be a son of Ibn Sā'īd's. But his political activity only began about 1551, so that either he must have been occupied with affairs of purely local importance during the first half of his life, or else he was born later than suggested by the aforementioned document.

We know that Ķānṣūh Beg paid substantial sums to the Ottoman central administration to secure his various appointments, even though he never held office in agriculturally productive regions. When at one point he fell into disfavour and wished to reestablish himself and obtain an appointment, he offered the government a hundred thousand gold pieces.[28] This was certainly an unusual situation, and the offer does not sound like a realistic proposition. But even when, under much more 'normal' circumstances, he was appointed governor of 'Adjlun and Karak-Shaubak, and commander of the pilgrimage caravan, Ķānṣūh Beg paid 5000 gold pieces directly to the Ottoman central administration; moreover, he promised to contribute 9000 gold pieces to the expenses of the caravan.[29] Thus the sale of offices, familiar to the historian of early modern Europe, was practised in the Ottoman Empire as well. The reasons in both cases were no doubt similar; governments were permanently short of cash and a bureaucracy regularly paid and remunerated according to performance criteria would have been much too expensive. In both cases, the taxpayer was the ultimate loser, as tax farmers and governors changed frequently and thus did not show much interest in preserving the population's ability to pay. In the regions close to the edge of the Syrian desert, the appointment of governors from locally prominent families somewhat mitigated these consequences.[30] In the sixteenth century, when the Ottomans were still in the process of consolidating their hold on the Syrian provinces, the appointment of governors with no local bases would have alienated a good many people and in most cases was therefore avoided.

Ķānṣūh Beg's power in Syria thus rested upon his positions as governor, tax farmer and commander of the pilgrimage, all of which he owed to the Ottoman government. At the same time, however, he maintained close relations with the Beduins. Ķānṣūh Beg belonged to the large faction of the Ķızıllu (Reds), which was opposed to the faction of the Aḵlu or Aḵili (Whites).[31] Some modern historians have surmised that the two terms, Turkish in origin, hide two much more ancient groupings, namely the Kays and Yaman of early Islamic history. Be that as it may, the conflict had practical repercussions as far as the pilgrims were concerned. If Ḵānṣūh Beg, as a Ḵızıllu, commanded the caravan, the danger that pilgrims might be attacked at the stopping points under the control of the Aḵlu was not to be denied. One of Ḵānṣūh Beg's opponents did, in fact, try to prevent the appointment by declaring that 35 stopping points were controlled by the Aḵlu, and only three by Ḵānṣūh Beg's own group. Needless to say, the petitioner, a certain Salāma, belonged to the Aḵlu faction himself. Ever cautious, the Ottoman administration appointed neither of the two competitors. But the same year, Ḵānṣūh Beg was made a governor of the province of Karak-<u>Sh</u>awbak, located directly on the pilgrimage road. The newly appointed official was enjoined to protect the pilgrims, and, as an additional safeguard, the governor of Damascus was ordered to reconcile Ḵānṣūh Beg and Salāma.

Among the documents, quite considerable in number, which deal with Ḵānṣūh Beg's tenure of office, a text from the year 1570–1 is particularly remarkable.[32] It constitutes an abridged version of an account of Ḵānṣūh's political career, which the governor himself must have presented to the central administration. Ḵānṣūh Beg declared that for a considerable time there had existed a state of enmity between himself and the Nu'aymo<u>gh</u>ulları, shaykhs of the Mafāridja Beduins.[33] There may have been many reasons for this hostility, but Ḵānṣūh Beg chose to stress the fact that, in his 35 years' service to the pilgrims, he had always tried to keep camel rents low. We may thus conclude that the Nu'aymo<u>gh</u>ulları hired out camels and therefore were alienated by Ḵānṣūh's policy. The governor claimed that camel rents had gone down by half, because he had managed to increase the number of animals offered. This he had achieved by inviting Beduin groups that had not furnished any animals in the past to begin supplying the pilgrimage caravans. But when the news spread that Ḵānṣūh would not be commanding the next pilgrimage caravan, the suppliers who had recently entered the market rapidly withdrew. Presumably these were small and weak groupings, who feared the wrath of their competitors once Ḵānṣūh Beg was no longer there to shield them. As a result, camel rents once again increased, and the long-time commander apparently felt that the Ottoman authorities would draw the consequences from this situation.

Ḵānṣūh Beg's career only ended with his death in Istanbul in 1591, where he had gone to protest his recent deposition.[34] This event probably had been occasioned by a major Beduin rebellion. A governor of Damascus had attacked two groups of Beduins when they presumed themselves in a safe place, and it was claimed that Ḳānṣūh Beg was behind this attack. The result was a minor civil war, and 70 to 80 villages in the vicinity of Ḳānṣūh Beg's fortress of 'Adjlun were burnt down. The old governor did not succeed in regaining control of the fortress which had been in his family's hands for so many years, and this effectively ended his political career. His successors temporarily regained control of 'Adjlun; but rivalries among the sons, nephews and grandsons of Ḳānṣūh Beg permitted the Druze prince Fakhr al-Dīn II to extend his control over the region previously dominated by Ḳānṣūh's family. After about 1624, the descendants of Ibn Sā'id were not even locally prominent any more.

NEGOTIATIONS AND CONFLICTS WITH THE BEDUINS

Negotiations to secure the safety of the pilgrims began in Damascus, shortly before the previous year's caravan had returned to the city. It was important to appoint the caravan commander as soon as possible, for many arrangements with the Beduins were made by the commander as an individual and ceased to be binding if another person came to command the caravan. The designated caravan commander in addition conferred with respected inhabitants of Damascus, among whom the merchants accompanying every caravan certainly played an important role.

Further negotiation became necessary after the caravan had started on its way. In order to influence the behaviour of the Beduins the commander might manipulate the amount of *şürre* paid to particular groups. In extreme cases, when the commander was particularly dissatisfied, he might refuse payment altogether, but then an armed conflict became likely.[35] Sometimes payments for services rendered to the caravan were changed at the last minute. At other times the commander took hostages from certain Beduin families, and, in the case of open conflict, might order the murder or execution of a Beduin leader. Attacks on the pilgrimage caravan were a frequent occurrence, and as long as the number of dead and wounded remained within limits, these events were not considered particularly remarkable. Only when relations broke down completely were there major attacks on the caravan which the chroniclers of the time found worth reporting. Ewliyā Čelebi mentions an attack which occurred in the early 1670s.[36] Even more serious, but outside the period treated in this volume, was the attack on the Damascus caravan returning from Mecca in 1757, in which a large number of pilgrims perished. In some cases Ottoman government officials engaged in bloody reprisals against the Beduins, which might be legitimized in religious terms because of the threat the latter posed to the pilgrimage caravan.[37]

Some of the negotiations between Ottoman governors and Beduins living close to the pilgrimage route have been documented in the Registers of Important Affairs. We will discuss them here as examples of negotiations that took a normal course. In one case we again encounter Nu'aymoghlu, the Mafāridja shaykh, whom we already know as the opponent of Ḳānṣūh Beg.[38] The latter had offered to accompany the Damascus caravan for a stretch of the road, which meant that he also intended to guarantee its safety. But his Beduin allies, for reasons that remain unclear, withdrew from the agreement, and now Nu'aymoghlu refused to take the risk upon himself. It also happened that the Beduins who had offered to guarantee the safety of the caravan went back on their commitments, particularly if their *ṣürre* was not paid out on time. Such events might result in a sharp reprimand of the caravan commander by the Istanbul authorities.[39]

Some Beduin leaders received Ottoman titles and other marks of honour in addition to their *ṣürre* and food subsidies. In the Ottoman realm, as in the medieval Middle East, the grant of robes as marks of honour, comparable to modern decorations, was common.[40] Provincial governors, and particularly the Sherifs of Mecca, often received such honours, so that the grant of a robe integrated Beduin leaders into the Ottoman *cursus honorum*. Mamluk titles such as the amir al-'Arab were also awarded, probably with the same aim in mind.[41] Thus a document dated 1576–7 reports that an assembly of Damascene notables had testified that the personage to be awarded the title of amir al-'Arab had supplied the caravan in a satisfactory manner and therefore was worthy of the honour about to be conferred on him.

Conflictual situations also tell us a good deal about the relationship of the Beduins and the Ottoman central power. The scholar 'Abd al-Raḥmān Ḥibrī, who lived in Edirne and wrote a history of his town still used as a primary source, undertook the pilgrimage in 1632, a year in which there was a good bit of unrest on the Arabian peninsula.[42] At this time a local dynasty had reestablished itself in Yemen after several decades of Ottoman rule, and attempts to reconquer the rebellious province failed.[43] Ottoman soldiers obliged to leave the country settled in Mecca and caused so much trouble that the central government entrusted the powerful Mamluk Riḍwān Beg with the task of dislodging the soldiers from the Holy City.[44] One effect of Riḍwān Beg's campaign, however, was to make the pilgrimage routes insecure. According to Ḥibrī, things were made worse by the fact that Ibn Farrukh, long-time commander of the Syrian pilgrimage caravan, happened to be out of office in 1632: fear of Ibn Farrukh supposedly had restrained many tribesmen up to this time.[45] It does appear, however, as if the excesses committed by the soldiers returning from the Yemen, and the loss of Ottoman authority which these events entailed, played the key role in triggering Beduin attacks. There was fighting at almost every major stopping point that year, and near the settlement of al-'Ulā, where the Syrian desert becomes the Arabian, the caravan very narrowly escaped catastrophe. The Beduins attacked with muskets, and could only be kept under control by the firing of cannon. Four pilgrims were killed that very night, and Ḥibrī calculated that the caravan had lost 125 loaded camels along a stretch of road that measured less than half the distance from Damascus to Mecca.[46] But, in spite of everything, the caravan reached the Hejaz and returned in good order. This success must have strengthened the Ottoman position at a critical time, when the young Sultan Murād IV was taking the reins of government into his own hands and the Ottoman court was shaken by factional strife.[47]

The second example of a well-documented open conflict between pilgrims and Beduins occurred during the Ottoman–Habsburg war of 1683–99, when the central administration concentrated its attention upon events in the Balkan peninsula and pilgrims, Sherifs and Beduins were little protected or supervised. In this case, events were recorded by the Palestinian scholar and mystic 'Abd al-Ghānī al-Nābulusī, who travelled to Mecca as a pilgrim in 1693–5.[48] Before his pilgrimage to Mecca, al-Nābulusī had intended to visit the grave of the Prophet in Medina. But the Sherif Sa'd b. Zayd declared that the Ḥarb Beduins had closed the road from Yanbu' to Medina, and that it was impossible to get through. The Palestinian scholar thus had the opportunity to watch Sherif Sa'd's manner of conducting a war, and the behaviour of his Beduin troops. One village was found to be empty, because the inhabitants had joined the war on the side of the Ḥarb. Sherif Sa'd not only burnt the houses down, but even destroyed the date palms, a measure of unusual severity in desert warfare.[49] But Sherif Sa'd, who according to Ewliyā Čelebi had tried to cut off the water supply of Mecca during a previous dispute with the Ottoman administration, had no doubt that his actions were justified.[50] After all, so he argued, the Prophet Muḥammad had not treated the unbelievers any differently. The assumption that Beduins troubling the hajj caravan were to be treated as if they were unbelievers is found in other seventeenth-century Ottoman sources as well. Thus Ewliyā occasionally makes remarks pointing in the same direction. Sherif Sa'd's violent measures were successful; after a short while, the caravan was able to continue on its way toward Mecca.

Further evidence concerning violent repression of Beduins can be found in an unexpected place, namely the biography of Mi'mār Meḥmed Agha, the architect of the Blue Mosque in Istanbul.[51]

Mi'mār Meḥmed Agha was one of the few Ottoman artists to be honoured by a full-scale biography during his lifetime; it was composed by his admirer Dja'fer Efendi, son of Shaykh Behrām. In his varied career, Mi'mār Meḥmed Agha had also been sent to Syria as second-in-command to the governor of Damascus, Khusrew Pasha.[52] Later he was posted to the Hawran as a local administrator. This was a difficult assignment for, as we have seen in the biography of Kānṣūh Beg, this area was quite rebellion-prone, and unrest in the Hawran was likely to affect the security of the Damascus pilgrimage caravan. Mi'mār Meḥmed Agha, on the other hand, as a product of the levy of boys (*dewshirme*), who had seen service mostly in the Balkans, lacked the local contacts which constituted the strength, and occasionally the weakness, of Kānṣūh Beg and other inhabitants of the desert edge.[53]

At the time when Meḥmed Agha served the governor of Damascus, the pilgrimage caravan was attacked by Beduins, and Khusrew Pasha undertook a punitive expedition. But after a one-month campaign he was obliged to withdraw without having achieved anything. Meḥmed Agha was left behind with a small force and implored the help of the saint Seyyid Shaykh Ibrāhīm, to whose mausoleum he paid a pious visit. There the shaykh appeared to him in a dream, announcing that he would find the robbers in their camp, fast asleep, and commanded Meḥmed Agha to kill them all.[54] Meḥmed Agha's soldiers did, in fact, encounter a camp of sleeping Beduins, but they were afraid since the number of people was quite large, and did not dare to attack. Meḥmed Agha then told them about his dream and promised them the aid of Seyyid Ibrāhīm. But at least as effective as this assurance of saintly support was probably the threat that he, Meḥmed Agha, would kill any soldier who attempted to escape. Most of the Beduins were destroyed in the following battle; only the commander, a man named Djum'a Kāsib, was taken prisoner with his immediate associates. When the prisoners proceeded to offer a weighty ransom, Meḥmed Agha decided that, if they were let go, they would soon be molesting pilgrim caravans again: he therefore had his prisoners slain. At first his deeds were celebrated in Damascus as a great victory. Later, however, Khusrew Pasha seems to have had doubts concerning the political wisdom of his second-in-command, and Meḥmed was transferred to another post.[55]

In Dja'fer Efendi's account, a remarkable religious aura surrounds this minor episode of desert warfare. The author aims at creating an image of Meḥmed Agha as a hero of the Holy War and a person directly inspired by God, and this story is but one of many episodes marshalled for the purpose. That the Beduins were themselves Muslims is quite secondary to Dja'fer Efendi, who presents the event as an example of an authentic Holy War, in which the Ottoman soldiers are supported not merely by a saint, but by God himself. This is all the more remarkable as a pious medieval writer, namely Ibn Djubayr, had been favourably impressed by the religious attitudes of the Beduins.[56] By the seventeenth century things had completely changed; now we find an Ottomanized upper stratum in Syria and occasionally even in the Hejaz, who often spoke Arabic as their native language but were complete strangers to the world of the Beduins. In this context, it may be of some importance that Sherif Sa'd had had a career in the Ottoman core lands, officiating in the Thracian sub-provinces of Kırkkilīse and Vize, and therefore belonged to this Ottomanized milieu.[57] Beduins attacking the pilgrimage caravan were easily placed on the same level as unbelievers because, from a cultural point of view, they were regarded as total strangers by the ruling elite.

WEAPONS AND SOLDIERS

Hibrī's caravan of 1632 was able to get through the desert without major disasters because it carried cannons. Every one of these valuable weapons was accompanied by a cannonier and transported by horses or occasionally camels.[58] The anonymous writer of the 1580s, who wrote about the Cairo caravan, reports that six cannons were transported by twelve camels.[59]

In the late sixteenth and early seventeenth centuries many Beduins owned firearms, mainly muskets. We know that there was a tax farmer in the Palestinian town of Zefat (Safed) who sold grain to European unbelievers, which at that time was strictly forbidden.[60] His illegal gains he invested in muskets, which he smuggled to the Beduins. Artillery, on the other hand, was the exclusive privilege of the Ottoman authorities. Thus the twelve cannons which the Syrian caravan usually carried were a reasonably effective deterrent.

During the last years of Süleymān the Lawgiver's reign, approximately in 1558–9, the Damascus caravan was accompanied by 150 janissaries and garrison soldiers and 100 cavalrymen[61]. Even though the janissaries were normally infantrymen, they could not traverse the long distance from Damascus to Mecca without mounts. When spies, whom the caravan commander regularly sent out to gather information on Beduin plans, reported suspicious movements, the number of accompanying janissaries was increased. In 1571–2, a detachment of 300 soldiers was considered indispensable even in 'normal' times.

Even under the Mamluk Sultans, camels, foodstuffs and

implements needed by the soldiers had to be paid for by the fisc.[62] A special bureau took care of these matters. Its mode of operation is known to us from the careful account of 'Abd al-Kādir al-Djazarī, who had worked in this office for many years, as had his father (see Chapter 2). After Syria and Egypt had been conquered by the Ottomans, the office continued to operate in the accustomed manner. But after the death of Süleymān the Lawgiver in 1566, his successor Selīm II (reigned 1566–75) attempted to save money.[63] The new Sultan ordered that all the holders of *timār*s (tax assignments) accompanying the pilgrimage caravan would have to take care of their own equipment, as there was no reason to grant them advantages not accorded to other *timār*-holders, who all needed to spend considerable sums of money on their horses and outfits. But this order proved to be unworkable in practice. The vizier Muṣṭafā Pasha objected that the Syrian cavalrymen's revenues were so insecure that he could not recommend burdening them with supplementary expenditures. Selīm II gave in, and the cavalrymen were assigned 25 gold pieces per person for their equipment (1567–8).

Even so, it proved to be difficult to find military men suitable for the protection of the pilgrimage caravan. In a sultanic rescript from the years 1571–2 the governor and finance director of Damascus were warned that many cavalrymen turned the money they had been assigned over to prospective pilgrims.[64] The men accepting the money agreed to shoulder the obligation to protect the caravan, but often they were quite old and no longer suitable for military service. This practice was sternly prohibited by the Sultan's council, but to enforce the prohibition was quite a different matter. In 1587–8 there were renewed complaints that older janissaries who sought to combine the protection of the caravan with a pilgrimage were unable to support the rigours of military service in the desert.[65] On the other hand, caravan commanders probably viewed the participation of elderly and sober soldiers with some favour; for on the long desert stretches inhabited only by Beduins, disciplinary problems were widespread.

Certain cavalrymen and janissaries sought to avoid service in the caravan because, in a time of rising prices, they were unable to support themselves on their tax assignments or soldiers' pay, and needed to work in a secondary civilian occupation as well. Those soldiers possessing a small amount of capital often farmed the collection of taxes. Thus Turkmen *timār*-holders from the province of Aleppo farmed taxes due from the nomads and semi-nomads in this province, and were unavailable when their services were needed by the caravan.[66] The Sultan's Council threatened to take away the *timār*s of those cavalrymen who neglected their official duties. But the authorities could not make up their minds to increase the soldiers' tax assignments.

Military men in the service of the caravan commander were frequently caught trying to increase their incomes in more or less illicit ways. Deliveries of foodstuffs to the caravan offered certain possibilities in this respect.[67] Beduins in receipt of *şürre* were obligated to deposit foodstuffs at prearranged stopping points, and pilgrims unable to transport large quantities of supplies depended on the possibility of purchasing them en route. Certain janissaries, however, met the Beduins in the desert and either robbed or purchased below market value the foodstuffs the latter had been carrying, which they then proceeded to resell at a hefty profit to the pilgrims. This kind of profiteering hurt the pilgrims in two different ways: not only did they have to pay high prices for necessities, but the Beduins in question were likely to make good their losses by stealing from the caravan.

Apart from the conflicts caused by the soldiers' insufficient pay, the rivalries between Syrian and Egyptian military men occasioned quite a few disturbances. The sixteenth-century historian and littérateur Muṣṭafā 'Ālī recounts an anecdote about a Cairo soldier who is congratulated by his friends upon his safe return from the pilgrim-age.[68] The man does not feel that there is any need for special felicitation; after all, he had gone to Mecca mainly to have a good fight with his Syrian rivals. Ewliyā also recounts a dispute between the soldiers of the Syrian and Egyptian caravans, when they encountered one another on a narrow stretch of road not far from Medina.[69] This rivalry was well known to the Ottoman central government, which had arranged the travelling schedules of the two caravans in such a way as to minimize contact. Apart from the fact that the market of Medina could not supply two large caravans at the same time, concern about brawls and fights determined route arrangements.

DESERT FORTIFICATIONS

Many stopping points in the desert were defended by small garrisons in charge of guarding the wells or reservoirs which contained the caravans' water supplies. In years of drought this was a major task, for Beduins in need of water for themselves and their animals were liable to take by force whatever was available.[70] Moreover, during desert fighting it was common practice to fill up or defile wells so as to render them unusable to the opponent. Pilgrim caravans might also be affected by this kind of warfare. According to Ewliyā Čelebi, the Damascus governor Ḥüseyin Pasha, who led the Syrian caravan to

Mecca in 1672, refused subsidies to rebellious Beduins whom he accused of having filled up wells, and had those who protested imprisoned and in some cases killed.[71]

New desert fortresses could not be built without the consent of the Ottoman central administration. Since the protection of the pilgrims was a major concern in Istanbul, provincial governors desiring to fortify this or that place usually adduced the needs of the pilgrimage as a motivation. When the governor of Egypt wished to build a fort in al-'Arish, at the provincial border between Egypt and Syria, he declared that this place was frequently visited by pilgrims and merchants, who often suffered from Beduin attacks.[72] If a fortress were to be erected in this place, these attacks would become much less frequent, and the state would save money on the pay of the soldiers now needed to protect the caravans. Pilgrims visiting the sanctuary of Ibrāhīm in Hebron and Jerusalem were to be protected by a fortress at the often unsafe stopping point of 'Uyūn al-Tudjdjār.[73]

Yet Ewliyā's account makes it clear that the security problem was not solved by the construction of a desert fort alone.[74] Frequently enough, these isolated fortresses were attacked by Beduins and ultimately given up by a discouraged garrison. Ewliyā has a good deal to say on the tricks and feints which reputedly formed part of desert warfare. In 1625–6 Beduins attacked the fort of Mu'azzama after having drugged the garrison with a sweetmeat into which a sleeping drug had been mixed. The garrison soldiers had been deceived by the blandishments of young Beduin maidens, who distributed the sweets as an offering in the name of a deceased person, to be accepted out of charity. Shortly after the lively and imaginative Ewliyā, the sober pilgrim Meḥmed Edīb enumerated all the desert forts he had encountered, but also described the elaborate precautions taken to protect the caravan while on the road.[75] Obviously Meḥmed Edīb also did not believe that the fortresses in the desert really guaranteed the pilgrims a safe trip.

IN SPITE OF EVERYTHING:
AN ACCEPTABLE DEGREE OF SECURITY

But even though the pilgrim of the sixteenth and seventeenth centuries had to expect a good deal of trouble and even danger, major attacks upon the pilgrimage caravan were not all that frequent during this period. Ottoman officials, historians and travellers have written a good deal about the disasters of 1670–1 and 1757; therefore, they would presumably have written about other catastrophes of this kind had they occurred.[76] Other indirect evidence points in the same direction: narrative as well as documentary sources of the time frequently mention merchants accompanying the caravans, who used the time that pilgrims spent in Mecca after the pilgrimage ceremonies to conduct a profitable trade. If the pilgrimage routes had been as insecure as some historians of the twentieth century would have us believe, traders would not have taken their valuable wares through the desert.[77] Admittedly, the alternative route through the Red Sea was difficult from a navigational point of view, and shipping scarce and of poor quality. But Egyptian and Syrian traders could have invested in better ships, and if they failed to do so it was probably because the desert routes remained reasonably safe.

Ottoman administrators considered it necessary to secure the route to Mecca by means of negotiation and if necessary by violent repression because, by so doing, they legitimized the domination of the Ottoman Sultan. Every unavenged attack on the pilgrimage caravan jeopardized the claim of the ruler to be the supreme protector of the pilgrims. This situation also explains why Ottoman commentators like Ewliyā Čelebi and Dja'fer Efendi made no attempt to understand the Beduins' point of view. In the eyes of Ottoman officialdom, the Sultan's control over the pilgrimage routes constituted a major aspect of his legitimacy as a ruler. When Beduins challenged this control, members of the Ottoman ruling stratum might easily assume that the rebels had lost even their claim to the status of Muslims.

4

The Finances of the Holy Cities

After the rapid collapse of Mamluk domination in Egypt, pilgrims and inhabitants of the Holy Cities, or at least those among them with a certain political standing, needed to determine their attitude toward the rule of the Ottoman Sultan. Ever since the times of the Ayyubids (1175–1250) and, especially, the Mamluks (1250–1517), the Hejaz had been tied to Egypt politically – the Abbasid caliphate having been eliminated by the Mongol conquest in 1258. To those inhabitants of Syria, Egypt or the Hejaz familiar with the international situation, the Ottomans were by no means unknown: in the fifteenth century, both Meḥmed the Conqueror and Bāyezīd II had waged wars against Mamluk Sultans. Those wars had not led to major Ottoman gains of territory, however, so that the rapid and total Ottoman victory in 1515–17 necessitated a complete reorientation of the Egyptian, Syrian and Meccan upper classes. This reorientation was made more troublesome by the fact that sixteenth-century Islamic writers on political questions had some difficulty legitimizing Ottoman rule in general.[1] Contrary to the Safawids ruling sixteenth-century Iran, the Ottomans never claimed descent from the Prophet Muḥammad, and therefore lacked an important element of religious legitimation. Moreover, down to 1517 these Sultans did not control the Islamic heartlands. Instead they ruled an extensive area which for the most part had been Christian territory before the conquest, namely the Balkans as far as Belgrade in addition to western and central Anatolia. The Ottoman Sultans thus abruptly relocated themselves from the periphery to the centre of the Islamic world.

Given these circumstances, the Ottoman administration must have considered it expedient to change as little as possible in the estab-

74

lished manner of supplying the Holy Cities. This conformed to Ottoman practice in other newly conquered territories as well; financial arrangements, particularly, were often allowed to subsist for decades before being adjusted to Ottoman practice, and, in some cases, taxes from pre-Ottoman times were even retained on a permanent basis.[2] But in the Hejaz the reasons for continuing Mamluk supply policies were more compelling than anywhere else; after all, the Ottoman Sultans sought legitimation not through descent, but through contemporary immediate political success. A policy of generosity toward pilgrims and inhabitants of the Holy Cities, which equalled and if possible surpassed the performance of the most brilliant Mamluk Sultans, constituted an effective source of legitimacy. Comparison with the Mamluks was facilitated if overall arrangements in favour of pilgrims and residents of the Hejaz were retained. However, as Ottoman administrators were to discover to their cost, certain Hejaz dignitaries were to continue regarding Mamluk Sultans such as Ḳā'it Bāy as the apogee of pious rule, to whom even Süleymān the Lawgiver came but a poor second.

SUBSIDIES AND THEIR RECIPIENTS

Since Mecca possesses almost no agricultural hinterland, it would have been impossible even in Abbasid times (750–1258) to feed a large number of pilgrims without subsidies from foreign rulers. In and around Medina, water resources were somewhat more abundant and agricultural production larger, but, on the other hand, demand was not insignificant either. Even before the Ummayads took power in 661, this city had developed into a centre for the study of all information concerning the Prophet's life and deeds, which was collected, subjected to critical study and taken down in writing.[3] It was the purpose of this activity to put together an image of the ideal Islamic community and present it to all Muslims as a model to be followed. This intimate concern with the life of the Prophet gave the city a special prestige, so that even in Abbasid times it was considered meritorious to settle there permanently. Moreover, wealthy Muslims who were not themselves in a position to retire to Medina, increasingly developed the inclination to support the inhabitants by donations, which would permit the latter a life of pious meditation. By the fifteenth century, donations for the poor of Medina were a popular form of charity throughout the Islamic world.

Support for the Sherifs of Mecca, who as a semi-independent local dynasty governed the Hejaz under Abbasid, Mamluk and ultimately Ottoman suzerainty, had more mundane reasons.[4] While the Sherifs were too poor to operate as fully independent princes, a ruler based in Baghdad, Cairo or Istanbul could not possibly control the Hejaz without the cooperation of the Sherifs. A member of this family who had fallen foul of his remote suzerain only needed to seek refuge with his Beduin allies in the desert, and from this all but impregnable position could make life very difficult for the pilgrims. Even in Ayyubid times it therefore had become customary to bind the Sherifs, and other Hejazi notables as well, to the Mamluk Sultans by means of gifts. As we have seen from Ibn Djubayr's account (see Chapter 1), in the twelfth century these gifts had not become institutionalized to any great extent, however.[5] Thus Ibn Djubayr does not mention pious foundations benefiting the inhabitants of the Holy Cities; these were not instituted on a large scale until the time of the Mamluk Sultans.

FOUNDATIONS AND GIFTS

By the fifteenth century, foundations benefiting the Holy Cities were not limited to Egypt, though that was where the most extensive foundations of this type were located. In the sparsely settled and politically fragmented Anatolia of that time, the Karamanid dynasty of Konya, at one point the ally of Venice against the Ottomans, established such foundations around the steppe town of Ereğli.[6] In the Balkans, newly conquered by the Ottomans, such foundations also began to operate quite early on, the oldest known Rumelian foundation dating from 1460–1.[7] High officials at the court of Sultan Mehmed the Conqueror appear to have been among the founders, and, by the sixteenth century, foundations benefiting the Holy Cities could be found in the Balkan borderlands of the rapidly expanding empire.

These foundations were supported by peasant taxes from villages originally owned by the founder and assigned to this purpose in perpetuity. In addition, the Holy Cities received grants from the Ottoman Sultans which appear in the yearly budgets (see Chapter 2) and which were financed by ordinary revenues; but, in this case, the Sultan could decide every year how much money he was going to send. We possess a list of gifts made by Sultan Bāyezīd II (reigned 1481–1512) to various recipients in the Hejaz: the poor of Medina received 14,442 gold pieces.[8] Apparently Mouradjea d'Ohsson, eighteenth-century dragoman to the Swedish embassy in Istanbul and author of a comprehensive work on the Ottoman Empire of his own time, must have seen either this document or else another one very much like it; for he reports that Bāyezīd II annually donated 14,000 gold pieces to the poor of Medina.[9] Table 3 lists the donations which

Table 3 *Bāyezīd II's Gifts to the Hejazis*

Recipients	akče	Ottoman gold coins
Pilgrims, in general	21,500	
Individual inhabitants of Mecca and Medina	3300	
'Beduins from Mecca'	10,400	
Messengers bringing gifts to the Holy Cities	25,500	
Inhabitants of Mecca		735
Inhabitants of Medina		1210
The poor of Mecca and Medina		831 14,422
Miscellaneous	5000	
Total	65,700	17,198

Since there existed different types of gold coins, the rate of exchange is approximate. A gold coin was worth about 50 *akče*, see Artuk and Artuk (1971, 1974), vol. 2, p. 494. This table does not include certain gifts to individuals identified as Meccans or inhabitants of Medina, as it is not clear whether they benefited as individuals or as inhabitants of the Holy Cities. Certain Arabs or Beduins from Mecca also mentioned in the register probably had come to the court as messengers; the largesse they received has therefore been included.

this Sultan, whom some chroniclers regarded as a saint, sent to Mecca and Medina in 1503–4. Among the recipients, we find the Hanefī *ḳāḍī*s of both the Holy Cities, a son of the amir of Yanbu', a teacher in a theological college and the descendants of certain well-known derwish shaykhs.[10] The mosque of the Prophet in Medina formed the subject of the Sultan's special solicitude; its employees received donations which were far more generous than those assigned to their counterparts in Mecca.

The gifts of 1503–4 probably did not constitute a unique case, but were repeated with slight variation from year to year. As an indicator of institutionalization, we may cite the fact that an envoy of the people of Medina appeared in Istanbul to collect the gifts on behalf of his fellow citizens. When regular recipients of the Sultan's bounty died, the ruler was informed of the fact by letter from the *ḳāḍī* of Mecca; then the place of the deceased was normally filled by a new beneficiary. Thus certain features of the Ottoman Sultans' gift-giving were established well in advance of the conquest of Cairo.

Table 4 *Expenditure for Pilgrims and the Holy Cities from the Central Administration's Budget*

Year	Expenditures in akče (a)	Total budget (b)	a/b as %
1527–8	4,286,475	403,388,322	1.1–1.2
1653	7,142,298	676,106,387	1.1
1660–1	10,898,778	593,604,361	1.8
1690–1	16,567,320	812,838,365	2

DONATIONS ON THE PART OF THE OTTOMAN CENTRAL GOVERNMENT

In the Ottoman financial accounts, which most historians are in the habit of calling budgets (see Chapter 2), we not infrequently find information concerning expenditure on the pilgrimage and the Holy Cities.[11] It is difficult, however, to determine to what extent the disbursements listed in Table 4 can be compared with one another, since a heading which remained more or less unchanged over the years might group expenditures which varied in nature in the course of time. For Ottoman finance officials, concerned with an overview of the past year's finances and not with long-term comparisons, this was irrelevant; for us, unfortunately, it is not. Moreover, the budgets did not record expenditures in an exhaustive manner, so that certain donations to the inhabitants of the Hejaz may have gone unrecorded. The figures we possess, therefore, should be regarded as minimal values. It is also often impossible to separate expenditures for the pilgrimage from those destined for the year-round inhabitants of the Holy Cities. In the present chapter, we will concern ourselves mainly with the latter. Under the circumstances it seems best to compare the percentages of pilgrimage and Hejaz-related expenditures with respect to the relevant totals, without according too much importance to minor discrepancies from one budget to the next.

Table 4 shows an increase in absolute terms which is largely due to the devaluation of the currency which occurred in the 1580s and thereafter.[12] There is also a notable increase in the percentage value of hajj- and Hejaz-related expenditures toward the end of the seventeenth century. This may be due to the fact that the central administration needed to make up the deficit which ensued when the Mamluks retained more and more Egyptian revenue sources for their own use.[13] Since the safe travel of the pilgrims was such a vital affair, payments were not interrupted even during the turmoil of the

Table 5 *Expenditure on Behalf of the Holy Cities According to the Egyptian Budget of 1596–7 (in* pāra*)*

For the caravan commander	400,000
Subsidies for the Holy Cities	1,327,040
Other	2,630,985
Total	4,358,025

Ottoman–Habsburg war (1683–99), a time when many other concerns were neglected.

PAYMENTS FROM EGYPTIAN BUDGETS

Even though Ottoman domination in the Hejaz became more costly to maintain with time, the load on the central administration's budget was not too great. Before the increasing political strength of the Mamluks allowed them to curtail the Egyptian contributions, and to some extent even beyond, Egypt was the main source of grain and funds for the pilgrimage. Grain prices in Mecca being always much higher than those in Egypt, an increased remittance of money at the expense of grain was always to the disadvantage of recipients in the Hejaz. According to the budget of 1596–7, subsidies sent to Mecca and Medina out of official Egyptian revenues amounted to at least 903,892 *pāra* or 22,597 gold pieces, and this total does not include the Beduin *ṣürre*s, some of which also went to the Hejaz.[14] Almost 10 per cent of the Egyptian budget of those years was spent on the support of the Hejaz, even though the revenues secured from the Egyptian public foundations almost certainly were not included in the totals.

From the money assigned to him the caravan commander had to purchase a variety of goods, on which in many cases he must have made a substantial profit. The same probably applied to other members of the provincial administration, for complaints on this score are routinely repeated in administrative records of the time, to say nothing of the bitter denunciations of the contemporary historian Muṣṭafā 'Ālī.[15] Some of these profits may have been hidden under a vaguely phrased heading which for the most part covered administrative and transportation expenditures. Admittedly, both grains and coin, the principal goods carried to the Hejaz, were both expensive to store and transport. Even so, the share of insufficiently identified and therefore possibly illicit expenses appears suspiciously high.

Even if the caravan commanders and their servitors made more or less illicit profits, genuine transport expenditures cannot be neglected.

Many camels died on the long march through the desert and needed to be replaced. Shipwrecks were common, and the construction of ships in an all but treeless environment was very expensive. In many cases, the Egyptian provincial administration must have subsidized transportation to the Hejaz of grain from the Egyptian foundations, whose budgets were notoriously insufficient.

Certain tendencies of the 1596–7 budget equally recur in seventeenth-century financial accounts, even though there was some variation from year to year which we can explain only in certain instances, while others remain somewhat opaque.[16] In 1601–2 there was probably a harvest failure, as remittances to the Hejaz were surprisingly low. On the other hand, in 1612–13 expenditures were much higher than in previous years, because the major costs of the extensive rebuilding projects of Sultan Aḥmed I (reigned 1603–17, see Chapter 5) were paid out of Egyptian revenues.[17] But the high costs of administration and transport and the amalgamation of genuine transportation expenditures with Beduin subsidies were permanent traits of the Egyptian Hejaz-related budget. For that reason the seventeenth-century budgets provide no better opportunity for checking official probity than the budget of 1596–7.

EGYPTIAN FOUNDATIONS BENEFITING THE HOLY CITIES

When Sultan Selīm I conquered the Hejaz in 1517, quite a few foundations providing grain to the Holy Cities and instituted by Mamluk Sultans and amirs were still in operation.[18] The latter were ultimately reformed and subsumed under the overall heading of the Greater Deshīshe foundation, whose core was made up of the foundations of Sultans Ḳā'it Bāy and Čakmak.[19] Sultan Süleymān the Magnificent and his successor Selīm II expanded these foundations by their own additions. Moreover, Murād III (reigned 1574–95) established the so-called Lesser Deshīshe foundation, which mainly remitted money. There were also two soup kitchens founded in Mecca and Medina by Sultan Süleymān in the name of his consort Khurrem Sultan, better known in Europe under the name of Roxolana; these were also funded out of Egyptian tax revenues.

All Egyptian foundations had been assigned villages whose taxes constituted their yearly revenues. In the sixteenth century, these foundations were frequently enlarged by the addition of new villages. In some cases, however, the newly annexed settlements merely made up the losses occasioned by the decline in revenues from the original villages. For even though it can be assumed that population and agri-

Table 6 *Expenditure on Behalf of the Holy Cities According to Early Seventeenth-century Egyptian Budgets (in* parā*)*[1]

Type of expenditure	1600–1	1601–2	1612–13
Payments to the inhabitants of the Holy Cities	194,525	unknown	less than 100,000
Transportation and administrative expenses	387,409	121,263	332,856
Other	1,312,355	unknown	ca. 4,000,000[2]
Total	1,894,289	1,393,423	4,392,331
Total (in gold coins)	47,107	34,835	109,808

1 MM 5672. See Shaw (1968), pp. 268–82 on the general background. It is not clear whether the totals include the prestations of the public foundations.
2 Largely construction expenditures in Mecca; in addition, this total probably includes the expenses of two subsequent pilgrimages.

culture in sixteenth-century Egypt expanded, individual villages were often ruined by natural or man-made calamities.[20] The Meccan chronicler Ḳuṭb al-Dīn, who wrote in the second half of the sixteenth century, believed that the new additions were insufficient to make up for a marked decline in the yield of old foundation holdings.[21]

That such losses did in fact occur is apparent from an account of the Greater Deshīshe foundation, which encompasses the period from July 1591 until November 1592.[22] Total income for that period amounted to 10,678,643 *pāra*, a substantial sum when compared to any one of the major expenditures in the Egyptian budget of 1596–7. But more than seven million were merely arrears from previous years, and even in 1591–2, the foundation still had 6.8 million *pāra* owed to it, presumably for the most part outstanding peasant dues. For its official purposes, the Greater Deshīshe had only been able to spend about two and a half million *para*. Nor had the foundation fulfilled its obligations in terms of grain deliveries; the Greater Deshīshe foundation owed the inhabitants of Mecca and Medina back deliveries for several years. A new administrator had just been appointed, who with some success tried to get the apparatus of the foundation moving again. But in the meantime the population of the Holy Cities must have suffered severe scarcities.

Contemporary documents mention some of the manipulations which resulted in the decline of foundation-sponsored grain deliveries. The tax collectors in charge of adjacent villages often usurped the revenues from villages held by the foundations.[23] Official corruption, frequently denounced in contemporary texts, also had a role to play – but the Ottoman policy of fighting corruption by a frequent change of foundation administrators was also quite often counterproductive. The confusion attendant upon frequent changes in personnel might result in a further decrease of grain and money deliveries.

ANATOLIAN FOUNDATIONS FOR THE BENEFIT OF MECCA AND MEDINA

A carefully executed register from the late sixteenth century informs us about the geographical distribution and financial resources of these foundations.[24] It was put together because of a dispute among high-level Ottoman functionaries, and to fully understand the nature of the data it contains, the background must be explained in some detail. Most Anatolian and Rumelian foundations had been established by private persons, but their annual proceeds were collected by the central administration and sent to the Hejaz en bloc. This was certainly the most economical solution in terms of transportation costs, but the danger that foundation-owned money was used for the daily needs of the Ottoman administration was not to be gainsaid. Now Ottoman officials disagreed over the question whether the administration should pay a standard sum to the population of the Holy Cities in place of the actual revenues of the many small private foundations which constituted their due, and which varied greatly in accordance with harvests and internal security conditions prevailing in their respective localities. The very diplomatic and polite formulations used in this text do not spell out the objection, which however must have been foremost in the minds of those officials opposed to the new dispensation, namely that the Ottoman government was likely to withhold some of the donations destined for the poor of the Holy Cities, and thereby violate the dispositions of the founders, sacrosanct in Islamic foundation law. Instead, those officials who preferred to continue with the old method pointed out that there was no precedent for the new arrangement, for an occurrence which previously had been proposed as a precedent after further investigation could no longer be regarded as such. Finally the case was submitted to Sultan Murād III (reigned 1574–95), who decided that the revenues of all foundations benefiting the Holy Cities should be handed over to their legitimate recipients and all violations of the donors' intentions scrupulously avoided.

Our text was probably written with much care, as it was meant to serve Murād III as a basis for his decision. In order to facilitate judgment of the case and later checking up on the activities of finance officials, the foundations were listed one by one. The inventory covers Istanbul, Edirne and Bursa, most of Rumelia and the Anatolian provinces of Anaḍolu, Ḳarāmān, Rūm, Mar'aṣh and Diyārbakır. Foundations in Syria, on the island of Cyprus and in Baghdad are also recorded, so that the inventory supplies a reasonably complete record of all Mecca and Medina foundations with the exception of those located in Egypt.

In 1588–9 the Anatolian and Rumelian foundations recorded 3,375,610 *akče* as their regular income. If we add once-and-for-all contributions and outstanding dues from previous years, the total is 4,206,142 *akče* or 35,051 Ottoman gold coins. This was a modest contribution compared to the prestations of the Egyptian foundations; for, in spite of all its problems, the Greater Deṣhīṣhe alone delivered about 64,600 gold pieces. Yet given the fact that so many of the founders were private individuals, the total was quite impressive nonetheless. After all, in provincial Anatolian towns during those years, a few thousand *akče* would buy a house, and in Istanbul during the last weeks and months of the sixteenth century, 355 grams of bread cost an *akče* and a chicken 14–16 *akče*.[25]

In the Ottoman capital, foundations benefiting the Holy Cities, and more particularly Medina, were very popular, though this does not mean that inhabitants of Istanbul necessarily chose the poor of the Hejaz as the prime recipients of their charities. But very often foundations were established to benefit specific people, such as the family or former slaves of the donor. When these beneficiaries had died, the foundation revenue was then transferred to the poor of Mecca or Medina. Members of the Sultan's family establishing pious foundations quite often reserved a sum of money for the inhabitants of the Hejaz from the very beginning. Thus the mother of Sultan Selīm I (reigned 1512–20) ordered the annual distribution of 1000 golden *eṣhrefīye* coins to the poor of Medina.[26] This money was to be taken from the fees paid by the users of the public bath of Sultan Bāyezīd II (reigned 1481–1512), which was (and still is) located in downtown Istanbul.

Many Mecca- and Medina-related foundations were strongly affected by the inflation of the later sixteenth century. For in the Holy Cities the *akče*, the principal Ottoman silver coin of this period, was not in use, so that gold coins were generally employed for the transfer of subsidies. But as the *akče* was devalued *vis à vis* the Ottoman gold coin, the value of Anatolian and Rumelian prestations sank accordingly. Some founders attempted to prevent this by fixing the height of their prestation in gold currency. We possess a record of the foundation of a certain Istanbullu named Meḥmed b. Aḥmed which contained a clause of this type.[27] But this did not solve the problem: when the *akče* was devalued by 100 per cent, the foundation was obliged to increase its revenue by the same amount, if it wished to abide by the donor's stipulation. In most cases, this would have been all but impossible.

On the Balkan peninsula outside of Istanbul, foundations benefiting the Holy Cities were concentrated in and around the former capital of Edirne. In the region of Salonica and Yenidje Vardar, the descendants of Ghāzī Evrenos, who had played an important role in the Ottoman conquest of the Balkans during the fourteenth century, established a foundation for the poor of Medina.[28] But foundations of this type were much more widespread in western and central Anatolia. Bursa, another former capital of the Ottoman Sultans, possessed a large number of such foundations, even though their value was much lower than that of their Istanbul counterparts. In the region of Amasya, Tokat, Sivas and Kayseri, but also in northern and central Anatolia, a number of wealthy foundations also served the poor of Mecca and Medina. This is all the more remarkable as these cities were of some commercial importance, but, except for Amasya, had not served as residences for princes and Sultans over any length of time. The foundations of Konya Ereğlisi in southern central Anatolia, on the other hand, owed their existence to the pre-Ottoman dynasty of the Karamanids, who had developed this stopping point of caravans into a small but active town. In the sparsely settled border regions of eastern Anatolia, however, foundations benefiting the Holy Cities were scarce, apart from the commercial centre of Diyarbakır. On the island of Cyprus, recently conquered from the Venetians, Ottoman governors had established some foundations of this kind.[29] The register also contains references to foundations in favour of Mecca and Medina located in Mosul and Baghdad. But no detailed information is available on these remote provinces, where Ottoman domination was as yet insecurely established.

We can thus group the foundations benefiting Mecca and Medina in two different categories. In Istanbul, and to a lesser extent in Edirne and the larger Anatolian cities, we find numerous small foundations, many of which had probably been instituted by local merchants and, occasionally, wealthy artisans. Outside of these larger urban centres, foundations in favour of the Hejazi poor were usually instituted by Ottoman officials, and sometimes by members of the Sultans' families. In newly conquered provinces, such as Cyprus with its recent Venetian past, these foundations probably symbolized the intention to establish a firm and durable bond with the religious centres of the Islamic world.[30]

THE INHABITANTS OF MECCA AND MEDINA:
A POPULATION ESTIMATE

Concerning the distribution of the pious gifts which Sultan Selīm I had assigned to the inhabitants of Mecca, we possess the account of the Meccan chronicler Ḳuṭb al-Dīn.[31] He describes how amir Muṣliḥ al-Dīn, Selīm I's envoy to the Hejaz, made a list of all the poor households in the city; his list included the names of their members, who were each assigned three gold pieces a year. By the later sixteenth century, payments were still being made according to amir Muṣliḥ al-Dīn's records. In addition (unfortunately we cannot tell whether before or after amir Muṣliḥ al-Dīn's count), the city's notables made a list of their own. This encompassed all occupied houses and all inhabitants of the city apart from merchants and soldiers – that is, women, children and servants in addition to the adult male population, a total of 12,000 persons. After registration, each of them received a share of the donations, which Ḳuṭb al-Dīn understood to be on the basis of a legal claim, and in addition a gold piece per person as a free gift. From Ḳuṭb al-Dīn's account, one may conclude that the city had 15,000 regular inhabitants at the very least, for the merchants, who had no claim to pious gifts, were usually numerous in Mecca, and many must have been heads of resident households. Unfortunately, Ḳuṭb al-Dīn tells us nothing either about them or about the soldiers.

We have no further data about the Meccan population in later years, but for Medina a few figures are available. In 1579–80 the Ottoman authorities assumed that 8000 people lived in the city in pious retreat (*müdjāvir*).[32] If each one of these people was in charge of a household of five persons, Medina should have had a population of at least 40,000 people, not counting merchants and soldiers with no claim to pious subsidies. On the other hand, many of the *müdjāvir*s of Medina must have been elderly people, who had smaller than average households. In 1594–5, 7000 inhabitants of Medina received subsidies from the Ottoman state.[33] If the criteria by which eligibility was determined had not changed in the meantime, the city's population should have contracted. A text from the mid-seventeenth century claims that during the reign of Murād III (reigned 1574–95) Medina's inhabitants totalled 6666 persons, which seems dubious in the light of previous and later figures. In 1641–2 23,200 inhabitants of the city received official support, though the authorities in Istanbul did suspect that this figure had been inflated by fraudulent manipulation.[34] A new count was therefore ordered, but no record of the results has been found. Medina probably contained more recipients of outside aid than Mecca, but this assumption is based on the fact that so much more is said in official documents about Medina, and of course there may have been other reasons, hitherto unknown, for this disproportion.[35]

THE DISTRIBUTION OF SUBSIDIES AND PENSIONS

When pensions and subsidies were distributed without incident, we know almost nothing about the process, for most of the documents relating to this issue are sultanic commands, designed to abolish this or that abuse. Usually complaints from pension recipients and local administrators preceded rescripts of this kind, but they have not survived; all that remains of the letters of complaint are the summaries at the beginning of the responses issued in the name of the Sultan. A frequent cause for complaint was the late arrival of grain deliveries, 1569–70 and 1578–81 being particularly bad years in that respect.[36] Outside of the pilgrimage season it was very difficult to earn money in Mecca, so that the late arrival of official subsidies caused distress so acute that pious inhabitants of Mecca could not afford to participate in the pilgrimage ceremony on 'Arafat, even though most of the Meccan population took part in this ritual every year.[37]

Even when subsidies finally arrived in Mecca or Medina a disappointment might be in store for the recipients, as the grain was often spoilt due to poor storage while in transit. A rescript from the year 1583 describes the *khān* located in Yanbu', the port of Medina, which was in such poor condition that, in the previous year, 3000 *irdeb* of wheat sent on behalf of the Deshīshe foundation had suffered water damage.[38] A thorough repair of the *khān* would have cost 3000 gold pieces, and the administrator of Jeddah, who had been ordered to take care of the matter had done nothing at all, protesting that everything in the Hejaz was very expensive. Moreover, the Beduins in charge of transporting the grain often stole some of it, mixing earth in the sacks so as to prevent detection of their pilfering; of course, knowledge of such tricks was not limited to Beduins.[39]

Other complaints concerned money remittances. Sometimes the Ottoman administration remitted not the coins most employed in the Hejaz, namely *pāra* and gold pieces, but a silver coin known as *shāhī* which, as its name indicates, originally was intended for the Iranian market. *Shāhī*s were minted by the Ottoman administration to make a profit from the outflow of silver to Iran, which in spite of all prohibitions could not be stopped. When coins were sent instead of bars or jewellery, at least minting dues could be charged. Somehow the *shāhī*s also became current in Syria, where peasants used them for the payment of taxes.[40] But this coin never gained acceptance in the Hejaz, and recipients of subsidies paid out in *shāhīs* had a lot of trouble in consequence. Money changers, however, certainly profited from this situation.

The conflict of interest occasioned by the employment of the *shāhī* for subsidies to the Hejaz was discussed by the *kādī* of Damascus.[41] This official explained that at the time of writing (1583) gold and gold coins were extremely scarce in Syria. Therefore it was unreasonable to demand that local peasants pay their taxes in money, although the *kādī* realized that the remittance of large quantities of silver coins was bound to create hardships for the poor of the Hejaz.[42] The administration tried to solve the problem by legislating the rate of exchange for the *shāhī*, with what consequences remains unknown.[43] At other times the Ottoman government attempted to keep the *shāhī* out of Mecca and Medina altogether, by demanding that these coins be exchanged for gold or *pāra* before remittance. If gold was scarce and expensive, however, the poor of the Hejaz were bound to lose, one way or the other.

Other conflicts arose because people who did not possess any rights to official aid managed to secure it nonetheless, or because people with political power assigned themselves much higher subsidies than those to which they would have normally been entitled.[44] Quite often, officials in charge of distribution kept a share of the subsidies for themselves. Sometimes *kādīs* and finance administrators made sure that people who did not even live in the Hejaz received grants from the foundations intended to benefit the poor of Mecca and Medina.[45] Thus a *medrese* teacher living in Damascus was being paid for teaching at the establishment founded by Sultan Süleymān in Mecca. As a result a colleague of his, who did in fact teach at the school, was unable to draw his pay.

In Medina there occurred a long drawn-out dispute involving the rights of a group of descendants of the Prophet Muḥammad known as the Banū Ḥusayn.[46] These influential families claimed one third of all subsidies sent to Mecca; they possessed a rescript from Sultan Murād III which assigned them grants-in-aid from the Deshīshe foundation. This was in itself remarkable. In the sixteenth century, when Ottomans and Safawids were frequently at war, the recipients of official subsidies normally had to be Sunnis, while the Banū Ḥusayn were Shi'is. The governor of Egypt opposed the Banū Ḥusayn's demands, pointing out that other legitimate claimants would then have to be denied their rights. For a while the opponents of the Banū Ḥusayn had the upper hand in Istanbul, and the Sultan's Council denied them official support of any kind. But the Banū Ḥusayn insisted and, in the long run, they seem to have been successful, for in the early seventeenth century we find them receiving subsidies out of the Egyptian provincial budget.[47]

AN ATTEMPT AT REFORMING THE DISTRIBUTION OF SUBSIDIES

Since complaints concerning the distribution of subsidies concentrated on Medina, an attempt at reform from the year 1594–5 also refers principally to this city. Various pious people with claims on the ruler's bounty had reported that, of 6000 *irdeb* of wheat delivered, one third was subtracted straight away (presumably this was the share of the Banū Ḥusayn); 1000 *irdeb* were reserved for the kitchen (probably the soup kitchen founded by Sultan Süleymān); and several hundred *irdeb* for administrative personnel and other expenses. This did not leave very much for the poor.[48] In the answer to this complaint, the Ottoman government laid down the principle that employees performing a service should receive a salary (*'ulūfe*), leaving all grants defined as alms for the genuine poor. When people in receipt of charities died, their rights to subsidies should not pass on to their heirs; rather, these vacant positions were to be entered into a special register for reassignment to other poor already residing in Medina. Candidates for official support could be native to the city or have moved there; what mattered was not their origin, but their piety and religious learning. Inhabitants of Medina who did not need the subsidies and invested them in trade were to be removed from the list of subsidy recipients. The same thing applied to people who were negligent in the performance of their daily prayers or whose lives were not above reproach. Slaves were to be excluded from all subsidies, presumably because their owners were responsible for their upkeep. Nothing is said about the claims of the Banū Ḥusayn, who had caused so much trouble in the recent past. Possibly the Ottoman administration hoped that the matter had resolved itself when Murād III increased the Medina subsidies by the amount of 5000 *irdeb*. Possibly the decrease of claimants discussed above should be connected with the edict of 1594–5 and the more stringent criteria ordered therein. But it is impossible to tell whether the stipulations of 1594–5 were effective for any length of time.

TOTAL EXPENDITURES IN FAVOUR OF THE PILGRIMAGE AND THE HOLY CITIES

Items of information about the different types of Ottoman expenditures in the Hejaz do not all date from the same year, and cannot therefore be used to put together a hajj-related budget for any given year. But to gain a rough overall impression nonetheless, we will add up a few figures referring to the major items of expenditure, both documented and estimated. We can assume that the Greater Deshīshe produced about 65,000 *akče* a year, and the Lesser Deshīshe about 10,000. From the foundations of Anatolia and Rumelia, about 28,000 gold pieces were obtained annually. Subsidies from the Egyptian provincial budget amounted to about 23,000 gold pieces, but often the sum really expended must have been a great deal higher, with an upper limit of about 109,000 gold pieces.[49] From the customs revenues of Jeddah, which the Ottoman administration had abandoned to the Sherif of Mecca, the latter in the 1580s could expect to collect about 90,000 gold pieces (see Chapter 7). We thus arrive at a total of between 216,000 and 302,000 gold pieces. In addition, there was the value of the grain sent to the Hejaz by the Egyptian foundations to be taken into account, while expenditures on behalf of the Syrian caravan amounted to about 80,000 gold pieces. Outside of grain deliveries, the pilgrimage thus cost the late sixteenth- and early seventeenth-century Ottoman administration anything between 300,000 and 385,000 gold pieces.

These figures become more meaningful when we compare them to other major expenditures of the Ottoman imperial budget. Between February 1606 and May 1607, 618,416 gold pieces were spent on the Ottoman war effort against the Habsburgs, excluding war matériel and a few other expenditures.[50] This is remarkable if we consider that, for the Ottoman Empire as for early modern European states, war was by far the most important item of expenditure. Of course these figures can do no more than indicate an order of magnitude, but it is still important that a sum of money roughly equivalent to one half or two thirds of annual campaign expenses was set aside for maintaining a measure of control over the Hejaz.

In return, the Holy Cities and the surrounding region produced no revenues for the Ottoman treasury, apart from the share of the Jeddah customs revenues not assigned to the Sherifs. Yet although at the end of the sixteenth and the beginning of the seventeenth century the position of the Ottoman treasury was quite precarious, as becomes obvious from the devaluations of this period, neither the Sultans nor members of their Council ever suggested that expenditures for the pilgrimage or the Holy Cities be cut down. Only in the late seventeenth century, when other wars against the Habsburgs put a severe strain on Ottoman resources (1660–4, 1683–99), do we observe attempts to cut down drastically on hajj-related expenditures.[51] By contrast, most sixteenth-century Sultans readily increased expenditures on the pilgrimage and the Holy Cities, which indicates their political importance.

The accounts also indicate that Egypt remained the source of most subsidies remitted to the Holy Cities; grain and other foodstuffs came almost exclusively from this source. Of the 300,000–385,000 gold pieces sent to the Hejaz every year, at least 120,000 or about one third were derived directly from Egyptian sources. In reality the percentage was no doubt higher: a significant share of the Jeddah customs revenues, for example, was paid by Egyptian merchants and shipowners in the first instance.

After about 1660, or 1670 at the very latest, this set of arrangements, which for one and a half centuries had enabled the Ottomans to maintain themselves in the Hejaz, was in deep trouble. The Mamluk tax collectors were less and less inclined to pass on Egyptian tax revenues to Istanbul, and after 1683 regular financing of the pilgrimage caravans became all but impossible. When, in the early eighteenth century after the war was over, Ottoman administrators attempted to reestablish control over the pilgrimage routes, it was necessary to rebuild not only *khān*s and fortifications, but, at least in Syria, the administrative structure as well.

The Istanbul authorities of the sixteenth and seventeenth centuries apparently reasoned that they needed to secure foodstuffs and a safe passage to the pilgrims, as well as subsidies to the inhabitants of Mecca and Medina, because any obvious failure delegitimized the Sultan himself. A flood of rescripts was therefore sent out to prevent corrupt practices and ensure that subsidies actually reached the intended beneficiaries:

> In the time of my late father, the ruler – may his grave be fragrant – [deliveries of money and grains on the part of different foundations as well as other payments] were not handed over on time, due to the negligence of the provincial governors and the avarice and lack of piety among supervisors and Beduin shaykhs. Arrears reached scandalous levels, so that the poor of the Holy Cities, the servitors [of the different foundations] and the pious inhabitants [of the Holy Cities] suffered great want. The Sultan has learned of their sorry plight . . . .[52]

Administrative reorganization and the appointment of a new Chief Supervisor were meant to secure that

> the Beduin shaykhs take note of the financial probity of the Supervisor and thereupon desist from their treason, and instead follow the path of justice. Then we will ensure that the wheat

deliveries of the Deshīshe, alms and salaries reach their destinations in full and on time. In this sense, my auspicious sultanly writ has been issued and my most noble order sent forth.

Quite obviously, the legitimacy of the Ottoman Sultan was at stake here.

5

In Praise of Ruler and Religion: Public Buildings in Mecca and Medina

When the Ottomans took over Mecca in 1517, they found the Great Mosque in the shape which it had received under the early Abbasids (750–86), apart from the Ka'aba which last had been rebuilt in early Ummayad times.[1] After the Ummayad governor al-Ḥadjdjādj had overthrown the Meccan caliph al-Zubayr in 693, he restructured the Ka'aba in such a fashion as to get rid of the changes which the defeated ruler had imposed. Thereafter, the Ka'aba was a rectangular building with a flat wooden roof, the ceiling of teakwood being supported by three wooden columns. The only door was located high above the courtyard and could be reached by way of a ladder.

The Great Mosque as a whole consisted of a courtyard bordered by galleries on all four sides, with the Ka'aba approximately in the centre. Within the courtyard proper, the area in which pilgrims performed their circumambulations was clearly marked off. This part of the mosque also contained a small monument commemorating the Prophet Ibrāhīm, the well of Zamzam, from whose water the pilgrims usually drink, in addition to a number of minor buildings. Some of the latter served the prayer leaders of the four schools of Sunni religious law, which in spite of differences in matters of detail are all considered equally orthodox. In the early days of Islam, the courtyard had been quite small, but since the time of the caliph 'Umar (634–44) it had slowly been extended by the purchase of adjacent houses. The gallery, which still retains the shape given to it by the Ottoman Sultans, was begun in the days of the Abbasid caliph al-Manṣūr (reigned 754–5). Al-Manṣūr's successors al-Mahdī (reigned 775–85) and al-Hādī (reigned 785–6) completed the structure, and also built the oldest of the seven minarets which were to grace the building in later times. The remnants of the palace which Ummayads and Abbasids had inhabited while visiting Mecca were also included in the gallery. At this time the latter possessed a flat roof, and the teakwood ceiling was partly gilt. Some of the columns were of marble, while the remainder had been put together out of different varieties of stone and covered with a coating of plaster. At the end of the twelfth century the Andalusian pilgrim Ibn Djubayr recorded 471 columns and piers.[2] About the middle of the nineteenth century, the English traveller Richard Burton counted 555 supports, the increase being probably due to Ottoman additions.[3] Until about 1950, when a new building campaign entirely changed the look of the Great Mosque, these Ottoman changes and additions determined its overall appearance.

In the Islamic world the Ka'aba is regarded as a sanctuary built by God and the angels and restored several times by different prophets. This explains why, throughout the centuries, changes to the building were kept to a minimum, though rulers of the first Islamic century had fewer qualms about making such changes than their descendants. But the veneration accorded the Ka'aba did not mean that the remainder of the Great Mosque was also considered sacrosanct; on the contrary, galleries and minarets have undergone major changes in the course of time.

A significant reason for public construction in Mecca has already been discussed: the prestige of a Muslim ruler to a not inconsiderable degree was due to the buildings which he put up to the glory of God and the welfare of the pilgrims. Aging and damage, too, have often occasioned both restoration and total rebuilding. The attempt to create a dignified and even magnificent environment for the pilgrimage ceremonies did not limit itself to the Great Mosque, but encompassed the entire city of Mecca. Making necessary allowances for the different requirements of pious visitors to Medina, the same thing applies to that city as well. The two cities also had a number of problems in common: water supplies and public hygiene, traffic and transportation had to be organized in such a way as to cope with major seasonal influxes of people and animals. As building in the remote and desert regions of the Hejaz was not only difficult but expensive as well, a ruler's decision to immortalize himself in this fashion amounted to a major political statement.

PIOUS FOUNDATIONS AND CONSTRUCTION ACTIVITY IN THE OTTOMAN EMPIRE

During the fifteenth and sixteenth centuries, and to a certain extent in the seventeenth as well, Ottoman Sultans, mothers of Sultans and high officials were very active as builders. Mosques were favoured by most donors, but the larger sanctuaries were associated with soup kitchens, schools for the elementary training of children but also for advanced theological study, libraries and many other institutions.[4] The funds needed to operate such a foundation were set aside by the donor, who either constructed shops, _khān_s, mills or public baths at the same time as the mosque or *medrese* which formed the core of the foundation. Or else the donor assigned previously existing enterprises to the upkeep of favoured charities. Highly placed personages, and particularly members of the Sultan's family, often could induce the ruler to grant their foundations taxes collected from villages. Thus a not inconsiderable transfer of purchasing power from the countryside to the city was effected. The size of the foundation indicated the rank of the donor; only the Sultan, thus, could build a mosque with two or more minarets.

Public construction was centred upon Istanbul and its immediate vicinity.[5] Muṣṭafā 'Ālī, sharp-eyed and sharp-tongued as ever, has concluded that the need for services in a given place was not considered when selecting the site of a new foundation.[6] In his view, high visibility and the donor's prestige were all that counted. But the larger and more important provincial cities such as Edirne, Damascus, Cairo, Mecca and Medina also received a large number of pious foundations. Relative to their rather modest permanent populations, the two Holy Cities were even particularly privileged in this respect.

CONSTRUCTION MATERIALS

Due to the lack of many materials needed in construction, building activities in the Hejaz demanded much more organization and preparation than construction in almost any other part of the empire. Building stone was available locally, but timber, iron, bricks and marble had to be imported from distant provinces. Timber at times was secured from the northern shores of the Black Sea; in 1609–10, a Christian sea captain asked for and received permission to buy timber in the province of Kefe (Feodosiya) and more particularly Balıklagu (Balaklava) for the needs of Medina.[7] Sometimes timber could be secured from the Ottoman arsenal, which possessed monopoly rights to large wooded areas of northwestern Anatolia, still heavily forested at that time. But wars in the Mediterranean were liable to cut off timber supplies, as happened in 1570–3 during the war with Venice over the possession of Cyprus. In the building of the Great Mosque of Mecca, large quantities of Indian teak were used – a wood so hard, according to some experts, that it could be used as a substitute for iron.[8] Only some of this teak consisted of recent imports. When older parts of the Great Mosque, presumably going back to the Mamluk period, were torn down in order to make room for Ottoman projects, quite a lot of the salvaged teak was still in good condition and was therefore reused in the Ottoman rebuilding of the gallery.

Iron was used for a variety of purposes: in many monumental buildings iron hooks held together large blocks of hewn stone, while doors had metal fastenings and windows iron grates.[9] Vaults were often strengthened by iron supports which, though they protruded in an obvious and inelegant fashion, secured the structure whenever there were doubts concerning the strength of the foundations. When vaults were added to the gallery of the Great Mosque of Mecca in the second half of the sixteenth century, iron (in addition to the teak already stored in Mecca) was employed for just this purpose.[10] Moreover, iron was needed for nails, and last but not least for the shovels and other implements indispensable for the functioning of any construction site.

Iron used in Mecca usually came from the smelting furnaces in the area of Samokov, in what is today southern Bulgaria. From there it was carried by caravan to Istanbul or to a port on the western shores of the Black Sea, and from there to Egypt. The use of iron in the Hejaz was made more difficult because the lack of fuel made it all but impossible to work iron at the construction site. Thus the Ottoman central administration sent ready-made nails to the Hejaz, even though the official in charge of this project warned that serious losses would be unavoidable.[11] After all, quite a few people could use nails. . . .

Many items needed for construction or repair of the Great Mosque were manufactured in Istanbul, so that upon arrival they only needed to be put in place. Manufactured items had to fit fairly stringent specifications, and coordination was made difficult by the length of time needed to get a response to a query or request. In 1611, when the walls of the Ka'aba needed strengthening, a regular public test of the items to be employed was held in the capital. Meḥmed Aḡa, Chief Architect and responsible for the construction of the Blue Mosque, had designed lavishly decorated iron props to support the Ka'aba from the outside. As Aḥmed I wished to see how the supports would work, they were set up outside the Edirne gate, at the site known as the estate of Davud Pasha. Other gifts to be sent to Mecca were also exhibited, and the Sultan attended the ceremony with the Grand Vizier, the Shaykh al-Islām and many other dignitaries.[12] To make sure that the supports would accurately fit the Ka'aba, drawings had been made previously, but, for good measure, a team of artisans was also sent to Mecca.[13]

Materials to be used in decoration were also brought in from afar.

Sultan Murād III sent a quantity of gold to gild the silver doors of the Ka'aba, but we do not know whether he used gold from the treasury in the Topkapı Palace or tax revenues from less distant provinces such as Syria, which could have been reassigned to Mecca.[14] Thus a multitude of deliveries from southern Rumelia, northwestern Anatolia and Istanbul had to arrive more or less punctually in the Hejaz for construction to proceed at a smooth pace. On the whole these arrangements seem to have worked reasonably well. This was a major organizational achievement, particularly since not only construction materials, but also workmen were in short supply and had to be brought in from outside.

CONSTRUCTION WORKERS

When Ewliyā was in Mecca in 1672, he noted that the city's inhabitants did not show any interest in the practice of crafts.[15] A similar observation can be found in the travel account of the Dutch scholar Snouck Hurgronje, who was in Mecca toward the end of the nineteenth century; at that time many services needed in the city were performed by immigrant Africans.[16] Similar evidence exists for sixteenth-century Medina; a report concerning the books in the library attached to the Prophet's mosque in Medina, dated 1578, states that these books were in urgent need of rebinding. But in the whole city there was no suitable bookbinder, 'and if we do find one he will charge a lot of money'.[17] The Sultan's Council therefore decided that it was better to bring in a bookbinder from Egypt. Apparently this was considered a cheaper solution even though the bookbinder's travel money would add to the cost of his work.

Qualified workers on Ottoman construction sites in the Hejaz often came from Syria or Egypt. An account concerning repair work undertaken in 1601–2 indicates that wages paid to such workers were at a medium level.[18] Compared to their colleagues working on an official construction site in the Aegean region they were not doing too badly, but they made considerably less than could be earned on a construction site in Saydā (Sidon) in the year 1616.[19] Given the instability of prices and exchange rates during this period, however, data from different times (even fifteen years apart) and places are risky to compare.

In all likelihood many Syrian and Egyptian construction workers did not leave their native provinces voluntarily, but were drafted by the Ottoman state. In some instances the opportunity to perform the pilgrimage must have been a motivating force. To date the best documented of all building projects of the Ottoman 'classical' period is the Süleymāniye construction site. If the Süleymāniye constitutes a typical case, few slaves were employed on Ottoman official building sites, and none are recorded for the construction of the Great Mosque of Mecca. Frequently, however, artisans were called up by local *kādī*s and assigned to work on public construction.[20] Sometimes the *kādī* was told to furnish a given number of stonecutters or masons, and sometimes artisans deemed especially skilful were even requested by name.[21] It was not easy to escape such a draft, though some craftsmen tried as best they could, and the cases in which they succeeded are also those about which we know least.

Wages in public construction were determined by the Ottoman government, and were probably lower than craftsmen could get from private employers. Some artisans, however, did attempt to better their situation. Concerning sixteenth-century Istanbul, we possess a document which shows that dissatisfied artisans demanded and obtained a raise; for this purpose, strikes and refusals to work were not unknown.[22] Some craftsmen employed on public building projects in the capital simply managed to 'disappear', taking up work for private persons or else leaving the area.[23] Similar tactics were employed in the Hejaz. Certain stonecutters and blacksmiths managed to enter the suites of influential pilgrims and thus return home, much to the dissatisfaction of the authorities.

BUILDINGS AND BUILDING EXPENDITURES

High food prices, lack of materials and labourers, losses in transportation, certainly also the difficulty of supervising officials in a remote locality – all contributed to the expense of construction in Mecca and Medina. We do not have any comprehensive accounts concerning the renovation of the Great Mosque of Mecca under Selīm II (reigned 1566–74) and Murād III (reigned 1574–95). Such isolated items of expenditure as are known show that the Ottoman government was able and willing to expend large sums. In 1571, when plans were being made for the renovation of the gallery, 40,000–50,000 gold pieces were set aside for the delivery of timber alone. Masonry domes were even more expensive.[24] The same text reports that to cover the gallery by rows of domes would increase the price to about 100,000 gold pieces. From a sultanic rescript dated 1568 we learn that 50,000 gold pieces had been spent on the four *medrese*s of Süleymān the Magnificent (reigned 1520–66), recently completed at that time.[25] Additional expenses may have arisen, moreover, for at the time the rescript was drafted, the previous owners of the land on which the *medreses* had been built had not yet been compensated.

Smaller repairs in Medina were also quite costly. In 1585 the Sultan's Council planned to spend 10,000 gold pieces on repairs to the outer wall of the courtyard of the Prophet's mosque in Medina.[26] The restoration of the minor fortress of Yanbu', where the grain stores for Medina were kept prior to transportation to the city proper, was to cost 50,000 gold pieces. Repairs to 63 hospices for the reception of poor pilgrims in Medina were estimated at 32,000 gold pieces all told, which means that repairs in Medina at the end of the sixteenth century ran to a total of 92,000 gold pieces. In 1564 renewal and extension of a single hospice was estimated at a thousand gold pieces.[27]

Large sums were also expended on the pipes which carried water from the 'Arafat plateau to Mecca. Since this water carried a large amount of sand and pebbles, the pipes were often clogged, and cleaning them caused considerable expense. New pipes were also added to improve the Meccan water supply. In 1571, 60,000 gold pieces were spent on this project alone.[28] Transmitting these large sums of money to Mecca on time caused the Ottoman fisc considerable difficulty. Some of the money was sent from Istanbul, while the Egyptian contribution was also substantial. Grain left over from last year's pilgrimage caravan equally was sold to defray expenses. A sizable amount of correspondence went back and forth between different Ottoman officials, and this doubtlessly increased the expense of the project yet further.

The costliness of building in Mecca and Medina as opposed to less out-of-the-way regions becomes apparent when we compare these figures to the building expenses of two major Istanbul mosques. The Süleymāniye complex – six colleges of law, religion and medicine, a hospice, a hospital and a public kitchen, as well as the magnificently decorated mausolea of Süleymān the Lawgiver and his consort Khurrem Sultan – cost 53,782,980 *akče* in the course of an eight-year construction period. This is equivalent to 896,383 Ottoman gold pieces. The Sultan Aḥmed mosque (built 1609–17) cost 180,341,803 *akče*, but as the *akče* had dramatically been devalued in the meantime, this corresponded to no more than 1,381,245 Ottoman gold coins. In size and elaboration, the two complexes were comparable: around the Sultan Aḥmed mosque clustered a major complex of buildings, including a reception pavilion (*ḳaṣır*) for the Sultan, a school, a place where drinking water was dispensed and numerous shops.[29] Apparently a vizier intent on building up his image in the manner criticized by Muṣṭafā 'Ālī, indeed would have been well advised to build in

Istanbul and not in the Holy Cities; he certainly got more value for his money.[30] But of course the very expense of prestigious construction in the Hejaz contributed to the prestige of the rulers who could afford to finance it.

The high cost of a building project could be used to legitimize the ruler initiating it, as becomes apparent from a description of the repairs which Ahmed I, also responsible for the Sultan Ahmed mosque, undertook in Mecca. The account of Ahmed I's repairs to the Great Mosque is found in Dja'fer Efendi's biography of the architect Mehmed Agha, who was in charge of both projects. The author recounts that Sultan Ahmed had a spout for rain water, made of pure gold, affixed to the roof of the Ka'aba.[31] As background information, he adds that the Abbasid caliphs, who originally had furnished the Ka'aba with a spout of silver gilt, did not possess the resources for a more valuable gift. Now this spout was in bad condition and needed to be replaced. According to Dja'fer Efendi, by contrast the Ottoman Sultan was so rich that he could easily afford not only a golden water spout but, if necessary, a golden wall all around the Ka'aba.

This willingness to employ costly materials is all the more remarkable in view of the sparing use of gold, silver and other valuables in the decoration of the great Sultans' mosques in Istanbul. In the foundation document of the Süleymāniye it is expressly stated that the ruler had decided against expensive decorations and in favour of a spacious and well-built structure.[32] In many other respects, however, the Ottoman Sultans when building in Mecca had introduced features characteristic of public construction in the capital. Therefore it is not a matter of chance if, in this particular instance, they disregarded Istanbul precedent in favour of a lavish use of precious materials. Mehmed Agha's biographer has attempted an explanation: for the Ka'aba he uses the image of the beloved, whose beauty is enhanced by her precious jewellery.[33] This simile and his description of the Ka'aba as a whole contain allusions to mystical poetry. Thus two sets of motivations apparently played a role when the decision was made to use a profusion of gold and silver in the decoration of the Ka'aba. On the one hand, the Sultan was to be legitimized by the display of his extraordinary wealth. On the other hand two holy sites, namely the Ka'aba as the centre of the world and the grave of the Prophet Muhammad in Medina, were to be confirmed as different in kind from any other place on earth, even the major Sultans' mosques in Istanbul. And yet at least one of the latter, namely the Süleymāniye, had been designed as a monument to the triumph of Sunni Islam.[34]

THE RENOVATION OF THE GREAT MOSQUE
OF MECCA

During the first fifty years of Ottoman control, major changes were made in the Great Mosque of Mecca. The place from which the Ḥanefī prayer leader directed the members of his law school at prayer was at first marked by a small two-storey structure. But soon this building, which had been erected by a governor of Jeddah, was torn down and replaced by a building domed in the manner characteristic of Ottoman monumental construction.[35] Sultan Süleymān also had four theological schools built in the immediate vicinity of the Great Mosque; to have *medrese*s form part of major mosque complexes was another element of Ottoman building tradition.[36] The number four was chosen because of the four schools of law recognized as orthodox by Sunni Muslims. But it was quite difficult to find suitable teachers for the Ḥanbalī and Shāfi'ī schools. Possibly this lack of personnel was the reason why the Ottoman administration later transformed the *medrese* of the Ḥanbalīs into a *dār al-ḥadīth*, that is a specialized school for the study of reports concerning the sayings and doings of the Prophet Muḥammad.[37] While the Ḥanbalīs were little represented in the Ottoman Empire, a *dār al-ḥadīth* was also the crowning feature of the educational system in Süleymān the Magnificent's Istanbul foundation (built 1550–7).[38]

Thus, even though the special traditions of the Holy City were initially upheld, specifically Ottoman institutions and building types soon appeared in Mecca. But to make the new *medrese*s operate was a difficult matter. Ewliyā Čelebi had noted that Meccans were not very enthusiastic about careers of study and teaching in religious law or theological studies, and for scholars from the Ottoman core lands Mecca proved too remote for comfort and career building.[39] Under these circumstances, it was difficult to prevent the buildings from being misused as residences for influential pilgrims, some of whom even stabled their mounts there. The central administration time and again was obliged to concern itself with complaints concerning the functioning of these *medrese*s.[40]

Süleymān the Lawgiver also renovated several of the Great Mosque's minarets. When he ascended the throne, the mosque was adorned by six minarets, one of which had been built by the Abbasid caliph al-Manṣūr (reigned 754–5).[41] In spite of its venerable age, Süleymān the Lawgiver had it torn down in 1524–5 and replaced by a new one. The same fate befell a minaret from the time of the Abbasid caliph al-Mahdī (reigned 775–85). Instead of the single gallery for the muezzin which had characterized the older building, the new minaret was furnished with two galleries; again, multiple galleries were typical of the Sultans' mosques in Istanbul. Toward the end of his reign Sultan Süleymān added a further minaret which struck the eye by its great height, thereby bringing up the total to seven. But around 1597–8, according to a note in the Arabic-language chronicle of Ḳuṭb al-Dīn which was translated into Ottoman at this time, possibly by the poet Bāḳī, the minarets of the Great Mosque suffered severe damage.[42] Unfortunately Bāḳī, or whoever else penned the note, does not specify what kind of damage this may have been. A fire seems the most likely possibility. Nor is there any information about subsequent repair work.

The most important undertaking of this period was the total renovation of the galleries surrounding the courtyard of the Great Mosque. As the Ka'aba had retained its shape since Ummayad times, the galleries and the minarets were the obvious focus for rebuilding. Moreover they determined the appearance of the mosque as a whole. A building with a large central dome, the most striking feature of Ottoman Sultans' mosques, could not be accommodated in the Great Mosque of Mecca. But it was possible to use a series of small-scale domes to cover the galleries.[43] This feature is also typical of the fully developed mosques of the Ottoman classical period, where the visitor walks from an exterior open courtyard into a second interior space lined by porticoes, where the ablution fountain is normally located.[44] Yet the strict symmetry of Ottoman interior courtyards could not be reproduced in Mecca, where a large number of ancient and highly decorative gates existed which could not be moved at will. Moreover, in consequence of the Meccan courtyard's great size, its character as an open space was a permanent feature, while in many Ottoman Sultans' mosques, and particularly in the Süleymāniye, a broad gallery combined with a small amount of unroofed space almost created the illusion of a closed room.

Due to the importance of this building project, which was executed in the reigns of Selīm II (reigned 1566–74) and Murād III (reigned 1574–95), there was a considerable amount of official correspondence, part of which has survived. The decision to build a domed gallery was probably taken during the Cyprus war (1570–3), when timber could not be imported and the Sultan still wanted to go through with the project as quickly as possible.[45] Therefore, locally available materials had to be used, particularly stone and mortar. Despite their haste, the Sultan and his advisers seem to have hesitated some time over the final shape of the gallery. In a rescript which postdated the first discussion of the domes by a few months, there were renewed references to a gallery in the 'old style', that is, with a flat roof.[46] In March 1573, however, the decision to build a domed gallery had finally been taken.[47] In the following year, the architect in charge of the project left Istanbul for Mecca.[48]

Unfortunately all we know about this personage is his name, Mehmed, and the fact that at the time in question he was a palace official (*čavush*). This is a different person from the Mehmed Agha who built the Sultan Ahmed Mosque in Istanbul at the beginning of the seventeenth century – and, as we have seen, was also later active in Mecca. If he had been involved in the building of the domed gallery in his youth, his admiring biographer Dja'fer Efendi would not have failed to mention the fact. Mehmed Čavush was not the first architect to work on the gallery project, however, as 34 domes had been built before he even left Istanbul.[49] At this time the Sultan's Council was still deliberating the number of domes to be erected. In a rescript dated 1573 the idea of a structure of 400–500 domes was ventilated; but in the end only 152 were actually built.[50]

The final shape of the gallery floor also was the subject of much deliberation. In Mamluk times the ground was covered with pebbles. The Ottoman structure at first followed the Mamluk example but, by about the year 1577, the authorities in Istanbul were debating a more magnificent solution.[51] As a reason for changing the traditional arrangement, it was claimed that most of the worshippers in the Great Mosque were poor people, who did not bring their own prayer rugs. For these people prostration in ritual prayer was most uncomfortable, as the sharp pebbles lacerated their legs. Certain descendants of the Prophet and other notables therefore applied to the *kādī* of Mecca, who passed on their wish for a more comfortable arrangement to the Ottoman central administration. Thereupon the Sultan ordered a floor covering consisting of marble slabs. But when the slabs had already been cut, certain inhabitants of Mecca strenuously objected to the new solution. Possibly the real reason was that the luxurious appearance of the gallery in its new form had aroused objections among the more piety-minded inhabitants of Mecca.

The authorities in Istanbul did not insist on putting in the marble slabs. According to the new order, the *kādī* of Mecca was to invite the inhabitants of the city (obviously the more prominent among them) and certain building specialists to a conference. After the participants had come to an agreement, the *kādī* was to notify the Istanbul authorities of the result. Thus the central administration attempted to secure the consent of the more prominent inhabitants of the city before new building projects were undertaken. This show of consideration must have been due to the religious prestige of Mecca on the one hand, and to the enormous distance from the centres of Ottoman power on the other. For no evidence of similar consultations has come to light where the cities of Anatolia or Rumelia were involved; at least in written texts, everybody pretended to believe that the Sultan only had to command for his order to be instantly obeyed.

In the following years, the reconstruction of the gallery proceeded apace.[52] Already in August–September 1576 the completion of the work was celebrated by a commemorative inscription. The text was written in Istanbul, but to have it inscribed on a slab of marble the authorities looked to a craftsman already present in Mecca or at least someone who could be brought in from Egypt. The whole affair was not without its political implications, for the *ḳāḍī* of Mecca was enjoined to find a master who could write a script that was not only elegant, but legible as well. 'But you [the *ḳāḍī* of Mecca and the administrator of Jeddah] must pay attention to the calligrapher and have [the text] written in such a fashion that nobody reading it has any doubts. The whole affair should be taken care of in this fashion. You should also write to us in which place the inscription has been put up.'[53] This may serve as some consolation to modern historians and epigraphers, who know the problems involved in deciphering a perfect-looking inscription; apparently contemporaries were in no better position. In the end the inscription was put up close to the gate of 'Abbās, a frequently used entrance into the Great Mosque.

LIGHTING, PERFUMING AND DECORATING THE GREAT MOSQUE

Chance has preserved a rescript from the last years of Süleymān the Lawgiver (1564–5), which gives us some idea of the manner in which the Great Mosque must have appeared to worshippers. Unfortunately, however, this text antedates the rebuilding of the gallery by a few years.[54] An official in charge of the Meccan water supply, by the name of Ibrāhīm, had complained to the central government that the six *ḳanṭar*s of wax assigned to the illumination of the mosque during night prayers were insufficient for the purpose. Therefore the mosque was only lit on dark nights, while at other times pilgrims were forced to rely on whatever light was available. This was not a desirable situation, as many pilgrims were elderly and handicapped, often even unable to see the *imām* in the dark. It therefore was suggested that the yearly allotment of wax be doubled. Some of this wax came in the shape of ten large candles, each weighing 10 *vuḳiye* according to the standard of Rūm, probably about 12.8 kg. Eight of these candles illuminated the Ka'aba, while the courtyard was lighted by small hanging lamps. These were probably similar to the ones seen on a European etching of 1719, where a ring of such lights is shown as surrounding the Ka'aba.[55] Throughout the mosque courtyard, 387 such lamps (*kandīl*) had been distributed; however, as olive oil recently had been in short supply, 285 lamps remained unlighted. There were also complaints about the fact that most of the mosque illumination was extinguished after night prayers, since visitors to the mosque kept coming at any time. The administrator therefore asked for a 150 *kantar* increase in the amount of olive oil allotted to the mosque.

In his response, the old Sultan emphasized his benevolent interest in all pilgrims, and promised to send ten large candelabras, as well as the wax and olive oil required for keeping the mosque lighted throughout the night. In addition, the text is interesting because it mentions the measures intended to prevent misuse of the Sultan's gifts: the *kādī* was to enter the donation into his register and future judges were enjoined to abide by the stipulations of the rescript. However, in the absence of the Meccan *kādī* registers, we have no way of knowing how long these instructions really were carried out. There seems to be some room for doubt, as a rescript dated March 1568 refers to golden candelabras sent to the Holy City as a gift. They had not been properly recorded and were now regarded as lost, while wax and olive oil also had not been used for their appointed purposes.[56]

In 1564–5 Ibrāhīm, the administrator of water resources already referred to, requested a donation of 250 gold pieces to pay for the perfumes which were twice a year sprinkled over the Ka'aba. Up to Süleymān the Lawgiver's last years, this ceremony had not in any way been supported out of official funds, and Ibrāhīm now suggested that sandalwood, rose water, amber and musk be supplied.[57] When committing himself to make this donation every year, Sultan Süleymān expressed the hope that this act of his be recorded among his meritorious deeds; presumably he had both this world and the next in mind. Yet his death apparently prevented these gifts from arriving with any regularity. In 1569–70 the new Sultan's Council had to concern itself with a petition by Mecca's influential Kādī Hüseyin, to the effect that for two years no money for perfumes had arrived from Jeddah, so that it had become necessary to borrow 500 gold pieces.[58]

The two texts establishing Sultan Süleymān's donations are remarkable for their discussion of motivation, which otherwise so often is absent from Ottoman official records. They show that religious motives and considerations of political legitimation were inextricably intertwined in the minds of the Sultans and their officials.

Discussions concerning religious and political aspects of the pilgrimage also occurred in connection with the various coverings used in the Great Mosque, the largest of which was the Ka'aba covering. Down to the reign of Aḥmed I (reigned 1603–17), this piece of fabric was sent from Egypt, as had already been the practice in Mamluk times. From the time of Aḥmed I, the lavishly decorated coverings sent whenever a new ruler ascended the Ottoman throne were made in Istanbul, leaving only the 'ordinary' coverings, which were prepared every year, to be manufactured in Cairo.[59] Generally the coverings were black, as had been the custom instituted in Abbasid times; for black was the colour of this dynasty. But in the late sixteenth century, the Ottomans for a while experimented with a white covering, for in the Meccan sun, black dye rapidly faded, giving the covering an unsightly appearance. Samples accordingly were sent to Istanbul, where it was decided to henceforth use black lettering on a white ground. No document so far has been located which explains why this eminently practical reason did not in the long run prevent a return to a black covering.[60]

Sixteenth- to eighteenth-century illustrations of the Ka'aba generally show a covering that is only slightly decorated, mainly by a band of cloth with an inscription mentioning the name of the reigning Sultan, although in the later sixteenth century Ottoman artists seem to have experimented for a while with a different design. From a rescript dated December 1577/January 1578, we learn that at this time it was customary to add a band decorated with versets from the Koran to the bottom of the covering. The Sultan's Council now ordered a change of design, however, which involved leaving out the Koranic inscription. The reasoning behind this prohibition was that when a large number of worshippers pressed around the Ka'aba, the inscription was bound to be trampled underfoot. Unfortunately we do not know whether at this time the covering was still white or had reverted to its original black colour.[61]

Other coverings used in the Great Mosque were those veiling the three columns bearing the Ka'aba ceiling. In 1566–7, the columns themselves had been in bad condition and the Sultan's Council had ordered their repair. Evidence from 1592–3 refers to the custom of renewing the column hangings at the accession of a new ruler. During the reign of Murād III, which by that time was already drawing to a close, this custom had been neglected. Now the ruler consented to pay for new hangings and for some other urgent repairs as well, but there obviously was some concern at the prospect of yet further expense.[62]

MECCAN FOUNDATIONS OUTSIDE THE
GREAT MOSQUE

In the second half of the sixteenth century, the Mamluk foundations of Sultans Ḳā'it Bāy, Ḳānṣūh al-<u>Gh</u>ūrī and Čakmak were still in existence, even though certain administrators supposedly had stolen most of the revenues. In the case of Ḳā'it Bāy's foundation, the deficit thus incurred amounted to 2000 gold pieces, while the *ḳāḍī* Hüseyin Mālikī, at that time also in charge of the Mālikī *medrese*, stood accused of having misappropriated 600 gold pieces. As a result, the foundations were operating at less than optimum efficiency, and certain services essential to the cleanliness of the area surrounding the Great Mosque were not being performed.[63] By the end of Murād III's reign, both the upper and the lower level of the *medrese* founded by Ḳā'it Bāy were in ruins, and the same applied to the rooms and chambers situated along the pilgrims' way between Ṣafā and Marwa, which belonged to the same foundation. But these buildings, along with other foundations dating back to the Mamluk period, were considered to be capable of repair, at least in part.[64] Nor was the foundation of the Mamluk amir <u>Dj</u>ānībeg in much better case. Three chambers belonging to this foundation were so ruinous that they were in immediate danger of collapse, and the reporting official felt that the structure endangered passers-by and might even place the Great Mosque in jeopardy.[65] In almost all these cases, the administration in Istanbul blamed the embezzling of foundation administrators, presumably Mamluks for the most part. With hindsight, their depredations may be viewed as part of an appropriation process, as a result of which Egyptian revenues increasingly were retained by the Mamluks, and which was to gather yet further momentum in the seventeenth century.

Rather more active was the soup kitchen which Süleymān the Lawgiver had established in the name of his deceased consort the <u>Kh</u>āṣekī <u>Kh</u>urrem. No information is available on its architectural form, but there were frequent discussions on the grain it was to receive from Egypt. In early 1589 there seems to have been a gigantic corruption scandal. Almost 700,000 *pāra* of Egyptian revenues pertaining to the foundation had not been collected; unjustified claims of shipwreck had been made to cover up irregularities by the administrators, who had been aided in their trickery by an organizational confusion which may well have been deliberate.[66]

We possess some evidence on the operation of the foundations established by the Grand Vizier Soḳollu Meḥmed Pasha (died 1579); a hospital he founded will occupy us in another context. But he was also the founder of a lunatic asylum, which he financed in an unusual manner: he had one of his ships sold, and obtained a promise from the Sultan that the provincial treasury of Egypt would lend him enough money to make up the total of available funds to 10,000 gold pieces. Meḥmed Pasha's foundation also contained a public bath, still functioning in the 1670s, although there had been complaints in connection with some 'funny business' concerning the replacement of the larger of the two boilers. The Grand Vizier had determined that any surpluses from the revenue-producing parts of his foundation should be spent toward the repair of the buildings. This rule and the overall wealth of the foundation may explain why, in spite of complaints concerning incompetent or corrupt administrators, the institution was able to function for a hundred years and more.[67]

Murād IV had been only moderately active in furthering public construction. But among his buildings in Mecca there was a lodge (*tekke*) held by members of the Naḳshbendī order of derwishes, who received stipends for praying for the Sultan's soul. In 1643–4, only a few years after the founder's death, there already were complaints that these stipends were not being distributed according to the register of official subsidies (*ṣürre*), and that people of political influence were using the foundation to reward their own adherents. By the middle of the seventeenth century, a Mewlewī derwish lodge was also in operation, founded by the Ḳapudān Pasha Mūsā. This lodge apparently received some of its support from faraway Bosnia, and the complaint was heard that local holders of military tax assignments retained the Mewlewīkhāne's revenues for their own benefit. According to the custom of Ottoman Anatolia and Rumelia, the foundation also received the interest from a sum of money that a benefactor had assigned to it; but in this case as well, the Mewlewī derwishes had difficulty obtaining what was due to them.[68]

ATTEMPTS AT URBAN PLANNING

With the completion of the gallery, which is in use to the present day, albeit dwarfed by the enormous additions of the 1950s and 1960s, financial means became available for another ambitious project. In the reign of Murād III (1574–95) it was decided to remove the town quarters immediately adjacent to the mosque; apparently an open square was meant to take their place. Here again, so it seems, the model of the great Sultans' mosques of Istanbul, Bursa and Edirne was at the back of Ottoman planners' minds.[69] For a 'classical' Ottoman mosque not only was flanked by *medrese*s, libraries, soup kitchens and similar institutions, but also possessed an outer courtyard where no houses could be built, although these areas sometimes were used as cemeteries. These outer courtyards isolated the mosque from the mass of urban houses and ensured its heightened visibility. The Great Mosque of Mecca, by contrast, had no remarkable façade apart from a number of monumental gateways, and often houses crowded in the immediate vicinity of the sanctuary. Thus Murād III's project aimed at creating a completely new urban form. It is not surprising that well-to-do Meccans who owned these houses, and during the pilgrimage season rented them to pilgrims at a good price, were less than enthusiastic about this project.[70] These people were able to mount a degree of opposition, the outlines of which can be dimly perceived through the surviving documentation. At the other end of the social scale, poorer pilgrims were also affected. Quite a few hostels serving the needs of this group had been located near the Great Mosque, and now they were demolished one by one.

House owners and administrators of pious foundations received compensations from the Treasury, as the Sultan would not have gained religious merit if the land and buildings in question had been acquired in a way regarded as unjust by Islamic law.[71] An estimate was made of the buildings' value, and the sum of 27,000 Ottoman gold pieces set aside for compensation purposes. Unfortunately nothing is known about the fairness or otherwise of the assessment process, nor can we tell whether the former owners could acquire new houses in other parts of the city. At first a mode of payment was adopted that placed poorer owners at a grave disadvantage, for the Egyptian finance administration was put in charge of compensation and effected payments in Cairo. People without contacts in Egypt were bound to suffer grave losses if they tried to convert documents issued by Cairene finance officials into ready cash locally. At the last moment, however, the central administration decided to effect payment in Mecca after all.[72]

WATER SUPPLIES

This wholesale restructuring aimed to provide the Great Mosque with an environment that was not only imposing but also clean and free from unwelcome smells. These were difficult problems in a hot, periodically overcrowded city where water was at a premium. The first precondition was an improved water supply, which involved both an increased volume of water to be brought into the city and a better distribution of the available water over the different parts of Mecca. The main water pipes, which led from the plateau of 'Arafat to the Great Mosque, were being repaired in 1564–5.[73] By April 1571, work was still continuing, as 3000 gold pieces had been earmarked for wages; at that time the Egyptian stonecutters and blacksmiths had not been paid for a full five years. Yet, during this period, the stonecutters had prepared enough stones to secure the completion of the project.[74]

Some of the delays were due to technical difficulties. A rescript from the year 1580 discusses the fact that the water channel had not been made as smooth as would have been necessary.[75] As a result, the water did not flow regularly but was collected in pools, and very little of it arrived in the Holy City. To rectify this mistake an important sum of money was set aside. But even if there were no technical defects, the pipes were liable to get clogged with the sand and gravel carried along by the water. In 1573, Ḳāḍī Ḥüseyin of Mecca pleaded in favour of the cleaning personnel employed by the water administration, whose modest pay was insufficient in a time of scarcity.[76] In addition, the foundation used slaves as cleaners. In 1573 there were 42 "Arab' (that is, presumably, black) slave women employed at this task, the remnant of a contingent of a hundred donated some time previously by an Ottoman princess; the remainder either had died or else run away. In addition, Süleymān Pasha on his voyage to India had acquired 40 "Arab' (in this case, probably, southern) Indians. Of these 40, 22 people survived at the time of the rescript; but since the text mentions their salaries (*'ulūfe*) they may have come to the Hejaz as free labourers, or else they were manumitted in the course of time. In 1573 the remaining slaves were also freed.[77]

Water was distributed to individual quarters with the help of special devices; in 1568 these were in the course of construction. We possess a sultanic rescript in which an Egyptian specialist in this art was ordered to travel to Mecca and participate in the task.[78] Certain quarters had been given pious foundations which allowed the inhabitants to make better use of the available water. In 1567–77 we find the Grand Vizier Soḳollu Meḥmed Pasha building a public bath, and the *ḳāḍī* of Mecca was instructed to aid him in this undertaking.[79] Previously Sultan Süleymān had established a foundation intended to supply the inhabitants of Mecca with drinking water. But by 1585 the Sultan's Council had to deal with a complaint that for 20 years this foundation had not been providing any water, which means it stopped working at about the time of the founder's death.[80] The foundation's employees, meanwhile, had not failed to draw their pay. In 1581 the Sultan and his Council expressed their dissatisfaction at the Meccan water supply: after so much treasure had been expended, a *kurna* full of water still cost four or five *pāra*.[81]

In addition to the establishment of Ottoman pious foundations serving the Meccans' need for water, those remaining from Mamluk times were restored. However, the amount of 15,000 gold pieces which was demanded for this purpose seemed excessive to the central administration; we do not know how much money was ultimately assigned.[82] In addition, there was the perennial problem of preventing well-to-do residents of the city from diverting the water to their own gardens and houses, an issue all to familiar from the Ottoman core provinces as well.[83]

Water supplies in Jeddah were even more precarious than in Mecca, and the inhabitants largely depended on cisterns. In 1573, there were plans to instal water pipes, as Sultan Süleymān had stipulated as much in his will, and his son Selīm II made an effort to honour his father's wishes. But the experts asked for their professional opinion were not sanguine. The pipe would have to be 79,910 *arshın* (63,768.18 metres) long, and some of it would have to be cut into solid rock. In addition, the land around Jeddah was saline and salt was liable to get into the water, making it bitter. As a result, the project was given up, and additional water reservoirs were commissioned as a palliative.[84]

OTHER URBAN SERVICES

A further precondition for keeping the streets of Mecca and particularly the mosque courtyard clean and orderly was to lodge even the poorest pilgrims in hostels of one sort or another.

> The poor people who come to pay a visit to the noble Ka'aba do not have a determined spot [in which to spend the night]. Therefore they settle in a corner of the noble sanctuary and this is dirtied, so that lice are propagated. . . . Therefore Her Highness the late princess had purchased a piece of land close to the soup kitchen she had established, and suitable for the construction of a hostel for the afore-mentioned people.[85]

This rescript from the year 1556 refers to a topic which was to gain importance in subsequent years, namely the construction of simple housing for pilgrims who otherwise would have spent the night outdoors or on the mosque premises themselves. When a poor pilgrim fell sick, the situation became particularly difficult.

> We hear that certain sick and helpless persons spend both day and night in the noble sanctuary because they do not have the force to leave [the premises]. Now my . . . Grand Vizier . . . has found a suitable house in the vicinity of the Great Mosque. It consists of a rectangular courtyard whose sides have been roofed

over. This he has purchased from the [previous] proprietor for a [suitable] price. Also, he has had a public bath built in the vicinity of the Great Mosque, and the income it produces should be spent on the things needed by these sick people. It should also be used to purchase shrouds for the dead.

However, the problem of finding appropriate lodgings for all pilgrims was made more difficult by the Sultan's ambitious project of restructuring, to which quite a few of the existing hostels had been sacrificed.[86]

Another difficult problem was the cleaning of the Meccan streets. This was important since the dirt, if not removed, in time found its way into the Great Mosque, located as it is in the lowest part of the city.[87] In 1577 the mosque courtyard had just undergone a thorough cleaning. 'But if people throw their garbage into the street, in the event of a flood the places just cleaned will fill up again, so that the cleaning has to be repeated.' Therefore the Sultan's Council ordered *ḳāḍī* and Sherif to make sure the inhabitants of Mecca deposited their garbage in a place outside the city limits designated expressly for the purpose. Unfortunately, we have no way of knowing how this worked out in practice.

Thus the Ottoman administration was concerned with both aesthetic and hygienic problems. However, these two categories are characteristic of twentieth- and not of sixteenth-century thinking. Ottoman administrators were simply trying to ensure that the pilgrimage took place in a dignified atmosphere consonant with the importance of the event. Apart from dirt and evil smells, quite a few other phenomena were regarded as inimical to the solemnity of the pilgrimage, such as high houses which afforded a view into the sanctuary, and particularly the use of the courtyard of the Great Mosque for purposes not immediately related to worship.[88] It seems that Ottoman administrators regarded casual and quasi-domestic use of the mosque courtyard as a sign of disrespect toward the sanctuary. That Iranian inhabitants of Mecca had a different view of proper use of the mosque courtyard only made the problem more intractable: 'Some Iranians known for their heretical views ... disturb the pious who have assembled for worship in the courtyard of the mosque. In the evening they come with their womenfolk and families, with their cushions and cradles to sit down in the mosque court, and there is no end to their inappropriate behaviour.'[89] In this respect at least we observe certain parallels to Christian Europe in the early modern period. Both churchmen of the post-Tridentine Church and Ottoman administrators were concerned about establishing a sharper division between the sacred and the profane areas of life, and ensuring that behaviour at holy places was marked by restraint and a show of respect and decorum.[90]

To permit pilgrims to concentrate on their religious experience, the Ottoman administration also needed to solve problems which today would fall within the province of the police. Traffic posed its own special difficulties. Thus the way between the hills of Ṣafā and Marwa, on which the pilgrims hurry to and fro in memory of Ibrāhīm's repudiated wife Hādjar/Hagar, had long since become an urban business street. Traders displayed their goods, and their stalls constituted a great obstacle to the movement of the pilgrims. To limit the damage, the Ottoman authorities prohibited the establishment of new shops.[91] But the previously existing shops continued to operate, and only in the twentieth century was the street between Ṣafā and Marwa incorporated into the sanctuary and reserved for the exclusive use of pilgrims.

Other problems were connected with the markets where 'cooks, sellers of cooked sheeps' heads, butchers and other people of dubious respectability assemble and try to attract the custom of the pilgrims. Sneak thieves also make use of the opportunity to steal the purses of the Muslims and rob them of their money.'[92] Yet the market was necessary, for the pilgrims could not have fed themselves without its existence. Therefore the Council of the Sultan merely decided to banish it to a locality remote from the Great Mosque. But in other parts of Mecca, too, makeshift huts and tents where food and coffee were offered for sale cluttered up the public thoroughfare and hindered the pilgrims at their devotions.[93] While the Ottoman central administration made every effort to keep the public thoroughfares open, the success of its efforts depended upon the cooperation of the Sherif and, last but not least, on that of the merchants themselves.

The available rescripts convey the impression that the Ottoman central government had a notion of what constituted a well-organized pilgrimage city, and was trying to realize this conception as a whole. Appreciable sums of money were invested in the city's infrastructure so as to create conditions allowing pilgrims to fulfil their religious duties in a dignified setting. By the creation of a city specifically geared to the needs of pilgrims and closely supervised by *kādī* and Sherif, the Ottoman political class attempted to legitimize the Sultan's rule. Unfortunately, and for reasons which at present remain unknown, almost all the evidence concerning Ottoman urban planning is confined to the second half of the sixteenth century. As to the seventeenth, the only project on which we possess evidence concerns the Great Mosque. However, here at least the available sources allow us to figure out the political considerations behind a major rebuilding project.

THE REBUILDING OF THE KA'ABA

The reconstruction campaigns of the sixteenth century had left the Ka'aba untouched. Apart from a few medieval repairs, this was still the building erected by al-Ḥadjdjādj after the defeat of al-Zubayr in 693. However, by the late sixteenth century the first warnings were heard that the Ka'aba was structurally in poor condition.[94] But some theological and legal experts were opposed to the idea of tampering with the building in any way, and the Ottoman administration accepted these views without demur. Only the young Sultan Aḥmed (reigned 1603–17), who was responsible for one of the last major mosques in the 'classical' style, decided to do something to support the greatly weakened structure of the Ka'aba. Even then the walls were left untouched. Instead, as we have seen, the building was supported from the outside by a set of braces, an iron belt on supports intended to contain the outward pressure of the walls.[95] Moreover, the rainpipe of the Ka'aba was replaced; this was not a merely utilitarian measure, as the spout is located at a place where the faithful prefer to pray and hope for the fulfilment of their prayers. In addition, most of the roof of the Ka'aba was replaced and damage to the walls repaired. Precious materials were used in abundance. Apart from the installation of a rain spout made of pure gold, already mentioned in another context, the three columns in the interior of the Ka'aba received a decoration made of gold and silver. Moreover a silver tablet over the entrance to the building was replaced by a tablet made of gold.

Even so the restoration of Sultan Aḥmed's time did not really strengthen the Ka'aba's structure. This became apparent in 1630, when Mecca suffered a serious flood.[96] While occurrences of this kind were quite frequent, this particular flood was so destructive that contemporary observers thought it without precedent. Due to its geographical location the Great Mosque of Mecca has suffered from flash floods down to very recent times. In many desert areas, rainwater does not enter the earth's crust but will flow down the surface in *wadı*s. The Great Mosque is situated in the middle of such a *wadı*, which is normally dry but fills up rapidly in case of precipitation. In 1630 not only the mosque courtyard but the entire lower city were under water, and many people were drowned. The chronicler Süheylī reports that the water came up to the key in the lock of the Ka'aba door, which is situated high above the ground.[97] For three entire days the water remained in the mosque courtyard and, when it finally withdrew, a mud layer as deep as the height of a man had been deposited. This mud soon dried and turned hard as stone, so that it had to be specially moistened before finally it could be shovelled away.

The walls of the 'Ancient House' were too weak for this additional stress and a subsequent investigation showed that it was about to collapse. Thereupon the Sherif called a meeting of the prominent inhabitants of the city.[98] While such assemblies of notables did not possess a corporate existence and at first glance seem quite informal gatherings, at least in Mecca they were frequently convoked and played an active role in the 1630s rebuilding of the Ka'aba. So we may assume that similar meetings had accompanied previous construction projects too. But, apart from the chronicle of Ḳuṭb al-Dīn, sixteenth-century sources are oriented toward the central administration and not toward local personalities, which explains why we only hear about assemblies of notables in connection with a later event, namely the restoration of the Ka'aba. Moreover, as changes of any kind to the building fabric of the Ka'aba were being challenged from a religious point of view, the Ottoman administration may have felt more need for consultation than in the case of earlier projects.

It was probably this assembly which decided to give the surveyor and construction expert 'Alī b. Shams al-Dīn the responsibility of saving the Ka'aba from collapse.[99] The administrator of Jeddah was requested to furnish some timber which happened to be in the port, and this soon arrived. According to a declaration by the supreme *müftīs* of the four schools of law, the restoration of the Ka'aba was a religious responsibility which the Sherif had to undertake in the Sultan's place. But representatives of the Ottoman central administration were approached directly as well:

> Sherif Mas'ūd hurried to send one or two messengers to the province of Egypt, in order to truthfully and in all the necessary detail notify Meḥmed Pasha, the governor of Egypt who knows no equals, as a representative of the Sultan. The messengers began their journey on Monday and reached Cairo at the end of the noble month of Ramaḍān. They were granted an audience with the governor, and submitted a statement by the inhabitants of Mecca and a petition by the Sherifs. After having informed himself about the situation, the aforementioned vizier forwarded the statement and the petition to the Sultan's palace and thus informed His Majesty, the ruler.[100]

But the governor of Egypt, due to his special responsibility for the affairs of the Hejaz, also took action independently. He ordered the remittance of further construction materials from Egypt and sent over Riḍwān Agha, the commander of his Circassian Mamluks.[101] To emphasize the importance of his mission, the latter was promoted to the rank of *beg*. At first Riḍwān Beg was meant to represent the governor merely until further orders were received from Istanbul. But later he was confirmed in office[102] and if Süheylī's account of the situation is more or less realistic, Riḍwān Beg should be considered the person actually in charge of the Ka'aba restoration.[103] This would mean that the decision not to attempt any further half-measures, but to take down the walls of the Ka'aba stone by stone, and then to rebuild the structure according to the old plan, was taken by Riḍwān Beg himself. Or, if the plan originally had been devised by someone else, he at least was responsible for its execution.

Riḍwān Beg was not an architect but an administrator and a political coordinator: he had to make sure that everything needed for the construction project was brought in from Egypt on time, and for that purpose needed to maintain good relations with the governor and the Mamluks of Egypt. But the consent of the Meccan notables was also indispensable and could never be taken for granted. Just when the mosque courtyard had been cleaned up to some extent, and the work of taking down the walls of the Ka'aba stone by stone was about to begin, the Shāfi'ī chief *müftī* voiced his objections.[104] In the latter's opinion, a step of this importance could only be undertaken after the Sultan had given his formal consent. Riḍwān Beg then proceeded to furnish himself with a legal opinion to the contrary, which certain Meccan scholars supplied in short order – there was even another Shāfi'ī *müftī* in this group. From the moment in which it was possible to fully assess the damage to the Ka'aba, many scholars had encouraged the authorities to proceed as rapidly as possible.

The technical aspects of the job concerned building experts and surveyors. We hear nothing of architects sent from Istanbul, who so often had been active in Mecca during the sixteenth century. Probably the experts consulted were Syrians or Egyptians who happened to be in Mecca at the time. Their main concern was to protect themselves from future recriminations by informing the notables as quickly as possible of every step taken. Thus a meeting was called before the walls of the Ka'aba had been taken down completely, in which Riḍwān Beg participated along with the Sherif of Mecca and other prominent personalities. Here the experts formally declared that even the remaining sections of the Ka'aba walls lacked solidity: 'Do not blame us in this matter and do not say: Why did you not tell us that before!'[105] However, certain scholars were still opposed to the dismantling of what remained of the Ka'aba. Riḍwān Beg responded by soliciting another legal opinion, which explicitly incorporated the opinion of the experts. Only when this latter opinion also favoured the project, did he allow the workmen to proceed. In the course of all this, building experts and surveyors appear to have played only a subordinate role. As a perusal of their biographies shows, people like

Sinān the Architect (about 1498–1588) or Meḥmed Agha, the builder of the Sultan Aḥmed Mosque, seem to have been assertive personalities with considerable self-confidence.[106] But nothing of the kind is apparent from the behaviour of the Meccan craftsmen.

Süheylī's chronicle reflects the administrative mechanisms which made possible the taking down and later rebuilding of the Ka'aba. He has also recorded the actual progress of the work in amazing detail.[107] As a first step, the Ka'aba was surrounded by a kind of fence. While pilgrims could continue to circumambulate it, the building remained invisible and was only unveiled when reconstruction had been almost completed. After demolition all elements of the building were preserved with great care. The more valuable pieces were guarded in a treasury, which had been installed in one half of the building known as the 'Drinking water room of 'Abbās'. At this time, the golden and silver decorations were taken off the iron braces which had supported the Ka'aba walls from the early seventeenth century until the flood of 1630. More than a hundred *baṭmān*s of gold and 120 *baṭmān*s of silver were recuperated in this fashion. Unfortunately, the *baṭmān* varies from one place to the next. But if we interpret these figures as meaning Egyptian *baṭmān*s, which is a distinct possibility given the Meccan dependence on Egypt, the decorations of Aḥmed I's supports should have contained 81 kilogrammes of gold and 98 kilogrammes of silver.[108] The iron was refashioned into supports built into the structure proper so as to give it greater solidity.

When the Ka'aba completely had been taken down, only the Black Stone remained in its original position. But as even the piece of wall supporting the Black Stone was not considered very durable, molten lead was poured into the cracks of the stones which had burst.[109] Then the rebuilding phase could begin; Süheylī claims that twenty rows of stone were needed before the level of the Ka'aba's interior ceiling had been reached, and four more courses were necessary to arrive at roof level. A twenty-fifth course served to complete the building. In every case Süheylī has recorded the time at which a new row was begun, and the section of the building at which the masons began their work. A few stones were replaced by newly cut ones, so that in the end, the builders were left with fifty stones from the old building.[110] Our chronicler has also recorded when the teakwood which served for the roofing of the Ka'aba was carried into the mosque courtyard, and the time at which the carpenters cut it into the size required for the building. He also recounts how the three columns supporting the ceiling were placed in the building along with their bases. Even the fastening of the iron holders for the lamps illuminating the interior was recorded, along with the reinstallation of the door and the two flanking colonettes.[111]

CHANGES TO THE BUILDING FABRIC OF THE GREAT MOSQUE

For no other building project of the Ottoman and indeed of the Islamic world do we possess quite such a detailed account. This is due to the fact that the Ka'aba in its original shape was regarded as a creation of God Himself, which later had been renovated by several prophets.[112] This view also explains why several religious and juridical scholars objected to the Ottoman restoration projects. As the ideal solution, most scholars and administrators alike regarded a restoration which stabilized the Ka'aba for future generations but kept interference with the venerable building to an absolute minimum. But a minority apparently considered that natural decay of the building should be allowed to run its course.

In all the discussions, the opinion of the building experts was important, since only they could decide whether a given piece of wall still was solid or not. But their opinion only became practically relevant when it had been accepted by a majority of juridico-religious scholars. Apparently Riḍwān Beg, who represented the Ottoman authorities at the building site, from the very beginning had decided in favour of complete reconstruction. He then made sure to get the appropriate legal opinions whenever he needed them. This proceeding, though comprehensible from a twentieth-century point of view, was not the only option available at the time. When at the end of the sixteenth century the Ka'aba's poor structural condition had first been discussed in Ottoman administrative circles, the people in charge made no prior commitment to reconstruction, and ultimately allowed themselves to be swayed by the opponents of restoration. And even though Riḍwān Beg favoured a radical solution, he apparently made no attempt to change anything in the arrangement of the Ka'aba itself, or, if he did change some minor detail or other, the chronicler was careful to pass it over in silence. In this part of the mosque, the standards applied were quite different from those encountered in the case of the gallery, where, as we have seen, Abbasid, Mamluk and Ottoman building styles could be applied in juxtaposition.

CEREMONIES ACCOMPANYING THE RESTORATION

Agreement between Sherifs, the *müftī*s of the four recognized schools of law, the generality of juridical and religious scholars, the other prominent inhabitants of the city and Riḍwān Beg, as a representative of the Ottoman administration, thus never could be taken for granted, but constantly had to be reestablished. This situation was reflected in a sequence of ceremonies which indicated the more important phases of the restoration process. Robes of honour were distributed at fairly frequent intervals.[113] The latter ultimately came from Sultan Murād IV, but were forwarded to Mecca by the governor of Egypt. Such robes were also distributed by the Sherif of Mecca, the most prominent recipient being Riḍwān Beg himself. The latter also distributed such robes in his own right, namely when the restoration of the Ka'aba had been completed and his own official duties terminated. Riḍwān Beg gave a robe to the Sherif and to a market overseer who presumably had directed Meccan administrative personnel.[114] In addition, the 'Opener of the Noble House' received a robe of honour; to the latter's family, the Banū Shayba, the keys of the Ka'aba had been entrusted from time immemorial. All these personages belonged to the inner circle of Meccan notables. More remarkable is the fact that the Sherif also honoured the surveyors and building specialists, who were of much more modest stature, while Riḍwān Beg distributed robes to both the chief mason and the chief carpenter.[115] This gesture is consonant with a declaration of Riḍwān Beg's at the beginning of the construction period, in which he promised satisfactory wages to all the people employed on the building project. However we have no way of knowing to what extent his promises were acted upon in practice.

The distribution of robes of honour was accompanied by public prayers for the Sultan.[116] But such prayers were a frequent occurrence and often took place without any distribution before or afterwards. Prayers for the Sultan marked off almost all the phases of the Ka'aba restoration, and were said for the continuation of the Sultan's rule and thereby for the continued existence of the Ottoman state. To refuse participation in such prayers was considered an act of rebellion. In his biography of the architect of the Sultan Aḥmed Mosque, Dja'fer Efendi tells us that rebels would be consigned to hell as they refused to pray for the ruler; while he was referring to the Ottoman–Iranian conflict and not to the Hejaz, the assertion tentatively can be regarded as valid in the Meccan context as well.[117] By participating in these prayers the Meccan notables recognized the rule of the Ottoman Sultan, and because the reconstruction of the Ka'aba politically was a disputed act, allegiance to a remote suzerain had to be reasserted over and over again.

In the scenario of the ceremonies legitimizing the rule of the Ottoman Sultan and the reconstruction of the Ka'aba, Riḍwān Beg had assigned himself a prominent place. Thus he personally concerned himself with the metal casing designed to protect the Black Stone from further damage. Later he examined whether the door of the Ka'aba had been inserted properly, and in person climbed on to the roof of the mosque (here the gallery probably is intended) to establish which parts of it needed to be repainted. When work on the Ka'aba had been completed, he in person ascended the roof in order to let down the covering which protects and veils the sanctuary. These gestures make visible the support of the Ottoman administration, whom Riḍwān Beg represented in Mecca, for the whole restoration project.[118] On a more personal level, this also was an opportunity for Riḍwān Beg to demonstrate his personal humility and piety. This latter element is stressed by the chronicler Süheylī, who states that after his term of office in Mecca had ended, Riḍwān Beg voluntarily renounced the title of *beg*, because whoever held it could not avoid shedding blood.[119] This highly placed Mamluk thus behaved in a way appropriate for a religious scholar, and it is interesting to see that the mixture of roles was viewed by Süheylī as a positive and not as a negative character trait.

Riḍwān Beg's key role in the restoration project is reflected in the fact that, at the end of his tenure of office, he received as a gift an entire covering of the Ka'aba, which had been used for a year but now had been replaced by a new one.[120] The Sherifs, the Banū Shayba as gatekeepers of the Ka'aba and other Meccan notables normally possessed the right to shares of this valuable silk brocade, which they had cut up and sold to well-to-do pilgrims. Thus in a sense they could be considered as the donors. Riḍwān Beg reciprocated by gifts of money to the Meccan notables. He did not retain the covering, however, but passed it on to the Sultan's treasury. This gesture presumably was meant to once again document the concord prevailing between the ruler, his representative Riḍwān Beg, and the more influential inhabitants of the Holy City. By donating their shares in the Ka'aba covering, the Sherif and the other Meccan notables also may have wished to acknowledge Riḍwān Beg's zeal and commitment, while at the same time recognizing him as a *primus inter pares*.

Sultan Murād IV (reigned 1623–40), who was not known as a great builder, only participated in this venture in an indirect fashion. When officials on the spot in Mecca needed help, not the Sultan but the governor of Egypt was their main recourse. Only a few documents from the Registers of Important Affairs refer to the project. As was customary in such cases, the commemorative inscription in gold and lapis lazuli put up in Mecca at the end of the building campaign, and mentioned by Süheylī, also records the name of the ruler.[121] More remarkable was the fact that the new inscriptions referred to the Sultan's predecessors who had taken an active share in the reconstruction of the Great Mosque, namely Murād III (reigned

1574–95) and Aḥmed I (reigned 1603–17). Two separate inscriptions were set up in their honour. In addition, there was a further inscription which mentioned all the rulers who had acquired religious merit in contributing to the building of the Great Mosque throughout its history. Thus Murād IV was placed at the end of a long and distinguished series of pious rulers and could not fail to derive additional legitimation from this fact.

Süheylī describes yet another ceremony which symbolically concluded the building campaign; the implements which had been used in the course of the work, and at a later date the scaffolding timber as well, were buried outside the city. It is a pity that the chronicler has not interpreted this ceremony for us; the only hint he gives comes from his use of the term 'pertaining to Süleymān, solomonic', which would seem to indicate that he was thinking of an analogy to the temple of Salomon.[122] The term 'salomonic' also reminds us of Süleymān the Lawgiver (reigned 1520–65), in whose symbolism Salomon played a major role. Probably the timber and implements were buried to preclude their use in any profane undertaking.

THE CASE OF MEDINA

Information on construction in Medina is a great deal more sketchy and, above all, limited to the last quarter of the sixteenth century. It is therefore probable that the specifically Ottoman character of Medina, which is apparent from nineteenth- and twentieth-century photographs, only came into being in later centuries. Repairs to the Great Mosque are first documented for 1575–6, when Ḳāḍī Ḥüseyin, at that time officiating in Medina, received a sultanic rescript complimenting him on the successful completion of a building project in the Prophet's mosque (*Ḥarem-i muḥterem*).[123] Unfortunately, our text does not indicate the type of work done. In 1580, urgent repairs had to be effected to the dome of the small building in the mosque courtyard, which for centuries had been used as a treasury, for the building fabric showed dangerous fissures.[124] This was one of the more ancient sections of the mosque, as due to its location in the courtyard it had been spared by the fires of 1256 and 1481. Another text from 1585 speaks about repairs to the mosque wall reaching as far as the Bāb al-Nisā, which had been put up in the time of the Ummayad caliph 'Umar b. 'Abd al-'Azīz. These repairs were to cost 10,000 gold pieces and therefore should have been substantial.[125] However, our text was written at the time when the financing was still being debated and actual work probably had not yet begun. Preparations in 1585 were well enough advanced for the *nakḳāshbashı*

Lutfullāh, described as having previous experience with official buildings in Medina, to be appointed as the person responsible for the project (*mu'temed*).[126] In the following year, discussion was still continuing. Now it was estimated that only 3000 gold pieces would be needed, which indicates that either the first estimate was unrealistically high, or that the project had been scaled down drastically.[127] By 1588, something concrete definitely had been undertaken, for we learn about timber brought in from (or rather by way of) Egypt, which had been used for repairs to the mosque wall.[128] Roofs also were leaking and urgently needed repairs at this time, and, even worse, the books in the library were being eaten by bugs so that a library room with wooden bookcases was deemed indispensable to limit further damage.[129] By 1588–9, construction was in progress, for the central administration had sent another *nakkāshbashı*, a certain 'Atā'ullāh, to supervise the undertaking as *emīn*.[130] His work was to be checked by a *nāzır*, a man of the Palace probably without specific skills related to construction. As this *nāzır* had been a finance director in his earlier career, in Medina he also must have been responsible for securing the necessary cash. Workmen apparently were secured by drawing them off from projects in Mecca; the *kādī* of this city was enjoined to send unskilled labourers, masons, stonecutters, blacksmiths and even an architect or skilled builder. Architects employed on the site were accorded 30 *pāra*s a day 'to pay for their meat', in addition to 10 *irdeb* of wheat every month. Masters and unskilled labourers were assigned a money wage (*üdjret*) of 12 *pāra* and a monthly food allotment of 5 *irdeb* (1588–9).[131] Further changes to the mosque compound are recorded for 1594–5. The area reserved for the reciters of prayer in the Rawḍa was broadened to accommodate two additional rows of people, and a school for the study of the Prophet's sayings and doings (*dār al-ḥadīth*) was built adjacent to the *kibla* wall of the mosque, not far from the gate of Bāb al-Salām.[132]

Not only the building fabric, but also the interior decorations were refurbished at this time. In 1577–8, the *shaykh al-ḥaram* pointed out to the central administration that the door curtains and the coverings over the Prophet's tomb and the graves of his associates all were in urgent need of renewal.[133] A list of all the textiles currently in the mosque was forwarded to Istanbul, where it possibly may still be found in one of the less accessible corners of the archives. In 1594–5 the covering for the Prophet's grave was manufactured in Istanbul, while the curtains and other items were ordered from Egypt.[134] Unfortunately it is impossible to determine whether in the intervening years the old decorations had continued in use or whether this was already the next renewal of the set.

Discussions about the financing of these different projects reveal some of the treasures possessed by the mosque, and which must have been donated over the course of several generations.[135] We learn that golden lamps weighing 697 *mithkāl* and silver lamps weighing 51,120 *dirhem* were no longer in a usable condition, and therefore should be sent to Egypt to be melted down. Once converted into money, these treasures could be used to finance further construction. Moreover there were donations from various Sultans, in the shape of both money and jewellery. In the last months of Murād III's reign (1594–5) the Sultan complained that his father had donated 40,000 gold pieces for the institution of various pious foundations, but that, after construction was completed, the remainder of the money found its way into the Egyptian provincial treasury.[136] It is most unfortunate that no archival evidence has been found to date on the gifts of treasure which Sultan Aḥmed I lavished upon the Prophet's grave, and which apparently remained there until the Ottoman–Wahabi war of the early nineteenth century.

On the extensive foundations of the Mamluk era there is little evidence. In 1588–9 a local administrator claimed to have spent a large sum on repairs to the foundation of Sultan Ḳā'it Bāy, but we do not know on what type of work.[137] A lunatic asylum bearing the name of Nūr al-Dīn Shahīd, presumably the ruler of Aleppo and opponent of the Crusaders (died 1174), was still operating in 1576. But there were complaints that for the last seven or eight years, the institution had been unable to obtain the medicines it needed; and the Sultan's Council believed that this might be due to the depletion of the foundation's Syrian revenues.[138]

We possess somewhat more documentation on a number of smaller sanctuaries, *medrese*s and other pious foundations which the Ottoman Sultans sponsored in Medina. Thus, in the first years of Selīm II's reign (1567–8), there was a plan to construct a residential courtyard surrounded by cells on the famous cemetery of Bāḳī, near the grave of the third caliph 'Uthmān.[139] The people residing there were to spend their time reading the Koran; possibly the site, which up to this point had been deserted and rather neglected, was chosen because the founder of the Ottoman dynasty bore the same name as the third caliph. Other negotiations concerned the wish of Meḥmed Agha, the head of the Black Eunuchs, to establish a pious foundation in Medina. The latter had selected a ruined school from Mamluk times, which he was planning to restore and complete. In the rescript which at present seems to be the only record of this foundation, the Sultan's Council stressed that, above all, the descendants of the founder or the administrators of the foundation would have to be consulted.[140] If the previous foundation was ruined beyond hope of repair, and the property in question could be acquired by way of exchange, well and good. If not, some other way should be found to enable the Chief Eunuch to set up his foundation.

More important from a practical point of view was the provision of places to sleep for the poorer visitors who crowded into the city on their way to and from Mecca, and who quite often elected to stay in Medina for the remainder of their lives. A rescript from the year 1579 describes their plight: as they were unable to find lodgings, they lived on the street, and in winter many of them perished.[141] It was now suggested that the courtyard of the storehouse where the city's grain was being kept was both vacant and suitable for the purpose, and that a room with a stove or fireplace could easily be added. Moreover, the land already belonged to the Ottoman state, and so the governor of Egypt was ordered to begin construction immediately. In 1585 there was talk of yet another project, namely to repair the 63 hostels (*rıbāt*) currently existing in Medina.[142] Unfortunately, no rescripts that have been located to date permit us to establish how much of this ambitious project actually was carried out.

Sultan Murād III, whose activity as a sponsor of public construction in Mecca has been discussed, was also active in Medina. His foundation consisted of a *medrese*, accompanied by other establishments. Ewliyā Čelebi mentions a public bath, while a rescript of 1586 records that the Sultan also had planned to build a drinking water fountain with its own special conduit.[143] But the depredations of a local shaykh, who claimed to have served on the project and lavishly remunerated himself for his services, rather held up the progress of the building. Certainly Murād III's *medrese* was functioning in 1607–8, when the foundation had been attached to the office of the *kādī* of Medina.[144] In return for teaching in the school, the *kādī*s received a supplement to their salaries from the Egyptian revenues of the foundation. In the reign of Aḥmed I (1603–17) the accounts were still conscientiously audited. At one time the Chief Black Eunuch, *ex officio* the supervisor of all foundations established by the Ottoman family, caught out a *kādī* who had collected his pay for days on which he had not actually taught, and reported him to the Sultan's Council. Disputes concerning the appointment of senior students as teaching assistants (*dānishmend*) and the assignment of living space to students prove that the *medrese* was still active in 1678.[145]

In addition, Murād III's foundation also boasted a public kitchen, and this too was operating in 1678, for at that time the foundation administration was deeply involved in a dispute with some of its neighbours concerning the disposal of waste water.[146] Complaining of the bad smell, the neighbours finally obliged the foundation administrators to construct a closed conduit for this water. By the time the rescript was issued, the latter were busily engaged in sabotaging this solution, claiming that it was too expensive and troublesome. The bread produced by the foundation originally had been intended for its servitors, but by the late seventeenth century, the right to procure it had become quasi-private property, an abuse the central administration had great trouble repressing. Partly this may have been due to the fact that the community of pious people Murād III had established in the village of Ḳubā', outside of Medina, was no longer very active. Although derwish lodges and similar communities normally were among his favourite haunts, Ewliyā Čelebi, who produced a vivid account of this village and its gardens as they appeared in the early 1670s, fails to mention Murād III's lodge.[147] At the end of the sixteenth century however, this particular foundation had been in much better condition; with a revenue of 15 gold pieces and a grain assignment, the foundation had managed to attract a scholarly shaykh who taught theological subjects, and was rewarded for his work by a very substantial supplementary income.[148] Probably the decay of Murād III's Ḳubā' foundation was due to the fact that Egyptian revenues were being withheld by the Mamluks, a problem which we have encountered in other contexts.

The mosque of Ḳubā' itself, which was visited by pilgrims because it had been founded by the Prophet Muḥammad when he first established himself in Medina, was also the object of the Ottoman Sultans' solicitude. In 1576 the mosque was in ruinous condition, and the order to estimate the cost of restoration indicates that ordinary repairs were not deemed enough, and that rebuilding of certain parts might well be necessary. Ewliyā Čelebi mentions the existence of domes and vaults, which may well date from this late sixteenth-century rebuilding.[149]

RELIGION, ART AND POLITICS

We have very little idea what impression pilgrims of the late sixteenth and early seventeenth centuries received when confronted with all this new construction. It is not easy to determine even how many people outside the Hejaz knew about the buildings. They were described in official documents, town chronicles and the biography of the architect Meḥmed Agha.[150] But the pilgrimage guide of Meḥmed Yemīnī from the seventeenth century has nothing to say about new construction in Mecca and Medina.[151] Except for the traveller Ewliyā Čelebi, few Ottoman authors of the time have produced extensive descriptions of the Meccan Great Mosque in its new shape.[152] We know very little about the reading habits of seventeenth-century Ottomans, but it is probable that short tracts of the kind written by Yemīnī were more widespread than the voluminous travel account of Ewliyā Čelebi, for instance, which only became famous in the nineteenth century. The Ottoman official documentation was totally inaccessible to contemporaries, of course. Thus most educated Ottomans must have found out about the buildings undertaken by Ottoman Sultans in Mecca only when they personally came to the city as pilgrims, or heard about them from friends and neighbours. This explains why the building inscriptions constituted a major source of information, and were regarded by the Ottoman central administration in this light.

The Ottoman government viewed its building projects as an opportunity to marshall the support of the influential families of the Hejaz, from the Sherif downwards. Much time and energy was spent on this matter, and the dissent of a single scholar was taken so seriously that major negotiations were undertaken for this reason alone. This applied particularly to the reconstruction of the Ka'aba, but the reorganization of the city's physical structure and its urban services likewise could only work if the notables of the Holy Cities could be persuaded to cooperate.

This situation differs in important ways from the practices we know from Anatolia and Rumelia, to say nothing of the Ottoman capital itself. For in the Ottoman core areas, where centralized political control was more intense, etiquette required the authors of official documents to pretend that the Sultan only needed to issue an order and it would be unquestioningly obeyed. Real-life situations were much more complicated, and political negotiations, between factions within the Ottoman administration but also between tax-paying subjects and officials, were by no means unknown. When an entire town quarter was moved to make room for the Yeñi Djāmi' in Istanbul, there must have been negotiations about relocations and compensations.[153] Complaints by inhabitants forced to move indirectly are reflected in the praise of Sultan Aḥmed I by the biographer of Meḥmed Agha, who lauds the Sultan for having selected a building site where he could establish his foundation without evicting too many people. But it is in itself remarkable that, in the extant documentation, these negotiations are only alluded to, and there is no explicit discussion of the subject as a whole.

If the Holy Cities thus received special treatment, this was due first and foremost to the great distance which separated them from Istanbul, and the expense of crossing great stretches of desert. As a result, Ottoman forces in the Hejaz remained modest, and control by the centre depended on factors which we today would call 'ideological' more than on the existence of a conventional military–administrative framework. Here the religious significance of the two cities came into play; because of their role in providing an infrastructure to the pilgrimage, inhabitants of the Holy Cities did not pay any taxes, and were subsidized by the public treasury and pious foundations. This arrangement made it possible for Ottoman power to maintain itself and, in this context, visibility was an important factor. Public building constituted a means of making the presence of the Sultan immediately apparent to visitors and residents of Mecca and Medina, and this must have been the political rationale for lavish spending in the Hejaz.

To create an environment in which the pilgrims might fulfil their religious obligations in a dignified manner and without encountering too many distractions, the Ottoman Sultans attempted to enforce a whole set of urban measures. Similar efforts otherwise were only undertaken in the Ottoman capital cities, that is successively in Bursa, Edirne and particularly Istanbul. Certain ideas about the city, such as the attempt to isolate a mosque from its environment by means of an open space, seem to have been transferred wholesale from Istanbul to Mecca. The same can be said of the dome, that characteristic element of Ottoman architecture. Attempts at applying Ottoman conceptions of design did not, however, extend to the Ka'aba, except for minor decorative features, such as the ornamentation of lintels or inscriptions.

On the other hand, the lavish use of precious materials, so characteristic of Ottoman projects in the Hejaz, was not a feature of the Sultans' mosques of Istanbul. Apparently, in the Holy Cities, where a visible sultanic presence was of paramount importance, it was considered necessary to emphasize the ruler's wealth and his willingness to spend it on lavish gifts to the sanctuaries. By thus inviting comparison with the rich buildings put up by the Mamluk Sultans, the Ottoman rulers attempted to legitimize their domination.

6

The Pilgrimage as a Matter of Foreign Policy

The pilgrims visiting Mecca every year came not merely from within the borders of the Ottoman Empire, but from all parts of the Islamic world, which reached from Tangier and the Niger all the way to China. In the sixteenth and seventeenth centuries, however, certain countries which today furnish large contingents of pilgrims were islamized only to a limited degree. Thus pilgrims from western Africa, Malaya or the Indonesian islands were not as visible in Mecca as they were to become in the nineteenth century. But subjects of the Shah of Iran and the Mughal Emperor of India were present in appreciable numbers, and this posed a special challenge to the Ottoman Sultan. On the one hand the pilgrimage was obligatory for every Muslim possessing the necessary means. Thus the Ottoman Sultan, whose claim to legitimacy to some extent depended upon the fact that he protected the pilgrims, was obliged to make and keep Mecca accessible to all Muslims.[1] This was also the image the Sultans presented to the outside world: 'No Muslim and believer in the unity of God', says one sultanic rescript, 'should be hindered in any way if he wishes to visit the Holy Cities and circumambulate the luminous Ka'aba.'[2]

At the same time, political considerations also had a role to play, as certain Muslim rulers might try to influence events in Mecca openly or in an underhand fashion, to say nothing of possible spies. In the period which interests us, this particularly concerns subjects of the Shah of Iran, a religious and political rival of the Ottomans with whom the Sultans of the time were frequently at war. Sheykh al-Islām Ebūssu'ūd Efendi, the foremost *müfti* of the Ottoman Empire and trusted adviser to Süleymān the Magnificent (reigned 1520–66) even

127

went so far as to deny that the Shi'is of Iran were Muslims.[3] When the Ottoman Empire and Iran were at war, Iranian pilgrims were not permitted to enter Ottoman territory and therefore unable to perform the pilgrimage. Even in peacetime the entries and exits of Iranian pilgrims were carefully checked by the authorities. A rescript from the time of Süleymān the Magnificent, dated 1564–5, expresses these intentions most graphically: 'It is not permissible to enter my well-guarded territories at any time outside of the [pilgrimage] season.' The same text also explains how the entering and exiting pilgrims were to be controlled in practical terms: 'May they all appear at the previously determined time. Their arrival should be reported to [the Ottoman authorities] so that [the pilgrims] can be met at the border.' The Iranian pilgrims then were to be taken to Mecca through sparsely inhabited territories. Whenever it was inevitable that they pass through inhabited regions, contact with the population was to be kept to a strict minimum.[4]

SAFE CONDUCTS FOR HIGH-RANKING PILGRIMS

Non-Ottoman pilgrims of some social status often made things easier for themselves by procuring an official *laissez-passer*. These documents in Ottoman parlance were called *yol emri* and, in many cases, copies were entered into the Registers of Important Affairs.[5] They constitute an important source for Ottoman policies toward distinguished visitors. As most of these texts conformed to a more or less standard format, divergences from the norm, which also occur occasionally, are of some interest. Normally the text explains that such-and-such a pilgrim, coming from Samarkand, Tashkent or some other remote place, was on his way to Mecca or else returning home. All *kādī*s, provincial governors and other administrators were requested to not cause the pilgrims any difficulty. In practice this meant that couriers on official business did not have the right to demand the mounts of the pilgrims and their servitors for their own use. Sometimes local authorities also were requested to furnish an escort along particularly dangerous stretches of road, as well as guides to show the way. Many travel permits also state that the pilgrims possessed the right to purchase foodstuffs in the localities along their route, and forbade local administrators to curtail this right under any pretext. This clause was probably aimed at *kādī*s and other officials in provinces where there was a scarcity for either natural or man-made reasons.[6] Especially prominent visitors sometimes were to be given an official reception. There were also *laissez-passer* which benefited not a group of individual pilgrims, but the inhabitants of an entire town.[7]

HIGHLY PLACED LADIES ON DIPLOMATIC MISSIONS

The foreign pilgrims whose *laissez-passer* we encounter in the Ottoman registers were all people of some standing, and often their position in spiritual or worldly hierarchies was recognized by the Ottoman authorities. Probably the special treatment often granted to them presupposed some research and verification of credentials on the part of the Ottoman government. But matters became even more delicate when members of ruling dynasties visited the Holy City as pilgrims, particularly if these visitors happened to be female. Thus Shah Ṭahmāsp of Iran sent his consort, the mother of Prince Ismā'īl, to the Hejaz.[8] Akbar, the Mughal emperor of India, was represented by one of his wives, Salīma, and by his aunt, the court historian and memorialist Gul-badan Bēgam.[9] Of course, the two ladies were accompanied by a numerous suite. Female members of the Ottoman dynasty also visited Mecca with some frequency, while no Sultan ever performed the pilgrimage. The only prince ever to do so was Prince Djem (1459–95), unsuccessful competitor of Bāyezīd II, who visited Mecca when he was already in exile, and the Hejaz still a Mamluk dependency.[10] Presumably the rationale was that the Sultan never should be too far away from the political centre of the empire and the Habsburg and Iranian frontiers. Princes, on the other hand, might have used the pilgrimage as an opportunity for political activity not readily controlled by their royal relative. Thus Ottoman princesses could be regarded as the politically least troublesome representatives of the dynasty.

In 1572–3 the Ottoman dynasty appeared in the Hejaz in the person of Princess Shāh Sulṭān, whose safe conduct specified that she wished to visit Jerusalem before proceeding to Mecca and Medina.[11] The governor of Damascus was enjoined to treat her as an honoured visitor and aid her in procuring the supplies needed for the journey. For the trip to Jerusalem, he was to furnish a special escort, and make sure that the princess was assigned a place in the first section of the pilgrimage caravan, the place normally favoured by distinguished travellers (see Chapter 2). While the governor, as the immediate superior of the pilgrimage commander, was requested to pass on this order through the regular channels, the commander also received a rescript of his own, in which his responsibilities were detailed once again. A notable difference between the two rescripts concerns the way in which supplies were to be procured. In the text addressed to the governor, much stress was placed on the honour and deference due to the princess and no mention was made of the manner of payment for her supplies. On the other hand, the order to the caravan commander was more matter-of-fact in tone, and explicitly stated that the princess would pay for her necessities. Quite possibly, the central authorities expected her to receive all supplies in Damascus, and here she probably paid very little, as even much less exalted personages received grants-in-aid toward their pilgrimages (see Chapter 2). On the other hand, last-minute purchases en route may well have been regarded as the princess's own responsibility.

Where foreign rulers were concerned, motives for sending a high-born lady as a pilgrim must have differed from case to case. Such visits already had a long history. The twelfth-century pilgrim Ibn Djubayr noted the presence of the 25-year-old wife of Nūr al-Dīn, ruler of Aleppo, who apparently attracted a good deal of attention by her magnificent suite and the number of her clothes, but also by the abundance of her charities.[12] Ibn Djubayr had many positive things to say about the Malika Khātūn, who in this context was very much a public personality. Seen from the political point of view, her visit was probably successful, as she had managed to bring her husband and father to the attention of the pilgrims, and made sure that the caliph al-Nāṣir did not monopolize the Meccan political stage.

Visits of high-born ladies from outside the Ottoman Empire presumably involved a gesture of trust toward the Sultan and also the Sherif of Mecca, as the honour of a foreign dynasty was entrusted to the Ottoman authorities for a few weeks or months. At the same time the household of a princess aroused less suspicion than that of a visiting prince, and such suspicion, even if once aroused, was more difficult to act upon; politeness demanded that no one pry too closely into the movements of a royal woman. This situation at times must have facilitated diplomatic contacts. A good example concerns an Iranian princess, who fell ill in the course of her pilgrimage and had to extend her stay. The Sultan's Council was unable to make out whether this was a real or a 'diplomatic' illness. While the authorities attempted to send the greater part of her suite home, basically there was little they could do, except await their visitor's recovery.[13]

The members of 'ordinary', non-royal embassies also sometimes combined the pilgrimage with their official duties. Thus the ambassador of the Khān of Tashkent in 1571–2 was given permission to travel to Mecca. His *laissez-passer* also specified that he should be assigned a safe place in the caravan, in this case in the very centre.[14] But otherwise we hear of no special privileges to be accorded to the ambassador.[15] Quite possibly the authorities in Istanbul regarded his ruler as a remote prince of minor importance, whose only merit was his proven Sunni orthodoxy. Ambassadors of more powerful rulers presumably were escorted to Mecca with somewhat more pomp and circumstance.

INDIAN PRINCES AND PRINCESSES IN MECCA

Ever since the Timurid prince Bābur (lived 1483–1530, ruler of India 1526–30) had brought all of northern India under his control, the Mughal court showed a close interest in the affairs of the Hejaz. The Indian court chronicler Badāōnī, a contemporary of Bābur's grandson Akbar, who lived in the second half of the sixteenth century, mentioned Bābur Khān's rich gifts to Mecca.[16] We possess a letter from Bābur's son Humāyūn (reigned 1530–56) to the Ottoman Sultan Süleymān the Magnificent; but this letter contains so many unrealistic assumptions that it is difficult to believe that it was ever sent.[17] Humāyūn, or whoever drafted the letter in his name, wrote about the Mughal prince's wish to meet Sultan Süleymān in Mecca, and embark upon a campaign with him against the Safawids. None of this ever materialized; neither Humāyūn nor Sultan Süleymān ever set foot in the Hejaz. Humāyūn, throughout his rule in India, was fully occupied in stabilizing his throne; and Süleymān campaigned against the Safawids without Mughal aid.

Humāyūn's son Akbar at first continued to show interest in pilgrimage affairs. In the 1570s he even announced that poor people wishing to perform the pilgrimage would receive a subsidy out of the ruler's funds.[18] He also founded a hospice for pilgrims in Mecca; certainly, a foundation bearing his name was seen by Ewliyā Čelebi in 1672.[19] In later years, however, the ruler moved away from Islam and invented a Hindu–Islamic syncretistic religion which became known as Dīn-i Ilāhī (Divine Religion). He also changed his mind with respect to the Mecca pilgrimage: the court chronicler Badāōnī reports that at this time highly placed personalities who demanded permission to undertake the pilgrimage had to brave the ruler's disfavour.[20] Only people whose attachment to Islam made them unwilling to adapt to court life under the new dispensation were sometimes told to travel to the Hejaz and stay there until further notice.[21] This was in accordance with what was by then an established Mughal custom; even in the reign of Humāyūn, political exiles had settled in the Holy Cities. They included the ruler's brother Kāmrān, blinded after an unsuccessful rebellion, and the latter's wife Māh Čiček Bēgam.[22]

While Akbar was still at least outwardly a Muslim, he also established a presence in the Hejaz by sending two prestigious female members of his family to Mecca as pilgrims. They stayed for several years, performing the rites of pilgrimage a total of four times, and only returned to India in 1582. This prolonged visit caused considerable apprehension in the Sultan's Council, and in 1580–1 a rescript referred somewhat obliquely to ostentatiously distributed alms and religiously dubious practices.[23] It appears that Mughal diplomacy regarded the Sherif of Mecca as a sovereign ruler with a multitude of political contacts, who controlled a territory which in a sense was common to all Muslims. Quite apart from accusations of heresy against many highly placed Indians, this situation explains the mistrust with which the visit of the two Indian princesses was regarded in Istanbul.

THE POOR INDIANS' TOWN QUARTER

Not only very highly placed, but also extremely poor people came to Mecca from India.[24] In all likelihood, not all the people who performed the pilgrimage due to Akbar's munificence ultimately returned home. We can draw this conclusion from a rescript dated 1578–9, which mentions that a large number of Indian pilgrims had arrived in Mecca in 1577 and 1578. The poorest of these pilgrims, for whom the authors of the rescript devised a number of vituperative epithets, had to spend the nights in the Great Mosque itself. Others settled in a quarter close by. That they were unwelcome to the Ottoman authorities is obvious; at least in part this must have been due to the resulting difficulties of provisioning. Moreover, the presence of a large number of destitute folk disturbed the plans which Sultan Murād III had made for the restructuring of the Meccan city centre (see Chapter 5). The plan was to pull down all private houses located within a certain distance of the mosque, and the poor and often smelly town quarter of the Indian pilgrims was a prime target. To the regret of the authors of the rescript, it was not considered possible to expel the Indians en masse; but at least they were to be transferred to a less centrally located part of the city, where the smells they generated would not waft into the Great Mosque. Unfortunately we possess no further evidence about the poor Indians and their town quarter, and thus cannot determine how many people were transferred, how they reacted to this traumatic event and where they finally reestablished themselves. It is even possible that they found local protectors, and the town quarter was left in place after all.

THE DANGEROUS JOURNEYS OF INDIAN PILGRIMS

Salīma and Gul-badan, in spite of their high status at the Mughal court, had to wait for quite some time before Akbar could secure the necessary Portuguese safe conduct; their return, too, was delayed by untoward circumstances, including a severe storm.[25] Many ordinary pilgrims, whose troubles no historian has recorded, must have lived through similar trials and tribulations. Ever since the Portuguese had established themselves in certain ports on the western coast of India (1498–1510), Indian and Arab shipowners, if they wished to avoid molestation, had to procure the same kind of safe conduct that Akbar tried to secure for the royal women – at one point through the (ultimately unsuccessful) mediation of certain Jesuit priests. Safe conducts were expensive, but shipowners found without one by a Portuguese man-of-war risked the loss of their ships. Muslim shippers in the Indian Ocean were more affected than Hindus or members of other religious groups, as Portuguese officials were accustomed to regarding Muslims of whatever background as their principal enemies. Economic motives also were of some importance, as in southern Asia traders on the high seas were mainly Muslims; thus measures taken against a Muslim merchant hit not only the Muslim but also the competitor.

To protect Indian pilgrims efficiently, a navy would have been necessary, but neither the rulers of south Indian port towns nor the Mughals were willing to spend money on such a venture. They therefore welcomed outside help; even Hindu princes were ready to cooperate with the Ottoman warships sent in 1538 by Süleymān the Lawgiver (reigned 1520–66) to drive the Portuguese out of the Indian Ocean. But this campaign ended in failure. In the first years of the reign of Süleymān's successor Selīm II (reigned 1566–74), before the decision to conquer Cyprus had been taken, projects for an active intervention in the Indian Ocean briefly revived. Plans were even made for a Suez Canal to link the Mediterranean and the Red Sea, and the justification for the whole undertaking was the protection of pilgrims. In the end, however, the war against Venice was given priority, and Ottoman presence in the Indian Ocean remained minimal. Indian pilgrims continued to suffer reprisals until the decline of Portuguese power in the seventeenth century forced the viceroys of Goa to seek good relations with the Mughal rulers: a prerequisite for such an improvement was the cessation of attacks on pilgrim ships on the part of Portuguese naval commanders.

As pirate attacks became more frequent in the seventeenth century, it is debatable whether Indian pilgrims gained very much from this new state of affairs. These pirates were English, Dutch or even Portuguese, and particularly attacked ships on the return voyage. For they were mainly attracted not by trade goods or potential slaves, but by the gold and silver which, due to the balance of trade constantly favourable to the Indian subcontinent, ships returning from Arabian or Persian Gulf ports were likely to carry (see Chapter 7). Even so, the overland route was not practicable for Sunni pilgrims, as the risks incurred in traversing Shi'i Iran were also quite high. In official correspondence between the Mughal emperors and the Shahs of Iran this matter was sometimes discussed, but the problem never received a workable solution.

If Mughal rulers abstained from any military intervention in order to increase the safety of Indian pilgrims, this abstinence also reflected the international situation. Throughout the sixteenth century, relations between Safawid Iran and the Uzbek khanates of Central Asia were quite tense, while, on the other hand, the Mughal rulers were concerned about possible attacks on the part of Uzbek princes against their vulnerable northwestern frontier. In order to maintain a political balance, the Shah of Iran therefore seemed a potential ally, and the closure of the land route to Indian pilgrims apparently formed part of the price paid for this alliance by the Mughal rulers.

IRANIAN PILGRIMS: A CASE OF POLITICAL MURDER

Even though the Ottoman administration regarded certain Indian pilgrims as a source of political instability, Iranian visitors to the empire were viewed with even graver suspicion. This is demonstrated by the tragic end which befell the pilgrimage of the Safawid vizier Ma'ṣūm Beg, who ventured onto Ottoman territory in 1568–9.[26] At that time the two rival empires were still at peace, and Ma'ṣūm Beg therefore had been accorded permission to visit Mecca. But Ottoman officials in eastern Anatolia soon informed the central power that the vizier had appointed functionaries of the Safawi order of derwishes, which at this time still played a role in the politics of the Shahs. From the Ottoman point of view, this activity was perceived as a major threat: before Shah Ismā'īl I made himself ruler of Iran in 1501, the Safawids had been a family of derwish shaykhs influential in eastern Anatolia as well as western Iran, both in the military and the political sense. Before losing eastern Anatolia to the Ottoman Sultan Selīm I (reigned 1512–20) after the battle of Çaldıran (1514), Shah Ismā'īl had controlled this area, and retained quite a few partisans particularly among the nomadic and semi-nomadic sector of the population. Ma'ṣūm Beg's attempt to integrate these partisans of the Shah into a formal organization therefore should be regarded as part of a deliberate and far-reaching policy.

The Ottoman central government countered this threat by having Ma'ṣūm Beg murdered. However, the peace with Iran was not to be endangered by this act of violence, and the governor of Damascus therefore staged an attack by Beduins, who could then be blamed for the fatal result. During the uncertain peace of those years, when a new war was soon to begin, other emissaries of the Shah to Anatolia suffered the same fate, but Ma'ṣūm Beg's high position ensured that his tragedy is better documented than most.

THE CLOSED ROAD FROM BASRA TO MECCA

As the story of Ma'ṣūm Beg's mission demonstrates, high-level Ottoman administrators were much worried about the possibility that Shi'i pilgrims to Mecca might make contact with the adherents of the Shah on Ottoman territory. This concern also is expressed in the very impractical route that many Iranian pilgrims were required to follow. For most Iranians it would have been easiest to travel to Baghdad and from there to the Iraqi port of Basra, which was in Ottoman hands. After crossing the Persian Gulf, the pilgrims would already have been on the Arabian peninsula, even though the latter needed to be crossed from east to west before reaching the Hejaz. But the alternative which the Ottoman authorities imposed upon the pilgrims was far longer and more dangerous. According to an exchange of letters between the Sultan's Council and certain notables of Basra, which is documented in a rescript dated 1564–5, all Iranian pilgrims were required to take the 'official' caravan routes by way of Damascus, Cairo and Yemen.[27] The notables of Basra lobbied for a caravan of their own, but their request was rather sharply turned down.

Apart from possible infiltration on the part of the Shah's emissaries, the Ottoman authorities presumably were concerned also about Portuguese expansion plans on the eastern coast of the Arabian peninsula. In Basra, al-Ḥasā and Bahrain, certain amirs supported the Portuguese as a counterweight to the Ottomans, and in this fashion hoped to preserve their independence. But while this was a probable concern of the central administration, it was never expressed in the rescripts which have been examined to date. It is nonetheless quite possible that the Ottoman authorities feared, rather than the Iranians, the expansion of the Bahraini Shi'is into the Hejaz, and that this constituted the major reason for the closure of the Basra route.[28]

On the other hand, the cessation of legal connections between Basra and Mecca generated political problems of its own. The notables of the province of al-Ḥasā, a fairly recent acquisition, no doubt suffered economic disadvantages due to this regulation. They therefore exerted pressure upon the Ottoman governor to have the route reopened. No doubt it was to the advantage of the Ottoman authorities to gain the loyalty of the influential families of this outlying border province. Moreover, the governor of the province also needed to establish his office as a recognized institution, for Laḥsā, as the Ottomans called al-Ḥasā, had been elevated to the status of a fully fledged province (*beglerbeglik*) only in 1554. The districts which made up the new province were controlled by local shaykhs, who had ruled the area before the coming of the Ottomans. If not won over to the Ottoman side, it was not unlikely that, at the next opportunity, they would go over to the Shah of Iran or even to the Portuguese. Given the need to find a compromise between these conflicting interests, the Sultan's Council experienced some difficulty in drafting a coherent policy. A rescript dated 1570–1 expresses the administration's hesitations with a frankness quite unusual in this type of document: after mentioning earlier pilgrim travel along the Basra–Mecca route, the text explains that it was later closed to shut out *Ḳızılbash*, that is, heretics from Iran or the Arabian Gulf coast, who were liable to cause disturbances among the pilgrims.[29] But whether a reopening really increased the danger of infiltration admittedly was open to some doubt. Sensibly enough, the authors of the rescript pointed out that it was mainly *bona fide* pilgrims who were kept away by the closing of the route. Real spies probably would find ways and means of insinuating themselves, no matter what precautions were taken. Financial considerations also were of some importance, as the pilgrims paid various taxes en route. Even though the rescript does not contain a clear decision, it seems that the Sultan's Council at this time was willing to risk the reopening of the Basra route.

In 1573–4 pilgrims from Basra finally could reach Mecca by direct travel.[30] This meant that certain groups of Beduins must have been willing to guarantee the safety of the pilgrims, and we do in fact learn that Beduins from Nedjd had protected pilgrims during previous years and were now offering their services for the coming year as well. But already by 1575–6, the pilgrims of Basra could no longer travel by way of Laḥsā. This measure was probably taken as a precaution. Shah Ṭahmāsp was known to be ill, and the continuance of the peace would be in doubt after the death of the ruler who had concluded it. Shah Ṭahmāsp did in fact die the following year and, by 1577–8, the two empires were again at war.[31] These events formed the backdrop to the closure of the Laḥsā route to all pilgrims, not only to Iranians. In one rescript, the Ottoman authorities even admitted that, under the present circumstances, it was all but impossible for pilgrims from the Gulf area to get to Mecca.[32] But it is unlikely that, before the end of the war in 1590, anything was done to solve the problem.

At the same time, the closure of the Basra–Mecca route quite obviously did not prevent Iranian spies from entering the Ottoman Empire. In 1580–1 a rescript refers to supposed Safawid agents, who were accused of having suborned military commanders at the frontier and sown trouble among the pilgrims assembled in Mecca.[33] The governors of Laḥsā and Basra were requested to employ their most capable counter-espionage agents in this affair, but also to make sure that ordinary traders were not molested. Unfortunately, the text does not tell us who these favoured merchants were. Since the war was still continuing, they must have been neutrals, probably Indians who brought spices and cottons into the country and purchased the famous pearls of Bahrain. After all, the customs duties paid by these merchants constituted an appreciable source of revenue.

The interests of merchants trading in Laḥsā were also defended by the local Ottoman governors, who had these customs revenues in mind. Before the Ottoman–Iranian war, the taxes of the province's principal port had been farmed out for three quarters of a million *akče*, but the interruption of pilgrimage travel also dried up this source of revenue. At least for a short time the provincial administrators were successful, for in 1580–1 the route was reopened to Sunni pilgrims.[34] But it is difficult to envisage how Shi'is could have been excluded in practice, particularly since many Iraqi Ottoman subjects as well as Bahrainis were Shi'i Muslims.

In later times the route from Basra by way of Laḥsā presumably was opened or closed according to political exigencies. Ewliyā Čelebi, in his pilgrimage account of 1672, explicitly mentions pilgrims from Basra. They had probably arrived by the direct route, because if they had made the enormous detour by way of Damascus, Ewliyā, who himself had travelled with the Damascus caravan, would not have failed to mention the fact.[35]

COMBINING TWO PILGRIMAGES

Shi'i pilgrims from Iran often combined their journey to Mecca with a visit to the Iraqi pilgrimage centres of al-Nadjaf and Karbalā'. In al-Nadjaf they visited the tomb of the caliph 'Alī (reigned 656–80), the Prophet's son-in-law and his fourth successor after the Caliphs Abū Bakr, 'Umar and 'Uthmān. Karbalā' is the site of the tomb of Imām Husayn, son of the Caliph 'Alī and the grandson of the Prophet by his daughter Fāṭima. Without ever ascending the throne, Imām Husayn was killed in an uprising in the reign of the Ummayad caliph Yazīd (reigned 680–3). In the Shi'i world view, these personages were the rightful heirs of the Prophet Muḥammad and leaders of the Muslim community. Given geographical proximity, there were probably more Iranian pilgrims to al-Nadjaf and Karbalā' than to Mecca. This can be concluded from the fact that, in the rescripts of the sixteenth century, the former are mentioned much more frequently than the latter.

In order to obtain an overall view of Ottoman official attitudes toward Muslim pilgrims, the two pilgrimages should be studied together.

A rescript from the end of 1568 or the beginning of 1569 makes it abundantly clear that the Ottoman authorities, even if they had wished to do so, often would have been unable to prevent Iranian pilgrims from visiting the graves of the Caliph 'Alī or Imām Ḥusayn.[36] In the case under discussion, a group of Iranian hajjis had returned from Mecca by way of Medina. After visiting the Prophet's tomb, they hired a guide and travelled to Baghdad. When the Sultan's Council was informed of this move, its members professed to be shocked. The Ottoman governor was reminded by special rescript that Iranians were forbidden to visit Baghdad. We have no other record of such a prohibition, and possibly it had been issued in a purely *ad hoc* fashion. But all of this cannot have had much of a practical effect; for, by the time the rescript reached its destination, the Iranians may well have completed their business and returned home.

The mother of Shah Ismā'īl II (reigned 1576–7), whose pilgrimage has already occupied us in a different context, also visited al-Nadjaf and Karbalā', probably in 1563–4.[37] Her visit, like that of other Iranians, was governed by a set of regulations probably taking shape at the time and officially issued in 1565, at the very end of Süleymān the Lawgiver's reign. The original version apparently has not survived, but we possess a confirmation from 1573–4, which probably reitcrates the principal stipulations of the original.[38] Semi-official representatives of the Shah seem to have resided both in al-Nadjaf and Karbalā', whose principal function it was to distribute alms – a manner of establishing a presence on the territory of a foreign ruler not unknown in Mecca. It was, however, not permitted to the two representatives to establish soup kitchens for the poor, even if only Iranians were to benefit from the Shah's largesse. In Istanbul it was argued that any pilgrim could take care of himself or herself for the span of five to ten days, and a longer stay was regarded as undesirable anyway. These regulations obviously were intended to keep down the Shi'i presence to an absolute minimum. Baghdad probably was regarded as an especially sensitive area; the city had only been conquered by the Ottomans in 1534, and presumably many Baghdadi Shi'is continued to sympathize with the Safawids.[39]

Certain Iranians, however, did settle in the Iraqi pilgrimage cities and even acquired houses and land. In 1578, when the Ottoman and Safawid rulers once again went to war after the death of Shah Ṭahmāsp, several of the Shah's subjects fled Karbalā', and their houses were confiscated by the Ottomans.[40] In Mecca there also existed a community of Iranian residents, who aroused the ire of the Ottoman authorities by their casual behaviour in the courtyard of the

Great Mosque (see Chapter 5).[41] But whether this community survived the Ottoman–Iranian wars of the late sixteenth and early seventeenth centuries remains unknown.

PIOUS GIFTS AS A SOURCE OF DIPLOMATIC RIVALRY

In times of peace Safawid rulers occasionally sent pious gifts to the major sanctuaries located in Ottoman territory. Such donations were made mainly to the mausolea of the Caliph 'Alī and his son Imām Ḥusayn, but gifts to the sanctuaries of the Hejaz, too, are documented. As the Ottoman rulers also sent gifts, rivalry between the two rulers occasionally ensued concerning the manner in which these gifts were to be exhibited. Thus a rescript dated 1573–4 informs us that the Shah, or else his active and influential sister the princess Perīkhān, had asked for permission to have the two Iraqi sanctuaries covered with carpets from Iran.[42] This demand was politely rejected; but when gifts from Iran did in fact arrive at a sanctuary, the Sultan's Council usually felt that it was not appropriate to reject them.[43] Thus a silver censer and a candelabra donated by Princess Perīkhān were consigned to the storehouse of the Iraqi sanctuaries.[44] Unfortunately, our sources do not permit us to determine whether they were ever exhibited in public.

PILGRIMS FROM CENTRAL ASIA

The Timurid principalities of Central Asia in the sixteenth century were governed by Sunni rulers, many of them in constant conflict with the Safawid Shahs of Iran. Due to the frequent wars between the Iranian ruler and the Khān of the Uzbeks, Sunni pilgrims could not travel to Mecca by the direct route, and all politically feasible detours were enormously long and difficult. Certain pilgrims reached Mecca by way of Istanbul, and returned to their Central Asian homelands by way of Delhi. Apparently one of these pilgrims was asked by the Ottoman authorities to deliver an official missive from Sultan Ahmed I (reigned 1603–17) at the court of the Mughal ruler Djihāngīr (reigned 1605–27). However, Akbar's son refused to recognize the credentials of this improvised ambassador.[45]

Central Asian pilgrims generally travelled from Bukhara and Samarkand through the steppe to the Caspian Sea. After a stopover in Astrakhan, they continued their journey through present-day southern Russia, until they arrived at one of the Ottoman ports of the northern Black Sea coast, such as Kefe (present-day Feodosiya) or

Özü (Ochakow).[46] If everything went well, the pilgrims then crossed the sea and ultimately arrived in Istanbul, where they could join the hajj caravan to Damascus. Some pilgrims might avoid the Istanbul detour and disembark in one of the ports of northern Anatolia, such as Sinop or Samsun.[47] But in that case they needed to traverse Anatolia from north to south, often on less frequented routes, to meet the Damascus pilgrimage caravan somewhere near Eskişehir or Konya. Given the bad state of the routes linking the Black Sea coast with central Anatolia down into the third quarter of the twentieth century, it is unlikely that the pilgrims who chose this route saved much time, quite apart from the much greater risk of being robbed on the way.

Before the Central Asians entered Ottoman territory in the narrow sense of the word, they needed to pass the steppes controlled, at least to some extent, by the Tatar Khān of the Crimea. This latter khanate was one of the successor states of the Golden Horde, which originally had been founded by Chingiz Khan and his sons during the thirteenth century. By the sixteenth century, the Crimean Tatars frequently were at war with the rulers of Moscow, and recognized the Ottoman Sultan as their suzerain, who appointed and occasionally dismissed their khāns. But the latter retained a good deal of political initiative, and among other things claimed to be the patrons and protectors of all Tatar pilgrims to Mecca. When one of the latter died en route, the Tatar Khān's representative, who accompanied every caravan setting out from Damascus, took charge of his effects, and the Ottoman official in charge of heirless property had no right to intervene (see Chapter 2).[48] At first this ruling probably applied only to the subjects of the Tatar Khān, but later it was extended to all Transoxanians.

As a protector of the pilgrims, the Tatar Khān at times intervened to protect them from excessive taxation. We possess a document dealing with a complaint from pilgrims to Mecca, of whom a prince of the Nogay Tatars had demanded high customs duties in the Black Sea port of Azak (Azov).[49] In response, the Ottoman provincial governor of Azak was ordered to bring the matter to the attention of the Tatar Khān. The authorities in Istanbul apparently assumed that the Khān would exert pressure on the Nogay princes and remind them of the Sultan's commands concerning the treatment of pilgrims. But it is difficult to determine to what extent this expectation was realistic, as the Nogay princes often regarded themselves as the opponents of the current Tatar Khān.

On the long route of the Central Asian pilgrims, Astrakhan was a much frequented stopover. In 1554–6 this city had been conquered by Czar Ivan IV and since then formed part of Russia.[50] When the

Czar attempted to stop the passage of pilgrims, the Ottoman Sultan intervened, partly because his title of caliph obliged him to concern himself with the problems encountered by all pilgrims, even if they were not subjects of the Ottoman state. Moreover, the ruler of the Central Asian khanate of Khiva had urged the Sultan to interfere in the region's political conflicts. A letter from the Khān of Khiva complained about the oppression that merchants and pilgrims suffered from both the Safawids and the Russian Czars; only if the Ottoman Sultan were to take Astrakhan, would these problems find a solution. This demand was taken seriously in Istanbul, since it immediately concerned the Sultan's prestige in the entire Islamic world. The problem of pilgrim transit through Astrakhan apparently contributed to the decision of Sultan Selīm II (reigned 1566–74) to lay siege to the city; but the Ottoman army failed to take it.[51]

Other factors doubtlessly contributed to the decision to go to war over Astrakhan. By the second half of the sixteenth century, Ottoman policy on the northern frontier involved maintaining a balance of power between the Nogay princes, the Tatar Khān and the Czars. Ottoman Sultans and viziers, even at this early period, may well have been worried about the possibility that the Czars would establish themselves on the Black Sea coast, and interpreted the conquest of Astrakhan in this sense. But even so it would be an error to underestimate the importance of pilgrim transit. The Ottoman Sultans could not legitimize themselves by their role in early Islamic history, nor could they put forth a claim, still of some importance in Turco-Tatar circles, of being descended from Chingiz Khan or Tamerlane. Thus their legitimacy depended on practical services to the Islamic community at large, and, among the latter, service to the pilgrims was of special importance.

Among the Central Asian pilgrims who got themselves a *laissez-passer* from the Ottoman administration, we find a good many derwishes. Some of the latter claimed descent from famous personages of Islamic history. Thus a shaykh from Bukhara supposedly was descended from the mystical poet Aḥmad-ı Yasawī, who lived in the twelfth century.[52] Another shaykh from Transoxania declared himself the descendant of 'Umar, the second caliph and successor to the Prophet Muḥammad.[53] This was a rich man, who travelled in the company of his family and sixty derwishes, who in turn had brought their own families along. This style of travel strongly differed from that of Ottoman pilgrims, who normally did not even take their wives. But the Transoxanian shaykh may have been special in other respects as well. His *laissez-passer* contains the clause that the provincial administrators of the regions he traversed should supply him with foodstuffs and camels, while no mention is made of any payment on his part. As most *laissez-passer* specify payment, it is quite possible that the shaykh made his pilgrimage as a guest of the Ottoman Sultan. Another guest of honour was the shaykh 'Abd al-Ḳahhār 'Ulvī; the rescript referring to his case specified that he was to receive high honours from both the Ottoman governor of Kefe (Feodosiya) and from the Tatar Khān as well.[54]

PILGRIMS FROM THE FAR WEST

In Ottoman documents from the sixteenth century, references to pilgrims from the North African provinces of the Ottoman Empire are rare, and the same applies to Morocco. This may be explained by the route followed by these travellers, who passed through Cairo and not through Istanbul, so that their problems were less likely to come to the attention of the Sultan's Council than those of the Tatar pilgrims. Seventeenth-century travellers often reached Egypt after a voyage on a French or English ship, for these offered better protection against attacks on the part of Maltese corsairs. There was also a caravan which traversed North Africa from west to east, and, after taking a rest in Cairo, pilgrims could join the annual pilgrimage caravan.[55] Among religious scholars of North Africa it was common practice to combine the pilgrimage with a visit to the major centres of the Islamic world, and even to produce a written account of their travels. Therefore we should not conclude merely from the scanty evidence in the Istanbul archives that few North Africans took the trouble to visit Mecca.

Some official information concerning pilgrims from Morocco can be gathered from two rescripts mentioning the name of Sultan 'Abd al-Malik (reigned 1576–8), who was a protégé of the Ottoman Sultan.[56] Like other Muslim rulers, he maintained an envoy in Mecca, whose job it was to distribute alms in the name of the Sultan. The Ottoman authorities accorded him the privilege of selecting the recipients without any outside interference. But the text also makes it clear that the Sultan's Council did not regard the envoy as a fully fledged ambassador, but as a simple servitor of the Moroccan Sultan.[57]

Within a short time after his arrival, the Moroccan envoy ran into trouble, probably due to the none too elevated standing of the ruler who had sent him. The Moroccan had acquired a house in Mecca, but Ḳāḍī Ḥusayn, former *ḳāḍī* of Medina and acting *shaykh al-ḥaram*, one of the most powerful men in the city, took it away from him under one pretext or another.[58] Thereupon the envoy complained to Istanbul, and the Sultan's Council apparently sympathized with his plight. But it is not clear whether Kāḍī Ḥusayn was in fact obliged to return the house.

A rescript protecting the heirs of deceased Moroccan pilgrims was probably due to the activities of the unfortunate envoy. This privilege resembles that issued to the Tatar Khān, assuring the Moroccan ruler that the estates of his deceased subjects would be turned over to the heirs and not confiscated. Given the atrocious reputation of the officials who farmed the collection of heirless estates (see Chapter 2) this exemption from their attentions constituted a significant advantage.[59]

POLITICS AND THE PILGRIMAGE

If politics consists of the skill of conciliating contradictory interests, Ottoman hajj policy did not deviate from the standard definition. An Ottoman Sultan who wished to fulfil the expectations of the political class, that is *'ulemā* and other public officials, needed to protect both domestic and foreign pilgrims from hunger, lack of water, Beduin attacks, hindrances imposed by foreign rulers and excessive taxation. In this context, the Ottoman rulers also acted as suzerains of the Sherifs. The Sultans were not the only Muslim rulers to maintain a presence in the Hejaz, however, as the Mughals and Moroccan Sultans sent envoys to oversee official almsgiving, to say nothing of the pilgrimages of members of different royal families. The Ottoman ruler's claim to preeminence might result in his controlling and limiting the charity of certain foreign rulers, especially if the latter's donations were so lavish as to imply a bid for support from Hejazi notables, particularly the Sherifal dynasty. But on the other hand, to limit the gifts of foreign rulers might lead to the disaffection of potential beneficiaries. This had to be prevented, often by the accordance of Ottoman largesse. For many Meccan families appreciably benefited from the donations of foreign rulers; in addition, the Sherifs passed on a sizable amount of the donations they received to the Beduins of the Hejaz. Under these circumstances, the hostility of politically active personages in Mecca or Medina might result in Beduin attacks on the pilgrimage caravans, and thus the attempt to secure Ottoman control indirectly might lead to a loss of legitimacy. The Sultan's Council and the relevant provincial governors therefore needed to proceed with circumspection.

Somewhat different political problems arose in connection with votive gifts. When the Ottoman Sultan or a foreign Muslim ruler donated carpets, candelabras, books or other items of value, these gestures must be understood as not merely religious but political as well. Between the Ottoman rulers and the Safawid Shahs these donations occasionally aroused a good deal of rivalry. Competition would have been even more intense if the Safawids had not preferred to concentrate their attention on the Iraqi mausolea of the Caliph 'Alī and his son the Imām Ḥusayn. To the Ottomans as Sunni rulers these personages certainly were venerable because of their relationship to the Prophet Muḥammad and their role in early Islamic history. But their graves were regarded as less important than the Prophet's mosque in Medina and the Great Mosque of Mecca. The Ottoman Sultans certainly attempted to establish a Sunni presence in Iraq by adorning Sunni sanctuaries, such as the grave of the derwish saint 'Abd al-Ḳādir al-Djīlānī; conversely the latter sanctuary was destroyed whenever the Safawids managed to conquer Baghdad and hold it for a more or less extended period.⁶⁰ But on the other hand, no Ottoman Sunni would have objected to the decoration of the mausolea which commemorated the graves of the Prophet's descendants in Iraq.⁶¹ Thus the different but not necessarily contradictory priorities of Ottomans and Safawids with respect to Islamic sanctuaries certainly kept diplomatic rivalry between the two ruling houses within manageable limits.

In the second half of the sixteenth century, Ottoman Sultans and their advisers showed a particular interest in the pilgrimages of derwishes and religious scholars from Central Asia. This again needs to be viewed against the backdrop of the Ottoman–Safawid conflict. Pilgrims from Central Asia could not take the closest route to Mecca, because the Safawids, locked in long-term conflict with the Uzbeks, prevented their passage. Detours through India or Istanbul were so difficult, however, that only people for whom religion was the dominant commitment, even in their everyday lives, were willing to take this burden upon themselves. Thus most Central Asian pilgrims who visited the Ottoman Empire were either religious scholars or derwishes. Such people in the eyes of their Ottoman opposite numbers must have appeared as heroic representatives of Sunni Islam *vis à vis* the heretic Iranians. Views of this kind probably explain why some of these Central Asian pilgrims were received with so much pomp and circumstance.

Pilgrims from Safawid Iran were affected by the conflict between the two great Muslim empires in yet a different fashion. Although no Ottoman rescript ever claimed that the pilgrimage route from Basra was closed in retaliation for the difficulties laid in the way of Central Asian pilgrims, it is not inconceivable that this motive had a role to play. On this issue, however, the Ottoman government again attempted to conciliate mutually incompatible interests. On the one hand the amirs of the Arabian peninsula in their desert fastnesses were to be prevented from establishing contacts with the Safawids, and possibly even with the Portuguese, in order to escape Ottoman control. At the same time, the wishes of the notables of Basra had to be taken into consideration, whose economic interests were at stake and who controlled a strategic port city of great importance to the Ottoman Empire. What at first glance appears as Ottoman indecisiveness, on further consideration turns out to be an attempt to find a viable compromise between these diverging political aims.

7

The Pilgrimage in Economic and Political Contexts

At all times, the pilgrimage was located at the intersection of several far-flung networks, primarily social and religious, but political and economic as well. Yet neither the Ottoman state, nor its predecessors dominating the Hejaz in the Middle Ages, fully controlled all these networks. Therefore the political elites, both Ottoman and Mamluk, were faced with a number of difficult tasks. As we have seen in the previous chapters, the safety of the pilgrims could only be assured if Ottoman administrators succeeded in satisfying, and where necessary intimidating, armed Beduins on the verge of famine, unruly janissaries and a local population accustomed to imperial largesse. As force could be used only in emergencies, the scope for various kinds of political action was considerable.

For this purpose a regional administrative apparatus was created, which, from the central government's point of view, was more difficult to control than its counterparts in the Ottoman core regions of Anatolia and Rumelia. The Sherifs functioned as the most important element. Accordingly, they demanded to be recognized as independent rulers, even if these claims were not accepted in Istanbul. To counter their ambitions, the Ottoman administration appointed the *kādī*s of Mecca and Medina, the administrator of Jeddah, the *agha*s of Medina, and lesser officials as well. Last but not least, the notable families of the Holy Cities, if handled with circumspection, might serve as a support for Ottoman power.

To maintain equilibrium, the Ottoman central administration had to take into account not only political relations, but also foreign trade. Here the possibilities for official intervention were severely limited. Yemeni traders in the Middle Ages, and southern Indians from the

146

seventeenth century onward, delivered foodstuffs and other necessities to the Hejaz. But the arrival or failure to arrive of these
merchants could be controlled only in a very limited sense by Sultans
and viziers, whether they resided in Baghdad, Cairo or later Istanbul.
Portuguese attacks, the activities of European pirates or bad rice
harvests in southern India could all endanger the supply of food in the
Hejaz, and the Ottoman administration possessed but limited means
to counter these threats.

In the present chapter, we will investigate the manner in which
politics and foreign trade affected different aspects of the pilgrimage.
We will be dealing with the attempt of a highly organized and
bureaucratized state of the early modern era to influence interregional
and international trade in the interests of pilgrims and permanent
inhabitants of the Hejaz, and thereby to legitimize its own existence in
the eyes of both domestic and foreign pilgrims. We will also discuss
both the cooperation and occasional resistance this official Ottoman
policy encountered from traders, local notables and the Sherifs
themselves.

THE SUBJECTION OF THE HEJAZ

In 1517 Ṭumān Bāy, the last Mamluk Sultan of Egypt, was hanged at
the gates of Cairo upon the orders of the Ottoman Sultan Selīm I
(reigned 1512–20).[1] Ṭumān Bāy's predecessor Kānṣūh al-Ghūrī
(reigned 1501–16) had been killed in battle; after 1516, Syria was in
Ottoman hands. These facts severely limited the options of the
Sherifs of Mecca who, as princes of local importance only, had
governed the Hejaz ever since the tenth century. A text from the year
1517 clearly demonstrates that, at the beginning of the sixteenth
century, the Meccan food supply closely depended on the arrival of
grains from Egypt. A short time previously the Portuguese had staged
an incursion into the Red Sea, with dire consequences for life in the
Hejaz. 'The situation in this place really is worthy of commiseration.
Before these accursed unbelievers arrived, a *ṭuman* of grain sold for
20 *ashrafī* coins. When the news arrived, the price increased to 30 on
the very same day, and to 40 a day later. It still continues to rise, and
people say that it will reach 100.'[2] This was the report of the Ottoman
naval commander Selmān Re'īs from Jeddah, and it explains why the
Hejaz submitted to Ottoman domination without a shot being fired.

The presence of the Ottoman fleet in the Red Sea equally
contributed to the rapid submission of the Sherifs.[3] In order to stop
the advance of the Portuguese into the Red Sea region, Sultan
Kānṣūh al-Ghūrī had asked the Ottoman ruler Bāyezīd II (reigned

1481–1512) for military and naval support. The Ottoman fleet, commanded by amir Ḥüseyin al-Kürdī, lost a battle against the Portuguese before Diu in 1509 and failed to drive them away from the western coast of southern India. But the amir rapidly fortified Jeddah, and this certainly influenced the last-minute decision of the Portuguese commander to leave the city in peace. Meanwhile relations between Ḥüseyin al-Kürdī and the reigning Sherif Barakāt seriously deteriorated, and, after a series of clashes, the Sherif had the Amir drowned near Jeddah. According to Meccan chronicles, Sultan Selīm himself had ordered the killing. But the Ottoman naval commander Selmān Re'īs, who was in Jeddah in 1517, felt that this act ran completely counter to Ottoman political traditions and was the sole responsibility of the Sherif.

MECCAN SHERIFS AND OTTOMAN GOVERNORS

Possibly Sherif Barakāt did not wish to discuss the killing of amir Ḥüseyin al-Kürdī with Sultan Selīm I, when the latter conquered Cairo in the same year.[4] In any case he did not in person travel to Cairo, but sent his very young son Abū Numayy to offer his submission to the Ottoman Sultan. Selīm I accepted this solution without ever travelling to the Hejaz himself, and the Sherifs were recognized as dependent princes. No Ottoman governors resided in Mecca or Medina, although small detachments of soldiers from Egypt were garrisoned there. In the second half of the sixteenth century, after Ottoman control had stabilized in the Hejaz and Egypt, a low-level provincial governor (*beg, sandjakbegi*) resided in Jeddah on the Red Sea coast and represented the Ottoman government *vis à vis* the Sherif of Mecca.[5] The hierarchical superior of the governor of Jeddah was the *beglerbegi* of Egypt, and later the equally remote governor of Ḥabeshistān (Ethiopia).

Given the great distances involved, the governor of Jeddah often possessed more room for manoeuvre than other Ottoman provincial governors. But many *'ulemā* and other well-connected personages, whose salaries were paid out of the revenues of the port, sometimes found this situation highly undesirable, and were able to limit the port administrator's freedom of action by calling on the central administration to intervene. In 1594, the Chief Black Eunuch was appointed *nāẓır* (supervisor) of the port of Jeddah, whose main job it was to make sure that the beneficiaries of official largesse did in fact receive their money. Since the Chief Eunuch continued to reside in Istanbul, a substitute was appointed who presumably came to reside in Jeddah itself. We do not know whether this arrangement was meant to be permanent, or limited to the frequent periods in which the governorship was vacant, as it had been when '*ulemā* and other beneficiaries allegedly were unable to collect their money. But whenever a new governor and port administrator arrived, coping with the Chief Eunuch's representative must have posed some delicate problems.[6]

The most distinguished holder of this position was probably the historian Muṣṭafā 'Ālī (1541–1600), who, even though he did not make the kind of career he considered appropriate to his merits, was appointed to governorships several times, and ended his career in 1600 as an administrator of Jeddah. 'Ālī had established amicable relations with the reigning Sherif, to whom he showed the literary work he was then in the course of completing, certain sections of which the Sherif was alleged to have endorsed with enthusiasm. These good relations also may have been due to the fact that 'Ālī was willing to regard the Sherifs as a sovereign dynasty.[7]

The Sherifs' attempts to be recognized as more or less independent princes have occupied us in another context (see Chapter 6); we now need to consider how the authorities in Istanbul reacted to such claims. Even though territorial limits in the desert were bound to be somewhat vague, the Ottoman administration had a working notion of the area the Sherifs were supposed to control, and distinguished this territory from provinces under direct administration. This is apparent from two rescripts dated 1573–4, which relayed instructions concerning the peasants of the oasis of Khaybar.[8] The latter had complained about mistreatment on the part of some 'rebellious Beduins', who came to the oasis at harvest time, allegedly robbed grain and dates, raped women and wounded or even killed some of the inhabitants. Now the peasants had offered to accept a garrison and in addition pay 2000 gold pieces to the provincial treasury of Damascus in exchange for protection. In the rescript addressed to the governor of Damascus, it is expressly stated that the responsibility for protecting the inhabitants of the oasis lay with the Sherif; only if the latter declared himself unable to do anything about the matter, would the central administration consider direct intervention. At the same time the Sherif received an official letter which reminded him that the local fortress commander was his own man, and that he would have to shoulder the responsibility of punishing the robbers.

Khaybar was a remote outpost, which even in the second half of the nineteenth century, the Ottoman government did not really control; and presumably the Sherif was enjoined to intervene because the administration did not wish to commit troops to this venture. Quite apart from practical considerations, it is noteworthy that the Ottoman government, even at the height of its power, did not claim that the Sherif's lands simply constituted Ottoman territory, where the nearest provincial governor could do whatever he considered necessary. At least in this limited respect, the Ottoman Sultan thus accepted the claims of the Sherifs to control a certain stretch of territory with minimum interference from the outside.

At the same time, the Sherifs of Mecca were appointed, usually for life, by the Ottoman Sultan.[9] In case of conflict, Sherifs could be deposed, but the successor had to be taken from the same family. Most Sherifs possessed a large number of brothers and nephews, and therefore had to be prepared for the eventuality of being ousted. It was not unheard of that a deposed Sherif might succeed in regaining office at a later period.

Among the Beduins the Sherif family had allies and thus could put together an armed force of its own. In 1585 the Ottoman central government did not contradict the Sherif's claim that from his revenues he must support 20,000 to 30,000 adherents and dependants.[10] Probably the Sherif paid subsidies to the Beduins, so as to have a claim on them in case of need. Given the difficulty of feeding large numbers of people in the Hejaz, a standing army would have been out of the question.

From the central administration's point of view, it was the function of this armed force to prevent attacks on the pilgrimage caravan. But a Sherif who got into trouble with an Ottoman caravan commander could make another use of his Beduin auxiliaries. Ewliyā Čelebi has given a full report of just such a case. In 1670–1, that is, a year before the traveller's visit, a newly appointed governor of Jeddah felt offended by the reigning Sherif, and serious conflict was the result.[11] Pilgrims engaged in their devotions in the courtyard of the Great Mosque felt so threatened that they closed the gates on the inside, while the Ottoman governor sent a small armed force to the mosque. The soldiers ascended the mosque roof, by which Ewliyā presumably meant the gallery surrounding the courtyard of the Great Mosque. But the Beduins in the service of the Sherif climbed the heights of Abū Ḳubays not far from the city centre, the *medrese*s immediately adjacent to the mosque itself and even the galleries of the minarets, firing into the courtyard. According to Ewliyā, two hundred dead and seven hundred wounded were the result. Even if we concede that his figures often were somewhat exaggerated, this incident shows that the Sherifs did not readily submit to Ottoman domination. As to the Sherif responsible, Ewliyā has left a somewhat comic account of his deposition; but ultimately the latter was able to reestablish himself as a ruler of Mecca.[12]

Thus the authorities in Istanbul possessed some experience of the troubles a Sherif might cause if so inclined. Accordingly they mostly used persuasion rather than force, and the rescripts addressed to the Sherifs often were replete with fulsome compliments. When certain tax collectors active in Jeddah aroused complaint, and the Ottoman administration decided to depose and banish them, the Sherif's cooperation was actively solicited (1575–6).[13] Another Sherif, who by his prudent intervention had managed to prevent a dispute between pilgrims and inhabitants of Mecca from getting out of control, received a robe of honour at the accession of the new Sultan Aḥmed I (reigned 1603–17). This was normal practice; but, amidst a formidable array of compliments, the Sherif was also informed that the current commander of the pilgrimage caravan had been stripped of his office. Although the text does not say so expressly, it does seem that the Sherif previously had intimated his dissatisfaction with this official.[14]

During the Ottoman conquest of the Yemen (1568–71), and in the following years, the Sherifs sometimes were requested to support the Ottoman war effort.[15] From the Ottoman point of view, the Sherifs benefited from the conquest of Yemen, as the latter secured their domain from a possible Portuguese attack. The lands under the control of the Sherif also increased, as some of the newly conquered areas were annexed to their domain. To the Ottomans, the Sherifs were important in this context mainly because they could furnish horses. Central Arabia at that time was already famed for these animals, which in the nineteenth century were to attract several adventurous English visitors. In 1579 the Sherif was requested to send three hundred horses against an appropriate payment; presumably he found these animals among his allies the Beduins.[16] At the same time, the Sherifs were to ensure communications between Yemen, where Ottoman rule always remained problematic, and the core areas of the Ottoman domain. On the caravan routes leading to Mecca, pilgrims and couriers travelled to the Hejaz and, along with them, news of recent political developments reached the authorities in Egypt and Istanbul.

Thus, in spite of their dependent position, the Sherifs constituted an important ally whose wishes had to be taken into account. The central authorities could never take the cooperation of these princes for granted, while tensions between the two powers could prove costly to the central government and very dangerous to the pilgrims. This explains why the Ottoman Sultans, in spite of their overwhelming military superiority, preferred to treat the Sherifs with circumspection.

OFFICIALS AND NOTABLES IN THE HOLY CITIES

Apart from the governors and port administrators of Jeddah, other centrally appointed Ottoman officials counterbalanced the activities of the Sherif. For these men, the Hejaz constituted a more or less extended stage in their careers, but not the site of their further official lives. Many indeed might hope to later achieve high office in Istanbul. The *ḳāḍī*s of Mecca and Medina had gone through the *cursus honorum* of teaching in a sequence of *medrese*s and officiating in ever more important cities as judges *cum* administrators. But, as we shall see, even these officials were sometimes absorbed into Hejazi society, and their ability to function as a counterweight to the Sherif could not be regarded as a matter of course.

In the judicial hierarchy, the rank of the *ḳāḍī*s of Mecca and Medina gradually grew more exalted. In the sixteenth century the two offices were not named among the highest-ranking *mewlewiyet* (provincial *ḳāḍī*ships), which allowed the incumbents nominal salaries of five hundred *aḳče* a day. Therefore, the judges of the Holy Cities seem to have ranked well below their colleagues of Damascus, Cairo and even Jerusalem. But by the middle of the seventeenth century, the *ḳāḍī*ships of the Holy Cities had been included among a small group of select and high-ranking offices, while most of the other sixteenth-century *mewlewiyet*s had fallen far behind. In the second half of the eighteenth century the rank of the *ḳāḍī*s of Mecca and Medina had become even more exalted; now the *ḳāḍī* of Istanbul was the only judge to precede them in the hierarchy.[17]

Presumably this development should be taken as one more indication of the growing official regard for religious law which we can observe in the Ottoman Empire of that time. In the sixteenth century, respect for the *sherī'at* had not precluded a wide scope for legal regulation based on the will of the Sultan (*'örf*).[18] From the seventeenth century onwards, however, the impact of religious law on crucial sectors of life such as the regulation of land tenure was clearly growing. Admittedly this widening application of the religious law was not a unilinear development; in other aspects of Ottoman life, the seventeenth and eighteenth centuries witnessed a measure of 'secularization' as well. Yet a growing respect paid to the *sherī'at* presumably induced Ottoman administrators to emphasize the role of the Holy Cities, and the *ḳāḍī*s benefited from this ideological trend in terms of a quite mundane increase in rank.

Even in the sixteenth century, the *ḳāḍī*ship of Mecca, at least, was occasionally granted to personages of the highest rank in the Ottoman juridico-religious hierarchy. Mīrzā Makhdūm had been a teacher of Prince Ismā'īl, the heir-apparent of Iran. He emigrated to the

Ottoman Empire in 1546 and returned home when his former charge ascended the throne. While in Iran, Mīrzā Makhdūm held high office, but, upon the death of Shah Ismā'īl, he returned to the Ottoman realm, where he was appointed *ḳāḍī* of Istanbul in early 1586. But when his mother died of the plague that same year, he decided to undertake the pilgrimage. While still on the way to the Hejaz, he was appointed *ḳāḍī* of Mecca with the honorary rank of army judge (*ḳāḍī'asker*) of Rumelia. Once in the Hejaz, he married off a daughter to a scion of the Sherif family, and when he died while in office there, he was publicly mourned with great solemnity.[19]

Mīrzā Makhdūm's political role did not even come to an end with his death. In 1588 the Sultan's Council responded to a declaration of the reigning Sherif to the effect that the *ḳāḍī* before his death had made no less than three wills, in all of which he had appointed the Sherif his executor.[20] The deceased's only heirs were his wife and his young daughter, who was still a minor and presumably identical with the bride who recently had entered the Sherifian household. This would explain the reigning Sherif's interest in the *ḳāḍī*'s inheritance, as the latter apparently had been a man of means. The story of Mīrzā Makhdūm is of interest for our purposes, as it shows that even Ottoman 'career' officials might form close social ties in the Hejaz, and thereby become less effective in their role as counterweights to the Sherif. But at the same time the personal prestige enjoyed by Mīrzā Makhdūm reflected upon his office and may well have enhanced Ottoman legitimacy. So it is quite possible that the tenure of office of this unusual scholar, whom his biographer clearly regarded as somewhat eccentric, was regarded as an asset rather than a liability by the Ottoman central government.

Apart from the *ḳāḍī*s, an important role, at least in Medina, was played by the *shaykh al-ḥaram*. This official sometimes was a member of the *'ulemā*, but at other times he was one of the eunuchs who served the Prophet's tomb. It was the *shaykh al-ḥaram*'s responsibility to appoint and dismiss the eunuchs and maintain discipline among them. A major part of this duty was to take charge of the court cases involving eunuchs (*aghāwāt*). This probably meant securing their appearance in court whenever this was demanded, for it is difficult to see what other involvement *shaykh al-ḥaram*s who were not members of the *'ulemā* could have had in judicial affairs explicitly connected with the religious law. If a member of the *'ulemā*, technically the *shaykh al-ḥaram* could have functioned as a judge. The closest analogy that comes to mind is that of a janissary commander who also had jurisdiction over his men. But it seems that the *shaykh al-ḥaram* punished recalcitrant *aghāwāt* primarily by taking away their positions.[21]

The _shaykh al-ḥaram_ also had other responsibilities. Thus he oversaw a number of Medina residents who every year were paid ten gold pieces out of official funds in order to perform the pilgrimage in the name and place of the Sultan, to whom they transferred the religious merit gained by this act.[22] Certain _shaykh al-ḥaram_s also took on financial responsibilities. A text from the year 1585 concerns complaints that revenues sent to Medina had not reached their destination, and the _shaykh al-ḥaram_ who authored the complaint was a provincial finance director by profession.[23] In emergencies the _shaykh al-ḥaram_ also took charge of public grains arriving in the port of Yanbu', had them remitted to Medina and then distributed among the inhabitants of the city. He also sent reports to Istanbul concerning the manner in which official donations of grain had been disposed of. Thus the _shaykh al-ḥaram_ had responsibilities extending not only over the Great Mosque proper, but over the city of Medina as well. Presumably he took over certain functions normally assigned to an Ottoman governor, as there was no such official in Medina, and the Sherif was represented only by a deputy of limited powers and responsibilities.

A balance of power in the cities of the Hejaz could be achieved if the Ottoman central authorities managed to forge links with high-ranking members of the local population, who might not always agree with the political tendencies of the reigning Sherifs. Certain administrative positions could be created _ad hoc_, and furnished opportunities for patronage; such advantages could be enjoyed both by people of local influence and by migrants to the Hejaz from the Ottoman core lands. Some of the latter came to the Holy Cities to retire from official life. But we do not hear of large numbers of former Ottoman courtiers fallen from favour, comparable to the Indian exiles of the sixteenth century. Presumably the Ottoman central administration regarded the establishment of malcontents in the Holy Cities as much too dangerous.

Numerous documents concerning the political and religious elites of Mecca and Medina record disputes concerning the allocation of officially granted revenues. It seems that these struggles for control over outside resources constituted the major element of political life in the Holy Cities. But this may be in part an optical illusion, as other processes, such as the formation and dissolution of family alliances, did not normally concern the Ottoman central government. We have already discussed the attempts of the Ḥusaynīs to retain a share of the _ṣürre_, and the at least temporary disadvantages they suffered on account of being Shi'is (see Chapter 4). Other distribution problems arose when deliveries were in arrears, and people close to the centres of political power made sure that they were served first whenever some grain or gold became available. When beneficiaries died, local administrators were not supposed to redistribute the all-important documents of entitlement (*berāt*) on their own initiative, and even less were these documents to be passed on to heirs. The Ottoman central administration quite obviously intended to reserve this source of patronage to itself.[24] But the frequency with which divergent practices were discussed in sultanic rescripts suggests that reality often must have been rather different from official commands. Thus several *kādīs* of Damascus were found out after they had assigned pensions ranging between ten and 50 gold pieces each to selected inhabitants of the Holy Cities, so that the pension fund no longer sufficed.[25] But even when officials duly reported candidates for the Sultan's bounty, they were not devoid of influence. Residing in faraway Istanbul, members of the Ottoman central administration had no means of knowing which candidates deserved official largesse, unless they received information from officials with local knowledge.

As a relationship to an Ottoman administrator had to be established before a person could successfully apply for imperial largesse, certain poor and pious people lacking such contacts automatically were excluded. In the rescripts emitted by the Sultan's Council, problems of this kind often were summarized in pithy phrases. We hear that 'wealthy people with power and influential backers' managed to get hold of official largesse, or that 'the vacant assignments are not given to the deserving poor but to the rich [or: to the notables]'.[26] Remarkably enough, the assignment of pensions to people already possessed of other resources was not considered an abuse unless there were poor people on record who thus were deprived of their rights.[27] Probably the alms granted to Meccans at least in part were meant to secure the loyalty of influential personages of the Holy Cities, and maybe even to cement their ties to individual Ottoman officials active in the Hejaz. Given the paucity of Ottoman military forces in the area, these links were essential if administrators were to function at all. At the same time, the unchecked use of religiously motivated alms for political purposes was bound to delegitimize the Sultans, and could not be countenanced either.

Another manner of discussing the conflicts between different candidates for sultanic largesse is connected with the statement that 'insiders' rather than 'outsiders' should receive positions and grants. In the political literature of the time variations on this theme frequently were encountered. A given author might demand the exclusion from the Sultan's service of this or that group of officials, because they had been recruited through channels of which he did not approve. In such instances, the writers of 'advice to princes' and similar texts normally championed meritorious 'insiders' over unqualified 'outsiders'. In the case of the sultanic alms remitted from Istanbul, the crucial 'in-group' consisted of 'the poor of the Holy Cities'. This term presumably denoted a residential group, although we cannot be too certain of its limits. And then there is the unsolved problem whether residence in the Holy City, the status of a freeman or freewoman, poverty and a life devoted mainly to pious purposes were sufficient to make a person a member of the in-group, or whether other conditions, less clearly spelled out but no less significant, had to be met as well. In the later sixteenth century, outsiders might pose their candidacy in a formal fashion. This was known as *mülāzemet*, due to an analogy to '*ulemā* who, temporarily out of office, applied for a vacancy in the judicial hierarchy. According to a rescript from 1576, such 'outsider' candidates had in fact been able to secure pensions in the past, but the practice was now forbidden since it hurt the interests of the established 'poor of the Holy Cities'.[28]

In addition, there were disputes over the control of *wakɪf*s, of the kind which frequently occurred in the Ottoman core lands as well. In 1567, the administrator of the Sultan's mother's Egyptian foundations in favour of the Hejazi poor had his books audited, and it turned out that he owed the foundation 10,000 gold pieces and 10,000 *irdeb* of wheat. Apparently the administrator had not used this gold and wheat for what we today would call 'private' purposes, but may have acted under duress. In Istanbul, it was assumed that some of the arrears were really the debts of certain Egyptian military men to the foundation. This probably means that the administrator had been using the foundation resources to improve his own political position.[29] A much later rescript, dating from the year 1657, relates accusations against the man in charge of the Syrian pious foundations on behalf of the poor of Medina, who supposedly had retained for himself a large share of what he should have paid to the beneficiaries.[30] In this case, we cannot even guess what happened to the money.

THE MECCAN SHERIFS AND THE CUSTOMS OF JEDDAH

The Sherifs collected one half of the Jeddah customs revenues, and this income constituted their financial base; the other half accrued to the Ottoman provincial governor.[31] How the Sherifs acquired this lucrative prerogative is open to debate. Sayyid Daḥlān Aḥmad and Ismail Hakkı Uzunçarşılı, two twentieth-century scholars, maintain that the Sherif actively supported the Ottomans when the Portuguese raided the port in 1542 and was granted one half of the Jeddah customs as a reward.[32] There exists, however, a much more colourful

account of these events, which we find in the chronicle of Ibrāhīm
Pečewī (1574–1649 or 1651).[33] According to the latter, the Grand
Vizier Sinān Pasha, who had a major share in the Ottoman conquest
of Yemen, visited Mecca in about 1570. Of the reigning Sherif Abū
Numayy b. Barakāt he demanded a letter to the Ottoman administration confirming his military successes in Yemen, but the Sherif had
been gravely offended by an earlier incident and was in no mood to
oblige him. Before embarking on his campaign, Sinān Pasha had paid
an earlier visit to the Hejaz, and had been received by the influential
Kādī Hüseyin in the name of the reigning Sherif. As a welcoming gift
he had been offered some rare cups and vessels, probably imported
from Iran, where Chinese porcelain was being imitated in the shape
of fayence, or even directly from China itself. But Sinān Pasha, of
whose harshness and lack of finesse his old enemy Muṣṭafā 'Alī also
had a great deal to say, had the costly pieces trampled underfoot by
his horse, and this insult was not forgiven by the Sherif. Only after
considerable hesitation did the latter allow himself to be persuaded to
write the letter to the Sultan which Sinān Pasha demanded of him,
and this act netted him the right to half the Jeddah customs. Ibrāhīm
Pečewī concludes his story with the remark that the dues demanded
from merchants doubled as a result.

No document found in the Ottoman archives allows us to
determine which one of these stories is true, or from what date
onwards the Sherif began to collect a share of the Jeddah customs
duties. But by 1575–6 he definitely was in possession. This is
apparent from a sultanic rescript responding to a complaint by the
Sherif about shippers and shipping on the Red Sea. If the Sherif had
not had a financial stake in this matter, he would scarcely have
bothered to correspond with Istanbul about it.[34]

In those years, when Ottoman power in the Yemen was still in the
process of consolidation, numerous Ottoman soldiers were stationed
in the area, who had to be supplied from overseas, mainly from Egypt.
As a result, there was a lot of boat traffic on the Red Sea, particularly
since many ships brought back to Egypt spices from India and South
Asia, which could be purchased in the ports of Yemen. In spite of all
attempts to eliminate Muslim shipping, the Portuguese, who in the
first half of the sixteenth century had established themselves on the
western coast of India and in 1511 conquered the port of Malacca on
the Malayan peninsula, had not been able to prevent the continuing
arrival of South Asian spices in the Red Sea region. The centuries-
old trade routes crossing the Indian Ocean continued to flourish.[35]
We know of contacts not only between the Yemen and India and
between Egypt and the Yemen, but also of more or less direct linkages between the Egyptian port of Suez and the western coast of India.

Direct connections, however, suffered from the actions of Ottoman provincial administrators operating in Yemen, who were anxious to have Indian goods unloaded in the ports under their jurisdiction, and thus to benefit from customs duties. Not only Suez, but even Jeddah lost traffic as a result of these policies. The Sherif countered by demanding an order from the Ottoman government forcing all shippers to put in at Jeddah. This the Sultan could not be persuaded to command, although the Sherifs were to renew their attempts in later years.[36]

TRADE AND TRAFFIC BETWEEN INDIA AND THE ARABIAN PENINSULA

If the trade of Yemen with the Red Sea ports had been insignificant, this dispute probably would not have arisen. Apart from the spice trade, the importation of Indian cotton fabrics increased the traffic of the Red Sea ports; in the course of the seventeenth century, these cottons were to become very popular not only in Europe, but in the Ottoman Empire as well.[37] We have no information on the quantities of textiles imported into Ottoman territory, but we know that in southern India whole villages specialized in production for the Arab provinces, while others worked for European, South Asian or Iranian customers. Indian terms for various textiles entered Ottoman Turkish as loan words, as happened in France and England. Jeddah was a major centre of the textile trade.

Fabrics exported from India to the Arabian peninsula were manufactured by weavers and spinners who did not themselves market their products, but depended on merchants.[38] Some scholars therefore have discussed the possibility that southern India possessed a proto-industry comparable to that which developed in certain parts of eighteenth-century Europe. Most researchers today prefer to emphasize the differences between the two cases rather than the similarities. Even so, the dominant role of merchants in the productive process is a feature which Indian textile manufacture shares with its European counterpart, while in Ottoman textile production, this type of control was much less widespread.

Certain Indian traders of the seventeenth century owned their ships, which they might send from the port of Surat on the Malabar coast to Mocha in Yemen. These shipowners did business in the grand style: the Surat merchant 'Abd al-Ghafūr in 1701 owned 17 ships, which among other places visited Manila and China.[39] 'Abd al-Ghafūr concentrated on the Surat–Mocha route, and it is probable that a significant share of the textiles arriving in this Yemeni port ultimately reached Mecca with the pilgrimage caravans. Armenian merchants resident in India also sent their ships to the Red Sea region; in the last quarter of the seventeenth century, the Surat trader Khodja Minas participated in this trade with ten ships of his own.[40] After 1650, Indian merchants began to invest in shipping on a large scale. In earlier years, that kind of investment had been something of a rarity; usually, Indian traders had freighted ships belonging to the major rulers of the subcontinent, but sometimes even to minor princes. Nor did ships belonging to Indian rulers disappear, even after 1650; in 1662, a ship owned by the queen of the southern state of Bijapur appeared in the port of Aden, carrying 1500 passengers and 400 bales of goods.[41] The bales were so large that they had to be carried into the city by a detour, as they did not fit through the harbour gate. The ruler of the city of Cochin, which also served as one of the more important Indian bases for the Portuguese trade toward the end of the sixteenth century, often sent ships to Jeddah, protected by a Portuguese safe conduct. But the most important shipowners were the Mughal rulers residing in Delhi and Agra.[42] Not only did they place ships at the disposal of merchants, they also participated in the Hejaz trade in their own right. The Emperor Shāhdjahān (reigned 1627–58) several times sent valuable goods; at one time his wares were worth 240,000 rupies. In 1650 he had invested 150,000 rupies in trade goods sent to the Arabian peninsula, and the Sultan of Gujerat also sent valuable goods to the Hejaz. These ware were sold at a high profit, one hundred per cent being not at all unusual. However, this profit did not return to India, but was distributed in the Hejaz in the shape of alms.

In spite of the distance, even rulers of states on the eastern coast of India quite frequently sent their own ships to the Arabian peninsula.[43] From 1580 onward, the Sultan of Golconda dispatched one ship a year from the southern Indian port of Masulipatnam, often with a cargo of 600 tons and more. Portuguese safe conducts for these ships demanded complicated negotiations; often they were issued in exchange for deliveries of rice to the Portuguese settlements of the Estado da India. Practical difficulties were numerous. When, at the beginning of the seventeenth century, the Dutch came to be active in the Indian Ocean and soon supplanted the Portuguese, the Sultan of Golconda declared that from now on it would be the responsibility of the Vereenigde Oostindische Compagnie to protect Jeddah-bound ships from Portuguese reprisals. The reasoning behind this demand was that the Sultan, who did not possess a navy of his own, had made enemies of the Portuguese by permitting the Dutch to trade.[44]

Between 1610 and 1620 the Golconda ship regularly visited the Arabian peninsula and returned without incident. As ballast it carried

a load of rice, which was distributed to the poor of Mecca in the name
of the Sultan. But in 1621 and 1625 the ship from Masulipatnam to
Jeddah was captured by the Portuguese. When the Sultan threatened
reprisals, the Dutch hurried to provide pilots and guards. But political
changes in Golconda from the 1630s onwards resulted in a change of
the ships' destinations; now they were dispatched to the Persian Gulf
instead. In the following decade, contact with the Arabian peninsula
was occasionally resumed. But from the middle of the century
onward, most Indian merchants began to freight English merchant-
men, whose captains seemed more successful in coping with the
numerous freebooters now scouring the Indian Ocean. After 1665
there is no further evidence for direct contact between Masulipatnam
and the Arabian peninsula, although the export of cotton textiles from
the area continued to flourish.

Aside from trade goods, the Indian rulers' ships transported
pilgrims to Mecca. Presumably most of the 1500 passengers on the
ship belonging to the queen of Bijapur had embarked with that aim in
mind. The ships belonging to the Mughal ruler were explicitly
defined as pilgrims' ships.[45] Even such ships, however, transported a
large amount of trade goods, as most pilgrims financed their journeys
by carrying wares they hoped to sell. Moreover, there was migration
in both directions. Thus several *seyyid* families from Hadramaut in
southern Arabia established themselves in India, and these family
links must have been useful in business as well.[46] In the sixteenth
century the port town of Calicut on the coast of western India boasted
a large group of Arab merchants, many of whom settled permanently
in the city and built themselves magnificent houses.[47] They differed
from other Indian merchants of this early period by owning ships,
which they used in the spice trade and the transport of pilgrims. But
the Arab immigrants of the western coast never succeeded in gaining
the position which Iranian migrants acquired in the seventeenth-
century sultanate of Golconda.[48]

Arab scholars and merchants also migrated to southeast Asia.
Portuguese writers of the sixteenth century demonstrate that even the
policy of the Estado da India, profoundly hostile to Muslims, did not
succeed in preventing this development. However, Muslim scholars
settling in the port of Malacca while it was under Portuguese control
often pretended to be merchants.[49]

TRAFFIC IN BULLION AND PRESSURE ON MERCHANTS

Trade balances in the sixteenth- and seventeenth-century Middle
Eastern trade with India were consistently unfavourable to the

Ottoman realm and Iran. Even though Arabian horses and Shīrāzī wine or essence of roses were sold in India, the demand for these goods could not possibly compare with the massive importation of textiles, spices, drugs and dies into both the Ottoman Empire and Iran. The resulting difference had to be paid for in bullion. Since European trade with the Ottoman Empire was equally unbalanced Ottoman merchants in their turn received considerable amounts of gold and silver. Much of the silver Ottoman merchants paid their Indian suppliers ultimately came from America by way of Europe. Or if we look at it differently, a considerable share of the silver entering the Ottoman Empire did not remain there, but was drawn off to India. This situation for Indian rulers seemed highly desirable, for there never was any lack of precious metals for minting, a serious difficulty for most other states of the early modern period.[50] After returning from Iran or from the Red Sea area, the Indian merchants could simply go to the nearest mint, and for a reasonable fee have their gold or silver transformed into coins.

Conversely the Ottoman political class regarded the loss of bullion as a great danger, even though the export of silver to Iran seemed more threatening than the loss resulting from trade with India.[51] Export of bullion, therefore, was frequently prohibited, but this was not done for the reasons which have become familiar from English or French mercantilist authors of the seventeenth century. In the Ottoman realm nobody advocated a policy of exporting as much as possible and importing nothing except raw materials. Quite to the contrary, down to the nineteenth century, most members of the Ottoman political class were in favour of encouraging imports as a source of customs revenues.[52]

Ottoman economic thinking has been characterized as 'provision-ism', incidentally a term applicable to many sectors of economic policy in pre-industrial Europe as well.[53] After the state had taken its share, raw materials and foodstuffs were to benefit primarily the inhabitants of the region where they had been produced. Ottoman administrators differed from mercantilist thinking in that they viewed exports at least potentially as a danger source, while imports eased the supply situation and were desirable for that very reason.

In spite of this generally positive view of imports, however, the Ottoman administration wished to prevent the outflow of gold and silver, for the consequences of a lack of specie for trade were well-known. Yet there never were any serious attempts to stop trade with India and replace it by other, less deficit-prone trades, even though the eighteenth-century historian Na'īmā suggested just such a course. Though as an official historian he was reasonably influential as a writer, his impact on practical politics remained minimal.[54]

In this context we must understand the admonitions and recom-
mendations which the Ottoman administration addressed to the
Sherif of Mecca in 1575–6, when the latter had complained about the
lack of ships putting in at the port of Jeddah. The authorities in
Istanbul disapproved of the violence exercised by local commanders
in Yemen, who forced merchants and shippers to visit the ports they
happened to control. A rescript to the governor of Yemen supposedly
had been issued with the express intention of preventing such
occurrences.[55] But the Sherif equally did not have the right to force
anyone to visit Jeddah, as all merchants could do business wherever
they preferred.

While taxes collected in Yemen were forwarded to Istanbul,
however, the temptation to use violence against shippers arriving from
India was built into the system. Instead of money, the provincial
governors sent spices either to Cairo or else to Istanbul, and that was
only possible when, by fair means or foul, enough spices could be
secured in the ports of Yemen. Considerations of this kind may have
induced the Ottoman central administration in 1582 to start
demanding money and not spices as taxes from Yemeni ports.[56] For
at a certain point the pressure on Indian shippers in order to secure
these spices came to be self-defeating: forced to sell their goods at
disadvantageous prices, merchants were liable to abandon trade with
the Arabian peninsula altogether.

Members of the Sultan's Council apparently assumed that the loss
of shipping in Jeddah had reasons similar to those with which they
were familiar in the case of Yemen. When the Sherif repeated his
complaint in 1590, the response from Istanbul was even more drastic
than that given in 1575–6: as the Sherif often had forced the
merchants to sell him their goods at low prices, it was not surprising
that there was now a loss in shipping.[57] Probably the Sultan's Council
realized that revenues due to the central treasury also suffered from
the Sherif's high-handed policies, as the Ottoman administration had
reserved one half of the Jeddah customs revenues for its own use.
However, the Sherifs often were quite successful in retaining even the
share they should have forwarded to Istanbul.[58]

A PORT IN CRISIS

While Mediterranean trade of the early modern period is documented
by a variety of Ottoman and European figures, we possess only very
few numerical data on Red Sea trade, and most of our information is

qualitative rather than quantitative.[59] The few figures extant all concern the activity of the port of Jeddah. Around 1590–1 the port administrator and governor of the province claimed that, in the past, yearly revenues had amounted to 90,000 gold pieces (*flōrī*).[60] However, it is impossible to determine whether by that figure he meant the entire revenues of Jeddah, or the 50 per cent share which theoretically should have accrued to the Ottoman central administration. To estimate the value of the goods which must have arrived in Jeddah at that time, we will base our calculation on the customs rate of 2.5 per cent demanded from Muslim merchants in many parts of the Ottoman Empire. Admittedly there is no guarantee that all traders doing business in Jeddah were Muslims, but the vast majority probably were. Under these circumstances we arrive at an estimate of goods worth 3,600,000 gold pieces. If the text refers not to the total revenue, but only to the central administration's share, it would be necessary to double this figure. But since we have no information on the customs rates actually applied, this is no more than a very rough estimate.[61]

In 1590–1 the Jeddah port administrator declared that he had been able to collect only 46,000 gold pieces during the past year; this means that, during the 1580s, the traffic must have dropped by half. Apparently the Sultan's Council assumed that this was a long-term development and not just a passing crisis, for its members tried to find alternative means of financing projects hitherto supported out of the Jeddah customs revenues.[62] Pečewı remarks that an additional load was placed on merchants doing business in Jeddah by granting the Sherif a share in the customs revenues, and thereby indicates that he was familiar with the port's difficulties.[63] In all likelihood, this chronicler also assumed that the abuses of officials had a share in the crisis.

It is doubtful that these abuses were the only reason. From a recent study of Indian trade during the early modern period, we learn that links between Masulipatnam and the Arabian peninsula were being forged in the 1580s.[64] If, in spite of this additional trade, the commerce of Jeddah was declining, we must assume that the newly developing trade with the eastern coast of southern India could not compensate for losses in trade with the western coast, particularly Surat and Calicut. European pirates certainly had a share in the decline of trade. Ottoman rescripts of the time mention the need to protect ships arriving from India from Portuguese attack.[65] It is also possible that Jeddah was losing trade to the ports of Yemen, and the Sherif may not have been altogether mistaken in accusing the Ottoman port administrators of that province.

MECCA AND CAIRO

As the Holy Cities depended on foodstuffs from Egypt, and Mamluk traditions continued to be important in many aspects of their inhabitants' lives, contacts between the Hejaz and Cairo were particularly close. The governor of Egypt, who at least for a while was the immediate superior of the administrator of Jeddah, was expected to keep himself informed of developments in the Holy Cities and pass on this information to Istanbul.[66] However, the distances involved and the relatively independent position of the Sherif made it impossible for the Pasha of Egypt to play a major role in the day-to-day events of the Hejaz.

Quite frequently the governor of Egypt was requested to make sure that the money and foodstuffs which the Ottoman Sultans sent to the Hejaz arrived on time.[67] The crucial aspect of the governor's role was to control abuses in the administration and taxation of the villages whose contributions financed life in the Hejaz (see Chapter 4). Very often, however, these attempts at control ended in failure, and peasants mistreated by tax farmers and provincial administrators fled, disorganizing the delicate supply system of the Hejaz. Once collected, foodstuffs and money were transported to Mecca and Medina under the governor's supervision. But complaints concerning failures in this area, such as delays and missing shipment, were not addressed to the governor but to the Sultan himself, in spite of the distances involved. The Sultan's Council examined the complaint and, if necessary, sent instructions and admonitions to the governor of Egypt. As a result, the central administration could easily check on the performance of one of its most important provincial officials. On the other hand, it often took a long time before the governor received orders to intervene in a particular issue.

TRADE IN FOODSTUFFS, RED SEA TRAFFIC AND THE PORT OF SUEZ

Connections between the Hejaz and Egypt were not limited to the official sector. Merchants also played a key role, as official subsidies were not sufficient to supply all the pilgrims and permanent residents of the Hejaz. Private trade is, however, very inadequately covered by the available sources; only the documents dealing with the problems of transportation on the Red Sea provide a certain amount of information.

Shipping on the Red Sea constituted one of the major bottlenecks;

for changing winds and numerous coral reefs only permitted ships leaving Suez to reach Jeddah, Yanbu' or one of the minor anchoring points at certain times of the year.[68] Shipbuilding was expensive due to the lack of timber, so that this basic raw material had to be imported from Anatolia, the territories north of the Black Sea or even India. Both owners and people leasing a ship therefore were tempted to earn back their expenses as quickly as possible by overloading. From the times of Ibn Djubayr to those of the Victorian traveller Richard Burton, we find numerous complaints about the avarice of ships' captains and their unwillingness to take responsibility for the safety of passengers and cargo.[69] To make a bad matter worse, boatbuilders had devised frames, which seem to have resembled those found on outrigger canoes, which made the ship wider and permitted the accommodation of even greater loads.[70] Under these circumstances shipwrecks were frequent, and the high rate of losses increased the price of goods marketed in Mecca and Medina.

Due to the lack of ships and boats, merchants came to compete for shipping space against the administrators of the Egyptian pious foundations, who delivered foodstuffs to the Holy Cities free of charge.[71] Theoretically this problem should not have arisen, as the larger foundations owned their ships. But often these ships were insufficient or unavailable, as they had been contracted out for jobs quite unrelated to the foundation's activities. For the foundations often ran out of cash, and then the rent for the use of ships paid by traders or even public officials was a welcome means of balancing the budget. Grain traders were not at all unhappy if the free food to be distributed by the foundations arrived late, for prices in the markets of Mecca and Medina increased in consequence.

Opportunities to create artificial scarcities in Mecca and Medina were abundant.[72] The key figure in such manipulations was the farmer of the Suez customs who, in theory, was also responsible for making the owners of Red Sea ships adopt elementary security precautions. About the farmers of the Suez customs, accusations of corruption were common enough. We thus hear of a farmer who supposedly had embezzled 7000 gold pieces.[73] Other complaints concerned Suez customs farmers who allegedly had given the order to unload grains belonging to Egyptian foundations from ships ready for the voyage to Jeddah, so that space became available for the wares of merchants.

In 1577–8 the key role of the *emīns* of Suez in the traffic to Mecca and Medina was given as the reason for entrusting only Muslims with that office. Previous Jewish holders of the position were accused of not supplying the pilgrims with the necessary ships, so that the latter were in danger of missing, or had already missed, the time of the pilgrimage. Given the welter of accusation and counter-accusation in the hotbed of intrigue that was the port of Suez, and the absence of documents concerning later years, it is difficult to place this event in its proper context.[74]

There was a major difference between Mecca and Medina, on the one hand, and all other Ottoman cities including Istanbul on the other: only in these two cities, and nowhere else, was a large portion of the food supply secured by mechanisms other than private trade. In ordinary Ottoman cities, the inhabitants depended on the services of merchants bringing in grain for their very survival, and this situation explains why Ottoman administrators, even if they controlled the activities of traders, still regarded them as necessary and therefore worthy of protection. Due to the special situation of the Holy Cities, however, the Ottoman administrators dealing with the Hejaz tended to regard private trade mainly as a potential source of abuses, to be supervised with suspicion.

Supplying the Holy Cities became somewhat easier when, from approximately the second half of the seventeenth century onward, Indian rice became available in sizable quantities – though rice still was not the item of mass consumption that it was to become in the nineteenth century.[75] In this early period we hear of rice distributed as alms in the name of the Sultan of Golconda, rather than of private dealers in rice. Quite possibly, the inhabitants of Mecca and Medina first became accustomed to the consumption of rice because it came as a free gift. Only after they had become familiar with this grain, and the possible ways of preparing it, were people ready to spend money on the purchase of rice, and only then did opportunities open up for commerce.

MECCA AND DAMASCUS

Where food supplies were concerned, the links of the Hejaz to Syria were far less important than those to Egypt. Politically speaking, the governor of Damascus also played a less important role down to the eighteenth century, as long as this official did not regularly appear in the Hejaz in person as commander of the pilgrimage. In exceptional instances, however, governors of Damascus were active in Hejazi politics in the seventeenth century as well, even to the point of deposing an unruly Sherif. Ewliyā Čelebi, no friend of that particular dynasty, witnessed such an event in 1672 and gave a long and elaborate description of an Ottoman expedition directed against Sherif Sa'd, who was invited to present himself before the pilgrimage commander and Damascus governor Ḥüseyin Pasha.[76] The Pasha and his entourage were kept waiting for quite some time, and Sherif Sa'd did not appear; he had taken flight and was duly deposed.

Damascus merchants certainly profited from the pilgrimage. But they had dealings mainly not with the Hejazis but with the pilgrims, who bought from them their mounts, riding utensils, clothes and foodstuffs. To gauge the volume of the business thus generated, we may evoke the train following Ewliyā Čelebi to the Hejaz, which had been assigned to him by the Damascus governor: several slaves, six camels, a mare, four camel litters, a tent, as well as food and fodder for men and horses.[77] Nor was this the ultimate in luxury; for while Ewliyā came from a family with connections at court, he himself had never held high office. Admittedly the governor of Damascus had not paid the full market price for the slaves, animals and travel gear he placed at Ewliyā's disposal, but no doubt other wealthy pilgrims paid the full price for comfortable travel. Of course the artisans and merchants of Cairo benefited from the Egyptian pilgrimage in similar fashion. As other trade opportunities were much greater in Cairo, however, the caravan trade probably was less prominent in the city's economic life than its Damascus counterpart.

Many pilgrims purchased their needs at the caravan fair of Muzayrib, a few stops to the south of Damascus on the route to Mecca.[78] In the nineteenth century this was to become a major commercial centre, and one of Syria's earliest train lines linked this locality with Damascus.[79] From a rescript dated 1637–8 we learn that the fair lasted ten days and that, at least in principle, goods acquired by the pilgrims for use on the journey were supposed to be exempt from taxes and customs dues. Things often were quite different in practice; in the 1630s, the governor of Damascus usually sent a market administrator and some soldiers to Muzayrib to collect taxes. The latter demanded dues from both buyers and sellers which amounted to 25 per cent of the purchase price. In addition, the administrator made the merchants pay 40–50 *ghurush* merely for the privilege of displaying their wares in a stall. As a result the fair was not much frequented, and this constituted a grave inconvenience to the pilgrims. Indirect evidence for this state of affairs is provided by the Edirne scholar 'Abd al-Raḥmān Ḥibrī, whose pilgrimage to Mecca fell in the year 1632. 'Abd al-Raḥmān Ḥibrī certainly travelled in style, but his entire outfit had been bought in Damascus; in Muzayrib he only rented the necessary camels.[80]

In the rescript of 1637–8 the Pasha of Damascus was held responsible for the sad state of the Muzayrib fair: to reactivate business, he was ordered to stop collecting taxes from the pilgrims' necessities. All other goods were to be taxed 'at the rate which has been customary for a long time'. This last remark is important for the modern historian, as here we have the oldest reference to the fact that things not immediately needed by pilgrims could be purchased in Muzayrib. Possibly the authors of the rescript were thinking of the well-known textiles of Damascus, which may have found a market in Mecca and Medina as well.[81] However, the sultanic rescript of 1637–8 apparently had little immediate effect. Ewliyā Čelebi, who visited Muzayrib in 1672, only noted that the place was fortified and that pilgrimage stores were kept there, and said nothing about a fair.[82] Derwish Meḥmed Edīb, whose pilgrimage report dates from the year 1682, very briefly mentions the locality, and thus probably did not notice anything remarkable either.[83] Muzayrib's revival must date from a much later period.

TRADERS IN MECCA AND THE MINA FAIR

As the centre of the hajj, Mecca was more specialized in its functions than any other city of the Ottoman Empire; the city lived off the pilgrims, the Sultan's subventions and trade. While almost all cities of the early modern period possessed an agricultural hinterland, this was absent in the Meccan instance. Even the gardens in the city's immediate vicinity were not very productive. Artisans were also in short supply, and our sources do not mention the craft guilds so characteristic of Ottoman towns, Cairo included. Craftsmen to work on the numerous Ottoman building projects usually were brought in from Syria and Egypt. Ewliyā Čelebi noted that the Meccans only applied themselves to commerce.[84] But the normal base for local trade was also missing, as there were no agricultural products of the immediate vicinity that could be marketed in Mecca, nor local manufactures. Meccan trade for the most part was long-distance trade.

Trade in Mecca took place in two locations:[85] in the city itself during the days which preceded and followed the pilgrimage ceremonies, and in the settlement of Mina/Munā, where the pilgrims spent several days on their return from the plateau of 'Arafat.[86] In Mecca two covered markets were at the disposal of traders, the smaller of these being known as the Syrian or Damascene market, probably because of the goods and traders to be found there. During the pilgrimage season, these covered markets were insufficient, and then the entrances of houses or, if sun shades could be installed, even the façades were turned into temporary shops. Ewliyā Čelebi claims that in this fashion the number of shops increased to six thousand, but his figures often should be taken with a grain of salt. Even if he does exaggerate, the pilgrimage season must have been the occasion for a good deal of petty trading, as many pilgrims sold a few wares to help finance their long and expensive journeys. Others for the same reason sought to purchase goods which they hoped to sell profitably in their home towns. Unfortunately, we know nothing about the way in which these 'amateurs' went about finding a market for their goods, whether they made use of brokers or other intermediaries, or whether Meccan merchants ever sold goods on commission.

The fair of Mina was held in the context of a general celebration, for at this time most of the prohibitions pilgrims had to respect while performing the rites of pilgrimage were temporarily suspended. Ewliyā has described the experience: officers of the pilgrimage caravan and public criers announced that buyers and sellers were under the protection of the Ottoman Sultan, and called upon the sellers to lay out their wares. The Sherifs, who owned a residence in this locality, had it illuminated for the occasion, and artisans and pilgrims decorated shops, coffee houses and tents in the same fashion. Many valuable textiles could be purchased in the shops, and Ewliyā claims that there he encountered people from all four corners of the Islamic world. Precious stones and aromatics were available in profusion; some traders even went so far as to decorate their shops with them.[87] As no dues were collected at this fair, many people may have been encouraged to exhibit their treasures. In the middle of this festive disorder, small boys from notable Meccan families were circumcised, the soldiers fired their guns into the air, and in the evening there were fireworks, at which the skills of Egyptian specialists were much admired.[88]

The combination of fair and public festivity is not unique to the Meccan pilgrimage, but is characteristic of many festivities in the Ancient World.[89] It was the trade in luxury goods which set Mina apart from other fairs with a strongly festive component, most of which were oriented toward local consumption. The great Balkan fairs of the seventeenth and eighteenth centuries, which Ewliyā also admired very much, were not accompanied by major festivities.[90] Perhaps the closest parallel to what happened in Mina is the festival of the Egyptian saint Aḥmad Badawı of Ṭanṭa, where a great fair also formed part of the celebrations.[91] Ewliyā claims to have encountered Indian, Yemeni, Iranian and Arab traders in Ṭanṭa, who sold their wares in huts or tents serving as temporary shops. Some of these visitors also frequented the *khān*s of the city. Presumably the festive atmosphere in Mina, which the merchants enhanced by generous offerings of perfumes, also was good for business.[92] This atmosphere of generalized goodwill was all the more important as many of the buyers and sellers were not professionals.

Apart from the Indian textiles, aromatics and precious stones traded in Mecca and Mina, special attention should be paid to the coffee trade.[93] Ewliyā mentions the existence of coffee houses in Mina, where Abyssinian slave women sang and played their instruments. But coffee was also a commodity which down to the beginning of the eighteenth century was grown uniquely in the Yemen, and therefore available in the Hejaz more readily than elsewhere. Taking a load of coffee to Cairo or Istanbul could be a lucrative deal for a pilgrim with money to invest. In Ewliyā Čelebi's time, the consumption of coffee had reached a level which permitted the major merchants to compensate without any trouble for the loss of the transit trade in spices to Europe, which was one of the most important reasons for the seventeenth-century decline of Venice. Even in the eighteenth century, when coffee produced on the Caribbean islands had begun to compete with Yemeni coffee, the coffee dealers were among the wealthiest merchants of Cairo. The consumption of coffee in the Ottoman Empire was frequently forbidden, however, particularly in the reign of Murād IV (reigned 1623–40). In justifying the prohibition, the effects of coffee were said to be comparable to those of alcohol; but the decisive factor was probably the sociability of the coffee house, in which people talked to one another and what they said was not always readily controlled by the authorities. Prohibitions generally were effective for short periods only; and Ewliyā Čelebi did not fail to purchase several loads of coffee, which he took along to Cairo.[94]

As well as coffee, Chinese porcelain could be obtained in Mecca more easily than in other parts of the Ottoman Empire.[95] We have already encountered a sixteenth-century Sherif who gave away Chinese porcelain (or an Iranian imitation in fayence) as an official gift. This was not an exceptional circumstance; Ewliyā Čelebi, who probably was less impressed by this novelty than Pečewī, once remarked, not without irony, that the Sherif gave away 'cups and saucers'.[96] At the Ottoman court there were connoisseurs of porcelain, and the Sultans of the period built up a major collection of sixteenth- and seventeenth-century Chinese porcelain. Certain pieces were elaborately decorated at the Ottoman court with gold and jewellery, but, given the state of our sources, we cannot determine whether this decoration was intended to enhance a highly esteemed piece or to compensate for the low intrinsic value assigned to this material.[97]

METHODS OF BARGAINING: AN INDICATOR OF CULTURAL CONTACTS?

Among Meccan merchants, a special form of bargaining was current, which Ewliyā apparently encountered in this city for the first time and which he has described at some length.[98] A customer desiring to acquire a certain piece of goods negotiated the price with the seller by mutually holding hands under a piece of cloth. The offer was made and accepted or refused by manual signs, while the parties to the purchase neither looked at one another nor said a word. Thus an outsider had no way of knowing the price agreed upon, or indeed if a purchase had been made, even if the deal concerned very large sums, this secrecy was deemed such an advantage that the risk of misunderstandings was not a deterrent.

Ewliyā calls this method of doing business an auction. Why it thus appeared to him can be better understood with the help of an older description of a similar practice, which we find in the account of the Bolognese traveller Ludovico di Varthéma.[99] The latter had become a Mamluk and visited Mecca in 1503; later he continued his travels to India. In the city of Calicut, on the southwestern coast of India, the traveller observed a method of bargaining by manual signs; only, in this case, a broker also was involved. Seller and broker, or at a later stage buyer and broker, without speaking, counted 'from one ducat to a hundred thousand', thus indicating the range of prices considered appropriate for the goods in question. Again the fingers were hidden under a piece of fabric, and when the two partners came to an agreement, they indicated this fact to one another by a sign of the fingertips. Probably Ewliyā also knew that the method of bargaining he had seen involved counting, and this fact reminded him of an auction.

We cannot be sure whether this custom was Indian or Arab in origin; given the frequency of commercial relations between the two coasts, either one of the two is possible. However, an Indian origin seems more likely. Probably, merchants perceived a twofold advantage in this proceeding; on the one hand, traders with no common language could negotiate with one another, although the example described by Ludovico di Varthéma shows that brokers might be employed nonetheless. In addition, by keeping the deal secret from outsiders, the merchants in question affirmed their membership of an exclusive commercial fraternity, one of the trading communities so characteristic of early modern India. Established merchants of Mecca also may have wished to emphasize that they were 'different' from the many 'amateurs' who crowded into the city during the pilgrimage season.

'INVISIBLE' TRADE

Although Mecca and the nearby fair of Mina constituted major centres of international trade, the Ottoman central administration paid very little attention to what happened there. Provincial records located in Cairo are slightly more explicit but, even so, Ewliyā's account still constitutes by far the most usable source, one which sometimes permits us to make sense of certain vague allusions in the Ottoman documents. In the last few decades, economic historians of India have also concerned themselves with trade relations between the Indian subcontinent and the Arabian peninsula. But the material at their disposal is largely Portuguese, Dutch and later English, and its perspective is defined accordingly. Reconstructing this trade, therefore, is something of a jigsaw puzzle. We can only hope that a few more pieces will be located in the future.[100]

Ottoman archives contain so little evidence on the trade of Mecca and Mina because the documents of the time so often were financial in character, and the Ottoman state collected scarcely any taxes in the Hejaz. The fair of Mina owed its liveliness to its exemption from all taxes. If market dues were collected in Mecca proper – and at present we have no evidence that they were – they filled the coffers of the Sherif. Thus, even if everything went well, the Ottoman administration benefited from Hejazi trade only to the extent that it collected one half of the Jeddah customs. The archive materials of early modern states concentrated upon war and the collection of taxes, and the Ottoman state was no exception to this rule. Thus the war in Yemen and the conflicts with the Portuguese are fairly well documented, while trade relations which did not immediately benefit the state treasury were passed over in silence.

Moreover, artisans' guilds, which constituted an important means of taxation and control in the Ottoman core lands of Rumelia and Anatolia, due to the special conditions obtaining in the Hejaz either did not exist at all or at least did not function in the manner known elsewhere. This is another reason for the lack of trade-oriented documentation. In most Ottoman cities, on the other hand, the local *ḳāḍī* registers and the record books of the central administration contain a fair number of complaints concerning the quality and prices of goods manufactured by local craftsmen, including disputes with merchants. Moreover, the Sherifs, who dealt with many issues which elsewhere would have been the responsibility of the local governor, do not seem to have kept many written records. All these features underline the special character of Mecca as a city which lived by and for the pilgrims, and in which Ottoman government was exercised only within narrowly circumscribed limits.

Conclusion

It has been one of the main aims of this book to depict the manner in which the Ottoman political class, which for four centuries organized many of the more visible aspects of the pilgrimage, viewed and depicted its own role in the Hejaz.[1] An attempt certainly has been made to analyse Ottoman rule in the Holy Cities with the aid of categories used in contemporary political discourse, and not that of the sixteenth or seventeenth centuries. But at the centre of the story we have placed the Ottoman authorities and, wherever possible, the pilgrims themselves.

If we were dealing with a chapter of European history, this would not need any justification. We have accustomed ourselves to studying the Spanish Reconquista between the thirteenth and sixteenth centuries from a Spanish point of view, or to regarding the integration of formerly Ottoman Hungary into the eighteenth-century Habsburg Empire from a Viennese perspective. But when Middle Eastern history is dealt with in Europe or North America, such an 'internalist' perspective does not go without saying: quite the contrary. Somehow authors will assume, at least subconsciously, that events within the Ottoman Empire receive their significance mainly from the impact which they have upon developments in Europe. Yet this is a narrow and unrealistic view. Over the centuries, political and economic processes of major importance, such as the securing of food supplies for pilgrims and permanent inhabitants of the Hejaz, took place without European rulers or merchants having any share in the undertaking. It should be the aim of any historical work concerning the Middle East to counteract the unfortunate tendency of regarding European–American history as the only 'real' history, to which every-

174

thing else is merely an adjunct.[2] Admittedly many historians do not see it that way, and even when an effort is made to present Middle Eastern history in its own terms, the attempt is not always successful.

INTERNAL VERSUS EXTERNAL PERSPECTIVES

There are other reasons why, in our imaginary travels through Istanbul, Damascus, Cairo and the Hejaz, we have taken for our guides not Richard Burton and John Lewis Burckhardt, but mainly the secretaries of the Sultan's Council, Ewliyā Čelebi and Süheylī. It is the principal task of historians to reconstruct the environments and historical processes of the past. But this is only possible if we familiarize ourselves with as many data from the relevant period as possible, so that, in a squeeze, we could have bought supplies at the fair of Muzayrib or participated in the festivities at Mina, without making undue fools of ourselves. To a somewhat lesser extent, this also applies to readers. Both sides will find their tasks easier if the writings of Ottoman authors are given priority. For if the account is built mainly on the observations of Burckhardt, Burton or Rutter, the danger of producing a variety of European social and intellectual history, instead of the Ottoman history we are aiming at, is very great indeed.

This statement has an affinity to historicist positions, and as such needs qualification.[3] For it should not be taken to mean that in explaining Ottoman hajj procedures, no categories should be used apart from those known to the participants themselves. That kind of an approach seems impractical, and to advocate it would be self-contradictory, as the key category of sultanic legitimation, upon which our entire account is constructed, was not employed by sixteenth- or seventeenth-century Ottomans. Moreover, in the minds of many historians, historicist positions are associated with a staunch political conservatism, and this connotation is certainly not intended either. Thus the position taken here is eclectic; reconstructions of human relationships connected with the hajj are undertaken on the basis of Ottoman material, and with a strong emphasis on the interpretations given to these events by the participants. But, at the same time, many crucial categories of analysis come from the arsenal of history writing in the late twentieth century.

The present study is conceived as a work of political and above all social history, which means that we focus upon changes within Ottoman society itself. Obviously, the pilgrimage could also be treated from totally different perspectives, a focus on religious practice constituting the most obvious alternative. Yet it seems that there is a strong explanatory force inherent in regarding ceremonies, buildings or literary texts as products of the societies in which they were created, and to explain what social and political needs were satisfied by putting up one kind of building rather than another, or by writing pilgrimage accounts and chronicles rather than novels or newspaper articles. This does not mean that we would advocate a reduction of all human activity to social and possibly even economic needs. Throughout the centuries, art, literature and religion have often developed in ways that owe as much to the internal dynamics of the field in question as to the social context, and the pilgrimage above everything else is a religious phenomenon which cannot be reduced (for instance) to commercial interests. But even though we admit that the history of religion, and thereby of the pilgrimage to Mecca, need to be studied on their own terms, that does not preclude close attention to the social and political context in which this phenomenon took place.

HISTORICAL CHANGE, RAPID OR SLOW-MOVING

Throughout the Ottoman period, the social and political structures which enabled pilgrims to get to the Holy Cities and back again, changed very slowly. Slow change does not mean no change at all. In the present study, we have attempted to show that the 'timeless Orient' of European travelogues and secondary studies is a construct with little relation to reality. In the course of our study, we have encountered a number of instances of historical change even in the Holy Cities, where existing arrangements often were legitimized by religious means, and change was correspondingly slow. Around the year 1600, the Ottoman administration in the face of appreciable local resistance attempted to impose its own ideas of what a well-organized pilgrimage city was supposed to look like. The attempt of Sultan Murād III to separate the Great Mosque from the surrounding urban tissue demonstrates the will of this ruler to impose new urban concepts upon the ancient city (see Chapter 5). It is therefore a grave methodological error to amalgamate data from the twelfth, sixteenth and nineteenth centuries, with the facile assumption that 'nothing changed much anyway'. For this proceeding renders invisible the slow but significant change the historian should try to track down.

The amalgamation of data specific to centuries far removed from one another at first sight may appear as mere sloppiness, but in reality it has a deeper significance.[4] Quite a few European and American students of the Ottoman Empire have tended to regard Ottoman state and society as the 'other' par excellence, incomprehensible and, moreover, scarcely repaying any effort at comprehension. To put it somewhat crudely, if European society has a history, the 'other', in this case the Ottoman, has none. In the political realm, however, the existence of change could not well be denied, and the most frequently used scheme of Ottoman history assumes a rapid 'rise' between about 1300 and 1520, a short period of 'florescence' (1520–1600), and a long period of decline from 1600 to the end of the empire in 1918–23. On the other hand, the society which *nolens volens* supported this state supposedly changed little if at all in the course of the centuries.[5] Agricultural techniques, religious notions, fashions and family structures remained all but immobile and, outside of the major cities, the changing tides of history had but a limited impact upon the lives of ordinary people.

During the last few decades, the work of Marc Bloch, Fernand Braudel and Emmanuel Le Roy Ladurie, in particular, has alerted historians to the importance of long-term, evenly paced secular change. If we transfer their insights into the Middle Eastern field – which unfortunately still happens but rarely – the notion that the social history of the Middle East was an area of 'slow' historical movement ceases to be usable as a feature by which to differentiate the history of this region from its European counterpart. Even in economically active regions of Europe such as northern and central Italy, certain aspects of feudal social structure survived even the Napoleonic period and, according to some authors, retained their vitality down to the middle of the twentieth century.[6] Where latecomers to industrialization such as the German territories are concerned, the survival of feudal structures and values into the twentieth century is not merely well-known to the specialist but forms part of general culture. We thus would do well to avoid the stereotype which contrasts a 'static Orient' and a 'dynamic Occident' and limit ourselves to the more modest statement that before the industrial revolution and its worldwide consequences, the pace of historical change throughout the world was a good deal slower than today.

The period covered by the present study may be considered 'medium length', amounting to somewhat less than two centuries. Long enough for historical change to occur, it allows us to point up the interplay between structural and conjunctural factors which constitutes the essence of social and economic history. At the same time it is still short enough to permit the researcher a reasonable grasp of the available sources. The relative brevity of the timespan from 1517 to 1683 also makes the problem of amalgamating, or not amalgamating, data from different periods somewhat easier to handle. While the use of historical evidence from different periods obscures intervening change, for periods where documentation is limited, we often are obliged to use texts from a previous or following decade, or even century, to make sense of the text we are trying to interpret. This contradiction can be held within manageable bounds most easily if the period studied is not too long.

When pointing out the dynamic aspects of Ottoman early modern social history we sometimes encounter the objection that this state was dynamic in its early days because it controlled the great international trade routes of the fifteenth and sixteenth centuries. When the Ottomans failed in their attempt to dislodge the Portuguese from the Indian Ocean, and when, in the early seventeenth century, the Dutch took over from the Portuguese as the principal European trading power in the Indian Ocean region, supposedly this dynamism was rapidly lost.[7] In this view, Ottoman dynamism is regarded as a result of a configuration basically external to the empire itself, and Ottoman–European trade relations in this context play an especially important role. But the present study has shown that the Ottoman administration of the sixteenth century made considerable efforts to change social arrangements in the Hejaz. As the Hejaz of this period was quite remote from European trade, and European political influence all but non-existent before the nineteenth century, it does not seem reasonable to link all change and dynamism in the area directly or indirectly to European intervention.

Initiatives originating with the Ottoman central administration were particularly visible in the built environment. The Great Mosque of Mecca was refashioned to conform to Ottoman models, and the attempt of Sultan Murād III (reigned 1574–95) to disengage the mosque from the surrounding houses may almost be regarded as a forerunner of twentieth-century urban solutions. Behind these initiatives, we discern the intention to impose a mode of behaviour in the sacred precinct which Ottoman bureaucrats considered appropriate, and which differed from the behaviour considered normal among the generality of pilgrims and townsmen. Unfortunately, the documentation unearthed to date does not permit us to figure out to what extent the Ottoman administration succeeded or failed in imposing its ideas in the long run.

If we try to set up an alternative model to the all but immobile society often referred to in the literature, it makes sense to imagine Ottoman state and society as a permanently growing complex of institutions and practices. This model implies that society, and particularly Ottoman society in the Hejaz, was not monolithic, so that not only consensus but also numerous contradictions existed between its different subsections.[8] A comparison of the Ottoman Empire after 1600 with *ancien régime* France seems appropriate; in both cases the creation of new institutions rarely involved the abrogation of the old ones, and the resulting complexity is often confusing to the outsider. A comparable overlay, only of even greater complexity, existed in the Hejaz; norms and social practices from the times of the Prophet Muḥammad and his immediate successors, buildings from the Abbasid period, a supply system which had assumed its most salient features in the period of the Mamluk Sultans, and Ottoman institutions for ensuring the security of the pilgrims all functioned at the very same time, and, as we have seen, friction resulting from this heterogeneity was not rare.

Political action in the Hejaz involved the reduction of this friction to manageable proportions at minimal cost to a remote central administration, usually hard pressed for funds. It would have been beyond the means of the Ottoman government to impose in this remote province, which largely lacked both a peasantry and urban artisans, the administrative structure characteristic of the 'core' provinces, with their tax grants, market tolls and craft guilds. There is no evidence that direct administration was ever considered. To mention a minor but characteristic example of this attitude: when Ewliyā Čelebi, after his adventurous travel to the Hejaz in 1672, expressed his annoyance at Sherif Sa′d who made life so difficult for the pilgrims, he did not say that he wished the Ottoman Sultan might punish his iniquities by fire and sword. This way of speaking, however, had come quite naturally to the pious and scholarly Ibn Djubayr, who in his time had felt wronged by a remote predecessor of Sherif Sa′d (see Chapter 1). Ewliyā limits himself to a gleeful enumeration of the humiliations to which the medieval Sherifs supposedly had been subjected by an irate Mamluk Sultan.[9] In Ewliyā′s view, the Sherifs formed part of the inescapable political realities of the Hejaz, who might be manipulated at times, but who for the most part had to be endured.

This is all the more remarkable as, by the end of the First World War, the situation had changed completely. When amir Ibn Sa′ūd took power in the Hejaz in 1925, he no longer felt bound by the centuries-old custom that a suzerain might depose a Sherif, but had to replace him by another member of the same family. Certainly the length and bitterness of the struggle by which Ibn Sa′ūd had come to power explains this radical innovation, but only in part. In all probability the amir felt much less compelled to come to an agreement with the Sherifal family, as his Wahabi convictions allowed him more radical departures from established political practices than had been true of the nineteenth-century political class of the Ottoman Empire.[10] After all, the Wahabi variety of Islam aimed at reshaping political conditions as far as possible according to the practice of early Islam. Given this outlook, there was no further need to seek accommodation with the Sherifs, who, after all, had established themselves well after the Abbasid rise to power. Thus it is not merely due to short-range considerations that the end of Ottoman rule in the Hejaz also resulted in the eclipse of the Sherifal dynasty, after about a thousand years of rule.

RELIGION AND CHANGING TIMES

It is remarkable that a religious movement which took the early Islamic period for a model should have been so much inclined toward radical innovation in the political sphere. This should induce us to reflect anew on the role of religion in historical change. In Islam, religious scholars will attempt to solve problems occurring in the course of time by referring to the Koran and to the Sunna – that is, the practice of the Prophet Muḥammad as recorded in his sayings, some of them real and others attributed.[11] This gives the impression that religious practice is immutable and monolithic, particularly since the freedom of interpretation allowed religious scholars is strictly limited. Here again, experience of European history should guard us against hasty conclusions. Even though the dogma of the Catholic Church changed little from the Council of Trent (1545–9 and 1562–3) to the Second Vaticanum (1962–5), the piety and world view of, for example, Teilhard de Chardin, differs profoundly from that of Ignatius Loyola. Not only are beliefs and ritual significant: at least as important are the attitudes both of religious scholars and ordinary believers toward their faith. To give an example: all Muslims concur in the belief that the Prophet Muḥammad was a human being and in no way divine. But while Ottoman Sunnis of the seventeenth or nineteenth centuries did not feel that visits to the Prophet's grave in any way contradicted this belief, many Wahabis of the nineteenth and early twentieth centuries found it very difficult to tolerate this practice. In their view, visits to the Prophet's grave might tempt fallible human beings to place a human being at the side of God, and thereby commit the sin of idolatry. Other examples abound. Thus many non-Wahabi Muslims of past centuries, would not have regarded the existence of a corpus of legends concerning the Prophet as detracting in any way from the humanity of the Prophet, even though many twentieth-century Muslims may see the matter in a different light. Nor was the respect accorded the descendants of the Prophet, including the Sherifs of Mecca, regarded as a culpable narrowing of the distance between God and mankind.

In a more mundane sphere, it seems that not all pilgrims shared the views of sixteenth-century Ottoman administrations concerning a clear separation of the sacred and profane, as evinced in the quarrel concerning the Iranians and their 'cradles and mattresses' (see Chapter 5). Wealthy pilgrims of the sixteenth century, and of later times too, apparently could not be convinced that there was anything reprehensible about houses whose windows overlooked the Great Mosque. Quite to the contrary, nineteenth-century accounts of the city record the existence of such houses; unfortunately, at present we do not know from what time onwards they were rebuilt. Thus, even if the basic features of the faith remain unchanged, the practice of religion, like most other human activities, shows something we might call a period style. Because religion had a strong impact on the daily lives of the Hejazis, and this religion was based upon immutable texts, it is tempting to assume that the politics and lifestyle of the inhabitants of Mecca and Medina also remained immutable over the centuries. But this assumption would still be an error.[12]

THE PILGRIMAGE AS AN INTEGRATIVE FACTOR

Apart from the interplay of a continuity and socio-political change, the present study has focused upon the pilgrimage as an integrative factor within Ottoman society, and the role of pilgrim protection in the legitimation of the Ottoman Sultan. The integration of state territories, that is the increasing mutual involvement of cities, regions and social groups within a given territory, has been a favourite topic of many historians ever since the nineteenth century. This scholarly interest has been conditioned by practical considerations, as from the late eighteenth century onward, the major states and societies of Europe forced the pace of integration by the creation of national markets, a system of roads and canals, and, ultimately, national educational systems.[13] Moreover, in the second half of the twentieth century, at least in western Europe, a further spurt of integration has been experienced, not only on the inter-state level, but also in terms of social organization. Many professional associations, political movements and clubs, which often succeed in arousing strong loyalties in their members, function on a supra-national level. These experiences no doubt constitute an important reason why a late twentieth-century historian regards the integrative potential of the pilgrimage as something crucially important.

In the nineteenth century, the Ottoman political class also pursued the integration of its remaining territory by means of railway construction, administrative reform and a new-style educational system.[14] This task proved beyond the means of a multinational empire plagued by outside intervention and a severe shortage of capital. Nonetheless, the legacy it left to its successor states, particularly in the form of a trained bureaucracy, proved significant. This state of affairs encourages us to search for policies pursued by governments and factors operating in favour of integration within the major empires of the preindustrial period as well. These factors often differ in kind from those to which we are accustomed today. But this does not mean that political integration was not pursued in preindustrial empires, and that the latter were held together exclusively by military force. Military might was not unimportant on the level of the empire as a whole, but the Ottoman administration in the Hejaz disposed only of a very minor military force, and had to depend on political solutions. This was possible because a whole web of interests had been created which tied different sections of the Hejazi population to the Ottoman state. The Beduins could only expect to receive their subsidies if the central administration was both able and willing to pay. By demonstrations of their 'nuisance value', which in extreme cases might include major attacks upon the pilgrimage caravans, they might attempt to increase their subsidies. But a withdrawal of the Ottoman central government from this area would have been a disadvantage and not an advantage to most Hejazi Beduins.

The inhabitants of Mecca and Medina, too, were integrated into the Ottoman system by pious foundations and subsidies. Throughout the centuries the townsmen have provided essential goods and services to pilgrims, for which they demanded and received high prices. Many of them rented their houses, permitted the installation of temporary stalls in their porches, and provided the pilgrims with food and water. Many inhabitants of Mecca and Medina acted as guides to the pilgrims, showed them the proper execution of the relevant rituals and helped them organize their journeys to Mina, Muzdalifa and 'Arafat. Apart from gifts and payments on the part of individual pilgrims, the official donations received by the townsmen enabled them to survive, and presumably they demanded less from individual pilgrims than they would have done if no official support had been forthcoming. Thus the pious foundations of Egypt, by their remittances of grain and money, contributed not only to the integration of the Hejazis, but to that of the pilgrims as well.

As to the inhabitants of the numerous Ottoman towns with a number of foundations benefiting the Holy Cities, they were included in a wider geographical horizon by the mere existence of these foundations. In a time in which travel was difficult and expensive, it must have been of some significance to experience a concrete link with Mecca and Medina, even though we do not know whether some Rumelians and Anatolians did not react with a degree of hostility against the outflow of locally needed resources. Whatever the reaction, horizons were widened to include the remote cities of the Hejaz, which most of the people concerned could scarcely hope to see with their own eyes.

Apart from the economic interests of certain groups of the population, the integrative function of the pilgrimage routes themselves should be taken into consideration. The routes travelled by pilgrims also functioned as trade routes, partly because pilgrimage caravans were used by merchants (see Chapter 2), partly because many pilgrims did some trading on the side. Trade routes, on the other hand, were at the basis of the economic resilience which the Ottoman Empire showed down into the eighteenth century. Crises, which outside observers often presumed would destroy the state, time and again were overcome, and between 1700 and 1760 Ottoman trade and crafts even went through a period of expansion.[15] In his monumental work on capitalism and the economy in the early modern world, Fernand Braudel has connected this remarkable resilience of the Ottoman polity with the fact that, down to the beginning of the nineteenth century, the government continued to control the trade routes leading through its territory.[16] Braudel's judgment does not refer to the international transit routes: some of the latter, particularly the route leading from the silk-producing regions of western Iran to Izmir and Istanbul, at the beginning of the eighteenth century were in a state of profound crisis.[17] But internal trade continued to flourish down to the 1760s, when it fell victim to the exigencies of almost constant war.

Among Ottoman internal trade routes, the connection between Istanbul and the Hejaz by way of Damascus was of major importance, and the same thing can be said of the overland route from Cairo to Mecca and Medina and the Red Sea route. The commercial activity along these routes was due not only to the supply trade of the Holy Cities, but also to the trade in coffee, which from the sixteenth century onward became increasingly popular in the Ottoman Empire. Down into the fifteenth century, as we have seen, coffee had been all but unknown outside of Yemen.[18] But by the year 1500, it was being brought to Mecca by pilgrims and merchants from the Yemen, and rapidly caught on. In the seventeenth century the coffee trade even became so profitable that Cairo wholesalers recouped their losses from the transit trade in spices to Europe, now in the hands of the Dutch, and did not experience the profound commercial crisis the Venetians suffered after losing the transit trade. Thus the pilgrimage routes contributed to the development of a new branch of commerce, which permitted Cairene traders to hold their own against European competitors down into the eighteenth century.[19] Moreover, the Hejaz, where previously money could only be made in connection with the pilgrimage trade, now turned into a significant coffee entrepôt.

THE SULTAN AS THE SERVITOR OF MECCA AND MEDINA

In a number of different contexts, we have discussed the role of the Ottoman Sultan as the protector of pilgrims and permanent inhabitants of the Hejaz. This role no doubt legitimized the ruler in the eyes of the Ottoman political class, and possibly in the eyes of foreign pilgrims as well; on this latter aspect, however, we possess little evidence. Probably the demonstrative protection accorded Central Asian pilgrims was intended to mobilize support for the Ottoman Sultan at the Sunni courts of Transoxania, as the *khān*s of this region formed a counterweight to the Shi'i Shahs of Iran (see Chapter 6).[20] At the present stage of our knowledge, it is equally hard to determine whether the Ottoman political class envisaged legitimizing the Sultan in the eyes of ordinary Ottoman tax-payers, or whether the latter's opinions were regarded as insignificant.

Ottoman Sultans frequently used the title 'Servant of the two Holy Places' (*Khādim al-Ḥaramayn*), and this surely was a means of legitimizing the ruler as the protector of the pilgrimage. More explicit uses of the same motif can be found in sixteenth-century rescripts. Thus it was certainly not by chance that, in the second half of the sixteenth century, an Ottoman Sultan opposed the expansion of the Czars into the steppes of what is today southern Russia with the argument that the pilgrimage routes had to be kept open for Central Asian Sunnis.[21] The effectiveness of this rhetoric was surely enhanced by the fact that it contrasted the Ottoman Sultan as a Sunni Muslim ruler not only with the infidel Czar but also with the Shi'i Shah – who, after all, had also placed major impediments in the way of Central Asian pilgrims.

Ottoman Sultans affixed numerous inscriptions to buildings in the Holy Cities, in order to commemorate a variety of construction and repair projects. These texts could be read by educated pilgrims both from outside the empire and from within: almost certainly they were drafted in Arabic, as sixteenth-century epigraphic texts in Ottoman Turkish constituted something of a rarity. We have seen that the Ottoman administration was greatly concerned about the visibility and legibility of such inscriptions, and that the texts at times were drafted in Istanbul (see Chapter 5). Probably the central government wanted to make sure that the Sherif did not claim a greater share of merit than the Sultan and his Council were ready to concede to him. It was also considered important to describe the Sultan who had ordered this or that construction project as a worthy successor to the prophets and distinguished personalities of Muslim history who had also embellished the Great Mosque in the course of its history.

As the Ottoman dynasty as a whole was legitimated by construction projects, rather than any Sultan as an individual, the sisters, daughters, mothers and consorts of Ottoman rulers could take on major roles as benefactresses of the Muslim community. This role recently has begun to interest historians with a feminist commitment, who concern themselves with the opportunities for political action open to women of the Ottoman political class, and particularly to royal women. For the most part, researchers have concentrated upon Istanbul, which did in fact house the majority of the royal women's foundations.[22] Often, however, Mecca, Medina and the stopping points along the pilgrimage routes were selected by Ottoman princesses as sites of their largesse. Apart from Khurrem Sultan (Roxolana), there is her daughter Mihr-ü-māh (died in 1578). A sister of Süleymān the Magnificent also contributed to the repair of the pipes which supplied Mecca with water. The number of princesses who went on the pilgrimage also appears to have been more important than assumed by previous researchers. Since Sultans and princes practically never appeared in the Hejaz, the occasional presence of royal women took on a strong symbolic connotation.

Apart from public construction, the Ottoman dynasty could be legitimated by gifts which were exposed to the public of Istanbul, Cairo or Damascus before expeditions to the Hejaz. Ahmed I (reigned 1603–17) appeared at a ceremonial showing of the newly fashioned support system for the Ka'aba and other decorative elements destined for the mosques of Mecca and Medina (see Chapter 5). At least in the eighteenth century, the remission of the Sultan's subsidies to the inhabitants of the Hejaz was celebrated by elaborate ceremonies.[23] As Sherifs, Beduin shaykhs and Meccan notables, by the acceptance of these gifts, admitted that they 'ate the bread of the Sultan', they also admitted the legitimacy of the ruler who had bestowed this bounty upon them.

Throughout the present study, we have emphasized the importance of negotiations which preceded the recognition of Ottoman legitimacy by the Sultan's more prominent Hejazi subjects. These negotiations were indispensable, as the distances involved, and Ottoman commitments in other parts of the empire, precluded the imposition of policies by military force alone. It would be a mistake, however, to assume that the Ottoman administration negotiated with the Hejazi notables merely because it had no other choice; for, after all, the Ottoman government was not necessarily obliged to commit itself heavily on the Rumelian and Iranian frontiers while establishing only a minor military presence on its southern borders. Therefore, the emphasis on negotiation should also be regarded as a political decision, and not merely a necessity imposed from outside.

It is necessary to emphasize these elementary truths because most twentieth-century historians dealing with the early modern Near East strongly emphasize the military dimension.[24] The *'ulemā* of this period, by accepting that even an unjust ruler was preferable to anarchy, supposedly capitulated *vis à vis* the power of any Sultan who might happen to stabilize his rule, so that there was no need for a special legitimating stance. But this view is scarcely applicable to the political situation of seventeenth-century Istanbul. Serious military defeats and a disadvantageous peace might destroy a Sultan's legitimacy and result in his deposition. To mention but a few examples: Meḥmed IV (reigned 1648–87) lost his throne after the failed siege of Vienna; Muṣṭafā II (reigned 1695–1703) was deposed after losing the battle of Zenta in 1697 and accepting the disastrous peace of Karlowitz in 1699.[25] Aḥmed III (reigned 1703–33) lost his throne due to further military failures, but also because, in the courtly celebrations of his time, the Ottoman elite indulged in the consumption of European-style luxuries in a manner that was all too provocative for many overtaxed Istanbul craftsmen, to say nothing of dissatisfied janissaries and *'ulemā*.[26] Ottoman Sultans therefore had every reason in the world to establish and confirm their legitimacy in a dialogue with those personages within and outside the court who could mount a challenge to their rule. The Hejazi elites belonged in this category, and their consent was actively sought.

PILGRIMS AND HISTORIANS

Thus we may hope the reader will conclude that there was nothing 'romantic' or 'exotic' about the pilgrimage, but that a great deal of hard work, sustained negotiations and complicated financial transactions went into its organization year after year. This more realistic perspective also coincides to some degree with that of sixteenth or seventeenth-century Ottoman officials, who corresponded at length about the political and financial ramifications of the pilgrimage. It must be admitted, however, that an interest in phenomena regarded in one way or another as 'exotic' was not completely alien to educated Ottomans of the early modern period. The accounts of an Ottoman ambassador who visited France in the early eighteenth century demonstrate this fact.[27] But the most obvious example is surely the travelogue of Ewliyā Čelebi, whose account of a visit to Vienna, and also his description of the Red Sea and its coast, suggest an interest in things that to an Istanbul gentleman appeared strange and yet not altogether unattractive.[28] The exotic is always in the eye of the beholder; it disappears when we reconstruct political and cultural processes by adopting, within certain limits, the perspective of the participants.

There is, however, no gainsaying that in this book the pilgrimage has been reconstructed by a rationalist historian of the late twentieth century, and that simple fact makes any attempt at an internalist perspective inherently problematic. For the tension between the vision of a sixteenth-century Ottoman pilgrim or bureaucrat and the view of a modern historian cannot be dissolved by even the most sophisticated form of historical analysis. But it is possible to keep this tension in mind and regard with respect the humanity of the people whom we have encountered at an often decisive stage of their lives. Historians are professionally tempted to misuse their advantage of hindsight, becoming authoritarian, domineering figures who claim to understand the authors of their sources better than the latter understood themselves. Another type of relationship is equally possible. Even while using the scholarly resources of our own age, we can and should take seriously the considerations which pilgrims and administrators had in mind when producing the texts on which we depend today. Better comprehension is the product of a permanent tension between immersion in the world of the sources and maintaining the critical distance of analysis.

Chronology

All dates refer to the Common Era (CE)

c570–632 CE	Life of the Prophet Muḥammad.
622	The Prophet Muḥammad and his companions leave Mecca and settle in Medina. This event, called the Hidjra, constitutes the beginning of the Muslim era.
630	The Muslims occupy Mecca; Islamization of the pilgrimage.
632	The Farewell Pilgrimage of the Prophet Muḥammad sets the standard for all future pilgrimages.
632–56	Medina the capital of the caliphal Empire. Conquest of Byzantine and Sassanian territory.
632–4	Caliphate of Abu Bakr.
634–44	Caliphate of 'Umar.
644–56	Caliphate of 'Uthmān.
656–61	Caliphate of 'Alī, the son-in-law of the Prophet.
661	Mu'āwiya establishes himself as the first caliph of the Ummayad dynasty.
680	Battle between Ḥusayn, son of 'Alī and grandson to the Prophet Muḥammad, and Ibn Sa'd, in the service of the Ummayad caliph Yazīd I. Ḥusayn's death in the battle of Karbalā takes on central religious significance in the belief system of Shi'i Muslims.

681–92	Caliphate of 'Abd Allāh b. Zubayr (Ibn Zubayr) in Mecca. Restoration of the Ka'aba.
692	Ibn Zubayr killed. Al-Hadjdjādj conquers Mecca for the Ummayad caliph 'Abd al-Mālik. Destruction and reconstruction of the Ka'aba.
747–50	Construction of a gallery in the Great Mosque of Mecca, some of whose elements remain visible today. An older gallery dating from 692–705 is no longer extant.
750	End of the Ummayad dynasty. The Abbasids establish themselves as caliphs in Baghdad.
after 777	Construction of the gallery of the Great Mosque of Mecca by the Abbasid caliph al-Mahdī (reigned 775–85) and his successors.
786–809	Caliphate of Hārūn al-Rashīd, who comes to Mecca several times as a pilgrim. His consort Zubayda has water conduits installed.
about 960	The Sherifs establish themselves as local rulers of Mecca.
before 929	Pilgrimage of Ibn 'Abd Rabbih.
1047	First pilgrimage of Naṣīr-i Khosraw.
1175–93	Reign of Saladin (Ṣalāḥ al-Dīn Ayyūbī) in Egypt, Syria and Palestine.
1183	Pilgrimage of Ibn Djubayr.
about 1200	Within the Sherifal family, the Katāda dynasty begins its period of rule.
1258	The last Abbasid caliph of Baghdad is murdered by the Mongols.
1260–1517	The Mamluk Sultans of Egypt and Syria control the Hejaz.
1468–96	Reign of Sultan Kā'it Bāy in Egypt and Syria. Repairs to the Great Mosque of Medina after a fire, and construction of a theological school in Mecca.
1453	Conquest of Istanbul (Constantinople) by the Ottoman Sultan Mehmed II (reigned 1451–81).
1481–1512	Reign of Sultan Bāyezīd II. Official gifts sent to Mecca and Medina.
about 1514	Jeddah threatened by the Portuguese.
1517	Ottoman conquest of Egypt by Sultan Selīm I (reigned 1512–20): the Hejaz enters the Ottoman realm.
1520–66	Reign of Süleymān the Lawgiver. Construction of soup kitchens in Mecca and Medina in the name

	of his consort <u>Kh</u>urrem Sultan (Roxolana). Repair of the Meccan water conduits and construction of a seventh minaret to the Great Mosque.
1538	Unsuccessful campaign of <u>Kh</u>ādim Süleymān Pasha against the Portuguese positions on the western coast of India.
1554–7	Exile of the Mughal prince Kāmrān in Mecca.
1566–74	· Reign of Selīm II. Reshaping of the gallery of the Great Mosque of Mecca, which in many places is tantamount to a rebuilding from the foundations upward. Construction of domes over the gallery.
1574–82	Pilgrimage of Salīma and Gul-badan, consort and aunt to the Mughal ruler Akbar (reigned 1564–1605).
1574–95	Reign of Murād III. The town quarter adjacent to the mosque is torn down.
1585–90	A direct link is established from the eastern coast of India (Masulipatnam) to the Arabian peninsula.
1582	The pilgrimage of Mi'mar Sinān, the 'Ottoman Michelangelo'.
1611–12	The Ka'aba supported by iron braces. The architect responsible is Me<u>h</u>med A<u>gh</u>a, who also built the Blue Mosque in Istanbul.
1630–31	Mutinying Ottoman troops occupy Mecca. They are defeated by the Mamluk amirs Ḳāsim and Riḍwān, operating in the name of Sultan Murād IV (reigned 1623–40). Destruction of the Ka'aba in a flash flood. Under the direction of Riḍwān Beg, the building is taken down stone by stone and largely rebuilt with the same materials
1632	Pilgrimage of 'Abd al-Ra<u>h</u>mān Ḥibrī.
1671	The Beduin chief Ibn Ra<u>sh</u>īd attacks the pilgrimage caravan of Damascus. Sherif Sa'd rebels in Mecca.
1672	Sherif Sa'd deposed by the governor of Damascus Ṣarı Ḥüseyin Pasha. Pilgrimage of Ewliyā Čelebi.
1683–99	Ottoman–Habsburg war.

Notes

INTRODUCTION

1. Compare the article 'Ḥadjdj' in the *Encyclopedia of Islam*, 2nd edition (London, 1954–), henceforth *EI*. A good summary of early Islamic history is found in Hodgson (1974), vol. 1, pp. 3–230.
2. Ibn Djubayr's pilgrimage account has been translated into both English and French (see Bibliography for details). I have mainly worked with the French translation by Maurice Gaudefroy-Demombynes, and am grateful to Dr Doris Behrens-Abouseif who checked quotations against the original. The English translation contains a biography of Ibn Djubayr (p. 15 ff.).
3. Faroqhi (1992).
4. MD 6, p. 562, no. 1222 (972/1564–5).
5. De Planhol (1958), pp. 113–14.
6. On gold and silver ratios in early modern India see Subrahmanyam (1990), p. 83 ff.
7. Ashtor (1986).
8. Wüstenfeld (reprint, 1964), vol. 4, p. 302.
9. Faroqhi (forthcoming).
10. Faroqhi (1991).
11. Shaw (1962), p. 253 ff.
12. Faroqhi (1992), p. 319.
13. Compare the *ḳāḍī* register of the district of Çorum, dated 1595–7, today probably preserved in the Library of Çorum. I do not know whether, in the past few months, this register has been transferred to the National Library in Ankara: fol. 58b.
14. Naṣīr-i Khusraw (1881), pp. 162, 167.
15. Ibn Djubayr (1949–51), pp. 148–9. For the practical problems that might

191

ensue if a foreign ruler wished to make a donation, see Wüstenfeld (reprint, 1964), vol. 4, p. 248.
16. Shaw (1962), p. 249.
17. For an analysis of this situation in the eighteenth century, see Barbir (1980), p. 97 ff.
18. About 800 rescripts were located in the Mühimme Defterleri (henceforth MD), called Registers of Important Affairs in the text of this study. I checked registers 3–96, in addition to the series Mühimme Zeyli 1–10 (henceforth MZ). Mühimmes 1 and 2 do not contain usable documentation. Accounts were found in the section Maliyeden Müdevver (henceforth MM). An Egyptian provincial account has been published and translated into English: Shaw (1968). Inalcık (1973) contains a comprehensive introduction to sixteenth-century Ottoman history and institutions.
19. Evliya Çelebi (1896–1938), vol. 9, pp. 565–842.
20. Süheylī (Süheilî) Efendi, 'Tārīkh-i Mekke-i mükerrime' also called simply 'Risāle'. I used the manuscript in the Vienna National Library, Flügel (1865–7), vol. 2, p. 125.
21. Ca'fer Efendi, ed. Crane (1987).
22. Meḥmed Edīb wrote at the end of the seventeenth century. Of his account there exists an early French translation: El-Hadj Mehemmed Edib, tr. Bianchi (Paris, 1825).

CHAPTER 1

1. Hodgson (1974), vol. 1, pp. 241 ff., 473 ff.; vol. 2, pp. 12–52; vol. 3, p. 69 ff.
2. Naṣīr-i Khusraw (1881). See also his biography in *EI*.
3. Bulliet (1972), *passim*.
4. The pilgrimage account given on the next few pages is based principally on the descriptions of Ibn Djubayr. In order to limit the number of notes, only a selection of page references has been included.
5. Masson (1911), p. 401.
6. Hanna (1983), p. 16.
7. Ibn Jubayr, tr. Broadhurst (1952), p. 64.
8. *Ibid.*, p. 66.
9. *Ibid.*, pp. 72–3.
10. *EI*, article 'Ḥadjdj'.
11. Burton (reprint, 1964), vol. 1, p. 141.
12. Evliya Çelebi (1896–1938), vol. 9, p. 676.
13. Ibn Djubayr (1949–51), p. 92.
14. Al-Ḥarawī (1957).
15. Ibn Djubayr (1949–51), p. 109.
16. Hartmann (1975), p. 121.
17. Ibn Djubayr (1949–51), p. 194.
18. Ibn Djubayr (1949–51), p. 197.
19. Evliya Çelebi (1896–1938), vol. 9, p. 685 ff.

20. Ibn Djubayr (1949–51), pp. 199–200.
21. Evliya Çelebi (1896–1938), vol. 9, p. 702.
22. Ibn Djubayr (1949–51), p. 206.
23. *Ibid.*, p. 208.
24. *Ibid.*, p. 156.
25. *Ibid.*, p. 177 f.
26. *Ibid.*, p. 157.
27. *Ibid.*, p. 137.
28. Hodgson (1974), vol. 1, p. 200.
29. Naṣīr-i Khosraw ed. Schefer (1881), pp. 163–5.
30. Ibn 'Abd Rabbihi ed. Shafī (1973), pp. 416–38.
31. *Ibid.*, p. 433.
32. Wüstenfeld (1860) gives an abridged translation of Samhūdī's work. For a critical discussion of the sources concerning the Prophet's mosque, compare Sauvaget (1947).
33. Wüstenfeld (1860), p. 67.
34. On history and institutions of the Mamluk period, compare the relevant article in *EI*. Wüstenfeld (reprint, 1964), vol. 4, p. 287, claims that a covering for the Ka'aba by Timur's son Shāhrukh was accepted, while Holt, in the *EI* article 'Mamluk', p. 324, expresses the contrary opinion.
35. Wüstenfeld (1964), vol. 4, p. 248.
36. *Ibid.*, vol. 4, p. 253 f.
37. *Ibid.*, vol. 4, p. 264 f.
38. *Ibid.*, vol. 4, p. 290 f.
39. *Ibid.*, vol. 4, p. 291 f.
40. Wüstenfeld (reprint, 1964), vol. 4, p. 292.
41. *Ibid.*, p. 302.
42. Mughul (1965), pp. 37–47.

CHAPTER 2

1. Jomier (1953), p. 85. However, this information concerns the early nineteenth century.
2. Compare the article 'Makka' in *EI* by A.J. Wensinck and C.E. Bosworth.
3. Al-Djazarī (1384/1964–5) p. 91 ff.
4. *Ibid.*, pp. 91–5.
5. *Ibid.*, p. 124.
6. MM 1645, p. 20. On the *sürre emīni*, compare d'Ohsson (1787–1824), vol. 3, p. 262 ff.
7. MM 927, p. 93, compare MD 28, p. 150, no. 351 (981/1573–4) on the duties of *ketkhüdā* and *mīrākhōr*.
8. And (1982) clearly demonstrates the public character of many Ottoman celebrations.
9. Evliya Çelebi (1896–1938), vol. 10, p. 424 ff.
10. *Ibid.*, vol. 10, p. 442 f.
11. *Ibid.*, vol. 10, p. 432. On the *maḥmal* see Jomier (1953), *passim*.
12. Evliya Çelebi (1896–1938), vol. 10, p. 427.

13. Inalcık (1973), p. 77 ff.
14. Evliya Çelebi (1896–1938), vol. 9, p. 570 f.
15. *Ibid.*, vol. 10, p. 441 ff.
16. Ḥibrī (1975), pp. 111–28; (1976), pp. 55–72; (1978), pp. 147–62. Ḥibrī's itinerary in: *Tarih Enstitüsü Dergisi*, 6, pp. 124–8. Compare Mehemmed Edib (1825), pp. 81–169, Burckhardt (1822), pp. 656–61.
17. MM 4108.
18. Taeschner (1924–6), map at the end of vol. 1.
19. Evliya Çelebi (1896–1938), vol. 9, p. 582.
20. See map in Inalcık (1973), p. 122 f.
21. MM 927, p. 93.
22. Al-Djazarī (1384/1964–5), p. 103.
23. Evliya Çelebi (1896–1938), vol. 9, pp. 575, 599. See also Burckhardt (1822),
    p. 660.
24. MD 27, p. 158, no. 364 (988/1575–6). Compare Kātib Čelebi (1145/ 1732) fol. 512b.
25. MD 23, p. 32, no. 65 (981/1573–4). There were however complaints concerning the misuse of foundation revenues.
26. MD 42, p. 334, no. 1021 (988/1580–1).
27. MD 40, p. 164, no. 358 (987/1579–80); MD 35, p. 225, no. 560 (980/ 1578–9). Evliya Çelebi (1896–1938), vol. 9, p. 565 describes the *wādjib al-re'āyet* as regular members of the Pasha of Damascus's suite. But documents such as MD 53, p. 27, no. 68 show that, at least in the sixteenth century, this cannot have applied to all beneficiaries.
28. MD 7, p. 525 f., no. 1506 (975/1567–8). In sixteenth-century documents, the Damascus support caravan was called *istikbāl* and its members *karshudju*. See MD 12, p. 168, no. 335 (978/1570–1); MD 7, p. 525 f., no. 1506 (975/1567–8); MD 12, p. 168, no. 355 (978/1570–1); MD 12, p. 445, no. 862 (979/1571–2); MD 24, p. 288, no. 781 (981/ 1573–4).
29. MD 12, p. 164, no. 348 (978/1570–1).
30. Evliya Çelebi (1896–1938), vol. 10, p. 438.
31. The Black Scribe and the Son of Djānbolāt were famous seventeenth-century rebels. See Griswold (1983).
32. MD 28, p. 142, no. 336 (984/1576–7).
33. MD 31, p. 256, no. 565 (985/1577–8).
34. MD 62, p. 256, no. 580 (996/1587–8).
35. Jomier (1953), p. 86.
36. *Ibid.*, p. 87. The anonymous source has been published by Hakluyt (1901), vol. 5, pp. 329–65. See also Beckingham (1977), pp. 75–80.
37. Jomier (1953), p. 87. On Ludovico di Varthéma, see Jones/Badger (1863), pp. 24, 37, 42. Compare also Anonymous (1901), p. 356.
38. Ali Bey (1814), vol. 2, p. 337.
39. Burckhardt (1829), vol. 2, p. 46.
40. MM 1003.
41. MM 1003, pp. 55, 57.
42. MD 28, p. 96, no. 225 (984/1576–7).

43. MD 40, p. 48, no. 103 (987/1579–80).
44. MM 4345, p. 65.
45. Bakhit (1982), pp. 53–68.
46. MD 26, p. 17, no. 48 (982/1574–5).
47. MD 14, p. 188, no. 269 (979/1571–2); MD 9, p. 24, no. 66 (977/1569–70). Compare also Bulliet (1975), pp. 165–178 and Faroqhi (1982), pp. 523–39.
48. MD 62, p. 52, no. 120 (995/1586–7).
49. MD 36, p. 23, no. 69 (986/1578–9).
50. MM 4345, pp. 16, 43 (1067/1656–7).
51. MD 5, p. 461, no. 1239 (973/1565–6); MD 36, p. 23, no. 69 (986/1578–9).
52. MD 36, p. 23, no. 69 (986/1578–9).
53. MD 7, p. 969, no. 2681 (976/1568–9).
54. MD 5, p. 206, no. 519 (973/1565–6).
55. MD 69, p. 15, no. 26 (1000/1591–2); MD 5, p. 208, no. 520 (973/1565–6).
56. Tresse (1937), p. 149 ff.
57. MD 29, p. 6, no. 12 (984/1576–7).
58. MD 69, p. 39, no. 76 (1000/1591–2).
59. MD 36, p. 23, no. 69 (986/1578–9).
60. MD 69, p. 69, no. 138 (1000/1591–2). On the official rate of exchange compare MD 73, p. 199, no. 462 (1003/1594–5).
61. Compare the unpublished paper of Anthony Greenwood, read at the annual convention of Middle East Studies Association, Chicago 1983. See also: Faroqhi (1984), p. 221 ff.; Mantran (1962), pp. 194–200; Cvetkova (1976), pp. 325–35.
62. Mantran (1962), p. 195, based upon Evliya Çelebi (1896–1938), vol. 1, p. 561 f.
63. See Kütükoğlu (1983) and the unpublished dissertation by Kafadar, 1986.
64. Tresse (1937), p. 149 ff.
65. MD 30, p. 28, no. 68 (985/1577–8); MD 9, p. 22, no. 58 (977/1569–70).
66. Rafeq (1970), pp. 53–9.

CHAPTER 3

1. Barkan (1953–4)(a), pp. 238–50. Majer (1982), pp. 40–63.
2. On Istanbul, see Sahillioğlu (1964), pp. 228–33. On Cairo, compare Raymond (1973–4), vol. 1, p. 17 ff. According to MD 73, p. 176, no. 413 (1003/1584–5), 1 gold piece (*altın*) equalled 120 *akče* and 1 ġuruš̱ 70 *akče*. Thus 1 *pāra* = 3 *akče*, but the rate of exchange was liable to fluctuation.
3. Shaw (1968), p. 158 ff.
4. Compare Başbakanlık Arşivi, Istanbul, Series Maliyeden Müdevver (MM): MM 5672, pp. 17 ff., 38 ff.; Shaw (1968), p. 165. MM 5672, p. 60 ff.; MM 5162, p. 14 ff.; MM 5658, p. 13 ff. According to MM 5162,

4,392,331 *pāra* equalled 44,851 *ḥasene* (gold pieces, *altın*) and 34 *pāra*. Compare also MM 5568, pp. 138 f., 146, 148 f., 151; MM 2520, p. 50; MM 86; MM 4901, pp. 2–6; MM 875.

5. Griswold (1983), p. 60 ff. Abu-Husayn (1985), pp. 67–128.
6. Sharon (1975), p. 26 ff.
7. MM 875.
8. Rafeq (1970), p. 55 ff. contains an extensive and most useful discussion of eighteenth-century pilgrimage problems as seen from Damascus.
9. Evliya Çelebi (1896–1938), vol. 9, pp. 565 ff. The editors claim, on p. 565, that Ewliyā visited Mecca in 1670–1. But that is highly improbable, as Ibn Rashīd's attack on the pilgrimage caravan occurred that year, and Ewliyā claims to have travelled a year later. See Rafeq (1970), p. 55 f. Cavit Baysun's biography of Ewliyā in *IA* also mentions 1082/1671–2 as the year of his pilgrimage. An edition of Hibrī's account can be found in: Hibrī (1975), pp. 111–28; (1976), pp. 55–72; (1978), pp. 147–62.
10. Shaw (1962), pp. 240–50.
11. MD 69, p. 34, no. 65 (1000/1591–2).
12. Al-Djazarī (1384/1964–5). I am grateful to Dr Humaydan for finding me a copy of this work.
13. Evliya Çelebi (1896–1938), vol. 9, p. 572 ff.
14. On the *maḥmal*, see Jomier (1953), *passim*.
15. Shaw (1962), p. 240. For a different opinion compare Holt (1961), p. 221. Holt believes that during the first ten years of Ottoman rule, Mamluks were appointed as commanders of the pilgrimage. According to MD 30, p. 275, no. 639 (985/1577–8) the commander was supposed to be one of the *ümerā* (see Shaw (1962), p. 199). But from MD 52, p. 297, no. 793 (992/1584) we learn that a wealthy Cairene merchant also might be awarded this honour.
16. MD 3, p. 525, no. 1553 (968/1560–1).
17. According to Shaw (1962), p. xxii an Egyptian 'purse' equalled 25,000 *pāra* or 60,000 *akče*. Later the Ottoman administration admitted that 16 purses were insufficient, and the commander was assigned 18 purses. Compare MD 12, p. 449, no. 868 (979/1571–2).
18. Concerning Özdemiroghlu, see Yavuz (1984), pp. 61, 99. MD 3, p. 525, no. 1553 (968/1560–1).
19. MD 14, p. 812 f., no. 1180 (978/1570–1); MD 30, p. 25, no. 90 (985/1577–8).
20. MD 43, p. 79, no. 161 (988/1580–1).
21. MD 14, p. 1149, no. 1692 (978/1570–1).
22. MD 61, p. 73, no. 190 (994/1585–6).
23. Yavuz (1984), p. 61.
24. Abu-Husayn (1985), p. 168 f.
25. *Ibid.*, pp. 164–71. On this milieu compare also Bakhit (1982) (b), *passim*.
26. See the article 'Adjlun' in *EI* (D. Sourdel).
27. MD 46, p. 1, no. 1 (989/1581).
28. Abu-Husayn (1985), p. 170.
29. MD 18, p. 28, no. 52 (979/1571–2); MD 24, p. 196, no. 522 (981/1573–4); MD 26, p. 156, no. 420 (982/1574–5).

30. Abu-Husayn (1985), *passim*.
31. In MD 47, p. 107, no. 272 (990/1582), Ḳānṣūh is referred to as a Beduin amir. On strife between the 'Reds' and the 'Whites', see Bakhit (1982), p. 214 and MD 14, p. 675, no. 973 (978/1570–1). Ḳānṣūh Beg's ties to the faction of the 'Reds' are alluded to; but not explicitly stated.
32. MD 14, p. 1023, no. 1515 (978/1570–1).
33. This version of the name is given by Bakhit (1982), p. 223. Hütteroth and Abdulfattah (1977), p. 169, refer to a tribe called 'Urbān Na'īm' living in the same area. It is thus not quite clear which group the rescript refers to. On the dispute between Ḳānṣūh and Nu'aym/Na'īm, see MD 14, p. 830, no. 1206 (978/1570–1).
34. Abu-Husayn (1985), p. 170 f. MD 64, p. 86 f., no. 252 (996/1587–8).
35. Rafeq (1970), p. 71.
36. The pilgrims were attacked while in the Great Mosque, unarmed and in pilgrims' garb – if Ewliyā's story is accurate. Even though the attack was instigated by the Sherif, the actual attackers were Beduins. Therefore this event may be regarded as another example of a Beduin raid against a pilgrimage caravan.
37. Barbir (1980), p. 10. On p. 200 f. there is a list of the most significant attacks upon the Syrian pilgrimage caravan. Between 1531 and 1671 no attacks are mentioned at all. However, Ibn Ṭūlūn and Ibn Ġum'a (1952), p. 198, refer to an attack in 1012/1603–4. See also Ca'fer Efendi, ed. Crane (1987), p. 39.
38. MD 3, p. 75, no. 189 (966/1558–9).
39. MD 29, p. 6, no. 11 (984/1576–7).
40. For the Ottoman realm, a good survey can be found in the article 'Hil'at' by Fuat Köprülü in *IA*.
41. Barbir (1980), pp. 99, 105. Bakhit (1982), pp. 200–4. MD 28, p. 17, no. 26 (984/1576–7).
42. On the role of Riḍwān Beg, see Holt (1959), pp. 225–9. Compare Raymond (1973–4), vol. 1, pp. 5–7, 264 and Holt (1961) p. 243 ff.
43. On the last years of Ottoman rule, compare Wüstenfeld (1884), pp. 52–6 and Uzunçarşılı (1972), pp. 80–4.
44. This campaign was commanded by Riḍwān Beg and his superior, Ḳāsim Beg.
45. Ḥibrī (1976), p. 58. On Ḥibrī's account of contemporary political difficulties, see p. 60 f.
46. *Ibid.*, p. 58.
47. Compare the article 'Murād IV' in *IA* (Cavit Baysun).
48. Al-Nābulsī (1986), pp. 316–26.
49. Uzunçarşılı (1972), p. 86 f.
50. Evliya Çelebi (1896–1938), vol. 9, p. 602.
51. Ca'fer Efendi (1987).
52. *Ibid.*, p. 9 f. For a listing of the Ottoman governors of Damascus, see Laoust (1952). The list contains two Pashas named K̲h̲usrew. The first officiated in 946/1539–40 and 970/1562–3, the second in 1004/1595–6 and 1007/1598–9 (pp. 183, 186, 194, 196). Probably our text

refers to the second K̲h̲usrew Pasha, but the second term of the earlier
personage also constitutes a possibility.

53. Ca'fer Efendi (1987), p. 7.
54. *Ibid.*, p. 38 f.
55. *Ibid.*, p. 41.
56. Ibn D̲j̲ubayr (1949–51), p. 156.
57. See Barbir (1979–80), pp. 68–81 for an overview of the problem.
58. MM 2520, p. 20; MM 932, p. 51 (1056/1646–7).
59. Hakluyt (1901), vol. 5, p. 342.
60. Heyd (1960), p. 82 f.
61. MD 3, p. 122, no. 317 (966/1558–9); MD 12, p. 478, no. 918 (979/1571–2).
62. Jomier (1953), p. 80 ff.
63. MD 7, p. 278, no. 786 (975/1567–8).
64. MD 14, p. 997, no. 1483 (979/1571–2).
65. MD 62, p. 255, no. 579 (996/1587–8).
66. MD 3, p. 370, no. 1094 (967/1559–60).
67. MD 52, p. 105, no. 258 (991/1583). It also happened that the soldiers
    occupied the water reservoirs and allowed the pilgrims access only after
    payment of a fee: MD 14, p. 540, no. 828 (978/1570–1).
68. Muṣṭafā 'Ālī (1975), p. 55 f.
69. Evliya Çelebi (1896–1938), vol. 9, p. 801. See also MD 78, p. 297, no.
    778 (1018/1609–10). In this rescript the Egyptian caravan is forbidden to
    stay in Medina for over three days.
70. An account of life in a desert fort in the year 1876 is found in Doughty
    (1979), vol. 1, p. 160 ff; vol. 1, pp. 1–255 contains a detailed description
    of the pilgrimage route from Damascus to the stopping point of Madā' in
    Ṣāliḥ.
71. Evliya Çelebi (1896–1938), vol. 9, p. 602.
72. MD 3, p. 203, no. 563 (967/1559–60); MD 23, p. 210, no. 443 (981/1573–4).
73. MD 46, p. 183, no. 380 (989/1581).
74. Evliya Çelebi (1896–1938), vol. 9, p. 590.
75. Mehemmed Edib (1825), pp. 128–32.
76. Evliya Çelebi (1896–1938), vol. 9, p. 776; MM 4345, p. 65. See also
    Barbir (1980), pp. 176–7.
77. Compare Sharon (1975), p. 18.

CHAPTER 4

1. Fleischer (1986), p. 253 ff.
2. Inalcık (1954), pp. 104–29.
3. Hodgson (1974), vol. 1, pp. 198–221, 320–6.
4. Wüstenfeld (1964), vol. 4, *passim*.
5. Ibn D̲j̲ubayr (1949–51), p. 146, mentions subsidies distributed to the
   Beduins by the vizier of the ruler of Mosul, but there is no mention of
   grants to the inhabitants of the Holy Cities.

6. Uzluk (1958), p. 54 f., Konyalı (1970), p. 401 ff.
7. Gökbilgin (1952), pp. 234 f., 317.
8. Published by Barkan (1979), pp. 1–380 as 'Defter-i müsevvedât-ı in'âm ve tasaddukaat ve teşrifât ve irsâliyât ve 'âdet ve nukeriye ve gayruhu vâcib-i sene . . . (909) (26. VI. 1503–13. VI. 1504). Location and call number of the document are missing. The edition begins on p. 296.
9. D'Ohsson (1787–1824), vol. 3, p. 258.
10. In Sunni Islam there are four recognized schools of law, which differ in certain points of law and ritual, but are all considered equally orthodox. Believers are free to choose their school of law, but in different regions of the Muslim world, one or the other predominates. In the Ottoman Empire as in modern Turkey, the Hanefis constituted the dominant school.
11. Budgets of the Ottoman central government have been published: Barkan (1953–4), pp. 251–329; (1957–8), pp. 219–76; (1957–8), pp. 277–332; (1955–6), pp. 304–47; (1955–6), pp. 225–303. Compare also Barkan (1953–4), pp. 239–50 and Majer (1982), pp. 40–63.
12. Kafadar (1986, 1989). On the *eshrefiye* see Artuk and Artuk (1971, 1974), vol. 2, pp. 494–504. When compiling the table, the *eshrefiye* has been counted as 50 *akče* throughout, even though in the early part of Bāyezīd's reign, 45 *akče* would have been more appropriate.
13. Shaw (1962), p. 5.
14. Shaw (1968), p. 155 ff.
15. Muṣṭafā 'Ālī (1975), p. 82 f.
16. MM 5672, p. 17 ff.; MM 5672, p. 38 ff.; MM 5162, p. 14 ff.; MM 5658, p. 13 ff.
17. Ca'fer Efendi (1987), p. 47 ff.
18. Shaw (1962), p. 269.
19. The term *deshīshe* originally signified 'porridge'.
20. Shaw (1962), p. 21.
21. Wüstenfeld (1964), vol. 4, p. 302.
22. MM 12784.
23. MD 70, p. 159, no. 312 (1001/1592–3).
24. MM 1806, p. 2.
25. On house prices, see Faroqhi (1987), pp. 116–46. On bread and chickens, see Kütükoğlu (1978), p. 22 f.
26. MM 1806, p. 5.
27. MM 1806, p. 9. On coins, see Artuk and Artuk (1971, 1974), vol. 2, pp. 494, 556.
28. MM 1806, p. 11.
29. MM 1806, p. 18.
30. In the Syrian provincial budgets we find very few data concerning the food supply of Mecca and Medina; the pilgrimage caravan definitely occupied centre stage. Foundations for the benefit of the Holy Cities seem to have been insignificant. In 1657–8, 169 inhabitants of Mecca and Medina received salaries or pensions from the Syrian budget. These payments totalled less than 600,000 *pāra*, while Beduin subsidies and other expenses connected with the pilgrimage amounted to almost nine

million *pāra*. It is difficult to estimate even roughly the amount of money which flowed from the Syrian exchequer in the direction of Mecca and Medina, but at least maximal (150,000 gold pieces) and minimal (55,000 gold pieces) figures can be suggested. However, in 1657–8, for reasons which remain unknown, about 220,000 gold pieces were spent (MM 956, p. 6 ff.). All these figures are dubious because, in cases of emergency, the caravan commanders borrowed substantial sums, which were only repaid much later, if at all. Thus expenditures were redistributed over the years, and the figures we possess give only a distorted picture of reality.

31. See Flügel (1865–7), vol. 2, no. 895, p. 123 f. This is a slightly abridged and updated Ottoman version of Ḳutb al-Dīn's chronicle, composed probably by the poet Bāḳī at the behest of the Grand Vizier Soḳollu Meḥmed Pasha (died 1579). The sections referred to here are on fols 223–5. For a German summary see Wüstenfeld (reprint, 1964), vol. 4, pp. 314–23.
32. MD 39, p. 115, no. 278 (987/1579–80).
33. MD 73, p. 460, no. 1015 (1003/1594–5).
34. MD 89, p. 26, no. 68 (1052/1642–3).
35. The Sherif received subsidies not merely for himself, but for his Beduin allies as well.
36. This impression is based on the Mühimme Registers of this period. But due to numerous gaps in our documentation, it may well be an optical illusion.
37. MD 43, p. 266, no. 490 (988/1580–1). On Meccan participation in the mid-nineteenth century pilgrimage compare Burton (reprint, 1964), vol. 2, p. 188.
38. MD 48, p. 318, no. 938 (991/1583).
39. Anonymous and Gölpınarlı (1958), p. 56, mentions a good example from Anatolia.
40. Sahillioğlu (1978), p. 10.
41. MD 49, p. 71, no. 249 (991/1583).
42. Masters (1988), pp. 147–51, discusses the results of a money famine in Aleppo.
43. MD 49, p. 71, no. 249 (991/1583).
44. MD 58, p. 277, no. 707 (993/1585); MD 60, p. 128, no. 308 (994/1585–6).
45. MD 75, pp. 8–9, no. 20 (1012/1603–4).
46. On the Ḥusaynīs of Medina (mid-nineteenth century) compare Burton (reprint, 1964), vol. 2, p. 3. The descendants of Ḥasan, the Prophet's other grandson, were Sunnis and often hostile to the Ḥusaynīs. Compare MD 47, p. 241, no. 578 (990/1582). On the Ḥusaynīs in general see MD 47, p. 241, no. 578 (990/1582); MD 39, p. 115, no. 278 (987/1579–80); MD 31, p. 267, no. 589 (985/1577–8); MD 6, p. 190, no. 409 (972/1564–5); MD 46, p. 100, no. 189 (989/1581).
47. MM 5672, p. 38 (1010–11/1601–3).
48. MD 73, p. 460, no. 1015 (1003/1594–5). It is hard to determine the equivalent of the *irdeb* or *ardeb*, because this measure varied from one

locality to the next. In early eighteenth-century Cairo, 1 *irdeb* corresponded to 6 *kile* of Istanbul, or 153.9 kg. See Shaw (1962), p. 79.
49. Compare the individual items mentioned by Shaw (1968), p. 154 ff. These were added, and the total (in *pāras*) then converted into gold pieces. From the document published by Shaw we learn that 1 gold piece then equalled 40 *pāra*. For the higher estimate compare Shaw (1962), p. 268. When converting *pāra* into gold pieces, the same exchange rate was again applied.
50. Finkel (1988), Appendix 10. On rates of exchange, see Sahillioğlu (1964), p. 233: in 1605, 1 gold piece was equivalent to 120 *akče*.
51. Compare the Syrian provincial account of 1075/1664–5 (MM 2394, pp. 5–9). Many later budgets show a similar tendency.
52. MD 75, p. 178, no. 350 (1013/1604–5). Sultan Aḥmed I reigned 1603–17. His deceased predecessor therefore was Meḥmed III reigned 1595–1603 .

CHAPTER 5

1. On the construction history of the Great Mosque in pre-Ottoman times see Gaudefroy-Demombynes (1923), pp. 26–154.
2. Ibn Djubayr (1949–51), p. 107.
3. Burton (reprint, 1964), vol. 2, p. 295.
4. On empire-wide practice, see Barkan (1962–3), pp. 239–96.
5. Kuran (1987), pp. 268–86.
6. Necipoğlu Kafadar (1986), p. 99.
7. Barkan (1972, 1979), vol. 1, pp. 386–93. MD 10, p. 253, no. 391 (979/1571–2).
8. MD 26, p. 297, no. 864 (982/1574–5); MD 27, p. 166, no. 381 (983/1575–6).
9. Compare Barkan (1972, 1979), vol. 1, pp. 361–80.
10. MD 23, p. 5, no. 7 (981/1573–4).
11. MD 23, p. 297, no. 644 (981/1573–4).
12. Ca'fer Efendi (1987), p. 57. At this time, golden keys for the Prophet's mausoleum also were remitted to the Hejaz.
13. 'Zübdet al-Tewā-rikh' by Muṣṭafā b. Ibrāhīm. The relevant section has been translated by Howard Crane in 'Ca'fer Efendi (1987), p. 57.
14. MD 28, p. 96, no. 226 (984/1576–7).
15. Evliya Çelebi (1896–1938), vol. 9, p. 779.
16. Snouck Hurgronje (1931), p. 11 ff.
17. MD 31, p. 369, no. 820 (985/1577–8).
18. MD 6, p. 604, no. 1332 (972/1564–5); MD 21, p. 205, no. 488 (980/1572–3).
19. MM 7222. For an interpretation of this text see Faroqhi (1986b), pp. 111–26.
20. Barkan (1972, 1979), vol. 1, pp. 132–7, points out that slave labour was rarely employed on the Süleymāniye construction site.
21. MD 7, p. 343, no. 200 (975/1567–8).

22. Barkan (1972, 1979), vol. 2, p. 292.
23. MD 5, p. 545, no. 1493 (973/1565–6).
24. MD 10, p. 253, no. 391 (979/1571–2).
25. MD 7, p. 314, no. 899 (975/1567–8).
26. MD 58, p. 277, no. 706 (993/1585).
27. MD 6, p. 45, no. 91 (972/1564–5).
28. MD 14, p. 954 ff., no. 1416 (978/1570–1). For construction costs of the Süleymāniye, see Barkan (1972, 1979), vol. 1, p. 41; for those of the Sultan Aḥmed Mosque, vol. 2, p. 276.
29. Ca'fer Efendi (1987), p. 33 ff.
30. Necipoğlu Kafadar (1986), p. 99.
31. Ca'fer Efendi (1987), p. 58.
32. Necipoğlu Kafadar (1986), p. 107.
33. Ca'fer Efendi (1987), p. 55.
34. Necipoğlu Kafadar (1986), p. 111 ff.
35. Ḳuṭb al-Dīn Muḥammad b. Aḥmad al-Makkī, 'Al-i'lām be-'alām balad Allāh al-ḥarām', tr. by Bāḳī (?) 1006/1597–8. See Flügel (1865–7), vol. 2, p. 123 f., fol. 225B.
36. MD 53, p. 172, no. 502 (992/1584).
37. MD 7, p. 169, no. 442 (975/1567–8). See also Wüstenfeld (reprint, 1964), vol, p. 314 ff. MD 26, p. 217, no. 616 (982/1574–5).
38. Barkan (1972, 1979), vol. 1, map facing p. 1.
39. Evliya Çelebi (1896–1938), vol. 9, p. 782.
40. MD 14, p. 412, no. 579 (978/1570–1).
41. Ḳuṭb al-Dīn, tr. by Bāḳī, fol. 254A ff. See also Wüstenfeld (reprint, 1964), vol. 4, p. 319.
42. *Ibid.*, fol. 255A. Esin (1985) gives an account of events according to Ḳuṭb al-Dīn's chronicle.
43. MD 23, p. 2, no. 6 (981/1573–4).
44. For a discussion of building types and their possible meanings, see Necipoğlu Kafadar (1986).
45. MD 10, p. 253, no. 391 (979/1571–2).
46. MD 12, p. 438, no. 849 (979/1571–2).
47. MD 21, p. 231, no. 553 (980/1572–3).
48. MD 22, p. 313, no. 624 (981/1573–4). See also Wüstenfeld (reprint, 1964), vol. 4, p. 316.
49. MD 22, p. 296, no. 587 (981/1573–4).
50. MD 21, p. 231, no. 553 (980/1572–3), Burton (reprint, 1964), vol. 2, p. 264.
51. MD 33, p. 1, no. 1 (985/1577–8).
52. MD 28, p. 188, no. 438 (984/1576–7).
53. MD 31, p. 386, no. 858 (985/1577–8).
54. MD 6, p. 48, no. 95 (972/1564–5).
55. For the equivalent of the standard Ottoman *vuḳiye* or *okka* see Hinz (1955), p. 24.
56. MD 7, p. 332, no. 955 (975/1567–8).
57. MD 6, p. 44, no. 90 (972/1564–5).

58. MD 9, p. 63, no. 169 (977/1569–70).
59. Uzunçarşılı (1972), pp. 65–7.
60. MD 16, p. 211, no. 407 (979/1571–2).
61. MD 33, p. 39, no. 82 (985/1577–8); MD 30, p. 17, no. 41 (985/1577–8).
62. MD 7, p. 874, no. 2400 (976/1568–9); MD 69, p. 130, no. 262 (1001/1592–3).
63. MD 7, p. 313, no. 896 (975/1567–8); MD 7, p. 169, no. 442 (975/1567–8).
64. MD 73, p. 282, no. 646 (1003/1594–5).
65. MD 26, p. 242, no. 693 (982/1574–5).
66. MD 29, p. 143, no. 352 (985/1577–8); MD 64, p. 217, no. 557 (997/1588–9).
67. MD 96, p. 59, no. 309; p. 60, no. 311; p. 60, no. 312 (1089/1678–9); MZ 2, p. 43 (date probably 982/1574–5).
68. MD 92, p. 22, no. 106 (1067/1656–7); MD 89, p. 86, no. 213 (1053/1643–4).
69. The Süleymāniye and Sultan Ahmed Mosques are good examples of this type of spatial structure. However, in Mecca, the open space was soon filled up by the temporary shelters of poor people: Wüstenfeld (reprint, 1964), vol. 4, p. 321.
70. Sultan Murād himself owned a house in this area: MD 26, p. 241, no. 693 (980/1572–3).
71. MD 30, p. 5, no. 14 (985/1577–8).
72. MD 39, p. 229, no. 458 (988/1580–1).
73. MD 6, p. 213, no. 456 (972/1564–5).
74. MD 14, pp. 954–6, no. 1416 (978/1570–1).
75. MD 43, p. 184, no. 336 (988/1580–1).
76. MD 22, p. 273, no. 535 (981/1573–4).
77. MD 23, p. 84, no. 173 (981/1573–4).
78. MD 7, p. 343, no. 990 (975/1567–8).
79. MD 28, p. 14, no. 30 (984/1576–7); MD 96, p. 60, no. 312 (1089/1678–9).
80. MD 58, p. 275, no. 699 (993/1585).
81. MD 42, p. 44, no. 244, (989/1581).
82. MD 40, p. 88, no. 200 (probably 987/1579–80). A *ḳurna* is a wash basin used in baths.
83. MD 43, p. 264, no. 503 (989/1581).
84. MD 23, p. 112, no. 227 (981/1573–4).
85. MD 3, p. 368, no. 1088 (936/1555–6). It is possible that the expression *Ḥaram-ı sheríf* ('Noble Sanctuary') refers to the territory of Mecca as a whole. But more probably, the Great Mosque is intended. Who is meant by the 'deceased princess' also is open to debate. Süleymān's consort Roxolana and his daughter Mihr-ü-māh can be excluded, even though both established foundations in Mecca. Roxolana died in 1558, while Mihr-ü-māh survived until 1578.
86. MD 28, p. 1, no. 2 (984/1576–7).
87. MD 31, p. 334, no. 744 (985/1577–8).

88. MD 26, p. 241, no. 693 (980/1572–3).
89. MD 26, p. 241, no. 693 (980/1572–3).
90. Delumeau (1977), p. 175 ff.
91. MD 64, p. 16, no. 44 (996/1587–8).
92. MD 35, p. 80, no. 194 (986/1578–9).
93. MD 33, p. 169, no. 339 (985/1577–8).
94. Ca'fer Efendi (1987), p. 54.
95. *Ibid.*, p. 57.
96. Süheylī (Suheilî) Efendi, 'Tārīkh-i Mekke-i mükerrime', also called 'Risāle'. The manuscript used here belongs to the Vienna National Library, see Flügel (1865–7), vol. 2, p. 125. An overview of Meccan inundations is found on fols 66A ff. According to Burckhardt (1829), vol. 1, p. 244, the flood which caused the collapse of the Ka'aba took place in 1626. An excellent account of the rebuilding of the Ka'aba, largely based on Süheylī but using official documents as well, can be found in Eyyüb Ṣabrī (1301–6/1883–9), vol. 1, pp. 514–60. On page 560 ff. a number of relevant documents have been published. I am grateful to Dr Christoph Neumann for pointing this out to me. On the water pipes of Mecca there is also an extensive account by Eyyüb Ṣabrī, *ibid.*, p. 738 ff.
97. Süheylī, 'Risāle', fol. 30A.
98. *Ibid.*, fols 30B–31A.
99. *Ibid.*, fol. 31A.
100. *Ibid.*, fol. 31B. A *müftī* is an official who profers opinions on the conformity of judicial measures with Islamic law.
101. Probably this is the same Riḍwān Beg who from 1631 to his death in 1656 commanded the Cairo pilgrimage caravan. His fame rests on the town quarter he founded in Cairo, the Kaṣaba Riḍwān. On his biography see Holt (1959), pp. 221–30 and Raymond (1973–4), vol. 1, pp. 5–7, 264. Strangely enough Süheylī does not call him commander of the pilgrimage, but it is hard to believe that two Riḍwān Begs should have held responsible positions in Mecca at the same time. The rescript from Istanbul ordering the renovation of the Ka'aba has been published: Feridūn Beg (1275/1858–9), vol. 2, p. 101.

When translating the text cited here, we are confronted with the problem that the word '*hidjdjān*' can mean both 'noble' and 'dromedary'. The context permits both translations. But in any case, messengers were sent to Cairo, and I have thus avoided taking sides in this thorny little problem of interpretation.
102. Süheylī, 'Risāle', fol. 32B ff. Apparently there was a dispute between Istanbul and Cairo officials, reflected in the chronicle of Muṣṭafā Na'īmā, which however was composed almost seventy years after the events discussed here. In his very extensive account, Na'īmā fails to mention Riḍwān Beg by name, although an anonymous official is probably identical with the celebrated Mamluk commander. On the other hand, a certain Seyyid Meḥmed, elder and controller of the Prophet's descendants, is mentioned as the person in charge of the Ka'aba restoration by Na'īmā, while Suheylī makes no mention of him.

It is improbable that these discrepancies are due to lack of information or negligence, particularly on Na'īmā's part, since the latter in his official position as imperial chronicler possessed the means for collecting an extensive documentation. It is much more likely that tensions between the Mamluks and the central power, which in Na'īmā's time were very much on the agenda, induced the latter to play down Riḍwān Beg's participation. Compare Muṣṭafā Na'īmā (n.d.), vol. 3, p. 44 f. On the circumstances of Na'īmā's history-writing, see Thomas (1972).

103. *Ibid.*, fol. 37A.
104. *Ibid.*, fol. 35B.
105. *Ibid.*, fol. 42A.
106. On Sinān, see Saî Çelebi (1988). On Meḥmed Agha, Ca'fer Efendi (1987), pp. 33–76. Sinān's year of birth is disputed, see Kuran (1987), p. 24.
107. Süheylī, 'Risāle', fols 60–64A.
108. *Ibid.*, fol. 41A.
109. *Ibid.*, fol. 45B. For the equivalents, see Hinz (1955), supplement 1, 1, p. 16.
110. Süheylī, 'Risāle', fol. 53A.
111. *Ibid.*, fols 49A, 50A.
112. *Ibid.*, fol. 6A ff. For historical information see *EI*, article 'Ka'ba' (A.J. Wensick, J. Jomier).
113. See Uzunçarşılı (1948), pp. 120–6.
114. In the Ottoman context, the *muḥtesib* mentioned here was in charge of policing the market and often farmed his office. See the relevant article in *EI* by Robert Mantran.
115. Süheylī, 'Risāle', fol. 54A.
116. *Ibid.*, fols 45A, 51A, 55A, 59A and many other examples.
117. Ca'fer Efendi (1987), p. 67.
118. Süheylī, 'Risāle', fols 46B, 48A, 54B.
119. *Ibid.*, fol. 38A.
120. *Ibid.*, fols 58B–59A.
121. *Ibid.*, fol. 62B.
122. *Ibid.*, fols 59A, 60A. Necipoğlu Kafadar (1986), p. 100.
123. MD 27, p. 174, no. 397 (983/1575–6).
124. MD 43, p. 70, no. 143 (988/1580).
125. MD 58, p. 277, no. 706 (993/1585); M23, p. 317 (984/1576–7).
126. MD 60, p. 25, no. 59 (993/1585).
127. MD 60, p. 297, no. 674 (994/1585–6).
128. MD 62, p. 236, no. 527 (996/1587–8).
129. MD 62, p. 236, no. 527 (996/1587–8).
130. MD 64, p. 4, no. 14 (997/1588–9).
131. MD 64, p. 45, no. 124 (997/1588–9).
132. MD 73, p. 394, no. 862 (1003/1594–5).
133. MD 31, p. 83, no. 212 (985/1577–8); MZ 3, p. 265 (984/1576–7).
134. MD 73, p. 562, no. 1226 (1003/1594–5).
135. MD 58, p. 277, no. 706 (993/1585).

136. MD 73, p. 368, no. 806 (1003/1594–5).
137. MD 64, p. 205, no. 524 (997/1588–9).
138. MZ 3, p. 333 (984/1576–7).
139. MD 7, p. 273, no. 772 (975/1567–8).
140. MD 35, p. 97, no. 941 (986/1578–9).
141. MD 36, p. 295, no. 782 (987/1579–80).
142. MD 60, p. 297, no. 674 (994/1585–6).
143. Evliya Çelebi (1896–1938), vol. 9, p. 643; MD 60, p. 279, no. 643 (994/1585–6).
144. MD 76, p. 118, no. 304 (1016/1607–8).
145. MD 96, p. 110, no. 552; p 108, no. 542 (1089/1678–9).
146. MD 96, p. 107, no. 536 (1089/1678–9).
147. Evliya Çelebi (1896–1938), vol. 9, p. 656 f.
148. MD 73, p. 214, no. 500 (1003/1594–5).
149. MZ 3, p. 316 (984/1576–7); Evliya Çelebi (1896–1938), vol. 9, p. 656.
150. For an illustrated document to demonstrate the completion of a pilgrimage, see Esin (1984), p. 179 ff.
151. Meḥmed Yemīnī, 'Kitāb-ı Faḍā'il-i Mekke-i muʻazzama', manuscript in the Vienna National Library, see Flügel (1865–7), vol. 2, p. 125 f., where the text is described as anonymous.
152. As an example, compare Evliya Çelebi (1896–1938), vol. 9, p. 750.
153. Nayır (1975), pp. 135–7.

CHAPTER 6

There is a distinguished study by Naimur Rahman Farooqi, 'Mughal–Ottoman Relations: A Study of Political and Diplomatic Relations between Mughal India and the Ottoman Empire, 1556–1748', PhD dissertation, Madison, Wisconsin 1986, now also available as a book. I owe a great deal to this work, but unfortunately I was not able to see it in its published form.

1. Evliya Çelebi (1896–1938), vol. 9, p. 682, seems to feel that the interests of the pilgrims were much more important than the deference to be accorded the Sherifs as the descendants of the Prophet. A Sultan might therefore earn his respect if he aided the pilgrims at the expense of the Sherifs.
2. MD 6, p. 17, no. 39 (972/1564–5).
3. Düzdağ (1972), pp. 109–11.
4. MD 6, p. 17, no. 39 (972/1564–5).
5. Compare MD 7, p. 271, no. 748 (975/1567–8); MD 7, p. 241, no. 671 (975/1567–8).
6. Thus in several sixteenth-century Balkan towns the slaughter of sheep was forbidden, so as not to endanger the meat supply of Istanbul.
7. MD 30, p. 182, no. 428 (985/1577–8) concerns the pilgrims of Fez and Marrakesh.
8. MD 6, p. 313, no. 665 (972/1564–5).
9. Compare the introduction by Annette Beveridge to Gulbadan und

Beveridge (reprint, 1972), p. 69 f. See also Abū al-Faḍl (1898–1939), vol. 3, p. 570f.

10. On Djem, see the relevant article in *EI* by Halil Inalcık.
11. Alderson (1956), p. 125 f. for the fifteenth and eighteenth centuries mentions several princesses who went on the pilgrimage, but gives no information for the sixteenth and seventeenth centuries. On Shāh Sultan, see MD 19, p. 203 f, nos 419–21 (980/1572–3).
12. Ibn Djubayr (1949–51), p. 211 ff.
13. MD 6, p. 313, no. 665 (972/1564–5).
14. MD 16, p. 375, no. 657 (979/1571–2); MD 75, p. 165, no. 304 (1013/ 1604–5). We learn that the envoy of the ruler of Bukhara intended to visit Egypt, Mecca and Yemen on his way home.
15. Ottoman officials on pilgrimage enjoyed similar privileges: MD 19, p. 203 f., nos 419–21 (980/1572–3).
16. Badāōnī (reprint, 1973), vol. 1, p. 443.
17. Riazul-Islam (1971/1982), vol. 2, p. 295 ff. Farooqi (1986), p. 27 is of the same opinion.
18. Badāōnī (reprint, 1973), vol. 2, pp. 217, 246.
19. Evliya Çelebi (1896–1938), vol. 9, pp. 772–3.
20. Badāōnī (reprint, 1973), vol. 2, p. 246.
21. *Ibid.*, p. 321 f.
22. See the article 'Kāmrān' in *EI* by H. Beveridge.
23. MD 39, p. 238, no. 471 (988/1580–1). For an extensive interpretation of this visit and its ramifications see Farooqi (1986), p. 35.
24. MD 35, p. 292, no. 740 (986/1578–9); MD 43, p. 54, no. 107 (988/ 1580–1); MD 43, p. 184, no. 336 (988/1580–1); MD 58, p. 260, no. 659 (993/1585). According to Farooqi (1986), p. 36, Akbar after this dispute broke off all relations with the Ottoman Sultans.
25. This whole section is based upon Farooqi (1988), pp. 198–220, who also discusses previous work on the subject. According to Farooqi (1986), p. 251 Princess Gul-badan had to turn over a village to the Portuguese to receive her safe conduct.
26. MD 7, p. 410, no. 1180 (975/1567–8); p. 910, no. 2491 (976/1568–9); p. 913, no. 1502 (976/1568–9), see also: Kütükoğlu (1962), pp. 11, 200, Kütükoğlu (1975), pp. 128–45. MD 7, p. 725, no. 1988 (978/1570–1).
27. MD 6, p. 355, no. 761 (972/1564–5).
28. On Ottoman influence in the Persian Gulf region compare Orhonlu (1967), Mandaville (1970), Orhonlu (1970), Özbaran (1971), Özbaran (1972), Özbaran (1977).
29. MD 14, p. 385, no. 542 (978/1570–1).
30. MD 23, p. 163, no. 341 (981/1573–4).
31. Hammer-Purgstall (1963), vol. 4, p. 52 ff.
32. MD 27, p. 115, no. 271 (983/1575–6); MD 31, p. 45, no. 115 (985/ 1577–8).
33. MD 42, p. 175, no. 553 (988/1580–1).
34. MD 43, p. 114, no. 211 (988/1580–1); MD 42, p. 176, no. 554 (988/ 1580–1); p. 282, no. 868 (989/1581).
35. Evliya Çelebi (1896–1938), vol. 9, p. 702.

36. MD 7, p. 980, no. 2717 (976/1568–9).
37. MD 6, p. 313, no. 665 (972/1564–5).
38. MD 6, p. 17, no. 39 (972/1564–5).
39. Niewohner-Eberhard (1975), pp. 103–27. In this context, the regulations concerning the burial of Iranian Shi'is near the mausolea of the Caliph 'Alī and Imām Ḥusayn, issued by the Ottoman administration in 1564–5 and 1570–1, are also of interest. Before the Ottoman conquest of Iraq it had apparently been customary to bury certain Shi'is in the courtyards of the two sanctuaries; this was prohibited by the Ottoman administration. The argument in favour of this new ruling was religious and not political: supposedly ordinary mortals could never have acquired sufficient merit to justify burial in the proximity of the great saints of Islam. Outside of the sanctuary court, burials remained permissible. But only important personalities, such as members of the Shah's family, were conceded such a privilege; in such cases, the relatives of the deceased could acquire a piece of land suitable for the construction of a mausoleum (MD 6, p. 17, no. 39). However, cemeteries and mausolea were to be located at a considerable distance from the sanctuaries (MD 12, p. 217, no. 450).
40. MD 30, p. 191, no. 449 (985/1577–8).
41. MD 26, p. 241, no. 693 (980/1572–3).
42. MD 24, p. 44, no. 124 (981/1573–4).
43. MD 24, p. 88, no. 234 (981/1573–4).
44. MD 24, p. 44, no. 124 (981/1573–4).
45. Riazul-Islam (1971/1982), vol. 2, p. 310 f. On Transoxania see Ott (1974). Sometimes Iranian pilgrims to Mecca also used the steppe route to the Black Sea. Compare Inalcık (1979–80), p. 464.
46. MD 7, p. 240, no. 667 (975/1567–8); p. 295, no. 838 (975/1567–8).
47. MD 7, p. 241, no. 671 (975/1567–8).
48. MD 27, p. 56, no. 142 (983/1575–6).
49. MD 24, p. 142, no. 389 (987/1579–80). On the Nogay, see Inalcık (1948), pp. 349–402, 360. See also Kurat (1966), *passim*. Inalcık (1948) also contains background information on Ottoman–Tatar relations. On the Nogay, consult also Benningsen, Lemercier-Quelquejay (1976), pp. 203–36. Inalcık assumes that in sixteenth-century Istanbul there was a well-developed 'northern policy', while Benningsen and Lemercier-Quelquejay assume that the Ottoman Sultans were little interested in Kazan and the Nogays. For a more recent restatement of Inalcık's opinions, see Inalcık (1979–80), p. 458 f.
50. Inalcık (1948), p. 368 f.
51. Inalcık (*ibid.*, pp. 391–5) discusses the preparations for a second Astrakhan campaign, which were broken off due to a disagreement with the Tatars. MD 7, p. 984, no. 2722 (about 976/1568–9) is an official letter of the Sultan to the Khan, which advocates a campaign against Astrakhan. The letter insists on the need to keep open the pilgrimage routes. Compare also MD 7, p. 295, no. 838 (975/1568–9). For the interpretation of this important text, see Inalcık (1948), p. 373.
52. MD 7, p. 271, no. 748 (975/1567–8).
53. MD 49, p. 72, no. 250 (991/1583).

54. MD 31, p. 192, no. 431 (985/1577–8).
55. On caravans traversing North Africa, see Raymond (1973–4), vol. 2, p. 470 ff.
56. Compare Hess (1978), p. 96 f.
57. MD 30, p. 182, no. 428 (985/1577–8).
58. MD 30, p. 219, no. 505 (985/1577–8). A safe conduct for all Moroccan pilgrims is found on p. 182 of the same register (no. 428).
59. MD 27, p. 56, no. 142 (983/1575–6).
60. Niewohner-Eberhard (1975), p. 116.
61. Compare MD 6, p. 17, no. 39 (972/1564–5). Niewohner-Eberhard (1975), p. 116.

CHAPTER 7

1. See the article 'Mamlūk' in *EI* by P.M. Holt.
2. Mughul (1965), p. 46.
3. Wüstenfeld (reprint, 1964), vol. 4, p. 300. Mughul (1965), p. 39.
4. Uzunçarşılı (1972), p. 17.
5. *Ibid.*, p. 26. Orhonlu (1974), p. 129 ff.
6. MD 73, p. 12, no. 27 (1003/1594–5).
7. Fleischer (1986), pp. 180, 184–5.
8. MD 23, p. 286, no. 615 (981/1575–6); MD 23, p. 287, no. 616 (981/1575–6).
9. Uzunçarşılı (1972), p. 19 ff.
10. MD 58, p. 201, no. 527 (993/1585).
11. Evliya Çelebi (1896–1938), vol. 9, p. 679.
12. Uzunçarşılı (1972), p. 87.
13. MD 27, p. 403, no. 965 (983/1575–6).
14. MD 75, p. 308, no. 645 (1013/1604–5).
15. MD 14, p. 440, no. 623 (987/1570–1); MD 7, p. 215, no. 595 (975/1567–8).
16. MD 39, p. 51, no. 119 (987/1579–80).
17. Uzunçarşılı (1965), pp. 95–100.
18. Barkan (1980), p. 316.
19. Faroqhi (1973), p. 211.
20. MD 64, p. 11, no. 30 (996/1587–8).
21. MD 91, p. 141, no. 447 (1056/1646–7).
22. MD 58, p. 279, no. 709 (993/1585).
23. MD 60, p. 294, no. 681 (994/1585–6).
24. MD 9, p. 80, no. 210 (972/1564–5).
25. MD 31, p. 245, no. 539 (985/1577–8).
26. MD 58, p. 23, no. 69 (993/1585).
27. MD 24, p. 119, no. 328 (981/1573–4).
28. MD 29, p. 224, no. 513 (984/1576–7).
29. MD 7, p. 81, no. 219 (975/1567–8).
30. MD 92, p. 51, no. 227 (1068/1657–8).
31. MD 17, p. 8, no. 13 (979/1571–2).

32. Uzunçarşılı (1972), p. 23.
33. Peçevî (1980), vol. 1, p. 484 f.
34. MD 27, p. 20, no. 60 (983/1575–6).
35. Braudel (1966), vol. 1, p. 495 ff.
36. Compare Faroqhi (forthcoming).
37. Inalcık (1979–80), pp. 1–66.
38. Arasaratnam (1986), p. 268 f.
39. Das Gupta (1988), p. 110 f.
40. Aghassian, Kévonian (1988), p. 166.
41. Serjeant (1988a), p. 72.
42. Farooqi (1986), pp. 205–9.
43. Subrahmanyam (1988), pp. 503–30.
44. Subrahmanyam (1988), p. 509.
45. Das Gupta (1988), p. 109 f.
46. Serjeant (1988b), p. 149 f.
47. Bouchon (1988), p. 53.
48. Subrahmanyam (1988), p. 510 ff.
49. Thomaz (1988), p. 42.
50. Arasaratnam (1986), p. 294 ff.
51. Sahillioğlu (1978), p. 13 f.
52. Masters (1988), p. 192.
53. The expression 'provisionism' for one of the basic components of Ottoman economic thinking was employed by Mehmet Genç at a lecture before the Congress for Turkish Social and Economic History, Munich, 1986. On 'provisionism' in late eighteenth-century France compare Vovelle (1980), p. 228 ff.
54. On the interpretation of this text see Inalcık (1970), pp. 207–18 and Masters (1988), p. 192 ff.
55. MD 47, p. 122, no. 308 (990/1582); MD 27, p. 20, no. 60 (983/1575).
56. MD 47, p. 123, no. 309 (990/1582).
57. MD 67, p. 111, no. 298 (999/1590–1).
58. MD 67, p. 113, no. 305 (999/1590–1).
59. Braudel (1966), vol. 1, pp. 383–421. On taxes collected in Yemeni ports, compare Sahillioğlu (1985), pp. 287–319.
60. MD 67, p. 131, no. 352 (999/1590–1).
61. Masters (1988), p. 194.
62. MD 70, p. 68, no. 141 (1001/1592–3).
63. Peçevî (1980), vol. 1, p. 484 f.
64. Subrahmanyam (1988), p. 505.
65. MD 6, p. 122, no. 256 (972/1564–5).
66. Shaw (1962), p. 253.
67. MZ 3, p. 179 (984/1576–7).
68. Shaw (1962), p. 261 ff.
69. Ibn Djubayr (1949–51), p. 79 f., Burton, vol. 1 (reprint, 1964), p. 209.
70. MD 6, p. 128, no. 269 (972/1564–5).
71. MM 5310 (1015–16/1606–8).
72. MD 58, p. 158, no. 418 (993/1585).

73. Faroqhi (forthcoming) contains a further discussion of Red Sea transportation.
74. MD 30, p. 299, no. 691 (985/1577–8).
75. Arasaratnam (1988), p. 534.
76. Evliya Çelebi (1896–1938), vol. 9, p. 716.
77. *Ibid.*, p. 966.
78. On sixteenth-century Muzayrib compare Bakhit (1982), p. 113. MD 88, p. 52, no. 123 (1047/1637–8). According to our text, buyer and seller both had to pay 15 *akče* for goods worth 1 *ghurush*, or a total of 30 *akče*. According to Sahillioğlu (1964), p. 229, in 1637–8 the Galata exchange rate was 120 *akče* to 1 *riyāl ghurush*. The equivalent for Damascus is unknown, so that we have used the Galata exchange rate: 30:120 equals 25 per cent.
79. Ochsenwald (1980), p. 22.
80. Hibri (1975), pp. 111–28; (1976), pp. 55–72; (1978), pp. 147–62. See particularly (1975), p. 125.
81. Evliya Çelebi (1896–1938), vol. 9, p. 554.
82. *Ibid.*, p. 570.
83. Mehemmed Edib (1825), p. 122.
84. Evliya Çelebi (1896–1938), vol. 9, pp. 779, 782. He also notes that Meccan women performed few household duties (p. 782).
85. *Ibid.*, p. 776.
86. *Ibid.*, p. 712.
87. *Ibid.*, p. 713.
88. *Ibid.*, p. 714 f.
89. Vryonis (1981), pp. 196–226.
90. Evliya Çelebi (1896–1938), vol. 9, p. 186. Mehlan (1938), pp. 10–49.
91. Evliya Çelebi (1896–1938), vol. 10, p. 612.
92. Evliya Çelebi (1896–1938), vol. 9, p. 713.
93. *Ibid.*, p. 713. Kissling (1975), pp. 342–55 and Hattox (1985).
94. Hattox (1985), p. 102 and Evliya Çelebi (1896–1938), vol. 9, p. 796.
95. Rogers, Ward (1988), p. 140 ff.
96. Evliya Çelebi (1896–1938), vol. 10, p. 445.
97. Rogers, Ward (1988), p. 140.
98. Evliya Çelebi (1896–1938), vol. 9, p. 776.
99. Pearson (1988), p. 462.
100. For the problems of foreign trade in general, compare Curtin (1984), Mehta (1974), Habib (1990).

CONCLUSION

1. A stimulating discussion of the problems touched upon here is İslamoğlu-İnan (1987), pp. 1–26.
2. This section owes a good deal to Said (1979). When reading Said's book, however, one may easily come to the conclusion that racism and ethnocentrism are inherent characteristics of European and American studies on 'the Orient', and that all attempts to escape this paradigm are

doomed in advance. The present author is less pessimistic in her assumptions, whether with justification or not is hard to judge at present. But if Said's assessment is totally correct, European/American historians and philologists dealing with the Middle East, who do not wish to comport themselves as racists and ethnocentrists, would be well advised to change their area of specialization. In any case, Said's work is a necessary corrective against naive assumptions about steadily progressing and 'value-free' scholarship.

3. This section owes a great deal to discussions with Halil Berktay.
4. Strangely enough, quite a few Turkish scholars, particularly of the older generation, seem to share these views. Compare Uzunçarşılı (1948), still a basic work of reference.
5. As one among many studies based on these assumptions, see Ward and Rustow (eds.) (1964).
6. An admittedly extreme example of this tendency is Romano (1980), pp. 22–75. See also Weber (1976).
7. For a coherent statement of these views, see Lewis (1968), p. 28. Lewis's statements are based on the work of Halil Inalcık, Fuat Köprülü and Sabri Ülgener.
8. I am grateful to Engin Akarlı for a stimulating discussion of these matters. See also Labrousse *et alii* (1970), vol. 2, particularly pp. 119–60 and 567–600; these sections are the work of Pierre Goubert. On the *ancien régime* in the Ottoman Empire see Cezar (1986).
9. On these issues compare Kortepeter (1979), pp. 229–46.
10. Rutter (1928) provides a vivid description of the transition from Sherifian to Sa'udi rule in Mecca.
11. Hodgson (1974), vol. 1, pp. 365–92.
12. Ochsenwald (1984) defends the view that in the Hejaz 'religion' determined 'politics'. However he strictly limits his claims to the seventy-odd years covered by his study.
13. For a recent treatment of this problem in a French context, compare Braudel (1986).
14. Shaw (1976–7), vol. 2, pp. 226–30.
15. Genç, 49/4 (1984), pp. 52–61, 50/5 (1984), pp. 86–93.
16. Braudel (1979), vol. 2, pp. 402–16. On the economic importance of the pilgrimage routes compare also Raymond (1985), p. 48.
17. Erim (1984, 1991). I thank the author for allowing me to read her unpublished dissertation.
18. Hattox (1985), Faroqhi (1986) (a).
19. Raymond (1973–4), vol. 1, pp. 143–6.
20. Farooqi (1988), pp. 198–220.
21. Inalcık (1948), pp. 349–402.
22. Dengler (1978), pp. 229–44; Bates (1978), pp. 245–60; Peirce (1988), pp. 43–82.
23. Uzunçarşılı (1945), p. 181 ff.
24. See Lapidus (1984), pp. 77 f. and 131. The author discusses the Mamluk period in Egypt and Syria; he does not, however, conclude that

the Mamluk rulers had no need for legitimation beyond the claim that
their rule averted anarchy.
25. Abou-El-Haj (1974), pp. 131–7.
26. Aktepe (1958), p. 41 ff.
27. Göçek (1987).
28. Kreutel (1948–52); Faroqhi (1991).

Bibliography

ARCHIVAL SOURCES

The documentation used in this book has been taken largely from the Başbakanlık Arşivi in Istanbul, also known as the Osmanlı Arşivi. The principal sections used were the Mühimme Defterleri (Registers of Important Affairs) and Maliyeden Müdevver ('Transferred from the Financial Office'). In the MDs all sultanic rescripts issued by the Sultan's Council (*diwān-ı humāyūn*) were entered; the members of this council were the viziers, the head of the Finance Office (*defterdār*) and the Chancellor (*nishāndjı*). The series of extant registers begins in the middle of the sixteenth century, although a few isolated specimens have been preserved from the first half of the century as well. These registers are richest for the late sixteenth and early seventeenth centuries, although even within this period, certain years are amply documented and the records of others must have been lost.

About 800 documents from the MDs were informative enough to merit a closer analysis. Almost all this material relates to the period 1565 to 1605. Remarkably enough, the restoration projects of Aḥmed I (reigned 1603–17) and Murād III (reigned 1623–40), which must have been the subject of ample correspondence, are passed over in almost total silence. Presumably from the seventeenth century onwards, more and more special purpose registers were created. Public construction was in all probability documented in a separate series, which later either was lost or may yet emerge in the course of future cataloguing. But even as things stand now, the documentation

214

is so ample that only a small part of the rescripts consulted could be mentioned in the notes.

Among the financial records of Maliyeden Müdevver, about 50 registers yielded usable data for our purposes. Most useful were the Syrian and Egyptian provincial accounts, also known as 'Budgets'. The Egyptian sources all concern the years around 1600, while the Syrian accounts are distributed over the entire seventeenth century. In both instances the accounts record only the money paid out for the 'official' sector of the caravan, that is for officers and men in addition to horses, camels and ammunition. Beduin subsidies have also been included. We also find several documents concerning foundations whose aim it was to succour the inhabitants of the Holy Cities. There is additional information on these foundations in the tax registers of the sixteenth century (section Tapu Tahrir of the Başbakanlık Arşivi in Istanbul). The foundation descriptions contained in these registers include information on beneficiaries, and the 1546 register of Istanbul foundations published by Barkan and Ayverdi (Istanbul, 1970) is especially rich in this respect.

The *ḳāḍī* registers of Balkan and Anatolian cities, by contrast, contain few court cases directly relevant to the pilgrimage. The court registers of Cairo and Damascus contain large quantities of hitherto unused information; unfortunately nothing is known of the where-abouts of the registers of Mecca and Medina.

Başbakanlık Arşivi, Mühimme Defterleri (MD): 3, 5, 6, 7, 9, 10, 12, 14, 16, 17, 18, 19, 21, 22, 23, 24, 26, 27, 28, 29, 30, 31, 33, 34, 35, 36, 39, 40, 42, 43, 46, 47, 48, 49, 51, 52, 53, 55, 58, 60, 61, 62, 64, 67, 68, 69, 70, 71, 73, 74, 75, 76, 78, 80, 81, 82, 85, 86, 88, 89, 90, 91, 92, 93, 94, 95, 96

Başbakanlık Arşivi, Mühimme Zeyli (MZ): 1, 2, 3, 4, 5, 6, 9

Başbakanlık Arşivi, Maliyeden Müdevver (MM): 7056, 5671, 5672, 5162, 5658, 5672, 3651, 6005, 5592, 1806, 7603, 4108, 2521, 1653, 1003, 2520, 5568, 880, 2916, 1308, 1286, 1290, 4895, 926, 927, 872, 86, 876, 2525, 932, 1647, 2530, 1644, 2459, 2535, 4345, 1645, 4345, 956, 2394, 2396, 952, 943, 1011, 4901, 941, 1007, 4475, 875, 4901, 241

Ḳāḍīregister, Çorum Belediye Kütüphanesi, Çorum: Register No 1741–2 (Çorum)

PRIMARY SOURCES

['Abd al-Karīm], *The Memoirs of Khojeh Abdulkurreem, A Cashmerian of Distinction*, trans. by Francis Gladwin (London, 1793)

[Abū al-Faḍl], *The Akbar Nama of Abu-l-Fazl*, trans. by Henry Beveridge, Bibliotheca Indica, 3 vols (Calcutta, 1898–1939)

Muṣṭafā 'Ālī's *Description of Cairo of 1599, Text, Transliteration, Translation, Notes*, trans. and ed. by Andreas Tietze, Österr. Akademie der Wissenschaften, Philosophisch-hist. Klasse, Denkschriften, vol. 120, Forschungen zur islamischen Philologie und Kulturgeschichte vol. V (Vienna, 1975)

Ali Bey [Domingo Badia y Leblich], *Voyages d'Ali Bey El-Abbasi en Afrique et en Asie pendant les années 1803–1807*, 2 vols (Paris, 1814)

Anonymous author, *Manakıb-ı Hacı Bektâş-ı Veli 'Vilâyet-nâme'*, ed. by Abdülbaki Gölpınarlı (Istanbul, 1958)

—— 'A description of the yeerely voyage or pilgrimage of the Mahumitans, Turkes and Moores unto Mecca in Arabia', in *The Principal Navigations, Voyages, Traffiques and Discoveries of the English Nation*, ed. by Richard Hakluyt, 12 vols (reprint, Glasgow, 1901), vol. 5, pp. 329–65

—— *Das Vilâyet-nâme des Hâdschim Sultan, Eine türkische Heiligenlegende*, ed. and trans. by Rudolf Tschudi (Berlin, 1914)

Mohamed Arkoun, Ezzedine Guellouz, Abdelaziz Frikha, *Pèlerinage à la Mecque* (Lausanne, Paris and Tunis, 1977)

'Abdu-l-qādir Ibni Mulūk Shāh, called al-Badāōnī, *Muntakhabuttawārīkh*, trans. by George S.A. Ranking *et al.*, A.D. Oriental Series, 3 vols., (reprint, Delhi, 1973)

Ömer Lütfi Barkan, '933–934 (M 1527–1528) Malî Yılına Ait bir Bütçe Örneği', *IFM*, 15, 1–4 (1953–4), 251–329

—— '1079–1080 (1669–1670) Malî Yılına Ait bir Osmanlı Bütçesi ve Ekleri', *IFM*, 17, 1–4 (1955–6), 225–303

—— 974–975 (M 1567–1568) Malî Yılına Ait bır Osmanlı Bütçesi', *IFM*, 19, 1–4 (1957–8), 277–332

—— '1070–1071 (1660–1661) Tarihi Osmanlı Bütçesi ve bir Mukayese', *IFM*, 17 (1955–6), 304–47

—— '954–955 (1547–1548) Malî Yılına Ait bir Osmanlı Bütçesi', *IFM*, 19 (1957–8), 219–76

—— 'Istanbul Saraylarına ait Muhasebe Defterleri', *Belgeler, Türk Tarih Belgeleri Dergisi*, IX, 13 (1979), 1–380: 'Defter-i müsevvedât-ı in'âm ve tasaddukaat ve teşrifât ve irsâliyât ve adet ve nukeriye ve gayruhu vâcib-i sene tis'a ve tis'a mie (909), (26.VI. 1503–13. VI. 1504), p. 296 ff.

Ömer Lütfi Barkan, Ekrem Hakkı Ayverdi, *Istanbul Vakıfları Tahrîr Defteri, 953 (1546) Târîhli*, Istanbul Fetih Cemiyeti Istanbul Enstitüsü 61 (Istanbul, 1970)

John Lewis Burckhardt, *Travels to Syria and the Holy Land* (London, 1822)

—— *Travels in Arabia, Comprehending an Account of those Territories in Hedjaz which the Mohammedans regard as Sacred*, 2 vols. (London, 1829)

Richard Burton, *Personal Narrative of a Pilgrimage to al-Madinah & Mecca*, 2 vols. (reprint, New York, 1964)

[Ogier Ghiselin von Busbeck], *Vier Briefe aus der Türkei von Oghier Ghiselin von Busbeck*, trans. and comm. by Wolfram von den Steinen (Erlangen, 1926)

[Ca'fer Efendi], *Risāle-i Mi'māriyye, An Early Seventeenth-Century Treatise on Architecture*, ed. by Howard Crane (Leiden, 1987)

Caïd ben Chérif, *Aux villes saintes de l'Islam* (Paris, 1919)

el-Hadj Nacir ed dine E. Dinet and el-Hadj Sliman ben Ibrahim Baâmer, *Le pèlerinage de la Maison sacrée d'Allah*, 2 vols (Paris, 1962)

'Abd al-Kādir al-Djazarī, *Durar al-fawā'id al-munazzama fī akhbār alhādjdj ve tarīk Makka al-mu'azzama*, (Mecca, 1384/1964–5)

Charles Doughty, *Travels in Arabia Deserta*, introduced by T.E. Lawrence, 2 vols. (reprint, New York, 1979)

M. Ertuğrul Düzdağ, *Şeyhülislâm Ebusuûd Efendi Fetvaları Işığında 16. Asır Türk Hayatı* (Istanbul, 1972)

Esat Efendi, introduced by Yavuz Ercan, '(Her yıl gelenek haline gelmiş olan) Sürre-i Hümayun Gönderme Töreni', *Tarih ve Toplum*, 3 (1985), 377–80

Evliya Çelebi, *Seyahatnamesi*, 10 vols. (Istanbul, 1314/1896–1938)

—— *Im Reiche des Goldenen Apfels, Des türkischen Weltenbummlers Evliya Çelebi denkwürdige Reise in das Giaurenland und in die Stadt und Festung Wien, anno 1665*, trans. and introduced by Richard Kreutel (Graz, Vienna and Cologne, 1957)

Ferīdūn Beg, *Medjmū'a-ı münshe'at-ı selātīn*, 2 vols. (Istanbul, 1275/1858–9)

Giovanni Finati, *Narrative of the Life and Adventures of Giovanni Finati, Native of Ferrara*, trans. and ed. by William John Banks Esq., 2 vols. (London, 1830)

[Gul-badan Begam], *The History of Humāyūn (Humāyūn-nāma) by Gulbadan begam (Princess Rose-body)*, trans. and introduced by Annette S. Beveridge (reprint, Delhi, 1972)

Abū'l-Hasan'Alī b. Abī Bakr al-Harawī, *Guide des lieux du pèlerinage*, trans. by Janine Sourdel-Thomime (Damascus, 1957)

Hassan Mohammed El-Hawary and Gaston Wiet, *Matériaux pour un Corpus Inscriptionum Arabicarum, Quatrième partie: Arabie, Inscriptions et Monuments de la Mecque, Haram et Ka'ba*, vol. 1, fasc. 1, revised by Nikita Elisséef (Cairo, 1985)

Colin Heywood, 'The Red Sea Trade and Ottoman Wakf Support for the Population of Mecca and Medina in the Later Seventeenth Century', in *La vie sociale dans les provinces arabes à l'époque ottomane*, ed. by Abdeljelil Temimi, 3 vols (Zaghouan, 1988), vol. 3, pp. 165–84

['Abd al-Raḥmān Ḥibrī], 'Menasik-i mesalik', ed. by Sevim Ilgürel, *Tarih Enstitüsü Dergisi*, 6 (1975), 111–28, *Tarih Dergisi*, 30 (1976), 55–72, *Tarih Dergisi*, 31 (1978), 147–62

[Ibn 'Abd Rabbih], 'A Description of the Two Sanctuaries of Islam by Ibn 'Abd Rabbihi (†940)', trans. and comm. by Muḥammad Shafī', in *'Adjabnāme, A Volume of Oriental Studies presented to Edward G. Browne*, ed. by T.W. Arnold and Reynold A. Nicholson (reprint, Amsterdam, 1973), pp. 416–38

[Ibn Djubayr], *Les voyages d'Ibn Jobair*, trans. by Maurice Gaudefroy-Demombynes (Paris, 1949–51)

[Ibn Djubayr], *The Travels of Ibn Jubayr*, trans. by R.C. Broadhurst (London, 1952)

[Ibn Malīḥ], *Labsal dessen, der bei Tag und bei Nacht reist, Ibn Mālīḥs (sic) Uns as-sārī was-sārib, Ein marokkanisches Pilgerbuch des frühen 17. Jahrhunderts*, trans. and comm. by Sabine Schupp, Islamkundliche Untersuchungen, vol. 106 (Berlin, 1985)

Ibn Ṭūlūn and Ibn Ǧum'a, *Les gouverneurs de Damas sous les Mamlouks et les premiers Ottomans (658–1156/1260–1744)*, trans. by Henri Laoust (Damascus, 1952)

Cassim Izzeddine, *Organisation et réformes sanitaires au Hedjaz et le Pèlerinage de 1329 (1911–12)* (Constantinople, 1913)

—— *Les epidémies de choléra au Hedjaz* (Constantinople, 1918)

Kātib Čelebi, *Djihānnumā* (Istanbul, 1145/1732)

—— *Fedhleke*, 2 vols. (Istanbul, 1286–7/1869–71)

H. Kazem Zadeh, 'Relation d'un pèlerinage à la Mecque en 1910–11', *Revue du monde musulman*, 6, 19 (1912), 144–227

T.C. Keane (Hajj Mohammed Amin), *Six Months in Mecca: An Account of the Mohammedan Pilgrimage to Meccah, Recently Accomplished by an Englishman Professing Mohammedanism* (London, 1881)

Ḳuṭb al-Dīn Muḥammad b. Aḥmad al-Makkī, 'Al-i'lām be-'alām balad Allāh al-ḥarām', trans. by Bāḳī (?) in 1006/1597–8. Compare Gustav Flügel, *Die arabischen, persischen und türkischen Handschriften der kaiserlich-königlichen Hofbibliothek zu Wien*, 3 vols. (Vienna, 1865–7), vol. 2, p. 123 f, No. 895

T.E. Lawrence, *Seven Pillars of Wisdom, a Triumph* (London and Toronto, 1935)

Vincent le Blanc, *Les voyages fameux du Sieur Vincent le Blanc, marseillois* (Paris, 1658)

Heinrich von Maltzan, *Meine Wallfahrt nach Mekka*, ed. by Gernot Giertz (reprint, Tübingen, 1982)

Henry Maundrell, *A Journey from Aleppo to Jerusalem in 1697*, introduced by David Howell (reprint, Beirut, 1963)

El-Hadj Mehemmed Edib ben Mehemmed, derviche, 'Itineraire de Constantinople à la Mecque (Extrait de l'ouvrage turc intitulé Kitab Menassik el-Hadj), trans. by M. Bianchi, in *Recueil de Mémoires de la Société de Géographie* (Paris, 1825), pp. 81–169

'Abd al-Ghānī al-Nābulsī, *Al-ḥaḳīḳa wa'l-madjāz fī'l-riḥla ilā bilād al-Shām wa Miṣr* (Cairo, 1986)

Na'īmā, *Tarīkh-i Na'īmā*, 6 vols. (n.p. [Istanbul], n.d.)

[Naṣīr-i Khosraw], *Sefernameh, Le voyage de Nassiri Khosrau, en Syrie, en Palestine, en Egypte, en Arabie et en Perse*, trans. by Charles Schefer (Paris, 1881)

Gérard de Nerval, *Reise in den Orient*, ed. by Norbert Miller and Friedhelm Kemp, trans. by Anjuta Aigner-Dünnwald, introduced by Christoph Kunze (Munich, 1986)

Carsten Niebuhr, *Reisebeschreibung nach Arabien und andern umliegenden Ländern* (Copenhagen, 1772)

—— *Description de l'Arabie, faite sur des observations propres et des airs recueillis dans les lieux mêmes* (Amsterdam, 1774–80)

Mouradgea d'Ohsson, *Tableau général de l'Empire Ottoman, divisée en deux parties, Dont l'une comprend la Législation Mahometane; l'autre l'Histoire de l'Empire Ottoman*, 7 vols. (Paris, 1787–1824)

Halit Ongan, *Ankara'nın İki Numaralı Şer'iye Sicili*, Türk Tarih Kurumu Yayınları, 14, 4 (Ankara, 1974)

Peçevî Ibrahim Efendi, *Tarîh-i Peçevî*, introduced by Fahri Ç. Derin and Vahit Çabuk, 2 vols. (reprint, Istanbul, 1980)

[Joseph Pitts], 'An Account by Joseph Pitts of his Journey from Algiers to Mecca and Medina and back', in *The Red Sea and Adjacent Countries at the Close of the Seventeenth Century, as described by Joseph Pitts, William Daniel and Charles Jacques Poncet*, ed. by Sir William Foster CIE (London, 1949), pp. 3–49

H. St John [Abdullah] Philby, *Forty Years in the Wilderness* (London, 1957)

Richard Pococke, *A Description of the East and Some Other Countries*, 2 (London, 1743), vol. 1 *Observations on Egypt*

Mehmed Rāshid, *Tārīkh-i Rāshid*, 5 vols. (Istanbul, 1282/1865–6)

Riazul-Islam, *A Calendar of Documents on Indo–Persian Relations (1500–1750)*, 2 vols. (Teheran and Karachi, 1971, 1982)

Ibrāhīm Rifa'at Pascha, *Mir'at al-Ḥaramayn*, 2 vols. (Cairo, 1344/ 1925)

Léon Roches, *Trente-deux ans à travers l'Islam (1832–1864)*, 2 vols. (Paris, 1887), vol. 2 *Mission à La Mecque, Le maréchal Bugeaud en Afrique*

Eldon Rutter, *The Holy Cities of Arabia*, 2 vols. (London, 1928)

Eyyüb Ṣabrī, *Mir'at al-Ḥarmeyn*, 3 vols. (Istanbul, 1301–6/1883–9)

Sa'd al-Dīn, *Tādj al-tewārīkh* (Istanbul, 1279/1862–3)

Saî Çelebi, *Tezkiretü'l Bünyan, Mimar Sinan'ın Kendi Ağzından Hayat ve Eserleri*, ed. by Sadık Erdem (Istanbul, 1988)

Ulrich Jasper Seetzen, *Reisen durch Syrien, Palästina, Phönicien, die Transjordan-Länder, Arabia Petraea und Unter-Aegypten*, ed. and comm. by Fr. Kruse (Berlin, 1854)

Stanford Shaw, *The Budget of Ottoman Egypt 1005–1006/1596–97)* (The Hague and Paris, 1968)

Azmat Sheikh, *The Holy Mecca and Medina – Saudi Arabia* (Lahore, 1980)

Silaḥdār Fındıḳlılı Meḥmed Agha, *Silaḥdār Tārīkhi*, ed. by Ahmed Refik, 2 vols. (Istanbul, 1928)

C. Snouck Hurgronje, *Mekka in the Latter Part of the 19th Century, Daily Life, Customs and Learning, The Moslims of the Eastern Archipelago*, trans. by J.H. Monahan (London and Leiden, 1931)

Süheylī (Suheilî) Efendi, 'Tārīkh-i Mekke-i mükerrime', see Flügel, *Handschriften Wien*, vol. 2, p. 125, No. 896

Sultan Jahan Begam, The Nawab, *The Story of a Pilgrimage to Hijaz* (Calcutta, 1909)

Ṭashköprüzāde, *Eš-Šaqâ'iq en-no'mânijje von Ṭašköprüzâde, enthaltend die Biographien der türkischen und im osmanischen Reiche wirkenden Gelehrten, Derwisch-Scheihs und Ärzte von der Regierung Sultan Otmān's bis zu der Sülaimân's des Grossen*, trans. and comm. by Osman Rescher (Istanbul, 1927)

Jean Thévenot, *Voyage du Levant*, ed. and introduced by Stéphane Yérasimos (Paris, 1980)

Abdel Magid Turki, Hadj Rabah Souami, *Récits de pèlerinage à la Mecque, Étude analytique, Journal d'un pélerin*, introduced by Lakhdar Souami (Paris, 1979)

Feridun Nafız Uzluk, *Fatih Devrinde Karaman Eyâleti Vakıfları Fihristi, Tapu ve Kadastro Umum Müdürlüğü Arşivindeki Deftere Göre*, Vakıflar Umum Müdürlüğü Neşriyatı (Ankara, 1958)

Ludovico di Varthéma, *The Travels of Ludovico di Varthéma*, ed. by

John Winter Jones, Georges Percy Badger, Hakluyt Society, I. Series No. XXXII (New York, 1863)

A[rchibald] J.B. Wavell, *A Modern Pilgrim in Mecca and a Siege in Sanaa* (London, 1912)

Johann Wild, *Reysbeschreibung eines gefangenen Christen Anno 1604*, trans. and introduced by Georg A. Narciss and Karl Teply (Stuttgart, 1964)

Meḥmed Yemīnī, 'Kitāb-ı Faḍā'il-i Mekke-i mu'aẓẓama', see Flügel, *Handschriften Wien*, vol. 2, p. 125 f., No. 897, who describes this work as anonymous.

SECONDARY SOURCES
(MECCA, MEDINA, THE PILGRIMAGE)

A. 'Ankawi, 'The Pilgrimage to Mecca in Mamluk Times', *Arabian Studies*, I (1974), 146–70.

C.F. Beckingham, 'The Date of Pitts's Pilgrimage to Mecca', *Journal of the Royal Asiatic Society*, (1950), p. 112 f.

—— 'Hakluyt's Description of the Ḥajj', *Arabian Studies*, IV (1977), 75–80

Mustafa Bilge, 'Arabia in the Work of Awliya Chalaby (The XVIIth Century Turkish Muslim Traveller)', in *Sources for the History of Arabia*, vol. I, part 2, ed. by Abdelgadir Mahmoud Abdalla, Sami Al-Sakkar, Richard T. Mortel, Abd Al-Rahman, T. Al-Ansari (Riyad, 1979), pp. 213–27

Mohammed Jamil Brownson, 'Mecca: The Socio-Economic Dynamics of the Sacred City', in *Hajj Studies*, vol. 1, ed. by Ziauddin Sarkar and M. Zaki Badawi (London, n.d.), pp. 117–36

Adil A. Bushnak, 'The Hajj Transportation System', in *Hajj Studies*, vol. 1, ed. by Ziauddin Sarkar and M. Zaki Badawi (London, n.d.), pp. 87–116

Dr Firmin Duguet, *Le pélerinage de la Mecque* (Paris, 1932)

Kurt Erdmann, 'Ka'bah-Fliesen', *Ars Orientalis*, 3 (1959), 192–7

Emel Esin, *Mekka und Medina*, trans. by Eva Bornemann, photographs by Haluk Doğanbey (Frankfurt, 1963)

—— 'Un manuscrit illustré representant les sanctuaires de la Mecque et Médine et le dome du Mi-Radj, à l'époque des Sultans turcs Selim et Süleyman Ier (H.922–74/1516–66)', in *Les provinces arabes et leurs sources documentaires à l'époque ottomane, partie française et anglaise*, ed. by Abdeljelil Temimi (Tunis, 1984), pp. 175–90

—— 'The Renovations Effected, in the Ka'bah Mosque, by the

Ottoman Sultan Selim II (H.974–82/1566–74)', *Revue d'histoire maghrébine*, 12, 39–40 (1985), 225–33

Richard Ettinghausen, 'Die bildliche Darstellung der Ka'aba im Islamischen Kulturkreis', *Zeitschrift der Deutschen Morgenländischen Gesellschaft*, 86–7 (NF 11–12) (1932–4) 111–37

—— 'Mughal–Ottoman Relations: A Study of Political and Diplomatic Relations between Mughal India and the Ottoman Empire 1556–1748', PhD dissertation, Madison, Wisconsin, 1986

Naim R. Farooqi, 'Moguls, Ottomans and Pilgrims: Protecting the Routes to Mecca in the Sixteenth and Seventeenth Centuries', *The International History Review*, X, 2 (1988), 198–220

Suraiya Faroqhi, 'Ottoman Documents concerning the Hajj during the Sixteenth and Seventeenth centuries', in *La vie sociale dans les provinces arabes à l'époque ottomane*, ed. by Abdeljelil Temimi, 3 vols. (Zaghouan, 1988), vol. 3, pp. 151–64

—— 'Anatolian Townsmen as Pilgrims to Mecca: Some Evidence from the Sixteenth–Seventeenth Centuries', in *Rencontres de L'Ecole du Louvre, Süleyman le Magnifique et son temps*, ed. Gilles Veinstein (Paris, 1992), pp. 309–26

Zaki M.A. Farsi, *Makkah al mukarramah, City and Hajj Guide* (Jeddah, 1408/1987–8)

—— *Map and guide of Almadinah almunawwarah* (Jeddah, n.d.)

Carol G. Fisher and Alan Fisher, 'Illustrations of Mecca and Medina in Islamic Manuscripts', in *Islamic Art from Michigan Collections*, ed. by Carol G. Fisher and Alan Fisher (East Lansing, Michigan, 1982), pp. 40–7

Maurice Gaudefroy-Demombynes, *Contribution à l'étude du Pèlerinage de la Mecque (Note d'histoire religieuse)*, PhD thesis, *l'Université de Paris* (Paris, 1923)

Gerald de Gaury, *Rulers of Mecca* (London, 1951)

Nejat Göyünc, 'Some documents concerning the Ka'aba in the 16th century', in *Studies in the History of Arabia*, vol. 1, 2, *Sources for the History of Arabia*, ed. by Abdelgadir Mahmoud Abdalla et al. (Riyad, 1979), pp. 177–81

Jacques Jomier OP, *Le maḥmal et la caravane égyptienne des pèlerins de la Mecque (XIIIe–XXe siècles)*, Publications de l'Institut Français d'Archéologie Orientale, XX (Cairo, 1953)

—— 'Le Maḥmal du sultan Qānṣūh al-Ghūrī (Début XVIe siècle)', *Annales Islamologiques*, XI (1972), 183–8

C.M. Kortepeter, 'A Source for the History of Ottoman–Hijaz Relations: The *Seyahatnâme* of Awliya Chalaby and the Rebellion of *Sharif* Sa'd b. Zayd in the Years 1671–72/1081–82', in: *Sources for the History of Arabia*, vol. 1, parts 1, 2, ed. by Abdelgadir Mahmoud Abdalla *et al.* (Riyad, 1979) pp. 229–46

David Edwin Long, *The Hajj Today, A Survey of the Contemporary Makkah Pilgrimage* (Albany, NY, 1979)

Ghazy Abdul Wahed Makky, 'Pilgrim Accommodation in Mecca: Spatial Structures, Costs and National Origins', in *Hajj Studies*, vol. 1, ed. by Ziauddin Sarkar and M.A. Zaki Badawi (London, n.d.), pp. 59–72

—— *Mecca, The Pilgrimage City, A Study of Pilgrim Accommodation* (London, 1978)

Ayyub Malik, 'Developments in Historic and Modern Islamic Cities', in *Hajj Studies*, vol. 1, ed. by Ziauddin Sarkar and M.A. Zaki Badawi (London, n.d.), pp. 137–61

Sulaiman Mousa, 'T.E. Lawrence and his Arab Contemporaries', *Arabian Studies*, VII (1985), 7–22

William Ochsenwald, *The Hijaz Railroad* (Charlottesville, Virginia, 1980)

—— *Religion, Society and the State in Arabia, The Hijaz under Ottoman Control 1840–1908* (Columbus, Ohio, 1984)

Francis E. Peters, *Jerusalem and Mecca. The Typology of the Holy City in the Near East*, New York University Studies in Near Eastern Civilization, No. 11 (New York, 1986)

A. Popovic, 'Le pèlerinage à la Mecque des musulmans des régions yougoslaves', in *Mélanges d'islamologie dédiés à la mémoire de A. Abel*, 2 vols. (Brussels, n.d., probably 1974), vol. 2, Correspondance d'Orient, No. 13, Publications du Centre pour l'Etude des Problèmes du Monde musulman contemporain, pp. 335–63

Abdul Karim Rafeq, *The Province of Damascus 1723–1783* (Beirut, 1970)

—— 'New Light on the Transportation of the Damascene Pilgrimage During the Ottoman Period', in *Islamic and Middle Eastern Societies*, ed. by Robert Olson (Brattleboro, Vermont, 1987), pp. 127–36

Augustus Ralli, *Christians at Mecca* (London, 1909)

William R. Roff, 'Sanitation and Security. The Imperial Powers and the Nineteenth Century Hajj', *Arabian Studies*, VI (1982), 143–60

Jean Sauvaget, 'Les caravansérails syriens du ḥadjdj de Constantinople', *Ars Islamica*, IV (1937), 98–121

—— *La mosquée omeyyade de Médine. Etude sur les origines architecturales de la mosquée et de la basilique* (Paris, 1947)

Stanford J. Shaw, *The Financial and Administrative Organization and Development of Ottoman Egypt, 1517–1798* (Princeton, 1962)

Christian Snouck Hurgronje, 'Een mekkaansch gezantschap naar

224 Pilgrims and Sultans

Atjeh in 1683', in *Verspreide Geschriften*, 7 vols. (Bonn and Leipzig, 1923), vol. 3, pp. 139–47

Sanjay Subrahmanyam, 'Persians, Pilgrims and Portuguese: The Travails of Masulipatnam Shipping in the Western Indian Ocean, 1590–1665', *Modern Asian Studies*, 22, 3 (1988), 503–30

René Tresse, *Le pèlerinage syrien au villes saintes de l'Islam*, PhD thesis, *Université de Paris* (Paris, 1937)

Ismail Hakkı Uzunçarşılı, *Mekke-i mükerreme Emirleri*, Türk Tarih Kurumu Yayınlarından VIII, 59 (Ankara, 1972)

Gilles Veinstein, 'Les pèlerins de la Mecque à travers quelques inventaires après décès ottomans (XVIIe–XVIIIe siècles)', *Revue de l'Occident musulman et de la Méditerranée*, 31, 1 (1981), 63–71

—— 'Les pèlerins de la Mecque à travers quelques actes du Qâdî de Sarajevo (1557–1558)', *Turcica*, XXI–XXIII (1991), *Mélanges Irène Mélikoff*, 473–94.

Ferdinand Wüstenfeld, *Geschichte der Stadt Medina, Im Auszug aus dem Arabischen des Samhūdī, Abhandlungen der historisch-philologischen Klasse der königlichen Gesellschaft der Wissenschaften zu Göttingen*, vol. 9 (Göttingen, 1860)

—— *Geschichte der Stadt Mekka nach den arabischen Chroniken*, 4 vols. (reprint, Beirut, 1964)

OTHER SECONDARY SOURCES

Rifa'at Abou-El-Haj, 'Ottoman Attitudes toward Peace Making: The Karlowitz Case', *Der Islam*, 51, 1 (1974), 131–7

—— 'The Social Uses of the Past: Recent Arab Historiography of Ottoman Rule', *International Journal of Middle East Studies*, 14 (1982), 185–201

—— *The 1703 Rebellion and the Structure of Ottoman Politics* (Leiden, 1984)

Abdul-Rahim Abu-Husayn, *Provincial Leaderships in Syria 1575–1650* (Beirut, 1985)

Doris Behrens-Abouseif, *Fêtes populaires dans le Caire du moyen-age*, Quaderni dell'Instituto Italiano di Cultura per la RAE (Cairo, 1982)

Michel Aghassian, Kéram Kévonian, 'Le commerce arménien dans l'Océan Indien aux 17e et 18e siècles', in *Marchands et hommes d'affaires asiatiques dans l'Océan Indien et la Mer de Chine 13e–20e siècles*, ed. by Denys Lombard and Jean Aubin (Paris, 1988), pp. 155–82

Münir Aktepe, *Patrona Isyanı (1730)*, Istanbul Üniversitesi Edebiyat Fakültesi Yayınları No. 808 (Istanbul, 1958)

Anthony D. Alderson, *The Structure of the Ottoman Dynasty* (Oxford, 1956)

Metin And, *Osmanlı Şenliklerinde Türk Sanatları*, Kültür ve Turizm Bakanlığı Yayınları: 529, Sanat Eserleri Dizisi 2 (Ankara, 1982)

Metin And, *Osmanlı Şenliklerinde Türk Sanatları* (Ankara, 1982).

Sinnappah Arasaratnam, *Merchants, Companies and Commerce on the Coromandel Coast 1650–1740* (Delhi, 1986)

—— 'The Rice Trade in Eastern India 1650–1740', *Modern Asian Studies*, 22, 3 (1988), 531–49

Ibrahim and Cevriye Artuk, *Istanbul Arkeoloji Müzeleri Teşhirdeki Islâmî Sikkeler Kataloğu*, 2 vols., TC Başbakanlık Kültür Yayınları III, 7 (Istanbul 1971, 1974)

Eliyahu Ashtor, 'The Wheat Supply of the Mamluk Kingdom', in *East–West Trade in the Medieval Mediterranean*, ed. Benjamin Kedar (London, 1986), pp. 283–95

Franz Babinger, *Die Geschichtsschreiber der Osmanen und ihre Werke* (Leipzig, 1927)

—— *Mehmed der Eroberer und seine Zeit, Weltenstürmer einer Zeitwende* (Munich, 1953)

—— *Osmanlı Tarih Yazarları ve Eserleri*, trans. and comm. by Coşkun Üçok, Doğumunun 100. Yılında Atatürk Yayınları 44 (Ankara, 1982)

M. Adnan Bakhit, 'Sidon in Mamluk and Early Ottoman Times', *Osmanlı Araştırmaları, The Journal of Ottoman Studies*, III (1982), 53–68 (a)

—— *The Ottoman Province of Damascus in the Sixteenth Century* (Beirut, 1982) (b)

Karl Barbir, 'From Pasha to Efendi: The Assimilation of Ottomans into Damascene Society, 1516–1783', *International Journal of Turkish Studies*, 1, 1 (1979–80), 68–83

—— *Ottoman Rule in Damascus, 1708–1758* (Princeton, NJ, 1980)

Ömer Lütfi Barkan, 'Osmanlı Imparatorluğu 'Bütçe'lerine Dair Notlar', *IFM*, 15, 1–4 (1953–4), pp. 238–50 (a)

—— 'Şehirlerin teşekkül ve inkışafı tarihi bakımından Osmanlı İmparatorluğunda İmâret sitelerinin kuruluş ve işleyiş tarzına âit araştırmalar', *IFM*, 23, 1–2 (1962–3), pp. 239–96.

—— 'Türk Toprak Hukuku Tarihinde Tanzimat ve 1274 (1858) Tarihli Arazi Kanunnamesi', in *Türkiye'de Toprak Meselesi, Toplu Eserler*, 1, ed. Abidin Nesimi *et al.* (Istanbul, 1980), pp. 291–375

Ülkü Ü. Bates, 'Women as Patrons of Architecture in Turkey', in *Women in the Muslim World*, ed. by Lois Beck and Nikki Keddie (Cambridge, Mass., 1978), pp. 245–60

Cavit Baysun, 'Evliya Çelebi', in *IA*, vol. 4, pp. 400–12

—— 'Evliya Çelebi'ye dair Notlar', *Türkiyat Mecmuası*, XII (1955), pp. 257–64

Alexandre Benningsen, Chantal Lemercier-Quelquejay, 'La Moscovie, la Horde Nogay et le problème des communications entre l'Empire Ottoman et l'Asie centrale en 1552–1556', *Turcica*, VIII, 2 (1976), pp. 203–36

Robin Bidwell, *Travellers in Arabia* (London, 1976)

J. Richard Blackburn, 'The Collapse of Ottoman Authority in Yemen, 968/1560–976/1568', *Die Welt des Islams*, XIX, 1–4 (1979), pp. 119–76

Geneviève Bouchon, 'Un microcosme: Calicut au 16e siècle', in *Marchands et hommes d'affaires asiatiques dans l'Océan Indien et la Mer de Chine, 13e–20e siècles*, ed. by Denys Lombard and Jean Aubin (Paris, 1988), pp. 49–58

Fernand Braudel, *La Méditerranée et le monde méditerranéen à l'époque de Philippe II*, 2 vols. (Paris, 1966)

—— *Civilization matérielle, économie et capitalisme, XVe–XVIIIe siècle*, 3 vols. (Paris, 1979)

—— *L'identité de la France*, 3 vols. (Paris, 1986)

Fernand Braudel, Ernest Labrousse *et al.*, *Histoire économique et sociale de la France*, 4 vols. (Paris, 1970), vol. II, *Des derniers temps de l'age seigneurial aux préludes de l'âge industriel (1660–1789)*

Martin van Bruinessen and Hendrik Boeschoten, *Evliya Çelebi in Diyarbekir, The relevant section of the Seyahatname edited with translation, commentary and introduction* (Leiden and New York, 1988)

Richard W. Bulliet, *The Patricians of Nishapur, A Study in Medieval Islamic Social History* (Cambridge, Mass., 1972)

—— *The Camel and the Wheel* (Cambridge, Mass., 1975)

Yavuz Cezar, *Osmanlı Maliyesinde Bunalim ve Değişim Dönemi (XVIIIyy dan Tanzimat'a Mali Tarih)* (Istanbul, 1986)

Philip D. Curtin, *Cross-Cultural Trade in World History* (Cambridge, 1984)

Bistra Cvetkova, 'Les registres des *celepkeşan* en tant que sources pour l'histoire de la Bulgarie et des pays balkaniques', in *Hungaro–Turcica, Studies in Honour of Julius Nemeth* (Budapest, 1976), pp. 325–35

Ashin Das Gupta, 'A Note on the Shipowning Merchants of Surat c. 1700', in *Marchands et hommes d'affaires asiatiques dans l'Océan Indien et la Mer de Chine, 13e–20e siècles*, ed. by Denys Lombard and Jean Aubin (Paris, 1988), pp. 109–16

Jean Delumeau, *Catholicism Between Luther and Voltaire: A New View of the Counter-Reformation*, trans. by Jeremy Moiser, introduced by John Bossy (London and Philadelphia, 1977)

Ian C. Dengler, 'Turkish Women in the Ottoman Empire: The Classical Age', in *Women in the Muslim World*, ed. by Lois Beck and Nikki Keddie (Cambridge, Mass., 1978), pp. 229–44

Michael W. Dols, *The Black Death in the Middle East* (Princeton, NJ, 1977)

Ross Dunn, *The Adventures of Ibn Battuta, A Muslim Traveler of the 14th Century* (Berkeley and Los Angeles, 1986)

Meşkure Eren, *Evliya Çelebi Seyahatnamesi Birinci Cildinin Kaynakları Üzerinde Bir Araştırma* (Istanbul, 1960)

Neşe Erim, 'Onsekizinci Yüzyılda Erzurum Gümrüğü', PhD dissertation, Istanbul, 1984

—— 'Trade, Traders and the State in Eighteenth-Century Erzurum', *New Perspectives on Turkey*, 5–6 (1991), pp. 123–50

Faḍlallāh b. Rūzbihān, *Transoxanien und Turkestan zu Beginn des 16. Jahrhunderts, Das Mihmān-nāma-yi Buhara des Faḍlallāh b. Rūzbihān Hunği*, trans. and comm. by Ursula Ott, Islâmkundliche Untersuchungen, vol. 25 (Freiburg, 1974)

Suraiya Faroqhi, 'Social mobility among Ottoman 'ulemā in the late sixteenth century', *International Journal of Middle East Studies*, 4 (1973), pp. 204–18.

—— 'Camels, Wagons, and the Ottoman State', *International Journal of Middle East Studies*, 14 (1982), pp. 523–39

—— *Towns and Townsmen of Ottoman Anatolia, Trade, Crafts and Food Production in an Urban Setting* (Cambridge, 1984)

—— 'Coffee and Spices: Official Ottoman Reactions to Egyptian Trade in the Later Sixteenth Century', *Wiener Zeitschrift für die Kunde des Morgenlandes*, 76 (1986), *Festschrift Andreas Tietze* ... pp. 87–93 (a)

—— 'Long-Term Change and the Ottoman Construction Site: A Study of Builders, Wages and Iron Prices', in *Raiyyet Rüsûmu, Essays Presented to Halil Inalcık* ..., ed. by Bernard Lewis *et al.* (Cambridge, Mass., 1986), pp. 111–26 (b)

—— *Men of Modest Substance, House Owners and House Property in Seventeenth Century Ankara and Kayseri* (Cambridge, 1987)

—— 'Red Sea Trade and Communications as Observed by Evliya Çelebi', *New Perspectives on Turkey*, 5–6 (1991), pp. 87–106

—— 'Ottoman Trade Controls and Supply Policies in the Red Sea Area (1550–1600)' in *The Reign of Süleyman the Magnificent*, ed. Cemal Kafadar (Istanbul, forthcoming)

Caroline Finkel, *The Administration of Warfare: The Ottoman Military Campaigns in Hungary, 1593–1606*, 2 vols., Beihefte zur Zeitschrift für die Kunde des Morgenlandes, vol. 14 (Vienna, 1988)

Cornell Fleischer, *Bureaucrat and Intellectual in the Ottoman Empire, The Historian Mustafa Âli (1541–1600)* (Princeton, NJ, 1986)

Gustav Flügel, *Die arabischen, persischen und türkischen Handschriften der kaiserlich-königlichen Hofbibliothek zu Wien*, 3 vols. (Vienna, 1865–7)

Mehmet Genç, 'XVIII Yüzyılda Osmanlı Ekonomisi ve Savaş', *Yapıt* 49/4 (1984), 52–61, 50/5 (1984), 86–93

Fatma Müge Göçek, *East Encounters West; France and the Ottoman Empire in the Eighteenth Century* (New York and Oxford, 1987)

Tayyib Gökbilgin, *XV–XVI Asırlarda Edirne ve Paşa Livası, Mülkler, Mukataaler*, Istanbul Üniversitesi Edebiyat Fakültesi Yayınlarından 508 (Istanbul, 1952)

Christina Phelps Grant, *The Syrian Desert, Caravans, Travel, Exploration* (London, 1937)

William Griswold, *The Great Anatolian Rebellion 1000–1020/1591–1611* (Berlin, 1983)

Ulrich Haarmann, 'Murtaḍā b. 'Ali b. 'Alawan's Journey through Arabia in 1121/1709', in *Sources for the History of Arabia*, vol. I, part 2, ed. by Abdelgadir Mahmoud Abdallah et al. (Riyad, 1979), pp. 247–51

Irfan Habib, 'Merchant Communities in Precolonial India', in *The Rise of Merchant Empires, Long-Distance Trade in the Early Modern World 1350–1750* (Cambridge, 1990), pp. 371–99

Joseph von Hammer-Purgstall, *Geschichte des Osmanischen Reiches grossentheils aus bisher unbenützten Handschriften und Archiven*, 10 vols. (reprint, Vienna, 1963)

Nelly Hanna, *An Urban History of Būlāq in the Mamluk and Ottoman Periods*, Supplément aux Annales Islamologiques (Cairo, 1983)

Angelika Hartmann, *an Nāṣir li-Dīn Allāh (1180–1225) – Politik, Religion und Kultur der späten Abbasidenzeit*, Studien zur Sprache, Geschichte und Kultur des Islamischen Orients (Berlin and New York, 1975)

Ralph Hattox, *Coffee and Coffeehouses, The Origins of a Social Beverage in the Medieval Near East*, University of Washington, Near Eastern Studies No. 3 (Seattle and London, 1985)

Andrew Hess, *The Forgotten Frontier, A History of the Sixteenth-Century Ibero–African Frontier* (Chicago and London, 1978)

Uriel Heyd, *Ottoman Documents on Palestine 1552–1615. A Study of the Firman according to the Mühimme Defteri* (Oxford, 1960)

Walther Hinz, *Islamische Masse und Gewichte, umgerechnet ins metrische System*, in *Handbuch der Orientalistik*, ed. by Berthold Spuler, suppl. vol. 1, 1 (Leiden, 1955)

Marshall Hodgson, *The Venture of Islam, Conscience and History in a World Civilization*, 3 vols. (Chicago, 1974)

David George Hogarth, *The Penetration of Arabia, A Record of the Development of Western Knowledge Concerning the Arabian Peninsula* (New York, 1904)

Sabine Höllmann, 'Ägyptisches Alltagsleben im 17. Jahrhundert: J.M. Wanslebens Reisenotizen als ethnologische Quelle', unpublished MA thesis, Munich, 1987

P.M. Holt, 'The Exalted Lineage of Riḍwān Beğ', *Bulletin of the School of Oriental and African Studies*, XII, 2 (1959), 221–30

—— 'The Beylicate in Ottoman Egypt during the Seventeenth Century', *Bulletin of the School of Oriental and African Studies*, XXIV, 2 (1961), 214–48

Wolf-Dieter Hütteroth, Kamal Abdulfattah, *Historical Geography of Palestine, Transjordan and Southern Syria in the Late 16th Century*, Erlanger Geographische Arbeiten (Erlangen, 1977)

Halil Inalcık, 'Osmanlı-Rus Rekabetinin Menşei ve Don-Volga Kanalı Teşebbüsü (1569)', *Belleten*, XII, 46 (1948), 349–402

—— 'Ottoman Methods of Conquest', *Studia Islamica*, II (1954), 104–29

—— 'The Ottoman Economic Mind and Aspects of the Ottoman Economy', in *Studies in the Economic History of the Middle East*, ed. by M.A. Cook (London, 1970), pp. 207–18

—— *The Ottoman Empire, The Classical Age 1300–1600*, trans. by Norman Itzkowitz and Colin Imber (London, 1973)

—— 'The Khan and the Tribal Aristocracy: The Crimean Khanate under Sahib Giray I.', *Harvard Ukranian Studies*, III, IV (1979–80), pp. 445–66

—— 'Osmanlı Pamuklu Pazarı, Hindistan ve İngiltere: Pazar Rekabetinde Emek Maliyetinin Rolü', *Türkiye İktisat Tarihi Üzerine Araştırmalar*, II, *ODTÜ Gelişme Dergisi*, (1979–80), pp. 1–65

Huri İslamoğlu-İnan, 'Introduction: Oriental despotism in world system perspective', in *The Ottoman Empire and the World Economy*, ed. by Huri Islamoğlu-İnan (Cambridge and Paris, 1987), pp. 1–26

Fahir Iz, 'Evliya Çelebi ve Seyahatnamesi', *Boğazici Üniversitesi Dergisi*, VII (1979), pp. 61–79

Cemal Kafadar, 'When Coins Turned into Drops of Dew and Bankers Became Robbers of Shadows; The Boundaries of Ottoman Economic Imagination at the End of the Sixteenth Century', PhD dissertation, McGill University, Montreal, 1986

—— 'Self and Others: The Diary of a Dervish in Seventeenth-Century Istanbul and First-Person Narratives in Ottoman Literature', *Studia Islamica 69* (1989), 121–50

Albert Kammerer, *La mer Rouge, l'Abyssinie et l'Arabie aux XVIe et XVIIe siècles et la cartographie des portulans du monde oriental, Étude d'histoire et de géographie historique, Mémoires de la Société royale de géographie d'Egypte*, vol. XVII (Cairo, 1947), part 1, *Abyssins et portugais devant l'Islam*

R.H. Kiermann, *L'exploration de l'Arabie, Depuis les temps anciens jusqu'à nos jours*, trans. by Charles Mourey (London, 1938)

Hans-Joachim Kissling, *Beiträge zur Kenntnis Thrakiens im 17. Jahrhundert*, Abhandlungen für die Kunde des Morgenlandes XXXII, 3 (Wiesbaden, 1956)

—— 'Zur Geschichte der Rausch- und Genussgifte im Osmanischen Reiche', *Südost-Forschungen*, XVI (1975) 342–56

Ibrahim Hakkı Konyalı, *Abide ve Kitâbeleri ile Ereğli Tarihi* (Istanbul, 1970)

Fuat Köprülü, 'Türk Halk Hikayeciliğine ait Maddeler, Meddahlar', in *Edebiyat Araştırmaları*, Türk Tarih Kurumu Yayınlarından VII, 47 (Ankara, 1966), 361–412

Klaus Kreisner, 'Zur inneren Gliederung der osmanischen Stadt', in: *XVIII. deutschen Orientalistentag . . . 1972, Vorträge*, ed. by W. Voigt, *Zeitschrift der Deutschen Morgenländischen Gesellschaft*, Supplement II (1974), 198–212

—— *Edirne im 17. Jahrhundert nach Evliya Çelebi. Ein Beitrag zur Kenntnis der osmanischen Stadt*, Islamkundliche Untersuchungen vol. 33 (Freiburg, 1975)

Richard Kreutel, 'Evliya Çelebis Bericht über die türkische Grossbotschaft des Jahres 1665 in Wien. Ein Vergleich mit zeitgenössischen türkischen und österreichischen Quellen', *Wiener Zeitschrift für die Kunde des Morgenlandes*, 51 (1948–52), 188–242

—— 'Neues zur Evliya Çelebi-Forschung', *Der Islam*, 48 (1972), 269–79

Aptullah Kuran, *Sinan, The Grand Old Master of Ottoman Architecture* (Washington, DC, and Istanbul, 1987).

Bekir Kütükoğlu, *Osmanlı-Iran Siyası Münasebetleri*, I (1578–1590), Istanbul Üniversitesi Edebiyat Fakültesi Yayınları No. 888 (Istanbul, 1962)

—— 'Les relations entre l'Empire Ottoman et l'Iran dans la seconde moitié du XVIe siècle', *Turcica*, VI (1975), 128–45

Mübahat Kütükoğlu, '1009 (1600) tarihli Narh Defterine göre Istanbul'da çeşidli eşya ve hizmet fiatları', *Tarih Enstitüsü Dergisi*, 9 (1978), 1–86

—— *Osmanlılarda Narh Müessesesi ve 1640 Tarihli Narh Defteri* (Istanbul, 1983)

Akdes Nimet Kurat, *Türkiye ve İdil Boyu (1569 Astarhan Seferi, Ten-İdil Kanalı ve XVI–XVII. Yüzyıl Osmanlı-Rus Münasebetleri)*, Ankara Üniversitesi Dil ve Tarih Coğrafya Fakültesi Sa 151 (Ankara, 1966)

Ernest Labrousse *et alii*, *Histoire économique et sociale de la France*, vol. 2, *Des derniers temps de l'age seigneurial aux préludes de l'age industriel (1660–1789)* (Paris, 1970).

Ira Lapidus, *Muslim Cities in the Later Middle Ages* (Cambridge, 1984)

Emmanuel Le Roy Ladurie, 'A Concept: The Unification of the Globe by Disease (Fourteenth to Seventeenth Centuries)', in *The Mind and Method of the Historian*, trans. by Siân Reynolds and Ben Reynolds (Chicago, 1984), pp. 28–83

Bernard Lewis, *The Emergence of Modern Turkey*, 2nd edn. (London, 1968)

Pierre MacKay, 'The Manuscripts of the Seyahatname of Evliya Çelebi', *Der Islam*, 52 (1975), 278–98

Hans Georg Majer, 'Ein Osmanisches Budget aus der Zeit Meḥmed des Eroberers', *Der Islam*, 59, 1 (1982), 40–63

Jon S. Mandaville, 'The Ottoman Province of al-Ḥasā in the Sixteenth and Seventeenth Centuries', *Journal of the American Oriental Society*, 90, 3 (1970), 486–513

Robert Mantran, *Istanbul dans la seconde moitié du XVIIe siècle, Essai d'histoire institutionelle, économique et sociale*, Bibliothèque archéologique et historique de l'Institut Français d'Archéologie d'Istanbul, XII (Paris, 1962)

Paul Masson, *Histoire du commerce français dans le Levant au XVIIIe siècle* (Paris, 1911)

Bruce Masters, *The Origins of Western Economic Dominance in the Middle East, Mercantilism and the Islamic Economy in Aleppo, 1600–*

1750, New York University Studies in Near Eastern Civilization No. 12 (New York, 1988)

Arno Mehlan, 'Die grossen Balkanmessen zur Türkenzeit', *Vierteljahresschrift für Sozial- und Wirtschaftsgeschichte*, XXI, 1 (1938), 10–49

M.J. Mehta, 'Some Aspects of Surat as a Trading Centre in the Seventeenth Century', *Indian Historical Review*, 1, 2 (1974), 247–61

M. Yakub Mughul, 'Portekizli'lerle Kızıldeniz'de Mücadele ve Hicaz' da Osmanlı Hâkimiyetinin Yerleşmesi Hakkında bir Vesika', *Belgeler*, II, 3–4 (1965), 37–47

Alois Musil, *The Northern Heğâz, A topographical itinerary*, American Oriental Society, Oriental Studies and Explorations No. 1 (New York, 1926)

Zeynep Nayır, *Osmanlı Mimarlığında Sultan Ahmet Külliyesi ve Sonrası (1609–1690)* (Istanbul, 1975)

Gülru Necipoğlu Kafadar, 'The Süleymaniye Complex in Istanbul: An Interpretation', *Mukarnas*, 3 (1986), 92–117

Elke Niewohner-Eberhard, 'Machtpolitische Aspekte des osmanisch-safavidischen Kampfes um Bagdad im 16.–17. Jahrhundert', *Turcica*, VI (1975), 103–27

Cengiz Orhonlu, '1559 Bahreyn Seferine Âid bir Rapor', *Tarih Dergisi*, XVII, 22 (1967), 1–16

—— 'Hint Kaptanlığı ve Pirî Reis', *Belleten*, XXXIV, 134 (1970), 235–54

—— *Osmanlı İmparatorluğunum Güney Siyaseti, Habeş Eyaleti*, Istanbul Üniversitesi Edebiyat Fakültesi Yayınları No. 1856 (Istanbul, 1974)

Salih Özbaran, 'XVI. Yüzyılda Basra Körfezi Sahillerinde Osmanlılar: Basra Beylerbeyliğinin Kuruluşu', *Tarih Dergisi*, 25 (1971), 51–72

—— 'The Ottoman Turks and the Portuguese in the Persian Gulf, 1534–1581', *Journal of Asian History*, 6, 1 (1972), 45–87

—— 'Osmanlı İmparatorluğu ve Hindistan Yolu, Onaltıncı Yüzyılda Ticâret Yolları Üzerinde Türk-Portekiz Rekâbet ve İlişkileri', *Tarih Dergisi*, 31 (1977), 65–146

—— 'A Turkish Report on the Red Sea and the Portuguese in the Indian Ocean (1525)', *Arabian Studies*, IV (1978), 81–8

Daniel Panzac, *La peste dans l'Empire Ottoman 1700–1850* (Louvain, 1985)

M.N. Pearson, 'Brokers in Western Indian Port Cities, Their Role in Servicing Foreign Merchants', *Modern Asian Studies*, 22, 3 (1988), 455–72

Leslie Peirce, 'Shifting Boundaries: Images of Ottoman Royal

Women in the 16th and 17th Centuries', *Critical Matrix, Princeton Working Papers in Womens' Studies*, 4 (1988), 43–82

Xavier de Planhol, *De la plaine pamphylienne aux lacs pisidiens, nomadisme et vie paysanne.* (Paris, 1958)

Ishwari Prasad, *The Life and Times of Humayun* (Bombay, Calcutta and Madras, 1956)

Donald Quataert, *Social Disintegration and Popular Resistance in the Ottoman Empire, 1881–1908, Reactions to European Economic Penetration*, New York University Studies in Near Eastern Civilization, No. 9 (New York and London, 1983)

Abdul-Karim Rafeq, 'The Law-Court Registers of Damascus, with Special Reference to Craft Corporations During the First Half of the Eighteenth Century', in *Les Arabes par leurs archives (XVIe–XXe siècles)*, ed. by Jacques Berque and Dominique Chevalier (Paris, 1976), pp. 141–59

André Raymond, *Artisans et commerçants au Caire au XVIIIe siècle*, 2 vols. (Damascus, 1973–4)

—— 'La conquête ottomane et le développement des grandes villes arabes. Le cas du Caire, de Damas et de Alep', *Revue de l'Occident musulman et de la Méditerrannée*, 1 (1979), 115–34

—— *The Great Arab Cities in the 16th–18th Centuries. An Introduction* (New York and London, 1984)

—— *Grandes villes arabes à l'époque ottomane* (Paris, 1985)

Saiyid Athar Abbas Rizvi, *Muslim Revivalist Movements in Northern India in the Sixteenth and Seventeenth Centuries* (Agra, 1965)

Saiyid Abbas Rizvi, Vincent J. Adams Flynn, *Fathpur-Sīkrī* (Bombay, 1975)

J.M. Rogers, R.M. Ward, *Süleyman the Magnificent* (London, 1988)

Ruggiero Romano, 'Versuch einer ökonomischen Typologie', in Ruggiero Romano ed., *Die Gleichzeitigkeit des Ungleichzeitigen, Studien zur Geschichte Italiens*, trans. and introduced by Eva Maek-Gérard (Frankfurt, 1980), pp. 22–75

Halil Sahillioğlu, 'XVII Asrın Ilk Yarısında Istanbul'da Tedavüldeki Sikkelerin Raici', *Belgeler*, 1, 1–2 (1964), 228–33

—— 'Osmanlı Para Tarihinde Dünya Para ve Maden Hareketinin Yeri', *Türkiye Iktisat Tarihi Üzerine Araştırmalar, ODTÜ Gelişme Dergisi*, special issue (1978), 1–38

—— 'Yemen'in 1599–1600 Yılı Bütçesi', in *Yusuf Hikmet Bayur Armağanı* (Ankara, 1985), pp. 287–319

Edward W. Said, *Orientalism* (New York, 1979)

Jean Sauvaget, *Alep, Essai sur le développement d'une grande ville syrienne, des origines au milieu du XIXe siècle*, Haut Commissariat de

l'État Français en Syrie et au Liban, Service des Antiquités, Bibliothèque archéologique et historique, vol. XXXVI, 2 vols. (Paris, 1941)
Afaf Lutfi al-Sayyid Marsot, *Egypt in the Reign of Muhammad Ali* (Cambridge, 1984)
James C. Scott, *Weapons of the Weak, Everyday Forms of Peasant Resistance* (New Haven and London, 1985)
Robert B. Serjeant, (a) 'Yemeni Merchants and Trade in Yemen, 13th–16th Centuries', in *Marchands et hommes d'affaires asiatiques dans l'Océan Indien et dans la Mer de Chine, 13e–20e siècles*, ed. by Denys Lombard and Jean Aubin (Paris, 1988), pp. 61–82
—— (b)'The Ḥaḍramī Network', in *Marchands et hommes d'affaires asiatiques dans l'Océan Indien et la Mer de Chine, 13e–20e siècles*, ed. by Denys Lombard and Jean Aubin (Paris, 1988), pp. 147–54
Moshe Sharon, 'The Political Role of the Bedouins in Palestine during the Sixteenth and Seventeenth Centuries', in *Studies on Palestine during the Ottoman Period*, ed. by Moshe Ma'oz (Jerusalem, 1975), pp. 11–30
Stanford J. Shaw, *Between Old and New, The Ottoman Empire under Sultan Selim III 1789–1807* (Cambridge, Mass., 1971)
—— *History of the Ottoman Empire and Modern Turkey*, 2 vols. (Cambridge, 1976–77), vol. 2 with Ezel Kural Shaw, *Reform, Revolution and Republic, The Rise of Modern Turkey 1808–1975*
Ashirbadi Lal Srivastava, *Akbar the Great*, 2 vols. (Agra, 1962, 1967)
Sanjay Subrahmanyam, *The Political Economy of Commerce: Southern India, 1500–1650* (Cambridge, 1990)
Franz Taeschner, *Das anatolische Wegenetz nach osmanischen Quellen*, Türkische Bibliothek, vol. 23, 2 parts (Leipzig, 1924–6)
Karl Teply, 'Evliya Çelebi in Wien', *Der Islam*, 52 (1975), 125–31
Lewis V. Thomas, *A Study of Naima*, ed. by Norman Itzkowitz, New York University Studies in Near Eastern Civilization No. 4 (New York, 1972)
Luis Filipe F.R. Thomaz, 'Malaka et ses communautés marchandes au tournant du 16e siècle', in *Marchands et hommes d'affaires asiatiques dans l'Océan Indien et la Mer de Chine, 13e–20e siècles*, ed. by Denys Lombard and Jean Aubin (Paris, 1988), pp. 31–48
Ismail Hakkı Uzunçarşılı, *Osmanlı Devletinin Saray Teşkilâtı*, Türk Tarih Kurumu Yayınlarından VIII, 15 (Ankara, 1945)
—— *Osmanlı Devletinin Merkez ve Bahriye Teşkilâtı*, Türk Tarih Kurumu Yayınlarından VIII, 6 (Ankara, 1948)
Ismail Hakkı Uzunçarşılı, *Osmanlı Devletinin İlmiye Teşkilâtı* (Ankara, 1965).

Michel Vovelle, *Ville et campagne au 18e siècle (Chartres et la Beauce)* (Paris, 1980)

Spyros Vryonis, 'The *Panēgyris* of the Byzantine Saint. A Study in the Nature of a Medieval Institution, its Origins and Fate', in *The Byzantine Saint*, ed. by Sergei Hacke (London, 1981), pp. 196–226

Robert E. Ward and Dankwart A. Rustow (eds.), *Political Modernization in Japan and Turkey*, Studies in Political Development, 3 (Princeton, NJ, 1964)

Eugen Weber, *Peasants into Frenchmen, the Modernization of Rural France 1870–1914* (Stanford, Cal., 1976)

Ferdinand Wüstenfeld, *Jemen im XI. (XVII.) Jahrhundert. Die Kriege der Türken, die arabischen Imame und die Gelehrten* (Göttingen, 1884)

Hulûsi Yavuz, *Kâbe ve Haremeyn için Yemen'de Osmanlı Hâkimiyeti (1517–1571)* (Istanbul, 1984)

Index

236

thinking of you

Jill Mansell

sourcebooks
landmark

Published by Sourcebooks Landmark, an imprint of Sourcebooks, Inc.
P.O. Box 4410, Naperville, Illinois 60567-4410
(630) 961-3900
Fax: (630) 961-2168
www.sourcebooks.com

Originally published in 2007 by Headline Review, an imprint of Headline
Publishing Group, a division of Hachette Livre UK Ltd.

Library of Congress Cataloguing-in-Publication data is on file with the publisher.

Printed and bound in the United States of America.
VP 10 9 8 7 6 5 4 3 2 1

Also by Jill Mansell

An Offer You Can't Refuse
Miranda's Big Mistake
Millie's Fling
Perfect Timing
Rumor Has It
Take a Chance on Me
Staying at Daisy's
To the Moon and Back
Nadia Knows Best
A Walk in the Park

To Charlotte Ash

And with many thanks to her husband Ian
for generously supporting Bliss.

Chapter 1

IF IT WAS SYMPATHY she was after, Ginny Holland might have known she'd come to the wrong place. Then again, it was early on a bright but blustery Saturday morning in October and her options were limited.

And it was only over the road from her own house, which was handy.

"I can't describe how I feel." She clenched a fist, pressed it to her breastbone, and shook her head in frustration. "It's just so... so..."

"I know exactly what it is. Bird's-nest syndrome," said Carla.

Ginny pulled a face because it was so screamingly apparent that Carla didn't have children. "Bird's-nest syndrome would be the name for the state of my hair. I have *empty*-nest syndrome. My nest is empty, my baby has flown away, and I just feel all hollow inside like... like a cheap Easter egg."

"Well, I think you're mad." Carla was busy executing Olympic-level sit-ups, her bare feet tucked under the edge of the cream leather sofa, her hair swinging glossily to and fro. "Jem's gone off to university. You're free again. You should be out there celebrating. Plus," she added as an afterthought, "Cadbury's Creme Eggs aren't hollow; they're full of goo."

"Unlike you," Ginny pointed out. "You're heartless."

"And you're thirty-eight, not seventy." Having completed her five millionth sit-up, Carla raised her legs in the air and, without even pausing for breath, began bicycling furiously. "I'm a year older

than you and look at me; I'm having a whale of a time! I'm in tip-top condition, men can't resist me, and sex has never been better. I'm a woman in my prime," she concluded. "And so are you."

Ginny knew her life wasn't really over, of course she did, but Jem's departure had nevertheless knocked her for six. She'd always been so happy and busy before now, so endlessly occupied, that this was a whole new experience for her. Nor did it help that it was happening as winter approached. Most of the jobs here in Portsilver were seasonal and she'd just spent the last six months being rushed off her feet working in a café down on the seafront. But the tourists had gone home now, Jem was in Bristol, and Ginny was finding herself faced with way more spare time than she was used to. To add insult to injury, two other female friends had separately moved in the last month, her favorite wine bar had been bought up and turned into a noisy haven for underage drinkers of alcopops, and the Latin American dance classes she'd so enjoyed attending had come to an abrupt halt when her dance teacher had slipped doing the samba and broken his hip. All in all, it hadn't been the best October on record. And as for Carla telling her she was a woman in her prime... well, she could end up being sued for false advertising.

Glancing at her reflection in Carla's glitzy over-the-top Venetian mirror, Ginny puffed away a section of overgrown bangs that were falling into her eyes. The aforementioned bird's-nest hair was long, blond, and wavy-with-a-definite-mind-of-its-own. Sometimes it behaved, sometimes it didn't, and she had no control over it either way. Face-wise, it wasn't as if she was a wrinkled old prune—if anything, Ginny knew she looked young for her age—but in glossy magazine world there was still plenty of room for improvement. It would be lovely to be as chic, groomed, and effortlessly femme-fatalish as Carla but, let's face it, she simply couldn't be doing with making all that effort.

"You need to get yourself together." Carla finished bicycling in the air, miraculously not even puce in the face. "Cheer yourself up; get out there and have an adventure."

"I'm just saying I miss Jem." Ginny hated feeling like this. She had never been needy in her life; the idea was as horrifying to her as suddenly developing a penchant for wearing puffball miniskirts.

"She'd want you to have an adventure," Carla said reasonably.

"I know." Ginny tugged at a loose thread on her sweater sleeve. "But I really want to *see* her."

"Fine. Go on then, if that's what you want to do. If you think Jem won't mind." Rising gracefully to her feet and automatically checking her sleek, serum-fed hair in the Venetian mirror—yep, still perfect—Carla said, "You've made a hole in that sleeve, by the way."

Ginny didn't care; it was a manky old sweater anyway. More importantly, she'd got what she'd come for. "Right, I will."

"Will what?"

"Drive up to Bristol to see Jem. It's a great idea!"

"Now? Shouldn't you give her a ring first? She's eighteen," said Carla. "She could be getting up to any number of naughty things."

To humor Carla, Ginny said, "OK, I'll call her. You have a lovely weekend and I'll see you tomorrow night when I get back."

"I always have a lovely weekend." Carla patted her flat brown stomach. "I'm a woman in my prime, remember?" Smugly she added, "Besides, Robbie's coming round."

Robbie was the latest in a series of interchangeable pretty young boys Carla favored for their fit bodies, floppy hair, and... well, unfloppy other bits. The last thing she was looking for was commitment.

"Right, I'm off." Ginny gave her a hug.

"Give Jem my love. And drive carefully on the motorway."

"I will."

As Ginny let herself out of the house, Carla said, "And don't forget to phone first. She might not be pleased to see you."

God, best friends could be brutal. If Ginny hadn't been so excited, she might have taken offense.

But that was Carla for you; she wasn't a mother so how could she possibly understand?

———

"Mum! I don't believe it—how fantastic that you're here!" Jem's face lit up as she launched herself like a missile into her mother's arms, hugging her so tightly she could hardly breathe.

Oh yes, that was a good one.

Or: "Mummy, oh my God, this is the best surprise ever… you don't know how much I've *missed* you…"

Whoops, mustn't make herself cry. Deliberately banishing the happy scenarios her imagination had been busily conjuring up, Ginny blinked hard in order to concentrate on the road ahead. The journey from Portsilver in north Cornwall up to Bristol took three and a half hours and so far they were on schedule to arrive at one o'clock. Luckily, Bellamy enjoyed nothing more than a nice long ride in the car and was lolling contentedly across the backseat with his eyes shut and his tongue out. Every time Ginny said in her excited voice, "Who are we going to see, Bellamy? Hey? We're going to see Jem!" he opened one eye and lazily wagged his tail.

If Ginny had owned one, she'd have been wagging hers too.

It was three weeks since Jem had left home. Ginny had braced herself for the worst but hadn't braced nearly hard enough; the aching void where Jem had once been was a million times worse than she'd envisaged. Her daughter was the most important person in her life; it was as simple as that.

As she drove toward Bristol, Ginny scrolled through some of her happiest memories. Marrying Gavin Holland on her eighteenth birthday… well, it may have been a mistake, but how could she possibly regret it when between them they had produced Jem?

Giving birth—gasping her way through ever more agonizing contractions and threatening to knock Gavin's teeth down his throat when he said plaintively, "Ouch, could you not squeeze my hand so hard? It hurts."

Holding Jem at long last and sobbing uncontrollably because the rush of love was so much more overwhelming than she'd imagined, particularly when you considered that the squalling creature you were cradling in your arms was covered in blood and gunk and slime.

Then later, tiny starfish fingers grasping the air... the first magical smile... the first day at school ("Mummy, don't leeeeave meeeee!")... and that look of blind panic on Jem's face after posting her letter to Father Christmas because what if he got her muddled up with the other Jemima, the one with sticky-out ears and glasses in Miss Carter's class?

Oh yes, there were so many perfect moments. Ginny's smile broadened as each one in turn popped into her mind. She and Gavin had separated when Jem was nine and that had been sad, of course it was, but it truly hadn't been the end of the world. Gavin had turned out not to be the settling-down-and-staying-faithful kind. Nevertheless, he'd always been a loving father and had never once let Jem down. And Jem had come through her parents' separation and subsequent divorce wonderfully well, taking the inevitable changes in her stride.

From that time on, Ginny and Jem had become truly inseparable, as close as any mother and daughter could be. Even the dreaded puberty hadn't managed to spoil their relationship and Ginny knew she'd got off lightly there; while other teenagers grew rebellious and sulky and slammed doors off their hinges, Jem had retained the ability to laugh at herself and hadn't lost her sparky, sunny nature. It had always been the two of them against the world.

At that moment a wet nose touched Ginny's left arm, and Bellamy, his head poked between the front seats, licked her elbow.

"Oh, sorry, sweetheart, I wasn't thinking." Concentrating on the road ahead, Ginny gave his ears an apologetic rub. "How could I forget you, hmm? The *three* of us against the world."

—*∿∿*—

The traffic on the motorway was light, and by ten to one, Ginny was on the outskirts of Bristol. Jem hadn't been keen on moving into the halls of residence. Instead, she'd got on the phone to local property agents, arranged a day of viewing back in September, and decided on a flat-share in Clifton with two other students. This was where Ginny had helped her to unload her belongings from the car three weeks earlier, prior to the arrival of the other flatmates.

Now she was crossing the Downs heading for Whiteladies Road, the location of Jem's flat on Pembroke Road indelibly printed in her mind and drawing her toward it like an invisible umbilical cord.

Actually, that conjured up a bit of a yucky image. Maybe not. Ooh, now that looked like an interesting Mexican restaurant over there on the left; maybe she and Jem could try it out this evening. And if Jem's flatmates wanted to join them, well, the more the merrier. As she indicated right and turned into Apsley Road, Ginny imagined them in the buzzy restaurant, all sitting and laughing to-gether around a table bristling with plates and bottles of ice-cold beer, the others exclaiming, "You're so lucky, Jem. I wish my mum was as much fun as yours!"

Whoops, mind that bus.

Chapter 2

THE FLAT WAS SITUATED on the second floor of what had once been a four-story Georgian house. Ginny waited until Bellamy had discreetly relieved himself against a tree in the front garden before ringing the doorbell. This was it; they were here and Jem was about to get the surprise of her—

"Yes?"

"Oh, hi! You must be Rupert!" Ginny did her best not to gush in front of the flatmate Jem had told her about. "Um… is Jem here?"

"No." Rupert paused. "And you are?"

"Oh, I'm her mum! And this is Bellamy, Jem's dog. How silly of me not to realize she might be out. I did ring a few times but her phone was switched off, and I just thought she was sleeping in. Er, do you know where she is?"

Rupert, who was wearing a pair of white shorts and nothing else, was lean and tanned. He shivered as a blast of cold air hit him in the chest. "She's working a lunchtime shift in the pub. Eleven till two, something like that."

Lunchtime shift? Pub? Ginny checked her watch and said, "Which pub?"

"No idea." Rupert shrugged. "She did say, but I wasn't paying attention. Somewhere in Clifton, I think."

Since there were about a million pubs in Clifton, that was a big help. "Well, could I come in and wait?"

He looked less than enthusiastic but said, "Yeah, of course. It's a bit of a mess."

Rupert wasn't joking. Upstairs in the living room there were dirty plates and empty cups all over the pale green carpet. An exotic-looking girl with short dark hair was sprawled on the sofa eating a bowl of CocoPops and watching a black-and-white film on TV.

"Hello!" Ginny beamed at her. "You must be Lucy."

The girl blinked. "No, I'm Caro."

"Caro's my girlfriend." Rupert indicated Ginny as he headed into the kitchen. "This is Jem's mother, come to see her."

Ginny wondered if she was supposed to shake hands or if that would be the ultimate uncool thing to do. Caro, through a mouthful of CocoPops, mumbled, "Hi."

OK, probably uncool.

"And this is Bellamy." Thank heavens for dogs, the ultimate icebreakers.

"Right." Caro nodded and licked her spoon.

Oh.

"So! Are you at uni too?" Nobody had offered her a seat so Ginny stayed standing.

"Yes." Caro dumped her empty cereal bowl on the carpet, rose to her feet, and headed for the kitchen.

Ginny, overhearing giggles and a muffled shriek of laughter, felt increasingly ill at ease. Moments later, Rupert stuck his head round the door. "Would you like a cup of tea?"

"Oh, thank you, that would be lovely!" OK, stop it, stop speaking in exclamation marks. "White, please, one sugar."

"Ah. Don't think we've got any sugar."

Ginny said, "No problem, I'll just have a glass of water instead."

Rupert frowned and scratched his head. "I think we've run out of water too."

Was he serious? Or was this their way of getting rid of her?

"Unless you drink tap," said Rupert.

Gosh, he was posh.

. "Tap's fine," said Ginny.

He grimaced. "Rather you than me."

"Just ignore him," said a voice behind Ginny. "Rupes only drinks gold-plated water. Hello, I'm Lucy. And I've seen the photos in Jem's room so I know you're her mum. Nice to meet you."

Oh, now *this* was more like it. Lucy was tall and slender, black and beautiful. Better still, she was actually smiling. Ginny was so overcome with gratitude she almost invited her out to dinner on the spot. Within minutes, Lucy had cleared away armfuls of plates, chucked a slew of magazines behind the back of the sofa, and installed Ginny in the best chair like the queen.

"Jem only got the job yesterday. It's her first shift today. Still, a bit of extra cash always comes in handy, doesn't it?" Lucy was chatty and friendly, the best kind of flatmate any mother could desire for her daughter. Having made a wonderful fuss of Bellamy, she brought him a bowl of water and gravely apologized in advance for the fact that it came from a tap.

Rupert and Caro stayed in the kitchen and played music, then Rupert emerged to iron a blue shirt rather badly in the corner of the living room where the ironing board was set up.

"I could do that for you," Ginny offered, eager to make him like her.

Rupert looked amused. "No thanks, I can manage."

"Jem's never been keen on ironing. I bet she's got a whole load that needs doing. Actually, while I'm here," said Ginny, "I could make a start on it."

"If I asked my mother to iron anything for me," Lucy said cheerfully, "she'd call me a lazy toad and tell me to do it myself."

Jem's room was untidy but clean. Ginny's heart expanded as she drank in every familiar detail, the happy family photos on the cork board up on the wall, the clothes, books and CDs littering every surface, the empty Coke cans and crisp packets spilling out of the

wastepaper bin. Unable to help herself, she quickly made the bed and hung all the scattered clothes in the wardrobe. This must be the new top Jem had bought in Oasis. Oops, and there was an oily mark on the leg of her favorite jeans; they needed to be soaked if that was going to come out. And was that nail polish on—

The front door slammed and Ginny froze, realizing that she was clutching her daughter's jeans like a stalker. Hastily flinging them back onto the bed, she burst out of the bedroom just as Bellamy began to bark. A split second later she reached the living room in time to see Jem and Bellamy greeting each other in a frenzy of ecstasy.

"I don't believe this! Mum, what are you *doing* here?" Jem looked up as Bellamy joyfully licked her face.

"Your mother's come all this way to see you," Rupert drawled and Ginny intercepted the look he gave Jem, clearly indicating how he felt about mad mothers who drove hundreds of miles to see their daughters on a whim.

Shocked, Jem said, "Oh, *Mum.*"

"No, I haven't," Ginny blurted out. "Crikey, of course I haven't! We're on our way to Bath and I just thought it'd be fun to pop in and say hello."

"Really? Well, that's great!" Letting go of Bellamy at last, Jem gave her mother a hug. Ginny in turn stroked her daughter's blond, pink-streaked hair. It wasn't quite the reunion she had envisaged what with Rupert, Caro, and Lucy looking on and her brain struggling to come up with an answer to the question Jem was about to ask, but at least she was here. It was better than nothing.

Oh, she'd missed her so much.

"Bath?" Jem stepped back, holding her at arm's length and looking baffled. "What are you doing going to Bath?"

Aaargh, I haven't the foggiest!

"Visiting a friend," said Ginny. *Quick, think.*

"But you don't know anyone in Bath."

I *know*, I *know*!

"Ah, that's where you're wrong," Ginny said gaily. "Ever heard me talking about Theresa Trott?"

Jem shook her head. "No. Who's she?"

"We were at school together, darling. I got onto that Friends Reunited website, left my email address, and in no time at all Theresa had emailed me. She's living in Bath now. When she invited me up to stay with her, I thought I couldn't drive past and not stop off here en route, that would be rude. So here we are!"

"I'm so glad." Jem gave her another hug. "It's lovely to see you again. Both of you."

"Your mother was about to start ironing your clothes," said Rupert, his mouth twitching with amusement.

Jem laughed. "Oh, Mum."

Deciding she hated him and feeling relaxed enough to retaliate now, Ginny looked Rupert in the eye and said, "Hasn't your mum ever ironed anything for you?"

"No." He shrugged. "But that could be because she's dead."

Damn, *damn*.

Dddddrrrringgg went the doorbell.

"You may as well get that, Jem," Rupert drawled. "It's probably your father."

Jem grinned and pulled a face at Rupert, then skipped downstairs to answer the door. She returned with a thin, dark-eyed boy in tow.

"Lucy, it's Davy Stokes."

Lucy was in the process of pulling her gray sweater up over her head. Tugging down the green T-shirt beneath, she said, "Hi, Davy. All right? I was just about to jump in the shower."

Ginny heard Rupert whisper to Caro, "I expect he'd like to jump in with her."

"Sorry." Davy, who had long dark hair, was clutching a book. "It's just that I promised to lend you this so I thought I'd drop it round."

"What is it? Oh right, John Donne's poems. Great, thanks." Lucy took the book and flashed him a smile. "That's really kind of you."

Blushing, Davy said, "You'll enjoy them. Um… I was wondering. There's a pub quiz on at the Bear this afternoon. I wondered if maybe you'd like to, um, come along with me."

Rupert was smirking openly now. Ginny longed to throw something heavy at him.

"Thanks for the offer, Davy, but I can't make it. Me and Jem are off to a party. In fact we need to get our skates on or we're going to be late. We're all meeting up at three."

Three o'clock? It was half-past two already. Ginny wondered if Lucy was lying in order to spare Davy's feelings.

"OK. Well, maybe another time. Bye." Davy glanced shyly around the room while simultaneously backing toward the door.

"Let me show you out," said Rupert.

He returned moments later, grinning broadly. "You've made a conquest there."

"Don't make fun of him," Lucy protested. "Davy's all right."

"Apart from the fact that he has no friends and still lives at home with his mum."

"So, what's this party you've been invited to?" Ginny put on her bright and cheerful voice and looked at Jem, whom she'd driven for three and a half hours to see.

"It's Zelda's birthday. She's on our course," Jem explained. "We're starting off at this new cocktail bar on Park Street. I'd better get ready. What time do you have to be in Bath?"

"Oh, not right this minute. I can drop you off at the cocktail bar if you like."

"Thanks, Mum, but there's no need. Lucy's driving and we're picking up a couple more friends on the way."

"Jem?" Lucy's disembodied voice drifted through from Jem's bedroom. "That black top you said I could borrow isn't here."

"It is! It's on the floor next to the CD player."

"The only thing on the floor is carpet." Popping her head round the door, Lucy said, "In fact all your clothes are missing."

"They're in the wardrobe," Ginny said apologetically. "I hung them up."

Rupert was highly entertained by this.

"Oh, Mum." Jem shook her head. "You'll be making my bed next."

Lucy grinned. "She's done that too."

"Checking the sheets," Rupert murmured audibly into Caro's ear.

"Well, I think we'd better leave you to it." Realizing that the girls had less than ten minutes in which to get ready and she was only in their way, Ginny clicked her fingers at Bellamy. She enveloped Jem in a hug and made sure it wasn't a needy one. "And you," she added, waggling her fingers in a friendly fashion at Rupert and Caro because, like it or not, they were a part of Jem's new life.

"What rotten timing," said Jem. "I've only seen you for two minutes and now you're rushing off again."

Ginny managed a carefree smile. So much for her wonderful plan to spend the weekend with the person she loved more than anyone else in the world. "I'll give you a ring in a few days. Bye, darling. Come on, Bellamy, say good-bye to Jem."

Outside it was starting to rain. As she drove off, waving gaily at Jem on the doorstep, Ginny felt her throat begin to tighten. By the time she'd reached Whiteladies Road the sense of disappointment and desolation was all-encompassing and she no longer trusted herself to drive. Abruptly pulling over, willing the tears not to well up, Ginny took several deep breaths and gripped the steering wheel so hard it was a wonder it didn't snap in two. It's not *fair*, it's not *fair*, it's *just not*—

With a jolt she became aware that she was being watched. She

turned and met the quizzical gaze of Davy Stokes. In the split second
that followed, Ginny realized she'd pulled up at a bus stop, it was a
bitterly cold, rainy afternoon and from the expression on Davy's face
he thought she'd stopped to offer him a lift.

Oh, brilliant.

But it was too late to drive off. And at least she wasn't in floods
of tears. Buzzing down the passenger window and reaching over,
Ginny dredged *that* voice up again and said chirpily, "Hello! You're
getting terribly wet out there! Won't you let me give you a lift?"

He was a kind-of-friend of her daughter. She was the mother of
a girl he was kind-of-friendly with. Just as she'd felt obliged to make
the offer, Ginny realized, so Davy now felt compelled to accept it.
Looking embarrassed, he said, "Is Henbury out of your way?"

Ginny had never heard of Henbury but after having driven two
hundred miles up here and with the same again to look forward to
on the return journey, what were a few more?

"No problem. You'll have to direct me, though. And don't
worry if Bellamy licks your ear, he's just being friendly."

"I like dogs. Hello, boy." Having climbed into the car and fastened his seat belt, Davy flicked his long dark hair out of his eyes and
said, "Can I ask you something?"

"Anything you like." *Yerk*, so long as it's nothing to do
with contraception.

"Did they talk about me after I'd gone?"

Ginny paused. "No."

He smiled briefly. "Shouldn't pause. That means yes. Do they
think I've got a crush on Lucy?"

"Um, possibly," Ginny conceded with reluctance. "Why?
Don't you?"

"Of course I do. She's gorgeous. But I kind of realize nothing's
ever going to come of it. I know I'm not her type." Wistfully, Davy
said, "I had hoped to win her over with my deadpan wit, kind of like

Paul Merton, y'know? Trouble is, every time I see Lucy my wit goes out of the window. I turn into a gormless dork instead."

Bless him. Ginny was touched by his frankness. "Give yourself time," she said soothingly. "Everyone gets a bit tongue-tied at first."

"To be honest, she's out of my league anyway. You won't mention any of this, will you? Can it be just between us?" asked Davy. "I've made enough of a fool of myself as it is."

"I won't breathe a word."

"Promise?"

"Promise. Shall I tell you something in return? I wasn't that taken with Rupert."

Davy's upper lip curled with derision. "Rupert's a prat and a dickhead. Sorry, but he is. He looks down his nose at everyone. Carry straight on over this roundabout."

"And you're still living at home, did somebody mention?" Lucky parents, thought Ginny as she followed the sign to Henbury.

"With my mother. Dad took off years ago. Mum didn't want me to move out," said Davy, "so I only applied to Bristol. Just as well I got a place really; otherwise I'd have been stuck."

Lucky, lucky mother. She'd asked her son not to move out so he hadn't. So simple, thought Ginny. Now why didn't I think of that?

"She might change her mind. Maybe Rupert will move out and you could take his place." Ginny was only joking but wouldn't it be great if that happened?

"Except Rupert's hardly likely to move out," said Davy, "seeing as it's his flat."

"Is it?" She hadn't realized that. "I thought they were all tenants."

Davy shook his head. "Rupert's father bought the place for him to live in while he's here at university."

"Oh. Well, that makes sense, I suppose. If you can afford it."

"From what I hear, Rupert's father can afford anything he wants."

"So the others are just there to help with the mortgage and keep Rupert company."

"Turn right here. And they just happen to be taking the same course." Davy's tone was dry. "He'll probably have them writing his essays for him before long. Now take the next left. That's it, and ours is the one there with the blue door. That's brilliant. Thanks so much; maybe we'll see each other again sometime." Twisting round in the passenger seat, he said, "Bye, Bellamy. Give me five."

He waited until Bellamy had raised a paw, then solemnly shook it.

"Good luck," said Ginny. "And you never know, things might work out better than you expect."

Davy climbed out of the car. "You mean tongue-tied good guy gets the girl in the end? Maybe if this was a Richard Curtis film I'd stand a chance." With a good-natured shrug, he added, "But I can't see it happening in real life. Oh well, at least it's character-forming. Everyone needs to have their heart broken some time."

Ginny watched him head into the house, the kind of modest, everyday, three-bed end terrace that Rupert would undoubtedly sneer at. Never mind other people having their hearts broken; hers was a bit cracked right now.

"Time to go home, boy." Patting Bellamy's rough head, Ginny said, "All the way back to Portsilver. So much for our weekend with Jem, eh? Sorry about that."

Bellamy licked her hand as if to let her know that he didn't mind and had already forgiven her. Ginny gazed lovingly at him. "Oh, sweetheart, thank goodness I've got you to keep me company. Whatever would I do without you?"

—⁓—

Bellamy died three weeks later. The cancer that had spread so rapidly throughout his body proved to be untreatable. He was unable to

walk, unable to eat, clearly in pain. The vet assured Ginny that putting Bellamy to sleep, letting him go peacefully, was the kindest thing she could do.

So she did it and felt more grief and anguish than she'd ever known before. Bellamy had been with them ever since Gavin had moved out. Someone had suggested getting a dog to cheer them up and that was it, a fortnight later Bellamy had arrived in their lives, so much better company than Gavin that Ginny wished she'd thought of it years ago. Gavin was unfaithful, a gifted liar, and emotionally untrustworthy in every way. Bellamy wasn't; he was gentle, affectionate, and utterly dependable. He never fibbed to her about where he'd been. His needs were simple and his adoration unconditional.

"You love that dog more than you ever loved me," Gavin had grumbled.

And when Ginny had replied, "Wouldn't anyone?" she had meant it.

Chapter 3

AND NOW BELLAMY WAS gone. Ginny still couldn't take it in, found it impossible to believe she'd never see his dear whiskery face again. This morning they had buried him in the back garden beneath the cherry tree. Jem had caught the train down last night and together they had sobbed their way through the emotional ceremony.

But Jem had lectures and tutorials back in Bristol that she couldn't afford to miss. Staying down in Portsilver wasn't an option. Red-eyed and blotchy, she had reluctantly caught the lunchtime train back to Bristol.

Ginny was pretty blotchy herself, not helped by having managed to jab herself in the eye with a mascara wand while she was doing her makeup. She felt bruised, emotionally drained, and wrung out but at the same time far too jittery to sit alone in an empty house gazing out at Bellamy's grave. Being miserable was alien to her character—she had always been the naturally cheerful type.

Set on distraction, Ginny drove down into the center of Portsilver and parked the car. At least in November it was physically possible to park your car in Portsilver. Right, now what little thing could she treat herself to? A gorgeous new lipstick perhaps? A sequined scarf? Ooh, or how about a new squeaky toy for—

No, Bellamy's dead. Don't think about it, don't think about it.

Don't look at any other dogs as you walk down the street.

And *don't cry*.

In a few weeks it would be Christmas, so how about making a start on some present buying instead?

Miraculously, Ginny began to feel better. Picking out stocking fillers for Jem, she chose a pale pink tooled leather belt and a notebook whose cover was inlaid with mother-of-pearl. In another shop she found a pair of blue-and-green tartan tights, acrylic hair bobbles that flashed on and off when you tapped them, and a ballpoint pen with lilac marabou feathers exploding from the top.

This was something she had always enjoyed, buying silly bits and pieces. Having paid for everything in her basket, Ginny left and made her way on down the street. A painting in the window of one of the shops further along caught her eye and she moved toward it. No, maybe not; up close it wasn't so great after all.

The next moment, glancing across the road, Ginny saw a woman she knew only as Vera and her heart began to thud in a panicky way. They weren't close friends but had got to know each other while taking their dogs for walks along Portsilver's main beach. Vera owned an elegant Afghan hound called Marcus who was at this moment sitting patiently while his owner retied her headscarf. She was the chatty type. If Vera spotted her, she would be bound to ask where Bellamy was.

Unable to face her today, Ginny ducked into the sanctuary of the shop. Inside, tables were decoratively strewn with china *objets d'art*, hand-crafted wooden animals, funky colored glass candelabra, and all manner of quirky gifts.

Quirky expensive gifts, Ginny discovered, picking up a small pewter-colored peacock with a jeweled tail and turning it over in the palm of her hand. The price on the label gave her a bit of a shock—blimey, you'd want real jewels for thirty-eight pounds. Then again, it wasn't her kind of thing but Jem might like it. Oh now, look at those cushions over there; she'd definitely love those.

Except Jem wasn't going to get the chance to love them because a surreptitious turning over of the price tags revealed the cushions to be seventy-five pounds each. Yeesh, this was a lovely shop but maybe not the place to come for cheap and cheerful stocking fillers.

Lurking by the table nearest the door, Ginny peered out to see if Vera was still there. Not that she disliked Vera; it wasn't that at all; she just knew that having to tell another dog lover that Bellamy was dead would be more than she could handle just now. And breaking down in public was the last thing she needed.

No, thankfully, the coast appeared to be clear. Glancing around the shop to double-check that there was nothing else she wanted to look at and might be able to afford—shouldn't think so for one second—Ginny became aware that she was the object of someone's attention. A black-haired man with piercing dark eyes, wearing jeans and a battered brown leather jacket with the collar turned up, was watching her. For a second their eyes locked and Ginny saw something unreadable in his gaze. Heavens, he was good-looking, almost smolderingly intense.

And then it was over. He turned away with an infinitesimal shrug that indicated he'd lost interest. Brought back to earth with a thump, Ginny gave herself a mental telling off. As if someone who looked like a film star was likely to be bowled over by the sight of her, today of all days, with her puffy, post-funeral eyes and tangled hair.

Dream on, as Jem would say with typical teenage frankness. And quite right too. Oh well, at least she hadn't made an idiot of herself and tried smiling and batting her eyelashes at him in a come-hither fashion. Relieved on that score, Ginny turned away as the door was opened by another customer coming into the shop. She ducked past them and left, still keen not to bump into Vera, and began heading swiftly in the direction of the car park. That was enough for one day; time to go home now and—

"I saw you."

Like a big salmon, Ginny's heart almost leaped out of her body. A hand was on her arm and although she hadn't heard him speak before, she knew at once who it was.

Who else could a voice like that belong to?

Whirling round to face him, she felt color flood her cheeks. Crikey, up close he was even more staggeringly attractive. And clearly intelligent too, capable of seeing beyond her own currently less-than-alluring external appearance. Like those scouts from model agencies who could spot a pale lanky girl in the street and instinctively tell that she would scrub up well.

"I saw you," he repeated.

He even smelled fantastic. Whatever that aftershave was, it was her favorite. Breathlessly, Ginny whispered, "I saw you too."

His gaze didn't falter. His hand was still on her arm. "Shall we go?"

Go? Oh, good grief, was this really happening? It was like one of those arty black-and-white French films where two people meet and say very little to each other but do rather a lot.

"Go where?" Steady on now, he's still a complete stranger; you can't actually go back to his place, tear off his clothes, and leap into bed with a man you've only just—

"Back to the shop."

Ginny's imagination skidded to a halt in midfantasy. (He had a four-poster bed with cream silk drapes that stirred in the breeze drifting in through the open window—because in her fantasy it was a balmy afternoon in August.)

"Back to the shop?" Perhaps he owned it. Or lived above it. Oh God, he was reaching for her hand; this was *so romantic*. If only she could stop herself idiotically parroting everything he said.

"Come on, do yourself a favor and give up. You might be good," he drawled, "but you're not that good."

What was *that* supposed to mean? Puzzled, Ginny watched him take hold of her hand, then turn it face up and, one by one, unfurl her fingers.

Her blood ran cold. The next second she let out a shriek of horror followed by an involuntary high-pitched giggle. "Oh my

God, I didn't even realize! How embarrassing! I can't believe I just walked out with it in my hand. Thank goodness you noticed! I'll take it straight back and explain…"

Ginny's voice trailed away as she realized that she was attempting to retrieve her hand and this man wasn't letting it go. Nor was he smiling at her absentmindedness, her careless but innocent mistake.

In fact he was gripping her wrist quite tightly, making sure she couldn't escape.

"Now look," said Ginny, flustered. "I didn't do it on purpose!"

"I despise shoplifters. I hope they prosecute you," the man said evenly.

"But I'm not a shoplifter! I've never stolen anything in my *life*. Oh God, I can't believe you even think that!" Hideously aware that people in the street were starting to take notice, some even slowing down to listen avidly to the exchange, Ginny turned and walked rapidly back to the shop still clutching the jeweled peacock and fighting back tears of shame. Because like a hammer blow it had struck her that while she had been mentally drooling over a man she ridiculously imagined might fancy her, she had completely forgotten about Bellamy.

That's how breathtakingly shallow and selfish she was.

Pushing open the door to the shop, she saw that there were a dozen or so customers wandering around, plus the woman who worked there. Hot on her heels—evidently ready to rugby-tackle her to the ground if she tried to escape—the man ushered her inside and up to the counter. Ginny pushed the jeweled peacock into the woman's hands and gabbled, mortified, "I'm so sorry; it was a complete accident. I didn't realize I was still holding it when I left."

"Sounds quite convincing, doesn't she?" The man raised an eyebrow. "But I was watching her. I saw the way she was acting before she made her getaway."

Was this like being innocent of murder but finding yourself on death row?

"Please don't say that." The tears were back, pricking her eyelids. Gulping for breath and aware that she was now truly the center of attention, Ginny clutched the edge of the counter. "I'm an honest person. I've never broken the law; I just wasn't *concentrating*."

"Obviously not," the man interjected. "Otherwise you wouldn't have got caught."

"Oh, will you SHUT UP? I didn't mean to take it! As soon as I'd realized it was in my hand, I would have brought it back," Ginny shouted. "It was an *accident*." Gazing in desperation at the saleswoman, she pleaded, "You believe me, don't you? You don't think I was actually planning to steal it?"

The woman looked startled. "Well, I…"

"See that sign?" The man pointed to a sign next to the till announcing that shoplifters would be prosecuted. "It's there for a reason."

Ginny began to feel light-headed. "But I'm not a shoplifter."

Gesturing toward the phone on the counter, the man said to the saleswoman, "Go on, call the police."

"It was a mistake," sobbed Ginny. "My dog died yesterday. I only b-buried him this morning." As she said it, her knees buckled beneath her. The tears flowed freely down her face as the saleswoman hastily dragged a chair out from behind the counter. "I'm sorry, I'm so sorry… everything's just getting too much for me." Sinking onto the chair, Ginny buried her face in her hands and shook her head.

"She's in a bit of a state," the saleswoman murmured anxiously.

"That's because she's been caught red-handed. Now she's trying every trick in the book to get out of it."

"Ah, but what if her dog's really died? It's awful when that happens. And she's looking a bit pale. Are you feeling all right, love?"

Ginny shook her head, nausea swirling through her body like ectoplasm. "Actually, I'm feeling a bit sick."

A large blue bowl with pink and gold daisies hand-painted on

the inside was thrust into her hands. The attached price ticket announced that it was £280. Breathing deeply, terrified that she might actually be sick into it, Ginny felt beads of sweat breaking out on her forehead.

"She looks terrible."

"That's because she's guilty."

"Hello, love, can you hear me? You shouldn't be on your own. Is there anyone we can call?

Pointedly, the man said, "Like the police?"

It was no good, even being thrown into a police cell and chained to a wall would be better than being gawped at by everyone here in the shop. Shaking her head, Ginny muttered, "No, no one you can call. My daughter's not here anymore. She's gone. Just get it over and done with and call the police. Go ahead, arrest me. I don't care anymore."

There was a long silence. It seemed that everyone was holding their breath.

Finally, the saleswoman said, "I can't do it to her. Poor thing, how could I have her arrested?"

"Don't look at me. It's your shop." The man sounded exasperated.

"Actually, it's not. The owner's gone to Penzance for the day and I'm just covering. But we've got this back." The clink of the jeweled peacock's feet against the glass-topped counter reached Ginny's ears. "So why don't we leave it at that?"

The man, clearly disappointed, breathed a sigh of resignation and said brusquely, "Fine. I was just trying to help."

The door clanged shut behind him. Ginny fumbled for a tissue and wiped her nose. Patting her on the arm, the saleswoman said kindly, "It's all right, love. Let's just forget it ever happened, shall we?"

"It was an accident," snuffled Ginny.

"I'm sure it was. You've had a rotten time. Are you OK to leave now? You need to take it easy, look after yourself."

"I'll be all right." Embarrassed and grateful, Ginny rose to her feet and prayed the Terminator wouldn't be waiting outside. "Thanks."

Chapter 4

"YOU'LL NEVER GUESS WHAT I did last week." Even as she said it, Ginny felt herself begin to blush.

"Hey, good for you." Carla, tanned from her fortnight in Sardinia, gave a nod of approval. "Welcome back to the real world and about time too. So where did you meet him?"

Honestly.

"I wasn't doing *that*," Ginny protested. "We're not all sex-crazed strumpets, you know."

"Just as well. All the more men for me." Amused, Carla said, "So tell me what you were doing instead that was so much better than sex."

"I didn't say it was better than sex." Entirely unbidden, the image of that cream four-poster bed with its hangings billowing in the breeze danced once more through Ginny's mind, accompanied by the shadowy outline of a tall, half-dressed figure. "It was horrible. I accidentally shoplifted something and got caught by this vile man who didn't believe I hadn't meant to do it. Don't laugh," she protested as Carla's mouth began to flicker. "It was one of the worst experiences of my whole life. I was almost arrested."

"I hate it when that happens. What were you trying to make off with anyway? Something good?"

Friends, who needed them? Aiming a fork at Carla's hand, Ginny said, "I wasn't trying to make off with anything. It was a miniature jeweled peacock. I didn't even like it."

"Never shoplift stuff you don't like. What were you thinking of?"

"That's just it, I *wasn't* thinking. It was after we'd buried Bellamy. And then I'd taken Jem to the station. I thought a spot of shopping might cheer me up." Ginny pulled a face. "Now I daren't even go into a shop in case it happens again. At this rate it's going to be tinned carrots and cornflakes at Christmas."

"You need to sort yourself out," said Carla. "Get your social life back on track, find yourself a new man. I mean it," she insisted. "Tinned carrots and a suspended sentence isn't the way forward."

"I know, I know." Ginny had heard all this fifty times before; her manless state was a continuing source of pain and bewilderment to Carla. "But not until after Christmas, OK? Jem'll be back soon."

"There, you see? You're doing it again. Putting your life on hold until Jem comes home." Swiveling around on her chair, Carla peered accusingly up at Ginny's kitchen calendar. "I bet you've been crossing off the days until the end of term."

"I can't imagine why I'm your friend. As if I'd do that," said Ginny.

As if she'd cross the days off on the kitchen calendar where Jem would see it when she got back; she wasn't that stupid. She was crossing them off on the other calendar, the secret one hidden under her bed.

"Anyway, enough about you. Let's talk some more about me," said Carla.

So far they were up to day eight of her eventful holiday in Sardinia. No man had been safe. "Go on then, what happened after Russell went home?"

"*Thank you.*" Carla's eyes danced as she refilled their wine glasses. "I thought you'd never ask. Well…"

Ginny smiled. Only nineteen more days and Jem would be back. She'd definitely drink to that.

~~~

It was the week after Christmas and Ginny was in the kitchen loading the dishwasher when Jem bellowed from the living room, "Mum! GET IN HERE!"

Ginny straightened up. Had a spider just galloped across the carpet? "Mum! *NOW!*"

In the living room she found Jem no longer draped across the sofa but catapulted bolt upright gazing at the TV screen. It was one of those daytime magazine-style programs and the presenter was talking chirpily about singles clubs. Ginny, her heart sinking, said, "Oh no, I'm not going to one of those, don't even try to persuade me—*oh!*"

The camera had swung round to reveal the person standing next to the presenter.

"I'm so embarrassed," groaned Jem. "Tell me you had an affair and he's not my real father."

Ginny, her hands covering her mouth, watched as the female presenter interviewed Gavin about the difference joining a singles club had made to his life. Gavin was beaming with pride and wearing one of his trademark multicolored striped shirts—some might call them jazzy; Ginny called them eye-wateringly loud. In his jolly way he chatted with enthusiasm about the fun they all had together and the great network of friends he'd made since joining the club. Never what you'd call shy, Gavin went on cheerfully, "I mean, I know I'm no Johnny Depp, but all I'm looking for is someone to share my life with, and I know the right woman has to be out there somewhere. That's not too much for a forty-year-old to ask, is it?"

"Forty!" Ginny let out a squeak of disbelief because Gavin—the cheek of the man—was forty-three.

"Uurrrgh, now he's flirting with the presenter!" Jem buried her face in a cushion. "I can't watch!"

Excruciatingly, the presenter and Gavin ended up dancing together before Gavin swept her into a jokey Hollywood embrace. Jem

was making sick noises on the sofa. Then that segment of the TV program was over and singles clubs were replaced by a three-minute in-depth discussion on the subject of cystitis.

"I can't believe I'm related to him." Finally daring to uncover her eyes again, Jem wailed, "God, as if it isn't bad enough having a dad who *joins* a singles club. But oh no, mine has to go one better and appear on TV to boast about it. Without even having the decency to have his *face* blurred." Reaching for her mobile, she punched out her father's number. "Dad? No, this *isn't* Keira Knightley; it's *me*. And, yes, of course we've just seen it. I can't believe you didn't warn us first. What if all my friends were watching? Why do *I* have to be the one with the embarrassing dad?"

"It's his mission in life to make you cringe," said Ginny.

Jem, having listened to her father speak, rolled her eyes at Ginny. "He says he's feeling a bit peckish."

"He's always feeling a bit peckish. That's why he has to wear big stripy shirts to cover his big fat stomach. Go on then," Ginny sighed, "tell him to come over."

"Hear that?" said Jem into the phone. She broke into a grin. "Dad says you're a star."

"He doesn't know what we're eating yet." Ginny wiped her wet hands on her jeans. "Tell him it's salad."

Chapter 5

GAVIN ROARED UP THE drive an hour later in his filthy white mid-life crisis Porsche and they ate dinner together around the kitchen table. Jem's efforts to shame him, predictably enough, failed to have the desired effect.

"Where's the harm in it?" Breezily unrepentant, Gavin helped himself to another mountain of buttery mashed potato. "I'm expanding my social life, making new friends, having fun. I've met some smashing girls."

Girls being the operative word. Ginny found it hard to believe sometimes that she and Gavin had ever been married. These days he was forever announcing that yet again he had met the most gorgeous creature and that this time she was definitely The One. Needless to say, Gavin was an enthusiastic chatter-upper of the opposite sex but not necessarily a sensible one. The girls invariably turned out to be in their twenties with short skirts, high heels, and white-blond hair extensions. These relationships weren't what you'd call a meeting of minds. They usually only lasted a few weeks. When Gavin had come round over Christmas he had spent all his time extolling the virtues of his latest amour, Marina. And now, ten days later, here he was extolling the virtues of a singles club.

"What happened to Marina?" Ginny dipped a chunk of bread into the bowl of garlic mayonnaise.

"Who? Oh, right. Her ex-boyfriend got jealous and kicked up a bit of a fuss. They're back together now."

"And you're back to square one," said Ginny. "Aren't the women at this singles place a bit older than you're used to?"

"So? Not a problem. Some of them have cracking daughters." Gavin was unperturbed. "And don't give me that look. You should try it yourself."

"What? Chatting up fifty-something women, then running off with their daughters?"

"The club. It'd do you the world of good. Jem's back at uni next week," Gavin went on. "You want to be getting out more. Come along with me, and I'll introduce you to everyone. It'd be fun."

"Are you mad? I'm your ex-wife." Ginny couldn't believe he was serious. "It's not normal, you know, to take your ex-wife along to your singles club. Even if I did want to go to one, which I *don't*."

Gavin shrugged. "You've got to move with the times. And think of what you're going to do with the rest of your life."

"Dad, leave it. This is like when you keep trying to persuade me to eat olives just because you love them. Mum's fine; she's not desperate like you."

"I'm not desperate." Gavin was outraged at this slur on his character.

"No, you're just a bit of a tart." Reaching over, Jem gave his hand a reassuring pat. "And that's not a criticism; it's the truth. But Mum isn't like that. She's happy as she is." Turning to Ginny, she added, "You never get lonely, do you, Mum? You're not the type."

"Um… well…" Caught off guard by what had clearly been a rhetorical question, Ginny wondered if this might perhaps be the moment to confess that sometimes, if she was honest, she did get a bit—

"Thank *God*," Jem continued with feeling. "And let me tell you, I seriously appreciate it." She shook her head in disbelief. "I mean, you wouldn't believe what some parents are like. There are some completely hopeless cases out there. Like Lizzie, one of the girls on

my course, her mum and dad ring her up almost every day; they have no idea how embarrassing they are. Everyone bursts out laughing whenever her phone rings—it's like her parents are living their whole lives through her. And Davy's another one—crikey, he's in an even worse situation. Poor Davy, his mother wouldn't even let him leave home. He's just, like, *stuck* there with her and everyone teases him. I mean, can't the woman get a grip? Doesn't she realize she's ruining his whole life?"

Poor Davy. Poor Davy's mother. Poor *her*. Feeling sick, Ginny drank some water. Part of her was relieved that Jem hadn't an inkling how utterly bereft she felt. The other part realized that, clearly, from now on, she was never ever going to be able to admit it.

"She doesn't mean to," Ginny protested on Davy's mother's behalf.

"Yes, but it's so… pathetic! I mean, it's not as if we're babies anymore." Jem waved her fork around for emphasis. "We're *adults*."

"It's not very adult to tease a boy just because he's still living at home." Ginny recalled how Jem, as a toddler, had sat in her high-chair imperiously waving her plastic fork in exactly that fashion. "I hope you haven't been mean to him."

"Oh, Mum, of course I haven't been mean. It's just a bit of a nerdy thing to do, isn't it? And it means he doesn't fit in. It's like if a crowd of us go out for a drink we always pile back to somebody's rooms or flat afterward for beer. But what can Davy do, invite everyone round to his mum's house? Imagine that! Sipping tea out of the best china, having to sit up straight and make polite conversation with somebody's *mother*."

Ginny winced inwardly. Why didn't Jem just stab her all over with the fork? It couldn't hurt any more than this.

"Don't bother with him. Just leave him to get on with it." Gavin, who was to political correctness what Mr. Bean was to juggling, said, "Concentrate on your other friends. That one sounds like a nancy boy, if you ask me."

Ginny was balanced on a stepladder singing along to the radio at the top of her voice when she heard the distant sound of the front doorbell. It took a while to wipe her hands on a cloth, clamber off the ladder, and gallop downstairs.

By the time she reached the hall, Carla was shouting through the letterbox, "I know you're in there; I can hear all the horrible noise. Are you crying again? Come on, answer the door. I've come to cheer you up, because that's the kind of lovely, thoughtful person I am."

Ginny opened the door, touched by her concern. "That's really kind of you."

"Plus I need to borrow your hairdryer because mine's blown up." Impressed, Carla said, "Hey, you're not crying."

"Well spotted."

"You're wearing truly revolting dungarees."

"Not much gets past you, Miss Marple."

"And there's bright yellow stuff all over your face and hands." Carla paused, considered the evidence, and narrowed her eyes shrewdly. "I conclude that you have been having a fight in a bath of custard."

"You see? That's why the police never take a blind bit of notice when you try and interfere with their investigations."

Carla grinned and followed her into the kitchen. "Any man having his 'investigations' interfered with by me is definitely going to take notice. So what's brought all this on? What are you painting?"

"Spare bedroom."

Carla, who was no DIYer, raised her eyebrows. "For any particular reason?"

"Oh yes."

"Am I allowed to ask why?"

Ginny made two mugs of tea and tore open a packet of caramel

wafers. "Because I've had enough of feeling sorry for myself. It's time to sort myself out and make things happen."

"Well, good. But I don't quite see where decorating the house comes in."

"Jem rang last night. She and Lucy were on their way out to a party. She sounded so happy," said Ginny. "They're having such fun together. Lucy got chatting to one of the boys from the rugby team and he invited her and Jem along to the match on Saturday."

"Poor Jem, having to watch a game of rugby." Carla, who liked her creature comforts, shuddered and unwrapped a caramel wafer. "I can't imagine anything more horrible."

"But that's not the point. She's making more friends all the time. And before you know it, she'll be meeting *their* friends," Ginny explained. "Once you start, it just carries on growing."

Carla couldn't help herself. "As the bishop said to the actress."

"So last night I decided that's what I should do too. Here's this lovely house with only me in it and that's such a waste. So I'm going to advertise for—"

"A hunky rugby player of your very own! Gin, that's a fabulous idea! Or better still, a whole *team* of hunky rugby players."

"Sorry to be so boring," said Ginny, "but I was thinking of a female. And preferably not the rugby playing kind. Just someone nice and normal and single like me. Then we can go out and do stuff together like Jem and Lucy do. I'll meet her friends, she'll meet mine, and we can socialize as much as we want. And when we don't feel like going out, we can relax in front of the TV, just crack open a bottle of wine, and have a good gossip."

Carla pretended to be hurt. Inwardly, she *felt* a bit hurt. "You mean you're going to advertise for a new friend? But I thought I was your friend. I love cracking open bottles of wine! I'm great at gossip!"

"I know that. But you already have your life exactly the way you want it," Ginny patiently pointed out.

"You'll like her better than you like me!" Carla clutched her hand to her chest. "The two of you will talk about me behind my back. When I turn up on your doorstep, you'll say, 'Actually, Carla, it's not really convenient right now. Doris and I are just about to crack open a bottle of wine and have a good old girly gossip. '"

"Fine." Ginny held up her paint-smeared palms. "I give in. You can be my new lodger."

Now Carla was genuinely horrified. "You must be joking! I don't want to live with you! No thanks, I like my own space."

"Well, exactly. But I don't. I hate it," Ginny said simply. "I'm used to having someone else around the house. And as soon as I get this room redecorated, I can go ahead and advertise." Brightening, she added, "And now you're here, fancy giving me a hand with the painting?"

"Are we still friends?"

"Absolutely."

"In that case I'm sure you'll understand," said Carla, "when I say I'd rather eat raw frogs than give you a hand with the painting. Why don't you just lend me your hairdryer and I'll leave you to it? Too many cooks and all that."

Ginny grinned as Carla rose to her feet and brushed wafer crumbs from her perfect black trousers. "Except you've never cooked anything in your life."

"Ah, but I have other talents." Carla experienced a rush of affection and gave Ginny a hug. "And you're not allowed to replace me. If a lodger's what you want, then that's great. But I'm your best friend and don't you forget it."

Chapter 6

"YOU DON'T HAVE TO do this, you know." Jem smiled at Davy Stokes, who had taken to dropping into the Royal Oak before closing time and walking her home after her shift.

"I know, but it's practically on my way." Davy shrugged and said mildly, "Sorry, is it embarrassing? I won't do it if you'd rather I didn't."

"Don't be daft. It's nice having someone to talk to. And when my boots are pinching my toes," Jem added because her new boots were undoubtedly designed to be admired rather than worn to work in, "it means you can give me a piggyback."

"In your dreams." Grinning, Davy dodged out of the way before she could grab his shoulders and jump up. "Should've worn trainers like any normal barmaid."

"But look at them! How could I leave them at home? They're so beautiful!" Jem's pointy pink cowboy boots were the new love of her life. "You're just jealous because you don't have a pair."

Together they bickered their way along Guthrie Road, shivering as a cold drizzle began to fall. On impulse, Jem said, "Kerry and Dan are having a party tonight. D'you fancy coming along?"

Davy reluctantly shook his head. "Thanks, but I have to get home."

Every Saturday after walking her to her door, he caught the bus back to Henbury. Feeling sorry for him, Jem urged, "Just this once. Come on, it'll be fun. Everyone's going. And you're welcome to crash at our place afterward." What with Davy's continuing crush on Lucy, if this wasn't an incentive, she didn't know what was.

He stuffed his hands into his coat pockets. "I really can't. Mum'll be waiting up for me."

"Davy, you're eighteen!"

Davy looked away. "I know, but she doesn't like to be on her own. Please don't start all this again. My mum isn't like your mum, OK?"

Jem slipped her arm through his and gave it a conciliatory squeeze. "OK, sorry. I'll shut up."

He relaxed. "That'll be a first."

"Anyway, I haven't told you about my mother's latest plan. I phoned her yesterday to tell her about my new boots," said Jem. "And that's when she told me, she's getting a lodger!"

"Crikey. Who?"

"No idea, she hasn't found one yet. She's just finished redecorating the spare room. Next week she's going to put an ad in the local paper."

"Wow. So how do you feel about that?"

"I think it's great. She wouldn't get anyone I didn't like, would she? Good for her, that's what I say." Jem was proud of her mother. "She's getting on with her own life, doing something positive. Now that I'm not there anymore she could probably do with the company. You know, you should suggest it to your mum. Then you could move out without feeling guilty about leaving her on her own."

Davy rolled his eyes. "You're doing it again."

"Sorry, sorry, it just seems such a shame that—"

"And again!" They'd reached Jem's flat; Davy checked his watch. "I'd better make a move if I'm going to catch my bus. You enjoy your party."

"I will. And thanks for walking me home. See you on Monday." Jem waved as he headed off in the direction of Whiteladies Road, a lone figure in an oversized coat from Oxfam, on his way home to share cocoa and biscuits with his mother. No wonder other people made fun of him.

Poor Davy, what kind of life did he have?

Jem let herself into the flat expecting it to be empty. It was midnight and Rupert would be out at some trendy club somewhere. Lucy was already at Kerry and Dan's party. All she had to do was quickly change her clothes, slap on a bit more eye shadow, and re-spritz her hair, and she would be on her way. This time in footwear that didn't pinch like delinquent lobsters.

But when she pushed open the door to the living room, there was Rupert lying across the sofa watching TV and with an array of Chinese food in cartons spread out over the coffee table.

"Crikey, I thought you'd be out."

Amused, Rupert mimicked her expression of surprise. "Crikey, but I'm not. I'm here."

"Why? Are you ill? Where's Caro?" As she shrugged off her coat—the great thing about Rupert was he was never stingy with the central heating—it occurred to Jem that Caro hadn't been around for a few days now.

"Who knows? Who cares? We broke up." He shrugged and reached for a dish of chicken sui mai.

"Oh, I didn't realize. I'm sorry."

"Don't be sorry on my account. She was boring. Spectacular to look at," Rupert sighed, "but with about as much charisma as a soap on a rope."

This was true, but Jem diplomatically didn't say so. In her experience, this was a surefire method of ensuring they'd be back together within a week, plus they'd then both hate your guts.

"So here I am, all alone, with more Chinese food than one person could ever eat. But now you're here too." Patting the sofa, Rupert said, "So that's good. Come on, sit down and help yourself. I've got a stack of DVDs here. How was work this evening?"

Jem hesitated. He'd never asked her about work before. She suspected that Rupert was keen to have company and more upset about Caro than he was letting on.

"Um, actually I'm supposed to be meeting up with Lucy. At Kerry and Dan's party. Why don't you come along too?"

"Kerry the bossy hockey player? And carrot-top Dan the incredible hulk? I'd rather cut off my own feet. You don't really want to go there," Rupert drawled. "All those noisy rugby types downing their own vast bodyweight in cheap beer. It's cold outside, it's starting to rain so you'd be drenched by the time you got there, and what would be the point of it all?"

He *was* lonely; it was obvious. And speaking of cutting off your own feet, hers were certainly killing her. Jem hesitated, picturing the party she'd be missing. She was starving, and the most anyone could hope for at Kerry and Dan's would be dry French bread and a bucket of garlic dip. Whereas Rupert didn't buy ordinary run-of-the-mill takeaways; he ordered from the smartest Chinese restaurant in Clifton, and all the food on the table looked and smelled like heaven.

"Maybe you're right." Giving in to temptation, she sank down onto the sofa next to him.

Rupert grinned. "I'm always right. Want a hand with those?"

Jem tugged off her left boot and heaved a sigh of relief as her toes unscrunched themselves. Having helped her pull off the right one, Rupert held up the boot and sorrowfully shook his head. "You shouldn't wear these."

What was he, a chiropodist?

"They're leather," Jem told him. "They'll stretch."

"That's beside the point; they'll still be horrible."

"Excuse me!"

"But they are. How much did they cost?"

"They were a bargain. Twenty pounds in the sale."

"Exactly."

"Reduced from seventy-five!"

"*Exactly*. Who in their right mind would want them?"

"*I* would," Jem protested, looking at her boots and wondering if he was right.

Smiling at the expression on her face, Rupert chucked them across the carpet. "OK, that's enough boot talk. Have some wine. And help yourself to food. Are you warm enough?"

The king prawns in tempura were sublime. Greedily, Jem tried the scallops with chili sauce. The white wine too was a cut above the kind of special-offer plonk she was used to. Closing her eyes and wriggling her toes, she said, "You know what? I'd rather be here."

"Of course you would. Staying in is the new going out." Wielding chopsticks like a pro, Rupert fed her a mouthful of lemon chicken. "Listen to the rain outside. We're here with everything we need. Turning up at some ropy old party just for the sake of it is what people do when they're too insecure to stay at home. They're just desperate."

Swallowing the piece of chicken, Jem thought how much chattier Rupert was when it was just the two of them together. While he and Caro had been a couple, their attitude had always been... well, not stand-offish exactly, but distant. Now, taking a sip of wine, she realized he was showing definite signs of improvement. Wait until she told Lucy that super-posh Rupert might actually be human after all.

Actually, better text Lucy and tell her she was giving the party a miss.

By half-past one they'd finished two bottles of wine. *Gangs of New York* wouldn't have been Jem's DVD of choice, but the food more than compensated. When the film ended, Rupert said, "Want to watch *The Office* next?"

"Ooh yes." Relaxed and pleasantly fuzzy, she beamed up at him. "You know what? I'm really glad I stayed in."

"All the best people do it. Unlike that rabble," said Rupert of a group of noisy revelers making their way along the road outside.

"Listen to them, bunch of tossers." Raising his voice, he repeated loudly, "*Tossers*."

Jem giggled. "I don't think they can hear you."

Rupert leaped up from the sofa and crossed the room. Flinging open the sash window, he bellowed, "TOSSERS!"

A chorus of shouting greeted this observation. Whistles and insults were flung up at him and a beer can made a tinny sound as it bounced off a wall.

"Close the window," Jem protested as cold air blasted through the room.

"Are you kidding? They tried to throw a beer can at me." Casting around the living room, Rupert searched for something to throw in return.

"No bottles." Jem swiftly grabbed the empty wine bottle before he could reach it. Then she let out a shriek as he snatched up her boots and flung the first one out of the window. "Not my boots!"

Chapter 7

"WANKERS," YELLED RUPERT, HURLING the second boot before she could stop him, then slamming the window shut.

"Are you mad? Go and get them back! They're *my* boots."

"Correction. They're horrible boots." Amused, he reached out and grasped Jem's arms as she attempted to dart past him. "And it's too late now; they've run off with them."

"You bastard! How dare you?"

"Hey, shhh, they've served their purpose. I'll buy you a new pair."

"That was the last pair in the shop!" Jem struggled to break free.

"And they were cheap and nasty. You deserve better than that. I'll buy you some decent boots." Rupert was laughing now. "Now there's an offer you can't turn down. OK, I'm sorry, maybe I shouldn't have just grabbed them like that, but I've done you a big favor. We'll go out tomorrow and find you a fabulous pair. That's a promise."

Jem stared past him, lost for words. Her beautiful pointy pink cowboy boots, the bargain boots she'd been so proud of, gone, just like that.

Had they really been cheap and nasty? Davy had said they looked nice.

Then again, Davy wasn't exactly known for his unerring sense of style.

"Come on." Rupert tilted her face up to look at him. "You know it makes sense." His gaze softened as he stroked her cheek. "God, you're a pretty little thing."

Jem knew he was going to kiss her. This wasn't something she had ever imagined happening. But now that it was, it seemed entirely natural. As his mouth brushed against hers, she felt warmth spread through her body. Rupert's fingers slid through her hair, then he drew her closer to him and kissed her properly.

It was great. Then he pulled away and cradled her face in his hands, his hazel eyes searching hers.

"What?" whispered Jem.

"Sorry, shouldn't have done that." He smiled briefly. "I just couldn't help myself."

Jem hesitated. Would it be too forward to suggest that he could do it again if he liked?

But Rupert was shaking his head now, looking regretful. "Probably not the best idea."

This was his flat, she was his tenant. Maybe he was right. Not hugely experienced sexually, one part of Jem was relieved that he wasn't launching himself at her, employing all his seduction skills and doing his level best to inveigle her into his bedroom for a night of torrid passion.

The other part of her wondered why not and felt, frankly, a bit miffed. Wasn't she attractive enough?

"Come on, let's watch *The Office*." Rupert affectionately ruffled her hair before turning away to sort through the pile of DVDs.

And that was what they did. For the next hour, Jem sat next to him on the sofa gazing blindly at the TV, completely unable to concentrate on what was happening on screen. Her mind was in a whirl; all she could think about was that kiss and the way Rupert had looked at her. Why had he stopped? And wasn't he feeling anything now? Her whole body was fired up, awash with adrenaline, and he was acting as if nothing had happened between them.

Had the kiss put him off? Had she done it wrong? Was Rupert regretting it now or did it genuinely not mean anything to him at all?

One thing was for sure, she wasn't going to be the one to ask.

Jem's heart broke into a gallop as Rupert moved, reaching forward for the remote control. He switched off the DVD and the TV, yawned widely, and said, "That's it. Time for bed."

Was that some kind of code? Hardly daring to breathe, she watched him stand up, yawn again, and stretch his shoulders. Turning briefly, he said, "Night then," before heading for the door.

OK, not some kind of code after all.

"Night," said Jem, confused and disappointed. All these months of sharing a flat with Rupert and she had honestly never thought of him in a romantic way, but that had been because he was so out of her league it had simply not occurred to her that anything could happen. Rupert's background, his gilded life and upper-class glamour, set him apart from the rest of them. He and Caro moved in elevated circles, whizzing up to London at weekends, staying with friends in country houses, and flying to Paris when the mood took them.

It was a different world. He'd kissed her.

And now he'd gone to bed.

Let's face it, nothing was going to happen. She'd been naive to even think it might.

———

Jem had been in bed for ten minutes when the knock came on her bedroom door. Before she had time to reply, the handle turned and the door opened.

Rupert stood framed in the doorway, wearing shorts and nothing else. "I can't stop thinking about you."

"What?" It came out as a quivery whisper. Her pulse was going for some kind of world record.

"I think you heard." It was dark but Rupert sounded as if he was smiling. "I can't sleep." He tapped his head. "You're in here. I've tried to get you out but you won't go."

Oh, that voice, that silky upper-class drawl.

Moving toward her in the darkness, he went on, "And I wondered if it was the same for you."

Jem's tongue was stuck fast to the roof of her mouth. She couldn't say no; she couldn't say yes; she couldn't say anything at all.

"Room for one more in there?" Rupert tilted his head to one side. "Or would you rather be on your own? If I've just made a horrible mistake here, I'll go back to my room."

Her fingers trembling, Jem reached for Barney Bear, the battered soft toy that had accompanied her to bed since she was five years old. Surreptitiously she dropped him down between the side of the bed and her chest of drawers, then lifted the duvet and pulled it back, moving over to make room for Rupert to join her.

"You're sure?" said Rupert as he slid into bed and took her into his arms.

"Yes," Jem whispered into his ear. She'd never been more sure in her life.

—⁓—

At four o'clock, Rupert climbed out of bed and located his shorts.

Jem pushed herself up on one elbow. "What are you doing?"

"Being discreet. Better if Lucy doesn't know about this." Combing his fingers through his hair, he said, "She might think three's a crowd, feel a bit of a third wheel. Easier all round if you don't tell her."

He had a point. This was Rupert's flat, she and Lucy were his tenants, and it could cause awkwardness.

That made sense.

Except... did it mean what they'd just done was a one-off, nothing more than a meaningless shag?

Was that *it*?

"Hey, don't look at me like that." Having pulled on his shorts,

Rupert bent over and kissed her. "It'll be fun. Like having an affair without all the hassle of being married to other people. It's more exciting when no one else knows."

Relieved, Jem wrapped her arms around his neck. "You're right. It's easier if we don't tell Lucy. It'll feel a bit funny, though. We tell each other everything."

"Well, this time you're just going to have to stop yourself." Straightening up, Rupert grinned. "We don't want this to be spoiled, do we? Trust me, some secrets are better kept."

Chapter 8

THE ADVERT HAD GONE into the classified sections of today's *Western Morning News* and the *Cornish Guardian*. Ginny had spent ages composing it, finally settling on, "Cheerful divorcee, 38, has lovely room to let in spacious home in Portsilver. Would suit lady in similar circumstances. £60 pw inclusive."

There, that sounded OK, didn't it? Friendly and appropriately upbeat? If she were looking for somewhere to live, she'd be tempted herself. Gazing with pride at the adverts in the papers—all fresh and new and filled with promise—Ginny felt a squiggle of excitement at the thought of the fun she and her new lodger would have, going shopping together and—

Yeek, phone!

"Hello?" She put on her very best voice.

"'Ello, love, you sound up for it. Fancy a shag?"

Oh God. Outraged, Ginny said in a high voice, "No I do *not*," and cut the connection. Her hands trembled. How completely *horrible*. Was this what was going to happen? Would she be harassed by perverts?

The phone rang again an hour later. This time Ginny braced herself and answered it with extreme caution.

"It's me. How's it going?"

Oh, the relief. Gavin. "Nothing so far. Except some vile pervert."

"What did you say to him?"

"I told him to fuck off."

"Listen, let me know when anyone's coming around to look at the room. I should be there. It's not safe, inviting strangers into your home when you're on your own."

Ginny relented. Gavin had offered before but she'd told him there was no need, seeing as she'd only be meeting women anyway. Now, though, she realized he was right. It was silly to take the risk. Gavin might be disastrous in many ways, but he did have his good points.

"OK. If anyone *does* call." Reluctantly, she said, "Thanks."

"No problem. I'm free this evening. You didn't, by the way."

"Didn't what?"

"Tell me to fuck off."

Ginny counted to ten. "That was you? Thanks a lot."

"Ah, but I got my point across. It might not be me next time."

Gavin was annoying enough when he was wrong. When he was right he was insufferable. Ginny, who hated it when that happened, said, "Fine then, but you can hide upstairs. I'm not having you sitting there like some minder while I'm talking to them."

"You spoil all my fun," Gavin protested. "Never pass up the opportunity to meet new women, that's what I say. Hey, what if a foxy young chick moves in and I start dating her? That'd be a laugh, wouldn't it? Would you be jealous?"

"No, just astounded by her bizarre taste in men." Ginny was patient. "And no, it wouldn't be a laugh either." Counting off on her fingers, she added, "And thirdly, I can promise you now, my new lodger isn't going to be a foxy young chick."

⁓

The doorbell rang at seven o'clock on the dot, heralding the arrival of the first of the three potential tenants who had phoned that afternoon. More nervous than she let on—heavens, was this what it was like to go on a blind date?—Ginny shooed Gavin upstairs and took a steadying breath before opening the front door.

"Hello, love, I'm Monica. I've just been having a look at your window sills; you know they'd benefit from a quick going over with a dab of bleach. Brighten them up lovely, bleach would. Ooh, and those skirting boards could do with a dust."

The trouble with blind dates was, it wasn't considered polite to take one look at the no-hoper in front of you and say, "Sorry, this is never going to work out, so why don't we just give up right now?"

But here she was, faced with the equivalent of a blind date with John McCririck, and Ginny knew she was going to have to be pleasant and chat politely to the woman because that was how these things were done. Even if this one had just criticized her window sills and she'd saw off her own head rather than allow her to move into this house.

Monica was short and squat, with permed gray hair and flicked-up spectacles. She looked like a short-sighted turtle. She also looked sixty-five years old. And she hadn't stopped talking yet.

"...that's what I do, love. My little secret. Just dab a toothbrush in vinegar and scrub away like billy-o—those taps will come up like diamonds! Here, you take my coat. Oh dear, haven't you got a hanger? Now, why don't we have a nice cup of tea and a good old chat before I take a look at my room, hmm? Then we can start to get to know each other. Ooh, I say, Gold Blend, that's a bit extravagant, isn't it? And washing-up liquid from Marks and Spencer, well I never. Nice and weak, please, love, we can share the teabag. No sugar for me, I'm already sweet enough."

Oh help, oh help, get me out of here. Ginny said, "Sorry, how old did you say you were?"

"Forty-two, love. That's why I knew we'd have plenty in common, what with being the same age."

"Ri-ight." Ginny considered calling Gavin down from upstairs to see if he might like to flirt with the woman.

"I'll tell you a bit about myself, shall I? Well, my hubby and I

are getting a divorce so we're selling our bungalow, which is why I'm looking for a place to rent. And sharing's nice, isn't it? Cozy, like. Between you and me I'm not that bothered about losing him. My hubby's a bit of a misery, quiet as a church mouse, never been the sort to join in with conversations. Used to spend all his time in his blessed garden shed when he wasn't at work, so I can't see me missing him much at all. Mind you, could have knocked me down with a feather when he said he wanted a divorce! Didn't see that one coming! Men are funny creatures, aren't they? I'll never work out what makes them tick. Silly old fool, how he thinks he's going to manage without me I can't imagine. Did you know there's a mark on the outside of your window? Some bird's gone and done its nasty business on the glass. You want to get that cleaned off, it doesn't look very nice. I could do it for you now if you like."

"She sounds perfect. When's she moving in?" As soon as the front door closed, Gavin came downstairs.

"Shhh, my ears hurt."

"Want me to give them a polish with Brasso? That'll bring them up a treat."

"What a nightmare." Ginny shuddered. "That was horrendous. I told her I had lots of other people interested in the room and that I'd let her know tomorrow."

"You've only got two more to see. What if they're worse than her?"

Dumping the coffee cups in the sink and thinking longingly of the bottle of white wine in the fridge, Ginny said, "There can't be anyone worse than Monica."

⁓

"Hi, come in, I'm Ginny."

"Zeee."

Ginny hesitated, wondering if the woman had a bumble bee trapped in her throat. "Excuse me?"

"Zeee. That's my name. With three *e*'s." There was a note of challenge in the woman's voice, as if daring her to query the wisdom of this. "Zeee Porter. You shouldn't have a table there, you know. Not in the hallway like that. Bad feng shui."

"Oh." In that case, Ginny longed to tell her, you shouldn't have grubby blond dreadlocks and earrings bigger than castanets emphasizing your scrawny chicken neck, and you definitely shouldn't be wearing purple dungarees and homemade leather sandals over woolly toe socks, because that's bad feng shui too.

Zeee Porter, she learned, was thirty-six and—incredibly for such a catch—still single. Currently the only man in her life was her spirit guide, Running Deer. During the summer months, Zeee surfed, worked as a henna tattooist, and just, like, generally chilled out. The rest of the year she just, well, generally chilled out and waited for summer to come around again. Yes, she'd had a proper job once, in a vegan café in Aldershot, but being told what to do and having to get up in the morning had done her head in.

"It was a bad vibe, man." Zeee shook her head dismissively. "I just don't need that kind of hassle in my life."

She evidently didn't need the hassle of shampoo or deodorant either. Ginny wondered if Running Deer wore a peg on his nose or if spirit guides weren't bothered by those kinds of earthly matters.

Heaven knows what Monica would make of her. She'd probably march Zeee out into the garden and set about her with neat bleach and a scrubbing brush.

Ginny dutifully showed her the room she wouldn't be living in then said brightly, "Well, I've got *lots* of other people to see, but I'll give you a ring tomorrow and let you know either way."

"I haven't got a phone," said Zeee. "Phones are, like, destroying the planet."

"Oh." Except for when Zeee had rung earlier to make the appointment, presumably.

"To be honest," Zeee went on, "I think we'll just leave it. No offense, but I wouldn't want to live here anyway. It doesn't really do it for me, know what I mean?"

Flabbergasted, Ginny said, "*Oh*."

"*Plus*, Running Deer's telling me I shouldn't move in. He wouldn't be comfortable here."

"Right." Awash with relief, Ginny sent up a silent prayer of thanks to spirit guides everywhere. Hooray for Running Deer.

Zeee flicked back her moth-eaten dreadlocks. "Plus, he says you have a muddy aura."

———

"God, what a stink. Open the windows," Gavin complained. "Who's next?"

Ginny wasn't getting her hopes up. The third and final prospective lodger was male. "His name's Martin. I told him I was looking for a female to share the house with, but he said I couldn't specify like that because it was sexual discrimination and I could be sued if I refused to even interview men."

Gavin's lip curled. "Sounds like a nutter. Just as well I'm here."

"Actually, he didn't sound like a nutter. He was quite nice about it. He's split up from his wife," said Ginny, "and just needs somewhere pretty fast."

"Probably because he murdered her and the police are on his tail."

Ginny was fairly sure Martin wasn't a murderer. "He apologized for being a man but said he really wasn't difficult to live with, he didn't play loud music and he was fairly sure he didn't have any annoying habits. So what else could I do but agree to see him? You never know, he might be all right."

"Soft, that's what you are. I'll keep an ax upstairs with me," Gavin said cheerily. "Just in case."

Chapter 9

MARTIN MASON DIDN'T LOOK like a murderer. He politely introduced himself, appeared happy with the room Ginny showed him, and complimented her on her decorating skills. In the kitchen he accepted a cup of tea and said, "Well, I expect you've got plenty of other people to see, but just to let you know, I'd be very interested in the room." Drily he added, "Although I daresay you'll end up choosing a female."

"I don't know. I'll decide when I've met everyone." Was her nose getting longer? He seemed pleasant enough, but Ginny knew she wouldn't be inviting this man to be her housemate, although she didn't doubt that he'd pay his rent on time. Sharing her home with a gray-haired, suit-wearing, fifty-year-old assistant bank manager wasn't what she'd had in mind at all.

"I'd appreciate a quick decision," said Martin. "I'm sleeping in a work colleague's spare room at the moment, you see. I don't want to outstay my welcome."

Ginny nodded, remembering that his marriage had just broken up. Poor man, it couldn't be easy for him; it must have come as a terrible shock.

"So what happened? Is your wife still living in your house?" Was it impertinent to ask this? Oh well, she was curious.

Martin blinked behind his owlish spectacles. "For now, yes."

"And she just kicked you out, told you you had to leave?" Ginny was indignant on his behalf; that hardly seemed fair.

"Oh no. I was the one who left." His tone was mild. "It was absolutely my choice. I just couldn't stand being married to my wife a minute longer."

Good heavens, she hadn't been expecting that. Ginny said with bemusement, "Why? What was it like being married to her?"

Martin's mouth curled up at the corners. Behind his steel-rimmed spectacles his eyes glinted with amusement. "Believe me, if you'd ever met Monica, you wouldn't need to ask."

"Monica's husband. Poor man," Ginny said with feeling. "No wonder he was glad to be out."

"Did you tell him she'd been here?"

Ginny nodded as she sloshed wine into two glasses up to the brim and handed one to Gavin. "He said, whatever you do, don't let her move in. She'd drive you demented."

"But you aren't going to be asking him to move in either. So that's it." Gavin shrugged. "You've seen all three and none of them fitted the bill. What happens now?"

"Re-advertise I suppose. Try again. Hope for better luck next time." Ginny made headway into her much-needed glass of wine, more disappointed than she cared to let on by the events of this evening. She had been so looking forward to meeting someone lovely, the two of them hitting it off from the word go. Now she knew how naive she'd been and the sense of disappointment was crushing. What if she kept on advertising and no one suitable ever turned up?

By eight o'clock they had finished the bottle and Gavin was preparing to leave when the phone rang.

"Hi," said a warm male voice, "I'm calling about the house-share. Is it still going, or have you found someone now?"

It was more than a warm voice; it was a gorgeous voice, the kind

that made you think the owner had to be gorgeous too. Wondering if maybe all might not be lost after all, Ginny said, "No, it's still free."

"Fantastic. Now it says here in the ad that you'd prefer a female..."

"Either. Really, I don't mind."

"As long as it's someone you can get along with." He definitely sounded as if he were smiling. "I know, that's the important thing, isn't it? My name's Perry Kennedy by the way. And your house sounds great, just the kind of thing I'm after. How soon could I come around and take a look?"

Giddy with hope and three hastily downed glasses of wine, Ginny said recklessly, "Well, whereabouts are you? If you want to, you can come around now."

Having expected so much, Ginny was relieved to see when she opened the front door that he wasn't a troll. Perry Kennedy was six feet tall, with wavy reddish-gold hair, sparkling green eyes, and a dazzling smile. He was also athletically built and wearing a dark casual jacket over a white shirt and jeans.

"It's really good to meet you." As he shook Ginny's hand he said, "I've got a great feeling about this place already. Hey, I love the way you've done the hall."

Twenty minutes later they were sitting together in the kitchen chatting away as if they'd known each other for years. Perry's current flat was too small; it was driving him crazy. He was thirty-five, single but with a great crowd of friends in Portsilver and he loved socializing. A year ago he had moved down from London to Cornwall, selling his flat in Putney and plowing the equity into a T-shirt printing business. He enjoyed jet-skiing and scuba-diving in his spare time. His favorite food was Thai. He drove an old MG and his all-time favorite film was *The Color Purple*.

"But I don't normally admit that to people," said Perry. "I don't know why I told *you*. That film always makes me cry." He shook his head confidingly. "This could ruin my street cred."

"I can't tell you how many times I've sobbed my way through *The Color Purple*," said Ginny.

"Yes, but that's allowed. I'm not supposed to, though, am I? I'm a man."

Ginny laughed at the expression on his face. He was perfect.

"Anyway, I'm taking up too much of your time. The room's great," said Perry. "And so are you. What shall I do, then? Leave my number and wonder if I'll ever hear from you again?"

Could she ask for anyone better? Ginny raced through everything she knew about him in her mind, searching for flaws and finding none. Perry was charming and brilliant company. OK, he wasn't a woman and they probably wouldn't spend a lot of time discussing nail polish, but other than that, were there any drawbacks at all?

"Or," said Perry with a smile, "do you think there's a chance we might have a deal?"

Three glasses of wine didn't make the decision for her, but they certainly played their part. Seeing no reason to prevaricate, Ginny threw caution to the wind. Her mind was made up. She beamed at Perry and said, "We have a deal."

He looked at her in delight. "You don't know how much this means to me. It'll make all the difference in the world. How soon would the room be available?"

"Whenever you like." Ginny watched him take out his wallet and count his way through a sheaf of twenty-pound notes.

"Would Saturday be all right?"

"Saturday? No problem."

"Here, one month's deposit and the first month's rent in advance." Perry pressed the notes into her hand and said cheerfully, "Before you change your mind. And you'll be wanting references of course. I'll bring them along on Saturday. Thanks so much for this." He fixed Ginny with the kind of look that made her insides go wibbly. "I'm so glad I met you tonight."

"Me too." She watched as he rose to his feet and reached for his car keys.

"I'd better get back. Saturday morning, OK? Elevenish, or is that too hideously early?"

Ginny shook her head. This was the start of her new life and as far as she was concerned Saturday couldn't come soon enough. "No problem. Eleven o'clock's fine."

The trouble with ex-husbands was you could always rely on them to notice things you'd much rather they didn't.

And, naturally, to take huge delight in pointing it out.

"Ha!" Gavin pointed a triumphant finger at her as he came down the stairs.

Ginny was determined to bluff it out. "What?"

"You fancy him."

"I do *not*."

"Oh yes you do. You fancy the pants off him. *And* you're going red."

"Only because you *think* that," Ginny protested. "Not because it's true."

"I don't think it, I know it. I *heard* you." Smirking, he launched into a wickedly accurate imitation of her, repeating random overheard phrases punctuated with girlish giggles and slightly too loud laughter.

Why couldn't she have an ex-husband who lived five hundred miles away? Or in Australia? Australia would be good.

"You were eavesdropping." Ginny curled her lip accusingly to let him know how she felt about such low behavior.

"I was making sure you were safe. It was my job to listen to what was going on. Fine chaperone I'd be," Gavin remarked, "if I sat upstairs with my Walkman clamped over my ears. You could be screaming your head off and I wouldn't hear a thing. I'd come down

to the kitchen just in time to see him stuffing the last bits of you down the waste disposal. Then you'd be sorry."

"Anyway, he's moving in on Saturday." Ginny was defiant. "And I don't fancy him, OK? He just seems really nice and we get on well together, that's all."

"Hmm." Gavin raised a playful eyebrow. "Very well indeed, by the sound of things. Good-looking, is he?"

"Average," said Ginny. "Better looking than the other three that came round here tonight. Four, actually." To get her own back she pointed at Gavin. "Including you."

He grinned. "This is going to be interesting."

Ginny felt a squiggle of excitement. *Interesting.*

She hoped so too.

Chapter 10

By ELEVEN O'CLOCK ON Saturday morning the house was all ready and, as if in celebration, the sun had come out. Perry Kennedy would be here soon. Ginny, working on not sounding as if she fancied him, had been practicing her laugh as she tidied around the kitchen, making sure it didn't get too loud or high-pitched. Of course, once Perry had settled in and they became more used to each other, things would hopefully settle down and she'd stop feeling so—

Oh God, that sounded like him now! Flinging the dishcloth into the sink, Ginny wiped her hands on her jeans and fluffed up her hair. The throaty roar of a sports car outside died as the engine was switched off. She went to the front door and opened it.

"Hi there." Perry was already out of the car and waving at her. Today he was wearing a dark blue sweater, cream jeans, and Timberlands.

"Hi!" Ginny watched as the passenger door opened to reveal a slender woman with a mass of long, red-gold curls and pale, freckled skin. She was staggeringly beautiful and wore a long black coat falling open to reveal a pale gray top and trousers beneath.

"This is Laurel." Perry ushered the slender woman toward Ginny. "My sister."

Oh, phew, of course she was. All that incredible red-gold hair—what a relief.

"Hi, Laurel, nice to meet you." Ginny shook her hand with enthusiasm.

Tonelessly, Laurel said, "Hello."

"Come on then, let's get this lot upstairs." Already busy unloading the MG's tiny boot, Perry said, "Laurel, you take these. I'll bring the rest of the bags."

"Give some to me." Keen to help, Ginny held out her arms. "I can carry those."

Perry looked across at Laurel and said, "See what I mean? Didn't I tell you how great she was?"

Ginny flushed with pleasure. She'd done the right thing.

Laurel nodded. "You did."

Once all the bags and cases had been taken up to the spare room, Ginny left them to it. In the kitchen she boiled the kettle and began making tea. After a couple of minutes, Perry rejoined her.

"Don't bother with tea."

"No? Would you prefer coffee?"

He shook his head and produced the bottle he'd been concealing behind his back.

"Woo, champagne. On a Saturday morning!" And Veuve Cliquot at that, none of your old rubbish.

"The very best time to drink it. Quick, glasses," said Perry as the cork rocketed out and bounced off the ceiling.

"Well, cheers." Ginny clinked her glass against his; he'd only filled two of the three she'd set out. "Isn't Laurel having any?"

"Laurel doesn't drink. Cheers. Here's to you."

If Gavin were here now, he would tell her that replying "here's to both of us" would be flirty beyond belief. So Ginny didn't; she just smiled instead and took a demure sip of the champagne. As they heard the sound of furniture being moved around in the bedroom overhead, she said, "What's Laurel doing? Doesn't she want to join us?"

"She's fine, best to leave her to get on with it." Perry's eyes sparkled. "She's just rearranging the room, getting her things unpacked. You know how it is."

"Sorry?" Ginny thought she must have misheard.

"What?"

Or it had been a slip of the tongue. Of course, that was it. Ginny smiled. "You just said she was getting *her* things unpacked."

Perry nodded. "Yes."

OK, hang on, had she fallen into some kind of parallel universe here? Her heart beginning to thump unpleasantly, Ginny said, "But… why would she be unpacking her things? She isn't the one moving in. I've rented the room to you."

Perry looked at her. "God, I'm sorry, is that what you thought? No, no, the room's not for me. It's for Laurel."

This couldn't be happening.

"But you were the one who came to see it! You said it was just what you were looking for!" Her voice rising—and not in an I-fancy-you way—Ginny said, "You said it was perfect!"

He blinked, nonplussed. "It *is* perfect. For Laurel."

Frantically, Ginny ran back through everything he'd told her. "No, *hang on*, you said your flat was too small…"

"It *is* too small. I mean, it's all right for me on my own," Perry explained, "but it's definitely a squash for two. Laurel moved in six weeks ago and, to be honest, it's been doing my head in."

Doing *your* head in! What do you suppose this is doing to *my* head? Still in a state of shock, Ginny repeated, "B-but I rented the room to *you*."

"I know you did. That's right. I paid the deposit and I'll be paying the rent," said Perry. "No need to worry about that. I'll set up a direct debit. Really, everything's going to be fine."

Fine? How *could* it be? Ginny's head was about to explode.

"You made me think it was you! You never once mentioned your sister. You *knew* I thought it was you."

Perry spread his arms. "Honestly, I didn't."

"But the whole point of interviewing people when they come to

look at the room is so that you can decide whether you want to share your house with them!"

"Is it?" Perry looked genuinely bewildered. "I didn't realize." He paused, then said eagerly, "But it doesn't matter, because you won't have any problems with Laurel. As soon as I met you, I knew the two of you would get on brilliantly. You're just the kind of person Laurel needs."

What?

What?

Ginny wanted to yell, "This isn't about what somebody else needs, you idiot; it's about what I need."

"Oh, and I've brought the references. You don't have anything to worry about with Laurel." Perry withdrew a couple of envelopes from his pocket. "She's honest, tidy, considerate—everything you could want in a housemate."

This was all going so desperately, horribly wrong that Ginny was struggling to think straight. She wished Gavin could be here to back her up because right now she appeared to be the only one who thought there was anything amiss. Except if Gavin were here, he'd be too busy laughing his socks off at the mess she'd managed to get herself into. Ha, that was what happened when you got carried away and were silly enough to think someone might actually find you attractive.

"Besides," Perry went on, "you did advertise for a female to share with. That was what you really wanted."

"So why didn't Laurel phone up the other night? Why didn't she come round to see the house herself?"

He sighed and refilled his glass with champagne. Offered the bottle to Ginny, who shook her head.

"Laurel was happy to carry on sleeping on my sofa. Finding somewhere else to live wasn't a priority as far as she was concerned. To be honest she's been a bit down lately. She broke up with her

boyfriend last summer and things haven't been easy for her since then. She lost her job in London. Her ex-boyfriend met someone else and got engaged, which didn't help. Laurel was pretty fed up. I told her she should move out of the city and the next thing I knew, she'd turned up on my doorstep." Perry paused, shrugged. "Well, it was fine for a few days. It was great to see her again. Except she's decided she wants to stay in Portsilver now and my flat really isn't big enough for the two of us."

"So move to a bigger flat."

"Oh, Ginny, I'm sorry. I didn't mean to spring this on you. But I'm used to living on my own. I like my own space. And when I met you, I just thought how fantastic you were, so chatty and bubbly, and I knew you'd be perfect for Laurel. Sharing a house with you is just what she needs to perk her up again."

Ginny shook her head. This wasn't supposed to be happening; it wasn't what she wanted. And she was going to have to tell him.

"The thing is, I—"

"Look, you'll have a great time with Laurel." Perry gazed at her. "And much as I'd like to be the one moving in here, that could never happen."

"Why couldn't it?" Ginny rubbed her aching temples; she didn't understand why not.

His eyes crinkled at the corners. "Come on, you must know the answer to that one. You're gorgeous. How could I live in this house when I fancy the landlady rotten? That would be... God, that would be impossible."

Oh. Ginny hadn't been expecting this. Talk about a bolt from the blue. So he *did* find her attractive.

"Sorry, was that a bit sudden?" Perry's smile was rueful. "Have I scared you witless?"

"No, no..."

"I'm usually a bit more subtle. But you did ask. If I'm honest,

I've been sitting here wondering if you'd consider coming out to dinner with me next week. But who knows if I'll have the courage to ask you?" He pulled a wry face and said, "It's a scary thing, you know, being a man. We always have to run the risk of inviting someone out and being turned down flat. You women don't realize how fragile our egos are."

Ginny was lost for words. As she was floundering for a reply, they both heard footsteps on the stairs. The next moment the door had swung open and Laurel entered the kitchen.

"I've unpacked."

"Great." Perry beamed at her. "Well, that didn't take too long, did it? Good girl."

Oh hell. Ginny took another gulp of champagne and found herself unable to meet Laurel's eye. If she was going to say something it had to be now, this minute. But how could she say it? How could she tell Laurel that she wasn't moving in after all, that she should get back upstairs and start repacking all her things?

"Is something wrong?" said Laurel.

Her heart beginning to gallop, Ginny mentally rehearsed telling her that there had been a terrible mistake, that she couldn't stay here because… well, because… um, because…

"Perry? What's going on?"

Perry looked at Laurel and shrugged.

"Look, I'm sorry," Ginny blurted out, "but I didn't realize you were the one who'd be moving in. There's been a bit of a misunderstanding here. I thought your brother was the one looking for a room."

Laurel frowned. "No. He's already got his flat."

"Well, I know that *now*." Her knuckles white, Ginny exclaimed, "But he didn't mention it before."

Laurel gazed steadily at her. "So what are you saying?"

Oh God, what was she saying? In a complete flap now, Ginny

felt the heat rushing back to her face. She was British, for heaven's sake. It wasn't in her nature to deliberately hurt another person's feelings. If she didn't have Laurel, she'd have to go through the whole advertising-and-interviewing rigmarole all over again and who was to say she'd get anyone better next time round? Plus, Perry fancied her anyway and was going to invite her out to dinner. Which was good news and almost better, in a way, than—

"Don't you want me here?" There were now tears glistening in Laurel's huge green eyes. "Do I have to go?"

That was it. How could she say yes and live with herself? Shaking her head, Ginny said, "No, no, of course you don't have to go. Everything's fine."

Laurel blinked back her tears and smiled a watery smile. "Thank you."

Perry beamed with relief. "Excellent."

Instantly, Ginny felt better, no longer twisted with guilt. There, she'd done it. And she had a first date with Perry to look forward to, so everything *was* going to be fine. Forgetting what he'd told her earlier, she seized the champagne bottle and said gaily to Laurel, "Let's celebrate!"

"I'm not allowed to drink." Laurel shook her head. "Because of my tablets."

Tablets. Everything was going to be fine, Ginny reminded herself. Aloud she said sympathetically, "Antibiotics?"

Laurel blinked. "Antidepressants."

Oh.

"Right, I'd better get back to the shop." Perry jumped up. "I'll leave you two girls to get to know each other. Bye."

Hastily, Ginny said, "I'll just show you out," and followed him to the front door.

"She's a lovely girl. You won't regret it." Perry kept his voice low. "Listen, I'll be in touch. If I manage to pluck up the courage to

ask you out to dinner sometime soon, do you think you might say yes?" His smile was playful.

Ginny replied flirtatiously, "I might."

"Great. I'll give you a call. Just do me a favor, don't mention it to Laurel."

"Why not?" Ginny was puzzled.

"Oh, it's just that she's been through a bit of a bad patch with men, you know? She's kind of anti-relationships right now. I told her you were divorced and she liked the idea of sharing a house with someone else in the same boat. If she knew we were meeting up with each other, she might feel a bit odd-one-out."

Ginny wondered if she really was doing the right thing here. Somehow, in the space of a morning, all her plans had been turned inside out. What had she let herself in for?

"Shhh, stop worrying." Evidently capable of reading her thoughts—or more likely the panicky God-what-have-I-done look in her eyes—Perry raised his right index finger to his lips then smiled and tenderly pressed that same finger against her own mouth. "You two'll have a great time. You're just what Laurel needs to get over her dip."

Brushing his finger like that against her lips had set off a deliciously zingy sensation in Ginny's knees. Crikey, if that was kissing by proxy, she couldn't wait for the real thing.

Anyway, of course she and Laurel would get on; hadn't she been through dips of her own in her time? Together they would bond and forge a real friendship.

"I really have to go." Perry was glancing at his watch.

Ginny opened the front door and said, "Bye then," her mouth still tingling from the proxy kiss.

Everything *was* going to be fine.

—⁓—

"I think Perry got fed up with hearing me talk about it," Laurel said tonelessly. "Men aren't into that kind of thing, are they? Especially brothers. Every time I mentioned Kevin he'd try to change the subject. But I *have* to talk about Kevin," she went on. "It's like a compulsion. I loved him so much, you see. *So* much. And I can't just wipe him out of my life because he's still here." She tapped the side of her head. "I think about him all the time. How can you forget someone who's broken your heart, smashed it into a million pieces?"

"Well," Ginny said uncertainly, "er…"

"Although he's probably forgotten me." Laurel wiped her eyes with a proper hanky. (Not even a tissue.) "Because I just don't matter to him anymore, do I? Kevin's moved on now; he met someone else in no time flat and loved her enough to ask her to marry him. I used to drive past his house, you know. One evening I saw them kissing on the front doorstep. I was so unhappy I thought I'd die. And you know what? She had fat ankles. Fat ankles, I swear! Really… *chubby.*"

Ginny did her best to look suitably shocked and sympathetic, but a terrible urge to yawn was creeping up her rib cage, threatening to make a bid for freedom the millisecond she relaxed the muscles in her jaw. For ninety minutes now she had been listening to the Story of Kevin. Ninety minutes was the length of an entire film. She could have watched *Anna Karenina* and been less depressed.

"I suppose I'm boring you," Laurel said flatly.

"No, no." Hastily Ginny shook her head.

"It's just that I thought we'd get married and have babies and be happy together for the rest of our lives, but he changed his mind and now I'm just left without *anything.* He'll probably have babies with her now instead. I can't bear to think of it. Why does life have to be so unfair?"

Oh dear, yet another unanswerable question. Slightly desperate

by now, Ginny said, "I don't know, but how about if you try to... um, stop thinking about him quite so much?"

Laurel gave her a pitying look, as if she'd just suggested switching off gravity. "But I loved him so much. He was my whole world. He still *is*."

Oh God.

Chapter 11

Despite having promised to be in touch, Perry Kennedy hadn't called and Ginny was in need of some serious cheering up. Carla, who hadn't said as much yet but already wasn't sure she trusted Laurel's smooth-talking brother, made an executive decision and said, "Right, I'm taking you out to lunch."

Ginny looked up, surprised. "When?"

"Today. Now. Unless you don't want to."

"Are you kidding?" Ginny's eyes lit up. "Of course I want to."

"Sure?"

"Yesss!"

Carla shrugged. "Because if you'd rather stay at home and have a lovely girly chat with your new best friend Laurel, I'd quite understand."

"Noooo!"

"No, really, I mean who in their right mind would want to come out to lunch with me when they could sit in their kitchen talking about Kevin Kevin Kevin…"

"*I* would," Ginny pleaded.

"Kevin Kevin Kevin Kevin… ooh, and then a teeny bit more about Kevin."

"Shut up and take me out to lunch."

⁕

Carla loved her job and was good at it. When potential clients contacted Portsilver Conservatories, she made an appointment to visit

them in their homes and employed her own special no-pressure sales technique to persuade them that if they wanted the perfect conservatory, then her company was the one for them.

And in almost every case Carla succeeded. She was great at charming the clients and enabling them to imagine the joy a sunny conservatory would bring into their lives. She traveled all over the southwest and often worked in the evenings and at weekends, but that was a bonus too because it meant she could take other days off whenever she liked.

Like today, which she was determined was going to be a memorable one because the last few months hadn't been easy for her friend Ginny. She deserved a break. Personally, Carla suspected that this sudden crush on Perry was largely down to the fact that it had been a long time since Ginny had been so comprehensively targeted by an attractive man. From what she could gather, Perry Kennedy had made quite a play for her and she had been flattered by the attention. For Ginny's sake, Carla hoped she didn't end up getting hurt.

Ginny was enjoying herself already. Here they were whizzing along in Carla's sporty black Golf, the sun was out, and she wasn't going to feel guilty about leaving Laurel at home cleaning the kitchen floor. She hadn't asked or expected her to, but Laurel had volunteered herself for the task, saying sadly, "I like doing housework; it makes me feel useful. I used to do the kitchen floor every day when I was with Kevin."

She had also, as Ginny was escaping the house, leaned back on her heels and said, "I do like living here. It's nice us sharing, isn't it?"

Ginny hadn't known how to respond to this. She could hardly announce that it was about as much fun as sharing a house with Sylvia Plath.

Anyway. Three blissful Kevin-free hours stretched ahead. Maybe this was the answer to all her problems; she would simply have to become one of those ladies who lunched, every day of the week.

Well, maybe if she won the lottery first.

"I wonder what he's doing now?" said Carla.

Instantly thinking of Perry, Ginny said, "Who?"

"Kevin."

"Don't. We mustn't make fun of her."

"I'm not making fun, I'm really wondering. I'd love to meet him," Carla said mischievously. "Drag him into bed. Find out what all the fuss is about, see if he's worth all the hoo-ha."

"Just as well he's living in London, then. So what's wrong with Jamie?"

"Nothing at all." Her boy toys didn't usually last four months, but Jamie had spent three of them away in Australia. "He's great, better than any keep-fit video," said Carla. "But you know me; I like to keep my options open. You just never know, do you, when you might meet someone that little bit more perfect. Ah, here we are." She indicated right and slowed down before turning into the driveway.

Ginny, reading the blue-and-gold sign, said, "Penhaligon's. It's supposed to be good here. We tried to book a table over Christmas but it was full."

"One of my clients recommended it. Lunch cost him two grand," said Carla, "and he still reckons it was worth it."

Two *grand*? Yikes. "I promise I'll just have the stale bread and tap water," said Ginny.

The restaurant was housed in a long, whitewashed, and ivy-strewn sixteenth-century farmhouse with a gray slate roof and a bright red front door. A series of smartly renovated interlinked out-buildings extended from one end of the farmhouse, forming three sides of a rectangle around the central courtyard. As Carla parked the car between an old dusty blue Astra and a gleaming scarlet Porsche, a black cat darted out of one of the outbuildings ahead of a middle-aged man carrying a small wooden cabinet. The man proceeded to

load the cabinet into the back of a van. The cat, tail flicking ominously slowly, looked as if it might be about to launch itself at the man's legs.

"It's a restaurant and antiques center," explained Carla, fairly pointlessly as there was a sign saying so above the door. "Quite a nifty idea. My client came here last week with his wife to celebrate their wedding anniversary. They got a bit tiddly over lunch, went to have a look around afterward, and ended up buying a Georgian chandelier for eighteen hundred pounds."

Ginny was out of the car gazing up at the buildings. Sunlight bounced off the windows, and the glossy tendrils of ivy swayed gently in the breeze. The smell of wonderfully garlicky cooking mingled with wood smoke hung in the air. Animated chatter spilled out of the restaurant, and from the antiques center came the sound of Robbie Williams singing "Angels." Well, it probably wasn't Robbie Williams in person. But wouldn't it be completely brilliant if it was?

The black cat took a swipe at the man who was now closing the van doors. Darting out of the way, he said, "Don't get pissy; it's mine now."

"Nnnaaarrh," sneered the cat, before turning and stalking off.

"Bloody animal," the man called after it.

"You've gone quiet." Having watched him jump into the van and drive off, Carla gave Ginny a playful nudge. "Cat got your tongue?"

And in a way it had. Well, maybe not the cat, but the sights and sounds and smells of Penhaligon's Restaurant and Antiques Center. Captivated by the unexpected charm of it all, Ginny felt as if she was falling a little bit in love at first sight.

"One more drink," Ginny urged, waggling the bottle of Fleurie at Carla. "Go on, you can have another."

"I mustn't, I'm driving."

"Leave the car. We'll come and pick it up tomorrow morning. God, I *love* it here. Why can't all restaurants be like this?"

For a Tuesday lunchtime in February, Penhaligon's was impressively busy. The restaurant, with its deep red walls covered in prints and original paintings, was eclectically furnished with an assortment of antique furniture. The atmosphere was unstuffily friendly and the food divine. Having guzzled her starter of scallops in lemon sauce, Ginny was now finishing her smoked beef main course. Not to mention the best part of a bottle of wine.

"Go on then, you've twisted my arm," said Carla. "Just don't let me buy anything next door."

One bottle became two. They talked nonstop for the next hour and watched through the window as the black cat stalked and intimidated visitors crossing the courtyard. A selection of music ranging from Frank Sinatra to Black Sabbath drifted across from the antiques center and every so often they could hear the kitchen staff joining in and singing along.

"Coffee and a brandy, please," Carla told the waitress when she came to take their order. "Gin?"

Ginny nodded in agreement. "Lovely."

The waitress looked startled. "Coffee and a gin? Crikey, are you sure?"

"Two coffees and brandies." Carla was grinning. "Her name's Gin."

"Oh phew! I thought it sounded a bit weird! Just as well I checked." The girl shook her head by way of apology. "Sorry, my brain's had enough today. Busy busy."

"Hey, Martha," one of the men at the next table called over. "On your own today, sweetheart? What happened to Simmy?"

"Simmy shimmied off to Thailand with her boyfriend. Well, three hours' notice—what more could we ask? So now we have to

find a new waitress before my feet drop off. If you fancy the job, Ted, just say the word."

Ted, who was in his sixties, said, "I'd make a rubbish waitress, love. Don't have the legs for it. Table six are asking for their bill, by the way."

"Thanks, Ted. Right, two coffees and two brandies. I'll bring them as soon as I can."

Martha hurried off and Carla shared out the last of the second bottle of wine. She looked over at Ginny.

Ginny gazed back at her.

"What are you thinking?" Carla said finally.

"You know what I'm thinking." A little spiral of excitement was corkscrewing its way up through Ginny's solar plexus. "I could work here. I'd love to work here."

"Are you sure? It's only February."

"I don't care." Working seasonally meant she was usually employed from April to October, but what the heck? Penhaligon's was calling her name. Last year she had worked in a tea shop down on the front, which had been busy but not what you'd call riveting. Currant buns and cucumber sandwiches lost their appeal after a while and practically their entire clientele—evidently attracted by the ruched cream lace curtains and the sign above the door saying Olde Tea Shoppe—had been over eighty. Ginny's toes had been run over by more recklessly driven wheelchairs than you could shake a walking stick at.

Her toes flinching at the memory, Ginny said, "It's got to be better than the Olde Tea Shoppe."

Nodding in agreement, Carla shuddered and said, "Not to mention Kid Hell."

It hadn't really been called that, but it should have been. Kid Heaven!—complete with jaunty exclamation mark—was the children's activity center where Ginny had worked as a face painter

two summers ago, struggling to paint animal faces on screaming, wriggling children who either had ice cream already smeared
around their mouths, lollipops they refused to stop licking, or
summer colds accompanied by extravagantly runny noses and
cheeks awash with… well, let's just say it played havoc with the
face paints.

Not that Carla had ever witnessed this debacle firsthand—she
was no fool and children were in her view quite pointless—but she'd
heard enough about it from Ginny to know that this was a job on a
par with sifting sewage with your bare teeth.

"I want to work *here*," Ginny repeated. "I've just got a feeling
about this place." Counting off the reasons on her fingers she burbled
excitedly, "It's only… what, three miles from home? And no problems parking, *that's* a bonus. And the only reason I've never done
proper waitressing before is because I didn't want to work evening
shifts while Jem was at home, but now she's gone it doesn't matter!"

"And you'd be getting away from Laurel," Carla drily pointed out.

"Oh God, that sounds terrible!"

"Terrible but true. You've gone and landed yourself with the
world's most boring lodger and any sane person would get rid of her.
But you're too soft to do that, so you're going to take a job to keep
you out of your own house because anything's better than having to
stay in it and listen to loopy Laurel droning on about Kevin."

This was only semitrue. OK, maybe she was soft—a *bit*—but
there was also Perry to be factored into the equation. Ginny sensed
that turfing his sister out into the street might not win her too many
Brownie points in his eyes.

Knocking back her wine with a flourish, she said, "Laurel or no
Laurel, it makes no difference. If I want to be a waitress, I *can* be a
waitress. I think this place is great, and I'd love to work here."

"*Would* you?"

"Oh!" Ginny hadn't realized Martha was standing behind her

with their drinks, patiently waiting for her to stop waving her arms around before putting the tray down on the table. Filled with resolve, she exclaimed, "Well, yes, I would. Definitely!"

"Hey, excellent." Martha's freckled face lit up. "I'll tell Evie, shall I? She manages the restaurant. She'll be thrilled."

"They're desperate; they're going to sign you up before you can say slave labor," Carla murmured as Martha hurried away. "This must be a hellhole of a place to work. Now don't go rushing into anything."

"I want to rush into it! Oh listen, now they're playing Queen." Ginny clapped her hands as the drumbeats of "We Will Rock You" rang out across the courtyard. "How can it be a hellhole when they play Queen?"

"Better stop talking about hellholes. And don't sing," Carla ordered. "Save the Freddie Mercury impression for later—the big boss is on her way over."

The manageress click-clacked across the floor in double-quick time. She was in her midfifties, tall, and as elegant as a racehorse, with tawny blond hair fastened up in a chignon and beautifully applied makeup including Bardot-style eyeliner and glossy red lipstick. Smiling broadly she held out her hand. "Hi, I'm Evie Sutton. Lovely to meet you. When you've finished your lunch, would you like to come and have a chat with me in my office, or…?"

"We're just drinking our coffee." Indicating the spare chair at their table and feeling deliciously proactive, Ginny said, "If you like we can talk about it now."

Twenty minutes later she had the job. Three lunchtime and four evening shifts a week, starting as soon as she liked.

"Tomorrow, if you want," said Evie as she handed her an application form. "Just fill this in and bring it with you, and we'll sort you out with a uniform then."

"Perfect." Ginny could hardly wait. "Thank you so much, I know I'm going to love it here."

"Oh you will, I can tell. We'll soon have you charming those customers. And you've certainly made my day." Evie's blue eyes danced. "There's nothing more depressing than having to interview a bunch of no-hopers."

Liking her more and more, Ginny said with feeling, "Tell me about it."

Chapter 12

"WE AREN'T GOING HOME yet. I want to see the antiques center."
Buzzing with excitement and with her inhibitions loosened by
alcohol, Ginny practically skipped across the sunny courtyard.

Inside the converted outbuildings, the stone walls were painted
emerald green and an Aladdin's cave of well-lit paintings, mirrors, polished furniture, and *objets d'art* greeted them. In the center of the main
room stood a magnificent jukebox currently playing Stevie Wonder's
"Superstition." Further along, in one of the interlinked rooms to the
right, they could see someone showing a couple of potential customers
a walnut bureau. On the sales desk by the window stood a mug of
coffee, a half-eaten KitKat, and an open copy of *Miller's Guide to
Antiques*. Just poking out from beneath it was the latest edition of *Heat*.

"Look at this." Ginny longingly ran her fingers over a bronze
velvet chaise longue. Turning over the price tag, she blanched and
abruptly stopped envisaging it in her living room.

"Never mind that, look at *these*." Twenty feet away, Carla held
up a pair of heavy silver Georgian candlesticks. "I love them!"

"Stop it." Ginny's eyes danced as Carla attempted to stuff them
into her cream leather handbag. "*Bad* girl. Put them back."

"Damn bag's not big enough. No forward planning, that's my
trouble. Ooh, now this is smaller." Picking up an enameled box,
Carla playfully waggled it.

"Antlers!" Ginny let out a shriek of delight and rushed over to
take a closer look. "I've always wanted a pair of real antlers."

"They wouldn't suit you. And you definitely couldn't slip those into your handbag." As she said this, Carla's gaze slid past Ginny.

"And I'd rather you didn't try it."

The moment she heard the voice behind her, Ginny knew. So did her skin, which came out in a shower of goose bumps, and her stomach, which reacted with a nauseous lurch of recognition.

"You can put that down too," the voice continued, this time addressing Carla.

Taken aback by his tone, Carla put down the decorative enameled box and said chippily, "I wasn't going to steal it, you know. We were just having a bit of fun. It was a *joke*."

"Good job you're not a stand-up comedian then. People might ask for their money back."

"Well, you're full of charm, aren't you?" Her eyes flashing, Carla demanded, "Is this how you treat all your customers?"

"Not at all." His reply was cool. "But you don't appear to be customers, do you? Call me old-fashioned but I'd class a customer as someone who pays for what she takes from a shop."

Ginny closed her eyes. This was awful, just *awful*, and Carla was practically incandescent with—

"How dare you!" Carla shouted, marching toward the door. "As if anyone in their right mind would even *want* to buy anything from your crappy shop. Come on, Gin, we're out of here. And don't worry; I won't ever be coming to this dump again."

But *I* will, Ginny thought in a panic.

"Excellent." Moving to one side, the man allowed Carla to stalk past him. "Mission accomplished."

"No, it isn't," Ginny blurted out. "Stop! Carla, come back, we're going to sort this out."

"*Ha*. The only way we could sort this out is if I gored him to death with his own antlers." Jabbing furiously at her phone, Carla said, "Hello? Hello? Yes, I want a taxi this minute…"

"We came here for lunch." Ginny turned in desperation to face the man. "We had a lovely meal."

"Did you pay for it?"

"Yes!"

His eyes glittered. "With your own credit card or with somebody else's?"

"Oh, for crying out loud, will you stop accusing me? We haven't—"

"Oh great, you're still here!" Evie appeared in the shop doorway, a bright smile on her face. "I just came over to tell Finn all about you, but I see you've already met. Finn, did Ginny tell you the good news?"

"No, I didn't," Ginny said hurriedly. "You see, there's been a bit of a—"

"We don't have to advertise for a new waitress!" Evie turned to Finn. "This is Ginny Holland, and she's coming to work for us; isn't that—"

"No, she's not," Finn said flatly. *Very* flatly.

"I'm coming to work for *you*," said Ginny, looking at Evie and praying she'd believe her when the whole sorry story came tumbling out.

"Maybe you thought you were," Finn countered, "but Evie only runs the restaurant. My name's Finn Penhaligon and I own it, which means you *won't* be working here because I say so."

Evie's expression changed. "Finn, could I have a private word with you outside?"

He actually looked amused. "Probably not the wisest idea. I'd prefer it if we were in here and these two stayed outside."

Ginny felt as if her head was about to burst with the unfairness of it all. She'd *so* wanted to work here, and it clearly wasn't going to happen now.

"It's him, isn't it?" Having worked out what was happening, Carla's lip curled with disgust. "He's the one from that shop who made you cry."

"I'd love to know what's going on here," said Evie, bewildered.

"I'm sure he'll tell you. Sorry about the job." Ginny swallowed hard. "I'd have loved to work for you." Following Carla to the door she checked she wasn't inadvertently holding some antique *objet* then opened her bag wide to demonstrate to Finn Penhaligon that there was nothing that belonged to him inside. Determined to retain at least a shred of dignity, she then met his gaze and said steadily, "I know you think you're right, but you're wrong."

"I know what I saw." Unmoved by her declaration, Finn shrugged. "You know what really gave you away? The way you looked at me when I stopped you outside that shop."

The way she'd looked at him. In any other circumstances, Ginny might have laughed. He would never know it, but that hadn't been guilt flickering in her eyes.

It had been lust.

It was midnight, clouds were scudding past the moon, and Ginny and Carla were on a mission under cover of darkness to retrieve Carla's car from the courtyard of Penhaligon's without being seen.

"What a *bastard*." Carla was still seething about the treatment they had received earlier at the hands of Finn Penhaligon.

Ginny concentrated on the road ahead. "I know."

"I mean, that man has a serious attitude problem!"

"I know." Nearly there now.

"You didn't tell me he was that good-looking."

Ginny knew that too. She hadn't told Carla that she'd fantasized about Finn Penhaligon. And since it was pretty irrelevant, she didn't see the point in telling her now. "Is this the turn, up here? God, what if he's there? We should have worn balaclavas."

"Balaclavas aren't my style. Besides, then he'd probably threaten us with a shotgun and I'd have to kill him with my bare hands. OK,

here we go." Carla leaned forward as they entered the courtyard and saw her green Golf parked on its own by the far wall. "Just swing round, pull up next to my car, and I'll jump out. We'll be gone in—fuck, what's that on the windscreen? If that sad git's given me a parking ticket…"

She was out of the car in a flash. As she wrenched the envelope out from under the windscreen wiper, a dark shadow darted across the yard, meowing loudly. For a couple of seconds the cat was caught in the beam of Ginny's headlights before it leaped forward again and disappeared from view. Oh brilliant, now it was probably under the car and if she tried to drive off she'd kill it.

Hurriedly buzzing down her window, Ginny hissed, "Where's the cat?"

"Don't know, but this is for you." Carla handed her the envelope. "Probably a restraining order warning you not to go within five miles of him."

"My pleasure." Ripping open the envelope, Ginny said, "Just see if that cat's under the car, will you?"

She was forced to switch on the interior light to read the note, which was from Evie. It was brief and to the point.

> *Dear Ginny,*
>
> *We need you! Sorry about today—Finn can be a grumpy bugger sometimes, but he's all right really. I've spoken to him now and sorted everything out. I really hope you'll come and work here. Please give me a ring.*

"What is it?" Carla was peering through the open window. "What does it say? God, what's that?" As a door suddenly slammed across the yard, she jumped and whacked her head on the window frame. "Ow, that hurts."

"It's him." Reading Evie's words was all very well, but Ginny

still had an overwhelming urge to stick her foot down and, tires squealing, make a high-speed Steve McQueen–style getaway.

Except it wouldn't only be the tires squealing if she ran over the damn cat. Stuck where she was, Ginny watched warily as Finn Penhaligon made his way across the courtyard. He was wearing a white shirt and dark trousers, and she didn't trust him an inch.

"On the bright side," said Carla, "he isn't carrying a gun."

"Unless there's one in his pocket." Ginny gave a nervous hiccup of laughter. "Although I can't say he looks pleased to see us."

"Damn, he's good-looking though."

Carla hadn't said it loudly but noise evidently traveled across an otherwise empty courtyard.

"Thank you." Gravely, Finn nodded at her, then turned his attention to Ginny. "Have you read Evie's note?"

"Yes."

"And?"

"And she's right." With a surge of reckless bravery Ginny said, "You are a grumpy bugger."

The look in his eyes told her he hadn't read the note himself, hadn't realized that this was what Evie had said about him. The next moment, to his credit, he smiled briefly.

"Well, maybe that's true. But I wouldn't necessarily call that a bad thing. What else did she say?"

"That she'd spoken to you and everything was sorted out." Ginny still couldn't quite believe this was happening, that she was here, in the early hours of the morning, sitting in her car, having this conversation. "And she still wants me to come and work in the restaurant. Well, officially, I'd be working in the restaurant. Unofficially, of course, I'd be fiddling the bills, pocketing all the tips, and cloning people's credit cards."

"I may have overreacted," said Finn. "When you're in this line of business, believe me, shoplifters are the bane of your life."

Furiously, Carla hissed, "Excuse me, she's *not* a—"

"OK, OK." Finn held up his hands. "Let's not get into all that again." Addressing Ginny, he said evenly, "Look, if you want the job, it's yours."

Ginny could hear her pulse thud-thudding in her ears. On the one hand it would be gloriously satisfying to be able to tell him to stick his magnanimous offer *and* his lousy rotten restaurant up his bum.

On the other hand it wasn't a lousy rotten restaurant, was it? And despite everything that had happened, she did still want the job.

Finally, Ginny said, "What did Evie say to make you change your mind?"

His eyes glittered. "Truthfully?"

"Truthfully."

"I told her about the first time we met in that shop in Portsilver." Finn paused. "And Evie told me that she'd once walked out of a department store holding a Christian Dior mascara. She didn't realize until she'd reached her car; she took it back to the store, and the saleswoman said not to worry, that she'd once left a shop carrying two bath mats and a toilet brush."

Ginny looked at him. "Is your cat under my car?"

He shook his head. "No, she shot past me into the flat when I came out. So how about this job then? What shall I tell Evie?"

Revving the car's engine, Ginny said cheerily, "Tell her I'll think it over." Then, because it wasn't often she felt quite this in control, she flashed Finn Penhaligon a dazzling, up-yours smile. "Bye!"

Chapter 13

GINNY'S HEART LIFTED WHEN she heard Jem's voice; a phone call from her daughter always cheered her up.

"Hi, Mum, how's it all going? Are you and Laurel having a blast?"

If only. What was the opposite of a blast? A tired phfft, perhaps. Expecting Perry and getting Laurel instead had been like setting out on holiday to Disneyland then having your plane hijacked and diverted to Siberia.

"We're fine!" Ginny was determined not to admit her catastrophic mistake to Jem. "Laurel's settling in. How about you? Everything OK?"

"Better than OK." Jem sounded on top form. "I'm having such a great time, Mum."

"Oh, darling, I'm so glad." Impulsively, Ginny said, "Listen, you haven't been home since Christmas. Why don't you and Lucy come down this weekend? It'd do you good to have a break, and Dad would love to see—"

"Mum, I can't. My shifts at the pub, remember? I'm doing Saturday evening and Sunday lunchtime."

Bloody pub.

"Well, I hope you're not wearing yourself out," said Ginny. "I could send a bit more money if you want. Then you wouldn't have to work so hard."

"I like working in the pub. Don't worry about me. And it's not long now until Easter, is it? I'll pop down then."

Pop? Ginny didn't like the sound of pop one bit. Her composure momentarily slipping, she said, "Pop? I thought you'd be back for the whole of the Easter break."

"Well, that was the plan, obviously. But the landlord's already asked me to work through Easter. If I tell him I'll be away for a couple of weeks I might lose my job. Oh God, is it half nine already? I've got a tutorial at ten. Mum, I'll ring you again next week; you look after yourself and give my love to Dad. Have fun! Bye!"

Ginny had always been a great one for singing in the shower but this morning she wasn't in the mood. She missed Jem so much it hurt. She missed Bellamy dreadfully too. Instead of a life-enhancing new lodger-cum-friend, she had Laurel. And instead of some form—*any* form—of love life, she had a big empty void. Perry Kennedy, needless to say, had reneged on his promise to call and arrange a date for dinner, which made her feel not only unattractive, but also a complete fool to boot, because she'd been gullible enough to believe he might.

Well, enough was enough. This was her life and it was up to her to be in charge of it. Ginny switched off the shower and wrapped herself in a blue towel, then wiped condensation from the bathroom mirror and gazed steadily at her reflection. She wasn't a doormat and the time had come, yet again, to prove it. This morning while she'd been in the kitchen making a cup of tea, she had seen squirrels chasing each other across the lawn and said aloud, "I bet they can't believe their luck, having the garden to themselves after all these years. Bellamy used to chase them nonstop."

Laurel, scraping margarine very thinly indeed over her slice of whole meal toast, had replied, "You won't get another dog, will you." It had been a statement rather than a question. "I don't like dogs."

"Why not?"

"They're dirty. They smell."

As offended as if she'd said, "*You're* dirty, *you* smell," Ginny had vehemently shaken her head. "Maybe some dogs. Not Bellamy."

But Laurel had simply shrugged and said, "Anyway, I still don't like them," before wandering out of the kitchen with her plate of toast.

Now, recalling this exchange, Ginny vigorously towel-dried her hair. It was too soon to replace Bellamy—she would feel as if she were betraying his memory—but if she told Laurel that she was getting another dog, would Laurel decide she could no longer live here? Could this be the answer to her prayers? OK, so it would be a lie, but infinitely easier than announcing to Laurel that due to the fact that she was boring and miserable and droned on endlessly about Kevin, she would have to move out.

Ginny brightened. Oh yes, this was an excellent idea, a fictitious dog.

And a smelly one at that.

———

"There you are." Radio Two was playing in the background and Laurel was in the kitchen making bread when Ginny headed downstairs, dressed and ready to go out. "You look great. I really like your dress."

"Thanks." Laurel had a disconcerting habit of being nice when you were least expecting it.

"Look, I'm sorry if I seemed a bit rude earlier. I didn't mean to imply that your dog wasn't clean. And I'm sure he was lovely."

"He was." Terrified that Laurel was about to announce that she adored dogs, Ginny said hastily, "Although he wasn't always clean, of course. Dogs will be dogs! Bellamy loved nothing more than splashing through muddy puddles or rolling in foxes' poo."

"Anyway, I'm sorry. And as soon as this bread's done, I'm going to make a cherry and almond cake. Your favorite."

"Right. Well, thanks." Guiltily, Ginny said, "You don't have to do that."

"I want to. You deserve it. Perry rang while you were in the shower, by the way. I told him how happy I was here."

Perry had rung! Ginny's cheeks heated up at the mention of him. Or should he be addressed by his full name of Perry Bloody Lying Bastard?

Kneading away at the dough on the table, Laurel went on, "He said could you give him a call when you've got a moment. Something to do with setting up the direct debit."

"Right, thanks." Did that mean he really wanted to talk to her about the direct debit? Casually, Ginny said, "Well, I'd better be off. See you later."

"Bye." Laurel's clear green eyes abruptly filled with tears and her chin began to tremble.

Oh God, what now? Bewildered, Ginny hesitated in the doorway. "Are you… will you be OK?"

"Yes, yes." Floury hands flapping, Laurel wiped her eyes with her thin upper arms and nodded at the radio, now playing the Osmonds' "Crazy Horses." "Sorry, it's this song. It just reminds me so much of Kevin."

Climbing into the car, Ginny told herself she'd phone Perry in her own good time. No need to appear overeager. She had lots to do today, *lots* to do, not least paying a visit to Penhaligon's to see Ellie and discuss—

Oh sod it.

The moment Ginny was round the corner and out of sight of the house she pulled up at the curb and dug her mobile out of her bag.

"Hi there! How are you?" Perry sounded delighted to hear from her. "How's everything going with Laurel?"

"Um, well…" Clutching the phone, Ginny cursed her inability to tell him the truth; it was all her parents' fault for drumming into her as a child the importance of being polite. "Fine."

"You see? Didn't I tell you it would be? And Laurel's so much happier now. You've done wonders with her."

Ginny's mouth was dry with anticipation. "Laurel said something about the direct debit?" Here was Perry's cue to laugh and reply, "Hey, that was just an excuse to speak to you about our dinner date."

Instead, he said, "Actually, that was just an excuse to speak to you about Laurel's tablets. The thing is, she'd hate it if she thought I was checking up on her but it's important that she keeps taking them. I thought maybe you could subtly remind her next week about dropping the repeat prescription into the pharmacy; otherwise, she'll run out."

And become even more depressed. It didn't bear thinking about.

"Right." Ginny bit her lip.

"Great."

Disappointment flooded through her. "Is that all?"

"Yes, I think so. Well, I'll leave you to get on…"

Buggering hell, that *was* all! The bastard! Sick to the back teeth of being polite—walked all over, more like—Ginny blurted out, "To be honest, I don't think this is going to work. Maybe you should start looking for somewhere else for Laurel to live. I did say that if things didn't work out I'd give you four weeks'—"

"Whoa, *whoa*." Perry sounded alarmed. "I can't believe you're saying this."

Ginny couldn't quite believe it either, but she just had. The words had come tumbling out in a rush like baked beans from a can.

"Ginny, where are you now? We need to talk about this. Look, I know you don't want to go out to dinner with me but could we at least meet up for a quick drink? Are you busy today?"

Flummoxed, Ginny heard herself stammer, "W-well no, I suppose not."

"How about the Smugglers' Rest? Around one-ish, would that suit you?"

One-ish. That was two whole hours away. Trying not to sound too eager, Ginny said, "One o'clock, the Smugglers' Rest. Fine."

———

Perry was already there when she arrived, waiting at the bar. Hesitantly, he greeted her with a handshake—a *handshake!*—and said, "It's good to see you again, you're looking... no, sorry, mustn't say that. What can I get you to drink?"

Ginny waited until they were seated opposite each other at a table by the window before uttering the question that had been rampaging through her mind for the last two hours.

"On the phone, why did you say you knew I didn't want to go out to dinner with you?"

Perry shrugged, glanced out of the window, looked uncomfortable.

"Because I could tell. Sorry, I really liked you and got carried away. Made a bit of an idiot of myself, I suppose. Not for the first time. Like I said, it's scary having to make the first move and risk getting it wrong. And I realized I had, that's all. It was pretty obvious you weren't interested." Clearing his throat, he took a drink. "Look, this is embarrassing for me. Could we change the subject?"

"No." Far too curious to leave it now, Ginny said, "I don't know what I did to make you think that. I thought everything was fine. You asked me if I'd like to go out to dinner and I said yes."

Perry shook his head. "You said you might."

"I *meant* yes."

A glimmer of hope shone in his eyes. "I thought you were just being polite, sparing my feelings."

"Well, I wasn't," said Ginny. "I've been waiting for you to ring, like you said you would. I wondered why you hadn't called."

Perry looked as if he didn't believe her. "Seriously?"

"Seriously."

"I got it wrong?"

Ginny loved it that he was so vulnerable. "Completely wrong."

He clasped his head in his hands. "I'm such a prat. It's that fear-of-rejection thing. If I'm not five thousand percent convinced that someone's interested, I back off."

"Well, you shouldn't."

"Easier said than done." Perry's smile was crooked. "When you've been traumatized as a teenager, it kind of sticks with you. I plucked up the courage to invite a girl to the school disco when I was fifteen. She said OK and I was over the moon. Then I knocked on her front door to pick her up and her dad told me she'd gone out."

"You poor thing!" exclaimed Ginny.

"So I went to the disco on my own and there she was, with all her friends, and everyone knew. It turned out she'd only said yes for a bet. I was the laughingstock of the whole school."

Ginny's heart went out to him; she could picture the scene, imagine the agony he must have endured.

"Children are so cruel."

"Still, I should have grown out of it by now. Just goes to show what a coward I am." Pausing then taking a deep breath, Perry said, "So if I asked you out to dinner, you'd really say yes?"

"I would."

"*Really* really? And mean it? Five thousand percent sure about that?"

Who would have believed such a good-looking man—and one who appeared so confident on the surface—could be so unsure of himself? "Of course I mean it," said Ginny. "Five thousand percent sure. Maybe even six."

A broad smile spread across Perry's face. "OK, before I lose my nerve again, how about tomorrow night?"

"I'd love that." Ginny found herself nodding to emphasize just how much she'd love it.

"Great. We'll go to Penhaligon's."

Ah.

"Maybe not Penhaligon's. I'm seeing them this afternoon about a waitressing job."

"Hey, good for you! They do fantastic food. OK, how about the Green Room on Tate Hill? I could meet you there at, say, eight o'clock?"

"Eight." Ginny was nodding again, happier than she'd imagined possible.

"Promise you won't stand me up?"

"I promise. So long as you don't stand me up either."

"No chance of that." Perry grinned and took her hand, gave it a quick squeeze. "You're incredible. No wonder Laurel's so happy living with you. She'd be distraught if she had to leave."

Oh God, that was true. Her conscience pricking, Ginny reached for her spritzer and took an icy gulp.

"So what's she done?" said Perry. "Is she untidy?"

"No."

"Doesn't do her share of the housework?"

"No, it's not that."

"Makes too much noise?"

Ginny squirmed. If anything, Laurel didn't make enough noise. She was quiet, thoughtful, considerate—technically, a model tenant with no annoying habits or antisocial tendencies.

"Does she break things? Use up all the hot water? Hog the TV remote?"

Laurel did none of these things. She just talked too much about Kevin, the man who had broken her heart.

"OK," Ginny conceded. "She can stay."

Perry's look of relief said it all. "Thank you. Really. God, I could… kiss you!" He glanced around the pub, which was filling up. "Well, maybe not in here."

"Chicken," Ginny said playfully.

"Is that a challenge?" He rose to his feet and pulled her up to meet him. The next moment he was kissing her—kissing her *properly*—right there in the middle of the pub with everyone watching.

Crikey, not so chicken after all.

"Bloody disgusting if you ask me." An ancient fisherman propping up the bar gave a snort of disgust.

"Wow. They're, like, really *old*," giggled a skinny girl in a Day-Glo pink tube top.

A waitress, emerging from the kitchen with two plates piled high, shouted, "One vegetarian tart, one king-sized sausage."

Cue sniggers all round.

Hastily collecting herself, Ginny took a step back. "Let's get out of here."

Perry looked amused. "Your fault. You dared me to do it." Men, they really were the limit.

"Only because I didn't think you *would*."

Chapter 14

WHEN GINNY ARRIVED AT Penhaligon's, Evie Sutton greeted her like a long-lost sister. It was three o'clock and lunchtime service was over. They sat together over a pot of coffee in the empty restaurant discussing the job, hours, and wages, and Ginny filled in an application form.

"The shifts can be flexible, can't they? I mean, we're allowed to switch shifts if something crops up?" Apologetically, Ginny said, "It's just that my daughter's away at university. If she decides to come down and see me one weekend, I'd hate to be working non-stop." Not that Jem was showing much sign of coming down any time soon, but she lived in hope.

"No problem." Evie nodded to show she understood. "My three are all scattered around the country now; they've got their own lives. But when I can, I grab the chance to see them…"

"Oh I know. I miss Jem so much it's embarrassing!" Recognizing a kindred spirit, Ginny said eagerly, "In fact I've got a couple of photos in my purse."

"Me too!" Delightedly, Evie fetched her handbag from the office and brought out photographs of her own children. As they pored over them together, Ginny wondered why someone more like Evie—or better still Evie herself—couldn't have replied to her ad for a lodger.

The phone rang in the office and Evie, in the middle of an anecdote about her younger son, went to answer it. Moments later the

door of the restaurant opened and Finn Penhaligon strode in, raising an eyebrow when he saw Ginny sitting there. "Oh. Hi."

"Hello." Ginny felt her mouth go dry; it was still hard to look at him without being reminded of a four-poster bed and ivory drapes billowing in the breeze. She really was going to have to knock that fantasy on the head, particularly seeing as she was the hussy who'd been kissed not two hours ago in front of a whole pub full of customers.

"Where's Evie?"

"In the office. I'm starting work here on Thursday, by the way. I'll be working three lunchtime and four evening shifts." Ginny indicated the filled-in form in front of her and watched him pick it up.

"Right. Fine." Scanning through it, he nodded then glanced at the photographs still on the table. "Who's that?"

"My daughter. Jem." With Evie she had felt free to glow with pride and extol her daughter's many virtues, but this time Ginny kept it low-key. Men were different.

Finn studied the photograph in silence. Finally, he said, "What happened to her?"

"What? Oh, the hair! It's blond, but she had the tips dyed pink."

"No, I mean…" He frowned. "Is this not the one who died?"

What?

"I don't know what you mean." Bemused, Ginny said, "Jem's my only daughter. She isn't dead!"

He shook his head. "You said she was. In the shop that day. That's why the woman couldn't bring herself to call the police."

"I swear to God I didn't say that! Why *would* I?"

"Who knows? To play on our sympathy and get yourself off a shoplifting charge?"

"You're making this up!" Her eyebrows knitted in disbelief, Ginny shouted, "That's a wicked thing to say!"

"You were hysterical. You told us you'd buried your dog that morning." He shrugged. "Maybe that wasn't true either."

"It *was* true. I loved my dog!"

"And then the woman asked who we could call and you said there was no one," Finn persisted. "You said your daughter wasn't here anymore, that she was gone."

The penny dropped. Mortified, Ginny realized that she had inadvertently misled them. "She was, but I didn't mean she was dead. Jem's alive and well and living in Bristol."

Finn surveyed her steadily. "And there we were, feeling sorry for you."

"You don't say. Well, excuse me if I didn't notice."

"Anyway, you weren't arrested. So it did the trick."

"Let me guess," Ginny said heatedly. "You don't have any children. *Do you?*"

He surveyed her for a moment, then shook his head. "No."

"Well, that's pretty obvious, because if you did, you'd know that no decent parent would *ever* tell such a terrible lie to get out of *anything*. I would *die* for my daughter."

"OK, OK. I'm sure you're right. Anyhow, can we put all that behind us?" Raising his hands, Finn said, "We got off to a shaky start. But now you're going to be working for me, so it'll be a lot easier all around if we can just get along together. Don't you think?"

Still outraged but realizing he was right, Ginny shook his outstretched hand and said, "Yes, I do."

"Good. Now if you'll excuse me, I need a word with Evie."

He disappeared through to the office. Ginny drank her lukewarm coffee and sat back, idly twirling the ends of her hair. This was where she would be working, in this sunny, eclectically furnished restaurant with its beamed ceilings and burnished oak floor. The paintings on the crimson walls were a beguiling mix of old and modern, the velvet curtains at the windows were held back with fat satin ropes and on every table stood an unmatched bowl or vase containing greenery and spring flowers.

Waiting for Evie to return and having nothing else to do other than study her surroundings meant that only a few minutes had elapsed before Ginny spotted the scrunched-up note on the floor.

Bending down and retrieving it from its position halfway under table six, she briefly considered tearing it into teeny tiny shreds.

That would teach him.

But twenty pounds was twenty pounds and she couldn't bring herself to do it. Instead, reaching into her handbag and taking out her purse—luckily she'd paid a visit to the ATM this morning—Ginny swapped the crumpled twenty-pound note for two crisp tens and replaced them under table six.

Minutes later, Evie burst back into the restaurant, followed by Finn.

"Sorry to leave you all on your own! Finn kept me talking."

I'll bet he did, thought Ginny, watching as Finn's dark eyes flickered in the direction of table six. When he saw the two ten-pound notes on the floor he almost—*almost*—smiled.

"Nice try," said Ginny as their eyes met.

"What?" Evie clearly hadn't been in on the impromptu test.

Finn shook his head. "Nothing. Right, I'll leave you to it. Looks like my New York dealer's arrived."

A long black car had pulled up outside the antiques center. Ginny and Evie watched as Finn strode across the courtyard to greet the dealer.

"Yikes, it's a female. She won't stand a chance." Evie looked sideways at Ginny. "Did he just have another go at you?"

"He tried, but I'm getting used to him now. In fact, I had a bit of a go back." Proudly, Ginny said, "He made one comment about Jem, and I told him it was obvious he wasn't a father."

"Ah. And what did he have to say about that?"

"Nothing. Well, he admitted he didn't have children."

Evie sat back down opposite her. "OK, seeing as you're going to

be working here, I'd better tell you. Finn was due to be married at Christmas. He and Tamsin had a baby last summer."

"Oh God!" Covering her mouth in horror, Ginny gasped, "Don't tell me the baby died!"

Evie shook her head. "No, nobody died. Mae was born in July, and she was the most beautiful thing you'd ever seen—well, with parents like that, what else would you expect? Finn was completely besotted, you can't imagine. He was just… lit up. You wouldn't credit the change in him. He'd just bought this place, and we were working night and day to finish the renovations and get the restaurant up and running. But he couldn't bear to tear himself away from Mae. She was always with him. You've never seen a happier man," Evie said sadly. "He was a born father."

Ginny was utterly mystified. "So what happened?"

"Oh God, it was awful. Finn was away one day at an auction in Wiltshire. I was here supervising the decorators in the restaurant when a taxi pulled up outside. This dark Italian-looking guy stepped out of the taxi, and I went over to see what he wanted. He said he'd come to collect Tamsin and Mae. The next thing I knew, Tamsin came running out of the flat above the antiques center—that's where she and Finn were living with Mae—carrying a load of bags. She told me they were leaving. I couldn't believe what was going on. She packed all her things and Mae's into the taxi and gave me a letter to give to Finn. Well, by this time I was *shaking*. I said, 'You can't take Mae away from Finn; he's her *father*.' And this Italian-looking guy, who *was* Italian by the way, just laughed at me and said, 'No, he isn't. I'm Mae's father.' Then he looked at his watch and told Tamsin to get a move on, the helicopter was waiting and he had to be back in London by three."

Ginny felt sick. What a terrible, terrible thing to happen. "And was it true? About him being the father?"

"Oh yes. Finn let me read the letter that night. Basically, Tamsin

had met this Italian—Angelo Balboa, his name was—in a nightclub one night while Finn was away on a buying trip. They had an affair that carried on for a few weeks then ended when Angelo had to go away to Australia on business. When Tamsin found out she was pregnant it was a toss-up which of them might turn out to be the father. And when Mae was born—well, Finn and Angelo both have dark hair and dark eyes, so she could have got away with it."

"So why didn't she?"

"For the first couple of months she did." Drily Evie made a whirly motion with her finger. "But maybe the mention of the helicopter gave you a clue? Angelo Balboa is seriously wealthy. His family made zillions in the olive oil industry. And Tamsin's always had a liking for the good things in life, especially good-looking zillionaires. I mean, Finn's done well for himself, but he's not in the same league as Angelo. And I imagine this swayed Tamsin's judgment. In the letter she told Finn that she'd had a DNA test done and that Mae wasn't his. Naturally, she'd then felt obliged to write to Angelo and let him know he had a daughter. And bingo, Angelo came up trumps! In the romantic modern way, he demanded more DNA tests to prove it. But as soon as they had, he did the honorable thing and announced that from now on, Tamsin and Mae were *his*."

"What a nightmare. Poor Finn." Now there was a sentiment Ginny had never envisaged herself feeling. Raking her fingers through her hair, she said, "What did he do?"

Evie shrugged. "What could he do? Nothing at all. Well, apart from drink himself stupid for a while. And cancel the wedding. And come to terms with the realization that he wasn't a father after all."

"God. And he hasn't seen them since?"

"Nope. They're in London with Angelo."

"When did it happen?"

"October."

October. And Mae had been born in July. So that meant Finn

had had three whole months in which to bond with this living, breathing baby, believing her to be his daughter and loving her more than life itself, before she'd been whisked away without even a chance to hold her in his arms one last time and say good-bye.

Imagining it, Ginny felt a lump form in her throat. She couldn't speak. How would she have felt if someone had tried to take Jem, as a baby, away from her?

"Maybe I shouldn't have told you." Evie looked worried.

"No, you should." Vigorously, Ginny shook her head. "God, I've already put my foot in it once. That's more than enough." Another thought struck her. "And it was only a few weeks after it happened that he saw me in the shop that first time. No wonder he wasn't in the sunniest of moods."

"Now you know why Finn's got such a thing about honesty and trust." Fiddling with the freesias in the vase in front of her, Evie said, "Can't blame him, I suppose. Up until Tamsin left, he'd always prided himself on being a great judge of character. It must come as a kick in the teeth when you realize you've got it so badly wrong about the woman you were planning to marry."

Well, quite. Lots of people later discovered they'd got it wrong when it came to choosing who to marry (mentioning no names... OK, *Gavin*).

But what Tamsin had done was beyond belief.

Chapter 15

WHEN SHE ARRIVED HOME at five o'clock, Ginny saw Gavin's white Porsche, muddier than ever, parked outside the house. She winced slightly, because this meant he'd introduced himself to Laurel without her being there to act as a buffer.

She winced even more when, upon letting herself in through the front door, the first thing she heard was Gavin saying, "... I mean look at your shoes, they're *ugly*. You're never going to get wolf-whistled at in the street wearing shoes like that."

Good old Gavin, as subtle and sympathetic as ever. Hastening into the living room, Ginny saw that Laurel was sitting bolt upright on a chair with a trapped-rabbit look in her eyes.

"Gavin, leave her alone."

"Me? I haven't laid a finger on her. We're just having a friendly chat." Gavin spread his hands. "I popped over to see you and you weren't here so Laurel and I have been getting to know each other. And let me tell you, I've learned a *lot*."

Ginny didn't doubt it. Asking impertinent questions was a specialty of Gavin's.

"He says I'm boring," said Laurel, her knuckles white as she clasped her knees.

Not to mention offering impertinent opinions, whether they were welcome or not.

"*Gavin*." Ginny shot him a fierce look. "You can't go around saying things like that."

"Yes, I can." Unperturbed, he turned back to address Laurel.

"You *are* boring. It's not rocket science. You're never going to get over Kevin until you meet someone else to take your mind off him, and you're never going to find someone else because all you do is talk about Kevin."

"How long have you been here?" Ginny wondered if a good clip round the ear would do the trick.

"An hour. A whole hour, and believe me it's felt more like a week. I've been telling her, it's time to move on. Put the whole Kevin thing behind her." Gavin made helpful, pushing-backward gestures with his arms. "And just move on. Which means getting out and socializing. And wearing shoes that won't send men screaming in the opposite direction."

Laurel was still looking shell-shocked. "Are you always this rude?"

"*Yes*," said Ginny apologetically.

"I prefer to call it honest. If you were wearing beautiful shoes, I'd tell you. And you're not a bad-looking girl," Gavin went on, sizing Laurel up like a racehorse. "Nice face, shiny hair, decent figure. I don't much go for redheads myself, but—"

"Good, because I don't go for men with double chins and receding hairlines."

"Fair point. Each to their own." Gavin wasn't offended. "But I'm serious about you needing to get over this ex of yours." He paused, looking thoughtful for a moment. "In fact, I bet I know someone you'd hit it off with."

Hurriedly, Laurel said, "No thanks!"

"See? Don't be so negative! I think the two of you would really get along."

"I'm not interested."

Despite her misgivings, Ginny said, "Who?"

"His name's Hamish. Lovely chap. Bit on the shy side, but a heart of gold. He's the sensitive type." Gavin was warming to his theme. "You know the kind. Writes poetry. Reads books."

Ginny stared at him. "How on earth do you know someone who writes poetry?"

"He's joined our club. It's a singles club," Gavin explained to Laurel. "Fabulous fun. We meet twice a week. What I could do is mention you to Hamish, put in a good word on your behalf, then when you turn up I'll introduce you to him, and Bob's your uncle."

Laurel's light green eyes widened in horror. "I'm not doing that."

"Oh, come on, live a little! You know, the more I think about it, the more sure I am that you two would be perfect for each other. He's tall and skinny, just like you. And quiet! Half the time he sits on his own in the corner and we hardly even notice he's—"

"*No.*" Vehemently, Laurel shook her head. "No way. Me, go to a singles club? Not in a million years."

"So you'd rather be miserable for a million years."

"I'm not going to a singles club," Laurel repeated flatly.

"Leave her alone," Ginny protested, but weakly because while Gavin might not be subtle, what he was saying made a lot of sense. It would be heavenly if Laurel were to meet a kindred spirit.

"You don't want to go on your own? Fine. Gin, how about the two of you coming along together?" Gavin the perennial salesman raised his eyebrows at Ginny, making an offer she couldn't refuse.

Maybe it would be worth it. "Well…"

"Tomorrow night."

"Oh." Tomorrow was dinner-with-Perry night. "I can't," Ginny apologized. "I'm busy."

"Doing what?"

"Seeing a friend!"

"Well, how about next week?"

"Excuse me, am I invisible?" Shaking back her hair, Laurel stood up and said impatiently, "I told you I wasn't going and I meant it, so will you please stop trying to make me do something I don't want to do?"

"If you met Hamish, you'd like him," Gavin wheedled.

"That's your opinion." As she stalked out of the living room, Laurel said, "If you ask me, he sounds like a complete drip."

Ginny met Perry the following night at the Green Room, the cliff-top restaurant on the outskirts of Portsilver. This time he didn't stand up and kiss her in front of everyone but the food was good, they talked nonstop, and she still felt that spark of attraction every time she looked at him.

"Your ex sounds like a character." Taking her free hand when she'd finished telling him about Laurel's run-in with Gavin, Perry idly stroked her fingers. "How long have you two been divorced?"

"Nine years." Ginny was finding it hard to concentrate; all of a sudden her hand had turned into an erogenous zone.

"Nine years. That's a long time. You must have had other relationships since then."

"Well, yes." Was he trying to find out whether she was a saucy trollop who bundled men into bed at every opportunity? "Not many. Just… you know, a few."

Perry raised a questioning eyebrow.

"OK, three," said Ginny.

He smiled. "That's good. Three's a nice ladylike number. I knew you were a lady."

It was a compliment, but Ginny wasn't sure she deserved it. If she had been free of responsibilities, her life, sex-wise, might have been far more eventful. But with Jem around, that kind of thing hadn't been a priority. Motherhood had come first and men had been a distraction she simply hadn't needed.

"You know, I appreciate that, I really do." Perry nodded and carried on stroking her hand. "It's more romantic when people take the time to get to know each other properly, isn't it? Too many

people just go from one one-night stand to the next. And that just cheapens everything for me." He gazed into Ginny's eyes. "I'm so glad you're not like that."

Bugger, thought Ginny. Just because she'd been like that in the past didn't mean she wanted to be like it now.

True to his word, when the meal was over, Perry kissed her in the car park then did the gentlemanly thing and helped her into her car—before Ginny could throw him over the bonnet and rip his shirt off, which was what she really wanted to do.

Oh well, it was flattering in its own way. If Perry thought she was a lady worthy of respect, that was... *nice.*

"You're gorgeous," Perry murmured. Cradling her face between his warm hands, he kissed her again, lingeringly, before pulling away.

See? That *was* nice. And a million times more romantic than being groped by some panting Neanderthal intent on getting inside your bra.

"I'll be in touch," said Perry. "Take care."

He really likes me, thought Ginny, happiness bubbling up inside her as she drove out of the car park.

Wasn't that *great*?

Chapter 16

GINNY STILL FOUND GOING for a walk without a dog a strange experience, like waking up on Christmas morning and finding your stocking empty. Even after all this time, she still found herself glancing around, expecting to see Bellamy either trotting along beside her or madly bounding around in circles in search of treasure.

Even more disconcertingly, at least for anyone who happened to be watching, she still sometimes picked up sticks and went to hurl them into the air before realizing Bellamy was no longer there to retrieve them.

That got you some funny looks from passersby.

The beach had always been their favorite place. Now, as she made her way along the shoreline, Ginny kept her hands stuffed firmly in the pockets of her black padded jacket. There, tangled in a skein of glossy wet seaweed, was a piece of driftwood ideal for throwing. (*Mustn't* pick it up, *mustn't* throw it.) A crab skittered across the sand heading for the shelter of a semi-submerged rock. One of Bellamy's favorite games had been snuffling after crabs, nudging them with his nose then leaping back like an outraged maiden aunt confronted by a male stripper when the crabs retaliated with their claws.

Oh God, she missed Bellamy so much. Strolling along the beach wasn't the same without him. Nor without Jem. For years it had been the three of them splashing through the waves, playing frenetic games, and collecting shells for Jem's bedroom windowsill.

Now it's just me, thought Ginny, gazing out to sea and watching a lone fishing boat chug along with seagulls swooping in its wake.

The phone rang in her pocket.

"Mum?"

"Hello, darling!" The sound of Jem's voice, just when she most needed to hear it, lifted Ginny's spirits in a flash. "How lovely to hear from you! What have you been up to?"

"Oh, you know, all the usual stuff. Buckets of work. Boring old essays, bossy lecturers... did you get my email yesterday?"

"I did." Jem had attached a photo to the email, of Lucy and herself on their way out to a party. "And I can't believe you weren't wearing your new boots." When Jem bought anything new, she had a habit of wearing it nonstop for the next three months.

Giggling, Jem said, "I was."

"I meant the pink ones. Oh, you naughty girl, don't tell me you've bought another pair."

"I didn't; Rupert did. He didn't like my pink boots so he threw them out of the window at some people who were annoying us." Still laughing, Jem said, "Then the next day he gave me the money to buy a new pair. Can you believe it? He gave me a hundred pounds!"

Ginny was incensed. "He just threw them out of the window? What kind of person does that? You *loved* those boots."

"And now I love these ones! Oh, Mum, it was *funny*; you should have been there. And mine were a bit cheap-looking. These are much nicer. I'm wearing them now. Rupert thinks they're great; he says I don't look like a hooker anymore."

Rupert was a prat and an arrogant one at that; if he'd tried chucking anything of hers out of a window, Ginny would have thrown him out after it. Hearing Jem, normally so sensible, leaping to his defense sent a faint chill down her spine.

"And is he still with his girlfriend? What's her name... Caro?"

"Nope. They broke up." At this, Ginny's sense of foreboding

increased. "Anyway," Jem went on, "I want to know how your new job's going. Is it good?"

Right. Change of subject. For the next few minutes, as the seagulls wheeled overhead, Ginny told Jem all about her first evening shift yesterday at Penhaligon's. Finn hadn't been there and she had enjoyed herself hugely; Evie and Martha were fun to work with, the kitchen staff was hardworking and cheerful, and she had enjoyed getting to know the regular customers.

Jem was delighted. "Hey, Mum, good for you. Maybe I should come down and meet them too."

"Except you're working." Ginny darted out of the way as a wave lapped against her trainers.

"Ah, but I'm not! That's why I'm ringing." Jem was triumphant. "The pub landlord called me this morning—a pipe burst in the roof last night and the place got flooded, so it's closed until next week. Which means I'm free," she went on gaily, "so I thought I'd shoot down for the weekend, if that's OK with you."

This time, Ginny was so overjoyed she didn't even notice the next wave breaking over both her feet. She wouldn't have noticed if a shark had reared up out of the water with a mermaid on its back.

"Of course it's OK with me. Oh, darling, that's *fantastic* news. I can't wait!"

"You can't do that." Rupert emerged from the kitchen as Jem came off the phone. "You mustn't go home. That's a complete waste of a weekend."

"How can it be a waste of a weekend? I'll be seeing my mum."

"I mean a waste for *us*." In the middle of the living room he slid his arms round her. "I'll be here all on my own. What'll I do with myself while you're gone?"

"You won't be on your own. Lucy's going to be here."

"She isn't. She's just told me she's off up to Manchester for some cousin's wedding."

"Damn." Lucy was in the shower; Jem gazed in dismay at the closed bathroom door. "I thought she'd be around so we wouldn't have the chance to... you know... *be* together."

"Well, she won't be. Which gives us all the time in the world to... you know... *be* together." As he mimicked her choice of expression, Rupert grinned wickedly and pressed his groin against hers. "I mean, think how much *being together* we could do."

Jem was torn. It was an opportunity they weren't often likely to get. If only she'd known twenty minutes earlier that Lucy would be away.

"Mmm," Rupert murmured, moving his hips. "Being together, being together..."

"I've told Mum now. She's expecting me."

"You're starting to sound like Davy Stokes. Hey, come on, you only told her five minutes ago. Call her back and say you can't make it." As he nuzzled her ear, Rupert said with amusement, "Just tell her something's come up. That wouldn't be a lie now, would it?"

Weakening, Jem imagined telling her mother that she would be staying in Bristol after all. Maybe think up a less lascivious reason than the one Rupert was suggesting, for decency's sake. Would her mum be disappointed, though?

"She sounded so pleased when I said I'd be coming down."

"That's what mothers do." Rupert shrugged. "They have to sound pleased; it's part of the job description. You wouldn't like it if she said, 'Oh God, do you have to?'"

Was that true? Actually, it was, come to think of it; she might be in the way. Her mum had a new job now and a new housemate. She had a busy, happy life. The last thing she needed, probably, was a nosy daughter arriving back to take up more of her time.

"If you leave me here on my own"—Rupert gave her a mournful

look—"I might have to go out and shag some ugly fat bird. And I'd really hate that."

Jem grinned and made up her mind. "You know what? I'd hate it too."

—⁓—

Ginny's phone rang again as she was standing in the queue at the delicatessen waiting to pay for her basket of luxuries.

"Mum? It's me again. Look, I'm not going to be able to make it after all—I've only just realized how behind I am with my essays. If I don't spend the weekend catching up, I'm going to be in big— *yeeek!*—trouble. So, that's all right, isn't it? I expect you're rushed off your feet anyway!"

Ginny's mouth was dry. Her heart sank. Jem was gabbling at warp speed, a sure sign that the excuse wasn't genuine. And she wasn't coming home. Disappointment flooded through her. And what had provoked that squeak?

"What just happened?"

"When?"

"The squeak. You were saying you'd be in big trouble, and you squeaked."

Jem giggled. "Oh, that was just Rupert mucking around. It's nothing. So is that OK then? I won't be around to interrupt your hectic life!"

The basket was suddenly far too heavy. Moving out of the queue, Ginny said carefully, "Fine, darling. It would have been lovely to see you, but it's your decision. If you need to catch up on your essays... well, that's what you have to do."

"I knew you wouldn't mind. OK, Mum, better go now. Love you!"

Having tucked the phone back into her handbag, Ginny retraced her steps around the delicatessen, emptying the basket. Back onto the shelves went the jars of stuffed olives, the packets of cashews and

macadamia nuts, the prosciutto slices and the marinated artichokes. All Jem's favorite things.

"Come out without your purse, love?" An older woman gave her a sympathetic look.

Ginny shook her head. "I thought my daughter was coming to stay for the weekend. She's just phoned to say she can't make it. Too busy."

"Tuh, heard that one before. Kids are selfish, aren't they? Mine used to do that to me." The woman clicked her tongue. "We had some arguments about it, I can tell you. Right humdingers."

Ginny didn't want to argue with Jem, but her disappointment was so great that she was willing to give almost anything a try. "Did it help?"

"I wouldn't recommend it, love." Heaving a sigh of resignation as she picked up a jar of pesto, the woman said sadly, "She married a man I didn't like. We had a few rows about that too. Then fourteen years ago they upped and immigrated to Australia."

Chapter 17

It was Saturday evening and the restaurant was busy. Finn was there, greeting new arrivals, working the tables like a pro, and attracting plenty of attention from the female diners. Watching him in action, Ginny saw the way they lit up and sparkled when he spoke to them, then chatted equally easily with the husbands of the married ones, ensuring they realized he wasn't a threat.

The single women loved that bit too. All the more chance for them. When a man as attractive as Finn Penhaligon moved into the area, it gave them all hope.

"Watching how it's done?" Evidently amused, Evie paused on her way to table six with two plates of mussels. "Can't you just *feel* all those flirty female hormones in the air?" With a wink, she added, "Good old Finn, he hasn't lost his touch."

"I can see that." As Finn crossed the room in order to answer the ringing phone, every female eye followed him.

"You'd better watch out. You could be next."

Ginny grinned because the idea was so ludicrous. "I don't think that's going to happen. He'd be too worried I might nick his wallet."

Finn beckoned her over to the desk a few minutes later.

"Relative of yours?"

"What?" Ginny peered down at the diary where he'd written the name Holland for nine thirty.

"Table for two. I've just taken the booking. She didn't say so, but I thought it might be your daughter."

Her heart leaping like a fish, Ginny wondered if it could be Jem. Had she come down after all, to surprise her? And a table for two... did that mean she'd brought someone with her?

If it was Rupert, Ginny vowed to be as nice to him as she knew how.

―――~~~―――

An hour later her foolish hopes were dashed as the door of the restaurant opened and Gavin walked in with a blond who looked as if her lifetime ambition might be to appear on page three of the *Sun*, adopting one of those "Good gracious, where *did* my clothes go?" pouts.

Clearly struggling to match this vision in four-inch sparkly stilettos with the photograph he'd seen of Jem, Finn said doubtfully, "Is that your daughter?"

"If it was, I'd tell her to get her roots done and wear a bra." Awash with disappointment at having even thought it could be Jem, Ginny said, "It's my ex with one of his lovely young things. At a guess I'd say he's probably not with her for her mind."

"Now now." Finn's mouth twitched. "Never judge someone on first impressions. You of all people should know that."

He was having a dig, but Ginny's thoughts flew immediately to someone else whom she had met and disliked on sight. Maybe she'd got it wrong about Rupert and he wasn't obnoxious after all.

"Except men pointing guns at you." She picked up a couple of leather-bound menus. "If they're doing that, it's generally best to go along with your first impression. And run like hell."

"Thought we'd surprise you," Gavin said cheerfully when Ginny went over to hand them their menus. "This is Cleo, by the way. Cleo, this is Gin."

"Hiya!" Cleo actually had a sweet and friendly smile, but with her gauzy low-cut top and missing bra, it wasn't likely that many men would notice.

"You did surprise me. When Finn said a girl had booked the table, I thought it was Jem."

Cleo giggled. "That was me. Gavin asked me to make the call while he was in the shower." She gazed around eagerly. "I've never been to a restaurant like this before; I'm more of a burger girl myself. Are these... serviettes?" She was pointing to the dark blue linen napkins.

Politely, Ginny said, "Yes, they are."

"Wicked! Fancy having serviettes that aren't made of paper!"

After their main course, Cleo tottered off on four-inch heels to the loo and Gavin beckoned Ginny over.

"Well? What do you think of her?"

"Nice enough. Pretty. Young." Ginny shrugged helplessly; what did he expect her to say? "Just don't marry her, OK?"

Gavin beamed; he never took offense. "She's fun. We're enjoying ourselves. Speaking of fun, how's the lodger? Still the life and soul of the party?"

"OK, OK." Ginny acknowledged that if she was going to have a dig at his choice of girlfriend, it was only fair that he should be allowed to have a go in return about Laurel.

"So, Wednesday. Bring her along to our singles do."

"Not that again. She won't go."

"Ah, but it's up to you to persuade her." Gavin looked pleased with himself. "And you know it makes sense. Now listen, because I've had one of my ideas."

"Would that by any chance be similar to the idea you once had about pouring a can of petrol on the barbecue to liven it up a bit? The idea that left you without eyebrows for the next three months?"

He ignored this disparaging reminder. "You have to tell Laurel that you want to go to the singles night, but that you're too shy to do it on your own. You beg her to go along with you for moral support. Brilliant or what?"

Transparent was the word that sprang to mind. Rather like Cleo's top. Ginny said, "And you'll be there?"

Gavin looked at her as if she'd just suggested the sea was pink. "Of course I'll be there!"

"But what about Cleo?"

"We're not joined at the hip, you know." His eyes twinkled. "Besides, Wednesday's her yoga night."

He was never going to change. When Gavin was eighty he'd be the scourge of the nursing homes; no still-sprightly widow would be safe.

"Everything OK?" Finn joined them.

"Wonderful, thanks. Great food." Patting his stomach, Gavin said cheerily, "I've just been persuading Ginny here to give the local singles club a try."

The temptation to grab hold of Gavin's chair, wrench it backward, and tip him to the ground was huge. Would a bruised coccyx be painful enough? Did her ex-husband seriously not realize that she might prefer it if he didn't blurt out this kind of thing in front of her new boss? The new boss who was struggling to keep a straight face.

"I'm not interested in singles clubs!" Ginny felt herself going very red.

"Sorry, of course you're not." Infuriatingly, Gavin winked and raised a finger to his lips, indicating that it was their little secret. "Wednesday, eight o'clock. You'll love it. OK, shhh, Cleo's coming back."

"Hiya!" Cleo trilled when Gavin had introduced her to Finn. "It's really nice here, isn't it?" Leaning closer and resting her hand on Finn's shirtsleeve, she whispered, "Only I hope you don't mind me telling you, but someone's made off with the towel in the ladies." I had to dry my hands on bits of toilet paper! I mean, you don't expect people to nick things in a posh place like this, do you?"

"I'll go and check," Ginny murmured hurriedly before either Finn or Gavin could come up with some oh-so-witty retort.

Twenty seconds later she was back. "They're all there." Then, because Cleo was looking baffled, "Dark green, in two piles on the shelf above the linen basket."

Cleo's expression cleared. "Oh *those*. But they're only little! I thought they were flannels in case you wanted to wash your face!"

Gavin roared with laughter and gave her shoulders a squeeze. "My little Eliza Dolittle. They're towels, darling. You dry your hands on them then throw them in the basket to be washed."

For a moment, Cleo looked flustered. "Oh! Well, that's very extravagant."

Poor Cleo. Feeling a stab of sympathy toward her, Ginny said, "I think it's extravagant too."

It was Wednesday night and they were actually here. Ginny still couldn't quite believe it. Yesterday, she had discovered, was the anniversary of the day Laurel and Kevin had first met. As a result, Laurel had been inconsolable, gazing helplessly at a battered photo of her former love and mournfully wondering aloud, over and over again, why she was bothering to carry on, because what was the point?

By the evening, Ginny couldn't have agreed more. If Laurel wanted to end it all by electrocuting herself in the bath, she'd have happily supplied the hairdryer and the extra-long flex.

"Sorry, I know how boring this must be for you." Laurel tugged the last tissue out of the box and wiped her eyes. "I just miss Kev so much, you know? It just feels like life isn't worth living. It's all right for you, you're completely over Gavin, you don't want him back. But I still want Kevin, more than *anything*."

"I don't want Gavin back," Ginny blurted out, "but I'd like a man in my life. In fact, I'd love to try that singles club Gavin was talking about. Except... I couldn't go on my own."

Laurel sniffed damply. "You could. Gavin would be there."

"Exactly! That's what makes it impossible. I wouldn't know anyone apart from my ex-husband!" Out of sheer desperation, Ginny pleaded, "But if you'd come along with me, just once, you'd be doing me the biggest favor. Tomorrow night. Would you? Please?

She didn't for a moment expect Laurel to say yes.

"All right then."

What?

Ginny gazed at her. "Really?"

"If it's what you want, I'll do it," Laurel said sadly. "I'll hate it, of course, but I suppose I owe you that much. If it makes up for me being a bit miserable sometimes."

A *bit*?

Stunned, Ginny said, "Well, thanks."

"Don't expect me to talk to any men though. Especially not that Hamish person Gavin was going on about."

"Absolutely not." Ginny crossed her fingers behind her back.

"And I'm only going the once."

"Absolutely." Bugger, now that meant she had to go too.

The singles club was held in the back room of the White Hart. Now, pausing in the doorway, Laurel said, "Are you sure you want to do this?"

"Of course!" Ginny flashed a bright smile. "This is exciting! Just think, I could be about to meet the man who'll change my life!"

Laurel looped a strand of long red hair behind her ear. "It must be nice to feel so hopeful. I hope he's in there."

Me too, thought Ginny. More to the point, I hope his name is Hamish.

Chapter 18

THE CLUB WAS BUSY, which was a relief. The music didn't stop nor did an eerie saloon-bar silence fall as they walked in. But heads turned, they had definitely been noticed. Aware of dozens of pairs of eyes upon her, Ginny realized she was being subjected to the lightning appraisal afforded each newcomer. The other women were sizing up the competition, their collective gaze flicking over her hair, her face, and her clothes. Gavin may have praised these people to the skies, assuring her that everyone was wonderfully friendly, but they weren't looking that thrilled to see her right now.

A quick glance around revealed that the women outnumbered the men in the club by about two to one, so their lack of enthusiasm was perhaps understandable. Ginny longed to run up to them and blurt out that it was OK, she wasn't here to snaffle their men.

But with Laurel at her side she could hardly do that.

Laurel said ruefully, "Well? Seen anyone you like?"

Poor Laurel. She couldn't wait to be out of here. If she had her way, Ginny would pick her man, twirl a lasso above her head, and bring him crashing to the ground. The sooner she'd captured him, the sooner they could go home.

"I think it might take more than twenty seconds." Ginny briefly scanned the males on display wondering if there were, in fact, any she did like the look of. There was a wide-ranging choice—fat men, tall men, ones with hair and some without, men in trendy clothes and others wearing the kind of outfits their mothers might have chosen for

them. Some were blessed in the looks department, while some… well, you could only hope they had sparkling personalities on their side.

But none, at first glance, made her heart beat faster. None of them was Perry-shaped.

However, there was one who was Gavin-shaped. Having spotted them, he made his way over. Her eyes narrowing, Laurel muttered, "He'd better not be rude to me."

Which was a bit like hoping that a man-eating tiger wasn't going to take a bite out of your leg.

"Girls, girls, you made it! Excellent." Gavin clapped Laurel on the back, almost flooring her. "You're going to enjoy yourselves."

"I won't. I'm only here because Ginny begged me to keep her company." Tetchily, Laurel said, "And don't call us girls. That's sexist."

"Oh God, are you starting already? Would you rather I called you a middle-aged misery?"

"Drinks," Ginny cut in hastily before Gavin *did* start calling her a middle-aged misery and Laurel stormed out. *Be nice*, she mouthed at her ex-husband.

"I am being nice," Gavin retorted. "She started it. I don't see what's so terrible about being called a girl. But anyway," he added as Ginny shot him another fierce look, "let's not bicker. We're all here to have fun, aren't we? Laurel, why don't I introduce you to a few of my friends…"

Wasting no time, he whisked Laurel off. Ginny approached the bar and ordered their drinks—an orange juice for Laurel and a vodka tonic for herself. In the mirror above the bar she could see Gavin introducing a clearly reluctant Laurel to a mixed group of people. Craning her neck, Ginny wondered if one of them was Hamish but since none of the men was wearing a kilt or brandishing a set of bagpipes, it wasn't possible to tell. Although he couldn't be that chubby one, surely, the one who looked like a Weeble, nor the guy in the orange cardigan who had to be sixty if he was a day.

"Are you Gavin's ex-wife?"

Turning, Ginny saw an attractive, interested-looking brunette of her own age, wearing a cream trouser suit.

"That's right. I'm Ginny. Hi." Shaking the proffered hand, Ginny said, "How did you know?"

"Gavin told us you'd be coming along tonight. He said you were very pretty, like a young Goldie Hawn. Which didn't go down too well with the female contingent, I can tell you." The woman smiled. "I'm Bev, by the way."

"Maybe I should have blacked out some of my teeth and stuck on a big wart." Ginny pulled a face. "Gavin did say everyone was friendly, but..."

"That's because everyone loves Gavin. He's our star performer. All the women want him and all the men want to be like him. But it doesn't work that way for us. And I know how it feels, believe me. The women aren't wild about me either."

"Because they want to keep all the men here to themselves?"

"Not *these* men. They just can't bear the thought that one night George Clooney might walk in and they won't get first go at him."

Entertained, Ginny said, "And is that who you're waiting for too?"

"Well, I wouldn't say no. But I've actually got a bit of a crush on one of the men here."

"Really?" Fascinated, Ginny scanned the room. Not that one, surely. Or him, or him. Definitely not him...

"It's Gavin," said Bev.

"Blimey."

"I know." Bev tilted her head in rueful acknowledgement. "It's hopeless. I'm forty! Maybe if I was ten years younger I'd stand a fighting chance, but I'm not. So I don't."

"He might come to his senses one day, sort himself out, and realize it's time to settle down with someone his own age. I wish he would," Ginny said with feeling.

"But you can't see it happening."

"To be honest, no. More chance of George Clooney walking in here."

"He'll just have to do, then. Poor old George, relegated to second prize. And you'll probably want him too." Bev's eyes danced. "I'd have to fight you for him."

If Ginny had her way, she'd never be coming here again after tonight. But she couldn't tell Bev she was only here because of Laurel.

"Speaking of George Clooney," Bev added in an undertone, "here comes someone who looks... absolutely nothing like him."

For the next ten minutes, Ginny chatted to Bev and an earnest bespectacled divorcé called Harold who was an accountant, forty-nine, and very keen on growing his own vegetables. He was even keener on explaining to her, step by step, how he grew them. After that they were joined by Timothy, a thirty-four-year-old butcher by day and would-be Elvis impersonator by night.

Elvis with a lisp.

"You might not think I look much like him now," Timothy said eagerly, "but jutht wait till you thee me in my wig and makeup!"

And—not for the first time, Ginny suspected—he proceeded to demonstrate his moves. Since Timothy had wispy blond hair and a round pink face like a fat baby, it was as surreal as Princess Anne pretending to be Freddie Mercury. His white Lycra Elvis jumpsuit, Timothy told her with pride, had been made to measure and he'd thewn on every thequin himthelf by hand.

Jim was next, a math teacher whose wife had died three years ago. His interests were rock-climbing and playing badminton. "But not at the same time!" With an ear-splitting guffaw, Jim clutched his sides. "That would be dangerous!"

After hilarious Jim came David the cattle farmer, who was quite handsome in a ruddy, outdoorsy way and seemed absolutely

charming but had an unfortunate saliva-spraying thing going on whenever he spoke.

"God, I'm so sorry, I've done it again." Apologetically, David fished a large cotton handkerchief out of his pocket and dabbed at Ginny's cheek. "It's because I'm nervous. I'm always doing it here, but when it's just me and the cows on the farm I'm fine." It was a relief when Gavin came over and reclaimed her. He had his drawbacks, but at least he'd never sprayed spit in her face.

"How's Laurel getting on?"

"Great guns. Hopeless with the men," said Gavin. "I warned her not to talk about Kevin but she couldn't help herself. Not the world's greatest chat-up line, telling men the reason you're not drinking is because you're on antidepressants because your boyfriend chucked you and you know you'll never get over him because he's the only man you ever loved. To be honest, they couldn't get away fast enough. Happily, I had the bright idea of introducing her to the three witches. Their husbands chucked them too," he explained when Ginny looked blank. "Bitter doesn't begin to describe them. They spend all their time huddled together muttering about how all men should be drowned in a bucket at birth."

"I thought this club was supposed to be friendly," Ginny protested.

"Oh, come on, it's hilarious. And they're being friendly to Laurel. Look." Gavin pointed them out, gathered around a table in the corner. Laurel was crying and talking and the three witches were nodding vehemently, evidently in agreement that Kevin was a bastard of the first order.

"So no joy with Hamish. Which one is he, by the way?" Ginny peered around hopefully.

"Not here. Hasn't turned up tonight."

Typical. After all the effort she'd put into dragging Laurel along in the hope that she and Hamish might hit it off, he hadn't even had the decency to show his face. Oh well, it had been a ridiculous idea

anyway, one of Gavin's mad notions. And since when had he shown an iota of talent for matchmaking?

Actually, speaking of matchmaking…

"Bev's nice, isn't she?"

"Bev's great." Gavin shrugged then caught the look in Ginny's eye. "Oh no, don't go getting any ideas. She's not my type."

Honestly, he drove her insane—was Gavin the most frustrating man in Cornwall?

"Because she doesn't wear skirts up to her knickers?"

He grinned. "That could have something to do with it."

Ginny looked at her watch. "Do you think Hamish might still turn up? He could just be late."

"He's always here by eight thirty."

That was that, then. "Brilliant. What a waste of an evening."

"Hey, don't get niggly. He'll be here next week."

"But we won't be. I'm not doing this again." Ginny couldn't face another evening here; people were starting to dance and some of them were people who should never be allowed to dance outside the privacy of their own bedrooms. This wasn't her kind of place. She could be out with Perry now, having a lovely time…

Except that wasn't quite true, sadly. She couldn't be out with Perry because he hadn't phoned her all week. And out of practice with dating though she might be, even Ginny knew it wasn't cool to ring the man and demand to know why he hadn't rung you.

"You know, you might not have to come back." Gavin turned her in the direction of the corner table. "Look at Laurel."

Ginny looked. Laurel was no longer crying. All four women were in hysterics, clutching each other and giggling like eighteen-year-olds.

"I didn't know she could laugh," Ginny marveled.

"She's joined the coven. You mark my words; she'll be back every week from now on." Modestly, Gavin said, "God, I'm brilliant."

Was he? Could he actually have done something right? Deciding

that he might have, Ginny gave him a grateful hug and was instantly aware of the waves of resentment being directed at her by all the single women in the room. Hastily she let go, stepping back and landing on somebody's foot.

"Ouch… thorry!" Wincing but putting on a brave face, Elvis Presley said, "I wondered if I could perthuade you to danthe?"

"Of course she will," Gavin said heartily before Ginny could open her mouth.

The coven beadily watched as Timothy led her onto the dance floor. Ginny's heart sank as the music changed. Over in the corner the witches were sniggering.

Timothy, his mouth millimeters from her left ear as he steered her around, crooned happily along to "Thuthpiciouth Mindth."

Thank goodness Jem wasn't here to see her now.

~~~

They drove home at eleven o'clock. Encouraged by the fact that the three witches appeared to have taken Laurel under their wing, Ginny said brightly, "Well? Not as terrible as you expected?"

Laurel looked shocked. "What makes you think that? It was *worse.*"

"But you made friends with the wi—um, with those women, didn't you? I thought you were getting on really well with them."

Laurel said flatly, "They were awful."

"I saw you laughing," Ginny protested.

"It's called being polite. Sitting with them was awful, but marginally less awful than having to talk to the men. That's the only reason I stayed where I was."

"So you didn't enjoy yourself."

"Of course I didn't enjoy myself! Did *you*?"

"I thought it was… good." Ginny gripped the steering wheel in order to lie with more conviction. "I mean, it's always a bit scary

going somewhere new for the first time, but maybe if you tried it again next week you might find yourself—"

"Oh no." Laurel shook her head with such determination that her long hair almost slapped Ginny across the face. "No, don't even *try* to persuade me."

"But—"

"I've done it once and that was enough. To be honest, I didn't realize you were this desperate to meet a new man." In the orange glow of the streetlamps, Laurel looked at Ginny as if she were a particularly slutty teenager and a severe disappointment to boot. "I'm sorry, but if you really want to go to that place again, you'll just have to go by yourself."

Chapter 19

"He still hasn't rung," said Ginny.

Carla was on her living-room floor doing sit-ups, her flat stomach sheeny with perspiration but her ability to speak unimpeded. "Have you called him?"

"I can't."

"So you're just going to wait?"

"What other choice do I have?"

Carla shrugged in mid-sit-up. "Call him."

"No! The thing is, I don't understand it. He's so nice when I do see him. He really seems to like me. He said he'd be in touch and he said it as if he meant it. So I believed him." Ginny heaved a sigh and glanced over at the TV, where a guilty-looking bearded character in an Aussie soap was being confronted by both his wife and his mistress. ("Noelene, ya don't understind, I kin explain ivrything...")

Following the direction of her gaze, Carla said, "Maybe he's seeing someone else."

This had already crossed Ginny's mind. "If he is, I wish he'd just tell me."

Carla finished her two hundredth sit-up. Reaching for the phone on the coffee table, she said, "What's his number?"

"Why?"

"Because you're my best friend and he's treating you like dirt."

"He doesn't," Ginny protested. "That's the thing; when we're together, he treats me like a princess."

"Are you working on Friday night?"

"No. Why?"

"Just give me the number."

Ginny was torn between stuffing her fingers in her ears—her own ears, not Carla's—and listening to Carla giving Perry a hard time.

"Is that Perry? Hi, my name's Carla James, I'm a friend of Ginny's." Carla was in brisk, don't-mess-with-me mode, pacing the living room as she spoke into the phone. "You remember Ginny; she's the one you haven't rung for the last week and a half."

Ginny flinched and stuffed her fingers in her ears. Sadly it didn't block out what Carla was now saying.

"So I was wondering, do you have another girlfriend taking up all your free time? Or a wife perhaps?" Pause. "Sure about that? OK, in that case, have you decided you don't want to see Ginny anymore?" Pause. "Well good, I'm glad to hear that, although I have to say I'm not sure you deserve her. If you were my boyfriend, I'd have chucked you by now." Pause. "Oh, don't give me that. We're all *busy*. If you want to see someone you just have to make time. So how about tomorrow night?"

By this time squirming for England, Ginny was amazed she hadn't disappeared down *inside* the sofa. Jumping to her feet she escaped through to the kitchen with the sound of an irate Aussie wife yelling, "Bruce, you're nothin' but a no-good lyin' *cheat*," echoing in her ears.

By the time she'd finished noisily unloading the dishwasher, Carla came through to the kitchen looking pleased with herself.

"All sorted."

"You bullied him into it," Ginny wailed. "That makes me feel so wanted and desirable."

"Hey, you gave me his number. You wanted to see him again and now you're seeing him. More to the point," Carla said crisply, "so will I."

"Why?"

"So I can check him out and give you my verdict. If I think he's giving you the runaround, I'll tell you. If I don't like him, you'll be the first to know. If I don't think he's trustworthy, I'll give it to you straight. Because you deserve better than to be mucked about by some smooth-talking bastard and I won't stand by and see you hurt."

This was Carla all over, in-control and no-nonsense. She had never had a dithery moment in her life.

"You'll like him. You couldn't not like him," said Ginny.

"Don't be so sure. So far he hasn't made the greatest impression. Anyway"—Carla took a bottle of Evian from the fridge and gulped half of it down in one go—"you're both coming along to the Carson Hotel tomorrow night."

The Carson was Portsilver's biggest hotel, reopening in grand style following a refurbishment that had taken eight months and cost many millions. It had been a coup for Carla, who had sold them the biggest conservatory her company had ever built. Ginny already knew no expense had been spared for tomorrow's bash. Hundreds of people had been invited. On the one hand, she didn't want Perry to be seeing her because Carla had forced him into it. Then again, it would be a spectacular night out.

Ginny had never been inside Perry's shop before. Every wall was covered with printed T-shirts. Behind the counter sat a gum-chewing girl with surfer's hair and a lip ring, wearing a T-shirt that said I'M CLEVERER THAN I LOOK. To prove it, a copy of Tolstoy's *War and Peace* lay open next to the till.

"Hi, is Perry around?"

"He's in the back."

After waiting for a couple of seconds, Ginny said, "So could I see him?"

"I expect so." The gum-chewing didn't falter. "What's your name?"

"Ginny Holland."

There was no flicker of recognition; clearly, Perry hadn't mentioned her to his assistant. Oh well.

"Just go on through." The girl tilted her head in the general direction of the door and yawned widely.

Maybe the copy of *War and Peace* belonged to someone else.

Perry was in the back room unpacking boxes of T-shirts in every color. He jumped to his feet when he saw Ginny standing in the doorway.

"Sorry, I know you're busy." Having rehearsed what to say, Ginny blurted the words out. "I just wanted to apologize for Carla; she gets carried away. And forget about tomorrow night, that's off too. So don't worry about it. Right, I've got to get to work and—"

"Whoa, hey, stop." Perry reached out and grabbed her arm as she turned to leave. "What's wrong?"

Only a man could ask that question.

"Nothing's wrong. I just don't need other people making arrangements for me. And neither do you," said Ginny. "So let's just leave it there, OK? I'm sorry Carla phoned you."

"Stop saying sorry. That's my job." Pausing, Perry studied her face. "I really have been busy, you know, getting ready for the start of the tourist season. But I should have phoned you. Your friend Carla was right to give me a hard time. And I would like us to go to the Carson tomorrow. Very much indeed."

Oh God, more confusion. When he was looking at her like this and sounding so genuinely regretful, Ginny no longer knew what to do or say. She'd come here to be strong and now she was weakening again, because she so badly wanted to believe him.

"Please?" prompted Perry, drawing her closer and smiling his twinkly irresistible smile. "Give me the chance to make it up to you. We'll have a fantastic evening, I promise. And I'll do my best to

prove to Carla that I'm not the heartless bastard she thinks I am. Is she as scary as she sounds, by the way?"

"Scarier," said Ginny. It was no good; she couldn't hide her relief that he was saying all the things she'd hoped he'd say. "OK, I'll see you there tomorrow night."

"Hooray." He kissed her. "You're gorgeous."

Oh, the bliss of his mouth on hers. "And I want you to win Carla over."

"You're the important one. As long as I've won you over, I'm happy." Perry's eyes danced. "Besides, what can Carla do to me?"

"Put it this way," said Ginny. "You might want to wear a bullet-proof vest."

—⁓—

It took Ginny, emerging from the restaurant kitchen, a couple of seconds to place the three women who had just arrived for lunch. Then it clicked. Eeurgh, the coven.

Worse still, Finn was greeting them and taking their coats because it was Evie's day off.

"I'm the duck, love. He's the crab."

"Oops, sorry." Ginny hastily switched the plates she'd just put down. Behind her, she could feel the witches turning their attention in her direction.

"Ginny, over here." Finn beckoned her over to the bar where they had congregated to order drinks. "These ladies are saying they recognize you from somewhere."

"It's Gavin's ex-wife, isn't it?" Up close, the head witch was heavily made up with lots of lime-green frosted eye shadow and an unpleasant gleam in her eye. "You came along to our club last night, dumped your friend on us. We didn't get a chance to speak to you, which was a shame." Turning to Finn, she explained, "It's a singles club; we're very friendly. But some people don't like to waste time

socializing with members of their own sex. Ginny here seemed far more interested in meeting the men. In fact I think you spent pretty much all evening talking to our men, didn't you? Nobody else got a look-in."

Ginny squirmed. On the other side of the bar, Finn's face was a picture. Of course it was; only last week she had been outraged by Gavin's suggestion that she might like to go along to the club.

Finn, the corners of his mouth twitching, said, "You didn't tell us you were going. What changed your mind?"

Blood pulsated through Ginny's face; she didn't need to look in the mirror behind the bar to know she was the color of Campari. "I wanted Laurel to meet someone. I only went along to keep her company."

The second witch smirked. "You didn't though, did you? You abandoned her. And she told us you were desperate to meet a new man, that's the only reason *she* agreed to go with *you*." She paused to light a cigarette, blew out a plume of smoke. "Well, you certainly met plenty, by the looks of things. Timothy seemed pretty smitten when you were smooching together on the dance floor."

Finn raised an eyebrow. "Sounds like you had a good night."

"He asked me to dance. It would have been rude to say no. And I didn't only meet men," said Ginny. "I talked to Bev."

"Oh well, *her*. She thinks she's a cut above the rest of us." The third witch shook back her oversprayed, overstraightened hair. "She's man-mad too. Nothing but a slut. Nobody likes her."

"I did." Ginny reached for the leather-bound menus and handed one to each of the witches. "But I won't be going back to the club."

"Shame," Finn drawled. "Sounds like fun."

"He's single, you know." Ginny eyed the coven who immediately perked up. "If he thinks it's fun, why don't you persuade him to go along?"

Bingo. The first witch's eyes gleamed beneath layers of caked-on

mascara. Clutching Finn's sleeve, she exclaimed, "Now that is an *excellent* idea."

"And you wouldn't have to worry about being on your own," Ginny told him breezily. "I'm sure these ladies would look after you."

———

"Thanks for that." Finn had waited until the restaurant was empty, the three witches having been the last to leave.

Revenge was sweet. Energetically clearing the tables, Ginny beamed at him. "My pleasure. You'll have a lovely time."

"I'd rather throw myself off a cliff. Not that there's anything wrong with singles clubs *per se*," Finn said quickly. "I just couldn't handle those three being there, following me around. But there's no shame in being on your own and wanting to change that."

Ginny contemplated explaining all over again then decided against it. The more she protested, the more of a desperate Doris she sounded. Instead she nodded and said, "I know."

"Now, this isn't a date," Finn announced when she returned from the kitchen to collect the tablecloths, "it's a straight offer. I've been invited to the reopening of the Carson Hotel tomorrow evening and I can bring a guest. If you want to come along with me, you can."

Talk about a turn-up for the books. Clutching the mound of tablecloths to her chest, Ginny said, "You want me to go with you to a hotel? Aren't you worried I might steal a few bathrobes?"

Finn smiled. "I'll just have to trust you to behave."

"I might not be able to. Will there be lots of single men there?"

"I'd say it's a possibility. That's why I thought you might enjoy it. And while you're talking to them, you can put in a good word for Penhaligon's."

Ginny considered this. "So I'd be allowed to plug your restaurant and chat up men at the same time?"

"Absolutely. As many as you like."

Maybe he meant to be helpful but she couldn't help feeling slightly patronized. Beaming at him, Ginny said, "That's really kind of you. But no thanks."

"No?" Finn looked taken aback, rather like a do-gooder whose offer to have a lonely pensioner round for Christmas has been rejected.

"Actually, I'm already going along to the Carson do tomorrow night. With my boyfriend." Was it yucky to call someone your boyfriend when you were thirty-eight? Oh well. "So I'll see you there."

"Fine." He looked amused. "Good for you. I just thought I'd offer."

"See? I'm not as much of a charity case as you thought."

"I didn't think you were a charity case," said Finn. "Anyway, you can still plug the restaurant while you're there."

"Of course I will." As she swept past him with her armful of tablecloths, Ginny flashed him a jaunty smile. "If I'm not too busy having fun."

Chapter 20

"YOU LOOK NICE," SAID Laurel.

Ginny was immediately overcome with guilt. Laurel was sitting on the sofa in her droopy dressing gown, half reading a novel with a depressing cover and half watching a documentary about alopecia. The title of the book on her lap was *How Can I Live without You?* Ginny couldn't help feeling that if Laurel needed cheering up she'd be a lot better off with some nice breezy chick lit.

"Thanks." She smoothed her lime-green silk dress over her hips and showed off the lilac shoes that matched her bag. "These are a bit high, to be honest. I'll probably tip over and break an ankle. It's a shame you couldn't have come along too, but…"

"I know. Carla only had one spare ticket." Laurel didn't seem too distraught. "Don't worry, I'm fine staying in."

"And you've made that great curry," Ginny went on with too much enthusiasm. "So there's that to look forward to!"

Ergh, now she sounded like a hospital visitor.

"I know. Actually, I thought I might ring Perry and invite him round. He likes curry." Catching the flicker of alarm in Ginny's eyes, Laurel said, "That's all right, isn't it?"

Oh God, more deceit.

"Of course it is! Well, I'll just—"

The phone in her bag was ringing. Praying it wouldn't be Perry, Ginny fished it out.

It wasn't, thank goodness. "Jem! Hello, darling, how are you?"

She waved, mouthed good-bye to Laurel, and headed out to the hall.

"Great, Mum. I'm just calling to say don't ring me tomorrow morning because we're having a party tonight here at the flat and lots of people will probably end up staying over, so we'll all be asleep until midday."

Ginny smiled, picturing the scene the morning after. The flat would be in a revolting state. "OK, sweetheart, I'll let you have your lie-in. And don't forget to rope in all those overnighters to help with the clearing up. Don't let them slope off leaving you with all the work."

Jem laughed. "No need for that. Rupert's already booked a team of cleaners to come and blitz the place tomorrow afternoon. One of the advantages of being rich—we don't have to do a thing."

"That's good news then. So you're all still getting on well together?" Since Jem had never volunteered any information about her relationship with Rupert, Ginny hadn't asked. Jem might regard it as prying, Ginny knew she wouldn't be able to pretend to be overjoyed, and the last thing they needed was to have a fall-out.

"Everything's great." Jem certainly sounded chirpy. "We're busy doing all the food. Lucy and I are burning sausages and chopping onions…"

"And Rupert?" See? She couldn't help herself.

"Oh, he's a lazy bum. He's in the bath!"

What a surprise. But Jem was laughing, too happy to mind that Rupert was supercilious, selfish, and not one of life's workers. Impulsively, Ginny said, "Have you invited Davy to the party?"

"Mum, I'm beginning to think you've got a bit of a thing about Davy." Jem giggled. "You're always going on about him."

That's because he's a nice boy, Ginny longed to say. Unlike some people I could mention.

Aloud she said, "Sorry."

"To be honest, Davy and Rupert don't like each other much. So it was easier not to. Anyway," Jem changed the subject, "I haven't asked how things are with you. What are you up to this weekend? Anything nice?"

"Very nice, thanks." Letting herself out of the house enabled Ginny to talk freely without being overheard by Laurel. "In fact I'm off to a party myself tonight. The Carson Hotel's reopening at last, having a bit of a flashy do to celebrate. Carla invited me along with a friend and we're hoping for better than burnt sausages and fried onions."

"Hey, Mum, brilliant. Who's the friend, one of Carla's boy toys?"

"Actually, he's someone I've been out with a couple of times. We get on well." Ginny said it casually, as if she'd been out with gazillions of men.

"Mum!" Jem, who knew she hadn't, was instantly agog. "Who *is* he?"

"Just someone nice. Don't get excited." It had been killing Ginny not to mention Perry before now but she still didn't dare give him a name. Never one for discretion, Jem had once loudly announced on a bus that Father Christmas wasn't real, reducing a dozen younger children to tears.

She'd only been ten at the time, but still.

"Don't tell me not to get excited. I *am* excited! Is he handsome? Has Carla met him yet? This is so cool!"

Ginny crossed the road as Carla came out of her house. "Yes, he's handsome. And Carla's about to meet him for the first time. In fact we're just off to the hotel now, so I'm going to say bye. Have a lovely time tonight, darling. Be good!"

Jem, sounding as if she was grinning, said, "You too."

"There he is." Pride welled up as Ginny pointed across the room to where Perry was standing, smartly dressed (hooray) and (double

hooray) handsomer than ever. His red-gold hair gleamed in the brilliant light from the chandeliers, setting him apart from every other man in the room. He was wearing a dark blue suit and a blue and white striped shirt, and when he spotted Ginny with Carla he broke into a smile that sent tingles of lust zip-zapping up and down Ginny's spine.

He joined them and she performed the introductions.

"It's good to meet you at last." Perry shook Carla's hand.

"Hmm," Carla said coolly. "You may change your mind about that."

Perry turned to Ginny. "You said she was scary. You were right."

"Ginny's my friend. I'm looking out for her." Carla's tone was crisp.

"Well, guess what? You don't need to."

Her eyes flashed. "When I start seeing a new man, he's on the phone day and night. He can't keep away. We see each other all the time."

"As long as they've done their homework and their mothers say they're allowed out," Perry retorted.

"OK, stop it." Ginny stepped between them—God, this was turning into a soap opera. "No mud-slinging. I want you to be nice to each other."

Perry shrugged. "She started it."

"What are you, a complete *wimp*?"

"Don't," Ginny pleaded.

"Fine. I'm sorry. I'm sure he's wonderful." Briskly, Carla nodded and glanced around the room. "Well, I have to network. I'll leave you two to chat." And she left them.

Alarmed, Ginny said, "She isn't usually like that."

"Don't worry, I know the type. Some women can dish it out but they can't take it. Look at her hair." Perry's tone was disparaging. "The outfit, the makeup. Hard as nails, desperate to prove herself.

That's why she goes for younger men, so she can boss them around, be the one who calls the tune. But deep down? She's insecure." He sounded so sure, so dismissive.

"Carla isn't insecure. She's—"

"Enough about Carla. You're here and that's all I care about." Perry gazed deep into her eyes. "We're going to have a good time tonight."

Despite the tricky start, Ginny was glad to see him again. Perry took two glasses of champagne from the tray of a hovering waitress and they clinked them together.

"Here's to you. Looking fabulous." He eyed her dress with appreciation. "Now tell me what you've been up to this week."

So she told him about working at Penhaligon's and taking Laurel to the singles club, and about Laurel sitting at home in her droopy dressing gown watching sad programs on TV. "She was planning to invite you over this evening," Ginny added. "I felt terrible."

"Don't. You're great with her."

"But she's still depressed about Kevin."

"Think how much more depressed she'd be if she didn't have you." Glancing past her left ear, Perry said, "We're being watched, by the way. Not one of your exes, is it?"

Ginny turned and saw Finn a distance away, talking to a luscious brunette but with his gaze flickering in their direction. "That's my boss."

Finn's attention was recaptured by the curvy brunette but Ginny, delighted he'd noticed them, found herself becoming more animated and moving closer to Perry, touching his arm as they talked. If Finn had been expecting her to turn up with some ordinary unprepossessing man, well, ha, she hadn't! She hoped he was impressed. Later, when the situation arose, they would wander over and she would introduce him to Perry. Ooh, more drinks coming around, lovely.

Carla had spent the last hour circulating, greeting people she knew, and introducing herself to those she didn't. The Carson Hotel was the only five-star hotel in Portsilver and its glittering reopening was a major event. Everyone was impressed by the Victorian-style conservatory, immaculately finished and commanding uninterrupted views over the ocean. Already she had been asked by three guests to supply quotes for extensions to their own homes or businesses.

So far, then, a successful evening. With one awkward but manageable exception.

On her way to the ladies' loos, Carla bumped into him. Without missing a beat, as smoothly as a conjuror executing a nifty magic trick, Perry pushed open a door leading off the long corridor and drew her into the empty room.

"What?" Carla demanded fiercely.

"Has this ever happened to you before?"

Her eyes narrowed. "You mean being kidnapped?"

"You know what I'm talking about."

He was looking down at her, holding her by the shoulders against the wall. Carla swallowed and realized she was trembling. "Let me go."

"You haven't answered my question."

"I don't have to."

"I think you should."

"If you're trying to scare me…"

"No need," Perry said with a smile. "You're doing an excellent job of scaring yourself. So, ready to admit it now?"

Carla's mouth was bone dry. "Ready to admit *what*?"

By way of reply he released one of her shoulders and laid the flat of his right hand over her sternum between the vee of her shirt and the base of her throat. Immediately—as if she needed reminding—Carla felt her heart thumping away, pounding as if she'd just run a marathon.

"Now, I'm no doctor," Perry's tone was intimate, "but I'd guess a hundred and twenty beats per minute."

She was losing. He *knew*.

"That's what happens when you're trapped in a room with someone." Attempting to press herself backward into the wall, she said, "Especially when it's someone you don't trust."

"Except it was happening before, wasn't it? When Ginny first introduced us back there in the ballroom. I saw it happen." Perry smiled again as he lightly brushed a forefinger over the frantically pulsating, all too visible vein in her neck.

This was terrible, a full-blown nightmare. Carla had always, *always* been able to hide her true feelings. It was a gift she prided herself on. Then again, had she ever experienced sensations as intense, as overwhelming as these before? The moment she'd clapped eyes on Perry Kennedy, her body had reacted independently of her mind. She didn't believe in love at first sight, but if she did... well, it would feel like this.

Except this man belonged to Ginny. And Ginny was her best friend. She *couldn't* allow herself to give in.

"It's the same for me," Perry whispered. "Exactly the same for me. You're the one; you're everything I ever wanted. Sorry, I know that sounds corny. But it's true."

"Let go of me. This isn't going to happen. I don't want to see you again." Lightheaded and gulping for air, Carla tried to push him away.

"You will; you have to. Look, I don't want to hurt Ginny either. And I know we can't do anything tonight, but I do need to see you again. Just give me your number, and I'll ring you. Can we meet up tomorrow?"

"No." This time Carla managed to free herself. Panting, she said, "*No*," and stumbled out of the room.

Dear God, why had this had to happen to *her*?

The ladies' cloakroom was thankfully empty. Locking herself in one of the cool marble cubicles, Carla sat on the loo with her head in her hands, covering her flaming cheeks and willing the last ten minutes to empty themselves from her mind. Delete. Rewind. Think of Ginny, think of Ginny, *don't* think of—

Brrrppp. Carla's phone trilled and she almost fell off the loo seat. Her hands shaking violently, she saw an unfamiliar number flash up. Leave it to go to voice mail, just leave it.

No, she couldn't.

"H-hello?"

"It's me."

She'd known it would be him. "I said don't ring me."

"No you didn't." Perry's voice was conversational, amused. "You said you wouldn't give me your number."

"So how…?"

"*Luckily* there's a table out in the conservatory with your company's brochures on it." He paused. "Not to mention a pile of your business cards."

"I don't want to speak to you. I'm hanging up."

"I live in the flat above my shop. Twenty-five B, Harbor Street. Eight o'clock tomorrow evening suit you?"

Carla closed her eyes, pressed her trembling knees together. "You're out of your mind. Ginny's my *friend*."

"Eight o'clock it is then."

"I'm going to tell her about this. I'm going to go out there right now and tell her what you're doing behind her back."

"Eight o'clock," said Perry.

Click.

Carla gazed at the phone. He had hung up.

Chapter 21

"HERE HE IS." GINNY was standing with Finn. Proudly she introduced Perry.

"Hi. Good to meet you." Shaking Finn's hand, Perry said, "Sorry to be so long. I got chatting to someone I know."

Ginny said gaily, "That's nothing. I've been chatting to lots of people I *don't* know, telling them why they should come to Penhaligon's! One couple is going to book a table for next week; they're looking for somewhere to hold their daughter's wedding reception."

"Wedding receptions." Perry shuddered. "Sorry, my idea of hell. Kids running around screaming, babies crying... do you have children?"

"No." Finn's jaw was taut.

"Sensible man. Don't go there. Can't see the attraction myself. Everyone tells you kids change your life... well, I don't want to change mine, thanks very much. I'd rather keep it just the way it is. Who needs all that grief?"

"Probably not the best thing to say," murmured Ginny when Finn had excused himself and moved away to resume his conversation with the luscious brunette. "His girlfriend had a baby last year. Finn assumed it was his, but it wasn't. She ended up leaving him and going off with the baby's father."

"That's what I call a lucky escape. Oh, come on; don't look at me like that." Perry grinned and slid his arm round her. "Kids aren't my thing, that's all. And trust me, there's nothing worse than a broody woman. I mean, look at Laurel. Half the reason she's taking

this whole Kevin thing so badly is because she thinks she won't find another man before it's too late. Her hormones are in panic mode, flying around like headless chickens." He gave her waist a squeeze. "That's what I like about you."

"What? That my hormones are flying around like headless chickens?"

"That they *aren't*." Perry's green eyes glinted with amusement. "You and Laurel are the same age, but you've already done your bit, got the whole breeding thing out of your system. Don't get me wrong; I think it's great that you have a daughter. I'm just not interested in having any myself."

"You sound exactly like Carla."

"God, don't tell me there's something we actually agree on. I'm not sure I'm happy about that."

"Carla's all right." Ginny so badly wanted the two of them to get along. "Wait till you get to know her better."

Perry pulled a face. "I'd rather not."

"Don't be mean. She's my best friend."

"She's a viper. Anyway, why are we wasting time talking about her? I haven't even kissed you yet."

With this audience? Alarmed, Ginny squeaked, "You can't do that in here!"

"I know, I'm not a complete heathen." Keeping his arm around her waist, Perry steered her through the crowded ballroom, acknowledging an unsmiling Carla with a friendly nod as they passed her in conversation with a potential client. "That's why I thought we might take a walk around the grounds."

"It's dark out there. I'll trip over something and land flat on my face."

"You won't, there's a full moon. And the gardens are floodlit." Opening the doors that led outside, Perry ushered her through. "Hang on to me. I won't let you fall."

Ginny loved the way he said it, like James Bond would. It made her feel safe.

———

Carla couldn't help herself. When she saw Finn Penhaligon at the bar, she went over and stood next to him. He raised an eyebrow in recognition.

"Can I ask you something?" God, her stomach was in knots. "What do you think of Ginny's bloke?"

"I only spoke to him for a minute. I don't like to make snap judgments about people." Pausing, Finn said, "Although in his case I'll make an exception."

"And?"

His tone was contemptuous. "The man's an arse."

This was what Carla wanted to hear. She picked up a cocktail stick and snapped it in half.

"And?" Finn mimicked lightly. Funny how such an outwardly attractive man could have zero effect on her, whereas... oh God, don't even go there, don't even *think* about Perry Kennedy.

Carla nodded and reached for another cocktail stick to snap. "I think so too."

———

The music was bouncing off the walls of the flat, making the floor vibrate. A rumbustious game involving seeing how long you could balance an open can of lager on your head before it fell off was in progress in the living room, with much shoving and spillage going on. The carpet was drenched and empty cans were strewn every-where. Jem, watching as one of Rupert's friends tackled another to the ground—splat—felt sorry for the cleaners from the agency when they arrived tomorrow to clear up.

A hand on her bottom made her jump. His mouth brushing her ear, Rupert murmured, "What are you thinking?"

"That if this lot are planning to sleep on this floor tonight, they might drown."

"Their problem, not mine. Are you wearing any knickers?"

"Yes!" Jem wriggled as his warm fingers roamed over the back of her jeans.

"Shame. Hey, no one would notice if we slipped away for a few minutes. Fancy a quickie?"

"We can't do that." Jem turned and grinned at him. "It's not polite to abandon your guests."

"Bugger the guests. It's my party, and I'll shag if I—"

"Rupert, can you do something about Tilly and Marcus?"

This time Jem jumped because Lucy had appeared out of nowhere behind them. Gazing hard at Rupert, she went on, "They've locked themselves in the bathroom and there are people desperate for the loo."

"Great minds think alike," Rupert whispered in Jem's ear before levering himself away from the wall. "OK, I'll go and sort them out. Spoil their fun."

When he'd gone, Lucy said in an odd voice, "What was Rupert saying to you?"

Oh God, surely she couldn't have overheard. Awkwardly, Jem said, "Nothing. We were just talking about the carpet getting wet with all the beer being spilled. Like that." She nodded across the room as another can of lager went flying, spraying froth.

"It didn't look like that to me." Lucy's hands were thrust stiffly into the front pockets of her low-slung jeans. "The way you were whispering together."

Jem's mouth was dry. At least Lucy hadn't seen Rupert groping her; thank goodness he'd been discreet.

"And did he have his hand on your backside?"

"No... well, he was just mucking around," Jem stammered. "It didn't mean anything."

Lucy frowned. "Is there something going on between you and Rupert?"

See? It was clearly bothering her. This was exactly why she couldn't admit the truth.

"*No.*" Jem looked astounded. "God, are you serious? No way! I can't believe you even thought that."

There, was that convincing enough? Exuding innocent outrage, she held her ground and prayed Lucy wasn't about to whip out a lie detector.

"OK," Lucy said levelly. "But you'd tell me if there was, wouldn't you?" Her words were brittle, like dry sticks. "I mean, I'd want to know."

Of course she would. And if she did find out? Then the easy, happy atmosphere in the flat would be spoiled, Lucy would feel like a third wheel, and the next thing you know, she'd be moving out.

Jem didn't want that to happen. Lucy was her closest friend here in Bristol and a perfect flatmate.

"I'd tell you if there was anything going on," said Jem, "but there isn't, I promise. Crikey, I'm not nearly posh enough for Rupert!"

A faint smile tugged at the corners of Lucy's mouth. "You could be his bit of rough."

"Charming!" Relieved that the interrogation was over, Jem pretended to tug at one of her friend's gaudy earrings. "Speak for yourself."

Lucy grinned back, equally relieved. "Can you smell sausages burning?"

Jem could. It was a wonder the smoke alarm hadn't gone off. Thankful that the crisis had been averted and eager to please, she said, "You've done loads of cooking; I'll take over in the kitchen now."

"And we need more onions chopping up."

"Fine, I'll do it."

Lucy tilted her head to one side and said lightly, "Guilty conscience?"

"No!" Jem made an attempt to grab her other earring. "As if! I just want first pick of the sausages so I get the ones that aren't burned to a crisp."

"I took them out of the oven," said Davy when Jem burst into the kitchen. The trays of sausages were smoldering on top of the hob and Davy, shirt sleeves rolled up, was busy peeling and chopping a mound of onions.

"My hero! I didn't even know you'd arrived!" Jem hugged him, delighted that Davy had been able to make it; following the phone call to her mother earlier, guilt had prompted her to send him a text inviting him to the party. Now she was extra glad she had. "And just in the nick of time too. You saved our sausages!"

"Not all of them. Some are pretty cremated."

"Trust me, this crowd won't notice. The state half of them are in, they'd eat lumps of coal if we served them up in bread rolls with a squish of ketchup. Here, try one of the unburned ones." Choosing the best sausage and breaking it in two, she popped half into Davy's mouth and the other half into her own.

Damn, it was hot.

"Aaarrgh." Jem let out a shriek of pain.

"Yeeesh." Davy, his hands otherwise occupied with half an onion and a chopping knife, held the sausage clamped between his teeth and waggled it at her like Groucho Marx.

"Hot-hot-hot," Jem gasped, flapping her arms and hopping from one foot to the other.

"You'll never get off the ground," drawled Rupert behind her.

"Mmpph." With her mouth full of sausage, Jem swung round.

Rupert said, "What's he doing here?"

Jem chewed and swallowed, fanning her mouth. "I invited him. And he's helping with the food."

"Not to mention eating it."

"I'll write you a check," Davy said evenly.

"Don't bother, it'd probably bounce. Anyway, I like to do my bit to feed the poor."

"Rupert! God, you can be such a pig sometimes." Jem turned to Davy. "He doesn't mean it."

Drily, Davy said, "Of course he doesn't. Don't worry; I'll leave you to it."

Jem was alarmed. "You're not going."

"No." Having rinsed and dried his hands, Davy smiled at her. "I'm not."

When he'd left the kitchen, Jem said, "I hate it when you do that."

Rupert grinned, moved toward her. "But it's fun."

"It isn't. And you mustn't do that either." Darting out of reach as he made a playful grab for her, Jem said, "Lucy saw us just now. She's getting suspicious."

"What did you tell her?"

"That nothing was going on, of course. I said you weren't my type. Which you *aren't*," Jem added pointedly, "when you're being mean to Davy. If you can't say anything nice about a person, don't say anything at all."

"Bloody hell, where's the superglue? May as well seal my mouth shut now. God knows how I'll be able to drink."

Rupert sauntered out and Jem dealt with the rest of the onions. When she rejoined the party twenty minutes later, a limbo contest was in noisy progress in the middle of the room. Rupert was laughing as Lucy collapsed in a heap on the floor. Hauling her to her feet, he had a go himself and somehow—miraculously—managed it. His boisterous friends clapped and roared their approval, finding it something of a challenge to stay on their feet even without the distraction of a limbo pole. Then they roared again, having spotted Jem and her tray of hot dogs. Within seconds they'd descended on her like a pack of wolves.

But friendly wolves, thank goodness. Slapping away a few

hands—not all of them after the hot dogs—Jem managed to save three and crossed the room to where Davy was chatting to a plump but pretty brunette.

The girl's name was Suze, Jem discovered, and she was Patty Carson's sister. Patty, on their English course, was currently smooching with one of the rugby boys. Suze, a nurse down from Birmingham for the weekend, seemed glad of Davy's company. Jem gave them each a hot dog and was pleased Davy had found someone nice to talk to.

"Door," bellowed several people as the bell shrilled, indicating yet more late arrivals. Realizing that no one else was planning to let them in, Jem rolled her eyes and excused herself from Davy and Suze. Task completed, she was about to head back to the party when an ear-splitting crash came from the kitchen.

"Oh, Jem, I'm really sorry." A red-faced Patty Carson clutched her arm. "Ben came over all masterful and got carried away. We knocked the big glass salad bowl off the kitchen table."

Patty and Ben, both of them many sheets to the wind, were more of a hazard than a help. After they'd each cut themselves three times, Jem banished them from the kitchen and embarked on clearing up the shards of broken glass herself. It was safer this way for all concerned, plus between them Patty and Ben had used up the last of the plasters.

"Don't come in," yelled Jem as the door handle turned.

"Only me." Davy let himself in anyway. "Need a hand?"

A sober hand, what a luxury. Jem nodded gratefully and said, "What about Suze?"

"She's giving Patty a good talking-to. There's a lettuce leaf in your hair, by the way."

"There's glass and lettuce everywhere. And oil. Mind the floor; it's all slippy with dressing. Patty and Ben looked as if they were having their first skating lesson." Jem pushed her bangs off her

forehead with one elbow. "I had to get them out of here before one of them severed an artery."

Together they cleared up the mess. When they finally rejoined the party, Rupert was talking to Suze Carson. Picking a bottle of lager out of the tub of melting ice cubes, Davy said, "That's me out of the picture, then."

"It doesn't mean anything. He's just being friendly."

"Hmm. Very friendly." Davy raised an eyebrow and when Jem glanced over again she saw with a jolt that they were kissing. Suze's head was tipped back and her arms were wrapped ecstatically round Rupert's neck.

Jem hurriedly looked away and took a gulp of wine. The next moment, Lucy shimmied over and grabbed her hand. "Let's dance," she shouted happily above the blaring music. "Come on, Davy, you too."

By four o'clock the party was on its last legs. People were crashed out on sofas and chairs; those not fast enough to bag them had to make do with the soggy floor.

"Bed," Lucy yawned, switching off the CD player and almost tripping over a snoring body behind the door. "Night, Davy. Night, Jem. Night, all you drunken bums."

Acting normally was almost killing her but Jem had spent the last few hours doing it and she wasn't about to give up now. Rupert had spent the evening flirting with and enthusiastically kissing Suze Carson. At two o'clock, Patty and her bowl-smashing rugby player had left the party. Shortly after that, Rupert and Suze had disappeared into Rupert's bedroom and she probably wasn't teaching him first aid. Jem had given her best impression of a single girl without a care in the world while her stomach had been busy tying itself up in one giant knot.

Now, utterly miserable, she looked over at Davy and said, "Want me to phone for a cab?"

Davy sounded hesitant. "Well, you did say I could crash out here if I ever needed to. And it is pretty late."

It was. She had. It was just so hard to concentrate when all you wanted to do was run down the hallway and hammer on Rupert's locked bedroom door yelling, "Stop it, stop whatever you're doing, STOP IT!"

Jem nodded. "Of course you can. Sorry, I just thought you'd be going home."

"I told my mum I'd be staying here. She was OK about it, considering. One small step for man." Davy's smile was self-deprecating. "One giant step for me."

"That's great, Davy." Jem wished she could summon up more enthusiasm for his triumph, because it was a big deal. "Good for you."

"Don't worry about where to put me." He gestured to a space on the carpet in front of the sofa. "I'll be fine here."

The carpet was squelching beneath his feet and Tommy Beresford-Smith was snoring like a walrus on the sofa; if he tried to turn over in his sleep, he'd roll off and squash Davy flat.

"You can't sleep there." Rubbing her tired, smoke-reddened eyes, Jem said, "Better stay in my room. The carpet's dry and I don't snore."

Chapter 22

It felt like five minutes later when Jem woke up but a glance at the alarm clock revealed that it was eleven thirty. Davy's impromptu bed of cushions and blankets on the floor was empty and the sound of male voices drifted through from the kitchen.

Jem crawled slowly out of bed, dehydrated and dry-mouthed with apprehension, just as the door opened and Davy walked in carrying two mugs of tea.

"Hi. I made these."

"Thanks." She took the steaming mug he handed her. "Is everyone else up?"

"Only Rupert."

"I need a glass of water. Back in a minute." Running her fingers through her slept-in hair, Jem made her way past Davy.

Rupert was in the kitchen looking disgustingly healthy and unaffected by the amount of drink he'd put away last night. He was wearing jeans and a wicked grin, and piling sugar into two cups of coffee.

"Morning, gorgeous." He winked at her. "Sleep well?"

Sick with jealousy, Jem closed the kitchen door so they couldn't be overheard and said, "Did you have sex with her?"

"With who?"

"Scarlet Johansson." Jem shook her head vehemently. "Who d'you think? That girl!"

"Oh, you mean Suze. *That* girl." Amused, Rupert said, "Of course I didn't."

Jem seized a pint mug, swilled out the dregs of last night's lager, and shoved it under the tap, managing to spray ice-cold water all over the front of her nightie. "I don't believe you."

He shrugged. "Well, I can't help that. But it's the truth. We just crashed out."

"You were kissing her." God, it was horrible sounding like a neurotic nagging shrew, but what else was she supposed to do? He'd been *kissing* her.

"I thought you'd be pleased," said Rupert.

"*Pleased!*"

"Lucy was suspicious about us. By taking Suze back to my room, I've put a stop to that. Stroke of genius."

Jem swallowed. "Is that why you did it?"

"Yep. Well, that was one of the reasons." Breaking into a grin, Rupert drawled, "The other one being to get her away from your pal Davy."

"Why?"

"Why d'you think? To piss him off."

"I still think you slept with her."

"Well, I didn't. But fine, think what you like. Anyway," said Rupert, "you can talk. What happened between you and Davy?"

"Nothing!"

He tilted his head. "So you say. But let's face it; he spent last night in your room, which has to be the first time he's ever stayed out overnight. What better way to celebrate?" There was a glint in his eye as he went on, "Bloody hell, what's his mother going to be doing now? She's probably spent the last six hours dialing 999. There'll be helicopters circling overhead, police divers searching the river."

"He told her he was staying here. And he slept on the floor. You *know* we didn't do anything," said Jem. "I *wouldn't.*"

"You mean I just have to trust you? Well, snap." Dropping a lazy kiss on her bare shoulder, Rupert carried the mugs past her. "But remember, it's thanks to me that you've got Lucy off your back."

She weakened. Even a passing shoulder kiss had the power to make her go weak at the knees. Watching him leave, Jem experienced a violent rush of longing. You knew you were a lost cause when you found yourself embroiled with someone who actually was sexier than Johnny Depp.

Back in the bedroom she drank her cooling tea and listened to Davy's brief telephone conversation with his mother.

"Yes, Mum, I'm still alive. No, I didn't take any drugs. No, the police weren't called. Mum, everything's fine. I'll see you later, OK? Yes, me too."

Jem sat down on the bed. How awful to have such a clingy, neurotic mother. She watched as Davy ended the call then keyed in another number.

"Hi, it's me. Where are we and what time do we start?" He listened, nodding, then reached for a purple felt-tip pen on Jem's dresser and began scribbling down an address.

He didn't get very far.

"Right," Davy said evenly. "I'll see you there."

When he'd switched off his phone, Jem said, "Going somewhere nice?"

He shrugged and held out the scrap of paper upon which he'd written down the first line of the address. Jem frowned. "But... that's *here*."

"Just my luck."

"I don't understand. Who are you meeting up with?"

Davy puffed out his cheeks and rubbed the back of his hair. Finally, he said, "The rest of the team from Spit and Polish."

Spit and Polish. The contract cleaning company hired by Rupert to come and restore the flat to some semblance of normality. More than a semblance, actually, given the prices they charged.

"I didn't know you worked for them," said Jem.

"I only started a couple of weeks ago. A few hours on a Saturday,

and again on Sunday. The money's not bad and it seemed like a good idea at the time." Heaving a sigh, Davy said, "Rupert's going to have a field day when he finds out."

~~~

Jem had done her best to chivvy everyone awake and get them out of the flat but it was like trying to shovel mud in a swamp. At twelve o'clock on the dot a bright orange van with Spit and Polish emblazoned in turquoise along each side pulled up outside the flat. Out jumped five ready-to-go cleaners in neon orange and turquoise boilersuits.

"Here they are then." Turning away from the bedroom window, Davy said, "And brace yourself. The one in the headscarf is Rhonda."

"Hello, my love, Spit and Polish at your service." When Rupert opened the door he was almost knocked sideways by a mini whirl-wind in a fluorescent orange headscarf. "Ooh, my Lord, cracking party by the looks of things, what a state, these walls are going to need some elbow grease." Barreling past him and beadily surveying the scene of post-party chaos with her head on one side, Rhonda patted Rupert's hand and said, "Never mind, love, we're here now to do all your dirty work for you, we'll have this mucky old flat spick and span again in no time. My word, you're a handsome lad, aren't you? Now what we really need is for everyone to clear out of here and leave us to get on, then when you come back at three o'clock you won't recognize the place, that's a promise!"

"We'll go and grab some lunch." Rupert counted the boiler-suited individuals piling into the flat armed with buckets and clean-ing paraphernalia. "I thought there were meant to be six of you."

"There are, love. The last one hasn't arrived quite yet but don't you worry, he'll be here in two shakes of a lamb's—oh my word, speak of the devil. Davy, love, you beat us to it after all! Janice, give the lad his overalls and we can get cracking."

Rupert struggled to keep a straight face as Janice threw the orange jumpsuit at Davy, standing in the doorway. Davy climbed into it and zipped it up to his neck.

"You work for this company?" said Rupert.

"Yes, I do."

"So you'll be cleaning my flat."

"Looks like it."

"Nice one. Don't forget to scrub the toilet, will you?"

"It'll be done," Davy said evenly.

"But I'd really like you to be the one who does it. That'd make my day."

From the kitchen, Rhonda yelled, "Goodness me, what a state! Davy, love, come and help me make a start in here."

Rupert smirked. "Better get a move on, Davy, love. The kitchen, eh? In that case let's hope for less of the spit and more of the polish."

—~~~—

Still on a high from last night, Ginny couldn't wait to ring Jem and find out how the party had gone. At one o'clock—surely it was safe to do it now; they couldn't still be asleep—she made the phone call.

It was picked up on the fourth ring. "Hello?"

Not Rupert. *Good.* Ginny said brightly, "Hi, is Jem there?"

"Sorry, no. Everyone's out."

"Oh. Right." Did the male voice sound faintly familiar? "But you're there."

"Yes." There was a moment's hesitation. "Is that Jem's mum?"

"It is." Caught off guard, Ginny said, "And who are you?"

"Davy Stokes. You probably won't remember, but you gave me a lift home to—"

"Davy! Of course I remember! How lovely to speak to you again. How *are* you?"

"Fine thanks."

"So you must have gone to the party last night. I was just calling to find out how it went." A thought popped into Ginny's head. "Oh my goodness, Jem isn't there but you are. Does this mean you and Lucy are an item?"

He sounded amused. "Wouldn't that have been good? Sorry to disappoint you. I reckon I'd have more chance with Claudia Schiffer."

"So what are you…?"

"Doing here? Rupert hired a cleaning team. I'm one of the team." Drily Davy added, "Which, it goes without saying, made Rupert's day."

"I can imagine." Ginny paused because she and Davy shared the same low opinion of Rupert; it was their guilty secret. On impulse, she said, "Can I ask you something?"

"Fire away. Something about Jem?"

"And Rupert." She chose her words with care. "Is there anything… well, going on between them?"

Davy sounded surprised. "You mean are they a couple? I don't think so. She hasn't said anything to me."

"No?" Ginny wished she felt more reassured. "But would she tell you?"

"Look, I'm sure there's nothing going on. I slept on her bedroom floor last night. Rupert was with someone else."

"Oh. Right." This was more like it; this was far more encouraging. "Have you asked her?"

"I haven't dared, in case she says yes. Anyway, you must be right if Rupert hooked up with another girl." Ginny breathed a sigh of relief. "Well, I'd better let you get back to work. Tell Jem I'll give her a ring later. And good luck with Claudia Schiffer!"

They said their good-byes—*such* a nice boy—and Ginny tried next to ring Carla, to see if she wanted to meet up for a spot of lunch. But Carla's mobile was switched off, which probably meant she was working, following up on all the leads she'd so assiduously collected last night.

Oh, well, never mind. Maybe head into town and go shopping for a new dress instead.

Or sit listening to Laurel relate the latest installment in the ongoing Saga of Kevin.

Ginny reached for her bag. Definitely go shopping instead.

Chapter 23

Rupert had brought them to Pink, the latest trendy restaurant to open on Whiteladies Road, and the weather was warm and sunny enough to sit outside. There were ten of them altogether, and the champagne was flowing, easing the pain of last night's hangovers. Jem was feeling more relaxed now although she'd feel better still if Suze would give up, accept defeat, and go back to her sister's flat, leaving the rest of them to carry on without her. It was painfully obvious that she was crazy about Rupert, sitting next to him with a besotted smile on her face, clearly fancying her chances with him later if she just hung around long enough.

But it was just as apparent that Rupert wasn't remotely interested in her. The banter being batted back and forth across the table excluded Suze. Rupert and his smart friends down from London were on top form and Jem and Lucy were joining in, part of the team.

"Uh-oh, here comes the big boss." Rupert grinned as the manager threaded his way between tables toward them. "Maybe he's going to kick us out."

Jem hoped not. "Are we being too noisy?"

Rupert, his eyes glittering, said, "I can be loads noisier than this."

"Me too." Suze smirked and wriggled her chair closer to his. Jem rolled her eyes at Lucy. Inwardly, she felt like pushing Suze off her chair.

But the manager hadn't come over to ask them to leave. He

explained to Rupert that a photographer from a glossy lifestyle magazine was here to take pictures to accompany a feature on upmarket restaurants in the southwest.

"Your table epitomizes our target clientele," said the manager. "OK with you if we have some photos taken?"

"Oh wow!" Suze looked excited and began fluffing up her hair. "Cool!"

Which just went to show how completely uncool she was.

"Fine by me." Rupert shrugged, glancing around the table. "Everyone else all right with that?"

The photographer joined them and Suze trilled, "Wait until my friends hear about this. I've never been in a magazine before! Ooh, I'd better go and re-do my makeup!"

How completely pathetic. Jem couldn't bear the possessive way Suze was clutching at Rupert's arm, emphasizing their togetherness. Everybody was probably a little bit excited about being featured in a glossy magazine but only Suze was making a show of herself by admitting it.

"Actually, could we move things around a bit?" The photographer swung into action, studying angles and indicating that a couple of chairs should be moved out of shot. Addressing Rupert, he said, "You stay there, I want you in the center of the shot. Now, I need a girl either side of you…"

"I fit that job description." Simpering, Suze stayed put.

"You and you, could you two move closer together?" The photographer indicated Lucy and one of Rupert's raffishly handsome London friends, then looked from Jem to Suze. "And could you two girls swap places?"

Yes, yes, yes! Jem could have kissed him. The smile slid off Suze's face like an iced bun melting in the rain. And now the photographer was getting himself into position, concentrating his camera on Rupert's side of the table. As Jem slid into the seat sulkily vacated

by Suze, Rupert draped an arm casually over her shoulder and murmured in her ear, "Welcome to the world of the beautiful people."

"Could we just move the ashtrays out of shot?" The photographer made vigorous clearing gestures with his hands. "And cover up
that wine stain on the tablecloth?"

"Where's Davy when you need him?" Rupert mockingly clicked
his fingers. "Dammit, you can't get the staff these days. Still, just as
well he isn't here—who'd want to bother taking our photos when
they could take Davy's?"

"Don't be mean." Jem said it automatically.

"I'm not mean. I'm just being honest. The guy's a loser." Rupert
lifted a bottle from the ice bucket and refilled their glasses. "I mean,
be fair. Life is for living. Which would you rather do? Sit out here
in the sun, drinking champagne, eating amazing food, and having
your photo taken for a feature in a glossy magazine, or dress up in an
orange nylon jumpsuit that frankly doesn't suit you and scrub out
someone else's toilet?"

Lucy said easily, "You're such an obnoxious git, Rupert."

He winked at her. "I know, but I'm a bloody good-looking obnoxious git. And I know how to have fun."

The photographer was busily snapping away now. Everyone else
outside the restaurant was watching them. Feeling special and glamorous and reveling in the attention, Jem shook back her hair—snap
snap—and took a sip of ice-cold champagne.

There was no getting away from it, Rupert had a point.

Penhaligon's had been taken over for the evening by a work party
celebrating their boss's fortieth birthday. Before they arrived, Finn
and Ginny put the finishing touches to the dining room, as specified, including tying a bobbing silver helium balloon to the back of
each chair.

Ginny tied the last one and stepped back to survey the effect. "It looks like a children's party."

"This is what they wanted." Finn shrugged. "And they're paying for it. Apparently it's a work tradition—they all unfasten the ends of the balloons after the meal, suck in lungfuls of helium, and sing 'Happy Birthday' in Mickey Mouse voices."

"Some companies have strange traditions."

"And this is a firm of chartered accountants. There, all done." Finn straightened a couple of chairs. "Let's hope they charged the balloons to expenses."

From where she was standing, Ginny had a clear view of the courtyard. A small van had just rolled up and a man now emerged carrying a vast cellophane-wrapped bouquet.

"Did the accountants say they'd arranged for flowers to be delivered?"

"No." Finn looked out of the window. "Could be for you, from that chap of yours."

There was something ever so slightly offhand about the way he said it. Niggled, Ginny replied, "His name's Perry. And if he were sending me flowers he'd have them delivered to my house." She managed to make it sound as though Perry sent her flowers at least three times a week, if not on a daily basis. Ooh, though, what if these were from him and he just didn't want to risk Laurel reading the accompanying slushy card?

"Hello, love." The delivery man addressed Ginny cheerily when she pulled open the door. "Sorry, we've been rushed off our feet today, but better late than never, eh? Could you sign for these?"

She scribbled her signature and took the flowers, an excitingly exotic arrangement of striking blues and oranges. Then turned over the accompanying envelope and saw the name on the front. Bum.

"They're for you." Ginny held them out to Finn, who raised an eyebrow.

"Why, thank you so much, how kind of you and how unexpected. Is this to thank me for being such a great boss?"

"Absolutely. Best ever. And these cost me a fortune, so a pay rise wouldn't go amiss." Ginny watched him open the envelope, skim the card. "Who's it really from?"

"Catherine."

"Zeta Jones? Now I'm impressed."

Finn's mouth twitched.

"So? Catherine *who*?"

"Nosy."

"Not nosy. Interested," said Ginny. "You can't say her name then not tell me who she is."

"You saw her. She was at the Carson last night. I just gave her a lift home, that's all."

The curvy, sexy-looking brunette. Picturing her, Ginny said, "Dark hair, white dress?"

"That's the one."

"And now she's sent you flowers? Must have been a hell of a lift."

"We aim to please."

Ginny knew she was being juvenile—he was single and presumably Catherine was too—but the faintly derogatory way he had referred to Perry had brought out her competitive side. "I'd say you succeeded. Will you be seeing her again?"

"Might do, might not. I haven't really thought about it. Actually, probably not." Pulling a face, Finn said, "It feels a bit odd, being sent flowers by a woman. That's never happened to me before. You can have them if you like." He was holding out the bouquet, offering it to her. It must have cost at least fifty pounds.

"No thanks. I don't want your cast-off flowers. Poor Catherine," said Ginny. "She must really like you. You'll have to phone and thank her."

He gave her a look. "Nosy *and* bossy."

"I'm serious. Honestly, single men can be horrible sometimes."

"Not speaking from experience, I hope." Finn's tone was light but she was almost sure he was having another dig.

"Not personal experience, no. And I'm very happy with Perry. We had a great time last night."

"Glad to hear it. Good for you. Well, looks like our party's arriving." As Finn spoke, a convoy of taxis streamed into the yard. "I don't know which one's the birthday girl."

Out of the second cab jumped a lively-looking blond in a bright red dress, wearing big plastic Mickey Mouse ears and a battery-operated flashing necklace proclaiming 40 TODAY!

"Call it female intuition," said Ginny, "but possibly that one."

"And she's their chief accountant," Finn marveled.

Ginny tut-tutted. "Making snap judgments again. You think accountants don't know how to have fun. That's such a job-ist attitude."

"You're right. I'll make it up to her." Finn went to greet the party at the door, kissing the chief accountant on both cheeks before presenting her with the bouquet.

"Oh, that's so kind of you. Really, these are beautiful." Delightedly the blond buried her nose in the exotic blue and orange blooms and came back up dusted with pollen. "So thoughtful! And you'll never guess what; my sister rang this morning and told me she'd met you last night! You gave her a lift home from the Carson, isn't that a coincidence?" Beaming, she went on, "Catherine said you were one of the nicest men she'd ever met!"

Chapter 24

IT WAS TEN PAST eight on Saturday evening. Ginny was out at work. Carla was standing in her kitchen determinedly not looking at her switched-off phone.

If she owned a pair of handcuffs she'd chain herself to the stove and swallow the key.

Oh God, this was unbearable. She was wavering badly. Last night she'd barely slept at all, her mind frenziedly replaying every second of the brief and fateful encounter with Perry Kennedy. And every minute of today had been filled with more of the same, because she couldn't stop thinking about him. If there was a switch to turn off, she would.

But there wasn't.

Twelve minutes past eight. She was winning so far. Meeting Perry mustn't happen, it just *mustn't*. He wasn't single; he was taken. More to the point, taken by Ginny. And Ginny was besotted with him, which made him so completely off limits it just didn't bear thinking about.

Dry-mouthed, Carla looked again at her watch. Twelve and a half minutes past now. He was there, waiting for her. And she was here. Which was the *right* place to be. And OK, maybe it was killing her but she only had another fifteen or twenty minutes to endure because surely if she hadn't turned up to meet him by eight thirty he would realize she wasn't coming and would go out.

Thirty minutes passed.

Forty minutes, then fifty. She was still here; she hadn't gone to Perry's flat. So why wasn't she feeling more relaxed?

At nine fifteen the doorbell shrilled and every nerve in Carla's body went into overdrive. This was why she hadn't felt more relaxed.

She opened the front door an inch, keeping the chain on, and hissed, "Go away. I'm not going to do this."

"At least let me in." Perry was wearing a hat as an attempt at a disguise and spoke in an anguished whisper. "I can't believe you made me come here. Laurel's just across the road; she could look out of the window at any moment and see me."

Oh God, oh God. "I can't let you in. I just can't."

"Carla, I'm not leaving." He clearly meant business. "This is too important. We need to talk, you know we do."

Carla trembled; she knew it too. But not here in her house, across the road from Ginny's.

"I'll come to your flat. You leave now. I'll follow in ten minutes." Would she? Wouldn't she? She didn't even know herself.

"Promise," Perry whispered.

"I promise." Was that another lie? Maybe, maybe not.

"Ten minutes," said Perry. "I'll be waiting."

"OK. Bye." Carla closed the door and saw his shadow recede through the hall window as he slipped away down the path to wherever he'd left his car.

She mustn't go, *she mustn't*.

She parked her car haphazardly at nine forty, too agitated and filled with self-loathing to even check her reflection in the rearview mirror because that would mean having to look into her guilt-riddled eyes.

The car park was two hundred yards from his flat. Hurrying along the narrow, darkened street, Carla reminded herself that she knew barely anything about Perry Kennedy. When you met someone

for the first time, you could be wildly attracted by their outward appearance, but that didn't tell you what they were like beneath the surface—they could have any number of wildly unattractive character traits that you had yet to discover.

OK, here it was, Perry's shop with its window full of printed T-shirts, and next to it the door leading up to his flat. Just an ordinary dark blue door with the 25B picked out in brass lettering that could do with a polish. See? She really didn't know him at all. Maybe a quick glance around Perry's flat would be enough to magically decimate any feelings she might have had for him, in less time than it took to squash a cockroach. He might live in utter squalor, for instance. That would be enough to turn her stomach. Or cat food bowls left soaking in the sink along with the rest of the washing-up—perfect. Or he might harbor a secret passion for train-spotting complete with model railway occupying pride of place in his living room. Or he could have the walls plastered with posters of topless girls reclining on motorbikes. Or maybe he liked to save all his toenail clippings and keep them in a glass jar in the kitchen.

Or better still, *other people's* toenail clippings.

Sick with excitement and shame, lust and fear, and hoping against hope that there would be *something* up there to put her off him, Carla rang the bell and prepared herself for Perry to answer the door.

She took a deep breath and waited. And waited.

Rang the bell again.

Waited some more.

Nothing, oh God, he wasn't even here. Carla's heart began to clamor as panic rose; how could he not be here now?

Still no sign of life. She couldn't ring the bell again—he wasn't in the flat and that was that. Or he was there and was determined not to come to the door. Or he was there but he'd slipped in the shower, knocked himself unconscious, and was at this moment bleeding tragically to death on the bathroom floor…

OK, so he'd deliberately gone out.

Carla turned to leave. That was that then, over before it had begun. Well, she should be glad that at least one of them had come to their senses and—

"Carla."

She spun round, saw him standing there in the doorway and let out a strangled cry of relief. The next moment Perry, now minus his absurd hat, was wrapping her in his arms, frenziedly kissing her face and squeezing the air from her lungs.

"I thought you'd changed your mind," Carla babbled helplessly.

"Never."

"You didn't answer the door!"

"I was up there." He pointed to the curtained first-floor window. "I wanted to see how long you'd keep trying."

"*Sadist.*"

"I needed to know if this means as much to you as it means to me." He paused, gazing deep into her eyes. "Does it?"

"You bastard, you know it does. Otherwise I wouldn't be here, would I? Ginny's my best friend, I *hate myself…*"

"Shhh, come on, let's get you inside." He bundled her through the doorway and led her upstairs, and Carla knew that nothing about his flat, not even toenail clippings in the kitchen sink, could put her off him now.

But it was still a relief to see that there weren't any. Perry, watching her swiftly explore his domain, said, "What are you doing?"

"Checking you out. Don't interrupt. This wallpaper is hideous, by the way."

"I know. I don't care. It's only a rented flat."

"Your pillowcases don't match the duvet cover."

"I'm anti-coordination."

Carla swept past him out of the only bedroom and into the living room. "How charming, a surfboard propped against the wall."

"Glad you like it."

"And a banana skin in the wastepaper basket. Banana skins should go straight into the *kitchen* bin," said Carla. "I *hate* the smell of bananas."

"Ginny did mention you were freakishly tidy."

"I am." She was investigating the bathroom now. "And proud of it. The blade in your razor is blunt, by the way."

"When it's time to slash my wrists I'll buy a new one. Shampoo meet with your approval?"

"It's all right I suppose." Carla smelled the contents of the shampoo bottle. "I'm not wild about hair smelling of coconut."

"Fine. I'll shave it all off."

"And blue loo roll is just tacky."

Perry had his hands on his hips, his head tilted to one side. "You're criticizing everything."

"This lot needs to be criticized."

"Why are you doing this?"

"You kept me waiting," said Carla, "standing outside like an idiot." She gestured briskly. "Well, this is me, getting my own back."

Perry half smiled. "That's the other thing Ginny told me about you. She said you gave your men a hard time."

"Could we please not talk about Ginny? I feel bad enough as it is."

"OK. In fact I've got a better idea. Why don't we not talk at all?"

Adrenaline whooshed through Carla's body as she moved toward him. In her whole life she'd never felt like this before. And she was here now; they'd kept each other waiting long enough.

Clasping Perry's face between her hands and gazing hungrily at his thin, beautifully carved mouth, she said, "Fine by me."

Their lovemaking was frantic, frenzied, and heightened by guilt. Carla had never known sex like it—and in her time she'd known a lot of sex. But now, instead of a purely physical connection, her

emotions were involved too. For the first time, Carla belatedly realized. The connection between Perry and herself was *there*, inescapable and so overwhelming she wanted to cry.

This was what she'd been waiting for all her life and she hadn't even known it.

It didn't matter that the pillowcases didn't match the duvet. Where were the pillows anyway? Carla leaned up on one elbow and peered over the side of the bed. There they were, scattered on the floor along with the clothes she and Perry had torn off each other. Her dress was linen and would look like a dishrag unless it was hung up.

Who cared?

She closed her eyes. They had more important things to worry about than a crumpled dress.

"What are we going to do?"

"Hmm?" Perry was kissing her shoulder, snaking his hand along her thigh. "I'll give you a clue… I may need a few minutes before we try it again."

"I mean about Ginny."

The hand stopped snaking. "I don't know."

"We have to tell her."

"We can't."

"We can. We have to. I'm an honest person," said Carla. "I don't lie to my friends."

"Did you tell her you were meeting me this evening?"

"No, because I haven't spoken to her all day. I've deliberately kept my phone switched off. But I won't deceive her. If you want to be with me, you have to tell Ginny it's over."

"Oh God." Perry rubbed his face in despair. "I *do* want to be with you. But… I just…"

More buts. Why was he hesitating? "OK," said Carla, "which of us do you prefer?"

"You!"

"Because we're alike. You know it and I know it. I don't even really *know* you." Her eyes filled with unexpected tears. "But I know we have to be together and I can't even believe I'm saying these things. Nothing like this has ever happened to me before, but it's happening now."

Perry nodded, clearly torn. "You're right. It is. Bloody hell, this is difficult." He turned his head to look at her. "Ginny's going to hate you."

"I know, and I hate myself. She'll be distraught," Carla said miserably. "And it's a double betrayal. Like being kicked in the teeth twice."

"Does she really like me?"

"*Yes.*"

"How much?"

Carla rolled her eyes. "A *lot*. Plus, she thinks you like her too."

"I do," said Perry. "She's beautiful and funny and great company. I *do* like her. Just… not in *that* way."

"Why not?"

"God, I don't know, do I? You can't help how you feel about people. Ginny's a lovely person. Maybe she's too nice for me. She's nicer than you," he added with a brief smile. "But that's irrelevant. You're my type; you're the one I want. And she's not."

They were going around in circles. Carla completely agreed with him that Ginny was a far nicer person than she was. She, Carla, was the focused successful saleswoman with the laser-sharp brain and body to match. Her wardrobe was super-chic, her life was just as she wanted it to be, and there was no aspect of it that she didn't like. Ginny, contrastingly, was warm and impulsive, disorganized and accident-prone. Clothes-wise, she was less than cutting edge. She was, as Perry had pointed out, beautiful and funny in a dizzy-blond kind of way, but she was also overwhelmingly maternal, cuddly, and

nurturing, and with a capacity for forgiveness that Carla knew she could never hope to achieve.

Although she suspected even Ginny might find this a betrayal too far.

"We have to tell her," Carla repeated.

"We can't."

"But you said it yourself; Ginny's not your type! I don't know why you even *started*—"

"Look," Perry interrupted, "there's Laurel to consider. I'm not proud of this, but I was pretty desperate. I charmed Ginny into taking my sister off my hands and the only way I could persuade her to let Laurel stay was by... well, I suppose you could call it emotional blackmail. But it worked. If I finish with Ginny, she'll chuck Laurel out; it's as simple as that."

Carla recognized in a flash how alike she and Perry were; he had behaved ruthlessly toward Ginny and now she was equally prepared to be ruthless where Laurel was concerned.

"So? She's not five years old anymore. She's a *grown-up*."

Perry heaved a sigh. "She's fragile. I know she's my big sister but she's always been the one who needs looking after. And since Kevin bailed out, she's been worse. She's depressed and clingy, and I know I shouldn't have to feel responsible for her, but I can't help myself. Going to live with Ginny was perfect, but if Ginny won't keep her anymore... well, I don't know what I'll do. Laurel will want to move back in here with me. God knows, it's not what I want to happen, but she'll beg and plead and I'll end up not being able to say no." He turned his head and said bluntly, "Because she doesn't have anyone else or anywhere else to go."

Oh God, this was turning into a nightmare. Carla couldn't bear to think about the trouble this thing with Perry was going to cause. Life would have been so much simpler if they'd never met.

But they had, and now she wanted to make love to him again

because one thing was for sure. Perry Kennedy had tipped her calm, ordered, super-efficient world off its axis and whatever else happened she knew she couldn't give him up.

Chapter 25

"I'm going to be in big trouble," said Finn as he poured red wine into three glasses. "And it's all your fault."

It was midnight and the noisy, happy accountants had finally hokey-pokeyed their way into the string of waiting taxis. Ginny, Evie, and Finn were gathered around one of the tables having a drink to celebrate the end of a successful evening.

"You can't blame me," Ginny protested.

"I can. You should have graciously accepted the flowers when I offered them to you."

"You shouldn't have offered them in the first place! Damn cheek! If you took someone out to dinner, you wouldn't like it if they walked out of the restaurant and handed their plate of food over to some stranger in the street."

"That's completely different. Catherine didn't ask me if I'd like her to send me flowers." Finn paused. "Maybe she won't find out what happened to them."

Ginny and Evie caught each other's eye, because only a man could think that.

"Oh, she will," said Ginny.

"And Catherine's feelings will be very hurt," Evie added helpfully. "She'll be furious. In fact, from now on you might want to check under your car for incendiary devices before you start the engine."

Finn took a slug of wine. "You're a big help."

"I could have been a big help." Evie's eyes danced. "You see,

I'm not as choosy as some people. I'll accept cast-off flowers from anyone. If you'd offered them to me I'd have taken them, then you wouldn't have been able to give them to Alex's sister."

"Alex?" Finn frowned. "Who's *Alex?*"

"Oh sorry, silly me, that's the name of the woman in *Fatal Attraction*. Glenn Close played her, remember? Got rejected by Michael Douglas and turned into a deranged stalker. Fancy me using that name," Evie said cheerfully. "Slip of the tongue! I meant Catherine."

"Thanks," Finn said drily. "And if you'd been around when the flowers arrived, I would have offered them to you. But you weren't here, were you? You were late."

Evie was unrepentant. "Ah, but for a very good reason. My darling daughter rang me as I was about to leave the house. She's just moved into a new flat in Salisbury and they're throwing a house-warming party tomorrow. So I'm going to be driving up there tomorrow morning!"

Ginny tried to suppress a stab of envy. Lucky Evie, off to see her daughter Philippa. She'd give anything for Jem to ring her up and say, "Hey, Mum, we're having a party, you'll come along, won't you?"

God, she'd be there in a flash, like Superman fired out of a cannon. *And* she'd provide gorgeous food and do all the washing-up afterward.

But there didn't appear to be any danger of that happening. The happy weekends she'd envisaged Jem and herself sharing in Bristol hadn't materialized and the ones here in Portsilver were woefully few and far between.

Lucky, *lucky* Evie.

"What's the flat like?" said Finn.

"Second floor, renovated Edwardian, two bedrooms. I can't wait to see it for myself. Ooh, you don't have a road atlas, do you?" Evie touched his arm. "My neighbor borrowed mine and lost it."

"There's one lying around somewhere. No idea where." Finn

frowned. "Salisbury, would that be the A36? I can look it up on the internet if you like."

"I know where it is." Ginny jumped up.

"What, Salisbury?"

"Your road atlas. I saw it the other day."

The atlas was in the second drawer down behind the bar, almost hidden beneath a pile of telephone directories. Feeling smug and efficient, Ginny produced it with a flourish, curtsied modestly, and said, "Thank you, thank you, it was nothing."

"I love it when people do that." Evie clapped her hands delightedly. "I'll have to bring you back to my house to find all my long-lost bits and pieces. There's a blue sandal somewhere that's been missing for years."

"What's that?" said Finn as something slipped out from between the pages and landed face down on the floor. Ginny bent to retrieve it.

"A photograph?" Evie guessed, because it was the right shape and size.

It was a photograph. Ginny only looked at it for a split second but the image remained imprinted on her mind. She glanced over at Finn and handed it to him without a word. Evie, her eyes widening with glee, exclaimed, "Finn, is it rude? Don't tell me it's a photo of you with some scantily clad girl!"

Ginny bit her lip and turned away, because in a manner of speaking it was. In the photograph Finn was sitting on a stone wall wearing jeans and a white T-shirt. It was a sunny, breezy day and the wind had blown a lock of dark hair across his forehead. In his arms he was holding a baby with equally dark hair and eyes. The baby, clad only in a tiny pink and white sundress, was beaming at Finn. And Finn was smiling back at her with a look of such love, joy, and utter devotion on his face that anyone who saw the photograph would get a lump in their throat even if they didn't know the full story behind it.

"What *is* it? Show me," Evie demanded, reaching for the photo in Finn's hand. Then she saw it and her expression abruptly changed. "Oh."

An awkward silence ensued before Finn took the photograph back from Evie and put it down on the table. Turning to Ginny, he said, "You must be wondering what this is about. The baby is the daughter of an ex-girlfriend of mine. Well, ex-fiancée."

Ginny wavered for a split second, then realized she couldn't tell him she already knew about Tamsin and Mae. Evie wasn't saying anything either; she had related the story in confidence and the chances were that Finn wouldn't take kindly to discovering he'd been gossiped about behind his back.

"Right." She braced herself; this was the kind of lying she found hardest to pull off. Assuming her I-know-nothing expression—a tricky balance between neither too wide-eyed nor too village-idiot—Ginny nodded and said innocently, "So you were… um, engaged."

Oh brilliant. *Mastermind* next. Then maybe a degree in astrophysics.

"I was." Finn paused. "I also thought Mae was my daughter. But it turned out she wasn't after all."

"Oh! How awful." Ginny put her hand to her mouth and shook her head in dismay. Act natural, *act natural*. "That must have been… so, um…"

He nodded. "It was. Tamsin got back together with Mae's father. They're living in London now. He's a very wealthy man."

"Is… is he?"

"But then you already knew that."

Whoosh went Ginny's face, faster than a Formula One car. Struggling to look as if she didn't have a clue what he was talking about, she raised her eyebrows and said, "H-how would I know that?"

"Let me hazard a guess." Finn glanced pointedly at Evie. "Someone told you. Because I have to say, you're the world's most hopeless liar."

"Yes, it was me." Evie came clean.

"Thanks a lot," said Finn.

"She wasn't gossiping about you," Ginny put in hastily. "She was just *explaining*. After that time I put my foot in it and said something awful about it being obvious you weren't a father. I felt terrible about that."

"OK." Picking up the photo once more, Finn said, "So what do I do with this now? Throw it away, I suppose."

"You can't." Ginny snatched it away before he could crumple it in his fist. "Not to a photograph like that."

A flicker of something crossed his face. "But it's based on a lie."

"You're still not throwing it away." To lighten the mood, she said, "For one thing, it makes you look human."

Finn said drily, "Thank you again."

"But it's true. Promise me you won't," said Ginny.

He rolled his eyes but put the photograph in his shirt pocket.

"Right, I'm off." Evie drained her glass and scooped up the road atlas. "Can I take this and bring it back on Monday?"

Ginny said enviously, "Have fun tomorrow."

"Oh, I will. I can't wait to see my baby again!" Too late, Evie realized what she'd said. "Finn, me and my big mouth. I meant Philippa. I know she's grown up but she's still my baby to me."

In a flurry of good-byes, Evie left and Ginny finished her drink too before collecting her things together.

When Finn showed her to the door, Ginny said, "I really am sorry about tonight."

"Not your fault." The corners of his mouth twitched. "For once."

"And I'm sorry about what happened with Tamsin and Mae. I can't imagine how that must have felt. You must have gone through hell."

For a moment, Finn didn't reply. Then he nodded, his face turned away in enigmatic profile. "I'd say that pretty much covers

it. Mae was the center of my world, the most important thing that had ever happened to me. One minute she was there and I would have died for her, literally. Then the next minute she's gone, and it turns out I was never even her father in the first place. She's alive but I don't suppose I'll ever see her again. And there's no reason why I should want to, but she's still the same child." He paused again. "Just not *my* child anymore."

It was the most unbearably sad story. The lump was back in Ginny's throat. If Finn had been anyone else she would have thrown her arms around him. Instead, clutching her car keys and handbag, she said awkwardly, "You'll meet someone else. The right person. And then you'll have a proper family of your own."

"I thought I had a proper family last time. And look how well that turned out." His dark eyes held hers for a second before he turned back to concentrate on the door handle. His tone dismissive, indicating that this conversation was now well and truly over, Finn said, "I'm not sure I'd want to try again."

———

Rolling over in bed, Carla reached for her mobile and peered at the screen. If it was Ginny, she definitely wasn't answering it.

"Make it stop," Perry groaned, burrowing under the pillows.

It was a number she didn't recognize, possibly a new client. Dredging up her efficient voice, Carla said, "Hello, Carla James."

"Woo, you make me want to buy a *huge* conservatory. Hi, Carla, it's Jem!"

Jem. For God's sake, it was months since she'd last heard from Jem. Instinctively turning onto her side, away from Perry, Carla said, "Well, this is a surprise. Everything OK, sweetie?"

"Everything's fine. I'm just bursting with curiosity about this new chap of Mum's and she's not giving me nearly enough information. I know he's nice and she really likes him but that's all I'm

getting. She just keeps saying it's early days," Jem complained good-naturedly. "But I can't help it; I want to hear more than that. And I know you met him on Friday night so I thought, ha, I'll ring Carla and find out what he's really like."

Carla's heart plummeted. It was Sunday morning and she was here in Perry's bed. How could she have sunk so low? What would Jem say if she told her the truth? How would Ginny, her best friend, react when she found out that—

"*Get off*," Carla hissed over her shoulder, covering the receiver and wriggling out of reach as Perry's hand trailed down her spine. Hot with shame, she said, "Jem, I only met him for a couple of minutes; I can't really tell you much. Like your mum says, it's not been going on long enough to get serious. I think they're just seeing each other every now and again."

"*Noooo*." Jem let out a wail of disappointment. "Not fair! You know what Mum's like, it's years since she's been keen on anyone," she protested, "so of course I'm interested. This could be my new stepdad, for heaven's sake. And now you're clamming up on me too! At least tell me if he's good-looking."

Perry overheard this. He tapped Carla on the shoulder and nodded.

"He's all right, I suppose." Carla winced as the taps turned into jabs. "OK, he's quite good-looking. For a redhead."

"And does he seem like a nice person?"

"I couldn't really tell. Nice enough."

"Hopeless," Jem scolded. "OK, if you met him at a party, would you fancy him?"

This was agonizing.

"I prefer my men younger." Carla slithered out of reach again as Perry, outraged, seized her arm in a pincer-like grip.

"Well, we all know that. You're not fooling me, by the way."

"What?"

"Not for a second," said Jem.

Carla almost stopped breathing. "Meaning?"

"I'm not completely stupid."

"Aren't you?"

"And I'm not five years old either. I know what's going on." She couldn't know. She just couldn't.

"What's going on?" Carla was dimly aware that she sounded like a parrot.

"You're pretending you're on your own." Jem's voice was playful. "But you aren't. You've got someone there with you."

Oh. "How could you tell?"

"You mean apart from me hearing you cover the receiver and tell him to get off?"

"Bit of a giveaway, I suppose," Carla admitted.

"And I bet there's something else I know about him too."

Carla's sigh of relief abruptly went into reverse. Sucking in air, she braced herself. "And what would that be?"

With an air of triumph, Jem said, "I bet he's a good ten years younger than mystery man Perry."

Chapter 26

Last week, Ginny had been envious of Evie. Now she no longer needed to be because it was—*tra-laaa!*—her turn. Jem was coming home at last for Easter week.

"I swapped my shifts at the pub," she told Ginny. "Rupert's off to the south of France and Lucy's going back to Birmingham so I thought why stay here on my own when I can come and see you?"

So Rupert would be abroad; was that what had prompted Jem's visit? If so, hooray for Rupert. Joyfully, Ginny said, "That's *such* good news. I can't wait to see you again. And you'll be able to meet Laurel at last."

"Not to mention Perry." Jem sounded mischievous. "I definitely want to meet him."

Hmm, if he was able to spare the time. It had occurred to Ginny lately that Perry might not be quite as besotted with her as he claimed to be; being busy at work was one thing, but she was beginning to suspect that something else might be up.

Still, asking him if he'd like to meet Jem might give her a chance to find out what that something might be. "Yes, but you'll have to be discreet. Remember what I told you about Laurel."

"I remember. Although I think it's pretty ridiculous, the two of you having to skulk around keeping it a secret."

Ginny thought it was pretty ridiculous too, but at the same time she could see that Perry had a point. Not that they'd been

doing much skulking around recently—he claimed to be so rushed off his feet at the moment they hadn't managed to meet up all week.

"I know, darling, but she's his sister and he's trying to spare her feelings. She's just been a bit depressed, that's all."

"Well, tell her I'm great at cheering people up. I'll be down on Friday evening. Mum, you know how much I love you…?"

"Shameless child." Ginny grinned, because this was a familiar grovel. "Of course I'll pick you up from the station."

"Yay. So you're free on Friday evening?"

"Absolutely."

"In that case," said Jem, "why don't we have dinner at Penhaligon's to celebrate me being back? My treat!"

"Jem, you can't afford it."

"Can't I? OK then, your treat! How about a table for three?"

"You, me, and Dad? That's a nice idea." Ginny made a mental note to ring Gavin; she wasn't sure if he was still seeing Cleo but he could surely bear to give her a miss for one—

"Actually, I've already rung Dad—we're meeting up on the Saturday. I was thinking more you, me, and Perry." Sounding pleased with herself Jem said gaily, "Clever eh? This way I'll get to meet all your lovely new friends in one go!"

<hr/>

Just the sight of the peeling blue front door had a magical effect on Carla, drawing her toward it like a drug she was unable to resist. She'd been coming here for twelve days now and the magic was more powerful than ever. She rang the bell and Perry answered it. From then on they were cocooned in their own little world with trespassers prohibited and it was a feeling like no other she had ever known before. Total love. Total security. Total happiness.

Until Ginny found out.

Carla hated what she was doing but she couldn't stop doing it. Raising her hand to the bell she rang it quickly, twice. Waited breathlessly for the sound of Perry running down the stairs. Felt her heart quicken as the door began to open.

He grinned at her, ushered her speedily inside. "Hello, you."

Here came the feeling again. Sheer bliss. How could anyone give up something so utterly perfect?

After they'd made love Carla sprang her surprise.

"Tomorrow night we'll be doing this in a four-poster bed."

"What?"

"I've booked us into Curnow Castle. Their best suite." At an eye-watering three hundred pounds a night, it had better be their best suite. Not that she regretted a penny of it—she'd wanted to make a splashy extravagant gesture, to celebrate how she felt about Perry. Stroking a damp tendril of red hair away from his forehead, Carla said, "You'll love it."

"I won't, because I can't go. You'll have to cancel."

"Why?"

He shrugged. "I'm seeing Ginny tomorrow night."

"What?" Carla sat upright in bed, ice forming in the pit of her stomach. "But *I* want to see you. Tell Ginny something's come up!"

Perry grinned at the choice of phrase, then regretfully shook his head.

"And I want to see you—of *course* I'd rather see you—but I can't. She wants me to meet her daughter."

"*Jem?*"

He clicked his fingers with relief. "That's the name. Jem. I keep thinking it's Jenny."

Carla listened with growing dismay as Perry patiently explained that Ginny had called him last night and invited him to join them at Penhaligon's. He had gently attempted to turn her down but Ginny had practically begged. Evidently Jem was keen to meet him and…

well, it had been an awkward situation. In the end he hadn't had the heart to say no.

"It means a lot to her," Perry concluded reasonably. "I couldn't let her down."

"Because of Laurel." Carla saw beyond the altruism in an instant. "Because you need to keep the charade going. To keep Ginny happy."

He spread his hands. "Exactly. Not because I want to see her."

"This is all wrong." Vehemently Carla shook her head. "Laurel's ruling your life, keeping *us* from being together."

"Hey, hey," Perry protested, "we *are* together."

"Are we? Hiding here in your flat like fugitives when we haven't even done anything wrong? I want us to be a proper couple!" Carla gazed at him in desperation. "I love you. We can't carry on like this. It's not fair on any of us. And you're making a fool of Ginny. She's my *friend*," her voice rose, "and she doesn't *deserve* this."

"I know. But we don't have any choice, not now at least. When the time's right I'll sort it all out." Perry's tone was soothing, willing her to trust him. "But not yet."

⁓

"Sure she's not too heavy?" said Finn.

"Not too heavy." As Ginny had been leaving the restaurant after a busy Friday lunchtime shift, Finn had pulled into the courtyard in the van. Back from a country house auction on Bodmin Moor, he'd proudly shown off the Victorian marble statue he had acquired. Since Tom, his assistant in the shop, was currently busy with a customer, Ginny had offered to help him lift it out of the van and into the shop.

Actually, marble was heavier than it looked. But today was Friday and Jem was coming home. Ginny was on such a high she was pretty sure she could lift the statue and the van single-handed, if required.

Luckily it wasn't.

"Got her?" Finn double-checked.

"Stop fussing. I'm stronger than I look." Shaking her hair out of her eyes, she grinned at him and wrapped her arms securely around the ankles of the female statue. Finn, at the other end, had his arms round the woman's bare chest. Together they moved backward across the gravel, negotiated the doorway, maneuvered the statue into an upright position… and breathed out.

"Well done." Finn gazed at Ginny appraisingly. "I thought you were going to drop her. You *are* stronger than you look."

"Just give me a telephone directory," Ginny said modestly, "and watch me rip it in half." She ran her hand over the cool, silky-smooth marble of the statue's shoulder, thinking idly how nice it would look in her garden. "How much are you going to be selling her for?"

"Three grand."

Yikes, maybe not then. Perhaps the home store did a cheaper version in fiberglass.

"Good job you didn't tell me that before. I'd definitely have dropped her."

"She's one expensive lady." Finn gave the statue's bottom an appreciative pat. "And older than she looks."

Ginny couldn't help wondering how it felt, having your bottom patted by Finn. Hastily she dismissed the thought, pulled herself together. "No cellulite though. She's taken good care of herself. Or else gone under the knife, had a bit of a nip and tuck. You could call her Cher." As Ginny said it, her phone began to ring and Carla's name flashed up on the screen. "Speaking of women without cellulite… hello, you! Where have you *been*?"

"Just… busy." Carla sounded more subdued than usual. "Hi. Listen, I'm at home and I'd really like to see you. What are you doing?"

"Just finished work." Intrigued, Ginny said, "You sound mysterious. What's this about?"

"Can you come over now?"

"I've got some stuff to pick up in town first, but I can be there in about an hour. Jem's coming home!"

There was a momentary pause before Carla said, "Is she?"

"I'm picking her up from the station at six thirty. I'm so excited I can't wait. And guess what? We're having dinner with Perry, the three of us together!"

"Great." Carla appeared to have other things on her mind. "Um, so you'll be here in an hour?"

Ginny checked her watch. "By four o'clock, I promise. I wish you'd tell me what this is about."

"When I see you."

She definitely wasn't sounding like herself. Catching Finn's eye, Ginny said, "Carla, have you done something naughty?"

Another pause.

"Yes."

"Tell me!"

"I can't," said Carla.

Ginny put the phone back in her pocket. "Carla's being mysterious."

"You'd better get off then. We'll see you tonight."

"Eight o'clock." Ginny beamed. "I can't wait for you to meet Jem."

"And she'll be meeting Perry as well. What if she doesn't like him?"

Was that a dig? Honestly, just because Perry had made one innocent, off-the-cuff remark about children and fatherhood. Couldn't he just be happy for her?

"She'll love him," Ginny said firmly.

Finn shrugged. "She might not."

"Two things. One, I know my daughter. And two"—her eyes danced because today of all days nothing was going to dampen her mood—"don't be such a pessimist."

Chapter 27

"RIGHT, I'M HERE. TELL me what's going on." The moment Carla opened the front door, Ginny threw her arms round her. It wasn't until she'd been driving back from the shops that it had occurred to her that Carla might be ill. She had asked jokily if she'd done something naughty and Carla had soberly agreed that she had. But what if she was referring to the fact that last year a letter had arrived in the post reminding her that her next cervical smear test was due, and work had been so hectic that she hadn't got around to making the appointment?

The moment this possibility had lodged itself in Ginny's brain she hadn't been able to think of anything else. And now Carla wasn't hugging her back, she was standing woodenly with—Ginny now saw—tears swimming in her eyes.

"Oh my God." Ginny gazed at her in horror, a sensation like wet cement settling in the pit of her stomach. Barely able to speak, she clutched Carla's hands tightly and felt her throat tighten with fear. "Is it… is it cancer?"

Carla abruptly turned away, heading for the kitchen.

"It's not cancer."

Oh.

"Well, *that's* a relief." Following her, Ginny exhaled noisily and patted her heaving chest. Then, to be on the ultra-safe side, she said, "So it's not any kind of illness?"

"No."

Now she was truly relieved. "Because you can't imagine what's been going through my mind."

"Ginny, I'm not sick." Carla turned to face her, and there was that weird edge to her voice again.

"Has someone died?"

Carla's perfectly symmetrical bob swung from side to side as she shook her head, but her lips stayed pressed together.

"Then you have to help me out here," said Ginny, "because I just don't know what this is about. I have no idea."

"I know you don't," said Carla.

"What's *that* supposed to mean? Why are you saying it like that?"

"Ginny, you mean the world to me. You're my best friend and I never wanted to hurt you." Carla gripped the edge of the granite worktop behind her as the words came out in a rush. "Believe me, I *never* wanted to have to do this. But it's Perry. He's seeing someone else."

The kitchen was silent; it felt as if all the oxygen had been sucked out of the air. Carla couldn't bring herself to say the rest of it just yet. One bombshell at a time. Her fingernails ached from gripping the worktop. This was hell, but it had to be done. Ginny was gazing at her, clearly lost for words and as shell-shocked as she had every right to be. God knows, she—oh, that *bloody* phone.

But when Carla looked at the bloody phone and saw who was calling, she knew she had to answer it.

"Hi, it's me. Listen, I'll be back by midnight at the latest," said Perry. "Wait for me at the flat."

"Actually, I'm at home. Ginny's here."

"Really?" He sounded impressed. "I thought you'd been keeping out of her way."

"Not anymore." Carla paused, heard her own voice echoing weirdly in her ears. "I've just told her."

"*What?* You're not serious! About *us*?"

"Yes." Well, near as dammit. She was about to.

"Jesus Christ, what have you done?" shouted Perry. "I told you not to say anything!"

And where would that have got them? It was a job that needed to be done. Evenly, Carla said, "Well, I have."

She switched off the phone. Ginny was staring at her, her eyes huge.

"Who was that?"

"I'm sorry."

"Was it Perry? What's going on? OK, so you saw him with someone." Ginny shook her head in bewilderment. "But maybe you got it wrong, made a mistake."

"I'm not wrong."

"So he admitted it? You know he's definitely seeing someone else? What a *bastard*." Her hands trembling, Ginny reached for a glass and ran cold water into it from the tap. "When did you find out? Where did you see them? Damn, I really liked him too." The glass clunked audibly against her teeth as she gulped down half the water in one go. "Why can't anything ever go right for me? Do you know, I really thought we had something. And it turns out he's just another filthy rotten cheat after all. Oh no, poor *you*."

"What? Why?" It was Carla's turn to be confused.

"Having to be the one to tell me. I bet you've been dreading it." Ginny's lopsided smile failed to conceal her disappointment. "It's always horrible being the bearer of bad news. But I'm glad you told me, really I am. Don't worry, I won't shoot the messenger!"

Carla couldn't speak. The last few precious seconds of their friendship were ticking away. There was an unexploded bomb right here in the kitchen and any moment now she was going to press the detonator.

"So did you actually see her?" Needing information, Ginny said, "I suppose she's younger than me. What does she look like?" Only

a couple of seconds left now. Carla's mouth was so dry she could hardly speak. "She looks… well, she looks like me."

"Complete opposite of me then. I might have guessed." Surveying her reflection in the window and running her fingers disparagingly through her tousled Goldie Hawn hair, Ginny said, "Nature's way of telling you it's time you went to the hairdresser." Then she patted her gently rounded stomach. "And possibly had a go at a few sit-ups."

"There's nothing wrong with you." Carla couldn't bear to see her running herself down. Fiercely, she said, "You're warm, funny, *beautiful*—"

"But not good enough for Perry, because he prefers someone who looks like *you*."

Carla's finger had been hovering over the detonator button for what felt like hours. She didn't have to do this; she could carry on seeing Perry in secret.

No, she couldn't. That would be deceitful.

She could stop seeing Perry. *No, she couldn't.* That would be impossible.

She could… she could…

No, she couldn't.

Carla pressed the detonator. "It's me."

"What's you?"

"Perry prefers me. I'm the one he's been seeing. And I'm so *sorry*," Carla blurted out. "I hate myself; I can't believe this has happened. But it has. And you're my best friend," she pleaded. "I wouldn't hurt you for the world, but I've never felt like this about anyone before… I met Perry and it was just… well, like an earthquake or something. If I could have stopped it, I would. But I just *couldn't*…" She ground to a halt, nauseous and mortified, her fists clenched in anguish. Forcing herself to meet Ginny's gaze, she whispered helplessly, "And I'm so, so sorry."

Ginny felt as if she was watching a film, one with a twist she hadn't been expecting, the kind that takes your breath away and leaves you wondering what on earth will happen next. Carla's face was chalk-white, taut with strain. She had said what she'd clearly planned to say. She was like a stranger or a character in *Doctor Who* peeling off her face to reveal the robot beneath. Because one thing was for sure, this was no longer the Carla she'd known and loved and trusted for the last fifteen years.

"You wouldn't hurt me for the world?" Ginny was privately amazed she could still speak. "I'm your best *friend*?" Her voice rose. "Well, that's fascinating. If this is how you treat your best friend, I'd hate to see what you do to your enemies."

Carla flinched. "I'm sorry."

"Will you stop saying you're sorry? It doesn't mean anything! If you were really sorry, you'd never have started seeing Perry behind my back, would you? You would have said thanks but no thanks, like any normal friend, and walked away. It's called loyalty." Ginny shook her head in disgust.

"I know and I *wanted* to do that. Believe me, I did. But I couldn't. I love him," pleaded Carla. "And he loves me. Sometimes these things just happen." As she said it, they both heard the sound of a sports car screeching to a halt outside. A door slammed and footsteps raced up the path. The doorbell rang.

"Prince Charming, I presume. Riding to the rescue. How sweet." Ginny's heart was hammering against her rib cage. "How masterful. I suppose you've been sleeping with him."

"Of course I've been sleeping with him." Carla went to get the door. "It's what normal couples do."

The knife twisted in her stomach. With a jolt of pain, Ginny realized she was right. All that so-called gentlemanly stuff about wanting to take things slowly and get to know her properly first hadn't been romantic after all. It had just been… bullshit.

And here he was, the bullshitter himself, bursting into the immaculate kitchen with a wild look in his eyes and his hair uncombed.

Suddenly he wasn't looking quite so irresistible anymore.

Which, under the circumstances, was handy.

"I'm sorry. Ginny, I'm so sorry."

Oh, for crying out loud, not that again.

"You're a wonderful person," Perry went on, "and I wouldn't hurt you for the world…"

And that.

"This is getting repetitive," said Ginny.

"But I wouldn't, I swear to God. I never expected anything like this to happen. Neither of us did. But… it has." Perry's hands fell to his sides, signaling defeat. "It was a… a *coup de foudre*."

"Right." Ginny fantasized about seizing the heavy glass fruit bowl and hurling it at his head.

"It means love at first sight," Perry added.

Patronizing bastard. He thought she was gullible *and* dim.

"Actually, it doesn't," said Ginny. "It means struck by lightning." Struck by lightning, struck by a heavy glass fruit bowl, she didn't mind which.

"Anyway. We love each other. You weren't supposed to find out like this but—"

"From the look of things you didn't want me to find out at all." Leaving Carla out of it for now, Ginny concentrated all her attention on Perry. "How long has it been going on?"

"Since that night at the Carson Hotel. We couldn't help ourselves. Took one look at each other and that was it. We just knew."

"How lovely. Very romantic. So did you shag her in the toilets or in the bushes outside?"

"I didn't." Perry frowned, offended. "I was with you."

"OK, the next night then. Carla isn't the type to hang about." From the expressions on their faces she'd guessed right. For good

measure, Ginny said, "Although you're a damn sight older than the ones she usually goes for."

"I'm sorry," Perry said *again*. "And I know this has come as a shock to you, but I hope we can still be friends."

It was the pleading, let's-be-reasonable tone of voice he used that confirmed what Ginny had already suspected. Perry Kennedy had fooled her from the word go, manufacturing a relationship purely in order to offload his sister into her care. As if Laurel were a bin bag of old clothes and Ginny was his local branch of Oxfam.

And now, from the look of him, he was terrified she was going to give the bin bag back.

Interestingly, Ginny found she was able to separate out her emotions, like sorting knives, forks, and spoons into a cutlery drawer.

Humiliation because she'd thought he liked her and he didn't.

Anger because Jem was on her way home and today was supposed to be such a *happy* day.

Humiliation again because the three of them were booked into Penhaligon's and she had boasted so freely to Finn that Jem would love Perry to bits.

Anger because Perry had regarded her as a pushover. And yet more humiliation because Finn would be hard pushed to hide his amusement when he heard what had happened.

So that was the spoons and forks accounted for. But what of the knives? Her stomach churning, Ginny realized that they were what Carla had been using to stab her in the back. Because anger didn't begin to describe how she felt about Carla, her supposed friend. Seething boiling fury was closer to the mark. And this was what hurt more than anything, because being betrayed by your best friend was a million times worse than being betrayed by a man.

With men, sooner or later you kind of deep down expected it.

Well, Carla and Perry were welcome to each other. More than

welcome. And—how sweet—Carla was getting herself a ready-made family.

"So do you want to tell Laurel or shall I?"

Perry was looking nervous. "Tell her what?"

"Oh, I think you know. You tricked me into taking your sister off your hands in the first place," said Ginny. "Well, I don't want her anymore. You can have her back."

He blinked rapidly. "Ginny, you *can't*—"

"The three of you can live together. Won't that be fun?"

"But she's happy with you," Perry pleaded.

"Irrelevant. Not my problem. Believe me; I'll be happy when she's gone."

"You wouldn't throw her out."

"Wouldn't I? Watch me." Ginny marched across the kitchen, pausing only to glance back in disgust at Carla. "And I never want to speak to either of you again as long as I live."

Chapter 28

IN TWO HOURS SHE had to pick up Jem from the station. As Ginny slipped back into her own house she prayed Laurel was out or asleep or upstairs listening to a Leonard Cohen CD.

No such luck. The second the front door clicked shut Laurel emerged from the kitchen.

"There you are! Now, does Jem like chocolate? Only I've made a lemon drizzle cake but if she'd prefer chocolate I can easily—*oh.*" Laurel looked concerned. "What's happened?"

"Nothing. Nothing's happened. Lemon's fine. Or chocolate. Jem likes any kind of cake."

"Only you look as if you've seen a ghost. Something's wrong."

To tell her? Or not to tell her? Ginny was saved from having to make the decision by Laurel moving past her, opening the front door, and peering out in search of whatever it was that might have caused the upset.

"That's Perry's car." She pointed across the road. "What's going on? Where's Perry?"

"OK." Closing the door and leading her back into the kitchen, Ginny said, "Would you be upset if I told you I've been… kind of seeing Perry?"

Laurel looked astounded. "You? And Perry? Seriously? But that's great! Why would I be upset?"

Exactly. Why would she have been? Tempting though it was to open a bottle of wine, Ginny grabbed a can of Coke from the fridge and sat down.

"Sorry, Perry said you wouldn't like it. Anyway, I'm not seeing him anymore." She yanked the ring-pull and watched foam spill over the top of the can. "It's over now."

"Oh phew, thank goodness for *that*."

Ginny looked up. "Why?"

"Because he's a *nightmare*." Laurel rolled her eyes. "For your sake, I'm so relieved it's over. I mean, don't get me wrong, I love him to bits, but Perry's relationships always end in disaster. Where women are concerned he has the attention span of a gnat. One minute he's crazy about them, the next minute they're history. Oh God"—she covered her mouth in dismay—"is that what he's just done to you?"

"No... no..." Ginny didn't have the heart to admit the real reason Perry had pretended to be keen on her. "Well, kind of, I suppose. He's seeing someone else now."

"Par for the course. To be honest, you're well rid of him." Laurel leaned forward, her forehead pleated with concern. "Are you devastated?"

Devastated. Ginny tried and failed to summon up devastation. She could do humiliation and anger—oh yes, plenty of that, no problem—but devastation over Perry wasn't an issue. Losing her best friend—her *alleged* best friend—was far more upsetting than losing Perry Kennedy.

She shook her head. "No. We only went out a few times. It wasn't serious."

This clearly wasn't the answer Laurel wanted to hear. Or else she simply didn't believe her. "You must be upset though. He's let you down. These things are bound to hurt." Earnestly, she said, "But I'm a good listener. You can talk about it as much as you want. It doesn't matter that he's my brother, you just let it all out, get everything off your chest, because I know there's nothing worse than feeling miserable and not being able to talk to someone about—"

"Actually, I don't do it that way." Ginny had a brainwave. "I

find endlessly thinking and talking about a failed affair makes things worse. I prefer out of sight, out of mind. In fact, you could really help me if you want to. Make sure I *never* talk about Perry."

"Of course I will! Don't you worry." Laurel shook her head eagerly. "I'll tell you the *moment* you mention his name."

"And... and it might help if you try not to mention Kevin's name as well," said Ginny. "Because if you do, it'll only remind me of Perry, and to be honest, the less I'm reminded of him the quicker I'll forget he ever existed." *Oh yes, brilliant.* Perry had his uses after all.

"Good point. OK, I'll do that. And don't worry; you've had a lucky escape. Think how much worse it would have been if the two of you had been together for as long as me and Kev—*oops*, sorry!" Laurel pulled an apologetic face. "Nearly did it then!"

"But you stopped *yourself*. That's excellent." Nodding encouragingly, Ginny said, "And we'll both get better with practice."

"I'm sure we will." As if the concept had never occurred to her before, Laurel straightened her shoulders and said with pride, "Out of sight, out of mind!"

"Oh. Just one thing before we start it properly. The reason Perry's car's outside is because he's seeing Carla now."

"Carla? Your best friend?" Laurel's light green eyes widened in horror.

"Well, she *was* my best friend." Ginny watched her fingers tighten around the Coke can. "They just told me."

"I don't believe it! You mean she stole him? What a *bitch*!"

"Thank you. I thought so too."

"At least you know it won't last." Laurel's tone was consoling.

"It might. This time it's different," said Ginny. "They're in love. Perry had a—"

"*Coup de foudre*?" Laurel gave an elegant snort of amusement. "God, not another one."

Ginny took another gulp of Coke, marveling at this revelation. It *was* a consolation to know it wouldn't last.

"One other thing." Overcome with curiosity, she said, "Why did you never tell me this about Perry before?"

Laurel looked surprised. "You never asked."

Right. Fair enough.

"He's my brother," Laurel went on. "And he's always been great to me. I'm not going to go around bad-mouthing him, am I? And I didn't know there was anything going on between the two of you." Vigorously, she shook her head. "If you'd mentioned it, I could have warned you."

"But Perry said—"

"OK, *stop.*" Laurel held up both hands like a traffic cop. "Stop it *now*. See what you're doing? You're leading the conversation around to Perry again, obsessing about what happened! And it's my job to make sure you don't. So just clear him out of your mind. Stop thinking about him. He isn't worth it."

Ginny struggled to keep a straight face. She'd never imagined Laurel could be so bossy and forceful. Obediently, she said, "Right."

"Trust me." Nodding wisely, Laurel broke four eggs into a bowl and began briskly beating them. "It's the only way."

<center>~~~</center>

The day may have been tainted but it hadn't been ruined. The moment Jem jumped down from the train, all thoughts of Perry and Carla flew out of Ginny's mind. For almost thirty seconds they just stood there wrapped around each other, hugging tightly. Jem, her baby, was home again, and that was all that mattered. Burying her face in Jem's blond, pink-tipped hair, Ginny inhaled deeply, delving beneath the trendy new perfume until she managed to locate the precious, infinitely subtle but familiar body smell that reassured her that this was her daughter.

Finally, grinning like idiots, they pulled away from each other.

"Oh, sweetheart, it's so good to see you again." Her heart aching with love, Ginny said, "You've had your hair cut."

Jem reached out and gave Ginny's overgrown blond hair a mischievous tug. "You haven't."

"And where are the sacks of washing? I thought it was in the student rules that you have to bring home at least a hundred-weight of dirty clothes."

"We've got a top of the range Bosch washer-dryer."

"In that case I'll bring my washing to you. How's Lucy?"

"Fine."

"Rupert?"

"He's fine too."

"And Davy?"

Jem shrugged. "He's OK. Busy cleaning other people's houses. Anyway, I'm here. Let's go. I can't wait to meet everyone." Tucking her arm through Ginny's as they made their way down the station platform, she added with a complicit squeeze, "Especially Perry."

"I still can't believe it. What a bastard. How could he prefer her to you?" Franz Ferdinand was blaring from the stereo and Jem had to shout to be heard over the noise. "And as for bloody Carla… I'm never going to speak to her again as long as I live. She's a complete *cow*."

Ginny was touched by her vehemence. It was eight thirty, they were on their way to Penhaligon's, and Jem was continuing to let off steam in the passenger seat. Since Laurel had banned them from discussing *that* subject in the house, Jem was now making up for lost time. Knowing how intensely proud Carla was of her perfectly geometric bob, the latest plan was to sneak into her house while she was asleep and hack off her hair with garden shears. And possibly perform a spot of reverse liposuction while she was there,

by injecting a few liters of wibbly-wobbly fat into Carla's tanned, super-toned thighs.

"I bet that's who she was with when I phoned her," Jem said suddenly. "I've only just realized. God, talk about two-faced… they were probably in bed together. She's such a slapper. In fact, I could quite easily slap both her faces."

"You won't," Ginny said firmly. "If we see her, we ignore her."

"Spoilsport."

"She's going to have her conscience to live with. And from what Laurel says, it won't last long. Perry will dump her. I'll look forward to that."

"And after it's over?" Jem was looking at her. "What then? Don't tell me you'll be friends with Carla again."

Ginny shook her head; her mind was made up on that score. "That's not going to happen."

"Good." Jem sat back, satisfied.

"So what do you think of Laurel?" Reaching forward and turning down Franz Ferdinand, Ginny changed the subject.

"I like her! She's really nice. You said she was depressed but she seemed really cheerful to me."

Ginny smiled to herself. This was true; the change in Laurel had been staggering. Who would have guessed that all Laurel needed to snap her out of her misery was another depressed person in the house? She was now positively reveling in her newfound role as chief cheerer-upper, even if Ginny wasn't mourning the loss of Perry quite as much as Laurel seemed to want to believe.

"And her cakes are out of this world," Jem added cheerfully. "That has to be a bonus."

"It is." Ginny nodded with relief because she might have told Perry she no longer wanted Laurel in the house, but in her heart of hearts she'd known all along that she would never actually kick her out.

"So hang on a minute, let's just get this straight. You thought Carla was a great friend and it turns out she's a complete witch." Jem was now counting on her fingers. "You believed Perry was perfect, the man you'd been waiting for all these years. And as far as you were concerned, Laurel was depressed. You know, I think it's a good job I'm here," she told Ginny. "Because, basically, you're pretty hopeless. You've been wrong about everyone so far."

Chapter 29

FINN EMERGED FROM HIS flat as Ginny was parking in the courtyard.

"Is that your boss? And you didn't tell me he was that good-looking either. For an older man," said Jem.

"Shhh, keep your voice down." But as he came over to greet them, Ginny suspected Finn had overheard.

"You must be Jem." He smiled and shook her hand. "We've heard a lot about you."

"Ditto. You're the man who tried to have my mother arrested."

"I hardly ever do that anymore," said Finn.

Jem gazed past him. "I'm being hissed at."

Ginny saw Myrtle, her tail swishing, staring disdainfully down from the high, ivy-strewn courtyard wall. The cat blinked and bared her teeth again.

"Her name's Myrtle. Not the world's friendliest cat," said Finn. "We think she's pregnant but nobody's been able to get near enough to find out for sure."

"If she's this touchy, it's a miracle she ever managed to get pregnant in the first place. I suppose it's like some women," Jem went on pointedly. "They don't look sex mad on the outside, but deep down, they're nothing but tarts."

Finn threw a questioning glance at Ginny, who felt herself turning red. Oh brilliant, did he think Jem meant her?

"And if Myrtle's pregnant she shouldn't be climbing high walls. It's dangerous." Moving past Finn, Jem held her arms up and made

kissing noises. "Come on, sweetie, it's all right, let's get you down from there, shall we?"

Myrtle looked at Jem as if she was deranged before haughtily turning her back on everyone and springing like Spider-Man from the top of the wall to the upper branches of the mulberry tree beyond it.

"Dr. Dolittle, I presume." Finn was amused by Jem's failure.

"I'm usually good with animals." Disappointed, Jem watched as Myrtle elegantly picked her way along the branch before leaping across to the next tree. "She doesn't look pregnant to me."

Inside the restaurant, Finn looked around and said, "No sign of Perry yet."

"Just as well," Jem retorted, "if he doesn't want to end up being stuffed into a food processor."

"He won't be joining us," Ginny put in hurriedly. Another raised eyebrow from Finn.

"Mum's been chucked. And guess who he's been seeing behind her back? Only her best friend," said Jem.

"Who, *Carla*?" Finn looked startled. "But she told me she didn't—"

"Like him? She lied. Could we change the subject now?" said Ginny. "My daughter's home and that's all I care about. We're here to celebrate."

"And get the teeniest bit drunk." Jem beamed at Finn, who was moving behind the bar. "So we'll have a couple of glasses of house white to start with. Bucket-sized, if you've got them."

"That's not celebrating." Taking a bottle of champagne from the fridge and removing the wire, Finn expertly uncorked it. "Here, on the house."

"Hey, I like this place!"

"Don't get used to it. Strictly a one-off."

Jem's smile broadened as he filled their glasses and scrunched the bottle into a bucket of ice. "You're nicer than I was expecting."

His mouth twitched. "You mean nicer *and* better looking?"

"Yes. Still single?"

"Jem!"

"Why?" said Finn.

Jem looked innocent. "No reason. Just asking."

After an hour, Ginny began to relax. Introducing Jem to Evie had been a joy, followed by Evie asking where Perry was and having to hear about what had happened, which wasn't. Then Evie had relayed the information to Martha who was even more outraged on Ginny's behalf. But after that it had got easier, helped along by the rest of the bottle of Moët—so much more delicious when you weren't paying for it yourself. And Dan the Van had come up trumps too, supplying the restaurant with sublime asparagus and artichokes, Jem's favorite vegetables in the world.

"That was so gorgeous. I want to lick my plate," Jem said longingly.

"Might be best not to. Finn'll turf you out."

"So he runs the antiques center by day and works here in the restaurant in the evenings. Isn't that an awful lot of hours?"

"They're his businesses. He wants them to do well. And the customers like having him around."

Jem watched Finn chatting to a table of eight. "But when does he get time off?"

"When he needs it." Suspicious of the direction her daughter's thoughts were traveling in, Ginny leaned forward and changed the subject. "Anyway, tell me what's been happening in Bristol. You haven't mentioned boyfriends for a while. Anyone exciting you want to tell me about?"

"Maybe the reason I haven't mentioned boyfriends is because I've been working too hard too." But Jem's blue eyes were sparkling, her tone playful. Relaxed by the champagne, she was clearly in the mood to spill some beans tonight.

"Don't believe you." Ginny waved her last spear of asparagus tantalizingly over Jem's empty plate.

"We-ell, maybe there is someone."

"And his name is...?"

Jem said, "Do I get the asparagus?"

"Depends. Maybe. And his name is...?" Wouldn't it be great if she were to say Davy?

"It's Rupert," said Jem. And blushed.

Right. Bugger. Well, it wasn't really a huge surprise.

"Rupert? Gosh, that's a surprise! You two, a couple." Ginny shook her head in amazement. "Wow!"

"He's great," Jem said eagerly, fencing the asparagus spear from Ginny's fork and snaffling it before she could change her mind. "Well, you've met him; you already know how good-looking he is. We've been seeing each other for the last few weeks." Energetically, she chewed and swallowed the asparagus. "The thing is, though, we haven't told Lucy. It's a bit awkward, you see, the three of us sharing the flat. Because we all get on so well together, she might feel left out if she knew. So for now it's our secret."

Déjà vu. Déjà vu clanging away like a big old bell. Was it some kind of inherited condition? Ginny wondered. Were she and Jem destined only to meet men who didn't want their relationships made public?

Carefully, she said, "Was that your idea or Rupert's?"

Jem considered this. "Well, both really. I mean, Rupert said it. But it just makes sense. I'd hate Lucy to feel like a third wheel. *I'd* hate it if I was the third wheel."

This was a fair point—indeed, a familiar point—but Ginny couldn't help feeling a sense of unease. So all they were doing, presumably, was sleeping together behind Lucy's back. How romantic.

"But you're happy?"

Jem beamed and took a gulp of champagne. "Very happy." Then she paused. "I thought you'd be happy about it too."

"Oh, sweetheart, I am. If you like him, that's... great. I suppose

I was just thinking about this keeping-it-secret business because it's what Perry said to me. I don't want you to get hurt."

"But that was completely different. Laurel is Perry's sister. To be honest, Mum, it was a dodgy excuse in the first place. You were a bit gullible. But Rupert's not like Perry; he's only doing it to spare Lucy's feelings. He's a nice person. And he's fun. Loads of girls at uni have a crush on him," Jem concluded with pride. "He could have anyone he wants. But he's chosen me."

"That's because he has good taste." Ginny reached across the table and gave Jem's hand a rub. Forcing herself to sound suitably enthusiastic she said, "He's a lucky boy. And I can't wait to meet him again properly. The two of you could come down and stay for a weekend, how about that? Everyone enjoys a trip to the seaside, don't they?"

"Mum, Rupert isn't eight." Jem rolled her eyes in amusement. "What would we do, have picnics on the beach and build sand castles?"

What was so terrible about a picnic on the beach? "Well, no, but…"

"He's in the south of France now, staying in his dad's villa. I've seen photos of it," said Jem. "It's the most incredible place you've ever seen. Joan Collins is a neighbor!"

Lucky old Joan.

"Rupert's gone down there with an old friend from boarding school." Leaning forward, Jem whispered excitedly, "And *his* father's a billionaire!"

Was that the problem? Did Jem think her house wasn't glamorous enough to impress Rupert? Because they didn't have a vast swimming pool, hordes of servants, and a panoramic view over St. Tropez harbor?

"Oh well then, that'll just have to be my next move," Ginny said lightly. "Marry Rupert's friend's father."

Jem giggled. "Don't be daft; you're far too old for him. He married his fifth wife last year, and she's twenty-two."

Their main courses arrived and Ginny ordered a bottle of wine. The conversation turned away from Rupert and they chattered instead, far more pleasurably, about clothes, shoes, Jem's customers at the pub, and the rich American who had come to Penhaligon's last Wednesday and ended up offering Finn half a million dollars for his jukebox (*yes*, he'd been drunk).

Just after nine thirty the door opened and a family of six piled in. One of the girls immediately spotted Jem and rushed over to their table.

"Jem Holland! You're back!"

Jem jumped to her feet and hugged Kaz Finnegan, her old school friend. "Kaz, so are you!"

"This is brilliant. Hi, Ginny! Someone told me you were working here."

"I am." Ginny was very fond of Kaz. "But Jem came home today so I'm having a night off."

"Working for dishy Finn. Lucky you. Now listen, it's my birthday next Tuesday." Kaz looked at Jem. "Will you still be here then?"

Jem nodded. "I'm back for a week."

"Yay, so you can come to my birthday party. We've hired a huge tent for the garden, and there's a band and everything. Loads of people invited." Persuasively, Kaz said, "And fireworks!"

Jem hesitated then looked over at Ginny. "What d'you think, Mum? Would that be OK with you?"

"And Niall's going to be there," Kaz went on. "He'd love to see you again."

Ginny smiled, because Jem and Kaz's older brother had had a teenage romance a couple of years ago and although the relationship had foundered when Niall had moved away to study for a degree in history at Manchester, she knew Jem still had a soft spot for him.

Ginny had a soft spot for him too, basically because he wasn't Rupert. "Go," she told Jem. "You'll have a fantastic time. I'm working on Tuesday evening anyway."

"With Finn Penhaligon." Kaz's eyes sparkled. "My mum has such a crush on him it's embarrassing. Is he fun to work for?"

At that moment, Finn walked past their table. "He's a nightmare," said Ginny. "A complete slave driver."

Without slowing down Finn said, "Some slaves need to be driven."

By the time the dessert menus arrived, Jem was sharing the last of the wine between their glasses. Dabbing at the drops she'd spilled on the tablecloth, she sat back and tilted her head to one side.

"What?" protested Ginny. "Why are you looking at me like that? If you're trying to hypnotize me into saying I don't want a dessert, it's not going to work."

"I wouldn't do that. I might try to hypnotize you into giving me your dessert." Jem beamed. "But that's not what I was thinking about."

"OK." To tease her, Ginny returned her attention to the menu. "Now I'm either going to have the orange crème brûlée or the double chocolate tart. Ooh, or the mango and lime cheeseca—"

"You're supposed to ask me what I was thinking about!"

"Go on then." Ginny was feeling thoroughly relaxed now; the day might have been traumatic but she was enjoying herself. It was so wonderful to have Jem, her beloved daughter, back at last. That was all that mattered.

"We-ell, he's good-looking. And Kaz's mum fancies the pants off him." Jem signaled with her eyebrows to let Ginny know who she was talking about, just in case Ginny might think she meant the fat bloke on table six. "So what I'm wondering is, have you given it any thought at all?"

OK, Ginny amended; *sometimes* it was wonderful to have her back.

"No." She shook her head, hastily blanking out the mental image of that four-poster bed and those cream curtains billowing in the breeze while a semi-naked—"No, never, not at all, God *no*."

"That's a lot of nos."

It was. Too many. Ginny forced herself to stop shaking her head, which had acquired a momentum of its own. "I just don't think of him in that way! He's my *boss*."

"That's a rubbish excuse," Jem pointed out. "Lots of people fancy their bosses."

"Well, I don't." Feeling a bit hot, Ginny took another slug of wine. Whoops, chin.

"Why not?"

Why not? Off the top of her head Ginny could think of a hundred reasons, chief among them the fact that her confidence had just taken the kicking of its life. Because, let's face it, she'd made an almighty fool of herself falling for Perry's lies, and given half a chance she would have leaped into bed with him before you could say floozy. But that hadn't happened because Perry hadn't been even remotely interested in sleeping with her, to the extent that he had resorted to the feeblest of excuses.

How much of an ego boost was that?

And basically, if Perry found her that unattractive, why on earth would someone like Finn be tempted? He could have anyone, for heaven's sake. Even Kaz's mother.

A beady-eyed Jem, meanwhile, was still waiting for an answer.

"Look, we get on well together," Ginny improvised. "And that's enough of a miracle in itself, considering what happened the first time we met. But it's only been a few hours since I found out about Perry and Carla. I really don't think I'm cut out for this dating malarkey. I'd rather just... you know, live without the hassle."

Jem looked disappointed. "But I think he's nice. And I want you to be happy."

Her heart swelling up like a giant marshmallow, Ginny reached across and clasped the hands of the daughter who meant the world to her. "Oh, sweetheart, how can I not be happy? *You're back.*"

"But only for a week. What about when I leave? Then you'll be all on your own again." Jem's face lit up. "I know! Why don't I have a quiet word with Finn, see if he fancies you?"

Ginny's fingers tightened around Jem's hands, then tightened again until she flinched. "Darling, that's so sweet of you. But you can't do that."

"I could! I'd be really subtle and—*ow*, Mum!"

"Because if you did do that," Ginny continued, her smile angelic, "I'd have to break both your legs."

Chapter 30

"THE THING IS, I look at you and I just want to *yawn...*"

"Dad, that is so rude! Honestly," Jem complained, "you're turning into a juvenile delinquent. You're just asking for a slap around the face."

"Luckily for him, I'm not into violence," Laurel said placidly.

"I'm so sorry about my dad," said Jem. "He's always been like this. He's so embarrassing."

It was Saturday afternoon and Gavin, just arrived, was being his usual shy, retiring self.

"You didn't let me finish." Undeterred, Gavin stretched out an arm and helped himself to the last slice of lemon drizzle cake. "I was talking about Laurel's clothes, the impression she makes on people when they meet her. Everything droops," he complained, waving the cake as he gestured at Laurel. "OK, maybe not the boobs, but everything else. Droopy skirt, droopy top, droopy *hair*. I'm just offering some constructive criticism. What's wrong with that?" he demanded as Jem rolled her eyes. "First impressions count. You want people to look at you and go, wow."

"Is that what they say when they see you?"

Gavin, who was wearing a multicolored striped shirt, black trousers, and a bright red waistcoat, said with pride, "Nobody looks at me and thinks I'm boring."

"No," said Laurel. "But nobody looks at me and thinks I'm fat."

There was a stunned silence. Then Gavin started to laugh. "That was funny."

Laurel looked bemused. "It isn't. Being fat is a serious health issue."

"You said something funny. I love it!"

"You should lose thirty pounds," Laurel retaliated. "Look at your stomach."

"You should stop offering me cakes then."

"I didn't offer you any cakes. You helped yourself."

Still grinning, Gavin eyed her with new respect. "Know what? You're getting better. Buy yourself a perky new outfit and you'll be unrecognizable."

"I don't want a perky outfit. I like my clothes the way they are."

Ginny, rejoining them in the living room, looked suspiciously at Gavin. "Are you giving Laurel a hard time?"

"Quite the opposite. I'm giving her an easy time, complimenting her on her sense of humor. She's making progress," Gavin declared. "Plus, I've been here ten minutes and she hasn't mentioned Kevin once, which has to be some kind of—"

"Shhh," Laurel said severely. "We're not mentioning that name. New rule."

"Excellent rule. Why didn't anyone think of that before? You're on a roll now. Hey, what are you doing on Wednesday night?"

Laurel's huge green eyes widened in horror. "Please don't ask me out on a date."

"Sweetheart, I said you were on a roll, not that you'd scooped the jackpot. I was just going to suggest you giving the singles club another go. I'll make sure Hamish turns up this time. You never know, you being more cheerful now could make all the diff—"

"Not in a million years," said Laurel.

"But I just know you two would hit it off. And," Gavin added persuasively, "we're having a quiz night. Any questions about droopy clothes and you'd clean up."

"Is that another joke?"

He grinned. "Yep. Well done for recognizing it."

"Thank you," said Laurel, "but I'm still not coming to your singles club. And you could still do with losing weight."

"So cruel." Gavin clasped his chest. "Like a dagger in my heart."

"You'd be better with one in your stomach." For the first time there was a glimmer of a smile around Laurel's mouth. "Then it might go down, like a popped balloon."

"I don't know how it got there." Mournfully, Gavin patted his stomach. "It crept up on me when I wasn't looking. I used to have a fine figure, didn't I, Gin?"

"You used to have lots of fine figures," said Ginny. "Sadly they all belonged to bimbos in miniskirts."

"There she is!" Jem, who had been gazing idly out of the window while the grown-ups got on with their bickering, shouted, "The bitch is back! Look at her, scuttling inside like a rodent. God, I'd love to go over there and tell that lying tart what I think of her."

"Well, you're not going to." Envisaging some hideous street brawl, Ginny said, "This isn't Jerry Springer. We're just going to ignore her, OK?"

"But that means she gets away with it!" Indignantly Jem said, "How can that be fair?"

"Hang on." Gavin was looking blank. "Is this Carla we're talking about? Gets away with what?"

Everyone congregated at the window to watch Carla hurry into her house, slamming the glossy black front door behind her.

"Gets away with *what*?" repeated Gavin, bewildered.

"I was about to tell you." There was a horrid tightening knot in Ginny's stomach as she filled him in on the situation. When she'd finished she put the question she knew she needed to ask. "Did anything like that ever happen with you?"

Gavin's face was a picture. "You mean did Carla ever make a play for me?"

"Or vice versa."

"Bloody hell, Gin, I can't believe you even think that!"

"I can't believe it either, but until yesterday I thought I could trust my best friend." Ginny shrugged. "And look how well that turned out."

"Well, nothing happened, and that's a promise. Carla never tried it on and I wouldn't sleep with her if you paid me." Straight-faced, Gavin said, "I'd rather sleep with droopy Laurel."

Droopy Laurel rolled her eyes. "You wish," she said.

Carla had evidently whizzed home to pick up a change of clothes. Within ten minutes the front door reopened and she emerged carrying a small suitcase, her gaze deliberately averted from Ginny's house as she hurried back to the car.

"I'm going to go over there and give her a piece of my mind," Gavin announced.

"Oh no you're not." Touched by his loyalty, Ginny nevertheless moved to the living room door to block his exit.

Which was a fairly pointless exercise, seeing as Gavin launched himself at the window instead, flung it wide open, and bellowed across the road, "Hey, Carla, has he told you he's got herpes?"

Carla didn't look up but a young postman, cycling past at the time, did an alarmed double-take and almost wobbled off his bike.

"Poor kid." Gavin watched with grim satisfaction. "Looks like she's had him too."

⸺∿∿⸺

For once all the diners had left in good time. By half-past ten the restaurant was empty, leaving only Ginny and Finn to finish clearing up.

"Early night for you," Finn observed. "You'll be pleased."

"Jem's gone out for the night. It's Kaz Finnegan's birthday do. Anyway, I've got that chef program to watch," said Ginny. "The one

about the French guy who bought the crumbling castle in Wales and turned it into a restaurant."

"Damn, I missed it. Everyone's been telling me about that."

"No problem, I recorded it." Ginny, collecting cutlery to lay a table for ten, said eagerly, "I can lend you the DVD."

Finn shook his head. "It's OK, don't worry about it."

"But it's supposed to be brilliant. You'll enjoy it!"

"Really, it doesn't matter." He turned his attention to counting the twenty-pound notes in the till.

Something about the way he said it aroused Ginny's curiosity.

"Don't you have a DVD player?"

Defensively, maybe even too quickly, Finn replied, "Yes, of course I do."

"So why don't you want to borrow the DVD?"

He paused in the middle of cashing up, looked over at her for a moment.

"Because the DVD machine's still in its box."

Mystified, Ginny frowned. "OK, I know this is a pretty radical suggestion, but how about... ooh, let's see, taking it out of the box and connecting it up to the TV?"

Another lengthy pause. Finally he gave in, exhaled slowly. "Because I tried that and I couldn't make it work."

Oh, brilliant. Ginny did her best to keep a straight face. "Right, so did you read the instruction manual?"

"Yes. But that just made everything worse; it kept going on about *scart* leads and... and *grinch* cables and stupid stuff that made *no* sense at all." Finn shot her a warning look. "And if you're laughing at me..."

"I'm not laughing." Heroically, Ginny bit her lip but she was only human. "OK, maybe smirking a bit."

"It's not funny," said Finn. "It's embarrassing. I'm a *man*."

"It's not as embarrassing as having to admit you're impotent."

Ginny said it without thinking, then hastily added, "Not that I'm saying you *are* impotent, of course."

"I'm not," Finn said gravely.

"But you have to admit, it is *quite* funny."

"We're not talking about impotence now, are we?"

Equally seriously Ginny shook her head. "No, because impotence is never funny."

Good grief, was she really having this conversation?

"I can't set up DVD players." Finn admitted defeat. "Or video recorders. Or TVs, come to that. It's a recognized phobia," he went on, "of electrical leads and sockety things and manuals that deliberately set out to confuse you."

He was hating this; she was loving it. Ginny's mouth was twitching uncontrollably now. "So, um, how do you usually deal with this?"

He looked slightly shamefaced. "Get a man in."

A man. Of course. Giddy with power, Ginny said, "Would a woman do?"

This time she definitely detected a flicker of amusement. "Would a woman do what?"

"Would you like me to set up your DVD player for you?"

He shrugged offhandedly. "If you want."

"Sorry. That's not good enough. Not nearly enough enthusiasm."

Finn gave in gracefully, broke into a broad smile, and pushed the till shut.

"OK, you win. Yes please."

Chapter 31

THEY MADE IT ACROSS the darkened courtyard without, for once, being ambushed by Myrtle. Upstairs in the flat, Finn brought out the DVD recorder, crammed haphazardly into its original packaging as if someone—*ahem*—had previously had a go and ended up losing his temper with it. The expression on Finn's face as he handed it over made Ginny smile all over again.

It took her less than fifteen minutes to sort patiently through the spaghetti-like tangle of wires, plug them into the relevant sockets, set up the recorder, and tune in the relevant channels.

"I don't know how you can do that." Finn watched as she sat back on her heels and expertly keyed in instructions via the remote control.

"It's easy. Look, let me show you how to set it in advance."

"Don't even try. I'll just press record when it's time to record something. That's as technical as I get." Holding out a hand, he helped Ginny to her feet. "But thanks, I appreciate it. Now, do you have to rush off or can I ask you another favor?"

She breathed in the scent of his aftershave, experiencing a tremor as his warm hand clasped hers. "You want me to fix your kettle?"

"The kettle's fine. I'll prove it to you. What I really want is for you to give me your honest opinion of this room."

Ginny gazed around at the decor. "I thought you'd never ask."

It had, she learned, been Tamsin's idea to hire an outrageously trendy interior designer, lure him down from London, and have him

transform the flat while Finn had been away on a buying trip. Upon Finn's return, he had been confronted with the mother of all make-overs involving aubergine-and-silver striped walls, a pistachio-green ceiling, and a sixties-style, pop-arty aubergine-and-pistachio carpet. The lighting was modern, verging on the futuristic. The sofas, sleek and uninviting, were upholstered in lime-green tweed flecked with silver.

Austin Powers would have thought it was shagtastic.

"You don't want to know how much it cost," Finn said with a shudder.

"Did you tell her you hated it?"

"Couldn't. It was my birthday present. And Tamsin was so thrilled, I didn't have the heart to hurt her feelings."

He must have loved Tamsin an awful lot. Whenever Gavin had bought her something horrific for her birthday Ginny had trained him to hand over the receipt at the same time. Then again, that was the beauty of coordinated outfits from Marks and Spencer. It wouldn't be quite so easy lugging an entire room back to the shop.

"So what happens now?"

"It has to go. The whole lot. I would have done it before but the restaurant had to take priority. It's been easier to just ignore it. But the other day I picked up some paint charts," Finn went on firmly. "And this time I won't be hiring a bloody designer."

He made coffee with the non-broken kettle. Ginny sat down on the sleek, slippery sofa and spread the paint charts over the brushed aluminum—brushed *aluminum!*—coffee table. For the next hour they debated wall colors, curtains, furniture, and accessories. Out with the new and achingly trendy, in with the unflashy and tradi-tional. Ginny sketched out ideas and drew the room with cream curtains billowing gently at the open windows.

"Not blue curtains?" said Finn.

"No, too dark. Definitely cream." Her mind was made up on that score; it might not be the bedroom but Ginny was adamant there would be cream curtains. And billowy ones at that. Oh yes, they would billow if she had to smash all the windows herself.

"So how are you feeling about Perry now?"

Thanks for reminding me. "Like an idiot."

"Well, you shouldn't. He's the idiot."

Acutely aware of Finn's proximity to her on the sofa—their shoulders were only millimeters apart—Ginny said, "I'm out of practice when it comes to dating. I should have realized what his game was, but I didn't. Maybe if I'd been out with more men I wouldn't have been so gullible."

"Don't blame yourself. You're better off without someone like that. Carla would probably be better off without him too, but now she's the one being gullible." Drily, he added, "And look how much practice she's had."

"You think I should feel sorry for her?" Ginny half smiled. "I can't see that happening."

"Maybe not. You just have to put it behind you and move on."

"Is that what you did?" She felt brave enough to ask him now. "After Tamsin left?"

Finn shrugged and this time his shoulder made contact with hers. "It's the only thing to do."

"But it's easier for some people than others. Like you with that girl Catherine," said Ginny. "The one who sent you flowers the other week. Why did she do that?"

He sounded amused. "Because I gave her a lift home?"

Ha, and the rest. Bluntly, Ginny said, "Did you sleep with her?"

There was a pause then Finn nodded. "OK, yes. I did."

"You see?" Vigorously Ginny shook her own head. "I'd love to be able to do that!"

Now he was definitely smiling. "You'd love to sleep with Catherine? Or with me?"

Oh Lord, what a thought.

"Neither! I *meant* I'd love to be the kind of person who could do that." Ginny felt the heat creeping into her cheeks. "I wish I could go out, see someone I like the look of, and... well, have a one-night stand, just for the hell of it. But I can't, because I'm not that kind of person and I never have been."

"Never?"

"Never. It's really annoying. Men do it all the time. And so do loads of women, I know that. But I've never been able to." Recklessly Ginny said, "If I told you how many men I'd slept with, you'd fall off the sofa laughing. Honestly, I'm pathetic."

Finn raised a playful eyebrow. "So you're saying you want to be like Carla?"

"God, no, nothing like that. Just... you know, once in a blue moon it'd be nice to think, oh sod it, why not?"

"Find someone you like the look of and just go for it?"

"Well, yes." Ginny knew her cheeks were on fire now; she still couldn't quite believe she was having this conversation, and with Finn Penhaligon of all people. But her pent-up feelings were spilling out uncontrollably like molten lava. "What are you doing?" she added, because he was now twisting round on the sofa, peering out of the window at something in the sky.

"Just checking if it's a blue moon."

Her breath caught in her throat. This, subconsciously or otherwise, was exactly what she'd wanted to hear him say. Maybe it was pathetic, but after having her confidence dented—more like *smashed*—by Perry, she was ridiculously flattered to know that Finn Penhaligon would be prepared to have sex with her.

Except, terrifyingly, he appeared to have made his offer and was now awaiting her response to it.

Except, aaarrgh, what if it hadn't been an offer at all? Maybe he was a keen astronomer genuinely interested in discovering whether the moon tonight might actually be blue?

"Well?" Finn prompted, his dark eyes questioning.

Hopelessly unsure and petrified of making a twit of herself, Ginny said, "Is it?"

"Take a look." He gently turned her round to face the window. "Tell me what you think."

There was an unromantic *thunk* as Ginny's ankle knocked against the edge of the coffee table, setting the coffee cups rattling against the metallic surface. Her heart hammering against her rib cage, she followed the line of Finn's pointing finger and saw the moon hanging low in the inky-black sky, partially obscured by the branches of a sycamore tree.

"So, does it look blue to you?" The words came out as a whisper, his warm breath circling her ear in such a way as to send Ginny's nervous system into a frenzy. But she still didn't know if this was all part of his seduction plan or simply an experienced astronomer asking a hopeless ignoramus an easy question.

"It looks... um, well... I think maybe it looks a *bit* blue."

"Really?" Now he sounded amused—oh God, was that the wrong answer?

"White with a hint of blue?" hazarded Ginny. "Sort of... very faintly... bluish?"

"Hmm." He nodded thoughtfully. "You know, I think you could be right."

"Yiawoooooow."

"What's *that*?" Startled by the unearthly noise, faint but clearly audible, Ginny's eyes widened.

"Sounds like Myrtle, somewhere outside."

"*Yiiaaarrrrlll.*"

"She's not happy. Oh God, what if she's been cornered by a fox?"

"Poor fox, he doesn't know what he's let himself in for. She'll rip him to shreds."

"*Mwwwwaaaaaoooowwwwww*," Myrtle yowled, sounding more outraged than Ginny had ever heard her before.

"She's being attacked by something. I'll go and let her in." Leaping up and slipping past Finn, she headed downstairs and opened the front door. "Myrtle? Come on, sweetheart, it's OK, come inside."

But although she heard another faint yowl, Myrtle didn't materialize out of the darkness and shoot past Ginny's ankles in a blur of indignant black fur. Finally, she closed the door and made her way back upstairs. If Finn had a torch, they could go in search of her.

But when she reached the landing, she saw Finn standing at the far end of it, his hand resting on the handle of a half-open door that, if she'd got her bearings right, had to lead into the master bedroom. His dark eyes locked with hers for a moment, his expression unreadable. Then he held out his other hand and slowly beckoned her forward. His voice low and with a husky edge to it, he murmured, "Come here."

Oo-er. Tingling all over, torn between finding a missing cat and being drawn into Finn Penhaligon's bedroom, Ginny hesitated. Then again, what had Myrtle ever done for her? Maybe the time had come to be selfish for once. If Finn had decided that the moon was blue, who was she to argue?

Wandering in a dreamlike state toward him, she imagined herself unbuttoning Finn's white shirt, removing the leather belt that held up his black trousers, undoing the zip in a sensual manner. Oh Lord, she was disastrously out of practice; she hoped she didn't show herself up. Socks, for instance. Would he take his own socks off before the trousers came down? Surely he wouldn't expect *her* to deal with them. Heavens, she couldn't remember how socks got disposed of; she was going to make a complete fool of herself and—

"Take a look at this." Finn noiselessly opened the bedroom door and drew her inside. As she held her breath, the first thing Ginny realized was that she wasn't going to have to wrestle with sock etiquette after all.

Not with Finn either, come to that.

Another realization was that as far as her long-cherished fantasy was concerned, she couldn't have got it more wrong if she'd tried. There was no four-poster, no cream hangings billowing gently in the breeze. The bed was king-sized and ultra-modern with a leather headboard and a heavy, expensive-looking dark blue suede bedspread.

Except it wasn't looking quite so expensive at the moment, what with all the gunk and slime smeared in the center of the bed over the supple, top-quality suede.

"Oh…" Ginny's hand flew to her mouth.

"*Yiaaaaaawwwwww,*" Myrtle yowled, furry paws extending and rib cage heaving as the next contraction gripped her body. As they watched, a silvery parcel emerged, slithering out of Myrtle and onto the bedspread only inches from the first blind mewling kitten. Twisting round, clearly relieved to have got a second one out, Myrtle used her sharp teeth to remove the covering membrane and bite her way—*eww*—through the umbilical cord.

"I didn't even realize she was here in the flat," Finn whispered. "She must have jumped across from the tree outside and climbed in through the window."

"Like a true cat burglar."

He grinned. "Give her a motorcycle and she'd out-leap Evel Knievel."

"Oh *looook*." Ginny tugged at his shirtsleeve as the first kitten, having staggered to its feet, promptly fell over the second. Struggling to get up again, it then slipped on a patch of dark green slime and landed on its back. It lay there mewing piteously until Myrtle took

pity on it and unceremoniously hauled it by the scruff of the neck over to her stomach.

"How do they know how to do that?" said Finn as the kitten, without a moment's hesitation, latched on and frantically began to feed.

"How did Myrtle know she had to bite through the cord?" Ginny shook her head in wonderment. "I'm glad I didn't have to do that when Jem was born."

Myrtle turned and blinked majestically, topaz eyes surveying her audience. For once she didn't snarl or hiss at them. "Maybe now she's a mother she'll turn into a nicer cat." Finn didn't sound too hopeful.

"Maybe she just has more important things on her mind right now, like bracing herself for the next contraction. How much did your bedspread cost, by the way?"

"Hundreds." Finn paused. "And hundreds. Tamsin chose it." Another pause. "Almost a thousand, I think."

Consolingly, Ginny said, "It'll probably dry-clean."

Since seduction was no longer on the menu—if it ever had been—they left Myrtle to get on with the task in hand and headed back to the living room. Finn made more coffee and paced the kitchen while Ginny perched on a high stool at the counter and surfed the Internet on his laptop.

"Sit down," she complained. "You're making me jittery."

"I am jittery. I feel like a prospective father."

"Well, you aren't." Ginny winced the moment she'd said it. What a thing to come out with. Luckily, typing "cats giving birth" into Google diverted her attention.

Yikes, cats giving birth wasn't the straightforward procedure she'd imagined.

"What?" Observing her look of alarm, Finn plonked a mug of coffee in front of her.

"Are you squeamish?"

"Why?"

"There's a whole list here of all the stuff you need when your cat goes into labor. A maternity bed."

"Well, she's already helped herself to that," Finn said drily. "What else? Gas and air?"

"A heating pad," Ginny read aloud. "Clean cloths or towels. A weighing scale."

"I've got bathroom scales." Finn frowned.

"Sharp scissors," said Ginny, pulling a face. "Disinfectant. A small syringe. And dental floss."

"Do I want to know why?"

"If the mother doesn't sever the umbilical cord, you have to do it yourself. You tie the dental floss round the cord before you cut it."

"Interesting use of the word 'you,'" Finn observed. "How about if we toss a coin?"

"I only fix DVD recorders." Ginny held up her hands "Besides, she's your cat."

He grimaced, then nodded at the computer screen. "So is that it, then?"

"Not quite. Petroleum jelly." Ginny read the accompanying instruction. "If the mother is having trouble giving birth, you need to put some petroleum jelly on her to help ease the kitten out."

"Fine. I'll put some on her ears."

"And we're going to need three tennis balls and a washed lettuce."

"*What?*"

"Joking." Ginny beamed.

"*Yaaaaiiiioooooooow!*"

As they hurried back to the bedroom, Finn said, "I don't think Myrtle found that joke funny."

By three o'clock in the morning it was all over. Myrtle had given birth to a litter of four kittens and, thankfully, hadn't required the

services of two incompetent human midwives. She had delivered her babies, chomped her way with relish through their afterbirths (*bleurgh*), and was now lying peacefully on the bed with all four babies curled up at her side.

Finn, busy making up the bed in the spare room seeing as Myrtle had nabbed his own, came out and saw Ginny yawning and collecting together her jacket, bag, and car keys.

"Are you off now? Drive carefully."

Not *the* most romantic of sentiments but understandable, considering the circumstances. It crossed Ginny's mind that he might even have given her a good-bye kiss if she hadn't been yawning off-puttingly, like a hippo.

"I will. Sorry, bit tired." She waggled her fingers at him. "See you tomorrow."

Who knew how their evening might have turned out if Myrtle hadn't chosen to give birth in Finn's king-sized bed? Oh well, it had been an experience.

"See you," said Finn.

Was that a note of regret in his voice or was she imagining it?

Cattus interruptus, thought Ginny.

Damn.

Chapter 32

Saying good-bye didn't get any easier. Jem was on her way back to Bristol and Ginny's throat was aching dreadfully with the effort of not making a public disgrace of herself. Having Jem at home again had been wonderful, but now their week together was up and she couldn't bear it.

To add insult to injury the train was on time. As it pulled into the station, there was a clap of thunder overhead and the first fat raindrops began to fall.

"Oh yuck." Having painstakingly straightened her hair and keen to avoid it going stupid, Jem threw her arms around Ginny and gave her a kiss. "Don't hang around out here, Mum, it's going to tip down."

"I don't mind. Text me when you reach the flat, just so I know you've got back safely." Ginny had to force herself not to stroke her daughter's face—"Mum, that's *embarrassing*"—as she had always done when Jem was young.

"Yes, Mum, and I promise to eat plenty of fruit and vegetables and always wear a coat when it snows."

"Don't make fun of me. It's my job to worry about you."

"Well, you don't need to because I'm a big girl now." Hauling her vast rucksack onto her shoulders, Jem moved toward the waiting train. With a grin she added, "And you have to behave yourself too. No getting up to mischief while I'm not here to keep an eye on you."

Without meaning to, Ginny's thoughts turned to Finn.

Chance would be a fine thing. Since the arrival of the kittens, there had been no more talk of blue moons. No flirtatious looks either, to the extent that she now wondered if she'd imagined them ever being there in the first place.

The heavens opened and with a squeal Jem leaped into her carriage. "Bye, Mum! See you soon!"

"Bye, sweetheart." Ginny blew a kiss as the train's doors slid shut and the ache in her throat gave way to tears. Thankfully the rain streaming down her cheeks disguised them and she kept a bright smile plastered to her face.

Jem blew extravagant kisses back, the train pulled out of the station, and moments later she was gone.

Back to Bristol, back to Pembroke Road in Clifton, back to Rupert whom Ginny just *knew* wasn't right for her.

But what could you do? Jem wasn't six years old anymore; Ginny couldn't simply forbid her to see him because, like skateboarding without a crash helmet, if she did, Jem'd only end up getting hurt. Jem had to be allowed to make her own mistakes now. And hopefully learn from them.

Like the rest of us, Ginny reminded herself, thinking of Carla and Perry and the sorry mess that was her own nonexistent love life.

Jem had texted Rupert on the train. He had flown back from Nice airport that morning. Letting herself into the flat, she called out joyfully, "Hi, honey, I'm home!"

"Hey." He appeared in the hallway, impossibly tanned and clutching a bottle of lager. "Honey, you shrunk your T-shirt."

Jem gazed down at her front; the storm had followed her all the way from Cornwall and rain was bucketing down outside.

Her cropped white T-shirt was now drenched and transparent, thanks to the long walk from the bus stop on Whiteladies Road.

"Don't try and cover yourself up. I like it." Grinning, he gave her a cool, beery kiss and trailed his hand down her chest.

"Is Lucy here?" Jem had to double-check.

"Not back yet. Which I have to say I'm quite happy about. So, good time?"

"Great." With an expert shoulder wiggle Jem released the straps of her wet rucksack and let it fall to the ground with a *thunk*. "I went to a party, met up with loads of old friends."

"Old friends, eh? Would that be old girlfriends or old boyfriends?"

"Both." Entranced by the idea that Rupert might be jealous, Jem said, "Actually, there was one old boyfriend there."

Rupert raised a playful eyebrow. "Should I be worried?"

"No. I don't fancy him anymore." It was the truth; bumping into Niall again had had zero effect on her. Compared with Rupert he'd just seemed so… ordinary.

"Good." And then Rupert was kissing her, and all thoughts of Niall Finnegan flew from her mind. It was too busy experiencing its own fireworks display instead.

"What about Lucy?" breathed Jem as he led her by her wet T-shirt in the direction of his bedroom.

"Relax. She won't be home for hours." As skillful as an ice dancer, he maneuvered her through the door, simultaneously unzipping her skirt and pulling the T-shirt off over her head. Jem didn't even care that he'd stretched it beyond repair.

"Anyway, what about you in the south of France?" Teasingly, Jem prodded his chest. "Surrounded by beautiful girls in bikinis? You must have been chatted up."

"The thing is, you call them beautiful girls in bikinis. I call them a bunch of old slappers. Of course I was chatted up," Rupert drawled. "But all they're interested in is bagging themselves a guy with money. The moment they spot your platinum credit card they're all over you

like a swarm of wasps. Not my idea of fun." Gently he pushed Jem onto his double bed, gazed down at her, and said with a smile, "That's why I'm here now. Because you are definitely my idea of fun."

Afterward, Jem ran her fingers through her disastrous hair. "I must look like a wet hedgehog."

"You look gorgeous." Rupert kissed the tip of her nose. "Sexily disheveled."

"Sexily disheveled." She wrinkled her nose doubtfully. "Is that flattering?"

"Now you're fishing. OK." Gravely he surveyed her naked body. "You have a great figure." He ran an experimental hand up her shin. "No stubble, always a bonus."

Jem giggled. "Cheek."

"Ah yes, glad you reminded me." Skillfully flipping her onto her side, Rupert carefully inspected her bottom. "Excellent, no cellulite either."

"Of course I don't have cellulite!" Jem dug her fingernails into his shoulder by way of protest.

"But you never know; it could arrive any day now. Just take up residence whether you want it there or not. Does your mother have cellulite?"

"No she does not!"

"Hey, I only asked. It's just that these things can be hereditary. We saw a few prime examples ourselves last week, let me tell you." Laughing, Rupert rolled out of reach before she could hit him. "Like mother, like daughter, wibble-wobbling along together across the sand. That's on the public beaches, of course. No gloopy cellulite allowed on the private ones."

"You're wicked," said Jem.

"But you love me." He flipped her back over, his hazel eyes glinting with intent.

Jem's stomach contracted with desire as one of his knees slid between hers. She wouldn't admit it for the world, but she was

beginning to think she did actually love him. Let's face it, he was gorgeous. And they got on so well togeth—

"*Shit*," hissed Rupert as the front door slammed.

Beneath him Jem froze. They heard the click-clack of high heels out in the hall, then Lucy called out, "Where are you?"

"Fuck fuck *fuck*," Rupert breathed. Eyes wide and brain racing, Jem glanced over at the wardrobe. Bulging with clothes, unread textbooks, tennis rackets, and in-line skates, there wasn't room for a hamster let alone a fully grown eighteen-year-old.

A *naked* eighteen-year-old.

A hysterical giggle rose up in Jem's throat. Oh well, maybe it was fate. Sooner or later Lucy was going to have to find out about them anyway.

"Shhh." Rupert, who wasn't laughing, lifted himself off her in one swift movement. "Hide under the bed."

Was he joking? Clearly not.

"Rupert?" Lucy was knocking on the door now.

"Get down there," hissed Rupert, rolling Jem to the edge of the mattress. Still grinning, she decided to humor him and dropped silently to the ground. Moments later, having hastily gathered up her discarded clothes, Rupert thrust them into her arms.

"Lucy? That you?" Yawning noisily, he called out, "What time is it? I've been asleep."

Under the bed and clutching her clothes, Jem came nose to nose with a semi-deflated blow-up sheep (a bachelor party prop rather than a perversion). The sheep had a dopey, crumpled look on its face.

"You lazy bum, it's four o'clock! Where's Jem?"

"No idea. I don't think she's back yet."

"She is. Her rucksack's on the floor." The bedroom door was flung open and Jem saw Lucy's emerald-green high heels. "You're not hiding her in here, are you?"

The bed creaked as Rupert sat up. "If she's not in her room she

must have gone out. Hang on, I'll get up. Why don't you make us some coffee?"

There was a pause. Jem held her breath. Then Lucy said, "I've got a better idea. Why don't I wake you up properly?"

Jem frowned. What was that supposed to mean? She watched the shoes move toward the bed; Lucy was so close now that if she reached past the sheep she could touch her ankles. That'd give her a fright.

"Don't muck about, Luce. I've got a headache."

"Now that's something I never thought I'd hear you say." The bedsprings creaked again and one of Lucy's shoes disappeared from view; in disbelief, Jem realized that she was now sitting *on* the bed.

"Stop it," said Rupert.

"Sorry." Evidently unfazed, Lucy murmured, "But I just don't think I can. Come on, what's the matter with you? Haven't you missed me?"

What? WHAT?

"Luce, will you—"

"Because I've missed you. Loads. In fact," Lucy paused then said silkily, "I'd say I missed you *this* much."

Jem felt as if she'd been plunged into a vat of dry ice. Logically, she knew what was happening, but her brain was refusing to make sense of it. She was in such a state of shock she wasn't even sure she could move.

"OK, that's enough." Rupert's tone was brusque. "Game over."

"What's the *matter* with you?" protested Lucy.

"Oh, I don't know," Rupert drawled. "Why don't you take a look under the bed and see if you can work it out?"

Jem couldn't believe he'd said it. Then again, Lucy hadn't given him much choice. She closed her eyes, bracing herself. Above her she heard Lucy say, "Don't tell me you've been playing about with that stupid blow-up sheep."

Chapter 33

WHEN JEM OPENED HER eyes again, she saw Lucy, crouching down, staring at her.

"No. No." Lucy shook her head. "Tell me this is a joke."

"I'll make the coffee myself," said Rupert.

"You've been shagging both of us? You bastard!" shrieked Lucy.

"Be fair, you pretty much threw yourself at me. It was fun while it lasted." He sounded bored. "But now it's run its course."

"You arrogant fucker! Get out of here," Lucy screamed at him. "I need to talk to Jem."

"Fine by me." Dragging on a pair of jeans, Rupert sauntered out of the bedroom.

"I don't believe this," Lucy exploded. "I just do not bloody believe it. He's been playing us for a couple of fools."

Jem, emerging from beneath the bed, said, "Could you look away while I get dressed?"

"Oh, for God's sake." Impatiently, Lucy turned away. "So this is what's been going on behind my back. Rupert must have thought it was hilarious." She was fuming, tapping her foot and shaking her head at the thought of it.

Hurriedly, Jem shook out her balled-up clothes and climbed into them, shuddering as the cold clamminess of the T-shirt hit her skin.

"Why didn't you say anything?" Lucy blurted out.

Stung by her tone, Jem shot back, "Why didn't you?"

"But you never asked me! I actually *asked* you. At the party

when I saw him groping your backside." Lucy's dark eyes flashed with anger. "I asked if there was anything going on between the two of you and you said there wasn't."

"Rupert didn't want you to feel left out."

"Funny, that's what he said to me too."

Jem took a deep breath. "I can't believe this is happening."

"I can't believe you lied to me! *Shit*," Lucy said vehemently, before holding up her hands. "OK, OK, I lied to you too. But Rupert lied to both of us. This is all down to him. Well, he's really blown it now. *Bastard*."

"I heard that." Rupert, leaning against the door, took a swig from another bottle of lager.

"Good." Lucy swung around. "And you can find yourself a couple of new flatmates. Because we are *out* of here."

Jem looked at her in alarm.

"You're leaving? Fine. In fact, excellent." Rupert shrugged, then in turn fixed his gaze on Jem. "But you don't want to leave, do you? Lucy never meant anything to me; it was only ever a casual fling. But you and me... well, it's different. Something special."

Jem's heart was racing; this was what she'd longed to hear for weeks.

"Forget it!" Incandescent with rage, Lucy yelled, "We're both going!"

"You know, bitter and twisted really doesn't suit you." Rupert raised an eyebrow. "A woman scorned is never a pretty sight."

"You make me sick," bellowed Lucy.

"Carry on like this and you'll give yourself wrinkles."

"Oh, fuck off."

"I think that's your job, sweetheart. You've already promised." Taking another swig of lager, Rupert smiled at Jem. "You know why Lucy's so mad, don't you? She's upset because I prefer you."

"You bastard!"

"Again? This is getting boring. Anyway, don't you have some packing to do?"

"Come on, Jem," Lucy ordered. "Let's go."

"She's not your pet dog," Rupert said coldly. "She doesn't have to do what you say." He turned to Jem. "It's up to you. I don't want you to leave."

"Oh shut up, you arrogant wanker."

"Jem?" Rupert tilted his head to one side.

"Jem!" snapped Lucy.

"I'm going to my room," said Jem, "to think."

She sat on her bed and buried her face in her hands. Everything had been going so well and now this. From next door came the crashings and bangings of drawers being yanked open and slammed shut as Lucy emptied them of her belongings. When her own door was pushed open she didn't look up.

"Don't go." As Rupert spoke, the mobile in his jeans pocket beeped, signaling the arrival of a text. "I want you to stay. It'll be just the two of us from now on. We can be a proper couple."

Jem's chest was aching so much she felt as if she was quite literally being torn in two. Her instinct in the past had always been to side with a girlfriend against a boy; it happened so automatically she'd never even questioned it. But this time was different; there was so much more at stake. Because, OK, Rupert had behaved badly but that was over now. And boys will be boys, after all. Especially boys with the kind of upbringing he'd had.

Far more important was how they felt about each other now that all the bad stuff was behind them. And she knew how she felt about Rupert. More to the point, she was realizing how he felt about her.

Jem trembled. Lucy, her friend, was exotic, sexy, and stunningly beautiful. Jem knew she herself was pretty enough in a ditsy, blond-hair-streaked-with-pink kind of way, but she couldn't

begin to compete with Lucy in the glamour stakes. Yet when it had come down to it, Rupert preferred her. How flattering was that, for heaven's sake?

No wonder Lucy was spitting teeth.

CRASH went the wardrobe doors next door, followed by the furious jangle of coat hangers.

Rupert finished reading his text. "My mate Olly's invited us to a party next weekend. Up in Scotland. Fancy that?"

Olly, Olly. Oliver MacIntyre-Brown. "Is he the one with the castle?" said Jem.

"The one with the bloody enormous castle. Olly says we can hitch a lift up there in his uncle's helicopter if we want."

Helicopter.

Castle.

She'd never been to Scotland before, not even on a train.

"Sorry," Rupert continued. "Jumping the gun. You might be about to call me a bastard and start emptying your wardrobe too."

Jem looked up at him. Life without Lucy would be horrible.

But life without Rupert would be infinitely worse.

"I'm not."

He broke into a wide smile. "Really?"

"Really."

"I'm glad." Rupert's gaze softened as he put down his phone and the bottle of Pils. "Very, very glad. Hey, you. Come here."

He kissed her and Jem knew she'd made the right decision. They were a proper couple now. And the way she was feeling, she suspected it might be the real thing after all.

If this wasn't love, she didn't know what was.

There was a sharp knock at the bedroom door. Bracing herself, Jem peeled herself away from Rupert and went to answer it.

Lucy, her shoulders rigid, said, "Well?"

"I'm staying."

"With him?" Her mouth twisted into a pitying smile. "You sad cow."

He chose me over you, Jem wanted to retort, but stopped herself. Lucy already knew that.

"Do you think he loves you?" Lucy demanded. "Is that it? Because if you really think that, you're even more stupid than—"

"Everything packed?" Rupert broke in coolly. "Called the taxi yet? Tell you what, I'll even pay the fare. No hard feelings, sweetheart. It was a good contest but the best girl won."

"You arrogant git."

"Ah, but a generous arrogant git, you can't deny that." Having pulled out his wallet, Rupert began counting out twenty-pound notes. "Here you go; one month's deposit back and an extra twenty for the cab. Lucky I went to the cashpoint."

"Does it not bother you, living off your father's money?"

"Funnily enough, not in the least. I love it. You should give it a go yourself sometime—oh sorry, I forgot your family doesn't have any money. Bad luck, sweetheart, you don't know what you're missing."

Jem knew he didn't mean it nastily; Rupert was always making flippant, derogatory remarks about his own family's wealth or other people's lack of it.

"I feel sorry for the pair of you." Lucy's eyes flashed as she uttered the words. The next moment she'd stalked out of the room.

"Obviously keener on me than she was letting on." Rupert shrugged. "*And* a bad loser."

"Don't." Jem felt a pang of guilt. "She's my friend."

"Not anymore she isn't." Sliding his arms round her waist he winked and said, "You're all mine now."

━━━

Lucy hauled her bags out of the taxi and looked up at the unprepossessing terraced house with its blue front door and neat,

pocket-sized front garden. The door opened and Davy came out to greet her.

It wasn't ideal, but leaving Rupert's flat in a rush during the Easter break hadn't given her a lot of choice. Most of her friends had gone home for the holidays. At least Davy was here.

And he understood.

"Davy, thanks so much for this. I couldn't stay there." Lucy hugged him. "She's lost her mind; she actually thinks he… he…"

"I know. Shhh, it's OK."

"Oh, Davy, I'm so *mad*. How can she be so stupid? It's not that I'm jealous." Dashing away angry tears, Lucy gibbered, "It's just… how could she find out what he's been doing and forgive him?"

"Come on, let's go in. Mum's waiting to meet you."

"Oh God. And here I am, pitching up and dumping myself on you. Is she angry?"

Davy grinned. "Are you joking? She's over the moon."

Rhona Stokes was making tea in the tiny kitchen. In her late forties, she was an older, female version of Davy with the same big dark eyes and shoulder-length dark brown hair. When she crossed the kitchen, Lucy saw that she walked with a slight limp.

"Hello, love, welcome. Crikey, Davy said you were a looker but he didn't tell me you were a supermodel." She beamed and kissed Lucy on both cheeks. "It's going to get the neighbors talking, having you here. They'll think our Davy's got himself a cracking girlfriend at last!"

Davy rolled his eyes. "*Mum.*"

"Oh, I'm only joking. Sorry, love." Turning back to Lucy, Rhona stage-whispered, "I know I'm an embarrassment."

"It's your house; you can be whatever you like. It's so kind of you to let me stay." Lucy gestured awkwardly at her pile of bags. "I'll be out of here as soon as possible, I promise, the moment I find another flat."

"No hurry at all. You're welcome to stay as long as you like. Here, drink your tea while it's hot and help yourself to biscuits. Then we'll

get you settled in your room. It's only weeny, I'm afraid—smaller than you're used to."

Lucy was overcome with gratitude. "I don't care about that. I'm just glad to be here, away from Pembroke Road."

"I'll carry your stuff upstairs," said Davy.

"It's the first time I've met one of Davy's university friends," Rhona confided when he'd gone. "He said you've always been kind to him."

Kind. "Well… why wouldn't I be?"

"Can I ask? Does he have many friends there? It's just, you know what boys are like," Rhona went on. "They keep quiet about things like that."

"I think he's fine." Lucy was diplomatic. "He always seems quite happy to me."

Rhona's dark eyes searched hers for clues. "Only I wondered if he ever gets teased, you know? For still living at home with his mum."

Lucy burned her mouth on the steaming tea. How was she supposed to answer a question like that without offending Rhona? She put down her mug. "Well, one or two people might have said something, but they're idiots. The rest of us just ignore them."

Well, what could she say? That Davy was a laughingstock?

"Oh, that's good news then." Relieved, Rhona picked up a Maryland cookie. "Not that Davy's ever said anything, but I did wonder."

"He's a nice person." Lucy meant it. How many books had he lent her over the past months? Not that she'd actually wanted to read them, but still. It was the thought that counted, and you couldn't ask for a more thoughtful person than Davy.

"He's the light of my life," Rhona said simply. "I do feel bad sometimes, keeping him here, but it's not as if I don't have a reason." For a moment she grew misty-eyed, then visibly gathered herself and gave Lucy's arm a pat. "Anyway, bless you for putting my mind at rest, love. I honestly don't know what I'd do if Davy moved out."

Chapter 34

"SHOULD HAVE THOUGHT OF this years ago," said Finn. "Inviting women to come up and see my kittens. Beats etchings any day."

"That's because etchings are boring," Ginny told him, "and kittens are unbelievably cute. The only problem is, the women are going to be so bowled over by them, they won't take a blind bit of notice of you."

Finn nodded gravely. "Story of my life."

"As if. I bet you've spent your whole life fighting them off."

Finn uncorked a bottle of wine and poured out two glasses. As he put one down next to her, he raised a playful eyebrow. "So does that mean you think I'm moderately attractive to the opposite sex?"

Luckily, Ginny had the distraction of a kitten on her lap. The kitten promptly obliged by letting out a minuscule stream of wee that missed the hem of her skirt by an inch. By the time she'd mopped up the dinky puddle and returned the perpetrator to Myrtle, the need to reply had passed. Instead she raised her wine glass and said brightly, "Here's to toilet training. Cheers."

"To toilet training." Finn paused. "Not the most glamorous toast I've ever heard."

"Sorry. I'm not in a glamorous mood." Ginny, who had spent the evening putting on a determinedly brave face, shook her head.

"Is it about Perry?"

"God, *no*."

"Jem then," Finn guessed.

She nodded. "Yes."

"You're missing her."

"Missing her and worrying about her. She's got herself involved with a boy I don't trust an inch." Ginny could recall this afternoon's breezy phone call from Jem practically word for word. Evidently, she and Rupert were a proper couple now; Lucy had moved out to give them some space, and everything was fantastic. When Ginny had said worriedly, "Lucy's gone? Won't you miss her?" Jem had laughed and said blithely, "Mum, why would I miss her when I've got Rupert? Everything's cool!"

Her laugh, Ginny hadn't been able to help noticing, had got a bit posher in the last fortnight.

"She's only eighteen. It probably won't last." Finn was doing his best to reassure her.

"Yes, but what if it does? They're living together." Ginny shuddered as she said it. "And he's not a nice person. Too much money, too little... heart. He thinks he's God's gift."

"Good-looking, then?"

"Very."

"Is that why you don't trust him?"

She nodded. "That and his personality."

"Then she'll see through him," said Finn. "Jem's not stupid. She's a bright girl."

"I didn't think I was stupid either," Ginny retorted, "and look at what happened to me."

"Well, that's over now. Ready for another one?"

For a split second she thought he meant another man. But no, he was only taking her empty glass. Crikey, two whole units of wine and she didn't even remember drinking them.

"It's just so hard, having to sit back and do nothing. I know I have to let her make her own mistakes but I'm her mother." Taking the refilled glass, Ginny said, "It's like standing by while a surgeon

operates on your daughter, knowing he's incompetent and doing it all wrong."

"Hey." Finn patted the empty space next to him on the sofa. "They're young. Give them a couple of weeks and it could all be over."

Ginny left the squirming kittens in the cat basket and joined him. The shirt he was wearing was her favorite, cobalt blue cotton and as soft as peach skin. Well, it looked as soft as peach skin; she hadn't actually touched it. Nor was she about to tell him it was her favorite.

"I hope you're right about that. She's smitten at the moment. He's whisking her up to a castle in Scotland this weekend. In a helicopter, for God's sake."

Drily, Finn said, "Sounds familiar."

"Oh bugger. Sorry." Too late, Ginny remembered how Tamsin had made her exit from Portsilver, whisked away by her wealthy Italian lover in a helicopter. She clutched Finn's arm. "I'm really sorry; I didn't mean to remind you."

Ha, the material of his shirt was as soft as peach skin.

He smiled slightly. "I hadn't actually forgotten."

"Wine's gone to my head. I was too wound up to eat earlier." Ginny patted her empty stomach by way of explanation. "Now I'll have to get a cab home."

"My fault for opening the bottle."

"Or mine for coming up to see your etchings. I mean kittens."

"Hey, you're here now. You've seen the kittens and the bottle's open. We may as well finish it."

It? Singular? Now that the alcohol was spreading nicely through her bloodstream, Ginny couldn't help feeling that one bottle between two people somehow wasn't quite... ooh, what was the word?

Oh yes. *Enough.*

Sensing her disappointment, Finn topped up her glass once

more and said good-humoredly, "Don't worry, there's another one in the fridge."

Myrtle and the kittens fell asleep. For the next forty minutes they drank wine, ate crisps, and discussed the restaurant. Evie had been chatted up earlier by an estate agent who had done his best to persuade her to give him her phone number.

"I don't know why she wouldn't." Finn frowned. "He seemed like a nice enough chap."

"Too nice." Ginny did her best to explain why Evie hadn't been remotely tempted. "Verging on oily. That man was a super-smooth operator. Yuck."

"He was handsome though, wasn't he?"

"Way too handsome. You wouldn't want to get involved with someone like that, not in a million years." Ginny dabbed at the crisp crumbs speckling her top and licked her fingers, then washed down the saltiness with more wine.

"I don't want to get involved with him," said Finn.

She gave him a nudge. "I meant no woman with an ounce of brain would want to. Good-looking men are nothing but trouble."

"First Rupert, now the guy from table six. They're good-looking so you automatically don't trust them." Finn paused. "Isn't that a bit prejudiced?"

"Absolutely. But it's also common sense. OK-looking men are OK, but really handsome men are a nightmare. Number-one rule: don't touch them with a barge pole."

"I see." Raking his fingers through his hair, Finn said thoughtfully, "Can I ask you a question?"

Ginny was in a generous mood. "Anything you like."

"Would you say I was good-looking?"

Yeesh, not *that* question.

"What?" She sat back, as if he'd asked her to calculate a tricky algebraic equation. Actually, an algebraic equation would have been easier.

"I'm interested. When I look in a mirror I just see me, the same me I've always been," said Finn. "Dark hair, straight not curly. Gray eyes. Scar on left temple from some kid at school hitting me with a discus. Nose got broken once playing rugby, but still in one piece. Jaw, generally in need of a shave. That's it, that's all I see." He gazed at Ginny. "But I have been told I'm a good-looking bloke. Quite a few times, to be honest. So I just wondered what your opinion was. Do you think I am?"

If he had the guts to ask, Ginny decided, then she had the guts to answer. Glad of the insulation provided by several glasses of wine she said, "OK, first things first, you really shouldn't have allowed your nose to go off and play rugby. And second, of course you're good-looking."

Finn tilted his head a fraction, still doubtful. "Really?"

Did he seriously have no idea? Ginny nodded and said, "Really." Then, because he clearly needed the reassurance, she added, "Very."

Finn studied his wine glass for a couple of seconds, but she began to suspect that he was struggling to keep a straight face. "So you're saying it doesn't matter how nice a person I might be or how much I might like you; you wouldn't be interested in me because of the way I look."

Oh, for heaven's sake, he'd been teasing all along. If she'd been sober, Ginny realized, she would be all of a fluster now. In fact, in a state of utter fluster.

But by a stroke of luck she wasn't, so she shrugged and said cheerfully, "Correct."

"That's discrimination."

"Don't feel too sorry for yourself. You don't do too badly. Plenty of women out there who wouldn't turn you down." Teasingly, Ginny added, "Flower girl for a start."

"But I'm not talking about other women. I'm talking about you. You're saying you wouldn't consider a relationship with someone like me, purely because of my external appearance."

Now Ginny was beginning to feel flustered but it was too late to back down. Anyway, he was only saying "someone like him." It wasn't as if he was actually referring to himself.

She didn't know whether to nod or shake her head. "Yes... I mean no... I mean, that's *right*."

"But that would be unfair. You'd be dismissing me without giving me a chance. So technically I could take you to court," Finn said idly. "I could sue you for unfair dismissal."

Decidedly hot now, Ginny took another glug of wine. "Fine. So sue me."

There was a glimmer of amusement in his eyes. "I'd rather try and persuade you to change your mind."

"That's bordering on smooth talk. If you carry on like that, you'll end up like Evie's estate agent."

"Sorry. Fate worse than death. So you're saying men like me are useless when it comes to long-term investments. We're only good for meaningless flings, have I got this right?"

"Pretty much." Ginny shrugged in agreement.

"And you were only saying last week how you wished you could have a meaningless fling."

OK, now there was no getting away from it. He was definitely suggesting what she thought he was suggesting. Her mouth drier than ever, Ginny said, "Was I?"

"Oh yes. You were." There was a note of playful challenge in his voice. "And I'm just saying, if you still feel the same way, I wouldn't object."

Yeek.

"That's very generous of you." Ginny paused. "But where would I find a good-looking man to have a meaningless fling with at this time of night?"

Finn laughed. Then he leaned toward her. "Close your eyes."

Yeeeeeek.

"Why?" As if she didn't know.

"Will you stop arguing and just do it?"

He wanted to. And he was gorgeous. What's more, she'd fantasized about this happening for months.

Casting all doubt aside, Ginny stopped arguing and just did it.

———

How could you regret an experience like that? God, how could anyone?

It was one o'clock in the morning when Ginny slid out of bed. The sex had been glorious, like losing her virginity all over again. Actually, that was a stupid comparison; tonight had been a million times better than her first time. But it was also, now, undeniably tinged with awkwardness because she had to keep reminding herself that she and Finn weren't in a relationship, that this *was* only a meaningless fling. So instead of the two of them lying in each other's arms, whispering and laughing together and, well, making plans to see each other again, she had to pretend to be a modern, no-strings kind of girl who'd had a great time but now needed to get home, put it behind her, and get on with her busy, single-girl life.

Like Carla.

Finn raised himself up on one elbow. "Going to the bathroom?"

In the darkness she could just make out the glitter of his eyes. If she could see him, did that mean he could see her? Hastily holding in her stomach and reaching for her shirt, Ginny said, "No. Home."

Just like Carla.

"Why?"

She was filled with sadness. "Because it's time to go."

"You don't have to," said Finn.

He was being polite, saying the gentlemanly thing. The last thing he wanted was for her to leap back into bed with a squeal of delight, crying, "OK then, I'll stay!" As far as men like Finn were concerned, girls who outstayed their welcome were the bane of their

lives. Their worst nightmare was finding themselves trapped with someone clingy and overkeen.

"Thanks, but I'd rather get home." Dressing at the speed of light, Ginny shot him a casual, unclingy smile. "We've had a nice time, haven't we? But now it's over. Time to leave. No need to get up," she added as he made a move to push aside the bedclothes. "I'll see myself out. And don't worry, I won't be sending you any flowers!"

Finn sounded taken aback. "Are you all right to drive?"

"Absolutely fine." She'd downed four glasses of wine earlier but that had been two hours ago. Now she'd never felt more sober in her life. Stepping into her shoes and hastily smoothing down her hair, Ginny bent and gave him a quick careless kiss on the cheek. "Thank you, that was fun. Bye."

After a pause, Finn said, "Bye."

And that was it. Easy.

If Carla could see her now, she'd be so proud.

Chapter 35

DAN THE VAN RATTLED into the courtyard in his mud-spattered green van at midday. Ginny, poking her head through the kitchen door, called out, "It's all right; he's here. I'll go and fetch them."

Dan had blotted his copybook this morning, forgetting the raspberries when he'd arrived earlier with the rest of the fruit and veg. As Ginny made her way out of the restaurant, he leaped out of the van looking harassed and burbling apologies. "I'm so sorry, I can't think how it happened, I could swear I ticked everything on the list, this has *never* happened to me before…"

"Dan, it's fine." Ginny attempted to calm him down; normally shy and retiring, Dan was the world's most conscientious delivery man. "You're here now and it's only twelve o'clock. Really, it doesn't matter a bit."

"I feel terrible though. You trusted me and I let you down. Do you think I should apologize to Finn?"

"There's no need; he doesn't even know about it. Hello, beautiful," cooed Ginny as Dan's dog whimpered a greeting from the passenger seat of the van. As sweet-natured and shy as Dan, Stiller was a lanky, tousled, slightly unhygienic mongrel with eyes like Pete Doherty and a curly tail.

"OK, if you're sure." Unloading the tray of raspberries and evidently still racked with guilt, Dan thrust them into her arms. "But if he finds out, please tell him I swear on my life it won't happen again."

"Don't worry, we know that." As Ginny took the tray, they both

heard a car coming up the driveway. "Sounds like our first customers arriving. I'll take these through to the kitchen."

"Don't forget to tell chef I'm sorry."

"Dan, stop apologizing, it really doesn't—"

"Hello? Excuse me? Where would I find Finn?"

Ginny turned to look at the owner of the voice, which sounded as if it had been dipped in golden syrup. Another of Finn's conquests or a business contact? Very pretty, certainly. In fact very pretty. The girl was tall and probably in her late twenties with glossy, almost waist-length brown hair and silver-gray eyes. She was wearing a black T-shirt and narrow white jeans with—

"Finn Penhaligon," the girl elaborated, clearly wondering if Ginny understood English. Pointing first to the antiques center then to the restaurant and enunciating slowly she said, "Is he here?"

Resisting the urge to enunciate back, Ginny said, "I think he's in the antiques center."

"Thank you." The girl opened the rear door of her black car and leaned into it, scooping out a baby in a scarlet sundress. She hoisted the baby onto her hip and began to make her way toward the honeysuckle-strewn entrance of the shop. Then, abruptly stopping, she thought for a moment before turning back to Ginny. "Actually, could you do me a favor? I'll wait out here and you take her in."

Ginny froze, because the baby had twisted around to look at her and there was no longer any question of who Finn's visitors were. "Sorry?"

"Take her in; tell Finn there's someone here to see him. Yes," Tamsin nodded, pleased with herself, "that's a much better plan."

"I can't do that."

"Of course you can. Don't worry, she won't cry. Just give the raspberries to him." Tamsin nodded at Dan the Van, who was so stunned he immediately took the raspberries from Ginny. "There,

you see? Not too difficult! And now you take Mae. This is important; I want Finn to see her before he sees me. There you are."

Ginny wanted to shout, "I can't do this; I slept with Finn last night!" But it was too late; Tamsin had already plonked Mae into her arms.

"I'll take the raspberries in." Dan the Van scurried off.

"And I'll stay here." Tamsin, her silvery eyes sparkling with anticipation, gave Ginny a gentle push in the direction of the shop. "Don't worry; he's going to love it. Off you go!"

But I'm not going to love it, Ginny thought. I slept with Finn last night. She shook her head and said, "I'm sorry, I really can't; it's not—"

"Oh, for heaven's sake, what is the big deal here? One little favor, that's all I'm asking!" Stepping away and raising her eyebrows in disbelief, Tamsin said, "What possible difference can it make to you?"

Inside the antiques center a dozen or so potential customers were browsing, the warm air was heavy with the scent of old, cared-for wood and beeswax polish, and "Unchained Melody" was playing on the jukebox. Ginny saw Finn standing with his back to her, chatting to a couple of Japanese tourists who had just bought a Georgian writing chest.

She waited for him to finish the conversation. Mae gazed around the Aladdin's cave with interest and spotted a life-size enameled parrot. Entranced by the bright colors she pointed and exclaimed, "Birdie!"

"I know," whispered Ginny, her heart hammering wildly. "Clever girl."

"BIRDIE!"

Finn smiled and turned to see who was making all the noise.

When he spotted Ginny his smile broadened but at the same time she could tell he was wondering what she was doing here. Then his gaze shifted and the expression on his face changed as he recognized the baby in her arms. The smile fell away, and in the split second that followed, Ginny glimpsed shock, anguish, and joy.

It was heartbreaking to imagine the pain he must have gone through.

"Birdiebirdie," babbled Mae, pointing at the ceiling and beaming over at Finn.

He excused himself from the Japanese couple and came over, his jaw taut. "What's going on?"

"Tamsin's outside. She asked me to do this. I didn't want to," said Ginny, "but she insisted. Here, I need to get back to the restaurant." Hastily, she handed Mae to him. Unperturbed by all the pass-the-parceling, Mae reached out with both hands and spread her fingers like tiny starfish against the sides of Finn's face. Maybe subconsciously she recognized him as having been a previous fixture in her life, because her smile was so dazzling, a lump rose in Ginny's throat.

"Bah!" cried Mae, her dark eyes luminous and her mouth opening wide to reveal pearly miniature teeth. "Kawawaaa," she babbled, happily kicking her legs against the front of Finn's white shirt. "*Birdie*."

For several seconds, oblivious to his surroundings, Finn stood there holding Mae in his arms. This was the baby he had witnessed being born and fallen in love with at first sight, the baby that had changed his world forever. For four months she had been his daughter and he would, without question, have died for her. Until the day in October last year when she had vanished from his life—had been summarily removed from it by Tamsin—and he had learned that she wasn't his daughter after all.

But love, as Finn had discovered to his cost, wasn't as fickle as a DNA test. His feelings for Mae hadn't dissipated. And although he had known, logically, that he'd probably never see the child who

wasn't his daughter again, it hadn't meant he'd stopped thinking about her or wondering what she looked like now or grieving for the loss of the child who had made his life complete.

Making his way out into the sunshine, Finn saw Tamsin waiting for him.

"What's this about?"

"Hello, Finn." Tamsin smiled, though there was a note of tension in her voice. "I thought you might like to see Mae again."

"Boobooboo," burbled Mae, delightedly waving her arms.

"And?" Finn said steadily.

"Boo*boo*booboo… boo*boo*."

"And?" Tears welled in Tamsin's silvery eyes. "Oh, Finn, I suppose I was kind of wondering if you might like to see me again too."

"I can't believe she's turned up!" Evie was agog, peering through the restaurant window, torn between indignation and glee. "The nerve of that girl. What do you suppose she's doing here? Damn, *why* did I never take up lip-reading?"

"Come away from the window." Ginny didn't have any idea what was going on either, but she knew she felt sick.

"I can't; it's not physically possible. Oh God, look at Mae, she's so gorgeous. I can't believe how much she's *grown*."

"Evie, they'll see you."

"Ha, you're joking. They wouldn't notice if we ran out there naked and did the Macarena."

Ginny flushed. Last night Finn had seen her naked. She'd seen him naked too.

"Tamsin's crying," Evie announced with relish. "She's wiping her eyes. Have we got any binoculars?"

"No, but we've got a table of eight arriving any minute, so maybe we should—"

"Damn, they're going!"

"Tamsin and the baby?" Unable to help herself, Ginny rushed up and hovered behind Evie, keen to see them getting back into the car. No such luck. When she peered over Evie's shoulder, she saw all three of them disappearing through the front door that led up to Finn's flat.

"Some people are so thoughtless." Evie heaved a sigh of frustration. "No consideration for others. Wouldn't you just love to know what's going on? I'm telling you, I'd give my right arm for a listening device."

———

"What's going on?" Finn looked at the girl he'd once loved, the beautiful girl he had planned on spending the rest of his life with. Unlike most people, Tamsin even managed to look beautiful when she was crying.

"Oh, Finn, you don't know how hard this has been for me. I made the biggest mistake of my life when I left you." Biting her lip, Tamsin said tremulously, "I've been such an idiot. Believe me, if I could turn back the clock, I would. I wish I'd never met Angelo."

"He's the father of your child. If you'd never met Angelo, you wouldn't have Mae."

"I know, I *know* that, but I'm trying to say I wish Mae was yours. I made one mistake." Tamsin held up a French-manicured index finger for emphasis. "One. You were away and along came Angelo. He made a fuss of me, flattered me, swept me off my feet. It was a moment of madness. I slept with him. He wanted me to dump you and become his girlfriend but I told him I couldn't because I loved you. And I thought that was the end of it. I said I couldn't see him again and I meant it, I truly meant it because you were the one I wanted to marry. So I *did* stop seeing him and yes, of course I felt guilty afterward, but it was just a one-off with Angelo and I learned

a valuable lesson. I told myself that as long as you didn't know about it, we'd be OK."

"And then you found out you were pregnant." Finn spoke without emotion.

"Yes." Fresh tears were now rolling down Tamsin's tanned cheeks. "But I convinced myself you were the father. I refused to even consider the possibility that it could be Angelo's. Because I just so desperately *wanted* it to be you."

Finn looked over at Mae, who had fallen asleep on the sofa. He could remember every moment of the night she'd been born. When their eyes had met for the first time, he had experienced a rush of emotion so overwhelming that he'd known life would never be the same from now on.

Well, that had been the truth.

"But it wasn't me."

"I know, I know. And you loved her so much." Tamsin wiped her eyes with the back of her hand. "I thought I could handle not knowing for sure, but once she was here I just couldn't. It was the guilt, I suppose. I couldn't bear the thought that I might be deceiving you. I just had to know the truth." She paused, swallowed. "That's when I had the test done. And then the results came through. Oh God, that was the worst day of my life. I'd so wanted it to be you. But I knew I had to tell Angelo. He had a right to know. I'm sorry, this is so difficult..."

"So you told him," Finn supplied. That day hadn't been great for him either. When Tamsin and Mae had disappeared, she had left him a letter but this was the first time he'd heard the explanation from her own mouth.

"I did. And he decided he wanted us to be together. He convinced me that I'd be doing the right thing and I was in such a state by then that I couldn't say no. Angelo's a forceful character; he organized everything and I just went along with it." Tamsin

shook her head. "I hardly knew what was happening. It was all a blur."

Finn looked at her. "And now?"

"Oh, Finn, I was wrong. So wrong. It's over between me and Angelo. The only person he cares about is himself." Shaking her head, Tamsin said wearily, "He liked the idea of having a daughter to show off, but you wouldn't catch him changing a nappy. Ask Angelo to look after Mae for an hour and you'd think I was telling him to chop off his own legs. We had a day nanny and a night nanny. Materially we had everything. But I knew I didn't love Angelo. And I don't think he really loves Mae."

"And now you've left him." Finn's tone was even. "You've brought Mae down here. But you still haven't told me why."

"You know why." By contrast Tamsin's voice was wobbling, her hand splayed across her chest as she struggled to breathe evenly. "Oh, Finn, you *know* why I'm here. I made the worst mistake in the world and I'm sorrier than I can ever say, but I never stopped loving you. And I know how much I must have hurt you, but we were happy together before, weren't we? You, me, and Mae were a proper family. So I suppose what I'm saying is, do you think there's any chance—for Mae's sake, if not mine—that you could ever forgive me and we could be happy again?"

Chapter 36

LUNCHTIME IN THE RESTAURANT had been an ordeal for Ginny, what with Evie's endless speculations and the nest of snakes squirming away in her stomach. Finally the last diners were dispatched, the dining room was in a state of readiness for this evening's influx, and Ginny was able to leave.

Finn emerged from his flat as she was about to unlock the car. At the sight of him heading toward her, the snakes went into frenzied wriggly overdrive. Ironically too, the shock of this new situation with Tamsin was far greater than when she'd found out about Carla and Perry, which just went to show how much less Perry had meant to her than she'd imagined at the time. Last night with Finn had been in a completely different league, Ginny realized. It wasn't helping either that she was still experiencing vivid flashbacks to last night when both of them had been naked and doing something considerably more intimate than the Macarena.

It was disconcerting to think Finn might be getting flashbacks too. Although to be fair he probably had more on his mind right now than yesterday's casual fling.

When he reached her, Ginny saw the signs of strain in his face. His hands were pushed into the pockets of his trousers and his shoulders were tense. Fixing a troubled gaze on her, he came straight to the point.

"Ginny, sorry about this but there's something we need to discuss. Obviously, Tamsin's turned up. Not what I was expecting,

but there it is. And there are issues to sort out." Finn paused, clearly hating every second of having to explain to her. "Now, last night was great, really it was, and I don't want you to feel... well, pushed aside or ignored, but now that Tamsin's here it's a bit of an awkward—"

"Look, it's fine." Ginny blurted the words out, unable to bear his discomfort for another second. He was being a gentleman again, doing his best to let her down gently, making sure she understood the situation. "You don't have to say anything. I completely understand. Crikey, there isn't even anything to apologize for! It's not as if we're in a relationship," she went on. "We're two adults who just happened to fancy a bit of, you know, fun. It was one night, it was what we both wanted at the time, but it didn't *mean* anything."

Finn looked slightly taken aback at the vehemence of her tone, startled but at the same time visibly relieved. "Right. Well, um, absolutely. So long as you're sure you're OK about it."

There was definitely a note of disbelief in there too. Oh God, did he think she might secretly be harboring strong feelings for him, laced with bunny-boiler tendencies? Keen to emphasize just how completely OK she was, Ginny vigorously shook her head and exclaimed, "Please, last night wasn't a big deal. In fact it was a very *small* deal! If you're hungry, you grab something to eat. Same with sex. But sleeping with someone doesn't have to mean anything. It doesn't automatically follow that you want to keep on seeing that person. Like last week I had a really great Chinese meal," she added. "King prawns, mushroom chop suey, and a spring roll. But it didn't make me think I had to sell my house, jump on the next plane, and go live in China."

Finn looked at her, possibly a bit stunned by the chop suey analogy. But Ginny felt she'd convinced him at last. He nodded and said awkwardly, "Of course not. Well, that's sorted then. Good, thanks for that. So we'll just... carry on as normal."

"Completely as normal. As if it never happened." Ginny nodded

firmly, because it was so clearly what he needed to hear. Then, unable
to contain herself a moment longer, she said, "But are you all right?
Am I allowed to ask what's going on? What are they doing here?"

Finn hesitated, finally shaking his head. "It's difficult to explain.
I can't really—"

"Oh God, she's coming out," Ginny yelped. Her heart leaping
with fresh guilt, she yanked open the car door. "I'll leave you to it."

But she was stopped by Tamsin hurrying over to them waving
one arm to attract Ginny's attention. "Hello," she called out, making
her way across the courtyard. "Don't rush off!"

But I *want* to rush off, thought Ginny, panicking that Tamsin
might somehow have discovered it was her who had spent time last
night in Finn's bed. Had she found a stray blond hair on the pillow
perhaps and carried out a quick DNA test? Or spotted a stray pair of
knickers and immediately deduced that there was only one woman
around here frumpy enough to wear sensible, black size tens from
a bulk pack? No, it couldn't be that; she'd definitely been wearing
pants when she'd left the flat.

"Can I ask you something?" Tamsin, who was surely a size four
La Perla thong girl herself, reached the car and touched Ginny's arm.

No!

"Yes." Cautiously, Ginny nodded, praying she wasn't about to
be asked if she could just give that DNA sample now.

"It's just that you were so good with Mae earlier, and Finn and
I *really* need some quality time together." Tamsin's smile was complicit, her tone confiding. "So I wondered if you'd be an angel and
babysit for a few hours this evening."

"Um…" Caught off guard, Ginny faltered. It was a terrible idea.

"We'll pay you, of course. Whatever the going rate is." Tamsin
gestured airily, signaling that she hadn't the least idea what the going
rate might be. "Sorry, I'm used to live-in staff; I'm going to have to
learn all this new stuff! But don't worry, Finn will sort you out."

Actually, he gave me a pretty good sorting out last night. Ginny wondered what would happen if she said this aloud. Instead she shook her head and said, "Sorry, I can't do it. I'm busy tonight."

"Really?" Tamsin looked shocked, as if Ginny had just turned down the offer of a week on Necker Island with George Clooney. "Are you sure? Isn't it something you could cancel?"

"No, it isn't." Ginny didn't have anything on this evening, but she was buggered if she was going to babysit.

"It doesn't matter," Finn cut in impatiently. "We don't need a babysitter. We're not going anywhere."

Tamsin said, "Oh, but—"

"Tamsin, just think about it. I haven't seen Mae for eight months." He shook his head firmly. "Why would I want to leave her here with someone else?"

Especially with *me*, thought Ginny.

Chapter 37

JEM DOODLED A SERIES of boxes in the margin of her legal pad to give the impression that she was working, although she hadn't taken a single note so far. It was Monday morning and the lecture theatre was stuffy and airless. The lecturer, droning on about Milton's *Paradise Lost*, could have been babbling in Swahili for all the difference it made. Right now nothing useful was permeating her brain.

Three rows in front of her, Davy and Lucy were sitting together, paying attention like model students, and industriously scribbling away. Passing her on the way into the hall, Lucy had flicked a dismissive glance in her direction before turning and whispering something in Davy's ear. Jem had pointedly ignored them; she might be here in Bristol, but she may as well be invisible. She told herself they were pathetic, acting like ten-year-olds, but the cold scrunched-up feeling in the pit of her stomach refused to go away. It wouldn't be so bad if Rupert could have been here with her, but he wasn't. Rupert was back at the flat, missing this morning's lecture in order to nurse his hangover and recover from what had, reportedly, been a truly epic weekend in Scotland.

Imagining the epic-ness of the weekend caused Jem's doodling pen to dig into the writing pad and tear the paper. In the end there hadn't been room in Olly's uncle's helicopter for two extra passengers. Rupert had gone on his own to Olly MacIntyre-Brown's party and Jem, who had spent practically the whole of last week casually mentioning to anyone who'd listen that they were flying up to

Scotland to stay in a castle, was forced to invent a debilitating attack of food poisoning as the reason she hadn't been able to go. This in turn had meant she couldn't leave the flat all weekend. Basically, she'd never watched so much television in her life.

The lecture ended and the day dragged on tediously. At four o'clock Jem arrived back at the flat. Letting herself in, she quietly pushed open the door to the bedroom in case Rupert, who could sleep for England, was still out for the count.

The bed was empty.

So was the rest of the flat. A flutter of disquiet made its way up through Jem's chest, although there was no need to feel anxious. Of course there wasn't. She took out her phone and rang Rupert's mobile, which went straight to the answering service.

Where was he? She needed a hug, needed—after a day of near ostracization—the comfort of his arms around her and the knowledge that someone was on her side. And being hugged by Rupert would more than make up for all the crap she was being put through by Davy and Lucy. Or, as Rupert had taken to calling them, Booty and the Beast.

Except he couldn't hug her because he wasn't bloody well *here*. Grimly ignoring the feelings of unease—Rupert hated being nagged about his whereabouts—Jem emptied her rucksack of textbooks and sat down on the sofa to get some work done. She had essays overdue, studying to tackle, end-of-year exams looming like thunderclouds. Right, think positive, use this time profitably. If Rupert didn't come home before six, it meant she had two hours in which to…

OK, she'd just make a coffee first. And have a toasted cheese sandwich because nobody could revise on an empty stomach.

In the kitchen, Jem tried Rupert's phone again. Still no joy.

She found a KitKat in the back of the fridge and ate it while the cheese sandwich toasted. Where was Rupert anyway?

Back in the living room, after flicking through a textbook, Jem

pushed it to one side and switched on the TV. After this quiz, then *Richard and Judy*, she'd get down to some work.

Definitely.

———

"It's a beautiful DAAAAAY." Rupert was back and he was singing, the bellowed words accompanied by Bono-style strutting and air-punching. Having burst into the bedroom and thrown himself onto the bed like an upturned beetle he played a set of imaginary drums and roared, "DAAA, DAAA, DA-DAAAAH, it's a beautiful DAYYYYYY."

Except it wasn't. It was midnight. Jem, who hadn't been asleep, was torn between indignation that he had put her through hours of stomach-churning anxiety and relief that he was home at last. Even if his crash landing on the bed had scored a direct hit on her left ankle.

"Where have you been?" She sat up and pushed her bangs out of her eyes.

"Out."

"Where?"

"Ah, the dreaded inquisition." Rupert rolled over and surveyed her with a playful grin. "Sweetheart, it was all completely innocent. I got up at three o'clock and I was hungry. There was no Parma ham in the fridge. So I went down to Chandos Deli to buy some, that's all it was. Then on the way back I happened to bump into Maz and he dragged me against my will into this wine bar. I didn't have any choice, I promise you. He *plied* me with drink."

"For nine hours?"

"No, no, *no*." Rupert gravely studied his watch. "Eight hours and eleven minutes, your honor. Not a second more than that."

"I didn't have any idea where you were," said Jem. "And your phone was switched off. You could have called and let me know."

"I could." He nodded in agreement, considering this point. "But then I thought, I'm nineteen years old and you're not my nanny. I'm

allowed out of the house on my own; I can even cross big roads if I'm careful and look both ways first. Plus, you said you had loads of studying, so I thought I'd be doing you a huge favor, keeping out of your way."

"You have loads of studying too," Jem pointed out.

"I know, I know. But it's so bloody boring. Now, have you stopped nagging me yet? Because I've got something to tell you."

He was winning her over, regarding her with amusement. Jem said, "What kind of something?"

"Two things actually. To make up for being a naughty boy and not phoning you, I'm going to take you to Byzantium tomorrow night. How about that?"

Byzantium was possibly the glitziest restaurant in Bristol, with magicians and belly dancers. Glowing and feeling loved—see? he was sorry—she hugged her knees. "What's the other thing?"

His eyes danced. "U2 are playing a concert in Rome this weekend. Maz has tickets."

Jem let out a squeal of delight. "You're joking!"

"I know, can you believe it? Talk about fate, bumping into him like that this afternoon. So we'll be flying out on Friday night."

Jem was beside herself, her mind in a whirl. "Oh my God, that is fantastic! I'm supposed to be working on Saturday, but I'll get someone to swap shifts; that won't be a—"

"Whoa, hang on, did I say it wrong?" Rupert held up his hands, forestalling her. "Maz has tickets for the concert. The two of us are flying out to Rome. The two of *us*," he explained. "Me and Maz."

Oh. Disappointed wasn't the word. Crushed was more like it. Or stupid, possibly.

"Sorry, sweetie, didn't mean to get your hopes up there." He patted her knee. "It's just, I knew you were working in the pub this weekend, which is why I thought I might as well go. Maz was supposed to be taking his girlfriend, but they broke up last week. When

he mentioned the spare ticket, I jumped at it. Chance of a lifetime. Hey, cheer up," said Rupert, playing imaginary drums on her thigh. "It's a beautiful daaaaayyyyy."

It wasn't; it had been a completely shitty one. Jem felt her bottom lip begin to lose control. Now she wouldn't be seeing Rupert this weekend either.

"Oh, look at you. Don't get upset." He abandoned the drumming and put his arms round her, patting her on the back like a baby. "I couldn't turn down an offer like that, could I?"

Jem shook her head; this was U2 they were talking about, after all. "No. I'm just going to miss you."

"But it's only for a couple of days." Pulling back the duvet, Rupert gave her hip a gentle prod. "See this?" Then he pointed to his own denim-clad hip. "And this? We're not joined. We don't have to spend every minute of every day in each other's company."

"I suppose not." Jem's voice was small. The thing was, when you loved someone, surely it was only normal to want to spend as much time together as possible? She couldn't help feeling that Rupert wasn't as emotionally involved in their relationship as she was.

"Hey, no need to get all girly about it. Don't cry," he warned as her eyes filled up. "We're off to Byzantium tomorrow, remember. Unless you don't want to go."

She forced back the tears.

"I do want to go."

"Good girl. Now give me a kiss." His mouth, warm and reeking of alcohol, came down on hers. Drunk or not, he still knew how to kiss. Finally, pulling back and flashing his naughtiest smile, he shifted on top of her. "Mmm, I'm starting to change my mind."

"About what?" Jem knew better than to hope that he might decide not to go to Rome after all.

Rupert began unfastening his jeans. "Sometimes there's nothing I like more than being joined at the hip."

Chapter 38

THE LAST TIME CARLA had seen Tess Whelan she had felt incredibly sorry for her. It had been four weeks ago and Tess, then nine months pregnant, was lumbering around her house like an exhausted elephant. As she'd made a pot of tea and flicked through the color brochures of conservatories, she had been massaging her aching back, complaining good-naturedly about not being able to paint her toenails, and giving Carla… well, far too much information, frankly, about practice contractions, piles, and the need to visit the loo roughly every twenty minutes because the baby's head was pressing down on her bladder.

What's more, Tess had been wearing a hideous T-shirt stretched over her grotesquely swollen belly and elastic-waisted trousers. She might have been pretty once but now she just looked knackered. Carla, feigning sympathy but inwardly repulsed, hadn't been able to get out of the house fast enough.

She hadn't been much looking forward to coming back again either. If Tess Whelan had been a wreck before giving birth, God only knew what she'd look like now with a wailing, puking baby in tow.

And if the house smelled of poo she was going to be in and out of there in ten minutes flat. Tops.

"Hi there! Lovely to see you again. Come on through."

Carla's jaw dropped open at the sight of Tess. Her blond hair was shining, her face glowed, and she was wearing size six jeans and a lacy pink cropped top.

"Good grief, what happened to your stomach?"

Tess grinned and patted her flat abdomen. "I know, isn't it great? Like a miracle. All thanks to breastfeeding, my health visitor tells me. And I'm eating like a horse but somehow everything just snapped back into place. Come on through and meet Alfie."

Carla was stunned. Tess's figure was fabulous, both front and back. The house didn't smell of poo either, which was a bonus. "So how's it going?" she asked as she followed Tess through to the living room.

"Fantastic. So much easier than I'd been expecting. You hear all these nightmare stories about having babies, don't you? But Alfie's so good, he's an absolute angel. I've never been happier." Tess paused then said, "To be honest, I was never the maternal type. Babies didn't interest me. But my husband was so keen I kind of felt obliged to go through with it. And now Alfie's here, I'd just die for him. I can't imagine life without him. He means the world to me, makes my life complete."

That's how I feel about Perry, Carla thought smugly.

"And here he is!" Tess's face lit up with love and pride as she presented her son for inspection.

Carla gazed down at the baby, awake but silent, lying on a squashy blue and white beanbag. Alfie was wearing a tiny white T-shirt and a nappy. His dark eyes were watchful, his hair grew tuftily on top of his head, giving it a pointed appearance, and his miniature fingers clenched and unclenched as he steadily returned Carla's stare.

Oh God.

Oh God...

"Are you all right?" said Tess anxiously.

"Fine," Carla croaked. "Fine." Then she said the four words she'd never said before in her life and had certainly never envisaged herself saying. "Um... can I hold him?"

It was extraordinary, an epiphany, beyond anything she'd ever experienced before. Tess bent down and picked up Alfie then tenderly kissed him before handing him over. Carla took him in her arms and felt as if... oh God, as if her life could at last become complete.

Not with Alfie obviously. He belonged to Tess. But with a baby of her own.

Hers and Perry's.

How could she ever have imagined she didn't want a child? Well, it clearly hadn't been the right time before now. And she hadn't met the right man.

Cradling Alfie, Carla bent her head and inhaled the blissful baby smell of him, an indescribable mixture of milk and warmth and newness. His skin was beyond soft, as soft and silky as the lining of a just-opened horse chestnut; she could happily have stroked it for hours. In truth Alfie wasn't the most beautiful baby in the world but when you looked at him and held him he made you think he was. When his tiny starfish hand closed around one of her own fingers, Carla wanted to explode with happiness.

This, *this* was what she wanted.

"Look at you." Tess nodded approvingly. "You're a natural."

"I've never held a baby before. Ever." There was a catch in Carla's voice. "Never wanted to."

"How old are you?"

"Thirty-six."

Tess smiled. "Tick tock."

"I didn't think I even had a biological clock," said Carla, blinking back tears of happiness. "I still can't believe this is happening to me. I feel as if I've just discovered the meaning of life."

And she didn't care if that sounded ridiculously sentimental. It was *true*.

—⁓—

"You what?" Perry started to laugh.

"I want a baby." It was like finding God, as pure and as simple as that. Carla had barely been able to concentrate earlier on closing the deal for the Whelans' new conservatory but somehow she'd managed it. Turning up at Perry's shop afterward, she had persuaded him to come for a walk with her along the beach.

"This is a joke, right?" He stopped and tilted his head to one side.

"It's not a joke."

"But you hate kids. You told me that. You said you'd never wanted children of your own."

"I know I did. But I was wrong." Carla couldn't contain her happiness, her certainty. "My body *told* me I didn't want them, because I hadn't met the right man. But now I have." She reached for Perry's hand, which had slipped out of hers. "And I want one more than anything, with you. Isn't it incredible? We'll be even *happier*… you won't have to miss out after all."

He looked genuinely flummoxed. "Miss out on what?"

"Having children! Oh, you were fantastic before, not saying anything." Carla shook her head, moved by his generosity. When she had explained—on that first momentous night, in fact—that she was anti-babies, Perry had accepted the news without an argument. It hadn't affected how he felt about her, thank God, although of course he must have been dismayed deep down. But that was a *coup de foudre* for you, Carla now realized. You took the rough with the smooth and it didn't make an iota of difference. If Perry had told her that if she wanted to be with him, she'd have to move to Iceland and live with him in an igloo, she would have accepted that too. Because so long as they were together, nothing else mattered, *nothing*—

"Hello? Earth to Carla? What makes you think I want children? Did I ever say I did?" Shaking his head in disbelief, Perry gazed at her as if… well, as if she'd just grown a pair of antlers. "I can't stand

bloody kids. I was delighted when you told me you didn't want any yourself. As far as I was concerned, it was the icing on the cake."

"But that was before today. I've changed my mind," Carla said urgently, "and so will you. Perry, this is so *right*. We love each other. It'll be perfect."

"I promise you, it won't."

Adrenaline was racing through her body. It was a blow, but she was a star saleswoman; she could win him around. Men often panicked at the prospect of fatherhood, but they succumbed in the end.

"If you hated the idea that much, you'd have had a vasectomy." Carla's tone was almost playful.

"Jesus. If there's one thing worse than babies, it's the thought of some quack advancing on my tackle with a scalpel." Grimly Perry shook his head. "I've heard enough horror stories to put me off that idea for life. Anyway, if you were so sure you didn't want kids, why didn't you get yourself sterilized years ago?"

Carla was triumphant. "Because *obviously* my brain was telling me that one day I might change my mind! And it was right!"

Perry's smile was long gone. He gazed past her, out to sea, his left hand rubbing his chin. Gazing hungrily at him, at the golden bristles on his jaw and the glossy red-gold of his hair, Carla envisaged the baby they would have. She would be able to change his mind; this was a deal she could definitely close. Men just needed a bit of gentle persuasion sometimes, that was all.

"When did this happen?" Perry spoke abruptly as seagulls wheeled overhead and waves slid up the beach.

"Today. This afternoon. I went to this house and saw—"

"So you've still got your IUD in."

Carla nodded, smiling slightly. Never one to hang around once her mind was made up, she'd already phoned her doctor and made an appointment for tomorrow morning to have it removed. She was thirty-six after all, with no time to lose. If she could have tugged it

out herself this afternoon she would have done, but the thought had made her toes tie themselves in knots.

"Hear that?" said Perry.

She listened to the sound of a baby wailing, turned, and saw an overweight, exhausted woman pushing a buggy along the hard wet sand.

"Look at the state of her. Do you want to be like that?"

"I wouldn't be." Carla was adamant.

"And that *noise*." Perry registered pain, because the baby was puce in the face, howling and kicking out like a maddened cat.

"Babies cry." Incredibly the sound of this one wasn't making her want to yank it out of the stroller and throw it into the sea. She wanted to rush over, pick it up, *comfort* it...

Actually, better not try that either. The mother weighed about three hundred pounds and looked as if she might pack a bit of a punch.

"Bloody hell, that's an ugly kid," Perry snorted.

"We wouldn't have an ugly one."

He looked at her, long and hard. Then he broke into a smile. "What are you trying to do to me?"

"Nothing horrible, I promise. Just show you how much I love you." Carla wound her arms round his waist, held him tightly. "It's the right thing to do, I promise you. You won't regret it."

Then Perry kissed her and she melted, almost feverish with longing for him. If the beach had been empty, she would have pulled him down onto the sand and ravished him there and then. But there were tourists all around, dogs bouncing in and out of the surf, teenagers playing football, and toddlers picking up shells.

"Shameless hussy," Perry murmured into her ear as she pressed herself against him.

"I can't help it." Carla's body was on fire, her breathing rapid. Prospective motherhood was turning out to be quite an aphrodisiac.

"Doesn't look like you can. I don't know; what am I going to do

with you?" Amused, he turned her toward the stone steps leading up off the beach. "If we don't want to be arrested, I think we'd better get back to the flat."

Chapter 39

"FINN, WHAT'S GOING ON?" Evie demanded when Finn appeared in the restaurant on Friday lunchtime.

"Me? I've spent the morning selling antiques."

"Don't give me that. You know what I'm talking about." Evie, who wasn't in awe of Finn, asked the questions no one else dared to ask. Ginny, polishing glasses behind the bar, watched the look of annoyance on his face.

"It's none of your business what's going on."

"But are you *crazy*? Tamsin messed up your life last year and now she's back. Does that mean you're going to let her do it all over again?"

It was early; none of the diners had arrived yet. Finn, clearly not in the sunniest of moods, squared up to Evie. "I don't have to explain myself to you. I'm an adult capable of making my own decisions."

"And trust me, you're making a bad one," she shot back.

"OK, just listen to me. When you had Philippa, how would you have felt if someone had come along when she was four months old and taken her away from you? Announced that you'd never see her again? Would you have handed your daughter over and forgotten her? Stopped loving her? Simply put her out of your mind because that was it, she was no longer a part of your life?"

Evie's eyes flashed. "No, but Mae isn't your child."

"I thought she was." Finn's voice was even. "She could have been mine. Plenty of men bring up other people's children and love them as much as if they were their own."

"So that's what you're going to do, is it? Never mind that Tamsin cheated on you and brazenly passed Mae off as yours, *then* buggered off with Mr. I'm-a-Billionaire without even telling you she was going. You've just forgiven her for that, have you? You're letting her get away with it scot-free? Well, how very *handy* for her!"

Ginny felt sick, but she couldn't stop listening, couldn't even escape to the safety of the kitchen because Finn was blocking her exit route. He was really pissed off now, a muscle going in his jaw as he gripped the bar. In fact now might not be the time to be thinking it, but he was actually looking incredibly sexy...

"Don't tell me how to live my life."

"Why not?" Evie retorted. "Someone has to try and knock some sense into you. And God knows everyone else can see that what you're doing is wrong." Gesturing toward Ginny, she said, "Can't we?"

Oh, for heaven's sake. Hastily Ginny said, "I don't want to get involved."

"But you *should.*" Evie was adamant, on a complete roll now. "We all work together! We're friends, aren't we? That's what friends are for. Bloody hell, if I said I was having an affair with a seventeen-year-old boy who'd asked me to marry him and wanted me to lend him a hundred grand to pay off his gambling debts, would you two stand back and let me do it?"

"Right now? Like a shot," said Finn.

"See? And now you're angry with me." Changing tack, Evie said, "But you shouldn't be, because we're only saying all this because we care about you."

Less of the *we*, Ginny thought in alarm.

"And I know you love Mae," Evie went on, "but I don't believe you still love Tamsin. And that's no basis for a relationship. OK, Tamsin's a beautiful girl. She's sexy, I appreciate that. But fancying a glass of milk doesn't mean you have to buy the cow. If it's sex

you're after, there are plenty of women around here who'd be only too happy to hop into your bed. I promise you, Finn, all you have to do is click your fingers and they'll be queuing up for a quick—*urk*."

"Oooh!" Appearing in the restaurant doorway with Mae in her arms, Tamsin surveyed them with amusement. "All of a sudden there's an awkward silence. Should my ears be burning?" Then, as her gaze settled on Ginny, her smile broadened. "Except if they were, they couldn't possibly be redder than your face."

Ginny wished she could sink down through the floor. It was the comment about not having to buy the cow that had done it. Finn, sensing her discomfort—or possibly feeling as if he were standing next to a furnace, on account of the heat emanating from her cheeks—said, "We were talking about work. Did you want something?"

"Just came to say good-bye."

This pronouncement caused Evie's eyebrows to shoot up into her hairline, and Ginny's hopes to rise in similar fashion. Tamsin, swaying over to Finn, said cheerfully, "We're off into Portsilver to buy Mae some new clothes and have a play on the beach. Back by three, OK?" She proffered Mae for a kiss. "Say bye-bye."

Beaming, Mae gave Finn a kiss on the cheek and said, "Ghaaaa."

Finn softened and stroked her silky dark hair. "Ghaaaa to you too. Have fun."

"Look at them." Clearly reveling in the sight of Finn and Mae together, Tamsin said with pride, "Look at her face. She's crazy about him!"

Ginny swallowed disappointment and thought, me too.

To make up for the hour she'd taken off to go to the doctor's office, Carla had been forced to work until eight. Now she click-clacked her way down Hudson Street and stopped outside Perry's front door. Ringing the doorbell, she experienced a thrill of anticipation. If last

night had been a night to remember, this evening was going to be even better.

And there were his footsteps on the stairs...

She was taken aback when the door opened to reveal Ally the dim Goth who worked in the shop.

"Hi, Perry's expecting me."

Ally blinked at her through a curtain of dyed-black hair. "Yeah, he said you might drop round. Come on up then."

It wasn't until they reached the living room that Carla realized there was definitely something not quite right going on here. For a start, there were disgusting incense candles smoldering in holders on the window sill. And there was a small mountain of assorted shopping bags stuffed with God knows what piled up on the sofa.

More to the point, there was no sign of Perry.

"Where is he?"

"Hmm? Oh, gone away." Peering round the room, Ally said vaguely, "Hang on, it's around here somewhere."

"Gone *away*?" Carla's stomach did an incredulous swallow dive. "Where?"

"No idea, he didn't say. Just told me he needed a break and put me in charge of the shop. Bloody long hours, but he said I could move in here while he's gone, so that makes up for it. Living with my mum's been doing my head in, you know?" Ally pulled a face, inviting sympathy, her blue lipsticked mouth turning down at the corners. "So I was well up for moving in here instead. Ah, here it is." She found the envelope she'd been searching for amid a pile of clutter on the coffee table and handed it to Carla.

How could Perry have gone away? In the space of... what? Eleven hours? He'd been fine when she'd left here this morning. Carla ripped open the envelope, turning away from Ally and her curious magenta-lined eyes in order to read the note.

Carla,

I loved you but you've scared me. I don't want kids now and I never will. I'm going away for a while to think things through. Don't bother trying to phone me—I won't pick up. I thought you were my ideal woman but now it's all spoiled. Your spare clothes are in the bedroom—take them with you when you leave.

Sorry, not much good at this. In future I'd better stick to women who've had hysterectomies!

Best, Perry.

Carla crumpled the letter in her fist and squeezed until her knuckles clicked. Best, Perry. *Best, Perry.* Yesterday he'd loved her but now it was over, in the past, switched off like a tap.

"Everything all right?" Ally tipped the contents of one of the bags—a lurid tangle of socks and knickers—onto the floor.

"Fine. Couldn't be better." Carla shoved the scrunched-up note into her bag and wondered if there was an extra-sharp knife in the kitchen drawer. Half of her wanted to slash her wrists but the other half—actually by far the bigger half—wanted to slash Perry's.

And maybe slice off another treasured appendage while she was about it.

If only she knew where he was.

Fury was uppermost but tears were threatening—which only made Carla more furious. Swallowing hard, she headed through to the bedroom and snatched up the pathetic pile of belongings he'd left for her to collect. One shirt, a spare pair of shoes, makeup remover pads, and a toothbrush. She stuffed them into her shoulder bag before checking quickly through Perry's wardrobe and chest of drawers. He'd taken most of his clothes. Bastard.

"Off now? See ya!" sang Ally when she returned to the living room.

"Right." Carla nodded, feeling like a city employee sacked

without warning and ordered to vacate the building. Jerkily, she said, "See ya."

—⁓—

Midnight and the pain had well and truly kicked in. In both senses of the word. The removal of the IUD had left Carla with griping cramps, requiring extra-strong painkillers, a hot water bottle pressed to her stomach, and a stiff Scotch. But it was nothing compared with the awful, aching emptiness in her heart. She'd lost Perry Kennedy, the love of her life. She had no one to blame but herself. And she couldn't do anything about it, because unbearable though it was to imagine a future without him, she still wanted a baby. More than anything. It was like a compulsion, a force of nature that refused to be denied.

And come hell or high water, she would have one. Just not with the man she'd chosen to do it with.

Oh God, why did it have to hurt so much?

Carla's head jerked up at the sound of a car pulling into the road and slowing to a halt. Her heart lolloping like a landed fish, she flung aside the hot water bottle and leaped—ooch—out of bed. Maybe it was Perry, come to his senses, turning up to smother her in kisses and beg her forgiveness.

Well, if this were a film it might have been Perry doing just that. Except it wasn't. Lurking like a spy behind the protection of the drawn curtains, Carla peeped through the gap and saw that it was Ginny, back from her shift at Penhaligon's. Dry-eyed, too hollow with misery even to cry, Carla watched as she climbed out of the car. Disappointment mingled with regret, because if anyone could comfort her now it would be Ginny. Her best friend. Ex-best friend. The best friend whose man she had stolen.

She shrank back from the curtains as her ex-best friend swung around and looked up, almost as if sensing her presence. For a

split second Carla longed to throw open the window and call out to her, to shout out that she was sorry and beg her to come over. Ironically, no one would understand how she felt better than Ginny. And she would console her, know just what to say to make her feel less wretched.

Except she knew she couldn't and it was too late anyway, Ginny had already disappeared into her house. The front door slammed behind her and the kitchen light came on. As Carla watched, she saw Ginny and Laurel chatting and laughing together in the kitchen. Who would have thought that Laurel could laugh? But she was doing it now.

I'm on my own, thought Carla, turning away and clutching her stomach as it was gripped by another spasm of pain. And it's all my own fault. Ginny's got a new best friend now.

Chapter 40

"Seven pints of Blackthorn, four white wines, and five Bacardi Breezers." Having shoved his way through the crowd to the bar, Spider-Man added in a friendly fashion, "You all right?"

Jem looked up. Oh yes, she was just tickety-boo. The beer pumps were playing up tonight and best bitter was splattered across the front of her white shirt. It was also dripping from her elbows, a sensation she hated. But Spider-Man was the first member of the costume party crew to say anything remotely friendly to her tonight, so she forced herself to smile.

"Great, thanks. Dry white?"

Spider-Man, aka Darren, grinned and said triumphantly, "I'd prefer wet."

Hilarious. When it came to razor-sharp ripostes, Darren was no Jonathan Ross. Then again, at least he'd been invited to Alex and Karen's party tonight, which was more than she had been. Jem got on with the business in hand, flipping the tops off the Breezers. All week she'd been hearing people chatting excitedly between lectures and tutorials about Alex and Karen's costume party, deciding what they were going to wear. Everyone was going apart from her and Rupert, who had announced that he'd rather sieve his intestines through a colander.

Jem began pouring the Blackthorn into pint glasses, the familiar sense of abandonment nestling in her stomach. Earlier this evening Rupert had made love to her and she'd felt wonderful, special, the

luckiest girl in Bristol. Then afterward, he had showered and changed and driven up to Cheltenham for the bachelor party of an old school friend's brother, absently kissing her good-bye and telling her he'd be back sometime tomorrow.

Déjà vu. First Scotland, then Rome, and now this.

Which left her, yet again, feeling like Macaulay Culkin in *Home Alone*. Except the way things were going, she'd welcome a couple of burglars into the flat with open arms. At least they'd be company.

There was a burst of laughter from the crowd a short distance from the bar. Involuntarily glancing up from the cider pump, Jem saw Davy and Lucy dressed as a pair of New York gangsters in sharp suits and fedoras. Once upon a time Davy had been the ignored one, the geeky outsider. Now, unbelievably, Lucy had moved in with him and was busy dragging him by the scruff of his neck out of his shell. They were living with Davy's mother—how sad was that?—yet, weirdly, appeared to be having a good time. Davy was beginning to be more generally accepted; somehow he was no longer regarded as the nerd on the sidelines. Lucy's friendship had imbued him with cool. Jem had to admit he looked good tonight; gangster-style suited him. And it went without saying that it suited Lucy, who looked spectacular whatever she wore.

Neither of them had so much as glanced in her direction. She might as well be invisible for all the attention anyone else was paying her. Ugh, and now cider was dripping onto her jeans.

"Last orders," bellowed the landlord, clanging the bell at ten to eleven.

Jem finished lining up the wines, the ciders, and the Breezers. She totaled the bill and took Spider-Man's credit card, ready to slot it into the machine.

"So you'll be finishing soon," Darren said bouncily, his mask pushed up to his forehead and his manner jovial.

"As soon as everyone's gone."

"Are you coming along to the party, then?"

Was it Jem's imagination or did the pub suddenly go a few decibels quieter? Either Clint Eastwood had just walked in, or Spider-Man had said the Wrong Thing.

She shook her head. "Um, no."

Darren, not the brightest spark in the firework box, was oblivious to his faux pas. "Why not?"

Because nobody wants me there. Everyone hates me, haven't you noticed? Jem didn't say this out loud. She hurriedly pushed the credit card reader across the bar and said, "I'm fine. Just put your PIN in, please."

"But that's daft if you're not doing anything else! Hey, Alex." Darren turned and grabbed Alex by the shoulder. "I've just been telling Jem, she should come along to the party, yeah?"

Jem felt hot and sick. Alex was looking embarrassed now while the rest of them were nudging each other and smirking, loving every minute.

"Er... the thing is, it's a costume party," Alex mumbled.

"And I have to get home," Jem blurted out, hideously aware of Davy and Lucy watching from a safe distance as the scene was played out for their entertainment. "But... um, thanks anyway."

Thanks for not inviting me to your party, Alex, and thanks to you too, Darren, for so efficiently drawing this fact to the attention of everyone in this pub.

It'd probably be front page news in tomorrow's *Evening Post*.

Ceris Morgan, whom Jem had never much liked and who she knew for a fact fancied Rupert, was dressed as a French maid. Unable to resist joining in, she adjusted her saucily low-cut top and said in a singsong voice, "We wouldn't be rich enough. Jem isn't interested in parties thrown by boring old *ordinary* people anymore. She's got Rupert."

Witch. Jem was sorely tempted to retort that Ceris too might

stand a chance with someone like Rupert if only she didn't have fat ankles and a silly, horsy face.

She'd have done it too if it wouldn't have meant being sacked on the spot.

—⁓—

"Six pints of Blackthorn, four glasses of white wine, three Bloody Marys, and two Bacardi Breezers," said Alex, flushed with triumph at having made it back to the pub. "Oh, and fifteen packets of cheese and onion crisps."

It was Sunday lunchtime, and the bedraggled survivors of last night's party, still in costume, were all set to carry on. By the sound of things it had been a resounding success. Jem, who hadn't heard from Rupert, silently bent down and began pulling packets of crisps from the box under the counter. At least Davy and Lucy weren't here, which would only have made things more stressful.

Sadly, Ceris was.

"Alex, I don't want cheese and onion! Get me ready salted." Her voice was louder than anyone else's and ear-splittingly shrill.

"Did you hear that?" said Alex, peering over the bar. Jem murmured, "I think the whole of Clifton heard it."

"And I don't want white wine on its own. God, my brain, I'm just soooo dehydrated." Clutching her head for dramatic effect Ceris shrieked, "Make mine a spritzer."

Jem straightened back up.

"Ooh, what a night. You missed out big-time." Ceris lit a Silk Cut and blew smoke through her horsy nostrils across the bar. "You really should have come along to the... oops, I forgot! You weren't invited!"

Flushing, Alex the peacemaker said hastily, "It's not that Jem wasn't invited. She just didn't have anything to wear."

"Oh, I don't know." Ceris smirked. "She could have come as a two-faced bitch; that wouldn't have needed any dressing up."

Sploooooosh went the fountain of soda water as Jem's finger squeezed the trigger on the mixer gun. Heavens, how had that happened?

"Aaaarrrgh!" Ceris let out a screech as piercing as nails down a blackboard, her maid's uniform instantly drenched. Now that she'd started, Jem discovered she didn't want to stop. Ceris was a spiteful bully who reveled in belittling others and deserved to be taken down a peg or two. And how better to do it than with a drenching? Feeling empowered and better already, Jem carried on aiming the gun at Ceris until every inch of her was dripping with bubbly, ice-cold soda water. An unexpected but welcome bonus was realizing that other people were stifling laughter, acknowledging that this was no more than Ceris deserved.

Jem smiled because last night she had heroically resisted the urge to insult her and now she was glad she had. This was way more fun.

"Stop it, STOP IT," screamed Ceris, mascara sliding down her face as she struggled to dodge out of reach.

"No." Jem was enjoying herself; this was better than the water-shooting gallery at the fair.

"Will someone stop her? She's gone mad! It's *cold…*"

"And you have fat ankles." For good measure Jem added cheerily, "And a face like a horse."

Oh well, if a job was worth losing, it was worth losing well.

"Put the gun down." The pub landlord's big hands closed over Jem's, prying her away from her new favorite toy.

"You complete bitch!" Spitting with rage and shaking soda water out of her hair, Ceris bellowed, "My dad's a lawyer; he's going to sue you!"

"No, he isn't." The landlord fixed Ceris with a look of weary distaste. "You're loud and you're drunk." Then he turned to Jem. "And you're fired."

At least she wasn't being ignored anymore; the whole pub was, by this time, agog.

"Great," said Jem, wiping her wet hands on a bar towel. "I've always wanted to go out with a splash."

—⁓—

Who cared anyway? There were a million other pubs in Bristol. Although she was beginning to wonder if she wanted to do bar work anymore, what with the way it messed up her social life. As Jem trudged back to the flat, it occurred to her that she could always take out another loan and just enjoy herself instead. Then she and Rupert would be able to see more of each other and he wouldn't go away so much. Wasn't that a better idea? Loads of people did it and didn't waste time worrying about being in debt. You just paid off what you owed at some stage in the distant future when it was more convenient. When you thought about it, a bigger loan made so much more sense.

Turning into Pembroke Road, Jem's heart leaped at the sight of Rupert's car parked outside the flat. Oh thank God, he was back. Her pace quickened. Rupert would roar with laughter when she told him what had happened and he'd tell her she'd done exactly the right thing. Best of all he would put his arms around her and make her feel loved, which after the last couple of days was exactly what she needed. To be cosseted and told she wasn't the worst person in the world.

She hadn't even told him yet about being called into her tutor's office on Friday afternoon, the shame had been too great. Except there was no need to be ashamed in front of Rupert—he'd find that funny too.

Jem ran up the steps, fitted her key into the lock, and pushed open the front door.

"Rupert!" Too bad if he was sleeping; she'd wake him up. Right now she needed him too badly to care.

But he wasn't asleep; she could hear the shower running in the bathroom. Just the thought of Rupert naked, lathering his tanned body with shower gel, produced a fizz of adrenaline and brought a smile to Jem's face. She kicked off one boot and stealthily tested the door handle in case Rupert had changed the habit of a lifetime and locked it. No, he hadn't. She levered off the second boot and peeled off her less than alluring purple socks. She'd never had sex in a shower before.

But Rupert had.

It seemed, in fact, he was doing it right now.

Jem froze on the threshold of the overheated bathroom as she saw too many arms and legs through the misted-up frosted glass of the shower cubicle. Intermixed with the roar of the water, she now heard groans and murmured words uttered by a female. Next, even worse, came Rupert's voice going, "Oh yes... oh yes..."

Oh no. Please no. Don't let this be real.

But they were getting louder now and body parts—a tanned buttock here, a splayed hand there—were pressing up against the glass. Before anything more conclusive could happen—having to witness that would truly be the ultimate insult—Jem raced over to the sink and turned the hot tap on full blast.

It did the trick, like hurling a bucket of water over a couple of fighting dogs. Now she knew the true meaning of "cooling their ardor."

"Fuck it," yelled Rupert as the water in the shower ran from steaming hot to stone cold in two seconds flat. "*Fucking* plumbing."

"*Waaaah*," screeched a female voice, frantically scrabbling to slide open the shower door. "Turn it off, turn it off!"

Jem grabbed the navy towels hung over the brass rail and bundled them into her arms. Moving back to the door she whipped out the key in the lock on the bathroom side and waited for Rupert and his companion to emerge from the cubicle.

"WAAAAAHHH." Having stumbled out and seen Jem standing there in the doorway, Caro let out an ear-splitting scream and stepped back, cannoning clumsily into Rupert.

Caro.

"Oh, for fuck's sake." Rupert looked over at Jem and exhaled. "You're supposed to be at work."

"Sorry to spoil your afternoon." The words were spilling out of Jem's mouth automatically. "I thought I'd come home early and surprise you. And guess what? I did." She turned to Caro. "Did Rupert tell you we're together now?"

"No." Exotic Caro smiled slightly. "He just said he'd been shagging you."

Caro had always had an intimidating, supercilious air about her. When you thought about it, so did Rupert.

"OK," said Jem.

"Look, I'm sorry." Moving toward her, Rupert held out a hand for the towels.

Jem took another step back. This was turning into quite some afternoon. "Actually, I don't think you are. But never mind." Her tone conversational, she added, "You will be."

Still clutching the collection of towels, she slammed the door shut and used the key to lock it.

From inside the bathroom, Rupert shouted, "Jem, don't be stupid."

"I'm not." Wiggling the key between her thumb and forefinger, Jem thought for a moment then said, "I've *been* stupid, but I'm over that now."

Was her plan too harsh? No, of course it wasn't.

Ten minutes later she banged on the bathroom door and sang out, "Right, I'm off. The key's in the kitchen bin. Don't you two catch cold now. Bye!"

Chapter 41

"Jem?" When Ginny opened the front door at ten o'clock that night she thought she was hallucinating.

"Oh, Mum." Jem's face was white, stained with tears, a picture of grief as she stumbled into Ginny's arms.

"Sweetheart, what's going on? What's happened?" Over the top of her daughter's blond head Ginny saw a taxi at the gate and a barrel-chested taxi driver coming up the path.

"OK, love?" The taxi driver had a kind face. "There you go, you're safe home now." He looked apologetically at Ginny. "She was crying when I picked her up from the station. Hasn't got any money on her. It's fourteen pounds fifty."

Nodding, numb with fear, Ginny somehow managed to disentangle herself and fetch her purse from the kitchen. Twenty pounds later she closed the front door and held Jem again while she shuddered and wept.

Please don't let her be pregnant.

"Is it Rupert?" she said gently some time later when Jem had reached the messy, sniffing, over-the-worst-of-it phase.

"Y-yes." Jem nodded, then miserably shook her head. "W-well, no. He's only part of it."

"OK, sweetheart, you're here now. Don't you worry. Whatever it is, we'll sort it out."

Jem wiped her eyes on the sleeve of her sweatshirt. "No need. I've already sorted it out."

Had she murdered him? "What do you mean?"

"It's all over. I'm not going back. Not ever."

Something about the flat tone of Jem's voice caused the hairs on the back of Ginny's neck to prickle in alarm. Had she really murdered Rupert?

"Jem, you have to tell me what happened." Would she turn in her own daughter? Call the police? Or would she protect her, lie for her, whisk her off to Argentina for a life on the run from the authorities?

Yes, Ginny knew this was what she'd do. Nobody deserved to go to prison for murdering Rupert.

"Oh, Mum, it's all been so horrible. Rupert's been seeing someone else. I caught him with her today. It's Caro, his old girlfriend. You met her that time you called in."

"I remember." Ginny hadn't liked Caro either. "What did you do?"

Jem told her. When it became apparent that she hadn't left the two of them dead, Ginny hugged her harder than ever. "Oh, darling, you'll get over him in no time. Everything's going to be fine. How will he get out of the bathroom?"

"Through the window, I suppose. He'll have to climb down the drainpipe naked and ring someone else's doorbell to be let back in." She paused and wiped her nose. "Shame not to catch it on a camcorder."

Even the feeblest of jokes was surely a good sign. Ginny stroked Jem's hair and handed her a clean tissue. "You just wait; when you get back, everyone'll be on your side. All your friends will rally round and—oh Jem, don't cry; when they hear what you did, they'll love you for it."

"They won't, they won't." Sobbing again, Jem rocked with misery against her.

"They will!"

"They won't because I'm not going back. Because I don't have any f-friends, Mum. Everyone hates me… they *do*…"

"Oh, now that's not true! What about Lucy?"

"Hates me." The words were muffled by Ginny's mauve lambs-wool cardigan. "She was seeing Rupert as well. When he chose me, she moved out."

Oh Lord. So much she hadn't known, so much Jem had been keeping from her. Determined not to give up, Ginny said, "Well, there's Davy."

"Ha, he hates me too. And he's best friends with Lucy now. That's where she moved to when she left the flat." Pulling her messy face away from Ginny's shoulder, Jem said, "I don't have anywhere to live anymore. I lost my job in the pub today. And on Friday my course tutor called me into his office and gave me this big long lecture on how disappointed he is with me because I've been falling behind with my work. He thinks I'm going to fail my exams. And he's right, I am going to fail them, so what's the point of taking them? I was so worried about it yesterday," Jem raced on, "I didn't know what to do, but now that everything else has happened I don't have to worry anymore. Because I've made up my mind: I'm not going back. There's no point, because I hate it there. I just don't want to be in Bristol anymore."

"Sweetheart, you can't—"

"Mum, I *can*." Nodding vigorously, Jem clutched Ginny's arms. "I gave university a try and it didn't work out. So that's it. I've decided. I'm going to do what makes me happy instead."

Backpacking across Australia? Lap dancing in Thailand? Faintly Ginny said, "Which is?"

"I'm going to get a job." Jem's grip tightened around her elbows, her eyes shining as she managed a watery smile. "Right here in Portsilver. And I'm going to move back in with you."

———

"Excuse me? I don't want to be a nuisance." The elderly female customer on table four tentatively touched Ginny's arm as she passed. "But, um, do you think I could have my credit card back?"

Oh God.

"What are you looking for?" Finn found her two minutes later, rifling through a pile of menus and the sheaf of credit card slips.

"Mrs. Black's credit card." Feverishly, Ginny began rummaging through the contents of the wastepaper basket. "She gave it to me and now it's gone. I've lost it."

"First rule of stealing credit cards," Finn observed. "Try not to let the rightful owner see who stole it."

"What did I *do* with the damn thing?" In desperation Ginny peered into the bowl of white roses on the bar.

"Panic over." Having opened the till, Finn held up the missing Visa card. "In with the tenners."

Ginny fanned herself vigorously. "Sorry, brain's gone AWOL."

"I'd already noticed."

Damn, so he'd spotted her earlier, trying to serve dessert to the party at table eleven waiting for their starters.

"They didn't mind." Defensively, she said, "They laughed about it."

"I know they did. It's not a criticism. I'm just saying you're a bit distracted."

"A lot distracted."

"Anything you want to talk about?"

"Yes please." Ginny nodded, grateful for the offer. Her brain was in such a muddle she badly needed an impartial opinion from someone she could trust.

"Look, it's ten past two. Can you hang in there until three? What's so funny?" said Finn.

"Whenever anyone tells me to hang in there, I feel like an orangutan dangling from a branch."

He gestured around the busy restaurant. "Well, try not to dangle from any branches in here. When everyone's gone we'll have a proper chat, OK?"

"I don't know what to do," Ginny concluded an hour later. They were sitting at one of the tables by the window, drinking espressos. She had told Finn everything. "I'm torn. I was so devastated when Jem left home… in one way this is a dream come true. I can't think of anything nicer than having her home with me again. But I want what's best for Jem and I'm not sure that's it. Bloody Rupert Derris-Beck," she said angrily. "Up until this thing happened with him she was loving university. And I don't want to force her to go back, but I don't want her to feel like a failure either. What if she leaves and regrets it for the rest of her life?"

Finn, having paused for a moment, resumed stirring sugar into his coffee. "She can take a degree when she's eighty-five. There's no age limit."

"I know, I know there isn't. But she'd like to do it now, if only everything else hadn't gone wrong. She's always been so happy and popular. Losing her friends has knocked her for six and she just feels so alone. It breaks my heart, it really does." Through the window Ginny saw Tamsin emerge from the flat with Mae on her hip.

"OK, this is only my opinion but Jem's almost finished her first year. Exams are coming up and it seems a shame not to take them," said Finn. "Then at least she's got the whole of the summer break to decide what to do."

Ginny experienced a rush of gratitude; he was being so kind. "That's what I think too."

"If she fails the exams, she can always resit them." Glancing across the courtyard as Tamsin and Mae disappeared inside the antiques center, Finn continued, "But you never know, she might still pass first time. And after that, it's up to her. She can find another flat to share, make new friends, carry on with the course. Or stay down here with you. Or she might decide to try something completely

different, take some time out and go traveling. Like Dan did." He pointed through the window at the green-painted van trundling over the gravel. "He spent two years going round the world after finishing his PhD. Said it was an unforgettable experience. You could ask him to have a chat with Jem."

"Dan has a PhD? In what?"

"Astrophysics."

Blimey. Ginny watched as Dan, lugging crates of fruit and veg out of the back of the van, loped off in the direction of the kitchen. She'd never known that about him. And he'd ended up as a delivery driver, so what did that tell you about astrophysics?

"Did you go to university?"

Amused, Finn shook his head. "Too busy working for a firm of auctioneers, learning about antiques before setting up my own business."

Ginny sighed. And he'd ended up doing all right for himself. "I still don't know what to do about Jem."

"What does her dad say?"

Tuh, Ginny had phoned Gavin this morning and he'd been no use either. "That it's up to Jem."

"Cheer up. Everything'll sort itself out." Finn's gaze softened, distracting her for a couple of seconds with the kind of thoughts she didn't allow herself to think anymore. "Give her a few days to work things through."

"That's the other thing Gavin said. I just wish—"

"Aaaarrrrgh!" The ear-splitting scream jolted both of them; in a split second Finn was out of his seat. Through the window Ginny saw Tamsin racing across the gravel in her tiny skirt and spindly high heels, to where Mae was sitting behind Dan's van being cautiously investigated by Stiller.

"Get away from her, you BEAST," Tamsin yelled as Stiller interestedly sniffed Mae's face. Swooping down like a bony eagle, she scooped Mae up into her arms. Stiller, disappointed at having

lost his new playmate, waggled his tail and licked hopefully at Mae's dangling feet.

"UGH! NO! *Filthy* animal! Are you out of your *mind*?" Tamsin roared at Reg as he rounded the corner of the restaurant. "Letting a dog run loose to attack an innocent *baby*?"

Poor Dan turned white with horror, searching for signs of blood.

Finn was out of the door now with Ginny inches behind him. "OK, calm down, nobody's been attacked."

"But they could have been," screeched Tamsin, long hair swinging as she inspected Mae for signs of injury. "That monster could have done anything!"

Gibbering with terror, Dan stammered, "I'm s-sorry, I didn't know, oh God I'm so sorry, I had no *idea*..."

"Dan, it's all right." Finn took control of the situation, gesturing with his palms down that Dan wasn't to get upset. "What I want to know is how Mae came to be on her own out here." He looked at Tamsin, who immediately tightened her grip on Mae and went on the defensive.

"Oh, so this is my fault, is it? I put my daughter down for two seconds because she didn't want to be carried. All I did was say hi to Tom and ask how things were going. The next moment I looked down and Mae had crawled out of the shop. In two *seconds*," Tamsin declared vehemently, holding her thumb and forefinger half an inch apart for added emphasis. "You know how fast she can scoot along when she wants to."

"I do," Finn nodded. "But not fast enough to get away if a car had driven into the courtyard."

Tamsin's voice grew shriller still. "I was listening out for cars! My God, do you think I want my baby to be run over? If I'd heard an engine, I'd have been there. But to let a dog loose is just... irresponsible."

Poor Stiller, alarmed by all the shouting, had by this time backed away and pressed himself against Dan's corduroy trouser legs.

Blissfully unaware of the kerfuffle she had caused, Mae clapped her hands together and burbled, "Dogga-dogga-bleuwwwww."

"OK, let's calm down." Finn was clearly keen to avoid a slanging match. "Mae's fine, nothing happened."

"Nothing *happened*? God, she reeks! Smell her," Tamsin ordered. "That bloody dog slobbered all over my baby—and it's not even a pedigree!"

Dan and Stiller were by now both quivering with shame. Rushing to their defense Ginny said, "Tamsin, Stiller's the sweetest, gentlest dog you could ever meet. I promise you, he wouldn't hurt anyone. Mae would never come to any harm with him." Her tone was placating, meant to make Tamsin feel better, but Tamsin was by this time beyond reassurance.

"No harm? Are you serious? A stinking filthy dog crawling with germs licks my daughter's face and you think that's *safe*?" Her eyes wide, she said hysterically, "My God, and I thought you were a competent mother! If that's how you feel I won't be asking you to babysit again."

Excellent, thought Ginny, because I wouldn't do it anyway.

And by the way, Finn deserves *so* much better than you.

Chapter 42

THE EXCITEMENT AMONG THE crowd was palpable, fans buzzing with growing anticipation as the hands of the clock moved toward seven thirty. It wasn't often that a genuine A-list Hollywood celebrity came to Bristol to sign copies of their autobiography, but Marcus McBride was on his way. Now forty, he had been a true star for almost twenty years, something of a hell-raiser early on in his career but talented and dedicated enough to get away with it. Not to mention in possession of buckets of sex appeal. With his dark, unconventional looks, undoubted intelligence, and quirky sense of humor, women all over the world had fallen for Marcus McBride's charms and many millions more had swooned over him from a distance. The opportunity to buy his just-published book, have it signed by Marcus himself, and actually get to shake his hand had been just too good to pass up.

"Look, I bet that's him!" Lucy pointed up at the gray sky and hundreds of pairs of eyes followed the direction of her arm as the faint winking lights of a helicopter appeared in the distance.

"And it's starting to rain." Davy pulled a face as a raindrop splashed into his left eye. "You know, we could always forge his signature, pretend we met him, and just go for a drink instead."

But he said it good-naturedly, knowing it wasn't an option. Lucy was looking forward to seeing Marcus McBride. And his mother would have his guts for garters.

"Poor Rhona, missing out on all this." Lucy was still watching as the helicopter grew larger. "She'd have loved it."

Davy smiled, because his mum had never made any secret of her crush on Marcus McBride. When she'd heard he was coming down to do a book-signing in Bristol, she had been beside herself with excitement.

It was just a shame she wasn't able to come down to the shopping center herself.

The helicopter landed somewhere behind the complex and everyone in the hundreds-long queue began mentally preparing themselves. Lucy checked her camera for the umpteenth time. "I'll take loads of photos," she had told Rhona, "of Marcus and Davy together when he signs the book."

"Bless you." Rhona had smiled, touched by her thoughtfulness.

"Your collar's crooked," Lucy told Davy now, busily straightening it. "There, that's better."

"I'm sure it'll make all the difference. Along with this." Davy ruefully ruffled his new haircut, still unused to it. Lucy had dragged him along to a trendy salon in Cotham, standing behind him like a prison warden until she was completely satisfied with the short, spiky cut the stylist had teased out of his previously long, straggly, determinedly unstylish hair.

"Stop moaning, it looks great."

"It cost a fortune." Six whole hours of cleaning, to be precise, which was crazy when he had a perfectly good pair of scissors at home.

"Get a move on," the man behind them murmured impatiently. "The queue's moving."

It was, but with several hundred people ahead of them, Davy wasn't holding his breath. Marcus McBride hadn't even made his entrance into the bookshop yet.

"Look at him, that's the kind of man I could go for." Now they'd shuffled along a bit further, Lucy was able to drool over a huge promotional poster of Marcus in the shop window. "You can't

call him handsome, can you? But he's better than that, more edgy and interesting than just handsome. And those eyes. I wonder what he'd do if I kissed him?"

"Nothing," said Davy. "It's only a poster."

"*You.*" Lucy dug him in the ribs. "I'm going to miss you when I leave." Tilting her head to one side she said, "Remember when you had that big crush on me? Whatever happened to that?"

"I don't know. Just kind of evaporated."

"And now you don't fancy me anymore. At *all.*" She pulled a tragic face. "It's not very flattering, you know."

"Sorry." Davy grinned. "Don't take it personally."

"But you were besotted with me."

He shrugged, equally bemused. "I used to play my Darkness CD all the time too. I thought it was the best album ever. Then after a couple of months I didn't play it quite so often. And now I don't bother listening to it at all. The magic just… wore off."

"If you're saying I sound like Justin Hawkins, I'll give you a Chinese burn."

"You don't sound like him." Straight-faced, Davy said, "Mind you, looks-wise…"

They had a bit of a tussle outside the bookshop, won by Lucy as usual. Davy was glad his inconvenient crush on her had subsided of its own accord, to be replaced by an easy camaraderie. Because he was no longer hopelessly tongue-tied in her presence, they were able to banter together like… well, best friends.

He inhaled a blast of the peppermint chewing gum being noisily chewed by the man behind them. Lucy had picked up a sheaf of details from a flat-letting agency on the way home this afternoon. He would miss her too.

Aloud Davy said, "You don't have to go."

She slipped an arm through his, gave it a grateful squeeze. "I know I don't have to. But I should. Your mum's fantastic and I love

her to bits, but I can't stay on forever. The whole point of leaving home and being a student is so you can live like a student and do studenty things."

"Making a mess, having all your friends round, getting drunk, sleeping with people your parents wouldn't approve of," said Davy.

"Arguing about who finished the milk and put the empty carton back in the fridge."

"Sorry, I forgot that one."

"Wondering where the terrible smell's coming from, then finally discovering an open tin of tuna under the living room sofa."

"That old classic." Davy shook his head sympathetically. "I can see why you miss it so much."

"There are good bits too. Like borrowing your flat mate's clothes," Lucy pointed out. "And sharing each other's makeup."

"That wouldn't really work if he was a rugby player."

They fell silent for a couple of seconds, both thinking.

"I wonder what's happened to Jem?" Lucy spoke at last. "No one's seen her all week."

Davy knew how hurt Lucy had been when the whole Jem and Rupert thing had come out, with Jem choosing to stay with Rupert rather than siding with her best friend. The two girls hadn't spoken since.

"Maybe she's ill." But they'd both heard about the mixer-gun incident and Jem's instant dismissal from the pub. "I could give her a quick ring," he suggested. "Check she's all right."

But Lucy was already shaking her head. "Don't bother. She's got Rupert to look after her." Pressing her lips together she said, "Anyway, let's not talk about them. Let's talk about whether this damn queue is ever going to move…"

At that moment, almost as if she had caused it to happen, a whoop of excitement went up inside the shop, indicating that Marcus McBride had made his entrance. Flashbulbs went off like

fireworks, people were jumping up and down to get a better view and a round of applause broke out.

"Wow." Lucy was impressed. "I've never met a real film star before."

"You're not going to meet him now," Davy pointed out. "This isn't a cocktail party. You're not going to end up snogging in the stockroom. He's got hundreds of books to sign and one hour to do it in. While he's signing ours, you'll have about two seconds to take the photo."

"You really know how to squash a girl's fantasies," said Lucy.

Over the course of the next thirty minutes the queue edged forward, into the back of the store at last. Shop assistants demonstrated how to hold open their already-bought copies of Marcus McBride's autobiography at the title page, ready for his pen to make its illegible squiggle. As they neared the front of the queue and the desk at which he was sitting, they saw him for the first time. Flanked by burly minders and uniformed security staff with high-tech earpieces, Marcus was squiggling away and flashing his famous smile with production-line regularity. Anyone who'd hoped to stand and chat for a minute or two was firmly moved along. Nothing was allowed to interrupt the flow.

More minty fumes indicated the arrival of a fresh piece of chewing gum in the mouth of the man behind them, ensuring he had nice breath for his fleeting encounter with Hollywood royalty. When the queue advanced a couple of feet further and Davy was slow to catch up, the man prodded him in the back and said irritably, "Look, if you're not interested, don't bother."

Lucy raised an eyebrow and Davy flushed, trying to pretend he hadn't heard. This was when he felt his confidence deserting him, when strangers said something uncalled for and a braver person would stand up for themselves without giving it a second thought. Davy had always been embarrassed by the rudeness of others and had never known how to react; consequently he never did react, which

was utterly pathetic. Had Lucy expected him to come out with some quick retort, some cutting comment that would have put the man behind them in his place?

Of course she had. Davy swallowed, ashamed of himself, and pretended to be engrossed in a shelf of Fiction for Teenagers. That was just the way he was, the way he'd always been, and there was nothing he could do to change it. Even if it did mean Lucy thought he was a complete wimp.

Almost there now. Marcus McBride was wearing a tight pink T-shirt, black jeans, and blue cowboy boots, because he'd reached the level of film stardom that meant you could throw on whatever you liked and not be laughed at. Which must be nice, Davy thought with feeling, as the overweight woman in front of him readied herself for her turn. Patting her permed hair and glancing over her shoulder at Lucy, she whispered longingly, "Ooh, isn't he gorgeous? If I was thirty years younger!"

"Got it open to the right page? Right, off you go," ordered the strict sergeant major type in charge at the head of the queue. The woman tottered up to the desk, said breathlessly, "You're my favorite actor!" and held out her book.

Smile, squiggle, smile, all over.

"Next," barked the sergeant major as Lucy readied herself to take the all-important photo.

"Hurry *up*," the man behind Davy hissed, blasting him with mint.

Davy moved forward, held out his book, and self-consciously half turned so that the camera wouldn't just get a shot of his back. He felt rather than saw the signature being scrawled on the title page of the book he was still holding and, glancing behind Lucy, noted that the man behind her was fidgeting in an agitated fashion with something in his trouser pocket. God, how embarrassing, he hoped the man wasn't doing what he appeared to be doing; then again, some people could get inappropriately carried away in the heat of the—

Flash went Lucy's camera, temporarily blinding Davy. He hoped he hadn't had a gormless expression on his face. The sergeant-major type made vigorous move-on gestures, indicating that their time was up. In the split second that followed, Davy glimpsed another flash, of metal this time. Blinking, he realized that Mint Man had pulled a knife from his pocket and was now gripping it tightly in his right hand, keeping it hidden from view beneath his jacket. Ever hopeful Lucy, flashing a dazzling smile at Marcus McBride, was making her way past the desk, and the sergeant major was making increasingly urgent sweeping movements with his arms. It was Mint Man's turn next.

"No!" yelled Davy, realizing that no one else had spotted the knife.

Mint Man shot him a look of wild-eyed fury and launched himself at the desk. Davy, who had always loathed rugby at school, flung himself at Mint Man and tackled him to the ground. God, it hurt. All the air was punched from his lungs, and Mint Man was now roaring like an enraged bull elephant. Dazedly realizing how right he'd been to hate rugby, Davy became aware that he was now being crushed beneath a scrum of bouncers and security guards. Next moment he felt himself being hauled to his feet and discovered that his legs had gone wobbly. He could hear screams of panic all around him, interspersed with barked orders from security and loud staccato cursing from Mint Man.

Someone yelled, "Oh God, he's been stabbed," and Davy stumbled toward Lucy, feeling sick at the thought that the knife had gone into the madman on the ground. Then he saw the look of terror in Lucy's eyes and heard her gasp, "Oh, Davy! Oh my God, *someone call an ambulance…*"

Chapter 43

"HE'S BEEN ARRESTED AND taken down to the police station. Long psychiatric history, it turns out." The sergeant-major type, who was actually Marcus McBride's PR manager, brought Davy and Lucy up to date in one of the offices behind the shop. "Apparently, Princess Margaret told him to do it."

"That woman, she's nothing but trouble. This was my best shirt." Davy stuck his finger through the slash in the heavily blood-stained blue-and-green-striped cotton and looked mournful.

"I'm sure we can come to some arrangement."

Lucy's tone was despairing. "You got it from Oxfam."

"So? It's still my best shirt."

"There." The doctor finished applying the last of the skin sutures and peeled off his surgical gloves. "You'll live."

"I'll call it my dueling scar." Davy inspected the cleaned-up knife wound inflicted by Mint Man's panicky response to being brought down. At twenty centimeters long it had bled profusely and looked spectacular but was actually far less painful than it appeared, which he didn't mind at all. If it had been a stabbing injury rather than a shallow slice across his chest, on the other hand... well, the thought of it was enough to make him feel a bit queasy.

As if to emphasize this point, the sergeant major said, "That was a brave thing you did, son. Incredibly brave and unbelievably stupid."

Davy agreed with the unbelievably stupid bit. He didn't even feel as if he'd been brave back there on the shop floor, simply because

he had acted without stopping to think first. If he had thought about it, he would certainly never have tackled a lunatic wielding a knife.

The door to the office opened then and Marcus McBride walked in, exuding charisma.

"Hey, kid. You did good." He shook Davy's hand and this time his smile was genuine. "You're a hero."

Embarrassed, Davy said, "I'm not really the heroic type."

Outside, they had to have their picture taken by a clamor of photographers. Davy, wearing his bloodstained shirt, stood awkwardly while Marcus McBride rested his arm across his shoulders. Still in a daze, Davy told the waiting journalists his name. They wanted to see the wound across his chest. When they asked him how he felt, he said, "Like a Page Three girl," and everyone laughed.

Five minutes later the press was dispatched. Marcus said, "Seriously, you did great. I don't know how to thank you. I'd offer you a signed copy of my book, but…"

"We've already got one." Lucy held up the shopping bag containing the copy Davy had flung aside before tackling Mint Man to the ground. Luckily it didn't have blood on it.

"We'll sort something out." The sergeant major consulted his watch. "Now, is your car here or do you need transport home?"

"We caught the bus," said Davy.

"No problem. I'll organize a car." Taking out his mobile phone, the sergeant major began rattling out orders. Marcus's helicopter was evidently waiting on standby to whisk him up to a TV appearance in Manchester. A car was summoned to take Davy and Lucy back to Henbury.

An idea had come into Davy's mind; he plucked up the courage to voice it. "Actually," Davy looked at Marcus, "you know you said you didn't know how to thank me?"

"Yes."

"Well, my mum would love to meet you. She couldn't be here tonight but she's only ten minutes away."

"Sorry, son." Having concluded his call, the sergeant major said firmly, "Can't do anything now, we're behind schedule as it is. Some other time, OK?"

Deflated, Davy said, "Oh. OK."

—⁓—

Rhona finished the washing up and took a cup of tea through to the living room. She switched on the TV and semi-watched a program about a woman so addicted to shopping for new clothes that she was on the verge of being declared bankrupt.

At least that was something that she was never going to suffer from. Even observing the woman on TV as she rushed through Marks and Spencer grabbing armfuls of dresses off the rails made Rhona feel jittery and nervous.

Oh well, never mind about that. It was a shame she hadn't been able to go down to the shopping center this evening but she couldn't help the way she was. Maybe in time the panicky sensations would subside of their own accord. And at least Davy and Lucy were down there getting a book signed for her, so she wasn't completely missing out...

When the doorbell rang some time later, Rhona padded out to the hall. She opened the front door and looked at Marcus McBride.

For several seconds she carried on looking at him, as if he were a crossword clue she couldn't quite work out. Because it couldn't *really* be Marcus McBride.

"Rhona?"

"Yes." How incredible, she could still speak. Well, just about.

"Hi, I'm Marcus." The visitor on the doorstep took her hand and gravely shook it.

"How... how, how... I mean, how...?"

"Davy happened to mention that you'd like to meet me. And I said great, because I wanted to meet you too."

Rhona wondered if she had fallen asleep in front of the TV and was in fact having a dream. Then again, her dreams had never been as good as this. Unsticking her tongue from the roof of her mouth, she said, "Davy?"

"Your son?" Marcus broke into a smile. "That's why I'm here. I want to tell you, he did a very brave thing tonight. I'm very grateful to him."

"*My* son did a brave thing?" Rhona closed her eyes for a moment; when she opened them again Marcus McBride was still there, waiting on her doorstep and looking incredibly *real*. Forgetting that she wasn't wearing any shoes, she said, "Um… where is Davy?"

"Over there in the car. With Lucy. Look, I can't stay long; my PR guy's giving me a hard time. But when Davy said you'd like a visit, how could I refuse? He's fine, by the way."

"Fine? What d'you mean, fine? Why wouldn't he be fine?"

And, surreally, Marcus McBride explained what had happened at the book signing. Rhona's stomach clenched with horror and disbelief and she ran barefoot down the path to the waiting car. Wrenching open the rear door she shouted, "Davy, how *could* you? You might have been killed! Oh my God, look at your *shirt*…"

Lucy used up the rest of the film in her camera taking photos of Rhona and Marcus McBride. Finally Marcus gave Rhona a kiss on the cheek then laughed at the expression on Lucy's face and kissed her as well.

"Now I really have to go. Thanks again." He shook Davy's hand and said, "You take care of yourself."

"Bye," said Davy.

The car pulled away. Still barefoot, Rhona clapped her hand to

her chest and said, "I don't know, I can't let you out of my sight for two minutes."

Davy rolled his eyes. "Mum, there's no need to fuss. *I'm OK.*"

Chapter 44

"OH!" EXPECTING THE POSTMAN and getting Finn instead came as something of a shock. Probably for Finn too, thought Ginny, clutching the front edges of her dressing gown together and praying her hair wasn't too scarily bed-heady.

Come to think of it, postmen had to be a hardy breed, trained not to flinch visibly at harrowing early-morning sights.

"Sorry. I was on my way into Portsilver and I wondered if you'd seen today's paper."

"It's eight o'clock. I haven't seen the kettle yet. Why, what's in there?" Ginny reached out for the newspaper he was holding but Finn hesitated.

"Your daughter's friends in Bristol, Lucy and Davy. What's Davy's surname?"

Ginny searched her brain. "Um... Stokes."

Finn looked relieved. "It is the right one then. I thought it must be." He handed over the folded newspaper and added, "Bit of excitement up in Bristol. I thought it might give Jem the excuse she needs to ring her friends."

The doorbell had evidently woken Jem too. Appearing on the stairs behind Ginny, she said evenly, "I haven't got any friends in Bristol."

"No? Oh well then"—Finn retrieved the paper once more—"you won't be interested in seeing this."

Jem looked truculent. "What's my mum been telling you?"

"That you've given up on university."

She nodded at the newspaper. "What's Davy done?"

"If he's not your friend, why would you care?"

"Oh, for heaven's sake, give it to me!" Bursting with curiosity, Ginny snatched the folded paper. "I want to know!"

Finn said with amusement, "Don't show Jem."

Ginny's jaw dropped as she found the piece on page seven. "Oh, good grief."

"OK, OK," grumbled Jem, peering over her shoulder. "I want to know too."

Finn left them to it. Together Jem and Ginny devoured the article.

"Thank goodness he's all right," said Ginny. "He could have been killed."

"Mm." Jem carefully stirred sugar into her tea.

"Sweetheart, Finn's right. You should give Davy a ring."

"I can't." Clearly emotional, Jem failed to control her wobbling lower lip. "There's no point."

"There's every point. You can congratulate him!"

"I might not get the chance," Jem said miserably. "He'd probably just put the phone down."

It was no good; Ginny did her best to reassure her, but Jem was adamant, convinced that any attempt at contact with Davy or Lucy would be met with a snub.

"Can we change the subject, Mum? I don't want to talk about it anymore."

Her unhappiness was so apparent, Ginny thought her own heart would break.

Twenty-six hours later and Ginny's forehead was taut with concentration. Famous for her feeble sense of direction, she was now testing it to the limit. It had been seven months since she'd last made the journey

up the M5 to Bristol and that time she hadn't needed to pay attention
to the first bit of the return journey because Davy had been sitting next
to her in the passenger seat instructing her when to turn left and right.

Now she was on her own, attempting to retrace the route
through Henbury on memory alone and it wasn't an easy task.
Had they turned right at the Old Crow pub or gone straight over
the roundabout? When they'd reached the junction past the petrol
station, had they turned left? Oh God, this was hopeless; at this rate,
come midnight, she'd still be driving around in circles.

It took a while—OK, another forty minutes of being lost—but
finally Ginny turned into a street she dimly recognized. This was
it, she was sure. And the one thing she did remember was the tidy,
pocket-sized front garden and the royal-blue front door. Trundling
along in second gear like a curb crawler, she passed brown doors, red
doors, white doors, green doors…

Ooh, there it was.

At last.

Would Davy even be in?

If he was, would he close the door in her face?

And would Jem ever speak to her again when she found out
what she'd done?

Oh well, Finn had given her the day off work and she'd driven
all the way up to Bristol for a reason. It would be silly to turn around
and go home now.

The front door was opened by an anxious-looking woman who
clearly didn't welcome the interruption. Glancing at her watch, then
up at Ginny, she said distractedly, "Yes?"

"Hi. Is Davy here?"

"Sorry, he's out. Are you another journalist?"

Ginny took a deep breath. "No, I'm Jem Holland's mum."

"Oh, thank goodness! Come on in, Davy's about to be on
the radio."

Not thank goodness she was Jem's mum, Ginny realized as Davy's mother bundled her into the house, but thank goodness she didn't have to miss hearing her son being interviewed.

And who would blame her? She'd have done exactly the same. Together they sat in the kitchen and listened in silence to the old-fashioned wireless on the kitchen table. After fifteen minutes it was all over.

"Phew, sorry about that. I'm Rhona," said Davy's mother. "Davy's never been on the radio before." Overcome with emotion she wiped the corners of her eyes with a tissue. "Was that presenter having a bit of a dig, d'you think?"

Ginny knew at once what she meant. To begin with, it had all been about what a hero Davy was, but toward the end of the interview the presenter had said slyly, "And I gather you still live at home with your mother, which seems extraordinary to me. Does that not set you apart from your fellow students?"

Davy, of course, had roundly denied it, but the interviewer had been unconvinced. "You have to admit, though, it's an unusual situation. Most young people starting university can't wait to grasp their independence. Did your mother not want you to move out, did she put pressure on you to stay, or was it your own decision? Are you a bit of a mummy's boy at heart?"

Now, with the radio turned off, Ginny wondered what she was supposed to say. She shrugged. "Honestly? Yes, I suppose he was having a dig. But who cares what he thinks? If Davy wants to stay at home, that's his choice."

Rhona nodded slowly, lost in thought. Then she looked over at her. "It was you who gave Davy a lift home once from Clifton, wasn't it? He told me you live in Cornwall. So you're up here visiting your daughter?"

"No. Jem's at home in Cornwall. She's broken up with her horrible boyfriend."

"Rupert." Rhona's lip curled. "I've heard all about him."

"Jem's eighteen. She made a big mistake. And now she's paying the price," said Ginny. "She wants to give up university, come back home, and live with me."

"How wonderful. But you don't seem that thrilled. Don't you want her back?"

Rhona clearly didn't understand. Ginny exhaled and twisted the bracelet on her wrist. "Of course I do, more than anything. But I want what's right for Jem, not what's right for me."

"Oh God," said Rhona. "You're so brave."

Ginny shrugged. "I don't feel it."

They sat together in silence for a while. Finally Rhona announced, "I had a brain hemorrhage you know, four years ago. In British Home Stores."

"You did?" Ginny was startled. "I didn't know that."

"No? Well, I don't suppose you would. Davy doesn't feel it's anyone else's business why he chooses to stay at home. But that's the reason, even though I was one of the lucky ones. Made a good recovery." Rhona tapped her left leg. "Apart from a bit of a limp. But it frightened the living daylights out of me, I can tell you. I've been terrified of it happening again and not having anyone around to help me. I get panicky in shops too, which isn't ideal. That's why Davy and Lucy were the ones queuing up to see Marcus McBride. Because I couldn't face it myself."

"I'm not surprised," exclaimed Ginny. "Oh, please," she added as Rhona's eyes filled with tears. "You mustn't blame yourself for what happened to Davy."

"I don't." Rhona fished up her sleeve for a tissue. "Well, I do, but it's not that. I love having Davy at home with me, but it's not fair on him, is it? I'm not an invalid, after all. And he's a young lad with his own life to live."

Ginny nodded in agreement. "He is."

"I can't do it yet." Rhona swallowed. "But I'll do it soon. I know it's nearly time to let him go."

"It doesn't mean he's going to stop loving you," said Ginny.

Rhona managed a watery smile. "He'd better not."

Davy arrived home fifteen minutes later. Rhona, greeting him at the door, hugged him hard and exclaimed, "You were brilliant on the radio. I was so proud! It sounded just like you!"

Then she murmured something Ginny couldn't make out and sent him ahead into the kitchen where she was waiting for him.

"Hello, Davy."

"Hello, Mrs. Holland."

Mrs. Holland. So polite. Ginny said, "You're looking… smart."

He rubbed a hand self-consciously over his head. "Lucy made me have my hair cut."

"It suits you."

"Thanks." He paused. "Is Jem all right?"

Would Jem ever forgive her for being an interfering mother?

"No." Ginny shook her head, a lump springing into her throat. "No, Davy, she's not."

———

"Any good?" said Davy.

"Disaster." Lucy flung down her pink jacket and a couple of shopping bags. Having replied to an advert in the *Evening Post* for a fun-loving fourth person to share a large flat in Redland, she was just back from visiting it. "In fact, nightmare. The flat was a health hazard, the room they're letting is the size of a dog kennel, and the whole place smelled of socks. Two hairy physics students and a beard-and-sandals geography teacher." She pulled a face. "Oh, and no music allowed in the flat because music distracts them from their studies."

Privately relieved, Davy said, "Are they sure they want someone fun-loving?"

"Are you kidding? They think they're hilarious! They have an imaginary pet cat. And they play tricks on each other by putting joke plastic cat poo in their bowls of All Bran. I tell you, my sides nearly split. Anyway, get that T-shirt off."

Davy's eyebrows went up. "Are you after my body?"

"I've bought you two new shirts." Lucy reached for the bags. "Come on, try them on."

"In a minute. We've got a visitor." Leading her into the kitchen, Davy pointed through the open window to where his mother and Ginny were sitting out in the sunny back garden.

"Who's that?" Lucy frowned, puzzled. "Is it…?"

"Jem's mum." He took the shopping bags from her, wincing as he saw that one of the shirts was an eyeball-searing shade of lime green. "She wants to talk to you."

It was five o'clock on Saturday afternoon and Jem was alone in the house, having spent the day with her father. Poor Dad, he'd done his best to cheer her up and probably thought he'd succeeded, but lovely though it was to see him again, she'd been glad to get back to the sanctuary of her old bedroom, released from the pressure of smiling and pretending to be fine.

Mum was still working at the restaurant, Laurel had gone shopping in Newquay, and it was a relief to be on her own, although watching *Moulin Rouge* on DVD probably hadn't been the best idea she'd ever had. Sprawled on the bed with a tin of Laurel's home-made biscuits, Jem's eyes brimmed at the thought of poor, gorgeous Ewan MacGregor and the heartbreak in store for him when Nicole Kidman finally died in his arms. Why couldn't she be adored by someone as wonderful as Ewan, who would never have had sex in the shower with an old girlfriend behind Nicole's back? How could she have been so stupid as to be taken in by Rupert's pseudo charms?

Why, *why* hadn't she marched out of the flat with Lucy? She must have been out of her mind.

Tears slid down Jem's cheeks and dripped off her chin as she gazed blindly at the TV screen. Ewan and Nicole were singing "Come What May," promising to be together until their dying day. Not long to wait there, then. Miserably helping herself to another biscuit, Jem wondered how many people apart from her family would be upset if she died. Nobody from Bristol, that was for sure.

Nicole was looking stunning while elegantly coughing up blood when the doorbell rang a while later. Without enthusiasm Jem brushed cookie crumbs off her T-shirt, hauled herself off the bed, and padded downstairs.

Lucy was on the doorstep.

Dumbstruck, Jem gazed at her. Past Lucy, perched on the front wall, was Davy wearing an extremely green shirt.

Jem's heart was pounding; she was hideously aware of her swollen, froggy eyes. At last she said, "What are you doing here?"

"Oh, Jem, look at the state of you. Why do you think we're here?" For a second it seemed as if Lucy might burst into tears as well. Holding out her arms and shaking her head she said, "We've come to take you back with us."

"Really?" Jem's bottom lip began to tremble.

"Really."

"Oh, Luce, I'm sorry. So sorry for everything."

"I know. Come here."

They hugged and laughed and cried a bit on the doorstep. Then Davy, ambling up the path, said, "I'm not really a huggy person," and gave Jem's shoulder an awkward pat instead.

"I can't believe you came all the way to Cornwall." Overwhelmed, Jem said, "How did you know this address? Did you catch the train?"

Lucy's dark eyes shone. "Your mum came to see us."

"My *mum*? When?" Did Ginny have a time machine she didn't know about?

"Today," said Davy.

"But she's working at the restaurant; they've got a wedding reception… oh…"

Lucy said gravely, "She lied."

"She's just gone to the shop to pick up some food. We're staying for the night. You can invite us in if you like." Davy rested his hand lightly on his chest. "It's not doing my terrible knife injury any good, you know, standing out here."

"Oh God, of course, come in!"

"He's having you on." Lucy rolled her eyes. "It's nothing more than a scratch. I could have done better with one of my fingernails."

"I want to hear all about it," said Jem as she ushered them inside.

"Ha, that's nothing. Wait till you hear what happened when your mum went to Pembroke Road to pick up the rest of your stuff."

Chapter 45

THE CHANGE IN JEM was unbelievable, heartwarming. For once in her life, Ginny discovered, she had acted on impulse and it had paid off. Jem, hugging her, had said, "Mum, I can't believe you did this. Everything's sorted out now. I'm so happy."

"She just couldn't bear the thought of having you back here with her," said Lucy. "She was desperate."

Ginny smiled at them, because every maternal fiber of her being longed to hold on to Jem for ever, keeping her safe from harm at home. They were young; they couldn't begin to understand that making it possible for her daughter to leave again was one of the most grown-up things she'd ever done.

But this time, she knew, Jem would be happy. Tomorrow evening she was driving them back up to Bristol. For the last few weeks of term all three would be staying with Rhona in Henbury. It was complicated but not impossible; Davy was moving into the tiny bedroom that had been Lucy's, and Lucy and Jem were taking over his old room. Together, they were going to put all their energy into revising for their exams and hopefully Jem would be able to put in enough work to pass. Then, after the summer break, Lucy and Jem would get a flat-share together, hopefully with someone less good-looking but with a far nicer personality than—

"Mum, you have to tell me what happened with Rupert!"

Oh yes, that had been fun. Just for a split second when he'd opened the front door, Rupert's face had been a picture.

———

"Hello, Rupert," Ginny said brightly. "So you managed to get out of the bathroom then. I've come to pick up the rest of Jem's things. And her deposit."

His lip curled. "You're welcome to take her junk away. I'm keeping the deposit in lieu of notice."

"Rupert, don't be like that. There's no need." Marching into the flat, Ginny gave him a pitying look. "Besides, I'm not leaving until you've paid me back the money. In cash."

Well, why not? Five hundred pounds was five hundred pounds. And she must have looked as if she meant business, because Rupert heaved a sigh and disappeared into his bedroom, returning a couple of minutes later with a roll of twenty-pound notes.

"You don't have to count them."

"Oh, but I will. Honesty hasn't always been your best policy, has it?" Having checked that all the money was there, Ginny went into Jem's room and collected the last of her belongings. When she reemerged, Rupert was standing in the living room, smoking a cigarette, looking out of the window at Davy in the car below.

"So you've got Stokes with you. Don't tell me he's given up the cleaning job to become your minder."

"Rupert, he's worth ten of you." Patiently, Ginny said, "I don't suppose you'll ever understand that, but at least everyone else does. And Davy's happy with himself."

Rupert smirked, exhaling a stream of smoke. "You think I'm not?"

"Oh, I'm sure you are now. You're living your own life, doing whatever you like and not caring who else gets hurt. But that's the kind of attitude that comes back to bite you. And when it does, you'll know how it feels to be the one on the receiving end."

He raised a laconic eyebrow. "Lecture over? Am I supposed to fall to my knees and beg forgiveness for my sins?"

"Not at all," said Ginny. "In fact I'm glad it happened. My daughter made a huge mistake, but she's learned her lesson. With a bit of luck she'll steer clear of boys like you in future."

"Boys like me." Amused, Rupert flicked his cigarette out of the window.

"Plenty of money, no morals. Not what most people want from a relationship." Annoyed by the cigarette thing, Ginny made the comment she'd been debating whether to mention. "I think your mother came to much the same conclusion, didn't she?"

The arrogant half smile disappeared from Rupert's face; he stiffened, instantly on his guard. "Excuse me?"

"Your mother. You told me she was dead, remember?" Ginny shook her head. "I felt terrible at the time. But you weren't actually telling the truth, were you?"

She watched him turn pale; God bless the Internet, and Finn too for dimly recognizing Rupert's double-barreled surname.

"She's dead as far as I'm concerned," Rupert said flatly.

"Your father had lots of affairs while they were married. He made her desperately unhappy, but she stuck it out because of you. Then, when you were thirteen and away at boarding school, she fell in love with another man. And when your father found out about this, he kicked her out."

"OK, said what you wanted to say? You can go now." Stony-eyed, Rupert lit another cigarette.

"In a minute." Ginny had no intention of stopping. "So you've refused to have anything to do with your mum ever since. But she's still with the same man and they're very happy together. He sounds like a lovely person."

"I wouldn't know." Rupert's jaw was taut. "Well, you've done your homework."

"Your mum must miss you terribly." Her tone gentler now, Ginny said, "I wish you'd consider seeing her again."

"No chance." A muscle flickered in his cheek.

"You've got two little half sisters you've never met."

"Who live in government housing in a tower block in Hackney. With my mother and a tattooed window-fitter called Darren. There, I've said it. Happy now?"

Ginny almost—*almost*—felt sorry for him.

"I'm fine. How about you?"

"Best day of my life." Flick went the second cigarette, sailing through the window and landing on the pavement below. "Congratulations. I suppose you've told Jem."

He was both furious and mortified. Ginny shook her head. "I haven't. But I might if I hear you've said or done anything to upset her. From now on, I'd just like you to keep away from my daughter and her friends, OK?" She gathered up the bags containing Jem's things and indicated that Rupert could open the front door. As he did so, she added, "And it wouldn't kill you to use an ashtray."

Since she wasn't a saint, it had almost killed Ginny to keep the story of Rupert's mother to herself. But a small part of her had known that publicly humiliating Rupert was unlikely to spur him into making contact with his mother.

Less altruistically, a far greater part of her had whispered that if softhearted Jem were to hear of it, she would only feel sorry for Rupert and might find herself being drawn to his new-found vulnerability.

That was the last thing they needed.

So she had heroically withheld the information. As far as Jem, Davy, and Lucy were concerned, she had simply given Rupert a coruscating piece of her mind and successfully wiped the smirk off his face.

"Which I did," she told Finn now, in the restaurant on Monday lunchtime. "Thanks to you."

He grinned. "My pleasure. Lucky he had an unusual name."

"Lucky you remembered it," said Ginny.

By delicious coincidence, Finn had actually met Elizabeth Derris-Beck eighteen months ago when she had come into his shop in London to sell her old engagement ring. Well-spoken, charming, and accompanied by her young daughters, she had relayed the whole story of her miserable first marriage and told Finn how deliriously happy she was now with her new man and new life. The ring had been a serious square-cut emerald flanked by top quality diamonds. When the necessary paperwork had been completed, Elizabeth had hugged her girls and said cheerfully, "That's us off to Lapland to see Father Christmas. And the rest goes toward a new car."

"She sent me a photo of the four of them in a sleigh outside Santa's house," Finn added. "And a note thanking me for buying the ring. She said they'd had the best holiday of their lives."

"Maybe next year you and Tamsin could take Mae." Ginny felt funny saying it; next year was a long time ahead.

"Maybe. So your weekend was a success."

"Wonderful. Davy and Lucy are fantastic. We had a picnic on the beach yesterday, and a sandcastle competition. Lucy and Jem went swimming. Davy's phone hasn't stopped with friends calling to talk to him about how he saved Marcus McBride's life. It's done wonders for his confidence. I feel as proud as if he were my own son. And then last night I drove them back to Bristol. Jem's going to be fine, I know it. They'll look after her."

"That's good news. You must be relieved," said Finn.

Ginny smiled and nodded, because he sounded as if he really cared. And he was right; it was a happy ending. But what she couldn't tell him was that arriving back in Portsilver at midnight had been a depressing experience; Laurel was upstairs asleep and the house

had seemed unbearably quiet. She had gone to bed feeling empty, lonely, and bereft all over again, unable to stop herself thinking, *What about me?*

Chapter 46

"STOP OGLING THE BOSS."

Ginny jumped, unaware that Evie had emerged from the restaurant kitchen. "I wasn't!"

"Yes you were." Evie's eyes danced. "Mind you, I can't say I blame you. Gorgeous shoulders. Spectacular bum."

"Shhh." Did Evie have to be quite so loud? Finn was only twenty feet away, showing out the last diners of the afternoon. And now he was closing the door, turning to see what all the shushing was about.

"What's going on?"

"Nothing." Evie, who had no shame, said, "We were just admiring your body."

"*You* were," said Ginny, glasses clinking as she indignantly gathered them up.

"Fine, I was admiring. You were ogling."

"I wasn't. I was thinking about Jem." Keen to change the subject, Ginny said, "She phoned this morning to tell me her tutor's really pleased with all the work she's put in over the last couple of weeks. He thinks she might scrape through her exams after all."

"That's great news." Evie knew how worried she'd been about Jem. "But I still know an ogle when I see one. I have an eye for these things."

Not to mention a mouth. What a shame it couldn't be zipped shut. "You want to get out more." Ginny, clanking past with her hands full of glasses, said, "Some of us have more important things to think about than men's bodies."

Finn raised his eyebrows. "Even mine?"

The kitchen was empty apart from Tom, the washer-upper, busy at the sink.

"You look hot." He surveyed Ginny's hectically pink cheeks.

She took extra care unloading the glasses, giving herself time to recover. "Just busy, Tom."

God, life would be so much easier if only she didn't have this overheating problem.

OK, life would be so much easier if only she could get over this hopeless, pointless, *ridiculous* crush.

As if to hammer the point home, just as she headed back to the dining room, the front door opened and Tamsin burst into the restaurant with Mae on her hip.

"I'm in love." Tamsin's eyes were shining.

Which was the kind of announcement that might have got Ginny's hopes up, except that in her free hand Tamsin was waving some kind of glossy brochure. Rushing over to Finn, she gave him a don't-smudge-my-lipstick kiss and said, "Darling, you have to see it. Six bedrooms, sea views, Clive Christian kitchen, and an en suite bathroom to die for. It's the house of our dreams, a proper family home. I told the agent we'd meet him there at five o'clock."

"Six bedrooms." Finn studied the brochure in alarm. "Jesus, have you seen how much they're asking for it?"

"That's only a guide price; we can make an offer." Eagerly pointing to the photos, Tamsin said, "Look at the billiard room. And that garden! And six bedrooms aren't so many when this is the rest of our lives we're talking about." She turned her bewitching smile on him. "After all, you know we don't want Mae to be an only child."

Ginny felt a bit sick, but there was no escaping their domestic bliss. Tamsin insisted on showing her and Evie the brochure, cooing delightedly over every detail of the house and explaining how unsuitable the flat was now that Mae was walking.

"We have to get it. It's just perfect." Swishing back her long hair, Tamsin gave Ginny a sympathetic look. "Yours is only semi-detached, isn't it? I bet you'd love to live in a house like this?"

Ginny wondered what Tamsin would do if she said, "Yes, but only if I could live in it with Finn."

Obviously she didn't say it. Heavens, what was the matter with her today? Half an hour ago she'd been quietly ogling Finn from a distance. (Wouldn't Evie be delighted to know she'd been right?) And now here she was, fantasizing about making smart remarks to her rival.

Except Tamsin wasn't a rival, was she? Tamsin was having a proper grown-up relationship with Finn, rather than a sad, not-proper-at-all fantasy one.

Dutifully Ginny said, "It looks wonderful."

"Dadadablaaa," sang Mae, clapping her hands at Finn.

"You want to go to Daddy? Here, you take her. She weighs a ton." Having passed Mae over to him, Tamsin gazed raptly at the two of them, then back at the photograph of the house. "How could any child not be happy, growing up in a place like this?"

───

Driving home from the restaurant, Ginny resolved to get a grip, put the whole Finn thing behind her, and get on with her life. Let's face it, she wasn't the first woman ever to have a one-off fling with her very attractive boss and she certainly wouldn't be the last.

Anyway, think positive, now it was time to move on. Absolutely. Make the most of what she had, which was a lot. Healthy happy daughter. A job she enjoyed. A nice house, even if Tamsin probably felt sorry for her having to live in such a shoebox. And there were so many other things to take pleasure in too, like art, books, walking on the beach, listening to music…

Feeling more positive already, Ginny buzzed down the car

windows and made a conscious decision to find joy in those small things in life that it was only too easy to overlook, like the sunshine warming her face and those delicious little white clouds dotting the sky. Cornwall was beautiful. She was wearing her favorite white angora sweater, which looked a tiny bit like a cloud and hadn't gone bobbly yet. David Gray was singing on the radio and she loved David Gray, especially the way he wobbled his head. Turning up the volume, Ginny was tempted to sing along, but that might spoil it; the last thing David needed was her caterwauling mucking up his beautiful, heartfelt vocals. She'd just listen instead and think of other miraculous things like the velvety smoothness of pebbles, the crumbly deliciousness of Laurel's lemon drizzle cake, the incomparable sight of dolphins frolicking in the sea off Portsilver Point, the smell of hot tarmac…

Oh yes, hot tarmac, one of the all-time greats. And what a good job she hadn't been bellowing along to the radio. Having rounded the bend, Ginny slowed to a halt and beamed at the middle-aged man holding the Stop/Go lollipop sign currently directing her to Stop. Little did he imagine what a lucky escape he'd just had, not having been forced to hear her singing voice.

Ahead of him, two more council workers busily got on with the business of tarmacking a rectangular patch on the left-hand side of the road. A bus and a couple of cars passed through on the other side.

"Lovely day," Ginny called over to the lollipop man, who was wrinkled and leathery from long years in the sun.

"Too nice to be working." He beamed back at her, evidently a cheery soul. Well, why wouldn't he be, able to enjoy the smell of fresh tarmac all day long? With a flourish he swiveled the lollipop sign round to Go and Ginny gave him a little wave as she set off, breathing in deeply in order not to miss a single lungful of the hot, tarry deliciousness.

All too soon the moment was past, the joy behind her. Sniffing

the air, desperate for one last hit and not finding it, Ginny was bereft. Half a mile further down the road and unable to bear it a second longer, she pulled into a driveway and rapidly reversed the car. It was no good; you couldn't open a bag of Maltesers and only eat one, could you? Exactly. And if she wanted to go back and experience the smell of tar again... well, was there anything wrong with that? Crikey, it wasn't against the law. And, unlike Maltesers, it didn't have any calories. It was one of life's harmless pleasures, for heaven's sake. What's more, it was free.

The lollipop man looked momentarily surprised when he saw her. As luck would have it, Ginny again found herself up against the Stop sign.

"You again?" He winked at her. "Are you stalking me? Look, I'd love to meet up with you for a drink but my old lady would have my guts for garters."

Ginny grinned, because guts for garters always conjured up a wonderfully bizarre image in her mind. Then she got on with the serious business of inhaling the tar fumes which were, if such a thing was possible, even more irresistible this time. In fact, would it be possible to buy some tarmac from these men? Would they think she was weird if she asked them? And if they said no, maybe she could come back after they'd gone, like tonight under cover of darkness, and just dig up a little bit of tar before it set solid?

"Forget something, did you?" Lollipop man nodded genially. "Bad as my old lady. She'd forget her head if it wasn't screwed on."

Jolly banter over, he swiveled the lollipop and waved Ginny through for the second time. She breathed in the addictive scent of the tar as she passed it being spread like glossy, sticky jam on the other side of the road.

Moments later the elusive sense of familiarity finally clicked into place in her brain and Ginny realized when she had last been enthralled by the smell, so long ago now that it simply hadn't registered

before. There had been major road repairs going on outside the offices she'd been working in at the time and everyone else had grumbled constantly about the disruption, the smells, and the noise. But she had loved it all so much that she'd taken to sitting outside on the wall during her lunch breaks, watching the goings-on and eating her sandwiches.

Actually, *guzzling* her sandwiches, because that was when she'd been...

When she'd been...

Oh no, no, surely not...

~~~

Somehow, on autopilot, Ginny managed to park the car at only a slightly wonky angle in the town's central car park. When she climbed out, her legs almost gave way. OK, collapsing in a heap would just waste time and be an embarrassment. Girding herself, she clutched her handbag and headed for the shops.

At the threshold of the pharmacy, she stopped. The assistants knew her here; she'd spent many a happy hour browsing in the aisles, trying eye shadows on the back of her hand, and choosing lipsticks. What would they think if they saw her come in and buy a... no, she'd have to go somewhere else.

There was another smaller pharmacy in St. Aldam's Square that didn't stock any makeup so she'd never visited it before. Having done the deed, Ginny emerged and hurried away, checking left and right as she went, making sure there was no one around who might recognize her and demand to know what was in her bag.

The public lavatories weren't ideal but getting home wasn't an option; that would take fifteen minutes and she had to know now. And they were at least very nice public lavatories, scrupulously clean and freshly painted, with bright hanging baskets of flowers outside.

Locking herself in the far cubicle, Ginny trembled as she

unwrapped the packet and read the instructions. She peed on the stick and closed her eyes, waiting for the chemicals to do their thing. Outside the cubicle she could hear a mother struggling with a baby in a stroller and simultaneously trying to persuade her young daughter to wash her hands.

"Come on, Megan, be a good girl, don't splash."

"It's water!"

"I know, darling, but Thomas doesn't like it. Just keep the water away from him."

Time was up. Ginny opened her eyes and looked at the stick thing.

Oh God.

Oh *God.*

Outside, a scuffle ensued, accompanied by the sound of vigorous splashing and the outraged wails of a small baby. Ginny gazed blankly at the gray door of her cubicle and heard Megan giggling in triumph, her mission accomplished. The baby, evidently drenched, emitted ear-splitting howls of protest.

Megan's mother said with resignation, "Oh, you silly girl, look what you've done now. *That's* not very clever, is it?"

You're telling me, thought Ginny.

Chapter 47

GAVIN DIDN'T MIND HAVING his bottom pinched. In fact he positively welcomed it. He just hadn't been expecting it to happen as he threaded his way along a crowded street in Padstow.

"Hello, stranger!" He threw out his arms and gave Bev a kiss, delighted to see her. "I was hoping it'd be someone young, female, and dazzlingly gorgeous."

Bev, her smile lopsided, said, "Oh well, one out of three isn't bad."

"Don't give me that. You wouldn't want to be twenty-one again. And for an older woman you're looking great." Gavin admired her shiny dark hair, scarlet dress, and voluptuous figure.

"And you still haven't signed up for those How to be a Diplomat evening classes."

He beamed. "I'm set in my ways. There's no hope for me. Anyway, fancy bumping into you here. We've missed you at the club."

Bev shrugged. "I gave up waiting for George Clooney to join. He must have had problems getting his visa. Anyway, you're looking well." She admired Gavin's suit. "Who'd have thought you could look so smart? I almost didn't recognize you without one of your loud shirts on."

"Business. Long boring meeting with a short boring client. How about you?"

"Much more fun. A very unboring meeting with a rather exciting new friend." Bev's eyes sparkled as she moved back to the table she'd been sitting at when she'd jumped up to surprise him.

"Excellent. Can I meet her?"

"Very funny. It's a male friend." Indicating with pride the empty beer bottle on the table next to her almost finished glass of wine, Bev said, "But you're more than welcome to stay and say hello. We're having a couple of drinks here before going on to dinner at the Blue Moon. He's just gone inside to buy the next round."

"So you've found someone you like at last." It was pretty obvious from the way her whole face was lit up that she was smitten.

"I know! Can you believe it? I stopped going to the club and told myself that from now on, if it was going to happen, it'd happen." Bev clicked her fingers and beamed at him. "And bam, a few weeks down the line, it did happen. Which just goes to show: you don't have to schlep along to singles evenings or join a gym or buy a dog and take it for walks so you can get chatting to other people with dogs. Guess how we met!"

"You took a job as a stripper."

"Gavin, you philistine, how did I ever fancy you? I was weeding my front garden! On my hands and knees with my big bum in the air, pulling up dandelions."

Gavin the Philistine wisely kept his thoughts to himself. But it was undeniably an enticing mental image.

"When this guy who was walking past stopped at my gate."

Of course he did, thought Gavin the Philistine.

"He was lost," Bev went on. "He asked me for directions to Lancaster Road."

Oh yes, classic maneuver.

"Which was back the way he'd just come from, so we had a laugh about that."

Naturally.

"And then somehow we just clicked." Bev clicked her fingers to demonstrate. "It was incredible; we just carried on talking and didn't stop. There was this incredible… God, *chemistry*."

Total pro.

"After about an hour, he asked me if I'd like to meet him for a drink that evening. And that was it. I said yes, of course. We went out and had the most amazing time. It was as if we'd known each other forever," Bev said dreamily. "At last, I'd found my perfect man. He's so kind and such a gentleman, so interested in *me*. It's almost too good to be true. This is only our third date—I can't believe it's only our third date!—but I've just got this *feeling* about Perry, I really think this could be—"

"Whoa," Gavin abruptly halted her. "What did you say?"

"It's only our third date. We met last Sunday."

"Never mind that. Is his name Perry Kennedy?"

"Oh my God, yes it *is*!" Bev clapped her hands in delight. "Do you know him?"

Up until that moment Gavin had simply recognized Bev's new chap as a fellow womanizer, a man after his own heart, and where was the harm in that? Now, like plunging into the sea in diving boots, it struck him that there *was* harm in it. He hoped he wasn't as bad as Perry Kennedy. He did it because he had the attention span of a gnat, but he'd never deliberately set out to deceive a woman. He'd never been cold and calculating in his life.

Bev, her smile wavering, said, "Why are you looking at me like that?"

"I know him. He's bad news. A fake." Since there was no kind way to say it, Gavin didn't waste time wondering how to soften the blow. "He went out with Ginny, duped her, played her for a fool. She found out he was shagging her best friend. And it turned out he's done it a thousand times before."

Poor old Bev, the smile had well and truly melted from her face. Shock radiated from her. And any minute now, Perry would emerge from the bar with their drinks.

"I hate him for what he did to Ginny," Gavin went on. "He

broke her heart"—OK, bit of an exaggeration—"and he'll break yours too."

God, he hoped she wasn't about to burst into tears.

But Bev was made of sterner stuff. She exhaled slowly, sat back in her chair, and said, "Fuck, fuck, *fuck it*."

"Sorry, darling. I couldn't not tell you."

"Story of my life. I suppose I should be used to it by now. If something seems too good to be true, it probably is. And there was me, thinking my luck had changed." She exhaled. "Thinking I was irresistible."

"Sweetheart, you are." For an older woman anyway, Gavin allowed. "All the more reason not to get involved with a bastard like that. Trust me; he's all pain and no gain. You need to cut and run."

Bev glanced down at her shoes. "Easier said than done in these heels."

She was wearing red strappy four-inch stilettos adorned with butterflies, the shoes of a woman out to impress the new man in her life. Quite sexy, actually.

Gavin said, "You could always take them off."

"Oh God, why does this have to happen to me?" Bev glanced over her shoulder to see if Perry was on his way out.

"It doesn't only happen to you. Men like him need teaching a lesson."

"Pot." Her tone was dry. "Kettle."

"Ouch. That's me put in my place." Gavin's eyes crinkled at the corners. "I'd better get off, leave you to it."

"Where are you going?"

"To get something to eat. Probably not at the Blue Moon." He paused, watching Bev make up her mind. "Why?"

She shrugged. "Could you do with some company?"

"Only if you promise not to keep nagging me about my terrible ways."

Bev slipped her feet out of her stilettos, stood up, and drained her glass of wine. "And you aren't allowed to keep saying you could quite fancy me if only I wasn't so old. Just for once, try and be nice to me, OK? I'm a woman in crisis."

Gavin winked and said, "My favorite kind."

———

The queue at the bar had been ridiculous. Having finally been served, Perry emerged with a drink in each hand. Bev was nowhere to be seen.

What was this, a clip from *You've Been Framed*? He paused, peering around. The table at which he and Bev had been sitting was now occupied by a family of four. Approaching them, Perry learned that it had been free when they'd got here.

He scanned the rest of the drinkers gathered outside. No one else was wearing a red dress. Had Bev gone inside to the loo and somehow managed to slip past him unnoticed?

Yet more waiting. She didn't return. Feeling increasingly foolish, Perry finally approached the group of office workers at the table behind the one now occupied by the family of four. "Um... excuse me, did any of you notice what happened to the lady who was sitting over there? Dark hair, red dress..."

"She pulled." A freckled, tufty-haired boy grinned at his friends.

"Warren." The girl next to him gave him a nudge. "You can't say that."

"Why not? It's true."

"What do you mean?" Perry's shoulders stiffened.

"She was sitting there on her own. Then this guy walked past. The next moment she jumped up and launched herself at him. Pinched his bum and everything. They were all over each other."

"They talked for a bit," the girl at his side elaborated, "then walked off together down the road."

"He was carrying her shoes," a second girl chimed in. "Kind of like Cinderella, only the other way round."

The freckled boy looked scornful. "So, not like Cinderella at all then. More like he's got some pervy fetish thing for shoes."

"She just went off with him?" Perry blinked in disbelief. "What did he look like?"

"Forties. A bit overweight. Losing his hair at the front. Not exactly Pierce Brosnan." The first girl shrugged then said thoughtfully, "He had a nice smile though. And sparkly eyes. He looked quite... fun."

The boy sniggered. "She obviously thought he was fun."

Perry was in a state of disbelief. Bev had abandoned him for another man who wasn't even that good-looking. Gone off with him just like that, without so much as a good-bye.

How could she?

He'd never been so humiliated in his life.

Bev was smiling to herself.

"What?" said Gavin.

"I've just realized something." She turned onto her side to face him. "I bet I'm the oldest person you've ever slept with."

"By a mile. But you know what? It wasn't as scary as I thought."

"Cheek!" Bev hooked one of her bare legs over his.

"It's a compliment. Seriously." In return Gavin pulled her against him. "You know a lot of tricks."

"Years of practice. Almost as many as you. And a man in his forties is past his sexual peak. Whereas *I*"—she trailed the tips of her fingernails in tantalizing circles along his inner thigh—"am a woman in my prime."

"Past my peak? Now that's a slur I'm going to have to disprove." He rolled her over, intent on making his point, but Bev wriggled away before he could pin her down.

"No time now. It's eight o'clock. I have to be at work by nine."

This was frustrating but true. Neither of them had expected last night to end the way it had. Following dinner in Padstow, Gavin had invited Bev back to his house in Portsilver for a nightcap. At first they had talked about Perry Kennedy. Then they'd stopped talking about him, because that was just depressing, and had moved on to other subjects instead. It was at this point that Gavin had realized how refreshing it was to be able to hold a flirtatious conversation with someone who had a brain, intellectual curiosity, and a quick wit. Bev was terrific company; she made him laugh and she didn't look blank when he mentioned Nixon and Watergate. She knew who Siouxie Sioux was. She remembered a world before mobile phones. When it came to singing Duran Duran, she was word perfect.

OK, not everything they'd discussed had been intellectual.

After that, the rest had just happened. He'd been making coffee in the kitchen and Bev had been spooning sugar into his cup. His hand had accidentally brushed against hers and she'd jumped, spilling sugar all over the work surface. Amused, Gavin had said, "Do I really have that effect on you?"

"Yes," said Bev. "You do."

"When we were outside that wine bar, you said you used to fancy me. Was that a joke?"

She shook her head. "No, it was the truth."

"You never said anything." Gavin was enchanted by her honesty.

"No point. I couldn't turn myself into a twenty-two-year-old."

The last twenty-two-year-old of Gavin's acquaintance had been talking about this summer's V Festival. When Gavin had proudly informed her that he'd been at the original Live Aid concert, she'd trilled excitedly, "Oh wicked, we learned all about that at school in history!"

The next thing he knew, he'd found himself kissing Bev. Sugar crystals had scrunched underfoot as they'd clung to each other. The

coffee had been abandoned; the spilled sugar was still there. Last night had been a revelation, all the better for being so unexpected. Sex with Bev was a joy.

A repeat performance would have been nice but she was out of bed now, hurriedly dressing in order to shoot home and shower and change before heading off to work.

In no time at all she was ready to leave. Gavin realized he didn't want her to go. When she gave him a good-bye kiss, he said, "What are you doing tonight?"

"Me? Nothing. Watching *Last of the Summer Wine*. Polishing my walker. Looking through my Thora Hird scrapbook." Bev shrugged. "How about you?"

"Well, if you could bear to give *Last of the Summer Wine* a miss, I could demonstrate that I'm not past my sexual peak."

Her eyes searched his face. "Would that be to prove it to me, or to yourself?"

"Hey, I want to see you again. I wasn't expecting this to happen and neither were you. But it has." He surveyed the tiny lines at the corners of her eyes and realized they gave her face character. Reaching up to touch the side of her jaw—at least she wasn't jowly; he *really* couldn't handle that—Gavin said, "And I'm glad it's happened."

"You're not just saying that to be kind, to cheer me up?"

"I promise you, I'm not that unselfish. So, Moneypenny, are you coming over here at seven o'clock tonight or not?"

"Coming over here for what?"

Gavin did his best Sean Connery impression. "I thought maybe rampant sex and toasted cheese sandwiches."

"Oh well, if you put it like that." Bev's dark eyes danced as she kissed him on the nose. "I suppose I could always record *Last of the Summer Wine*."

Chapter 48

THE POSTMAN HAD DELIVERED a hat trick of envelopes together with a small recorded delivery parcel addressed to Laurel. Ginny carried them through to the kitchen and opened the first envelope.

Electricity bill, fabulous.

The second was water rates, great.

The third was a bank statement. As ever, Ginny fantasized that this would be the one containing an outrageously vast sum that had accidentally been credited to her account instead of somebody else's, but—and this was the best bit—the person who should have received the money was so rich that he never realized he hadn't. Like when Sting, eons ago, hadn't noticed several million pounds being fraudulently siphoned from his account. Imagine that. And who was to say that a completely innocent computer blip couldn't do the same for her?

Sadly a quick skim through the statement revealed that yet another month had passed and it hadn't happened.

Even more sadly, her balance was less than it should have been. Checking through more carefully, Ginny saw what was missing.

"Laurel?"

Laurel appeared in the doorway. "Yes?"

"Your rent hasn't gone through yet. Could you have a word with Perry, see what's happened?"

"Oh." Laurel shifted awkwardly, not meeting her gaze. "Um… he can't afford to pay it anymore."

"Excuse me?"

"Sorry. I meant to tell you." Laurel's tone was defensive; she'd clearly known for a while.

"So who is going to be paying it?"

"I don't know."

Ginny shook her head in disbelief. As if she didn't have enough to worry about. The past couple of weeks had seen Laurel slipping back into her old neurotic ways as the date of Kevin's birthday had approached. Laurel had for some reason convinced herself that Kevin would choose this date to come back to her. When it didn't happen, her misery had been of epic proportions. That had been a week ago and Ginny had done her best to sympathize, but now her patience was running out.

"Look, I have bills to pay." The words came out clipped and irritated. "Jem isn't working anymore so I'm having to help her too. You can't expect me to say, 'Oh well, never mind, maybe we'll have a lucky night at the Bingo.' If Perry's not paying your rent anymore, you'll have to pay it yourself."

With her pale green eyes, Laurel had never looked more like Ophelia. "But I don't have any money."

The knicker elastic of Ginny's patience finally snapped. "Then you'll just have to do what normal people do and get yourself a job!"

Laurel flinched as if she'd been slapped. "I can't."

"You *can*," Ginny shot back, "you just don't *want* to. And I'm sorry, but if you don't pay your rent, you aren't staying here. Because you aren't the only one with problems, OK? Things are pretty crap for me as well right now, but somehow or other I have to get on with it, because that's life."

Laurel welled up. She glanced at the small parcel on the kitchen table.

"That's yours. It came just now." Ginny eyed it jealously; how come Laurel got sent a parcel while all she got was stinking rotten bills?

"Thanks."

"Open it, then."

"Later."

Oh, for heaven's sake, what was the great mystery? It wasn't big enough to be a vibrator. Too het up by this stage to even care that she was being unreasonable, Ginny barked, "Open the damn parcel!"

Miserably Laurel did as she was told. Her chin began to wobble as the wrappings came off.

Ginny's eyes widened. "Somebody's sent you a Gucci watch!"

"No."

"You mean you bought it for yourself?" Bloody hell, how much did a Gucci watch cost?

"If you must know," Laurel blurted out defensively, "I bought it for Kevin. I thought it would make him love me again. He's always wanted a Gucci watch." She unfolded the accompanying note, scanned the few lines, and crumpled it in her hand. "But not from me. I can't believe he sent it back. Oh God, why can't I ever get *anything* right?"

Ginny's own hormones were jangling. "Look, I thought you'd stopped all this. It's crazy, Laurel. Kevin's never going to love you again. He's never going to come back. It's over and you have to accept that." Before Laurel could start sobbing, she added hastily, "And look on the bright side. You can take the watch back to the shop and get a refund."

And pay your rent with it hopefully.

"I can't." Laurel sniffed and gazed mournfully down at the watch.

"You can! Unless it's a fake one." Ginny peered more closely; actually, if it was a fake she wouldn't mind one for herself.

Laurel was outraged. "Of course it's not a fake! What kind of person do you think I am?"

Was she serious? "Well, obviously the kind of person who spends hundreds of pounds she doesn't have on someone who doesn't want

anything from her. For crying out loud, just take it back to the shop and get a refund!"

"I told you, I can't. I bought the watch three weeks ago." Laurel fiddled with the dangly, too-long sleeves of her sage-green cardigan. "They only give you your money back if you return it within fourteen days."

God. Exasperated, Ginny said, "Next time, go to a department store and buy him a pair of socks."

"I'm sorry. I love him." Tears were once more sliding down Laurel's colorless cheeks. "I just don't know what to do anymore."

"Don't you?" It was knicker-snapping time again. With an embryo in her stomach and bills strewn across the kitchen table, Ginny felt the elastic go *twaannggg.* Her voice spiraling, she yelped, "Seriously, don't you? Because I can tell you. You have to forget Kevin and stop feeling so sorry for yourself. You need to sort out your life and start acting like an adult. And if you want to carry on living in this house, you have to get out there and find yourself a job."

Ginny took a deep breath. Crikey, had she really just said all that? From the way Laurel stifled a horrified sob, ricocheted off the doorway, and stumbled out of the kitchen, it rather seemed as if she had.

Upstairs in Jem's bedroom, Ginny sat in front of the computer scrolling through images of embryos in the womb. Her own, she discovered, had by now developed fingers and toes and a face of sorts—albeit with huge alien eyes and low-slung ears. It also had a sense of smell (how could they *tell?*), a pituitary gland in its brain, and a tiny heart pumping away in its chest.

Oh God, she really was having a baby. One reckless moment and this was the life-changing result, how could she have been so—

"Um, hello?" A cautious tap was followed by Laurel pushing open the bedroom door. Ginny pounced on the mouse and fired frantically at the page-closer like a demented person on a rifle range, finally managing to clear the screen a millisecond before Laurel came into the room.

Prickling with adrenaline, she said, "*What?*"

Laurel flinched. "Sorry. Um, I'm just going out to the pharmacy to pick up my prescription. I wondered if there was anything you wanted while I was there."

Well, let's see, how about some nipple cream and a tube of that stuff that stops you getting stretch marks on your stomach when it's the size of a beach ball? And how about a box of breast pads, a thousand packs of nappies, and some teething biscuits? Oh God, actually she quite fancied a couple of Farley's rusks...

"No thanks."

"Oh. OK." Pause. "I'm really sorry about... you know, the rent."

Ginny steeled herself; Laurel knew she was a soft touch. Well, not this time. Stiffly she replied, "So you keep saying."

Her ploy evidently thwarted, Laurel's face fell. "Anyway, I'll be back in half an hour." She twisted the doorknob this way and that. "And I'm going to sort everything out. I promise."

Talk about emotional blackmail. Ginny refused to give in. Turning back to the computer she said, "Good."

Three hours later there was still no sign of Laurel. Ginny unloaded the washing from the tumble dryer and carried the basket of dry clothes upstairs. It was unlike Laurel to be gone for so long, but it hadn't been an ordinary day; maybe she'd gone into town to visit the Job Center or to see Perry.

By the time she'd finished sorting out the clothes, Laurel still hadn't returned. Her conscience by now beginning to prick, Ginny

let herself into Laurel's bedroom in search of a clue as to where she might have gone.

The sunshine-yellow room was incredibly neat, like something out of a show home. Apart from the handbag on the bed, nothing was out of place. Laurel's handbag. Ginny frowned at the sight of it; surely when you left the house to go to the shops you took your handbag with you? Unless Laurel had decided to swap handbags for coordination purposes (which was, frankly, unlikely) and had emptied the contents of this one into another that went better with her sludge-brown dress and green cardigan?

But no, picking up the handbag, she discovered it was full of Laurel's things. *All* her things, including her purse and credit cards.

That was a bit weird, wasn't it?

Her heart beating a little faster, Ginny pulled open the drawers of the chest next to Laurel's bed. The first drawer contained underwear, ironed and folded and in no way resembling the tangle of bras and knickers that comprised Ginny's own collection. The second held tights and petticoats, again arranged as pristinely as if they were part of a shop display.

The bottom drawer contained several framed photographs of Kevin (who was so not worth all this angst and grief); the box containing the Gucci watch; an old, navy, man-sized lamb's wool sweater with holes in both elbows; and a pale gray leather-bound diary.

Ginny swallowed. Should she? Shouldn't she? She had sneaked a look at someone else's diary once before. It hadn't been a happy experience, learning that: "Mum thinks she's a good dancer but she's really embarrassing, all my friends were laughing at her at the school Christmas dance." Followed by: "I wish Mum would buy proper name tapes for my school uniform; I'm the only one with my name in marker pen. Mrs. Hegarty (I hate her) was all sneery and said doesn't your mother know how to sew?"

Ginny prickled with shame at the memory. By the time she'd

finished sewing on thirty-two Cash's name tapes and ended up with fingers like pincushions she had hated Mrs. Hegarty too.

And after the way she'd lost her temper with Laurel this morning, she was unlikely to read anything complimentary about herself now. More like: "Ginny Holland is a cold, selfish, money-obsessed bitch who never dusts her skirting boards or irons her knickers."

Either way, this was Laurel's private diary, and she really shouldn't read it. Moving over to the bedroom window, Ginny peered out; nothing would make her happier than to see Laurel making her way down the street, heading home. Then she could put the diary back where she'd found it and avoid having to read uncomplimentary remarks about herself.

But the road was empty; there was still no sign of Laurel in her long dress and droopy cardigan.

She'd been gone for more than three hours. Without her handbag.

Feeling increasingly uneasy, Ginny opened the diary, flicking through dozens of densely written pages until she reached the most recent entry.

There were splodgy teardrops on the paper. Laurel had written:

> *Kevin sent back the watch with a letter telling me not to contact him again. Ginny found out about the rent not being paid and went mad. I know she doesn't want me here anymore. She said if I don't get a job I'll have to move out, but how can I get a job when I feel like this? She doesn't understand. No one does.*
>
> *It's pointless. I can't carry on like this. I hate the person I've become. I know what I have to do and now's the time to do it.*
>
> *Good-bye, Kevin, I loved you so much. Enjoy your life. And don't worry, I won't be bothering you again.*

Chapter 49

GINNY COLLAPSED ON THE perfectly made bed, shaking. Her mouth was so dry she couldn't swallow and there was a loud drumming noise in her ears. Oh God, this was so much worse than she'd imagined. The tear stains on the page were dry; Laurel had written these words over three hours ago, before leaving the house empty-handed.

Her heart clattering against her rib cage, Ginny reread the words. There was no mistaking Laurel's intention. She could be dead already, floating in the sea or lying in a battered heap at the foot of the cliffs. Or she could have gone to the pharmacy to collect her prescription for antidepressants and be taking them right now, grimly swallowing every last tablet in the bottle...

God, how could she have shouted at someone who'd been prescribed antidepressants? Snatches of what had been said zip-zapped accusingly through her brain.

Stop feeling sorry for yourself. Sort out your life. Kevin's never going to come back. He doesn't *want* you. Next time go to a department store and buy a pair of socks.

And what had been Laurel's last words to her before miserably leaving the house?

"I'm going to sort everything out. I promise."

Shakily, Ginny realized that she might as well have handed over the loaded gun herself. Laurel had come to her expecting sympathy and understanding, and had got yelled at by an over-hormonal harpy instead.

Ginny stood up, hyperventilating and feeling sicker than ever. She knew what she had to do now.

—∿∿—

Ner-ner-ner-ner-ner-ner-ner.

Come on.

Ner-ner-ner-ner-ner.

Oh please, please don't do this now. Just start, damn you.

Ner-ner-ner, ner-ner, ner-ner, ner-ner.

Ginny wiped a slick of perspiration from her upper lip and frenziedly pumped the accelerator, her stomach clenching as the rate of the ner-ners decreased.

Ner... ner... ner... ner...

Click.

Oh fuck. Fucking bloody thing. Panting, she leaped out onto the pavement and tried to figure out what to do next. But what else was there to do? She jumped back in and tried again, praying that her car would take pity on her and summon all its energy for one last go.

Click.

Bastard car. Ginny thumped the steering wheel and closed her eyes in despair.

A knock on the driver's window made her jump. Her heart plummeted when she saw who was standing next to the car.

"I've got a charger if you want to borrow it."

"What?" The unexpectedness of the encounter had caused Ginny's brain to go temporarily blank.

"Your battery's flat," said Carla. "You left your headlights on last night."

"What?" Ginny stared at the switch on the dash and realized it was true. "You mean you *saw* my headlights were on and you did *nothing*?"

Carla stiffened. "You said you never wanted to speak to me again. I only came over here now because you look a bit agitated."

A *bit* agitated? "Oh fine. So if you'd seen me being run over by a bus last night you'd have left me lying in the road? Thanks a lot. You knew I'd have a flat battery today but you just… just…" Ginny bashed the steering wheel again, unable to look at Carla with her swingy geometric bob, pink power suit, and flawless makeup.

"Look, I said I'd lend you my charger."

"That's no good, that'll take hours. I need the car"—another thump—"*now.*"

"OK, if it's that urgent, I'll give you a lift. Where are you going?"

"I DON'T KNOW." Ginny let out a bellow of panicky despair. "That's the thing: you can't give me a lift because I don't know where I'm going. I just know I've got to try and find her before… oh God, before it's too l-late…"

"Right, get out of the car." Carla snatched the keys from the ignition, hauled Ginny out onto the pavement, and said briskly, "We'll go in mine and it doesn't matter how long it takes. Is she in Bristol?"

"What?" Ginny found herself being propelled across the road and into Carla's car; half of her didn't want this to be happening, while the other half acknowledged she didn't have a lot of choice. "Why would she be in Bristol?"

Carla looked at her. "Is this not Jem we're talking about?"

"No, no. It's Laurel." Shaking her head, Ginny spilled out what had happened this morning.

Carla, having listened in silence, said, "Shouldn't you phone the police?"

"I did! But Laurel hadn't written 'I am going to kill myself' so they just said wait and see if she turns up. You can't report an adult as missing until they've been gone for twenty-four hours. It's all right for them," Ginny said with frustration, "but how do they think I feel? It's all my fault."

"Don't blame yourself. If it's any comfort," said Carla, "I'd have pushed her off a cliff months ago. So where to?"

She was all ready to begin the search. Helplessly Ginny said, "Anywhere. Everywhere. The pharmacy, I suppose. The doctor's office. The Job Center, maybe."

"Tuh." Carla snorted in disbelief as they set off down the road. "In your dreams."

"Don't say that." Oh God, what if Laurel was already dead? With a shudder Ginny went on, "We could drive up to the cliffs. Or try the beach, ask the lifeguards if they've seen her. She was wearing her brown dress when she left the house."

"Long thin female, long red hair, long brown dress."

"And I suppose we should check with Perry. She could be with him." Ginny felt sick at the thought of explaining to Perry what had happened if Laurel wasn't there. Carla could do that.

"He's not living in Portsilver anymore. And he's changed his number." Carla paused then said bluntly, "It's over between me and Perry. I haven't seen him for weeks."

"You're kidding." For a second Ginny forgot about Laurel. "Why, what happened?"

"It's just over, that's all. I'll tell you later." Keeping her gaze fixed on the road ahead, Carla said, "For now let's just concentrate on finding Laurel."

They didn't find her. The four hours she had been missing became five, and five stretched into six. No one had seen Laurel anywhere; she hadn't been to the pharmacy to collect her pills, and there had been no sightings of her either along the cliff top or on the beach.

"Well, that's good news," said Carla, attempting to cheer Ginny up. "At least they haven't pulled any bodies out of the sea."

But this was no consolation. Laurel was still missing and in a

desperately vulnerable state. Having left a message on the kitchen table for Laurel to call her mobile the minute she got back, Ginny nevertheless punched in her home number for the hundredth time and listened to it ringing in an empty house. It was hideously selfish and she was ashamed of herself for even thinking about it, but if Laurel was dead and the police read what was written in her diary, would she be held partly to blame for the tragedy, possibly even charged with manslaughter?

"Do you need the loo?"

Ginny realized she had her hand resting on her stomach. Abruptly banishing the mental image of herself giving birth in prison—in handcuffs and without pain relief—she snatched it away. "No, I'm OK."

"Where next?"

"Sadler's Cove, we haven't tried there yet."

"Right," Carla announced an hour later, "that's enough. I could have carried on longer, but not in these shoes."

Her impeccable black leather high heels were dusty and scuffed from scrambling down the narrow stony path to Sadler's Cove. Clouds had obliterated the sun and everyone was now leaving the beach for the day. Hollow with fear, it occurred to Ginny that when they arrived back at the house, there could be somber-faced police officers on the doorstep waiting to break the worst possible news.

But when they finally reached home there was no police car outside. Instead, mystifyingly, Ginny gazed at the battered green van parked behind her own broken-down car and said, "That's Dan."

Carla raised an eyebrow. "New boyfriend?"

"Hardly. Dan the Van, he delivers to the restaurant. What's he doing here?" Even as she was scrambling out of the car, Ginny could see the van was empty. How bizarre. Was Dan here visiting one of her neighbors?

"Oooh, you gave me a fright!" Laurel clutched her bony chest as

the kitchen door crashed open. "What's the matter? You look as if you've seen a ghost!"

Wild-eyed and panting, Ginny surveyed the scene. Laurel and Dan the Van were sitting cozily together at the kitchen table, drinking tea and making inroads into the orange drizzle cake Laurel had baked yesterday. Like a small boy, Dan guiltily brushed cake crumbs from his wispy beard and attempted to stand up.

"Sit *down*," Ginny barked, causing him to hurriedly resume his seat. "What are you doing here?" Turning back to Laurel she said, "For God's sake, where have you *been*?"

Laurel looked alarmed. "Out. Why?" Then her expression changed as she saw Carla in the doorway. "What's *she* doing here?"

"I'm sorry." Dan the Van was clearly terrified. "Maybe I should go—"

"No you will not," Ginny and Laurel chorused.

"I'll tell you what I'm doing here." Carla, her eyes flashing, advanced into the kitchen. "I've been helping Ginny to look for you. Or, more accurately, to help her look for your dead body. Oh yes," she went on as Laurel blanched, "we've spent most of the day trawling the cliff tops and beaches, wrecking my shoes while we searched for your corpse. We called the police and spoke to the lifeguards and I've had to cancel three important appointments with clients, so God knows how much money you've cost me. It's just a shame you never learned to *read*." Reaching across the table she snatched up the note Ginny had left and shook it in Laurel's horrified face. "Because Ginny's been frantic, going out of her mind with worry, and all you had to do was pick up the phone and tell her YOU WEREN'T DEAD."

Ginny raked her fingers through her hair. "OK, let's all calm down."

"Why would you think I was dead?" Laurel was perplexed.

Carla glared at her. "Because you wrote all that stuff in your diary about how you were going to end it all."

"*What?* You mean you went up to my room and actually read my diary?" Laurel's voice rose. "My *private* diary? Well, thanks a *lot!*"

"You selfish, ungrateful *dimwit*," Carla shot back. "You should be thankful Ginny bothered, because I'm telling you now, if you lived in my house, I'd—"

"Stop this, stop it." Ginny held up her hands like a football referee because too much was happening at once and all this shouting wasn't getting them anywhere. To Laurel she said, "I'm sorry I looked in your diary, but you said you were only going out for half an hour. You were upset. You didn't even take your handbag with you. Once I saw what you'd written, I was worried sick. That's why I left the note asking you to call me as soon as you got home."

"We only got back twenty minutes ago. I did try to ring you, but your phone was busy. I would have called again, but we were talking about… things. And then you burst in through the door like a tornado."

Carla shook her head. "So you've been out all day."

Mortified, Dan said, "It's all my fault."

"No it isn't. I just jumped to the wrong conclusion." Desperate for a cup of tea, Ginny filled the kettle and gestured for Carla to sit down. "Anyway, panic over. You can tell us what you've been doing. How did you meet Dan?"

Laurel looked blank. "Who's Dan?"

This was surreal. Surely Dan didn't have an identical twin brother. Ginny said, "Dan, help me out here. Am I going mad?"

Perplexed, Laurel turned to stare at Dan. "What does she mean? What's going on?"

He shrugged, embarrassed. "Everyone calls me Dan the Van because of my job. But it's just a joke. My real name's Hamish."

Chapter 50

OVER CUPS OF TEA and crumbly slices of orange drizzle cake, Ginny and Carla heard the whole story. Having taken Ginny's outburst to heart and realized that the time had indeed come to get her act together, Laurel had left the house in order to pick up her repeat prescription, pondering her future en route. The queue at the pharmacy had been epic, practically trailing out of the shop, so she'd wandered down the road for a bit to give the pharmacist time to catch up—anything was preferable to being sandwiched between two competitive pensioners discussing the various qualities of their bowels and piles.

There was a bit of a queue in the bakery too, but this time Laurel waited in line. When it was her turn, she plucked up the courage to tentatively ask the baker if by any chance they had a vacancy for a part-time cake-maker.

The baker hadn't needed to be quite so blunt. Scornfully he informed Laurel that making bread and cakes involved getting up at three o'clock in the morning and finishing at six in the evening. It was hard physical work. Their particular specialty here was lardy cake, and no, they didn't have any vacancies anyway.

Humiliated by his rudeness, Laurel hurried out of the shop. Behind her she heard a man protest mildly, "That was uncalled for."

She was on her way back to the pharmacy—irritable bowels and piles like blackcurrants were preferable to being sneered at—when someone tapped her on the shoulder. Turning, she saw the man who had been standing behind her in the queue.

"Don't let Bert upset you. His wife walked out on him last week."

"I'm not surprised." Her sympathizer was on the scruffy side, lanky and tall, but he had gentle eyes and a kind face.

"Look… um, I don't know if you'd be interested, but there's a woman in St. Austell who sells cakes at the farmers' market. I happen to know she's looking for help."

St. Austell was miles away, right down on the south coast of Cornwall. Tempted to say no outright, Laurel nevertheless found herself hesitating, reluctant to end the conversation. If anything, this man seemed almost shyer than she was.

"Would she bite my head off?"

He smiled and his whole face lit up. "Her name's Emily Sparrow. Can you imagine anyone called Emily Sparrow biting anyone's head off?"

"You lost your place in the queue." Laurel realized he'd left the bakery empty-handed.

"Hey, their pasties aren't that great. There's another shop a bit farther down the road. Do you have a pen on you?"

Laurel indicated her bagless state; all she'd come out with was her house key and the doctor's prescription in her cardigan pocket.

"Me neither. Never mind, I've got one in the van."

He had a nice voice too, reassuringly gentle and well spoken. Laurel found herself walking with him to the next shop, where he bought three pasties. Then they made their way back to his parked van and he explained that he'd been out on his delivery rounds since seven o'clock. She jumped when he opened the van's passenger door and a big hairy dog scrambled out.

"Don't worry about Stiller; he's a softy. We always have a break around now. Are you hungry?"

"Actually, I am." Laurel hadn't realized until now how enticing the hot pasties smelled. "Did you buy that one for me?"

"I did. Although if you don't want it I'm sure it wouldn't go to waste. I'm Hamish, by the way."

Hamish? Hamish! Good grief, surely not the Hamish who wrote poetry and who'd failed to turn up at the singles club that night all those months ago. The one Ginny's ex-husband had insisted would be perfect for her.

The three of them entered the park where benches were dotted around, and Hamish shared the pasties out.

"Are you married?" The words came tumbling out; she had to know.

He smiled and shook his head. "No. Why?"

"Just… um, wondered." Laurel hastily bit into her pasty to stop herself asking if he was a poet. Since Gavin was unlikely to have said complimentary things about her, it was surely better if Hamish—if this *was* the same Hamish—didn't know who she was.

But her brain clearly had other ideas. As soon as the mouthful of pasty had been swallowed, she heard herself blurting out, "Do you know someone called Gavin Holland?"

Hamish looked astonished. Then he went red and nodded. "Yes. Why do you ask?"

All of a sudden Laurel felt extraordinarily brave. She looked directly at him and said, "You stood me up."

He stared at her. "I did? Oh God, you mean that time at the club? I lost my nerve at the last minute, chickened out. You mean…?"

She smiled and nodded, no longer afraid. "My name's Laurel."

It had all become more extraordinary after that; it was as if several protective outer layers had fallen away, leaving them able to discuss anything and everything without embarrassment. There was a connection between them that Laurel had never experienced before, not even with… no, she wasn't even going to think about Kevin. Before she knew what was happening, they were back at the van and Hamish was writing down the name and address of the woman in St. Austell who ran a cake stall at the farmers' market. Then he looked at Laurel and said shyly, "I know this

is awfully presumptuous, but if you're free, I'm on my way back there now."

And that had been that. Together the three of them had driven down to St. Austell and Hamish had introduced her to Emily Sparrow who, as promised, wasn't shouty at all. He offered to pick up the supply of cakes Laurel made each Tuesday while he was on his rounds, so they could be sold at the Wednesday market. It was all so simple and straightforward that tears of relief had sprung into her eyes. OK, it wasn't a full-time job, but it was a start.

To celebrate, they had taken Stiller for a long walk on the beach. The conversation didn't falter once. When Laurel asked Hamish if Gavin had described her as boring, Hamish was perfectly honest. "Yes he did, but have you seen his girlfriends? Giggly airheads in miniskirts." With a shudder he added, "Gavin's a nice enough fellow, and each to his own and all that, but his taste in women would be my idea of torture."

After three hours on the beach, they had driven back to Hamish's cottage and dropped off an exhausted Stiller. When Laurel had rubbed his ears and said good-bye, Stiller had gazed up at her with such a look of pleading in his liquid brown eyes that she'd found herself saying, "Don't worry, boy, I'll see you again soon." Then, realizing how presumptuous that sounded, had abruptly shut up and glanced at Hamish to see if he'd noticed.

"I hope so," said Hamish.

"Excuse me," Ginny interjected when she and Carla had been brought up to date. "You hate dogs."

Laurel looked genuinely hurt by this slur. "I don't."

"You do. You told me you hated *all* dogs, that they were messy and horrible." Pointing accusingly with the last slice of cake, Ginny said, "You said all dogs *smell*."

Laurel stared at her as if she'd gone mad. "I said some dogs smell. But Stiller doesn't."

This was so blatantly untrue that even Hamish said apologetically, "He does a bit."

"Well, I don't think he does *at all*. Stiller's perfect."

Which just went to prove, Ginny discovered, that love wasn't only blind: it had a peg-on-your-nose effect as well.

Chapter 51

"WAIT TILL GAVIN HEARS about this." Having watched from the window as Hamish gallantly helped Laurel into the van's passenger seat, Ginny rejoined Carla at the kitchen table. "He's going to be unbearable."

"No change there then." Carla's smile was tentative. "Just kidding. How is he?"

"Same as ever. Gavin's never going to change." Pausing, Ginny dabbed up cake crumbs with her finger and popped them into her mouth. "So, how about you?"

This was what they'd both been waiting for. Carla visibly braced herself.

"It was the biggest mistake of my life, the worst thing I ever did. And I'm sorry." Abruptly her eyes filled. "Oh, Gin, I'm so sorry. And I've missed you so much. Can you ever forgive me?"

Carla, who never cried, now had tears running down her cheeks. Quite suddenly, what would have been unthinkable twenty-four hours ago became the natural, the only thing to do. Plus, Ginny realized, if Lucy had been able to forgive Jem, then she could do the same with Carla.

Some men simply weren't worth losing a best friend over.

And Perry Kennedy was no loss to either of them.

"It's forgotten," said Ginny, and Carla threw her arms round her.

"Thank you, thank you… oh God, it's just been so *awful* without you. It's like when someone dies and you keep picking up

the phone to ring them, then realizing you can't do it anymore. You wouldn't believe how many times I did that."

"Me too." There was a lump in Ginny's throat now; the last few weeks hadn't exactly been uneventful. "So tell me what happened with you and Perry. Did you chuck him or did he go off with someone else?" Despite having forgiven Carla, she still hoped it was the latter; saintliness was all well and good but there was something far more comforting about tit for tat.

"Neither. I told him I wanted a baby and that was it. He took off."

The word "baby" gave Ginny a bit of a jolt. Recovering herself, she said incredulously, "What on earth made you tell him that?"

"Because it was true."

"*What?*"

"I wanted a baby."

Ginny shook her head. "Is this a joke?"

"No! All my hormones exploded at once. It happened just like *that*," Carla clicked her fingers, "and took me over. Like being abducted by aliens. I couldn't think of anything else. I couldn't even sleep, I was so busy thinking about it." She leaned across the table and confided, "It's like when you see the most perfect pair of shoes in the latest copy of *Vogue* and just know you have to have them, even if it means driving up to London at four o'clock in the morning so you can be there when the shop opens its doors."

Ginny had never been tempted to do this, although she had once seen an advert on TV for a new kind of Magnum ice cream and had driven to the nearest supermarket, only to discover that they'd sold out.

"Shoes don't wake you up in the night. They don't puke on your shoulder. When shoes get a bit boring, you can give them to a charity shop. The people who work in charity shops hate it when you try to give them your baby."

"I know, I know." Carla sighed and buried her face in her hands.

"So you told Perry you wanted a baby, and…?"

"He panicked. I wasn't safe anymore. When I went round to his flat the next day, he was gone." Her smile crooked, Carla said, "You must be glad."

"For all our sakes. And how do you feel now?" The thought of unmaternal Carla wrestling with a colicky infant was as bizarre as Martha Stewart wrestling in the mud with a crocodile. "Do you still want a baby?"

"Kind of. I don't know. Sometimes I think I do and other times I wonder if I'm mad. It comes and goes in waves," Carla admitted. "When I'm being sensible, I think it's a terrible idea."

"Just don't rush into anything until you've really made up your mind." The cake had long gone but Ginny could still smell the oranginess of the last few crumbs in the tin; would Carla think it odd if she finished them up?

"The nappy thing could be a problem." Ever fastidious Carla wrinkled her nose.

"Nappies are the pits."

"And then there's the vacation thing. I mean, what happens when you want to go out at night and enjoy yourself? Babies can be such a *tie*."

"They can." A glass of orange juice would be nice. "It's a shame you can't leave them at home, put them in the baby equivalent of kennels."

"Exactly! I was *thinking* that! Oh, you." Realizing she was being made fun of, Carla jumped up and gave Ginny another massive hug. "I'm so glad we're OK again. We should be celebrating! Is there wine in the fridge?"

"Sorry. We've got orange juice." Lovely fruity *orangey* orange juice…

"No wine at all? That's terrible! What's the matter with you?"

Carla had by this time opened the fridge in disbelief, affording Ginny a tantalizing glimpse of the orange juice carton. The longing was now so fierce she was salivating.

"Never mind, I've got some." Closing the fridge—it was like slamming the front door in Johnny Depp's face—Carla said, "I'll zip home, bring back a couple of bottles, and we'll have a lovely catching-up session. You can tell me what's been going on with you."

"You're kidding."

"No," said Ginny.

"Oh my *God*."

"I know."

Carla was so stunned she almost slopped red wine over her pink skirt. "What are you going to *do*?"

"Ah well. That I don't know." Ginny clutched her almost empty pint glass of orange juice. "It's all a bit of a mess. There I was, worried sick that Jem might get pregnant. And instead it's happened to me."

"Maybe subconsciously you did it on purpose," Carla offered. "You know, you missed Jem so much that you wanted another baby to replace her."

"I did not do it on purpose. And we weren't irresponsible either." Ginny shook her head in frustration; she'd been through that night in her mind a thousand times. "We used something, OK? The bloody thing just didn't bloody work."

"So. Are you keeping it?" Carla was ever practical.

Ginny, who wasn't, said, "I can't get rid of it."

"You'll have to tell Finn."

"I definitely can't do that!"

"Look, I know men are stupid," said Carla, "but sooner or later he's going to notice."

Was it the pint of orange juice or the thought of Finn finding

out she was pregnant that was making her feel sick? Ginny took deep breaths. "Not if I leave the restaurant."

"But he should know!"

"As far as Finn's concerned, it was a one-night stand that meant nothing. God"—Ginny's face reddened at the memory—"he was practically doing me a favor. He's got Mae and Tamsin now. This is the last thing he needs." Realizing that Carla was gazing at her with an odd look on her face, she said defensively, "What are you thinking?"

"You've got a baby in there!" Dreamily Carla pointed at her stomach. "An actual real baby! When it's born, I'll be able to hold it as much as I want. And play with it and talk to it and... and *everything*."

"Ye... es."

"But don't you see how fantastic that is?" Triumphantly Carla said, "Now I don't have to worry anymore about having one of my own!"

Maybe it was just as well. As she watched Carla knocking back her fourth glass of wine, Ginny said drily, "So glad I could help."

Chapter 52

IT WAS A FLIMSY excuse but the best he'd been able to come up with at short notice. Finn felt like a teenager as he drove to Ginny's house, and it wasn't a sensation he was comfortable with.

Well, it hadn't featured in his life until recently. Having to work alongside her in the restaurant wasn't helping; his feelings for Ginny were flatly refusing to go away. It was killing him, not knowing if she felt anything for him in return. And now he'd made up his mind; he *needed* to know if there was any chance at all of some kind of future for them.

He pulled up outside Ginny's house, aware that it was a risky thing to do. The situation he now found himself in with Tamsin was impossible; he knew he didn't love her. Except there was Mae, whom he *did* love, to consider as well.

Shit, what a nightmare. But he was here now and he was going to tell Ginny the truth. Just like spotting a rare antique in an auction, you could maintain a poker face and apparent indifference for so long, but once the bidding started, sooner or later it became necessary to declare an interest. After that it was up to her; she could laugh in his face and tell him to get lost. Or she could say yes.

Either way, at least the agony of not knowing would be over.

Right, here goes. Finn switched off the car's engine and reached for the cardigan on the passenger seat. His stomach was clenched, his mouth dry, and he was about to make the riskiest bid of his life.

He rang the bell and watched through the distorted glass as a

blur of pink approached the door. Recognizing Ginny's dressing gown, he pictured her naked beneath it before hastily banishing the image from his mind.

Talk about tempting fate.

Then the door opened and—*Jesus.*

"Hey, Finn. Good to see you!"

Completely wrong-footed, Finn found himself succumbing to Gavin Holland's enthusiastic handshake. As if mistaking Gavin for Ginny wasn't terrifying enough, he was now forced to make conversation with a man wearing a lace-trimmed pink dressing gown that failed to conceal his hairy chest.

"Excuse the outfit. I've just had a shower." Gavin, evidently unconcerned, said cheerfully, "So what brings you here?"

Thank God he had his flimsy excuse. Finn held up the pale green angora cardigan and tried not to look at Gavin's bare feet. "Er... Ginny left this behind this afternoon. I was just passing and thought she might need it. Is she, um, around?"

"Upstairs, having a bath. We're going out to dinner tonight."

We? Hoping he'd misunderstood, Finn said casually, "With that girl you brought to the restaurant that time? What was her name? Cleo?"

"No, no. Long gone, that one. My bimbo days are over now. I've seen the error of my ways."

"Oh." Ginny was upstairs in the bath and the ex-husband with whom she'd always remained friendly was wearing her pink dressing gown and announcing that he'd seen the error of his ways. And they were on their way out to dinner together. Fuck it, what was there to misunderstand? Swallowing that kicked-in-the-teeth feeling and marveling that he could sound so normal, Finn said, "Ginny didn't mention any of this."

"Typical woman, she's not sure it'll last. I've blotted my copybook too many times before for her liking. But I'm working on

proving her wrong. It's taken me a while to come to my senses but this time it's for good, I just know it is." Gavin paused, his eyes sparkling. "This is my chance to do the decent thing at last and I'm not going to waste it. Those pretty young creatures are all very well, but sometimes the more mature woman just has... you know, that edge." He broke into a grin. "And if she heard me calling her a more mature woman she'd rip my head off."

"Right." Finn was out of here. "That's great," he lied. "I'm pleased for... both of you."

And then he left before he ripped Gavin's undeserving head off himself.

Ginny emerged shivering from the bathroom wrapped in a towel.

"When I said you could use my shower, I didn't mean you could use all the hot water. That bath was *lukewarm*."

"Sorry." Gavin, whose boiler had broken down, appeared at the foot of the stairs. "Anyway, how do I look?"

She softened, because the change in Gavin in the last couple of weeks had been a revelation. Whether it would last was anybody's guess—personally, Ginny was giving it two months, max—but he was certainly making an effort for Bev. "Very handsome. In an overweight, thinning-on-top kind of way."

"Charming. Sometimes I wonder why I divorced you. Then I remember."

"I divorced you," Ginny retorted. "Hot-water hogger. But I like your shirt."

Pleased, Gavin adjusted the cuffs of the smart, dark blue shirt he'd bought specially for tonight. It was the most ungarish one he'd ever owned.

"Bev said blue was my color."

"Bev said this, Bev said that," Ginny teased, because he was at

that besotted stage where he liked to include her name in every conversation. "Who was that at the door earlier?"

Gavin was now busy admiring his smartened-up appearance in the hall mirror. "Hmm? Oh, just Finn. He dropped off the cardigan you left at work. Hadn't you better get ready? Bev's going to be here soon."

Following a business meeting in Exeter, Bev was coming straight to the house before the three of them went out to dinner together. Ginny said, "Are you sure I won't feel like a third wheel?"

"Of course you won't. We'll have a great time."

"No lovey-doveyness then. You have to promise."

"My hands shall remain above the table at all times." Gavin waggled them to illustrate. "Mind you, can't make any promises about other body parts."

Ginny headed for her bedroom, combing her fingers through her wet hair, but not before flicking a playful rude hand gesture at Gavin in the hall below. He was in love—again—and it wasn't his fault she was jealous. She *would* enjoy the evening once she got her happy head on; it was just the mention of Finn that had knocked her off kilter. Sitting at a table for three was fine in its own way, but if her life could have been different, how much lovelier it would be to have someone of her own and be part of a table for four.

Chapter 53

GINNY DIDN'T KNOW WHAT she was missing. Carla, sipping ice-cold Moët, watched as Lawrence deftly worked his magic on her hair. Still desperate to make up for her previous transgressions, she had done her utmost to persuade Ginny to come along to Lawrence's for the cut of a lifetime, her treat.

But Ginny, blinking her bangs out of her eyes and too impatient—as ever—to wait for an appointment, had taken the kitchen scissors up to the bathroom and performed her usual snip-and-hack job. Annoyingly, her hair had looked fine afterward.

"See?" Ginny had executed a happy twirl, showing off her habitual no-style style. "Look how much money I've just saved you!"

Frustrated didn't begin to describe how Carla felt. "But think how much more fantastic it would have been if Lawrence had done it."

Ginny had been unrepentant and Carla had given up. What Ginny didn't know—couldn't begin to understand—was that coming here to Lawrence's was about so much more than just perfect hair. His tiny one-man salon was possibly her favorite place in the world, rose-pink and womb-like, and Lawrence himself was a psychiatrist, therapist, and counselor rolled into one. You could tell him anything and he wouldn't be shocked. He loved to talk but never gossiped. Once upon a time he'd been married with children; now, in his early fifties, he was gay and happily ensconced with a policeman called Bob. Lawrence was funny and wise, adored by

everyone, and a magical stylist; what more could you want from any man than that?

And he served champagne. Oh yes, Ginny definitely didn't know what she was missing.

"You're better off without him, darling," he said now. "Men like that? Professional heartbreakers, take it from me. And if you'd had a baby, what kind of a father would he have been?"

"I know that now. I was just so overwhelmed with the idea of it." Carla took another sip of champagne. "I wanted a baby; it didn't occur to me that he wouldn't feel the same way."

"Lots of men don't. After our first two, Linda wanted a third and I wasn't so keen." Wagging his scissors at Carla in the mirror, Lawrence shook his head and said ruefully, "I tell you, never argue with a woman whose hormones are raging, because you'll never win."

Carla knew he had three children, all grown up now, to whom he was extremely close. "So how did she get you to change your mind?"

"Fait accompli. She came off the pill without telling me. Oh darling, bless you for looking shocked!" Lawrence chuckled. "You're new to this game. It's what women do."

"But how did she know you wouldn't leave her?" Until the Perry debacle, Carla had always prided herself on her honesty; it hadn't occurred to her not to tell him her plans.

"I loved my kids. Linda knew that once I was used to the idea I'd be fine. And of course she was right. Anyone ready for a top-up?" Lawrence added another inch to Carla's glass and refilled the one in front of the girl having her lowlights baked under the heat lamp.

Entertained, the girl said, "So it all worked out in the end?"

"Ask me what I'm doing tonight," said Lawrence.

She glanced over at Carla in amusement. "What are you doing tonight?"

"Babysitting two of my grandchildren. The ones that belong to my youngest daughter." His face suffused with pride, Lawrence

said, "I have the best family in the world and I couldn't imagine life without them."

"Oh God," Carla wailed, "now you're making me want to have a baby again."

"But pick a better bloke next time." Lawrence shook a finger at her. "Find one who doesn't hate kids for a start."

"Then what? Just go for it?"

"Darling, exactly. But in a subtle way."

Pleasantly relaxed by the champagne, Carla grinned across at Lawrence's other client. "So announcing that I'd made an appointment to have my IUD whipped out probably wasn't my cleverest move."

The other girl and Lawrence looked at each other in horror and gasped, then burst out laughing.

"But I thought he'd be pleased!" said Carla.

"Such a novice." Lawrence patted her shoulder fondly. "Next time, subterfuge. Remember, you're the woman. You call the shots."

"Unless it's condoms." Carla pulled a face. "Not much you can do about them."

"Yes there is." The other girl winked. "That's easy. You just have to be discreet."

Carla snorted into her glass; this was why she *loved* coming here. "Come on! You mean slip it off halfway through and hope he won't notice?"

"When I wanted another baby, my fiancé said it was too soon. Same as you did." The girl pointed at Lawrence. "But my hormones were all over the place, and I *knew* I wanted another one. So I took this really fine needle and stuck it through every condom in the box." She grinned. "All twenty-four of them."

Carla clapped her hands in delight; she'd never have thought of that. "And he couldn't tell?"

"I didn't use a knitting needle. Just a teeny weeny one from a hotel sewing kit. And then you smooth over the hole in the wrapper with

your finger so it's hardly visible." Warming to her theme, the girl said, "Trust me: by the time you've got a man reaching for a condom, he's not going to be stopping to examine it under a microscope."

"Did it work?" Carla was enthralled.

The girl waved her free hand and said airily, "Well, things changed. You know how it is. But hey, it could have worked."

It could. Carla marveled at such subterfuge; it was reassuring to know she wasn't the only one seized by that desperate, primeval urge to procreate. And this girl had a child but hadn't let herself go, which she also definitely approved of. Her figure was fantastic and she was wearing casual but definitely expensive clothes.

"Right, that's you done." Lawrence finished cutting and laid down his scissors with a flourish. "Now just give me ten minutes to deal with these lowlights and I'll be back to do the blow dry. There's a piece in here you'll love," he went on, handing Carla a glossy magazine. "Irish woman gives up her baby for adoption, twenty years later the daughter traces her but the mother's only got days left to live— it'll break your heart."

Carla took the tissues he was offering her. Unlike most hairdressers who just dumped a mountain of magazines in your lap, Lawrence scoured them himself and singled out all the best articles for his clientele. He loved—and knew that they all loved—a good old tearjerker.

Lawrence led his other client over to the sink and began removing the dozens of foil wrappings from her head while Carla buried herself in the story. It was a tearjerker, so much so that she barely noticed the ringing of the girl's mobile phone. God, imagine realizing you were dying of cancer and not knowing if you'd get the chance to meet your long-lost daughter again before you kicked the bucket, then hearing the doorbell go one day and looking up from your sickbed to see—

"Oh, *hi*, so you got my text! How have *you* been?" The girl's

tone was flirtatious; she wasn't speaking to her maiden aunt. Carla attempted to shut out the sound of her voice in order to concentrate on the magazine article. She was just getting to the really good bit.

"Of course I'm fine; why wouldn't I be? Everything's great. I just thought we could meet up, seeing as I'll be in London for the weekend anyway."

This was someone she was definitely keen on. Carla carried on reading, tissues at the ready.

"Absolutely. It's a date." The girl was triumphant. "I knew you'd want to. Now, shall I bring Mae? Ha, thought not! No, no problem, I'll leave her here. God knows I deserve a couple of days off. What would you like me to wear?" She paused then gurgled with laughter at his reply. "Why am I not surprised to hear you say that?"

Carla frowned. She'd been doing her damnedest to concentrate on the magazine article but a part of her brain hadn't been able to help semi-listening to the one-sided phone conversation going on behind her.

Had the girl just said Mae? And if she had, why did the name ring a faint but somehow significant bell?

Mae, Mae…

Carla froze, placing it at last. Bloody hell. *Mae.*

Chapter 54

IT HAD BEEN AN eventful morning so far, what with saying good-bye to Laurel and now this. Ginny drummed her fingers on the steering wheel and inhaled the smell of fresh-cut grass while the drivers of the two cars yelled at each other and pointed increasingly dramatically at their dented fenders. Nobody had been hurt; it was only a minor accident, but they were blocking the road, and now she was going to be late for work.

Who'd have thought it? Laurel had actually gone, moved in with Dan the… no, not Dan the Van; she had to get used to calling him Hamish now. It just went to show, though, didn't it? As Gavin's granny had always said, there was a lid for every pot. And Hamish was Laurel's lid. They were perfect together, besotted with each other and so well suited that it didn't even seem strange that after so short a time they were going to be living together in Dan the—*Hamish's* tiny farm cottage. With Stiller, for crying out loud, to whose smelliness Laurel remained magically impervious.

Hamish had rattled up in his van this morning and lovingly loaded Laurel's possessions into it. Ginny, half guilty and half relieved, had hugged Laurel good-bye and waved them off, delighted that Laurel was happy once more and envying them for having found each other. She might not particularly miss Laurel, but she'd definitely miss her cakes.

A car horn hooted behind Ginny as another driver grew impatient. A door slammed and a woman shouted, "Oi! Shift those cars out of the way!"

The two men ignored her and carried on arguing. Ginny heard the tap-tap of irritated high heels. Next moment a woman peered into her car and said, "I'm not waiting here for the next hour, watching these two slug it out. If you give me a hand, we can bounce that Renault out of the way."

Ginny had seen cars being bounced before; it was a strenuous business. For a split second it crossed her mind that such energetic activity could precipitate a miscarriage, and that maybe it wouldn't be the worst thing in the world if it did. This could be her chance to make all the complications go away.

Except it wasn't an option. She looked at the woman and said, "Sorry, I can't. I'm pregnant."

Gosh, it felt funny saying the words aloud to a stranger. Almost as if it was really happening.

Bloody hell, I'm having a *baby*.

"Oh." The woman looked disappointed.

"Hang on." Ginny opened her door, clambered out, and approached the arguing men. "Hi, we need to get past. If you won't move your cars, we'll have to shift them ourselves. But I'm a little bit pregnant so I'd rather you did it."

The younger of the two men, with a shaved head and a body awash with tattoos, turned and looked her up and down. Finally, he heaved a sigh of resignation. "You sound just like my missus when she's trying to get out of the washing up."

Ginny was just pulling into Penhaligon's courtyard when her phone rang. Having squeezed between a Datsun and a Range Rover, she parked and flipped open her mobile. Carla.

"Hi there, I've only got time for a quickie."

"That's what got you into trouble in the first place."

"I'm late for work!"

"Never mind that." Carla sounded gleeful. "I've just found out a couple of things you might like to hear."

"What kind of things?" Hurriedly Ginny leaped out of the car; the restaurant was fully booked this lunchtime.

"OK, number one. I think I know how you got pregnant."

"Carla, I did biology at school. I *know* how it happened."

"Will you listen to me? Tamsin was desperate for another kid straight after she'd had Mae. I'm guessing it was because she wasn't sure Mae was Finn's and wanted one that definitely was."

"What? *What?*" Flummoxed, Ginny stopped racing across the gravel.

"But Finn *didn't* want another one, which was a bit of a pain," Carla machine-gunned on. "So Tamsin sabotaged his condom supply, punctured every last one of them. Except then the whole Italian-billionaire thing started up again and she left for London. But she forgot to tell Finn what she'd done."

Ginny frowned as the door of the restaurant opened. "Carla, is this what happened *in a dream*?"

"No! It's real! And she's gone shopping this afternoon so the coast's clear if you want to check it out. She has an IUD now so any condoms should still be wherever he keeps them."

Finn was standing in the doorway with Mae in one arm and a handful of folders in the other. "Ginny, you're late."

I know where he keeps them.

"Sorry, sorry, two cars crashed in front of me and the road was blocked."

"But, Gin, that's not all; you'll never guess what else I—"

"Come on, there are customers waiting in the shop, *and* I'm supposed to be phone-bidding at Sotheby's."

"Brrraaa brrraaaaa!" Mae waved her hands in the air like a demented bidder.

"I have to go," Ginny muttered into the phone.

"No! You can't! Wait until you—"

"Get the sack?" Aware of Finn's pointed gaze, Ginny said hastily, "I'll call you later," and cut Carla off in midsquawk.

"Are you OK?" Finn touched her arm as she rushed past him.

Oh God, why did he have to touch her? "Of course! Why wouldn't I be?"

"You look a bit pale."

"I'm fine." At least it made a change from being traffic-light red. Bloody hell, was that how it had happened? Really?

Mae kicked her bare feet against Finn's jeans-clad hip and babbled triumphantly, "Brrraawaaabrrra."

It was no good; she knew where he kept them and she had to find out if Carla was right. Lunch in the restaurant had gone on for what felt like weeks. At three thirty, Ginny lurked outside the entrance to the antiques center peering—without appearing to peer—through the crack in the door until she saw that Finn was occupied with a couple of potential customers.

He paused and looked up when she rushed in.

"Sorry, I brought something over for Myrtle and the kittens. I didn't realize you were busy... doesn't matter..."

"You could just leave it by the front door," said Finn. "I'll take it up later."

Nooooooo. Ginny clutched the foil-wrapped parcel of smoked salmon trimmings she had cadged from the kitchen. On the jukebox the Eurythmics were belting out "Would I Lie to You?"

"Or," Finn added as an afterthought, "you can take it up yourself if you wanted to see them."

Yessssss. Beaming with relief, Ginny said, "Thanks, I'll do that. Just for five minutes."

But first things first. Once up the stairs she turned left along the landing and made directly for the master bedroom.

Oh God, this was mad. The outcome was the same, whether or not Tamsin had sabotaged the condoms. But the compulsion to know the truth had her in its grip. Panting, Ginny headed for the chest of drawers on Finn's side of the bed and slid open the uppermost drawer. There was the box, right at the back, lying on its side with some of the packets spilling out amid a jumble of old belts, books of matches, pens, penknives, swimming goggles, and sunglasses. Scooping up a handful of packets, she realized it was too dark here in the bedroom to examine them properly and too risky to turn on the light. Closing the drawer she hurried through to the living room, ignoring the excited squeaks of the kittens. OK, over by the big window would be best. Ginny held the first one up to the light, her hands trembling as she ran the tips of her fingers over the plastic-coated foil. God, her heart was racing so hard it was impossible to—

"OW!" She let out a shriek as without warning something heavy landed on her shoulder. The condom packet flew out of her grasp and Ginny spun round in alarm. Bloody Myrtle, what a fright. Disentangling Myrtle's claws from her white Lycra top, she plonked the cat down and bent to retrieve the dropped condom.

Bugger, what were the odds? Ginny gazed in dismay at the packet, clearly visible but unreachable, in a deep gap between polished oak floorboards. You could fling five hundred condoms up in the air and not one of them would fall into one of the gaps between floorboards. And she couldn't leave it there; that would be just too bizarre.

OK, think, think. Stuffing the rest of the condoms into her bra, Ginny raced into the kitchen and yanked open the cutlery drawer. A knife? A fork? Grabbing one of each, she returned to the living room and fell to her knees in front of the window. The floorboards smelled gorgeous, of honey and beeswax, but that wasn't what she was here

for now. The knife was useless, the fork no better. Damn, why did these packets have to be so slippy? It was like trying to hook out a strand of overcooked spaghetti, and the more often it slid back down into the gap, the more her hands shook and the sweatier her palms became. OK, deep calming breaths and try again, and this time—

"Ginny, what are you *doing?*"

Chapter 55

GINNY FROZE, KNIFE AND fork in hand. Slowly, very slowly, she looked over her shoulder. Finn had a point; what *was* she doing?

"Eating woodlice for lunch?" Finn suggested.

"Um… um…" It was no good; he was crossing the room now.

Finn paused with his hands on his hips, gazing down. Reaching out and taking the fork from Ginny's grasp, he bent and deftly hooked out the condom packet in one go.

Typical.

"Right. Thanks." Ginny snatched it up and said, "Sorry about that! It just… well, Myrtle ambushed me and I jumped a mile… it just flew out of my pocket, and of course I couldn't *leave* it there…"

Finn frowned. "It flew out of your pocket?"

"Yes!"

"Your jeans pocket?"

Bugger, nothing else she was wearing *had* pockets. As she cast about in desperation, Finn raised a hand signaling that he'd be back in a moment. Returning from the master bedroom an uncomfortable thirty seconds later, he said, "How strange, I could have sworn I had a box of condoms in my bedside drawer. But the box is empty. They've all gone."

Ginny's mouth was as dry as sand. OK, here was her chance to come clean, to explain everything, to tell Finn that she was pregnant…

"What's that noise?" Finn was listening intently.

Superaware of the rapid rise and fall of her rib cage, Ginny said, "My breathing."

"That crackly sound."

"I can't hear it." She tried to stop breathing completely.

"Kind of plasticky and crackly." Finn's gaze was now fixed on her chest. "One side of you has gone a funny shape."

Ginny looked down. Her right breast was smooth and normal. The left one resembled a Christmas stocking. It looked as if... well, almost as if she'd stuffed a handful of wrapped condoms into her bra. Slowly she reached into the V-neck of the thin Lycra top, scooped out the offending packets, and handed them over. "I'm sorry."

Finn gave her an odd look; frankly she couldn't blame him. "I don't get it. Can't you just go to a shop and buy your own? Or ask Gavin to do it?"

Definitely, definitely time to tell him now. Flustered and searching for a way to begin, Ginny said, "Look, I can explain, there's a reason for... for..."

"Carry on," Finn prompted when her voice trailed away.

But it was no good; from where she was standing by the window, Ginny had seen the car pull into the courtyard. She shook her head. "Tamsin's back."

He heaved a sigh, glanced down at the condoms in his hand. "I'd better put these back in the drawer."

Ginny braced herself; she'd endured this much humiliation, what harm could a bit more do? Clearing her throat as Finn turned away, she said, "Could I have one?"

He stopped. "Excuse me?"

You heard. "Could you just... lend me a condom? OK, not *lend*," Ginny hurriedly amended as his eyebrows shot up. "But I'll pay you back."

"Sure one's enough?" There was a definite sarcastic edge to his voice.

What the hell. "Better make it two." Oh God, what kind of a conversation was this to be having with the father of your unborn child?

Without another word Finn dropped two condoms into her outstretched hand before heading through to the bedroom. He reemerged as Tamsin ran up the stairs. Having jammed the two condoms into her jeans pocket—so snug that nothing short of a nuclear explosion would dislodge them—Ginny said hastily, "Hi, you've had your hair done! It looks great!"

"I know." Tamsin smugly shook back her glossy-as-a-mirror, chestnut-brown locks. "What are you doing here?"

Well, I *was* about to tell Finn that I'm having his baby.

Which would probably have captured Tamsin's attention, but Ginny couldn't quite bring herself to say it. "I brought some salmon trimmings up for Myrtle."

Not that grumpy, lethal-clawed Myrtle deserved them.

"What, *those*?" Tamsin eyed the still unopened, foil-wrapped parcel on the window ledge.

"And I needed to discuss next week's shifts with Finn."

"Thrilling." Losing interest, Tamsin waved her armful of glossy shopping bags at Finn. "Darling, wait until you see what I've bought. I've had such a lovely time! Where's Mae?"

"Martha's taken her out in the stroller for a couple of hours. We've been pretty busy today."

If Finn meant to make Tamsin feel guilty, it whizzed over her head.

"Great, maybe she'd like to babysit this weekend. My friend Zoe's invited me up to stay for a couple of days." Her hair swinging some more, Tamsin dumped the bags on the floor and began rummaging through them. "And I got you a fab shirt… hang on, it's in here somewhere."

Ginny made her excuses and left before Tamsin could find the fab shirt and make Finn try it on.

—⁓—

"About bloody time too." Carla was out of her house a nanosecond after Ginny arrived home.

In the sunny kitchen each of them held a wrapped condom up to the window.

"Three holes," Carla pronounced.

"Four in this one." The needle marks were practically invisible to the naked eye, but you could just feel them if you ran your fingertips over the plasticized foil. And concentrated hard. No wonder Finn hadn't noticed.

"So that's it. Now you know."

"Tamsin got me pregnant." Ginny pulled a face. "Sounds like the kind of headline you'd read in the *News of the World*, all about turkey basters and lesbians."

"*Anyway*," said Carla, like a saleswoman going in for the kill, "you haven't heard the other thing yet. She's going up to London this weekend."

"I know. To see her friend Zoe. I was there when she told Finn."

"Hmm. I was there when she arranged it." A knowing smile played around Carla's perfectly lipsticked mouth. "And I'm telling you now. If that was a girl she was speaking to on the phone, I'm a banana."

—⁓—

It was another hectic night in the restaurant. Ginny hadn't meant to say it this evening, but she was being sorely provoked. Finn had spent the last two hours being decidedly offhand and shooting her filthy looks from a distance. It was both disconcerting and hurtful. When her pen ran out and she went through to the office to pick up another, he stopped her in the corridor on her way back.

"Sorry, we don't keep extra supplies of condoms in this office."

If his mood had been better, it could have sounded lighthearted, even playful. But it wasn't, so it didn't.

"My pen ran out." Ginny held up the new one. "The old one's in the bin if you want to check. And I've already said sorry about earlier." Deep breath. "Look, I still need to talk to you about the… um, condoms."

Finn's jaw was set. "No need. But as far as I'm concerned, you're making a massive mistake."

"Am I?" Whatever he meant, it was clearly unflattering. Fury bubbled up and Ginny blurted out, "Well, maybe I'm not the only one. Because I'd double-check who Tamsin's seeing this weekend if I were you."

Yeek, she'd said it. Well, Finn *should* know.

He stood there, motionless. "What?"

"You heard." Ginny instantly wished she'd kept her mouth shut. What was that expression, shoot the messenger? Finn was certainly looking as if he'd like to shoot her.

"What makes you say that?"

"Don't ask me. Ask Tamsin."

Without another word Finn turned and left. God, what a mess; what an absolute balls-up. Shaking, Ginny realized that now he would accuse Tamsin of seeing someone else. Tamsin, in turn, would deny it and heatedly demand to know who was spreading these lies. And then what? Without any concrete evidence, it was Tamsin's word against hers…

It was too horrible a prospect to even contemplate. There was only one thing to do. Ginny braced herself, clutched her new pen, and went back to work.

Waitressing was showbiz; you had to smile smile smile.

Chapter 56

Tamsin had just had a bath and was wrapped in a turquoise robe, painting her toenails shell pink. When Finn entered the living room she looked up and smiled. "Hi, darling. Mae's asleep. What are you doing back so early?"

She was beautiful. Any man would lust after Tamsin. If what Ginny had said was true, it would be the best news he'd heard in months.

"I've been working too hard. Time for a break," said Finn. "We're going up to London together this weekend. I've booked us into a suite at the Soho."

For a second there was silence.

"Oh, Finn, I'd have loved that." Tamsin was filled with regret. "But I can't. I promised Zoe I'd stay with her. The thing is—and this is top secret—she's just had a facelift and looks a complete fright. I'm just going along to cheer her up and take her mind off the fact that she looks like Frankenstein's ugly sister."

"Right." Finn held her gaze, the confident unwavering gaze of a woman who could lie about the paternity of her child and not let it trouble her.

"But some other time," Tamsin beamed up at him. "Definitely. In fact, how about next weekend? Then we can—what are you *doing*?"

"Borrowing your phone. That's all right, isn't it?" Finn scooped up the tiny mobile that Tamsin never let out of her sight and began deftly scrolling through the list of names. "Ah, here we go…"

"That's *my* phone!" Tamsin leaped up in a panic as he held it to his ear. "Look, you can't just—"

"Zoe? Hi, this is Finn Penhaligon. How are you? Now listen, this is just a preliminary call, but I'm ringing Tamsin's friends to see who might be able to make it along to a surprise party for her at the Connaught this Saturday evening." He paused, listened, then said, "Well, that's great news," before handing the mobile over to Tamsin. "Here, you can speak to her now. Zoe's thrilled. She says she'd love to come."

―ᗷ―

Ginny jumped a mile and almost dropped the sticky toffee desserts she was carrying through from the kitchen when Tamsin burst into the restaurant. She was wearing jeans and a white T-shirt and had a face like thunder as she stood in the center of the noisy, crowded room beadily eyeing each table in turn. Evie, raising her eyebrows at Ginny, approached Tamsin and said, "Are you looking for someone?"

"I'm seeing who's here." The words came rattling out like marbles. "Finn wouldn't tell me, but it has to be someone in this restaurant." Tamsin continued to scan the diners before turning to blurt out, "You won't *believe* what they've just done to me, some petty, spiteful... jealous..." Her voice trailed away as her gaze came to rest on Ginny. Slowly, incredulously, Tamsin drawled, "Or maybe you would believe it. Look at your face! Fucking hell, what is going on here? You know exactly what I'm talking about, don't you? Who told Finn?"

Ginny stared back. OK, this was now officially a nightmare. Licking dry lips, she said, "I did."

"You! *How?* My God, I might have guessed. You interfering bitch." Tamsin's voice rose and her features narrowed. "Let me guess, you were jealous because I had Finn and you don't have a man of your own. You can't bear to see other people happy so you have to stir up trouble by poisoning their minds!"

Close, thought Ginny. I'm jealous because you have Finn and you don't deserve him. You're cheating on him, which is something I'd never do. God, look at everyone *watching* us.

Levelly she said, "I didn't lie."

"You've probably got a crush on him." Tamsin's upper lip curled, revealing catlike incisors. "Is that what this is about? Is that why you were upstairs in the flat this afternoon, hoping he'd take some notice of you?"

"Right, that's enough." Evie ushered Tamsin toward the door. "You're upset; let me take you back to—"

"No!" bellowed Tamsin, wrenching free. She grabbed a carafe of white wine from the nearest table, spun around, and hurled the contents straight at Ginny. "You bitch, you've ruined my life!"

Everyone in the restaurant gasped. For the second time in three minutes Ginny almost dropped the sticky toffee desserts. Then, blinking wine out of her eyes, she saw that they'd been caught in the onslaught too, which meant they couldn't be served to paying customers. Oh well, waste not, want not...

"Aaarrrgh!" Tamsin, who clearly hadn't been expecting a mere waitress to retaliate, let out a shriek and leaped back. She gazed in disbelief at the brown sludgy gunk sliding down the front of her white T-shirt and jeans.

"It's not your day, is it?" said Ginny. "First your life is ruined, now your outfit."

Incandescent but unable to escape Evie's iron grip, Tamsin stamped her feet and let out another ear-splitting howl of rage. At various tables people began to whisper and giggle.

The husband of the couple who had ordered the sticky toffee desserts looked at Ginny and said tentatively, "Were those ours?"

Ginny's knees were trembling, but she managed to keep her voice steady. "I'm so sorry. And there aren't any more left. But I can really recommend the chocolate torte."

By some miracle she managed to drive home without ending up in a ditch. It was only nine o'clock, which had Carla running across the road shouting, "Oh my God, what happened?"

Ginny was incapable of sitting down. Revved up and hyperventilating, she paced around the kitchen. Finally she finished relaying the showdown in the restaurant and shook her head. "That's it, I've lost my job. I'm going to move to Scarborough."

"Sit down. Calm down. So he still doesn't know you're pregnant." Banging kitchen cupboard doors open and shut, Carla said, "Bloody hell, I'm trying to get you something to drink here and all I can find is hot chocolate." She took down the tin and gave it a shake. "Have you even been to Scarborough?"

"We went there on holiday once when Jem was a baby. It has a nice spa thingy. And it's a long way from here." Ginny's stomach lurched as the phone burst into life. Oh God, this couldn't be good for the baby.

"Don't answer it if you don't want to," said Carla.

But caller ID showed that it was Jem.

"Yay, Mum, you're there! You'll never guess what!"

Even when she was having a crisis, hearing Jem's voice cheered her up. Glad of the distraction, Ginny said, "What won't I guess?"

"Marcus McBride's got a beach house in Miami. He's just emailed Davy and said if we want a vacation in July, we're welcome to use it. And it's, like, the coolest house on the planet!"

"Gosh." Ginny wondered how much the plane tickets would cost.

"*And* he's taking care of the flights," Jem went on excitedly. "Isn't that amazing? We won't get to see him—he's going to be away filming in Australia while we're there—but when Davy said there'd be three of us, he was fine. He even said the more the merrier and why didn't Davy's mum go along too?"

"And is she?"

"No! Rhona said it was our trip and she'd stay at home. Which is serious progress, because she and Davy have never been apart before. That's OK with you then, is it? If I go to Miami in July?"

"Of course it is, sweetheart." Ginny's throat swelled; she and Jem had both had flings with unsuitable men. And to think she'd worried about Jem being the one ending up pregnant.

"I'd better get off now. Everyone's going to be so jealous when they hear about it! So, everything all right with you, Mum?"

"Yes, yes, fine. Carla's here. She's just pouring me a drink."

"Let me guess, a huge glass of ice-cold Frascati!"

Ginny looked over at Carla, frustratedly trying to stir lumps of cocoa powder into microwaved hot milk, and said, "How did you guess?"

"That's someone else you're going to have to tell before the baby actually pops out." Carla was nothing if not full of useful advice.

"I know. Don't nag." Ginny put down the mug of hot chocolate which was vile and lumpy.

"It feels like we're waiting for the world to end. You'd think somebody would have phoned by now, even if it's just to tell you you're sacked."

"If Tamsin phones, it'll be to tell me I'm dead." A kind of hysteria struck Ginny. "She could call the police, have me done for assault with a deadly dessert. Oh God, what if she hasn't been cheating on Finn? What if I made a—"

Drrrrrrinnnggg. The sound of the doorbell caused both of them to jump off their chairs.

"This really isn't good for me." Ginny pressed a hand to her breastbone.

"I'll go and see who it is."

"No." Shaking her head, Ginny said, "This is my mess. It's up to me to sort it out."

Her heart went into overdrive when she saw Finn, who clearly wasn't in the mood to waste time.

"Can I come in?" Already over the threshold before Ginny could reply, he stopped dead when he saw Carla. Brusquely, he said, "Could you leave us?"

"No I couldn't."

"Carla." Ginny tilted her head helpfully toward the door. "Please."

"Please what?"

"Go home."

"But he might chop you up into tiny pieces and feed you to that she-devil cat of his."

"Out," said Finn.

"Spoilsport," Carla muttered as she left.

Chapter 57

"I'm not sorry about the sticky toffee dessert, so don't expect me to apologize for that. And I'm leaving the restaurant, which saves you having to sack me." The words came tumbling out; until that moment Ginny hadn't even known she was going to say them.

"I wasn't planning to sack you," said Finn. "You don't have to leave."

Ha, he didn't know the half of it.

"I'm still going to." Her fingernails dug into her clenched palms. She was; it was the only way. Far better that he didn't discover the truth.

"It's all over, by the way. They've left." Finn's expression betrayed the way he felt. "Tamsin and Mae."

Oh God, how awful for him.

"I'm sorry." This time Ginny meant it. He must be devastated.

"It had to happen." Finn shrugged. "Getting back together with Tamsin was never going to work. I wanted it to, because of Mae. But it's no way to live. Tamsin wasn't the one who left Angelo, by the way, before she arrived back down here. He chucked her. It all came out tonight. She's been angling to get back with him for weeks. And was just about to, if she had her way." Surveying Ginny, he added, "She still doesn't know how you found out."

There was no reason not to tell him now. "Carla was at the hairdressers. She overheard Tamsin arranging it on the phone this morning."

"Carla again. I might have guessed. Anyway, it's over. They've gone. I don't imagine I'll be seeing them again."

How he must be feeling beneath the calm exterior didn't bear thinking about. Feeling horribly responsible, Ginny said, "But you could if you wanted to."

Finn shook his head. "It's over, dead and buried. As far as I'm concerned it was over between Tamsin and me long ago." He paused. "And Mae isn't mine. I know that now. Saying good-bye hurt like hell, but it's not like last year. This time it's been kind of inevitable."

"Really?" Well, that was a relief.

"Really. If I'm honest, I was looking for a way out. And for Mae's sake it's better that it happens sooner rather than later. So that's it. All over." Finn shoved his hands into his pockets. "Life doesn't always turn out the way you expect, does it? You think you're in control, but you're not. It's like getting on a plane to Venice, then getting off and finding yourself in Helsinki."

Ginny's stomach was in knots.

Tell him you're pregnant.

I can't, I can't do it.

Just *tell* him.

I really can't. God, news like that, tonight of all nights, could finish him off for good.

Aloud, she said, "Gavin and I went to Venice for our honeymoon. Maybe I should have gone to Helsinki instead."

It was meant as a flippant remark to make him smile, but clearly Finn wasn't in the mood. Almost angrily he said, "And did you think that at the time?"

Ginny was taken aback by his vehemence. "No, of course not. I knew what Gavin was like, but I was young and stupid. I thought I could change him."

"And now?"

She shrugged. "Now I'm old and stupid. But this time he tells me he's changed."

"Do you believe him?"

Did a leopard ever really change his spots? Who knew? But when you saw Gavin and Bev together, they certainly seemed happy. "I'm a romantic," said Ginny. "I want to believe it."

Finn looked at her as if there was plenty more he wanted to say. Ginny pictured his face if she blurted out the truth.

Tell him.

No.

"Right." Abruptly Finn said, "Well, good luck."

"Thanks." That was it, then. Resignation accepted. She wasn't going back to work.

"Bye." He turned and left the house, closing the front door without so much as a backward glance.

God, what a night. Ginny rubbed her face, then her hair. Too traumatized for tears, she picked up the phone to dial Carla's number even though Carla was doubtless, at this very moment, watching Finn get into his car.

The next moment the doorbell rang again. Speak of the devil. Padding barefoot down the hall, Ginny pulled open the door and—

"You're mad. I can't believe you're being so gullible."

"What?"

"Gavin." The look Finn gave her was fierce. "He's going to break your heart."

Mystified—yet at the same time ridiculously pleased to see him again—Ginny said, "Not my heart. What are you talking about?"

Finn was visibly taken aback. "So you're not seeing Gavin?"

"Bloody hell, *no*! We've been divorced for nine years. I went out to dinner last night with him and his new girlfriend. Her name's Bev and she's lovely." Ginny realized she was babbling. "And get this; she's as old as me!"

"I thought you and Gavin were back together." Frowning, Finn said, "When I dropped your cardigan off, Gavin was wearing your dressing gown."

"His boiler broke down." Gavin would think it was hilarious, Ginny realized, to answer the door in a girly dressing gown. "I said he could use my shower, that's all. God, if I ever thought of getting back with Gavin I'd have myself certified."

"Sorry. I can't believe I got it wrong." Finn shook his head, his expression unreadable. "So... um, will it work out, d'you think, with this Bev?"

"Truly? I shouldn't think so for a minute. Bev's great, like I said. But Gavin's never going to change. This is a novelty for him. Personally I give it a couple more weeks." It was a pretty irrelevant conversation but Ginny pressed on anyway. "And deep down, I think Bev does too. She said something last night about if it doesn't work out, at least she'll have got Gavin out of her system."

There was a long pause. Finally Finn said, "Not necessarily."

"Why not?"

He shrugged. "Doesn't always work that way."

"Well, they're adults." Ginny felt herself getting hot, unnerved by the intensity of Finn's gaze. "Why are you looking at me like that?"

Because if he knew, she would just *die*.

"Probably because I slept with you and didn't get you out of my system."

Ginny's knees almost buckled. "Wh-what?"

"Sorry. Being honest. You did ask." Finn raked his fingers through his hair. "And I know you only wanted a one-night thing, but I haven't been able to forget it. At all. Obviously, I couldn't say anything before, and maybe I shouldn't be saying it now." He swallowed and Ginny heard the emotion in his voice. "But it's been a hell of a day and I needed you to know how I feel about you. If I'm honest, it's how I've felt the whole time Tamsin's been back."

Seconds passed. Ginny was speechless. Finally, she stammered, "M-me too."

It was Finn's turn to look stunned. "Really?"

"Oh yes. *God*, yes. Really."

He kissed her and she'd never felt so alive nor so terrified. Pulling away, Ginny blinked and said, "There's something else I have to tell you."

Finn wasn't in the mood to take her seriously. "Don't tell me you were born a man."

Hardly. Ginny braced herself. "I didn't mean it to happen."

"Didn't mean what?"

Her courage failed. "I can't tell you."

Yes you can.

No I can't, can't, *can't*.

But you *must*.

"OK," said Finn. "Is it good or bad?"

"I don't know."

"I love you. Does that help at all?"

Tears sprang into Ginny's eyes. "I'm pregnant."

Finn was motionless. "You are?"

"Yes." She saw the look on his face, realized what he was wondering, and burst out, "It's yours, I swear. I haven't slept with anyone else—not for years. I'm sorry!"

To her relief Finn relaxed visibly, half smiling. "No need to apologize. I'm glad you haven't slept with anyone else." Glancing at her stomach he added, "Is everything OK?"

"With the baby? Oh yes. I've had a scan."

"Were you ever going to tell me?"

"No. I thought I'd move to Scarborough." Ginny was still in a daze of happiness. "Until this afternoon, you had a family."

Finn pulled her into his arms. "I had a child who wasn't mine and a girlfriend I didn't love." His gaze softened. "Even worse, I was *in* love with someone who worked for me, but couldn't tell her because she was back with her ex-husband... hang on, so what was all that with the condoms?"

At last, a question she could answer. The two she and Carla had examined earlier were still in the fruit bowl on the kitchen table. Reaching over and fishing them out, Ginny said, "Tamsin wanted another baby last year, but you weren't so keen. So she stuck a needle through every packet in the box."

"Good job the vicar didn't call round this evening." Finn raised an eyebrow at the fruit bowl, then ran his fingers over the packet in his hand. "Just as well it didn't work."

"Except it did. Right result," said Ginny, "wrong womb."

"Are you kidding? Tamsin finally did something that turned out well." Pushing her wayward hair back from her face, Finn said, "This could be the happiest day of my life. In fact, I think we should celebrate."

Ginny trembled with pleasure as he kissed her again, then regretfully pulled away. "I should phone Carla. She'll be wondering what's going on."

"Carla's a grown-up." Finn surveyed her with amusement. "I'm sure she can hazard a guess."

"But she hates not knowing things. It drives her insane. Plus," said Ginny, "she'll come over and start hammering on the front door."

Her mobile was still lying on the kitchen table. Picking it up and locating Carla's number, Finn rang it.

Carla, evidently waiting on tenterhooks, snatched it up on the first ring. "I saw him leave and then go back in. This is killing me! You're either shagging him or having the most almighty row."

"Well done," said Finn. "Your first guess was correct."

"Waaaah!" Carla squealed.

"Thanks. We think so too. So we'd appreciate it if you didn't come rushing over here because Ginny and I are going upstairs now."

Ginny, seizing the phone, added happily, "And we may be gone for some time."

The next morning it was necessary to make another phone call, this time to Jem.

"Hi, darling, how are you?"

"Great, Mum. Did you get the photos I emailed you?"

"I did." Ginny smiled, because Jem's happiness was infectious and the photos of her with Davy and Lucy attempting to roller-skate had been hilarious. "Listen, there's something I have to tell you. It might come as a bit of a shock."

Jem's tone changed at once. "Oh God, are you ill?" Fearfully, she said, "Is it serious?"

"Heavens no, I'm not ill!" Looking over at Finn, squeezing his hand for moral support and feeling him squeeze hers in return, Ginny said, "Sweetheart, I'm pregnant."

Silence. Finally Jem said soberly, "Oh, Mum. I don't know what to say. I suppose it's Perry Kennedy's."

"Good grief no, it's not his!"

"Mother!" Stunned, Jem let out a shriek of outrage. "Excuse me, but do you even remember that big lecture you gave me before I left home to start university? And now you're telling me you've gone and got yourself pregnant? How many men have you been sleeping with? And do you have the *faintest* idea who's the father?"

Jem was screeching like a parrot. Aware that Finn was able to hear everything, and that he was finding her daughter's reaction hugely amusing, Ginny offered him the phone.

"Oh no." Finn grinned and held up his hands. "This time I'm leaving it all up to you."

Chapter 58

SUMMER WAS OVER, AUTUMN had arrived, and red-gold leaves bowled along the station platform, threatening to get on the line and cause untold havoc with the train schedule. Ginny's mind flew back to this time last year, when she would have given anything for that to happen. Then she blinked hard, because although mentally she might be more able to accept it this time around, hormonally, any excuse for a well-up and she was off.

Luckily, distraction was at hand.

"Stop it," said Jem.

"Stop what?" Gavin looked innocent, which was never a good sign.

"Ogling that girl over there."

"I wasn't."

"Dad, you were. And the one who works in the ticket office." Jem looked at Ginny. "You were chatting her up. We both saw you."

"It's called being friendly," Gavin protested. "Can't you lot *ever* give me the benefit of the doubt?"

After twenty years? Frankly, no. Ginny rolled her eyes and felt sorry for Bev. Their relationship had lasted four months, which was longer than anyone in their right mind would have predicted. But now, like a *Big Brother* contestant clinging on by her fingernails, narrowly managing to avoid being evicted each week, Bev's time was pretty much up. She knew it, but just hadn't the courage to make the break and walk away.

Gavin was never going to change.

"The train's due in five minutes." Jem was gabbling into her phone, excited to be on her way back to Bristol. "I've got three bottles of wine in my case, and two of Laurel's cakes. Are we having pasta tonight?"

Ginny watched her, suffused with love and pride. Still deeply tanned after the three-week holiday in Miami, Jem was every inch the confident, vivacious nineteen-year-old looking forward to her second year of university. And she had plenty to look forward to, not least sharing a three-bed flat in Kingsdown with her two best friends. Poor Rhona. It hadn't been easy, but she'd finally accepted that the time had come for Davy to leave home and—

"Ginny, is that you?"

Swinging round, Ginny came face to face with a large, florid woman in a too-tight tweed coat who clearly knew her from somewhere.

"My goodness it is!" The woman let out a cry of delight. "How amazing! How *are* you?"

Always a nightmare. Ginny hated it when this happened. Pretend you recognize them and attempt to bluff it out, or admit defeat and hurt their feelings?

"I'm *fine*! Gosh, fancy bumping into you here!" Since it was already too late to come clean, Ginny submitted to being enveloped in scratchy tweed and kissed on both cheeks.

"I'm just catching the train home! I've been visiting my aunt in Tintagel. It's so good to see you again… you haven't changed a bit!"

You have, thought Ginny, frantically attempting to peel back the years and picture the woman as she might have looked. To make matters worse, Jem had now finished her phone call and was making her way over.

"My daughter's catching the train too."

"Your daughter? Well I never!" Beaming at Jem, the woman said, "And what's your name?"

"I'm Jem." Jem turned expectantly to Ginny. "Mum? Who's this?"

Bugger, *bugger*. Ginny said, "Darling, this is... ooh, excuse me..." Pressing her hand to her mouth she failed to stifle a tickly cough, then another one, then another...

"Lovely to meet you, Jem. And I'm Theresa Trott. Your mum and I were at school together, ooh, *many* moons ago!"

Jem said brightly, "Oh! Friends Reunited."

"Well." Theresa looked bemused. "I suppose we are."

Ginny cringed, wishing her daughter didn't have the memory of an elephant when it came to names.

"No, I mean the website. You're the one who contacted Mum last year." Jem was delighted to have made the connection. "She drove up to Bath to meet you."

"That was someone else," Ginny said hurriedly.

"No it wasn't! It was Theresa Trott!"

By this time thoroughly bewildered, Theresa said, "But I don't live in Bath; I live in Ealing."

"What's going on?" Gavin joined in.

"Dad, do something with Mum. She's lost her marbles."

"OK, I'm sorry." Ginny held up her hands. "I lied."

Startled but determined to carry on as if nothing had happened, Theresa shook Gavin's hand and said, "So you're Ginny's husband, how nice to meet—oh, I say!" Her eyes widened as Ginny's voluminous white jacket parted to reveal the unmistakable bump beneath.

"Bloody hell!" Gavin stared at it too. Indignantly, he said, "Where did that come from? It sure as hell isn't mine."

He thought he was so funny. At that moment something snuffly brushed against Ginny's left ankle. Relieved, she turned and scooped the little dog up into her arms and said, "Rescue me."

Finn rose to the occasion like a pro. Back from taking Rocky for a discreet pee on a patch of grass outside the station, he fixed Theresa Trott with a winning smile. "Shall I explain? Gavin is Ginny's

ex-husband. I'm her future husband and the baby's mine. The dog is ours as well. His name is Rocky. The baby's due in January, and Ginny's marrying me soon after that."

"He's going to be my stepfather." Jem grinned, sliding her arm through Finn's.

"How lovely." Dumbfounded but clearly entranced by Finn, Theresa said brightly, "Well, congratulations. And there's me, never been married at all!"

Ginny shot Gavin a warning look, daring him to announce that this could be because she was fat, frizzy-haired, and wearing a coat that made her look seventy.

"Ah," said Finn, "but you never know when the right one's going to come along. It could happen at any time."

See? Ginny glowed with love and pride; that was the difference between Gavin and Finn. She'd definitely made the right choice this time.

Theresa, her chins quivering with gratitude, beamed up at Finn. "That's what Mummy and Daddy keep telling me." She blinked eagerly. "So how did you and Ginny meet?"

As the baby kicked inside her, Ginny heard the train approaching in the distance.

"Actually, I caught her shoplifting," said Finn.

About the Author

With over 5 million copies sold, *New York Times* and *USA Today* bestselling author Jill Mansell is also one of the hottest selling authors of women's fiction in the UK. She lives with her partner and children in Bristol and writes full time. Actually, that's not true; she watches TV, eats gum drops, admires the rugby players training in the sports field behind her house, and spends hours on the Internet marveling at how many other writers have blogs. Only when she's *completely* run out of ways to procrastinate does she write.